Interpersonal Skills
in Organizations

Interpersonal Skills in Organizations

Second Edition

SUZANNE C. DE JANASZ, Ph.D.
University of Mary Washington

KAREN O. DOWD, Ph.D.
James Madison University

BETH Z. SCHNEIDER, MBA
George Mason University

Boston   Burr Ridge, IL   Dubuque, IA   Madison, WI   New York   San Francisco   St. Louis
Bangkok   Bogotá   Caracas   Kuala Lumpur   Lisbon   London   Madrid   Mexico City
Milan   Montreal   New Delhi   Santiago   Seoul   Singapore   Sydney   Taipei   Toronto

McGraw-Hill
Irwin

INTERPERSONAL SKILLS IN ORGANIZATIONS

Published by McGraw-Hill/Irwin, a business unit of The McGraw-Hill Companies, Inc., 1221 Avenue of the Americas, New York, NY, 10020. Copyright © 2006, 2002 by The McGraw-Hill Companies, Inc. All rights reserved. No part of this publication may be reproduced or distributed in any form or by any means, or stored in a database or retrieval system, without the prior written consent of The McGraw-Hill Companies, Inc., including, but not limited to, in any network or other electronic storage or transmission, or broadcast for distance learning.

Some ancillaries, including electronic and print components, may not be available to customers outside the United States.

This book is printed on acid-free paper.

3 4 5 6 7 8 9 0 QPD/ QPD 0 9 8 7 6 5

ISBN 0-07-288139-9

Editorial director: *John E. Biernat*
Senior sponsoring editor: *Kelly H. Lowery*
Editorial assistant: *Kirsten L. Guidero*
Executive marketing manager: *Ellen Cleary*
Producer, Media technology: *Mark Molsky*
Project manager: *Trina Hauger*
Production supervisor: *Gina Hangos*
Designer: *Kami Carter*
Media project manager: *Betty Hadala*
Supplement producer: *Gina F. DiMartino*
Developer, Media technology: *Brain Nacik*
Cover image: *© Corbis*
Typeface: *10/12 Times Roman*
Compositor: *Interactive Composition Corporation*
Printer   *Quebecor World Dubuque Inc.*

Library of Congress Cataloging-in-Publication Data

De Janasz, Suzanne C.
    Interpersonal skills in organizations / Suzanne C. De Janasz, Karen O. Dowd, Beth Z. Schneider.—2nd ed.
        p. cm.
    Includes index.
    ISBN 0-07-288139-9 (alk. paper)
    1. Organizational behavior. 2. Psychology, Industrial. 3. Interpersonal relations. I. Dowd, Karen O. II. Schneider, Beth Z. III. Title.
HD58.7.D415 2006
158.7—dc22

                                                                    2004060992

www.mhhe.com

Dedication

From Suzanne:

To my children, Gabby and Alex, who make me proud. To my husband, Chris, and my parents, Stan and Mary, for always believing in me. To my brother, Brad, who is gone but not forgotten.

From Karen:

To Tom and Peggy Dowd, for their support and unconditional love.

From Beth:

To my husband Jeff, sons Andrew and Nicholas, and my mother Dorothy Zuech, who help me keep moving forward. To my sister Julie, the little teacher who gave me an early jump on reading and writing.

About the Authors

Suzanne C. de Janasz, Ph.D., is an Associate Professor of Leadership and Management at the College of Graduate and Professional Studies at the University of Mary Washington in Fredericksburg, Virginia. Previously, as a member of the faculty of James Madison University, she taught Interpersonal Skills (undergraduate), Organizational Behavior (MBA), and Global Interpersonal/Managerial Skills (Salamanca, Spain). Suzanne earned her Ph.D. and MBA from the Marshall School of Business at the University of Southern California (USC). She moved west after earning a music degree from the University of Miami. She also worked for five years as an internal consultant in the aerospace industry.

Suzanne's research on mentoring, work–family conflict, leadership, and pedagogy appears in such journals as *Academy of Management Executive, Journal of Organizational Behavior, Journal of Vocational Behavior,* and *Journal of Management Education.* In 2002, her significant contributions to management education were recognized by the Organizational Behavior Teaching Society (OBTS) with the New Educator Award. Dr. de Janasz participates and serves in various leadership roles in the Academy of Management, Southern Management Association, and OBTS. She is also a part-time faculty member at the University of Virginia McIntire School of Commerce.

Karen O. Dowd, Ph.D., is an educator, writer, consultant, and trainer. She is on the Management faculty of the College of Business at James Madison University, Harrisonburg, Virginia, where she teaches Interpersonal Skill Development and Staffing and Selection. She is the co-author, with Sherrie Gong Taguchi, of *The Ultimate Guide to Getting the Career you Want (and What to Do Once You Have It)* (New York: McGraw-Hill, 2003). Her research interests are faculty careers, performance appraisal effectiveness, employee attitudes, and candidate and employer choice factors. Her background includes management consultancy for The Empower Group (now Right Management Consultants) for 9 years, director of career services for the University of Virginia's Darden Graduate School of Business for 11 years, and design and delivery of numerous management training programs on the topics addressed in this book. She is a member of the Academy of Management and the National Association of Colleges and Employers (NACE). Karen has earned a doctorate degree from the University of Virginia (Charlottesville), a master's degree from Indiana University (South Bend), and a bachelor's degree from Saint Mary's College, Notre Dame (Indiana).

Beth Zuech Schneider is an Instructor in Marketing at the School of Management at George Mason University. She is the course coordinator and professor of record for the Business Models/Communications keystone course. Beth is the faculty advisor for Delta Sigma Pi and the faculty secretary for Beta Gamma Sigma. She earned an M.B.A. from the University of Central Florida and a B.A. in Pre-Law/Social Science from St. Bonaventure University.

Prior to coming to George Mason, she was a lecturer at the College of Business at James Madison University (1996–2002), an adjunct instructor in the Department of Business and Accountancy at the University of North Carolina at Asheville, and an instructor at Blue Ridge Community College in Hendersonville, North Carolina. Beth also was president and manager of restaurant operations in Winter Park, Florida, and owner and manager of two catalogue companies in North Carolina.

Beth wrote the *Interpersonal Skills for the Manager* training manual for the Institute of Certified Managers, and her research interests include diversity, women in the workplace, and entrepreneurship.

Contents in Brief

Contents

Unit 2 Interpersonal Effectiveness: Understanding and Working with Others

Chapter 5   Understanding and Working with Diverse Others   90

Chapter 6   The Importance and Skill of Listening   112

Chapter 7   Conveying Verbal Messages   127

Chapter 8   Persuading Individuals and Audiences   145

Preface

What's New in the Second Edition?

Thanks to our students, faculty colleagues, and reviewers, we have become aware of what works well in the first edition and have focused our efforts on making meaningful improvements for this second edition. We describe these improvements—which fall into three main categories—below.

Reordering and Reorganizing

The first major change relates to the overall mission and organization of the book. Based on feedback from others and our own self-reflection, there was a need to more clearly define for the reader an overall map of the book that specifies both the journey and the major stops along the way. These stops include intrapersonal effectiveness (understanding yourself), interpersonal effectiveness (understanding others), understanding and working in teams, and leading individuals and groups. As these unit goals differ somewhat from the first edition, we have reorganized the chapters and included them in units where they fit best. Finally, we provide a clear description of the map, journey, and the stops in the introduction, and we offer unit reminders that reinforce where we've been, where we are, and where we are going.

Improved Topic Combinations

Authors are frequently challenged to provide comprehensive yet concise coverage of material suitable for a semester-long class. In an attempt to achieve these mutually exclusive goals, we combined topics in the first edition, such as mentoring and coaching (Chapter 13 in the first edition). However, it became clear that combining coaching and providing performance feedback (Chapter 7 in the first edition) made more sense from both a teaching and learning perspective. We feel strongly that this and other topic recombinations (such as decision making and problem solving—Chapter 14 in this edition) will reduce redundancy and improve clarity, resulting in a more logical and useful text.

Topic Expansion

Another of our challenges centered on a long-standing debate over the main thrust of the book—that is, whether our focus should be on interpersonal skills or on managerial/ leadership skills. In this edition, we've decided to set aside this arbitrary distinction and add coverage of two topics not previously included in the first edition: leadership and power. In the current business environment, any employee who wants to be successful must demonstrate leadership capabilities. Even employees whose position carries no supervisory or leadership responsibilities can and should exhibit self-leadership. For example, effective communication in work groups requires self-direction and appropriate leadership from each individual to make the group effective. Chapter 18's coverage of leadership and self-leadership provides a solid foundation on which to build the practices of effective empowerment and delegation. In addition, we have supplemented the coverage of politicking (newly separated from networking) in Chapter 15 with a discussion of the use and importance of power.

Overall, each of the chapters has been upgraded and updated with the latest research, business examples, and some new (some improved) exercises. For instance, a new four-session module on negotiation (Chapter 9) using a union–management example has been added to make the lessons of effective communication in negotiation highly engaging for all participants. The application of concepts through experiential activities has been and continues to be a necessary strength of our approach, and we continuously search for and create exercises that facilitate skill acquisition. As with the first edition, we believe this second edition remains very content-rich, informative, practical, and immediately accessible and applicable. We are excited about these strengths and improvements and hope you find them as valuable as we believe they'll be.

Acknowledgments

As is true of any substantive effort such as writing a book, there are many people to thank—more than can be listed here individually. Many thanks to all our teachers, colleagues, friends, and family members, from whom we learned what interpersonal skills are (and aren't!). Special note needs to be made of several individuals and groups. Our editors and production staff, ably headed by Andy Winston. Our colleagues at our respective schools for their support and ideas. Our associates at The Empower Group in New York who kept us current with today's workplace realities. Also, we would like to thank Monica Forret and Ted Rosen for their textual input and advice.

Special mention needs to be made of our reviewers, who gave us substantive, honest feedback that strengthened the final product. They include:

Blake Beck, ISU College of Technology

Elizabeth Cooper, University of Rhode Island

Joe Downing, Southern Methodist University

Walter Freytag, University of Washington, Bothell

Lynn Hamilton, University of Virginia

Cynthia Larson-Daugherty, National University

Laurie Levesque, Ph.D., Suffolk University

Joseph Seltzer, LaSalle University

Taggart Smith, Ed.D., Purdue University

Gregory K. Stephens, Texas Christian University

Dr. Mona Ternus, Old Dominion University

Robert J. Van Dellen, Baker College of Cadillac

Nancy Adams, West Virginia University

Susan Taft, Ph.D., Kent State University

Scott Homan, Purdue University

Our many academic friends, especially those in the Organizational Behavior Teaching Society, the Academy of Management Careers Division, and the National Association of Colleges and Employers, who provided a sounding board for our ideas about the book. Our families and friends, especially Chris, Alex, and Gabby de Janasz; Tom Dowd; and Jeff, Andrew, and Nicholas Schneider, for supporting our work. Most importantly we wish to acknowledge our terrific students, who keep us honest and are a joy to work with.

Introduction

Every journey needs a map . . .

Imagine that you are finally able to take a much-needed vacation. Two whole weeks . . . wow! If you're like most people, you will take time to plan your trip—the route you'll take, the places you'll stay, the activities you'll experience. You want to get the most out of this opportunity to relax, refresh, and renew.

What if the journey you were about to take were different? Longer? More meaningful? More impactful? Such is the journey to personal development: an exciting journey with a winding path toward an evolving destination and wonderful sightseeing opportunities. Some of the stops might be short visits, while others are like family and good friends who always leave the light on.

As with any planning for a journey, we first need to take time to consider where we've been and where we want to go. Then we envision all the wonderful places we might want to visit, honing in on a place that would bring us the most happiness. Finally (even if our desired destination were Disneyworld), we'd have to create a plan and devise a route for how we would get there. We can take the scenic route, stopping along many points along the way. We could also take a plane, and fly in to the Orlando airport. Before we leave, we will also need to select from numerous lodging options and make reservations.

This journey of personal development is no different. In Unit 1, we offer an opportunity for you to assess what (skills, values, traits) you have. By taking inventory, we are better equipped to select where we want to be (clarifying target areas for improving personal and professional effectiveness). The different stops along the way—Units 2, 3, and 4—offer an assortment of options that, individually and collectively, promise to provide an interesting and enlightening journey on your way to personal and professional success.

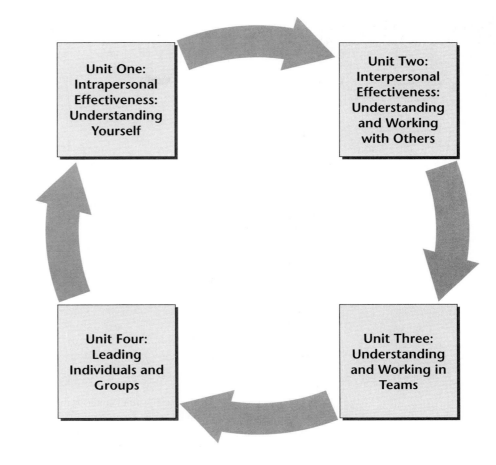

Interpersonal Skills in Organizations

UNIT 1

INTRAPERSONAL EFFECTIVENESS: UNDERSTANDING YOURSELF

1. Journey into Self-awareness
2. Self-disclosure and Trust
3. Establishing Goals by Identifying Values and Ethics
4. Self-Management

UNIT 2

INTERPERSONAL EFFECTIVENESS: UNDERSTANDING AND WORKING WITH OTHERS

5. Understanding and Working with Diverse Others
6. The Importance and Skill of Listening
7. Conveying Verbal Messages
8. Persuading Individuals and Audiences

UNIT 3

UNDERSTANDING AND WORKING IN TEAMS

9. Negotiation
10. Building Teams and Work Groups
11. Managing Conflict
12. Achieving Business Results through Effective Meetings
13. Facilitating Team Success
14. Making Decisions and Solving Problems Creatively

UNIT 4

LEADING INDIVIDUALS AND GROUPS

15. Power and Politicking
16. Networking and Mentoring
17. Coaching and Providing Feedback for Improved Performance
18. Leading and Empowering Self and Others
19. Project Management

Unit 1

The first leg of your journey toward self-development begins with an opportunity to take inventory of what you have and what you still need. This first unit is devoted to intrapersonal effectiveness—**understanding yourself** (and your goals, strengths, weaknesses, style, biases), and **improving self-management** skills, such as time management and stress management. As you'll discover, "knowing yourself" may not be as easy as it sounds. However, we give you the tools to facilitate this process. By visiting each of the four chapters in this unit, you increase the odds in achieving intrapersonal effectiveness, and ultimately, personal and professional success and satisfaction. This first leg provides a solid start to your journey, as well as a strong foundation on which to build interpersonal, team-based, and leadership skills in the units that follow.

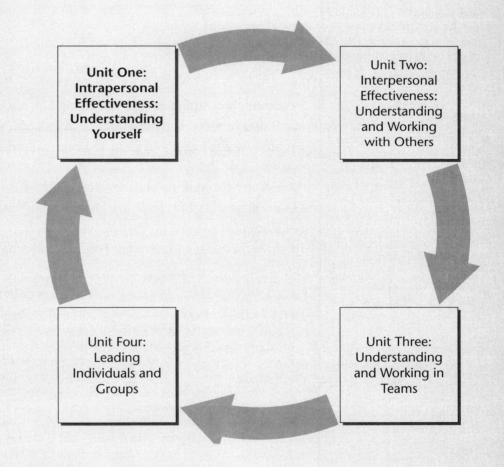

Unit One: Intrapersonal Effectiveness: Understanding Yourself

Unit Two: Interpersonal Effectiveness: Understanding and Working with Others

Unit Three: Understanding and Working in Teams

Unit Four: Leading Individuals and Groups

1

Journey into Self-awareness

Learning Points

How do I:

- Determine my strengths and understand how they might guide me in personal and professional choices?
- Figure out what motivates me in order to find personal and professional success?
- Assess my limitations and develop a plan for improving in these areas?
- Gain understanding and insight into my personality, attitudes, and behaviors?
- Identify the biases I have that preclude my understanding and appreciating others?

Marjorie Morgan, age 22, was excited about her first job out of college. She had worked summer jobs and one internship, but never in an environment as professional as the bank for which she'd work upon graduation. After taking some time off in the summer, she began work in August. Eager to show she was worthy of having been hired, she worked hard the first six months on the job. She enjoyed her co-workers, got along well with her manager, and was even involved in a technology project through which she was able to meet people from other departments of the bank.

The project objective was to develop a new system through which customer complaints could be handled. The present system barely met the needs of the bank's customers and was inefficient and costly to run. Over a period of several weeks, Marjorie and her project team members worked diligently to study the problem and develop a solution.

The team consisted of Marjorie plus five co-workers: two people were about her age and the other three were considerably older. Four of the five were college educated and all but one team member had greater tenure than she had. Of the six-person team, four were Caucasian and two were African American. The team did not have an official leader. Things ran smoothly for several weeks, until the time came for decisions to be made. As soon as a deadline was imposed on the group Marjorie became aware of some significant personality differences within the project team. Two members, who had always arrived late to meetings, were procrastinating on their assignments for the project. Two others who had attended the meetings began to spend more time socializing than working. One person who had been reluctant to state his opinion about the data that had been collected now said he thought the group needed more time before it would be ready to make a decision. Marjorie had been very task oriented all along and was eager to finish the project and move on to other projects within the bank. She was very frustrated with the lack of progress being made by the group and was concerned about being part of a team that wasn't going to meet its assigned deadline. Yet she was reluctant to speak up. She felt she was too young and hadn't been at the bank long enough to be credible with her teammates and take charge of the project. She didn't think she could approach her boss about the situation. She was perplexed about why the group was experiencing so many problems. Marjorie thought to herself, "Why can't they get along? Why can't everyone on the team be more like me? I work hard and have pride in how this project is going to turn out. Why don't the others?" She began to wonder if this was the right place for her.

1. Why is Marjorie upset?
2. In what ways are the work styles of Marjorie's teammates different from hers? What causes those differences?
3. Can these differences be resolved? Why or why not?
4. How would you handle the situation if you were Marjorie?

"Know thyself"

Socrates

As early as the time of Socrates, we have known about the importance of self-awareness. Understanding oneself is key not only to our ability to succeed, but also to our ability to work effectively with others. Studies show that the best managers are those who are keenly aware of their own strengths—*and* their weaknesses.[1] They are able to capitalize on their strengths and either improve their weaknesses or work with others whose qualities complement theirs. They are able to understand others—their motivation, needs, style, capabilities, and limitations—and use this information to motivate and get results from them. They also understand the importance of keeping current with self-knowledge and regularly engage in self-assessment exercises and experiences that allow them to continually learn about and improve themselves. This chapter describes self-awareness: what it is, why it's important, and how to improve your level of self-awareness. It also addresses how strong self-knowledge can enhance your ability to manage and work with others and provides a number of exercises that enable you to assess yourself and develop improvement plans.

What Is Self-awareness?

Self-awareness is knowing your motivations, preferences, and personality and understanding how these factors influence your judgment, decisions, and interactions with other people.[2] Through self-awareness one becomes attuned to present realities and surroundings and gains understanding of how awareness of these experiences impact our lives.[3] Internal feelings and thoughts, interests, strengths and limitations, values, skills, goals, abilities, leadership orientation, and preferred communication style are just a few of the elements that self-awareness comprises.

Benefits of Self-awareness

Self-awareness or self-knowledge is the starting point for effectiveness at work. As Machiavelli, the cunning author and statesman, wrote, "To lead or attempt to lead without first having a knowledge of self is foolhardy and sure to bring disaster and defeat." Self-awareness has many benefits, among them:

- Understanding yourself in relation to others.
- Developing and implementing a sound self-improvement program.

- Setting appropriate life and career goals.
- Developing relationships with others.
- Understanding the value of diversity.
- Managing others effectively.
- Increasing productivity.
- Increasing your ability to contribute to organizations, your community, and family.

For example, knowing what you are good at and what you enjoy doing may help in selecting a career or job that is professionally satisfying and therefore financially and personally satisfying. Relying solely on others' thoughts or beliefs about what is best for you can lead to personal and professional unhappiness. It makes no sense to spend one-third (or more) of your precious time doing what you abhor! By knowing yourself—your strengths, weaknesses, likes, and dislikes—you'll know where you belong.[4]

Self-awareness is also important for managers and organizations. Managers who have attained heightened states of self-awareness tend to be superior performers. Awareness of self often leads to a greater understanding of others. Managers who can relate to or empathize with co-workers tend to be more trusted and are perceived as being more competent. Because self-aware managers are in tune with the concerns of others, they are also able to reduce the potential for conflict and are more likely to be open to feedback. Self-aware managers who listen to feedback and make positive modifications to personal behavior are able to create trusting and productive work environments. Working effectively with others will therefore increase managerial and organizational effectiveness.[5]

"There are three things extremely hard: steel, a diamond, and to know one's self."

Benjamin Franklin

How to Gain Self-awareness

The first step to becoming aware of ourselves is to recognize our weaknesses, strengths, biases, attitudes, values, and perceptions. There are many ways to enhance our self-awareness. Some of these include analyzing our own experiences, looking at ourselves through the eyes of others, self-disclosure, acquiring diverse experiences, and increasing our emotional intelligence.

Self-analysis

Self-analysis requires people to examine themselves as an object in an experience or event. It requires a person to step back and observe (as objectively as possible) the positive or negative impact that may have influenced behaviors, attitudes, thoughts, or interactions.[6] Self-analysis is not always an easy process, yet it is a necessary skill for synthesizing information relevant to professional and personal effectiveness.

The self-analysis process should begin with reflection on and exploration of thoughts and feelings associated with affective events. By reflecting on these feelings and thoughts, individuals can obtain new perspectives relevant to their lives based on these learning experiences. From obtaining new knowledge and perspectives, individuals can become more effective by implementing new behavioral and cognitive changes in future situations.[7] For instance, Marjorie, from the chapter's opening scenario, has an opportunity to gain self-awareness from her dysfunctional team experience. Through reflection, she would be able to see that her current behavior of remaining silent has not aided the team in its process. Gaining awareness of the impact of her action, or lack of action, should lead to a new perspective regarding teaming and her part in the process and to positive behaviors and attitudes in her current and future team projects. This learning will not only help Marjorie in her professional life, but will enhance overall team and organizational effectiveness.

One means to gain insight into ourselves is through reflecting on, examining, and analyzing our behavior, personality, attitudes, and perceptions.

Behavior

Behavior is the way in which we conduct ourselves—the way in which we act. Our behavior is influenced by our feelings, judgments, beliefs, motivations, needs, experience, and the opinions of others. Patterns of behavior develop through our reactions to events and actions over a period of time. Behavior consists of four components:[8]

1. **Motivation**—the drive to pursue one action over another. What underlying factors move you to make a particular decision or choice? For example, what drives you to do a good job? The answer might be a competitive nature, strong achievement orientation, or a difficult childhood experience. Being aware of your core drivers, those things that motivate you—positively and negatively—can help you understand the roots of your behavior and make adjustments as necessary to modify your behavior.

2. **Modes of thinking**—the way you process the various inputs received by the brain. How do you analyze information and make judgments about how to use and apply that information? For example, do you process information quietly by reflecting on your own, or do you process information out loud by talking with others? Being aware of how you take in and make sense of information can help you understand how you make judgments and decisions that lead to choosing one behavior or course of action over another.

3. **Modes of acting**—the course of action you apply in a given situation. What approach do you choose to apply in response to stimuli, events, people, thoughts, and feelings? For example, when someone does something that offends you, do you react in anger? Or do you react quietly, assessing your options before acting? Being aware of how you express your reaction to the things that happen to and around you can help you understand the alternatives available to you when certain events arise.

4. **Modes of interacting**—the way in which you communicate and share ideas, opinions, and feelings with others. Whom do you feel comfortable relating to? How do you typically share your thoughts, feelings, and ideas with others? For example, are you comfortable in large groups of people? In team situations? Or do you prefer to work on your own? Being aware of how you talk to and work with others can help you understand how your preferred style meshes with those with whom you work and live.

Figure 1–1
Means for Obtaining Self-awareness

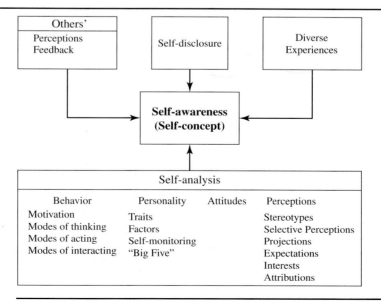

Personality

Personality describes the relatively stable set of characteristics, tendencies, and temperaments that have been formed by inheritance and by social, cultural, and environmental factors.[9] These traits determine how we interact with and react to various people and situations. Some aspects of our personality are believed to be a result of nature—those traits with which we are born and that we possess through heredity. Other characteristics of our personality are thought to be a result of our environment—those factors that we acquire through exposure to people and events in our lives.

Personality traits are enduring characteristics that describe an individual's attitude and behavior.[10] Examples are agreeableness, aggression, dominance, and shyness. Most of these traits have been found to be quite stable over time.[11] This means a person who is cold and uncaring in one situation is likely to behave similarly in other situations. Through a significant amount of research over time, psychologists believe the basic structure of human personality consists of five broad factors referred to as "The Big Five Model."[12] Even though some of these factors are inherited, some factors can be modified through training, experience, and a conscious attempt to change.

1. **Extroversion** represents the degree to which an individual is social or antisocial, outgoing or shy, assertive or passive, active or inactive, and talkative or quiet. A person who rates high for the first traits in these pairs is extroverted, while someone who rates high for the second traits is introverted. Extroversion or introversion, in itself, is not necessarily bad, but extremes at both ends of the spectrum can be equally dysfunctional. A person who is too outgoing could be perceived as overbearing and a person who is too reserved would lack the skills to relate to others.

2. **Agreeableness** measures the degree to which a person is friendly or reserved, cooperative or guarded, flexible or inflexible, trusting or cautious, good-natured or moody, soft-hearted or tough, and tolerant or judgmental. Those scoring high on the first element of these paired traits are viewed as agreeable and easy to work with, while those rating low are viewed as more disagreeable and difficult to work with. Being too agreeable could cause a person to be too accommodating, however, and others may take advantage of this weakness.

3. **Emotional stability** characterizes the degree to which a person is consistent or inconsistent in how they react to certain events, reacts impulsively or weighs options before acting, and takes things personally or looks at a situation objectively. Those who rate high on emotional stability are viewed as generally calm, stable, having a positive attitude, able to manage their anger, secure, happy, and objective. Those who rate low are more likely to be anxious, depressed, angry, insecure, worried, and emotional.

4. **Conscientiousness** represents the degree to which an individual is dependable or inconsistent, can be counted on or is unreliable, follows through on commitments or reneges, and keeps promises or breaks them. Those who rate high on conscientiousness are generally perceived to be careful, thorough, organized, persistent, achievement oriented, hardworking, and persevering. Those who score lower on this dimension are more likely to be viewed as inattentive to detail, uncaring, disrespectful, not interested or motivated, unorganized, apt to give up easily, and lazy.

5. **Openness to experience** characterizes the degree to which people are interested in broadening their horizons or limiting them, learning new things or sticking with what they already know, meeting new people or associating with current friends and co-workers, going to new places or restricting themselves to known places. Individuals who score high on this factor tend to be highly intellectual, broad-minded, curious, imaginative, and cultured. Those who rate lower tend to be more narrow-minded, less interested in the outside world, and uncomfortable in unfamiliar surroundings and situations. Professionals who are open to experience are more willing to reflect on feedback for personal development.

What are the characteristics of your personality? How do you know this? (See Exercise 1–B.) Which aspects of your personality do you like, and which would you like to modify? While it's true that some of these factors are very ingrained, few of these factors are fixed in stone. It's up to you to identify those qualities that are working well for you and worth keeping, as well as those qualities that aren't working well for you that you should change or abandon.

Self-monitoring is the tendency to adjust our behavior relative to the changing demands of social situations.[13] It is many times studied in conjunction with the five broad factors of personality to examine how varying situations will affect a person's desire or ability to control aspects of their personality. The concept of monitoring our own personality can help us come to grips with both those qualities we view as positive and those we would like to change. By being aware of the role of self-monitoring, we can assess our own behaviors and attitudes, diagnose which elements we are satisfied with, and identify and develop plans for addressing those aspects we want to change. When self-monitoring, it is important to want to set personal standards in accordance with certain accepted norms. High self-monitors are very sensitive to external cues and constantly adapt (and often hide) their true selves to conform to a situation or set of expectations. Low self-monitors are more consistent, displaying their feelings, attitudes, and behaviors in every situation. In an organizational setting, it is probably best to avoid the extremes. You don't want to be a high self-monitor (solely concerned with what others think) or a low self-monitor (not at all interested in what others think). Always trying to please everyone or conforming to gain everyone's approval—while it might facilitate getting what you want in the short-term—can be harmful to you in the long-term. Conversely, never adjusting your behavior relative to the audience or situation can be disastrous. (See Exercise 1–C.)

All of the personality dimensions can have a significant impact on job performance and interpersonal relationships.[14] By understanding the meaning of these factors, you can pinpoint areas for personal and professional development and growth. Knowledge of our ratings on each of these dimensions can also help us in selecting a career. Much research in the area of person/job fit demonstrates that individuals who select professions that suit their personality are more likely to be satisfied and productive.[15] Finding work that matches our personal preferences may require a fair amount of investigation; this investment in time and resources pays big dividends—success and happiness. For example, a person who is low on the extroversion and agreeableness factors would probably not be happy (or successful) as a traveling sales representative. The sheer nature of the job requires an outgoing, friendly individual in order to contact and build a rapport with clients. A poor fit between one's personality and job can be a recipe for disaster.

Attitudes

Attitudes are evaluative statements or "learned predispositions to respond in a consistently favorable or unfavorable manner with respect to a given object."[16] As human beings, we can choose how we think and feel about a situation or event. Imagine you are on an airplane that has been diverted to another airport due to bad weather. You can choose to become irritated and show your anger to the flight attendant, or you can be patient, acknowledge that nothing can be done to change the situation, and take out a good book to read while waiting for your flight to land. The emotions we choose to act on determine our attitude. This in turn is reflected in our behavior.[17]

Attitudes are narrow in scope. They can vary from situation to situation. For example, we might have a positive outlook when we are with our friends, feel negatively about our work, and have a neutral attitude toward our academic experience. Attitudes are derived from parents, teachers, peers, society, and our own experiences. Attitudes are one of the less stable facets of our personality, which means they are easier to influence and change than our behaviors or values.[18] Some can change at will depending on the situation, the people involved, other events that occurred to us in a particular day, how we're feeling as a situation unfolds, and how we respond as events evolve over time.

Strong attitudes can have an impact on our professional and personal relationships.[19] As students and managers, it is helpful to remember how much of a role our attitude can play in our success. Our demeanor, whether we're with others or grappling with an issue on our own, can make a significant difference in what behaviors we choose to exercise and in the outcomes of our efforts. Have you heard the saying "she takes lemons and turns them into lemonade"? This is an example of the power of one's attitude. Our attitude can determine whether we think positively and take control of a situation or think negatively and feel helpless about our ability to change or respond to a situation. Our attitude is an important component of our ability to be productive at work or in school. Our attitude can influence those around us. Being aware of our own attitudes, and making choices about which attitude to display to others, is very important for us as individuals and as managers. Our attitude can affect our job behavior as well as our interactions with others. Our friends, significant others, family members, co-workers, and others are definitely influenced by our thoughts and feelings toward situations. As managers, it is also important to recognize that our employees are affected by the attitude we display toward them and toward the work that needs to get done.[20] A manager's attitude is a large factor in how people feel about their jobs. If a manager is upbeat most of the time and supportive of his or her colleagues, employees will generally respond well and work hard to produce the desired results. On the other hand if a manager is pessimistic and belittling toward his or her employees, staff morale will suffer and, ultimately, so will the expected outcomes.

Perceptions

Perception describes the process by which individuals gather sensory information and assign meaning to it.[21] When we encounter a person or situation, we use our senses to absorb various inputs. Next, our brains select aspects from stored information in order to process and organize these inputs. Finally, our brains interpret and evaluate the person or situation. Perception is person-specific—no two people will take in, organize, and evaluate inputs the same way. Your perspective on a situation can be entirely different from the way another looks at the exact same situation. Two friends walking by the window of a crowded restaurant spot a couple engaged in conversation. One friend, taking notice of their mannerisms and gestures, concludes that it "looks like they're breaking off their relationship." The other friend vehemently disagrees. "No, they're probably discussing a plan to spend more time together." Which friend is right?

Individual perception may not always be consistent with reality; it is only the perceiver's interpretation of reality. For example, when you go to a movie with a group, your opinion and those of your friends might differ. You each perceived the same event through a different set of lenses. One might have seen the movie as an action film, another as a romance. There's probably some element of truth in both perspectives. What's reality for you is based on your interpretation of the event. Your reality can be shaped and impacted by learning about others' perceptions of the same incident. For example, checking your perception with others, and sharing yours with them, might change your opinion of the movie or increase your understanding of it. At work, the best managers are those who augment their own perspective with the views of others. Our perceptions can—and should—change based on new inputs.

It is important to be in touch with our perceptions—what they are and how they're being formed. Equally important is being aware of the perceptions of others. Others'

Figure 1–2

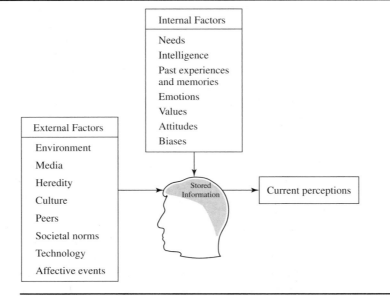

behavior toward you is heavily influenced by their understanding of the situation, and your behavior toward others is equally dependent on your assumptions about them and the situation. It is crucial to understand and disclose your own perspective as well as to solicit information from others about their understanding of the same situation.

Our perceptions are influenced by many factors, such as our culture, environment, heredity, the media, peers, past experiences, intelligence, needs, emotions, attitudes, and values. Perception can be a result of multiple causality: Many factors from a variety of sources may simultaneously impact individual perception. This makes it even more important to be fully aware of the factors that influence our perception. This way we can check ourselves to ensure that our own experience and perspective are not distorting our perceptions of reality.

As human beings, we tend to form perceptions based on our biases. If we are not aware of our biases and don't check our understanding with others, we may miss out on important information and situations by relying on distorted perceptions. Some of the more common filters that influence our perceptions are stereotyping, selective perception, projection, expectations, and interest.

■ **Stereotyping:** making assumptions about an individual or a group based on generalized judgments rather than on facts, or a means to make assumptions when there is little or no information. Many who stereotype others do so on the basis of observable demographic characteristics, such as race or ethnicity, gender, age, disability, religion, and sexual orientation. For example, some companies are reluctant to hire older workers for certain job roles for fear that they lack the energy and stamina to perform at a desired level. Stereotyping is a convenient but faulty way to make assumptions about a person's behavior and abilities. Rather than relying on a stereotype that is probably largely false, it is best to check your own perceptions and come to an event or meet a new person with an open mind. This will allow you to form your own perspective rather than rely on biases that have been shaped by judging and attributing certain behaviors to all members of a group.

■ **Selective Perception:** interpreting information for meaning and accuracy, and discarding information that is threatening or not relevant. We are constantly bombarded with stimuli. This has always been true but even more so today thanks to the availability of the Internet, downloadable newspapers, 24-hour news channels, cell phones, e-mail, and fax machines. In an effort to reduce the breadth and impact of continuous stimuli, our brains attend to information according to our own experiences, interests, attitudes, and background. This means we are constantly "filtering"—absorbing and processing only those inputs we think we can handle, or want to handle, at any given time. For example, people tend to dislike thinking about their own mortality so they avoid the subject of wills and funeral planning. A college student whose main concern is graduating is probably not likely to be thinking of retirement plans. A manager with a project deadline is probably not going to read information for a meeting that's scheduled for next month.

Selective perception provides a useful purpose, but it hinders communication with others. Rather than automatically "tuning out" information with which you disagree, it is best to keep an open mind, being open to all new views about a situation before prematurely developing your own perception.

■ **Projection:** the attribution of one's own attitudes, characteristics, or shortcomings to others. For example, someone who cheats and lies might make the assumption that everyone cheats and lies. This validates our own perceptions of the way things are, or at least the way we think things should be. However, projecting our beliefs onto others denies them the opportunity to provide us with a unique and fresh perspective. Rather than transferring your own experience and feelings to another, it is best to consider each new situation and person in your life as unique, paying attention to *their* features and characteristics rather than yours.

■ **Expectations:** forming an opinion about how we would like an event to unfold, a situation to develop, or a person to act, think, or feel. We tend to perceive, select, and interpret information according to how we expect it to appear. For example, when proofreading a paper you have written, you may pass over mistakes because you know what you intended to say, so you perceive it to be correct. Actually, the best way to proofread your own copy is to read it backwards! That way you're not preconditioned to see a word as you perceive or expect it; you see a word as it really is (try it!). By understanding what our expectations are and viewing a situation with a clear slate—minus preconceived notions about what to expect—we are better able to approach situations and people and form our own opinions based on actual experience rather than on assumptions.

■ **Interest:** basing our activities and inputs on things that are likeable or appealing to us. We tend to focus our time and attention—consciously or subconsciously—on those things that are enjoyable and meaningful to us. For example, if we are in the market to buy a new home we will notice "for sale" signs in front of houses that previously would have gone unnoticed. If you have an interest in people, you might focus on a career in teaching or counseling, while ignoring other subjects such as computer science. The tendency to be drawn to things that interest us can be positive, in that it helps conserve our energy for the things that matter to us. However, as you increase your own self-understanding, it is important to reach out to things that go beyond what interests you at the time. By doing this we can broaden ourselves and our understanding of the things that are important and meaningful to others.

By understanding ourselves, we can begin to change our perceptions that are often affected by the biases described above. It is imperative for us to understand and confront our biases. By doing so, we will increase our level of self-understanding and will be more understanding of others and their perspectives. The workplace is increasingly global and diverse. Companies are now involved in developing new business models. We will be better able to compete in this world and better equipped to formulate and embrace these new models—by expanding our self- and other-awareness. This will help us to be better managers and, just as important, better people.

Attribution Theory: A percentage of our perceptions are derived from what we attribute to the causes of behavior in ourselves or others. The **attribution theory** demonstrates that individuals tend to determine that a behavior is caused by a particular characteristic or event.[22] We make these attributions or judgments about what caused the resulting behavior based on our personal observation or evaluation of the situation. For instance, after being fired from a position one might blame the dismissal on an internal factor or personal characteristic such as being an incompetent worker. Or the individual might blame the dismissal on an external factor such as a declining economy. Understanding how and why we make these attributions is important because several achievement theories stress that future decisions and behaviors are based more on our perception of why something happened rather than on the actual outcome.[23] Therefore, we tend to reinforce our beliefs of ourselves and others based on the perceptions we gain from these experiences.

It is also important to evaluate whether these judgments are attributed more to internal or external factors. Attributing outcomes to controllable factors tends to be a stronger indicator of future behavior than attributing them to uncontrollable factors.[24] For instance, if a person attributes the loss of a job to internal or controllable factors, she or he might feel shame, which could have one of two effects: hampering attempts to get a new position or pushing the individual to become a more effective employee in the future. However, if she or he blames the job loss on an external or uncontrollable factor, it may lead to anger. Perceptions in turn determine behavior in future situations based on the amount of personal control those involved believe they have over the situation.

The accuracy of our attributions is important because they may impact our future actions positively or negatively, yet personal biases have an impact on making attributions. Our own behavior or perception of ourselves has an impact on attributions. The **self-serving bias** causes us to overestimate internal factors for successes and blame external factors for failures. This may cause us to incorrectly evaluate our personal strengths and weaknesses. Another bias is related to the **fundamental attribution error,** which causes individuals to tend to overestimate the impact of internal factors and underestimate the influence of external factors when evaluating the behavior of others. We are more likely to judge people who lose their temper as unable to control themselves than to blame the situation. It would therefore be important as managers to remember to evaluate both internal and external factors before jumping to conclusions.

Others' Perceptions

Self-awareness is also gained through understanding how others view us and understanding how we are shaped by others' opinions of us. Stephen Covey refers to this concept as the **"social mirror."**[25] Covey explains that we gain perceptions of ourselves as a result of what other people say about us or how they react to us. We adopt a view of ourselves based on other people's views. How do others view us? How do we change our actions as a result of what we think others are thinking about us? These are the questions to ask to get a handle on how we are shaped by others' perceptions. By seeing ourselves through others' eyes, we can learn about our strengths and also about areas in which we can improve.

Learning to read accurately how others see us enhances our "self-maps," our images and judgments of ourselves. For example, you might say to yourself, I'm not a creative person or I'm an athletic person after hearing comments from others about our artistic or athletic ability. The social mirror is based on our memory of how others have reacted toward us or treated us. Through feedback from others we can gain more insight or perspective into aspects of ourselves and our behaviors.[26] However, our potential may not be based accurately on this information. The social mirror can be wrong or only partially correct. For example, an overbearing parent might say something negative such as "You'll never amount to anything." In this case, be very careful to first assess the statement—is it true? If the statement is not a reflection of reality, then work hard to dispel this image of you in your own mind, if not for the person who said it to you. Negative self-statements can be very damaging to one's esteem. The social mirror is designed to help you learn about yourself, but you shouldn't accept everything that others say to you as reality.

Self-disclosure

Another means of gaining self-awareness is through **self-disclosure**—sharing your thoughts, feelings, and ideas with others. Talking with others allows us to share our feelings and responses. Self-disclosing is a key factor in improving our self-awareness; we must disclose information and interact with others to further clarify our perceptions.[27] Through verbalizing our perceptions, we verify our own beliefs, affirm our self-concept, and validate data received from an objective source. For example, if you've received a low grade on an exam, it's helpful to discuss this with someone else. They can listen to your concerns and give you feedback. They might empathize with the fact you've received a low grade, then offer to problem-solve; for instance, identifying a test-taking strategy you can use in the future. They might also remind you that in general you do well in school. This helps you to maintain perspective even while going through a hard time about the exam.

Diverse Experiences

Another way of increasing self-awareness is through acquiring multiple experiences in diverse situations and with diverse others. For example, living or studying in a country other than your home country, learning a new language, traveling, reading books on new subjects, and acquiring broad work experience are ways to broaden our experience base. Even negative situations such as having to face a life-threatening illness, going through your own or your parents' divorce, and overcoming a personal problem such as dyslexia can provide enormous learning and enhance your experience base.

As we encounter new situations, we use skills and acquire new ones, meet people and develop friendships, see new places, and learn first-hand about things we might have only read about. Being open to new experiences broadens our horizons. It helps us to see ourselves in a new light while giving us new information about ourselves and our ability to interact with the world. This boosts our confidence level and encourages us to reach out to further our experiences even more. It makes us more open to new ideas and diverse people with varying ways of living, working, and thinking. Expanding our experience base puts us into situations that test our abilities, values, and goals. This greatly aids in increasing our level of self-awareness.

Summary

Self-awareness is an essential skill for developing personally and professionally. If you have a high degree of self-awareness, you'll be able to capitalize on your strengths and develop plans for improving or compensating for your limitations. Part of being self-aware is being able to monitor and change our behavior. By concentrating on self-improvement, we demonstrate to others our willingness to learn and grow, increasing the likelihood of being able to develop close relationships and success in a profession.

Key Terms and Concepts

Agreeableness	Motivation
Attitudes	Openness to experience
Attribution theory	Perception
Behavior	Personality
Conscientiousness	Projection
Emotional stability	Selective perception
Expectations	Self-awareness
Extroversion	Self-disclosure
Fundamental attribution error	Self-monitoring
Interest	Self-serving bias
Modes of acting	Social mirror
Modes of interacting	Stereotyping
Modes of thinking	

Endnotes

1. Daniel Goleman, "What Makes a Leader?" *Harvard Business Review,* Nov.–Dec. 1998, p. 93.

2. Robert Cooper, *Executive EQ: Emotional Intelligence in Leadership and Organizations* (New York: Berkley Publishing Group, 1998).

3. Mary Ellen Kondrat, "Who Is the 'Self' in the Self-Aware: Professional Self-awareness from a Critical Perspective," *The Social Service Review* 73, no. 4 (Dec. 1999), p. 451.

4. Peter F. Drucker, "Managing Oneself," *Harvard Business Review,* March–April 1999, pp. 65–74.

5. John J. Sosik, "Self-other Agreement on Charismatic Leadership: Relationships with Work Attitudes and Managerial Performance," *Group & Organization Management* 26, no. 4 (2001), p. 484.

6. Kondrat, "Who Is the 'Self.'"

7. J. M. Scanlon and W. M. Chemomas, "Developing the Reflective Teacher," *Journal of Advanced Nursing* 25, no. 5 (1997), pp. 1138–43.

8. Patricia A. Hoffman and Gene Powell, "The Aura of a Winner: A Guide to Behavioral Hiring," *Journal of Property Management* 61, no. 5 (September–October 1996), pp. 16–20.

9. This definition is adapted from S. F. Maddi, *Personality Theories: A Comparative Analysis* (Homewood, IL: Richard D. Irwin, 1980), p. 10.

10. A. H. Buss, "Personality as Traits," *American Psychologist,* November 1989, pp. 1378–88.

11. Barry M. Staw, Nancy E. Bell, and James A. Clausen, "The Dispositional Approach to Job Attitudes: A Lifetime Longitudinal Test," *Administrative Science Quarterly* 31, pp. 56–77.

12. Murray Barrick and Michael Mount, "The Big Five Personality Dimensions and Job Performance: A Meta-analysis," *Personnel Psychology,* Spring 1991, p. 11.

13. M. Snyder, *Public Appearances/Private Realities: The Psychology of Self-Monitoring* (New York: Freeman, 1987).

14. Barrick and Mount, "Big Five Personality Dimensions."

15. Charles A. O'Reilly III, Jennifer Chatman, and David F. Caldwell, "People and Organizational Culture: A Profile Comparison Approach to Assess Person Organization Fit," *Academy of Management Journal* 34, pp. 487–516.

16. M. Fishbein and I. Ajzen, *Belief, Attitude, Intention and Behavior: An Introduction to Theory and Research* (Reading, MA: Addison-Wesley, 1975), p. 6.

17. Barry G. Smale, "The Power of Positive Attitude," *Fund Raising Management* 25, no. 8 (Oct. 1994), p. 24.

18. Gregory R. Maio, David W. Bell, and Victoria M. Esses, "Examining Conflict between Components of Attitudes: Ambivalence and Inconsistency Are Distinct Constructs," *Canadian Journal of Behavioural Science* 32 (April 2000), pp. 71–83.

19. Andrew E. Schwart, "How to Handle Conflict," *The CPA Journal* 67, no. 4 (April 1997), p. 72.

20. Adrian Furnham, "Managing Demotivated People Is a Tough Task," *Business Day,* August 22, 2000, p. 19.

21. David W. Johnson, *Reaching Out: Interpersonal Effectiveness and Self-actualization* (Boston: Allyn & Bacon, 1997), p. 4.

22. B. Weiner, "An Attributional Theory of Achievement Motivation and Emotion," *Psychology* 92 (1985), p. 548.

23. Jacquelynne S. Eccles and Allan Wigfield, "Motivational Beliefs, Values, and Goals," *Annual Review of Psychology* 53 (2002), p. 109.

24. B. Weiner, *Human Motivation: Metaphors, Theories, and Research* (Newpark, CA: Sage, 1992).

25. Stephen R. Covey, *Seven Habits of Highly Effective People: Powerful Lessons in Personal Change* (New York: Simon and Schuster, 1989).

26. Don L. Bohl, "360-Degree Appraisals Yield Superior Results," *American Management Association Compensation and Benefits Review* 26, no. 5 (Sept. 1996), pp. 16–19.

27. S. Harris, *Know Yourself? It's a Paradox,* Associated Press, 1981.

Exercise 1–A
The Big Five Locator
Questionnaire

1. Participants are to complete the Big Five Locator Questionnaire. On each numerical scale indicate which point is generally more descriptive of you. If the two terms are equally descriptive, mark the midpoint.

2. Complete the scoring sheet, following the instructions.

3. Place the scores on the Big Five Locator Interpretation Sheet.

Source: The Big Five Locator is a quick assessment tool to be used with an instructor and willing learners. Care should be taken to follow up this profile with a more reliable personality assessment instrument. This instrument was developed by P. J. Howard, P. L. Medina, and J. M. Howard "The Big Five Locator: A Quick Assessment Tool for Consultants and Trainers," from *The Annual, Developing Human Resources*, by J. William Pfeiffer and David Leonard Goodstein, Vol. 1, "Training," 1996, pp. 119–22. Copyright © 1996 by John Wiley & Sons, Inc. Reprinted by permission of John Wiley & Sons, Inc.

The Big Five Locator Questionnaire

Instructions: On each numerical scale that follows, indicate which point is generally more descriptive of you. If the two terms are equally descriptive, mark the midpoint.

1.	Eager	5	(4)	3	2	1		Calm
2.	Prefer Being with Other People	5	4	(3)	2	1		Prefer Being Alone
3.	A Dreamer	5	4	(3)	2	(1)		No Nonsense
4.	Courteous	5	(4)	(3)	2	1		Abrupt
5.	Neat	(5)	4	3	2	1		Messy
6.	Cautious	5	4	3	(2)	1		Confident
7.	Optimistic	5	(4)	3	2	1		Pessimistic
8.	Theoretical	5	4	(3)	2	(1)		Practical
9.	Generous	5	(4)	3	2	1		Selfish
10.	Decisive	(5)	4	(3)	2	1		Open Ended
11.	Discouraged	5	(4)	3	(2)	1		Upbeat
12.	Exhibitionist	5	4	(3)	2	1		Private
13.	Follow Imagination	(5)	4	3	2	(1)		Follow Authority
14.	Warm	5	(4)	3	2	1		Cold
15.	Stay Focused	(5)	4	3	2	(1)		Easily Distracted
16.	Easily Embarrassed	5	4	(3)	(2)	1		Don't Give a Darn
17.	Outgoing	(5)	4	(3)	2	1		Cool
18.	Seek Novelty	5	(4)	3	(2)	1		Seek Routine
19.	Team Player	(5)	(4)	3	2	1		Independent
20.	A Preference for Order	5	(4)	(3)	2	1		Comfortable with Chaos
21.	Distractible	5	(4)	3	2	(1)		Unflappable
22.	Conversational	5	4	(3)	(2)	1		Thoughtful
23.	Comfortable with Ambiguity	5	(4)	3	2	(1)		Prefer Things Clear-Cut
24.	Trusting	5	4	(3)	2	(1)		Skeptical
25.	On Time	5	(4)	3	2	(1)		Procrastinate

Scoring The Big Five Questionnaire

Instructions:

4 2 4 3 4
3 4 3 3 3

1. Find the sum of the circled numbers on the *first* row of each of the five-line groupings (Row 1 + Row 6 + Row 11 + Row 16 + Row 21 = __17__). This is your raw score for "emotional stability." Circle the number in the EMOTIONAL STABILITY column of the Score Conversion Sheet that corresponds to this raw score.   12

2. Find the sum of the circled numbers on the *second* row of each of the five-line groupings (Row 2 + Row 7 + Row 12 + Row 17 + Row 22 = __16__). This is your raw score for "extroversion." Circle the number in the EXTROVERSION column of the Score Conversion Sheet that corresponds to this raw score.   20

3. Find the sum of the circled numbers on the *third* row of each of the five-line groupings (Row 3 + Row 8 + Row 13 + Row 18 + Row 23 = __19__). This is your raw score for "openness to experience." Circle the number in the OPENNESS TO EXPERIENCE column of the Score Conversion Sheet that corresponds to this raw score.   6

3 3 5 4 4
4 4 4 4 3

4. Find the sum of the circled numbers on the *fourth* row of each of the five-line groupings (Row 4 + Row 9 + Row 14 + Row 19 + Row 24 = __19__). This is your raw score for "agreeableness." Circle the number in the AGREEABLENESS column of the Score Conversion Sheet that corresponds to this raw score.   16

5. Find the sum of the circled numbers on the *fifth* row of each of the five-line groupings (Row 5 + Row 10 + Row 15 + Row 20 + Row 25 = __13__). This is your raw score for "conscientious." Circle the number in the CONSCIENTIOUSNESS column of the Score Conversion Sheet that corresponds to this raw score.   22

5 3 1 3 1

6. Find the number in the far right or far left column that is parallel to your circled raw score. Enter this norm score in the box at the bottom of the appropriate column.

7. Transfer your norm score to the appropriate scale on the Big Five Locator Interpretation Sheet.

Tiger

5   2   2   2   1   =   12
4   5   4   5   2   =   20
1   1   1   2   1   =   6
3   3   4   5   1   =   16
4   5   5   4   4   =   22

Big Five Locator Score Conversion Sheet

Norm Score	Emotional Stability	Extroversion	Openness to Experience	Agreeableness	Conscientiousness	Norm Score
80						80
79			25			79
78						78
77	22					77
76			24			76
75						75
74						74
73	21		23			73
72		25				72
71				25		71
70	20	24	22			70
69					25	69
68				24		68
67		23	21		24	67
66	19					66
65		22		23	23	65
64			20			64
63					(22)	63
62	18	21	(19)	22		62
61					21	61
60		(20)				60
59	(17)		18	21	20	59
58						58
57		19				57
56			17			56
55	16	18			19	55
54			16	(19)		54
53						53
52		17			18	52
51	15					51
50		(16)	15	18	17	50
49						49
48	14	15			16	48
47			14	17		47
46		14			15	46
45			13			45
44	13			(16)	14	44
43		13				43
42			12			42
41				15	(13)	41
40	(12)	12	11			40
39						39
38				14	12	38
37		11	10			37
36	11					36
35		10		13	11	35
34			9			34
33	10	9			10	33
32				12		32
31			8			31
30		8			9	30
29	9			11		29
28		7	7		8	28
27				10		27
26		6			7	26
25	8		6			25
24				9	6	24
23						23
22			5		(22)	22
21	7	5				21
20				8		20

Enter Norm Scores Here: Adj = ____   S = ____   O = ____   A = ____   C = ____

(Norms based on a sample of 161 forms completed in 1993–94.)

Name __Michelle__   Date __Jan 9, 2006__

Big Five Locator Interpretation Sheet

Scores:

Emotional Stability	59	40
Extroversion	50	60
Openness to Experience	62	26 —
Agreeableness	54	44
Conscientiousness	41	—64

Strong Emotional Stability: secure, unflappable, rational, unresponsive, guilt free	Resilient Responsive Reactive 35 45 55 59 65	Weak Emotional Stability: excitable, worrying, reactive, high-strung, alert
Low Extroversion: private, independent, works alone, reserved, hard to read	Introvert Ambivert Extrovert 35 45 50 55 65	High Extroversion: assertive, sociable, warm, optimistic, talkative
Low Openness to Experience: practical, conservative, depth of knowledge, efficient, expert	Preserver Moderate Explorer 35 45 55 62 65	High Openness to Experience: broad interests, curious, liberal, impractical, likes novelty
Low Agreeableness: skeptical, questioning, tough, aggressive, self-interest	Challenger Negotiator Adapter 35 45 55 54 65	High Agreeableness: trusting, humble, altruistic, team player, conflict averse, frank
Low Conscientiousness: spontaneous, unconcerned with deadlines, adaptable, fickle, impulsive	Flexible Balanced Focused 35 41 45 55 65	High Conscientiousness: dependable, organized, disciplined, cautious, stubborn

Note: The Big Five Locator is intended for use only as a quick assessment for teaching purposes.

Source: The Big Five Locator is a quick assessment tool to be used with an instructor and willing learners. Care should be taken to follow up this profile with a more reliable personality assessment instrument. This instrument was developed by P. J. Howard, P. L. Medina, and J. M. Howard. "The Big Five Locator: A Quick Assessment Tool for Consultants and Trainers," from *The Annual, Developing Human Resources,* by J. William Pfeiffer and David Leonard Goodstein, Vol. 1, "Training," 1996, pp. 119–22. Reprinted by permission of John Wiley & Sons, Inc.

Exercise 1–B
Self-monitoring
Questionnaire

For the following statements, indicate the degree to which you think the following statements are true or false by circling the appropriate number. Use the following key as a guideline for scoring:

5 = Certainly, always true

4 = Generally true

3 = Somewhat true, but with exceptions

2 = Somewhat false, but with exceptions

1 = Generally false

0 = Certainly, always false

1. In social situations, I have the ability to alter my behavior if I feel that something else is called for.	5	4	3	2	1	0
2. I am often able to read people's true emotions correctly through their eyes.	5	4	3	2	1	0
3. I have the ability to control the way I come across to people, depending on the impression I wish to give them.	5	4	3	2	1	0
4. In conversations, I am sensitive to even the slightest change in the facial expression of the person I'm conversing with.	5	4	3	2	1	0
5. My powers of intuition are quite good when it comes to understanding others' emotions and motives.	5	4	3	2	1	0
6. I can usually tell when others consider a joke in bad taste, even though they may laugh convincingly.	5	4	3	2	1	0
7. When I feel that the image I am portraying isn't working, I can readily change it to something that does.	5	4	3	2	1	0
8. I can usually tell when I've said something inappropriate by reading the listener's eyes.	5	4	3	2	1	0
9. I have trouble changing my behavior to suit different people and different situations.	5	4	3	2	1	0
10. I have found that I can adjust my behavior to meet the requirements of any situation I find myself in.	5	4	3	2	1	0
11. If someone is lying to me, I usually know it at once from that person's manner of expression.	5	4	3	2	1	0
12. Even when it might be to my advantage, I have difficulty putting up a good front.	5	4	3	2	1	0
13. Once I know what the situation calls for, it's easy for me to regulate my actions accordingly.	5	4	3	2	1	0

Scoring Key:
Add up the circled numbers, except reverse the scores for questions 9 and 12. On those, a circled 5 becomes a 0, 4 becomes a 1, and so forth. High self-monitors are defined as those with scores of 53 or higher.

Source: Based on R. D. Lennox and R. N. Wolfe, "Revision of the Self-monitoring Scale," *Journal of Personality and Social Psychology,* June 1984, p. 1361. Copyright © 1984 by the American Psychological Association. Adapted with permission.

Exercise 1–C
The Social Mirror

To recognize the potential inaccuracy or incompleteness of the "social mirror," or others' opinions about you as a person, take a moment to reflect on how the social mirror has affected you. Use the questions as a guide. Reflect back on all aspects of your life: personal (dealing with family and friends, roommates, neighbors, significant others), academic (teachers, coaches, classmates), and professional (bosses, co-workers, subordinates, mentors) to examine what influences others have had on your self-image and other areas of importance to you (community, religion, sports, etc.).

1. What would others say about you that is generally positive?

   _____

   _____

   _____

   _____

   _____

2. What "constructive suggestions" would others offer to help you improve or change?

   _____

   _____

   _____

   _____

   _____

3. What do you most like about yourself?

   _____

   _____

   _____

   _____

   _____

4. What do you most dislike in yourself and would like to change?

   _____

   _____

   _____

   _____

5. What beliefs do you have about yourself that limit you?

   _____

   _____

   _____

   _____

6. How might these beliefs have been created or influenced by your social mirror?

   _____

   _____

   _____

   _____

7. Since it is possible—perhaps even likely—that these weaknesses or limitations are more imagined than real, what could you do to turn them into strengths?

_____

_____

_____

_____

Source: This exercise is adapted from Stephen Covey's *Seven Habits of Highly Effective People,* Leadership Training Manual.

**Exercise 1–D
Selective Perception**

How does selective perception affect the interpretation of what we see and hear?

_____

_____

_____

Your instructor will read two scenarios. Following the reading of each situation, write in the appropriate column what you see and hear from the description (what picture comes to mind?), what judgments you make or conclusions you draw about the situation, and what (if any) actions you would take.

Scenario One:

_____

_____

_____

Scenario Two:

_____

_____

_____

What I see/hear:	My judgment:	What actions I would take:
1.		
2.		

Questions to be considered individually and discussed in small groups:

1. Why do we interpret the same scenario differently from others?

2. What impact does this have on developing relationships?

3. What if in scenario one the person you "met" was a woman? How would your interpretation of the situation change?

4. What if in scenario two, the person with the daughter was her mother instead of her father? Or perhaps the discussion was between a father and his son? How would your interpretation of these situations change?

5. Why is it important to know what our biases are?

6. Let's say it's three years in the future. You've been working for a *Fortune* 500 firm as a member of a product development team. The meeting is about to start when a man matching the description in scenario one walks in. What's your judgment? Why?

7. As the meeting proceeds, he's about to open his mouth. Before he speaks, do you assume that he is credible or not credible until proven otherwise?

8. How do our biases help/hinder us in the workplace?

Exercise 1–E
Journal Writing

Journal writing has been used by educational disciplines, career coaches, and analysts for years. Developing reflective skills can lead managers and students to increased self-awareness, responsibility, and accountability as well as aid students to relate concepts and theories to practice.

In a separate notebook, keep an ongoing journal to record your thoughts, perceptions, insights, and goals for future interpersonal development. An entry should follow each class session or topic area. Your instructor will select the entry format and inform you of the collection dates.

The length of the entry is up to you. You should not be writing to impress; this is for your own personal learning and development. Write whatever you want, your ideas, feelings, and reactions relevant to the interpersonal skill being discussed. Your entry may be either negative or positive, as long as you try to be genuine and authentic. What you write should represent what you felt, thought, or learned that seemed important to your development. Entries might include such areas as these:

- Insights gained or concepts being explored.
- Reactions to the instructor, course, or other participants.
- Feelings/thoughts about yourself related to the course content, participants, and so on.
- Questions raised, resolutions made, things tried, risks taken.

Begin your first entry by doing a personal analysis based on your current perceptions of your interpersonal skills. Answer the following questions to give yourself a basis to compare your future development.

1. How would you describe your overall interpersonal effectiveness?

2. How would you describe your interpersonal relationships? Write about your best and worst relationship.

3. What are your personal strengths regarding interpersonal skills usage?

4. What are your weaknesses regarding interpersonal skills usage?

5. What are your goals for interpersonal development?

Every subsequent journal entry should include the following:

- The date.
- The interpersonal area being covered.
- A reevaluation of your strengths and weaknesses.
- What you have learned regarding the skill area or yourself or personal improvements obtained.
- Goals and action steps for future growth and development.

Source: From Robert Loo and Karran Thorpe, "Using Reflective Learning Journals to Improve Individual and Team Performance," *Team Performance Management* 8, no. 5/6 (2002), pp. 134–40. Reprinted with permission of Emerald Group Publishing Limited.

Exercise 1–F
Expanding
Self-awareness

1. Identify a behavior of yours that you would like to change. Practice a different form of that behavior for one week. For example, if you constantly interrupt others, try to go a week without interrupting others. Keep a record of every time you change this behavior. Reward yourself at the end of the week for being conscious of the need to change. Attempt a different behavior in week two. And so on.

2. Observe a person you admire at work or in school off and on for several days. How would you describe their attitude? What evidence do you have of this? What can you do to emulate their positive qualities?

3. Write on a sheet of paper adjectives that you wish could describe your personality. Identify some ways in which you could make changes to incorporate these qualities into your interactions with others.

4. Ask a few close friends for feedback about you as a person, your strong qualities, and areas you could change.

5. Reflect upon the last time you found yourself under a lot of pressure. How did you react? Respond? Behave? Develop a plan to help you think clearly in future situations to have a more controlled and less emotional response. For example, if you usually have a physical response when you get angry, think of an alternative means to handle your anger.

Exercise 1–G
Reflection/Action Plan

This chapter focused on self-awareness—what it is, why it's important, and how to acquire and increase the degree to which you possess it. Other elements which comprise the self, including personality, attitude, and emotional intelligence, were also discussed. Complete the worksheet below upon completing all reading and experiential activities for this chapter.

1. The one or two areas in which I am most strong are:

_____

_____

_____

_____

2. The one or two areas in which I need more improvement are:

_____

_____

_____

_____

3. If I did only one thing to improve in this area, it would be to:

_____

_____

_____

_____

4. Making this change would probably result in:

_____

_____

_____

_____

5. If I did not change or improve in this area, it would probably affect my personal and professional life in the following ways:

_____

_____

_____

_____

2

Self-disclosure and Trust

_____ ## Learning Points

How do I:
- Improve my relationships by sharing my thoughts and feelings?
- Learn to trust others, especially when trust has been broken?
- Determine the appropriate amount to disclose to others?
- Use situational cues to guide self-disclose and trust?
- Share my feelings about and reactions to people and situations, in addition to facts?
- Demonstrate that I am worthy of others' trust?

Mary Townsend has been on the fast track at the investment firm for which she has worked for five years. She entered graduate school shortly after graduating with honors from an elite university in the northeast. While in graduate school she interned with an investment firm in New York City that was at the time coheaded by John White, a close friend of the family. During her tenure at the firm, she exceeded all performance expectations and rose to the rank of vice president within three years. Now in line for another promotion, her performance has slacked off. Her record is inconsistent. One minute she appears to be at the top of her game, the next she is preoccupied and unreliable.

Her immediate supervisor, Jane Montgomery, has tried to talk with Mary about her inconsistent performance, to no avail. Jane, a director in the firm, placed a call to John White. John no longer heads the firm but often serves as a sounding board to senior management on important personnel and client issues in his role as senior partner. Jane has requested that John meet with Mary.

After an initial greeting, John praises Mary for her past performance with the firm and then expresses concern over her current performance. Mary responds by revealing that she feels she is in over her head. "Promise not to tell anyone," she pleads, and begins to discuss numerous personal incidents that are affecting her performance such as the breakup of a long-standing romance, financial problems brought on by overextending her credit, and a falling out with her family over their concerns about her lack of interest in getting married, having children, and settling down.

While sympathetic, John is dismayed at what he learns from Mary about her troubles. He concludes Mary's personal problems are detracting from her ability to focus on her job. John recommends to Mary's supervisor that she be let go as soon as a "legitimate" opportunity presents itself. One such opportunity is the upcoming announcement that due to the growth of online investment companies, the firm will be less reliant on the individuals at Mary's level.

1. What could Mary have done to minimize the degree to which her personal problems spilled over into work?

2. Did Mary disclose too much about herself, setting herself up for a negative recommendation from John? How would you have handled this situation?

3. Did John overstep his bounds in his conversation with Mary about her performance? What about the promise he made to her?

"Trust no one. Not your closest advisors, your spouse, your brother, your God. Trust only yourself, or you will face pain every day of your life."

These harsh words were spoken by the Egyptian king portrayed by Yul Brynner in the epic Cecil B. de Mille movie, *The Ten Commandments.* Fortunately, times have changed and we now know better! While it is good advice to not be too trusting early on in a relationship, the best relationships—in life and in business—are those that are built on mutual trust. Trust is built through a combination of shared experiences over time and willingness to talk with others about aspects of yourself that are relevant to your relationships. This chapter discusses self-disclosure and trust, their meaning and importance in life and in business.

What Is Self-disclosure?

Self-disclosure is the process of letting others know what you think, feel, and want. It is revealing to another how you are reacting to the situation and sharing experiences that are relevant to that situation.[1] By revealing information about yourself, others with whom you associate are better able to understand what makes you tick—your motivations, fears, work style, strengths, and weaknesses. This knowledge helps others to determine strategies for working effectively with you. In addition, as you self-disclose, others reciprocate, enabling you to better develop strategies for understanding and working effectively with them. To be effective, self-disclosure includes these elements:[2]

■ Feelings more than facts—When you share your feelings about or reactions to others, let them get to know the real you. Saying you have three co-workers is interesting information, but revealing the kind of relationship you have with them helps others get to know you better.

■ Greater breadth and depth over time—Have you ever cared about someone but felt uncomfortable sharing your feelings? In order for self-disclosure to facilitate building a relationship, it has to grow gradually in depth (becoming more revealing about your feelings toward a particular issue or set of issues) and breadth (expanding discussion to cover more issues, such as work, family, leisure, and religious beliefs).[3]

■ A focus on the present rather than the past—While sharing about your past might help explain why you behave the way you do, it is not advisable to share all your past skeletons. Doing so might feel cathartic, but it also might leave you feeling vulnerable, especially if this disclosure is not reciprocated. Stay in the present.

■ Reciprocity—To the degree possible, try to match the level of self-disclosure offered by people with whom you become acquainted. Be careful not to overdisclose prematurely, before the relationship has had time to build familiarity and trust. At the same time, if others are not forthcoming, it is not necessary to hold out until they self-disclose. Don't be afraid to take the first important step to building a relationship. Lead by example, and others will follow suit. If they don't, pull back.[4]

Self-disclosure is different from self-description. **Self-description** is the disclosure of nonthreatening information such as age, address, major, or organization for which you work. Self-disclosure is revealing selected information about yourself that is not easily transparent to others, such as how you feel about issues that are important to you. Not surprisingly, self-disclosure has an element of risk. At times, you may share information that might affect others' perceptions and acceptance of you as a person. For every action, there is a reaction, and in the case of self-disclosure, the benefits far outweigh the risks. People who engage in healthy, give-and-take dialogue with others are good managers of other people and of their relationships with others.

Benefits of Self-disclosure

The many benefits to self-disclosure accrue to both individuals and the relationships between individuals. Individuals who self-disclose reap psychological and physiological benefits. By self-disclosing and reciprocating others' self-disclosure, we can improve our communication and relationships with others.

■ Sharing with others about ourselves or problems we are facing often brings an enormous sense of psychological relief. Think about a time you did poorly on an exam or ended a relationship with a significant other. How did you handle the situation? Some go for a long walk, cry, sleep, or exercise; most will eventually talk to a friend or loved one. Through disclosing to others, we gain an added perspective that helps us see our disappointment or frustration in a different light.

■ Disclosing to an appropriate person (one who is sympathetic, supportive, trustworthy, and a good listener) can help us validate our perceptions of reality. By hearing ourselves talk, we process thoughts that are in our heads that help us to better understand the current situation in which we are involved. Often this brings with it a self-validation that tells us that either our thoughts are on the right track or our thoughts and perceptions need some tweaking. Imagine you are distraught over a strained customer interaction and fear that the customer will cease to do business with your firm. Being new to the firm, you are unsure how management will respond to this "error" and decide to get a co-worker's opinion on the situation. You disclose the situation and your concerns with her; she responds by not only agreeing with how you handled the situation but also by providing information that this customer has a reputation for "being difficult." You can see how self-disclosure can open us up to new information about ourselves that improves our ability to look at the world through realistic—rather than idealistic—lenses.

■ Self-disclosure can also help reduce stress and tension. By "getting things off your chest," you feel as if a burden has been lifted. If a customer was verbally abusive toward you or a co-worker took credit for your contributions, you are likely to bottle up your feelings in the interest of appearing professional. However, should these feelings remain unexpressed, you might explode! By sharing your problems or concerns with others, you might find ways to resolve them. Even if you find no resolution, you might feel relieved that you are not alone in your feelings—misery loves company. This intimacy brings us closer to others and increases our comfort in knowing that stress reduction through self-disclosure is available now and in the future in our relationships.

■ Self-disclosure also improves us physiologically. By sharing ourselves with others, our stress levels go down, lowering anxiety and altering vital signs such as heart rate and blood pressure. By positively affecting the mind–body connection, the case can be made that self-disclosure actually can lead to better physical—and emotional—health. This concept is one of the core tenets of counseling and hot-line/crisis-prevention programs.

■ Self-disclosure can result in clearer lines of communication with others. By showing our willingness to self-disclose, and encouraging others to share self-information with us, we improve our ability to understand diverse perspectives and viewpoints. We become more confident in our ability to clarify others' intentions and meanings, and in giving feedback and having open discussions that minimize uncertainty and confusion.

■ Self-disclosure can lead to strengthened, enhanced relationships. As co-workers get to know each other, disclosure leads to liking, which leads to more disclosure, which leads to more liking—a cyclical effect. Without self-disclosure, the level of intimacy and trust will be lower than in a group that discloses freely and appropriately. With disclosure comes trust, and with trust comes collaboration among co-workers.[5] Such collaboration and trust is essential to innovation, which is critical for organizations to compete and survive.[6]

■ Research shows that the more co-workers enjoy working together, the more productive they can be on projects and in team situations. For example, when working as a team under a tight deadline, knowledge of each other's work styles can help a team pull together and produce a top-quality project even when operating under time pressure. Conversely, a team that has not gotten to know each other will have difficulty pulling together on a tough assignment. This explains why team-building—processes and activities undertaken to help team members identify with each other and the team as a whole—is strongly endorsed by many organizations.[7]

■ Self-disclosure can create a trusting environment that is conducive to promoting long-term relationships with employees, customers, and suppliers. By building relationships through mutual self-disclosure, employees and management will develop open lines of communication. Open communication is essential in dealing with and managing conflict, making effective decisions, and enhancing organizational culture. Self-disclosure between customers and suppliers will open the doors to long-term relationships critical for the future viability of an organization.[8]

We are accustomed to sharing information with people in our lives with whom we are intimate: our parents, loved ones, and close friends. The lesson here is that even in work situations, it is important for project team members and co-workers to get to know each other personally. Naturally there are limits to what is expected and to what is appropriate. There is no need to disclose information of such a personal nature that it becomes awkward or embarrassing for you or your co-worker. And given the prevalence of sexual harassment incidents, we are all well-advised to restrict our disclosing to "safe" subjects. A rule of thumb to use is this: If the information would help a co-worker or colleague better understand how to work with you in the present, then the information is probably relevant and should be disclosed. If the information has little or nothing to do with the project you are working on, your ability to do the job, or your work style, it is probably less relevant and does not need to be shared.

Fears Associated with Self-disclosure

Only recently has self-disclosure been encouraged in business. As organizations become less hierarchical and more team-based, employees have less structure and fewer authority figures to rely on, increasing their need to work collaboratively in making decisions and getting things done. In other words, we can't rely on bosses to issue directives and achieve results based on sheer possession of authority. Collaboration depends to a certain extent on trust. And trust is fostered through self-disclosure.

What does this mean for those who are shy or reserved? Or who come from families in which self-disclosing was frowned upon? Or who are afraid to disclose themselves to others? Or for people who have been hurt by disclosing information to others who have used it against them?

There are several reasons why individuals are uncomfortable or hesitate to disclose information about themselves to co-workers. First there is uncertainty about how the information is going to be received and utilized. Will it be used against them in a performance appraisal? Will it be revealed to others outside the immediate work situation? Some are afraid of being judged harshly by others, concerned that things said in one context might be repeated in an unrelated context. Others have had previous negative experiences with self-disclosure in personal situations, affecting their willingness to be open in work situations. It is quite common early in an intimate relationship to reveal much about oneself before the other person is willing to open up. One says "I love you" and the other, now feeling threatened by the implied commitment, says nothing, causing the original discloser to withhold any further disclosure. Or, perhaps you revealed something personal to someone only to have that person violate your trust by disclosing the information to someone else.

Sometimes managers fear self-disclosure because they are concerned that others, especially subordinates, will perceive their willingness to share as a weakness or a shortcoming, leaving them vulnerable. Paradoxically, those managers who are willing to self-disclose are usually viewed very favorably by their co-workers. This happens because subordinates are able to see the manager as more human—complete with strengths and vulnerabilities—than before, allowing subordinates to feel closer to and interested in their manager.[9]

The benefits of self-disclosure far outweigh the concerns. If you are not used to talking about yourself to others, you will want to start slowly and with people you can trust. As you get to know a person or members of a group, gradually reveal information that helps others understand how to work effectively with you. As they disclose to you, you can increase your level of disclosure accordingly. By following your instincts about what is appropriate and relevant you will eventually find that it feels quite natural to talk about yourself with others. Soon you will find your project team members and co-workers will appreciate getting to know you, and that together you will be able to produce results beyond what was possible when you—and they—were more reserved.

Some Guidelines for Self-disclosure

- Discuss situations as they happen; don't wait until they are old news. The impact of your disclosure will be greater and more understandable within the context of your relationship when you share your thoughts and reactions to situations at the time instead of days, weeks, or months later. For example, if you are a member of a team evaluating a new computer system for potential adoption, withholding your concerns about the viability of this new system might prove problematic. On the one hand, you are concerned that others may look at you as too rigid or unable to accept change. However, you may have information or concerns that, if shared, would completely alter the decision-making process—in a way that would benefit your organization.
- Choose the appropriate time and place. Just as you may not choose to propose marriage in a crowded bar or noisy restaurant, you wouldn't want to tell your boss of your need for personal time right after he shares news that the department is being downsized.
- Choose the appropriate level of disclosure. Similar to the time and place, you need to match the depth and breadth of your disclosure to the situation. You would be ill-advised to reveal your innermost dreams and fears to your boss on the first day of your new job.
- Share feelings and thoughts rather than facts—move from self-description to self-disclosure as appropriate.

The Role of Self-disclosure in Increasing Self-awareness

We have discussed the many benefits of self-disclosure in the business world. While it is important to disclose to others, it is equally important to be honest with ourselves about our strengths and weaknesses. Sometimes this is difficult because we see ourselves differently than others see us or because we're not completely in touch with our inner selves—who we really are, what we believe, and how we come across to others. A concept that explains why this is true is the Johari Window.[10] Created by Joseph Luft and Harry Ingram, the **Johari Window** helps us understand how well we know ourselves and how much of ourselves we let others know. The Johari Window is depicted in Figure 2–1 in a grid that is divided into four regions, which represent the intersection of two axes:

1. Degree to which information about you (values, attitudes, beliefs) is known to or understood by you, and

2. Degree to which information about you is known to others

The basic premise of the Johari Window is that our personal and professional relationships can be greatly improved through understanding ourselves in depth and then selecting those aspects of self that are appropriate to share with others. The authors believe that the more

Figure 2–1
The Johari Window

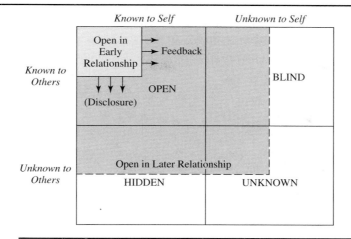

we share of ourselves with others, the more we can develop high-quality relationships. In order to complete this exchange, we must be fully aware of those aspects of ourselves that are "hidden" from view and those that we neither see nor know ourselves.

The **open area** consists of information about us that is known to us and to others, such as our name, job title or role, level in the organization, and possibly something about our personal life such as our marital status or the college from which we graduated. When we first begin a relationship, the open window is relatively small. We begin with safe information, such as the weather, school, and sports. As we build a relationship, we disclose more facts and feelings about ourselves and our beliefs, and the window enlarges vertically, reducing the hidden area. The larger the open area, the more productive and mutually beneficial the interpersonal relationship is likely to be.

The **hidden area** comprises information that we know about ourselves but is hidden from others. This information can range from our concerns about a boss or job to financial, family, or health problems. Not sharing hidden information can create a barrier that protects a person in the short-term. Over time, this lack of sharing can lead to distrust and miscommunication. In business this can have negative consequences such as reduced trust and morale. As we increase our comfort with and practice disclosing more and more information about ourselves through shared experiences with others, the hidden area shrinks. If we are more reserved, this area will remain rather large, resulting in relationships that aren't likely to develop beyond the acquaintance level.

The **blind area** denotes information that others are aware of but we are not. For example, we might have an unknown nervous habit of tapping a pencil or wiggling a foot during meetings when we are feeling stressed or bored. We might see ourselves as patient and helpful, yet our subordinates see us as micromanagers. As we receive feedback from others on their observations of our personalities and behaviors, the blind area will decrease and the open area will become more complete. The more we understand our strengths and weaknesses and are open to others' views of us, the better managers we can be of our personal and work lives.

The **unknown area** contains information that is unknown by us and by others. This window is unknown due to our lack of experience or exposure to various situations, or due to our inability to process difficult events that occurred earlier in our lives. Until we have experienced certain things in life, we will not fully know how we will react or feel. Until others have seen us in certain situations or we have disclosed to them how we behaved or felt, this information will remain unknown to them. For example, the first time you felt you loved someone (other than a family member), you may have found those feelings hard to express. How you express love may be unknown to you and to your significant other. This unknown window can also contain information that is forgotten or purposely suppressed. This window can become smaller over time as we grow, develop, and learn. Personal growth is a process. Self-awareness allows us to assimilate our experiences and move beyond them, rather than being unaware of, or worse, paralyzed by them. It also allows us to move forward in a positive way as we experience life and learn from both our successes and our mistakes.

What Is Trust?

By adding trust to self-disclosure, we are able to complete the relationship equation. The two elements form a cycle: the more you trust the more you disclose, and the more you disclose the more you trust. How do we define trust? **Trust** is a multifaceted concept that captures one's faith or belief in the integrity or reliability of another person or thing. In business, as in life, trust is an essential building block in developing relationships with customers, colleagues, and business associates. Think of a relationship you've had where trust has been broken. Perhaps a promised raise didn't materialize, a client misrepresented his or her financial situation, or a friend informs you that your significant other—who was attending a conference in another state—was seen with someone else. Isn't it difficult to relate to that person now or believe that person's promises? Does the lack of trust make you less inclined to make plans or have anything to do with this person?

Trust is essential for mature relationships. According to Schindler and Thomas, trust is composed of five elements.[11] (See Figure 2–2.) You are more likely to be seen as trustworthy if you demonstrate these characteristics:

- **Integrity**—honesty and sincerity. In short, you say what you mean and mean what you say. Integrity also relates to your ability to honestly disclose and share your thoughts, beliefs, and feelings.

- **Competence**—knowledge and ability. You are aware of your strengths and limitations, offering help where you can and seeking resources and assistance when needed.

- **Consistency**—conformity with previous practice; good judgment in handling situations. When you are consistent, for example, you do what you say you will do; friends and associates believe in your ability to follow through and do the right thing in a given situation.

- **Loyalty**—faithfulness to one's friends and ideals. A trustworthy person supports friends and associates both within and outside their presence. One who sings your praises in front of you but then spreads rumors behind your back is not only duplicitous but also untrustworthy.

- **Openness**—not closed to new ideas; willing to share ideas with others. This component of trust suggests that you are aware of yourself and comfortable sharing and disclosing with others. In addition, when someone shares with you, you encourage them and offer acceptance and support, as opposed to judgment and ridicule.

Figure 2–2
Five Elements of Trust

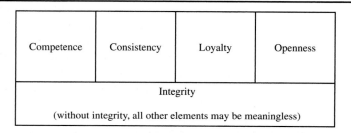

Competence	Consistency	Loyalty	Openness
Integrity			
(without integrity, all other elements may be meaningless)			

Personal Trust-Builders   There are some tangible things we can do to build up others' trust in us. Some of these include the following:

- Follow through on promises and commitments made; and its converse—don't promise what you can't produce.
- Don't reveal confidences told you in private.
- Avoid participating in unnecessary gossip about specific individuals.
- Don't make self-flattering or boasting statements about your capabilities.
- Develop a reputation for loyalty—a willingness to stand by, protect, and save face for others.
- Be consistent: reliability and predictability help others build faith in your ability to deliver on promises made.
- Be realistic: don't overcommit to the extent that you break promises.
- Develop personal competence; when you improve your knowledge and skills people can count on you to hold up your end of the bargain.
- Gain a reputation for honesty and truthfulness: "say what you mean and mean what you say."
- Make sure your actions are consistent with your spoken words: "walk the talk."

While an essential component of good relationships, trust does not come without some element of risk.[12] The riskiness of trust is evident in the following definition: Trust is the "willingness of a party to be vulnerable to the actions (whether words, conduct, or decisions) of another party based on the expectation that the other will perform a particular action important to the trustor."[13] Trusting is a two-way street. The person who places confidence in an individual must rely on that person to treat the information that was given in confidence. The element of risk is compounded by the inability of the truster to monitor or control the other party. For this reason trust is best when built up over time. As we gain experience with the judgments and behaviors of others, we can gradually build confidence in their ability to follow through on commitments and keep their word.

The development of trust in relationships may be affected by the attribution theory (discussed in Chapter 1).[14] As defined, the bias of the fundamental attribution error causes individuals to overestimate the influence of internal factors on the behavior of others. Since trust in relationships is directly impacted by the behaviors of others, we tend to determine that a trustworthy or untrustworthy action by a friend or co-worker was controlled by them rather than the situation. Because this bias greatly impacts individual perception, it is easy to see how quickly trust can be destroyed. Managers must be aware of their judgments and attributions to clearly determine if a perceived untrustworthy behavior warrants the loss of trust in a co-worker. Perhaps it had nothing to do with your relationship and instead simply resulted from the situation.

The Role of Trust in Organizations

Trust is essential in the work environment. Clients and customers need to be able to rely on information obtained from a company and its employees. Subordinates need to be able to trust their managers, managers need to be able to trust senior management, and everyone needs to be able to expect consistent reactions from their co-workers and associates. Trust is—and trustworthy behaviors such as those listed above are—a necessary foundation for a healthy work environment. Without trust, employees become overly protective of themselves and their immediate work environment, choosing to withhold information and avoid taking risks.[15]

Trust impacts the effectiveness of internal and external communication and influences the actions of organizational stakeholders. Since we argue that trust belongs in interpersonal relationships, we must examine the development of trust in organizations by looking at two levels of impact: individual and organizational.

■ *Individual impact*—The role of trust in organizations begins at the individual level. Trust is what binds leaders and followers together. In order to build trust, communication and action must be consistent. By demonstrating trustworthiness through open and honest communication, establishing a framework for organizational values and ethics, and creating a strong vision and purpose for the organization, leaders can foster trust.[16]

■ *Organizational impact*—All the current corporate scandals have led to distrust of corporate America. In truth, it is not the organizations that are untrustworthy (we cannot trust an institution); rather it is the individuals working for the organizations that cannot be trusted. When organizational members violate trust with stakeholders, organizations lose confidence from stakeholders.[17] Losing confidence and integrity can lead to the eventual demise of the institution.[18] In order to regain the trust of employees, stockholders, and the general public, leaders must first prove they are trustworthy, hence regaining integrity and confidence for their organizations.

Organizational Trust-builders

Organizations with low or no trust are susceptible to high turnover, rumor-mongering, low productivity, and increased absenteeism. These behaviors often exist in organizations going through a merger or acquisition. As the products, services, employees, and cultures of two or more companies are joined together, clashes inevitably result. The more openly and effectively each company can communicate with its employees about the changes as they occur, the better the employees will be able to adjust and move forward in their work on behalf of the newly merged organization. Research shows that those companies that make information available to their employees are more successful at achieving their business goals than are those companies that keep their employees in the dark or misrepresent information to them.[19] Organizational cultures associated with trust emphasize[20]

■ Depth of relationships.

■ Understanding of roles and responsibilities.

■ Frequent, timely, and forthright communication.

■ Member self-esteem and self-awareness.

■ High levels of skill competence.

■ Clarity of shared purpose, direction, and vision.

■ Honoring promises and commitments.

Ten Managerial Tips for Developing Trust[21]

1. Practice what you preach—narrow the gap between your intentions and your behavior.
2. Open lines of communication—declare your intentions to others and invite feedback on your performance.
3. Accept disagreements, differences of opinion, and conflict—when things go wrong and problems arise, seek out solutions.
4. Keep confidential information confidential.
5. Let others know what you stand for and what you value.
6. Create an open environment—make it safe for others to be with you and to share with you.
7. Maintain a high level of integrity and honesty.
8. Know yourself and how others perceive you and your actions—build on your competencies and accept your limitations.
9. Build credibility with others by being consistent and reliable.
10. Avoid micromanaging—this sends the message that "I don't trust you."

A Note of Caution

Trust is not a right; it is earned. Trust is person-dependent. That is, we do not automatically trust every individual in every situation. Perhaps we might trust certain but not all aspects of a person. If your co-worker supports you, is loyal to you, and holds sensitive issues in confidence, you will trust her. However, if your co-worker reveals that she has been unfaithful in her relationship with her spouse, suddenly her trustworthiness becomes suspect. Perhaps you have faith in your boss's wisdom and leadership, but the idea of him watching your pet while you're out of town makes you uneasy.[22]

Our ability to trust is also situation-dependent. Trust depends on our having the information and experience needed to make good judgments in a given situation or situations.[23]

Trust is earned. It evolves over time, based on past successful experiences that build on each other to eventually build a climate of trust. Trust is fragile. It is easier to destroy than it is to build. Consider the couple who have been married for 10, 20, or more years. One untrustworthy act could destroy decades of trusting behaviors, with trust likely never to fully return. By valuing and fostering trust and trustworthiness in your personal and professional relationships, you will be able to build mutually satisfying, long-term relationships in both your work and life.

Summary

Self-disclosure and trust are two mutually reinforcing skills that, when practiced with the appropriate persons at the right time and place, can serve to deepen and improve personal and professional relationships. By letting another person know your values and your beliefs about and reactions to a situation, you not only improve your own understanding and concerns about a situation, but also improve the quality of communication, collaboration, and performance with that person. There are fears and risks associated with disclosure, however; knowing what, when, and how to disclose can serve to mitigate the fears and risks.

By letting others know you, you pave the way for them to develop trust in you. When others trust you, they are more likely to disclose to you. The mutually reinforcing nature of disclosure and trust forms the basis of healthy personal and professional relationships. Organizations that are characterized by a lack of trust, such as the case during times of change (i.e., downsizing and mergers), become primed for employee gossip, absenteeism, and turnover. By practicing the tips and techniques we shared, you can improve your comfort level and skills in self-disclosure and trust.

Key Terms and Concepts

Blind area

Competence

Consistency

Hidden area

Integrity

Johari Window

Loyalty

Open area

Openness

Self-description

Self-disclosure

Trust

Unknown area

Endnotes

1. David W. Johnson, *Reaching Out: Interpersonal Effectiveness and Self-actualization* (Boston, MA: Allyn & Bacon, 2000), p. 46.

2. Johnson, *Reaching Out,* pp. 46–47.

   3. Irwin Altman and Dalmas A. Taylor, *Social Penetration: The Development of Interpersonal Relationships* (New York: Holt Rinehart and Winston, 1973).

   4. Valerian J. Derlega and J. Grzelzk, "Appropriateness of Self-Disclosure" in *Self-Disclosure: Origins, Patterns, and Implication of Oneness in Interpersonal Relationships,* ed. G. J. Chelune (San Francisco: Jossey-Bass, 1979), p. 151–76.

   5. B. H. Sheppard, "Negotiating in Long-Term Mutually Interdependent Relationships among Relative Equals," in R. J. Bies, R. J. Lewicki, and B. H. Sheppard (Eds.), *Research on Negotiation in Organizations* 5 (Greenwich, CT: JAI Press, 1995), pp. 3–44.

   6. Deborah G. Ancona and David F. Caldwell, "Demography and Design: Predictors of New Product Team Performance," *Organization Science* 3 (1992), pp. 321–41.

   7. Jon R. Katzenbach and Douglas K. Smith, "The Wisdom of Teams," *Small Business Reports* 18, no. 7 (July 1993), pp. 68–71.

   8. Richard S. Jacobs, Michael R. Hyman, and Shaun McQuitty, "Exchange-specific Self-disclosure, Social Self-disclosure, and Personal Selling," *Journal of Marketing Theory and Practice* 9, no. 1 (Winter 2001), p. 48.

   9. Irvin D. Yalom, "It's Lonely at the Top—Isolation as a Problem for CEOs," *Inc.* 20, no. 5 (April 1, 1998), pp. 39–40.

   10. Joseph Luft, *Of Human Interaction* (Palo Alto, CA: National Press, 1969).

   11. P. L. Schindler and C. C. Thomas, "The Structure of Interpersonal Trust in the Workplace," *Psychological Reports,* Oct. 1993, pp. 563–73.

   12. N. Luhmann, *Trust and Power* (New York: John Wiley, 1979).

   13. R. C. Mayer, J. H. Davis, and F. D. Schoorman, "An Integrative Model of Organizational Trust," *Academy of Management Review* 20 (1995), pp. 709–34.

   14. Donald L. Ferrin and Kurt T. Dirks, "The Use of Rewards to Increase and Decrease Trust: Mediating Processes and Differential Effects," *Organization Science* 14, no. 1 (Jan./Feb. 2003), p. 18.

   15. Robert D. Costigan, Salem S. Ilter, and J. Jason Brown, "A Multidimensional Study of Trust in Organizations," *Journal of Managerial Issues* 10, no. 3 (Fall 1998), pp. 303–18.

   16. Carol Stephenson, "Rebuilding Trust: The Integral Role of Leadership in Fostering Values, Honesty and Vision," *Ivey Business Journal Online,* Jan/Feb 2004, p. 1.

   17. Linda R. Weber and Allison Carter, "On Constructing Trust: Temporality, Self-disclosure, and Perspective Taking," *International Journal of Sociology and Social Policy* 18, no. 1 (1998), p. 7.

   18. Simon Webley, "Risk, Reputation, and Trust," *Journal of Communication Management* 8, no. 1 (2003), p. 9.

   19. Costigan, Ilter, and Brown, "Multidimensional Study of Trust."

   20. Jeffrey Cufaude, "Creating Organizational Trust," *Association Management* 51, no. 7 (July 1999), pp. 26–35.

   21. Robert Glaser, "Paving the Road to TRUST," *HR Focus* 74, no. 1 (Jan. 1997), p. 5.

   22. The complexity of trust explains why U.S. public opinion was divided during the 1999 Clinton impeachment hearings. Many believed in Clinton's competence as a leader but questioned his morals and integrity.

   23. Keith J. Blois, "Trust in Business to Business Relationships: An Evaluation of Its Status," *Journal of Management Studies* 36, no. 2 (March 1999), p. 197.

**Exercise 2–A
People Hunt**

Mill around the classroom and identify people who can help you complete the following chart.[1] Write the names of the people you identify in the "match" columns. Try not to use the same person more than three times in your chart. Challenge yourself to meet and talk with as many people as possible.

Information	Match 1	Match 2	Match 3
Same height as you within two inches: _____			
Uses the same toothpaste as you. Toothpaste brand: _____			
Uses the same shampoo as you. Shampoo brand: _____			
Has the same color eyes as you: _____			
Same favorite fast food: _____			
Same favorite color: _____			
Same number of siblings: _____			
Same hometown or country: _____			
Same favorite TV show: _____			

After completing the chart, answer the following questions:

1. In what ways did this exercise help you get to know others better?
2. What did you learn about yourself from this exercise?
3. What things do you and don't you have in common with others?
4. What additional items can be asked to uncover other similarities between you and others?
5. How can you apply this exercise to improving your relationships with others?

[1]If this is a distance learning class, students should use whatever means available to identify people who match your information.

**Exercise 2–B
Icebreakers**

Name, Face, and Fact

Participants sit in a circle and the first person states his or her name and a fact related to him or her. Facts can include items from the following categories: favorite food, hometown street name, college major, favorite color, favorite book, favorite travel destination, and so on.

Name Repetition

Participants stand in a circle and, taking turns, each person says her or his name. Participants then throw a ball to another member in the circle, each stating her or his name first followed by the name of the person to whom she or he is throwing the ball. Each time a person receives the ball, his or her name is stated as well as that of the person who threw the ball.

Name Tags

Participants write their name in the center of a piece of paper. In each corner of the paper participants write personal information such as where they are from, their college major, their ideal job, their favorite travel destination, their favorite movie/TV show/book, and so on. Participants mill about the room and introduce themselves to as many others as possible in the time allowed, being sure to listen intently to what each person is disclosing to others.

Show and Share

Participants bring in a personal item—an item that reveals something significant about their personal "essence" or identity. The item can be something the participant enjoys, carries at all times, is of sentimental value, or that holds some personal meaning. Participants show and discuss the meaning behind the object. Others give feedback on what they think the item says about the participant as well as share how they can personally relate to the other's show-and-share item.

Multiple Introductions

Participants stand and mill about the room, introducing themselves to one new person every two minutes. The instructor asks the class to concentrate on one question at a time per person met. After two minutes, the instructor calls time and the participants introduce themselves to a new partner and engage in a two-minute discussion about the next topic on the list. Suggested topics, which can be written in advance on a board, include these:

1. Your college major and why you chose it.
2. What you did last summer (and what you wished you had done instead!).
3. Why you chose the college you're attending or attended.
4. Your first job and what you liked, disliked, and learned about it.
5. A favorite hobby or nonschool, nonwork activity.
6. What you would do (and in what priority order) if you won the lottery.
7. Your favorite book, TV show, Broadway play, or movie and why.
8. Your favorite travel destination.
9. What you would do if you didn't have to work for a living.
10. What you liked about this exercise—and what you didn't—and why.

Exercise 2–C
Fishbowl

A fishbowl is a clear glass container we can see through and into from every angle. The fishbowl exercise is designed to help participants identify personal things that others can see and that they feel comfortable disclosing to others. This activity may be done in small groups or in front of the class.

Inside the fishbowl is an assortment of small cards, each containing a topic. Participants select a card and present a short (1–2 minutes) impromptu talk regarding an experience they have had relating to the topic. Participants use as many descriptors as possible to allow everyone to be able to understand and relate to the situation. Participants should be as expressive as they can be, telling a story, emphasizing their feelings and those of the other people involved in the story, and including their and others' reactions to what was occurring. Participants should include this information:

- A description of the players—all those involved in the situation.
- Information about the setting, atmosphere, surroundings, and so on.
- Details about the situation as it occurred.
- Thoughts and feelings they had about the experience as it unfolded.
- Outcomes, including lessons learned, awareness gained, and others.

Note: If this exercise is being done outside of a classroom, participants should pair up with a friend at school or work and take turns sharing stories as explained above.

Sample fishbowl questions (your instructor has more):

- Your happiest/saddest holiday memory.
- Your most/least enjoyable travel experience.
- An accomplishment you worked hard to attain.
- A lesson you learned in childhood that remains with you to this day.
- A time when you felt angry/happy/embarrassed/lucky.
- A memorable experience from grade school.
- A time you realized you were more like your mother/father than you care to admit.

Exercise 2–D
Johari Window
Questionnaire

Friendship Relations Survey

This questionnaire was written to help you assess your understanding of your behavior in interpersonal relationships. There are no right or wrong answers. The best answer is the one that comes closest to representing your quest for good interpersonal relationships. In each statement, the first sentence gives a situation and the second sentence gives a reaction. For each statement indicate the number that is closest to the way you would handle the situation.

5 = You *always* would act this way.
4 = You *frequently* would act this way.
3 = You *sometimes* would act this way.
2 = You *seldom* would act this way.
1 = You *never* would act this way.

Try to relate each question to your own personal experience. Take as much time as you need to give a true and accurate answer for yourself. *There is no right or wrong answer. Trying to give the "correct" answer will make your answer meaningless to you. Be honest with yourself.*

	Never				Always
1. You work with a friend, but some of her mannerisms and habits are getting on your nerves and irritating you. More and more you avoid interacting with or even seeing your friend.	1	2	3	4	5
2. In a moment of weakness, you give away a friend's secret. Your friend finds out and calls you to ask about it. You admit to it and talk with your friend about how to handle secrets better in the future.	1	2	3	4	5
3. You have a friend who never seems to have time for you. You ask him about it, telling him how you feel.	1	2	3	4	5

4. Your friend is upset at you because you have inconvenienced him. He tells you how he feels. You tell him he is too sensitive and is overreacting.   1 2 3 4 5

5. You had a disagreement with a friend and now she ignores you whenever she's around you. You decide to ignore her back.   1 2 3 4 5

6. A friend has pointed out that you never seem to have time for him. You explain why you have been busy and try for a mutual understanding.   1 2 3 4 5

7. At great inconvenience, you arrange to take your friend to the doctor's office. When you arrive to pick her up, you find she has decided not to go. You explain to her how you feel and try to reach an understanding about future favors.   1 2 3 4 5

8. You have argued with a friend and are angry with her, ignoring her when you meet. She tells you how she feels and asks about restoring the friendship. You ignore her and walk away.   1 2 3 4 5

9. You have a secret that you have told only to your best friend. The next day, an acquaintance asks you about the secret. You deny the secret and decide to break off the relationship with your best friend.   1 2 3 4 5

10. A friend who works with you tells you about some of your mannerisms and habits that get on his nerves. You discuss these with your friend and look for some possible ways of dealing with the problem.   1 2 3 4 5

11. Your best friend gets involved in something illegal that you believe will lead to serious trouble. You decide to tell your friend how you disapprove of his involvement in the situation.   1 2 3 4 5

12. In a moment of weakness, you give away a friend's secret. Your friend finds out and calls you to ask about it. You deny it firmly.   1 2 3 4 5

13. You have a friend who never seems to have time for you. You decide to forget her and to start looking for new friends.   1 2 3 4 5

14. You are involved in something illegal, and your friend tells you of her disapproval and fear that you will get in serious trouble. You discuss it with your friend.   1 2 3 4 5

15. You work with a friend, but some of her mannerisms and habits are getting on your nerves and irritating you. You explain your feelings to your friend, looking for a mutual solution to the problem.   1 2 3 4 5

16. A friend has pointed out that you never seem to have time for him. You walk away.   1 2 3 4 5

17. Your best friend gets involved in something illegal that you believe will lead to serious trouble. You decide to mind your own business.   1 2 3 4 5

18. Your friend is upset because you have inconvenienced him. He tells you how he feels. You try to understand and agree on a way to keep it from happening again.   1 2 3 4 5

19. You had a disagreement with a friend, and now she ignores you whenever she's around you. You tell her how her actions make you feel and ask about restoring your friendship.   1 2 3 4 5

20. A friend who works with you tells you about some of your mannerisms and habits that get on his nerves. You listen and walk away.   1 2 3 4 5

21. At great inconvenience, you arrange to take your friend to the doctor's office. When you arrive to pick her up, you find she has decided not to go. You say nothing but resolve never to do any favors for that person again.   1 2 3 4 5

22. You have argued with a friend and are angry with her, ignoring her when you meet. She tells you how she feels and asks about restoring the friendship. You discuss ways of maintaining your friendship, even when you disagree.   1 2 3 4 5

23. You have a secret that you have told only to your best friend. The next day, an acquaintance asks you about the secret. You   1 2 3 4 5

call your friend and ask her about it, trying to come to an
understanding of how to handle secrets better in the future.

24. You are involved in something illegal, and your friend tells you   1 2 3 4 5
of her disapproval and fear that you will get in serious trouble.
You tell your friend to mind her own business.

Friendship Relations Survey Answer Key

In the Friendship Relations Survey there are 12 questions that deal with your willingness to
self-disclose and 12 questions that are concerned with your receptivity to feedback. Transfer your scores to this answer key. Reverse the scoring for all questions that are starred; that
is, if you answered 5, record the score of 1; if you answered 4, record the score of 2; if you
answered 3, record the score of 3; if you answered 2, record the score of 4; and if you
answered 1, record the score of 5. Then add the scores in each column.

Willingness to Self-disclose	Receptivity to Feedback
*1. ____	2. ____
3. ____	*4. ____
*5. ____	6. ____
7. ____	*8. ____
*9. ____	10. ____
11. ____	*12. ____
*13. ____	14. ____
15. ____	*16. ____
*17. ____	18. ____
19. ____	*20. ____
*21. ____	22. ____
23. ____	*24. ____
Total ____	Total ____

On the Friendship Relations Survey Summary Sheet, add your score and your group's
average score for receptivity to feedback and willingness to self-disclose.

Friendship Relations Survey Summary Sheet

Draw horizontal and vertical lines reflecting your (Part *a*) and the group's (Part *b*)
receptivity to feedback and willingness to self-disclose scores. The results should look
like the Johari Window.

	Your Score	Group Average Score
Receptivity to Feedback:	_____	_____
Willingness to Self-disclose:	_____	_____

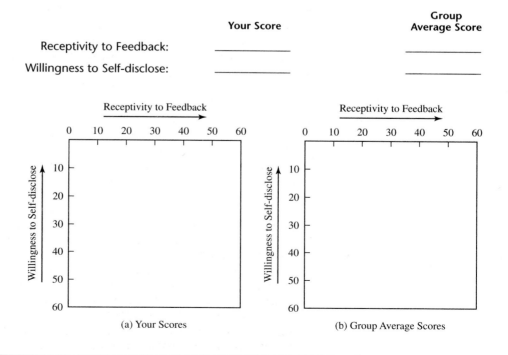

(a) Your Scores   (b) Group Average Scores

Exercise 2–E
Circle of Friends

It is important to examine our interpersonal relationships to determine whether the levels of disclosure and trust we have enhance the relationships we value.

1. In the first column, list the people closest to you in different categories: family, friends, co-workers (include classmates, teammates, or professors), and others (anyone with whom you have a valued relationship and are in frequent contact).

2. In the second column, rate your level of trust with each individual on a scale of 1–5, with 1 having very little trust and 5 having a high degree of trust.

3. In the third column, rate your level of disclosure with the individual on a scale of 1–5 with 1 being very low, dealing with trivial and nonthreatening information, and 5 being a high level of highly personable and sensitive information.

4. In the fourth column, write comments as to the quality of the relationship, such as a comparison on congruency between trust and self-disclosure and notes as to what you want and need to do to improve the relationship.

Name of Individual	Level of Trust (1–5)	Level of Self-disclosure (1–5)	Comments on the Relationship
(Family Members)			
(Friends)			
(Co-workers)			
(Others)			

Look over your completed chart and answer the following questions:

1. Is there a correlation between the level of self-disclosure and the level of trust? Why or why not?
2. How satisfied are you with the level of trust and disclosure in your relationships?
3. In what ways are the relationships progressing the way you want them to?
4. How can you improve the level of disclosure or trust in each of the most important relationships?

Exercise 2–F
Trust-building
Activities

The following two activities are designed to expose participants to—and build their comfort level with—trusting others.

Blind Walk

Working in pairs, participants will take turns leading each other around. One member closes his or her eyes, with his or her eyes remaining closed for the entire turn. The other member leads him or her around by the arm. The member should take the participant to as many different places as possible, incorporating other sensory experiences such as touch, smell, and hearing. Participants should then alternate and allow the other member to experience being "blind."

Trust Meal

In pairs, participants share a meal while one member is blindfolded. The sighted member leads the blindfolded partner through the meal, explaining and/or answering any questions or concerns. The blindfolded person may choose to request assistance or attempt to eat without help.

Questions

1. What was comfortable/uncomfortable about each of the above exercises?
2. What were your feelings as you were going through each role in each exercise?
3. What did you learn about yourself and others through each exercise?

Exercise 2–G
Ideal Cards: A
Self-disclosure
Activity

1. Students get into groups of five to seven members.
2. The instructor distributes play money and two Ideal Cards to each participant.
3. The instructor explains the following ground rules for buying, selling, or trading Ideal Cards before the exchange phase is begun:
   a. Each individual *must* sell or trade at least one of his/her Ideal Cards sometime during the entire experience.
   b. Each individual *may* buy, sell, or trade Ideal Cards within his/her group. Cards may be bought or sold for any mutually agreed-upon price or traded outright.
4. Participants trade cards within their subgroups.
5. When the trading within subgroups is completed, the instructor announces that participants may exchange cards (in accordance with the rules) with any other person in the room.
6. Following the activity, reflect silently on the following questions:
   a. What were the original Ideal Cards you received? Why did you want to keep/trade them?
   b. How much money did you have at the end of the experience?

    c. Were you more interested in obtaining meaningful Ideal Cards or in accumulating the most money possible?

    d. Which Ideal Cards did you most wish to obtain? Why?

    e. Are you satisfied with the Ideal Cards you now have? Why or why not?

7. Now discuss your reactions to these questions in your original group.

8. The instructor leads a discussion of the entire experience.

Examples of Ideal Cards

1. To persevere in what I am doing.
2. To be honest.
3. Never to be worried about having enough food.
4. To be a member of the opposite sex.
5. To be needed and to be important to others.
6. To have better feelings about myself.
7. To have a better relationship with God.
8. To be a good conversationalist.
9. To have my opinions respected.
10. To develop my potential.

Your instructor has more.

Source: J. Pfeiffer & J. E. Jones, *The 1975 Annual Handbook for Group Facilitators,* University Associates, 1975. Copyright © 1975 by John Wiley & Sons, Inc. Reprinted by permission of John Wiley and Sons, Inc.

**Exercise 2–H
Disclosure and
Trust in Action**

1. Watch a television show or movie (or read a book) in which trust plays a large part—perhaps trust is broken (e.g., *The Little Mermaid, Working Girl, Liar Liar, The Firm*) or is built over time (e.g., *You've Got Mail,* the Helen Keller story). Describe the role that self-disclosure and trustworthiness played in either the building or destroying of trust. What are some lessons that could be learned and applied in your own life from these depictions? What are behaviors to be avoided?

2. Take someone with whom you would like to enhance your interpersonal relationship to your "special place" (somewhere you feel special, peaceful, content, or comfortable). Discuss with that person what is going on in your life and your feelings and reactions to the situations. Encourage the other person to take you to a special place to discuss what is going on with him or her.

3. Practice "trust-building." Be aware of trust behaviors you are trying to incorporate into your daily interactions with others. Once a week for a month, record the times you have consciously or unconsciously done things that build others' trust in you. Examples can include returning money you've found in a public place to the appropriate office, planning your time so as to be able to follow through on commitments, and keeping a secret told you by a good friend from a mutual acquaintance.

Exercise 2–1
Reflection/Action Plan

This chapter focused on self-disclosure and trust—what they are, why they are important, and how to increase your comfort and skill in using them. Complete the worksheet below upon reading and finishing the experiential activities for this chapter.

1. When do you think it is appropriate to receive feedback from and self-disclose to others?

_____

_____

_____

2. How comfortable are you with self-disclosure? What aspects are most difficult for you?

_____

_____

_____

3. How does trust affect your receptivity to feedback and willingness to give feedback?

_____

_____

_____

4. In what ways is your current use of trust and self-disclosure effective in your relationships with friends and loved ones?

_____

_____

_____

5. What specific changes about your self-disclosure and trusting behaviors would you make that would enhance relationships with your friends?

_____

_____

_____

6. If you made the changes listed above, what impact would this have on your relationships? Explain.

_____

_____

_____

3 Establishing Goals by Identifying Values and Ethics

Learning Points

How do I:

- Implement goal setting to achieve personal and professional goals?
- Clarify what is important to me: my values and needs?
- Develop a personal mission statement?
- Write effective goals?
- Make progress toward my goals, especially when I hit a roadblock?
- Evaluate options concerning ethical dilemmas?
- Know if I am making ethical decisions?

Marsha Smith was enjoying her work as an associate at a leading investment bank in New York. The hours didn't bother her. As the first person from her family to attend college, she was used to working hard for what she wanted in life. She had worked part-time all the way through high school and college to pay for tuition, room, board, and other immediate expenses. Now in her third year, she was contemplating her next career step. Most of her friends had moved on to graduate business school, but her boss had convinced her to stay on. With all the excitement over "new economy" growth clients, there was plenty of interesting work to go around. She was traveling overseas frequently, had a great set of friends, had a terrific boyfriend, and was enjoying her current situation. So what was troubling her? In the back of her mind Marsha realized she wasn't sure what she should do next. For possibly the first time in her life she didn't have to focus single-mindedly on one goal, such as paying for college. She now had multiple priorities in which she was interested. But she didn't have a clue as to how to start making plans to attain any one of them. Besides, she thought, "I'm always working anyway. How would I have time to even think of anything else? So it doesn't really matter that I'm not sure where I'm headed." Or does it?

1. What are the issues that Marsha is facing?
2. Should Marsha follow the rest of her friends to graduate business school?
3. Why is it difficult for her to set new priorities for herself?
4. What steps does Marsha need to take?

5. What advice would you offer Marsha?

6. How can Marsha set new goals and work toward them while fulfilling her obligations to her present position?

"If you don't know where you are going, you'll probably end up someplace else."

Yogi Berra

These words provide the premise for and reasoning behind setting goals. If we don't have a plan to direct our lives, where will we end up? Effective goal setting gives us direction and purpose while providing a standard against which to measure our performance. It also allows both individuals and organizations to have a clear understanding of what they are trying to accomplish. This chapter describes personal goal setting and values clarification: what goals and values are, the benefits of being aware of your goals and values, and how to improve your ability to set meaningful goals that are aligned with your core values. We also address how effective goal setting can help you set objectives and make plans for achieving these objectives in both your personal and your work life. At the end of the chapter are a number of exercises that enable you to assess your goal-setting skills and develop improvement plans.

What Is Goal Setting?

Goal setting is a means of identifying our work/life priorities and developing strategies for attaining personal and professional objectives. Consider the lives of successful people. Do they seem to have a strong commitment to their plans? Are they organized, efficient, confident, or well prepared? Most likely you answered yes to most if not all of these words. Successful individuals and organizations have learned that the key to achieving meaningful results is through effective goal setting.

For example, Jack Welch decided, shortly after graduating from college, that one day he wanted to be the CEO of General Electric (he achieved this goal 20 years after setting it!). Bernie Carlson, who anchored CNN's news desk for 20 years, decided at the age of 13 he wanted to be a network news anchor. Jerry Garcia, the infamous lead of the rock group The Grateful Dead, said he knew as a youngster he wanted to head a rock band. And Scott Adams, the successful "Dilbert" cartoonist, claims to have envisioned himself as the world's greatest cartoonist.

Contrast these goal setters with those who are unable or unwilling to set goals and achieve them. Consider people you know who seem to set goals frequently but never attain them. Are they realistic about what they can achieve? Do they have the required resources to attain their goals (e.g., time, money, or support from others)? Do they have the necessary capabilities, training, and education? Chances are they may not have one or more of these resources that are so important to success.

Why Is Goal Setting Important?

The goal-setting process has several benefits:

■ Morale/Esteem—Achieving goals gives you an internal reinforcement of your personal abilities. Successful goal completion broadens your belief in what you can accomplish.

■ Purpose/Direction—Establishing written goals formalizes our dreams and wishes. Through the process of careful examination and self-analysis, we begin to understand what we want to achieve. Goal setting defines the destination point while providing the map to lead us there. Writing goal statements and developing an action plan gives our life purpose and direction. These statements provide us with short-term motivation and long-term vision. Whether or not you are aware of your goals or strategies, they are affecting your life's direction. Once you bring them into consciousness and formalize them, you can guide your life more strategically.[1]

- Motivation—Goal setting helps us to build internal momentum. Through goal setting, we direct our actions toward fulfilling our dreams and ambitions. Usually this process starts by setting incremental steps to achieving a goal. If you want to run a marathon, you start your training by running in small amounts that increase over time. Momentum begins to build as soon as you set your goal, and continues as you take steps toward achieving it. To borrow from a physics principle, a person who sets goals becomes "an object in motion [that] remains in motion." Directing your life toward fulfilling dreams motivates you to achieve continual success.

- Productivity—Goal setting gives us a way to measure our success. Systematically setting goals provides balance and perspective to our decisions about how to allocate our time and resources. Having a clear plan of action greatly focuses the expenditure of time, money, and energy. Goal setting boosts performance to a higher level and helps in overcoming challenges. Up to a point, performance also increases with the level of goal difficulty, provided the individual working to attain the goal is committed to achieving it.[2]

Key Behaviors for Effective Goal Setting

The approach you use to set goals greatly affects your ability to be successful in attaining your goals. A few fundamental behaviors underpin most successful goal-setting efforts:

- Being Realistic—be honest with yourself about your skills and abilities and in evaluating all related conditions needed to attain your goals. You can only influence or change things over which you have control. Understand that there will be setbacks. Continually search for means to overcome obstacles and secure all necessary resources.

- Being Positive—we face obstacles and challenges in everything we do. The ability to maintain in the face of adversity is a key success factor in goal setting. Adopting an optimistic "can-do" attitude can give you the boost to continue the uphill climb. It is also helpful to describe goals in a positive tone; focus on achieving a positive rather than trying to eliminate a negative. For example, say, "I want to master this new version of a software program" rather than saying, "I need to improve my miserable computer skills."

- Starting Small—begin with smaller, simpler, more manageable goals. Successfully completing small goals will build confidence and create momentum toward future goal-setting behavior. Setting incremental benchmarks for marking your progress will make broader, long-term goals seem attainable.

- Taking Full Responsibility—even though you may need to solicit the help and support of others, you are in control of your actions. Set your goals with the understanding that you have the power to direct your energy toward personal productivity.

- Persevering—effective goal completion requires the ability to maintain strong forward motion. Perseverance is essential for successfully reaching every goal you want to achieve.

> *"Success is not measured by those who fought and never fell, but by those who fought, fell and rose again."*
>
> (Anonymous)

Clarifying Values

To determine what goals you want to achieve, start by clarifying your own values, those things in life that are most meaningful to you. **Values** are personalized views or deeply held opinions that guide chosen courses of action or judgments of outcomes. Our individual set of values is a result of learning and personal experiences. Values are influenced by family, friends, peers, religious beliefs, community, and even the organizations in which we are associated. Many of our values are deeply set and we make decisions or judgments without consciously reflecting on the source. Values can become a matter of habit.

Identifying your values will help you answer the question, "What do I want to achieve with my life?" How can you begin your career planning process without knowing your lifestyle preferences or having a clear sense of what values provide you with the most motivation? A recent survey showed that over half of the MBAs "would not work for a tobacco company for ethical, social, and political reasons."[3] Your values can have a direct affect on your behaviors, attitudes, and decisions. Setting and achieving goals that are congruent with your values will lead to increased satisfaction and positive personal feelings.

Once you determine your values and why they are important to you, you can then work on a plan for achieving your goals. For example, Marsha, in our case study, might write down some of the things that are important to her. These might include continued learning, spending time with family and friends, and being secure financially. This might explain why going to graduate school has not been her uppermost priority. She might be concerned about having to borrow money to pay the tuition, or about the time it would cause her to spend away from friends and family.

According to Milton Rokeach, a *value* is "an enduring belief that a specific mode of conduct or end-state of existence is personally or socially preferable to an opposite or converse mode of conduct or end-state of existence."[4] In other words, we work toward what we value—and our values guide our behavior. Rokeach identifies two general types of values contained in an individual's belief system: instrumental values and terminal values.[5]

- **Instrumental values** are the hows of goal setting—the standards of behavior by which we achieve desired ends. Courage, honesty, compassion, and loving are examples of instrumental values.

- **Terminal values** are the whats—the end states or goals that we would like to achieve during our lifetime. Such values include wisdom, salvation, prosperity, or sense of accomplishment.

Personal values are also tangible and intangible.

- **Tangible values** are things that you can see, feel, or hold, including the kind of car you want to drive, the level of income you want to have, the size of the house you want to own. Tangible values consist of the material things you want to possess.

- **Intangible values** deal with concepts rather than things. Freedom, independence, happiness, friendship, and love are intangible values and can be defined differently for each person. Intangible values consist of ideals you wish to strive toward or pursue.

Try This: Take a minute and write your definition of personal satisfaction. What are the behaviors you'll use to achieve this satisfaction? What will bring you enjoyment or fulfillment? Is this short term or long term? Which values are terminal, the things you must have accomplished? Which aspects of satisfaction are derived from your instrumental values? What aspects are tangible or intangible?
Now write your definition of success. What will you need to accomplish or attain in order to say you are a success in your life? Set these definitions aside for later reflection.

Writing Effective Goals

Developing personal goals begins with creating written goal statements. Written goal statements are the aims or the targets you want to achieve. These goal statements deal with various aspects of your life such as career, personal, financial, and so on. Objectives or an action plan should accompany every goal statement. The plan should specify the strategies needed or means for reaching your ends. For instance, our case example

Marsha could have as a goal "To achieve the level of vice president within the next two years." Her action plan could include talking with her boss about potential career options within the firm, taking extra courses at night to develop the technical skills needed to advance, and networking with several alumni from her college who work at the firm who are in senior positions to gain their support and advice.

One system used successfully by managers and others who wish to incorporate goal-setting principles into their lives is the "SMART" system.[6] *SMART* refers to a goal that is specific, measurable, attainable, realistic, and time-bound. By ensuring your goal statements are SMART, you create a system for managing action steps and increase the likelihood that these goals are attained. Use this approach as a checklist for writing your goal statements and action plan.

"SMART" Goal Writing

- Specific—write your goals, including as many details as possible, leaving no room for misinterpretation. Rather than writing, "I would like to be in better shape," define what "in better shape" means to you. Say "I want to lose 10 pounds," or "lower my cholesterol by 20 points," or "lower my blood pressure by 15 points." Specific goals are focused and incremental, giving clarity to your direction and purpose. Research has shown that individuals who set specific goals are more likely to develop plans for idea generation and subsequent actions.[7]

- Measurable—provide a means to measure your progress, a way to measure actual performance against desired performance standards. Set up checkpoints to evaluate your progress from the time you start to the time you expect to attain your goal. Write your goals in quantifiable terms, to determine to what extent you completed each goal and fulfilled each objective. For example, "I will write one essay per week to improve my writing skills."

- Attainable/Believable—set an actionable, believable goal. In addition to being fully dedicated, you also need the resources and capabilities required for attaining a goal. Goals that are believable have a much higher probability of success. Make sure you have secured all necessary resources and that you anticipate and develop a strategy for dealing with any obstacles that could bar your success. For example, say "I will raise my G.P.A. from a 2.5 to a 3.0. To do this I will get tested at the Learning Center to see if I have a learning disability."

- Realistic/Achievable—write your goals with consideration for your capabilities and limitations. A goal should be challenging enough that you stretch your abilities to gain attainment, but not so difficult that it is impossible to fulfill. Studies show "that given an adequate level of ability and commitment, harder goals will lead to greater effort and performance than easier goals."[8] Goals should also have realistic deadlines. Closely tied to the notion of realistic goals is the aspect of control. Only set goals that are within your means to achieve. Say "I will contact 10 percent more potential clients this week than usual," rather than "I will sell 10 percent more than usual this week." The former statement reflects things that are within your control as well as realistic. The latter reflects a desire about something that may not be totally within your control.

- Time Bound—develop a specific deadline for meeting each of your goals; otherwise they will remain dreams and never become reality. Setting a deadline creates a commitment to begin and pursue a goal until it is attained. Saying "I'd like to lose 10 pounds" is specific, measurable, and realistic, but without a target date for completion, you might find yourself continuously repeating "I'll start my diet tomorrow." Time bound also relates to attainable, as some goals may be unattainable within a compressed time frame, yet possible within a longer time frame. In fact, when setting goals that span a longer time horizon, it is best to establish incremental time frames to make long-term timeliness more manageable and acceptable. Plan a schedule or time frame for goal completion that is sufficient to allow you to achieve the goal, at the same time not allowing for so much slack time that you lose interest or focus.

Another important criterion that can be added to **SMART goals** is to make sure the goal is yours. Personal goals are just that, personal. You will be less likely to accept and complete goals that someone else gives you.[9] Goals should be a direct reflection of your values, aspirations, and life mission, not someone else's like your friends' parents', or roommates'. If you are pursuing an accounting degree because a parent believes it's a good solid career, yet you just don't see yourself as an accountant, you may want to reevaluate this goal. You are more likely to stick with and attain goals you desire than goals set for you by others. Likewise, when you are in a position to influence others such as subordinates or children, encourage them but let them set their own goals. When individuals set their own goals, they have a greater amount of intrinsic motivation to accomplish the goal, which leads to a higher percentage of positive results.[10]

Goal-setting Strategies

There are several strategic steps you can take to overcome potential pitfalls while ensuring progress toward achieving your goals.

1. *Visualize the outcome*—imagine being at the completion point of your goal. State your goals as if you have already accomplished them. Say things like "I am the owner of a Cadillac" or "I am the executive vice president of my advertising firm." Positive self-talk will reinforce your belief in your ability to live your dreams.

2. *Strive for performance, not outcomes*—throughout the process, you should strive to give 100 percent effort and to perform to the best of your ability. This will allow you to feel confident and proud of your smaller accomplishments. Barry Goldberg, the prominent TV producer (*Spin City, Family Ties*), says he has always focused on creating the best television program possible, seeking first and foremost to produce high-quality entertainment; money and success resulted as a by-product.

3. *Develop a support network*—determine the resources that will be necessary for you to achieve your goals. Obtain support and commitment from individuals who will be essential in ensuring your success. Associate with people who will support you in attaining your goals. If someone in your network is hindering your ability to accomplish your goals, reevaluate whether continued association with this person is desirable.

4. *Limit the number*—focus on a limited number of goals at a time. Having too many goals will only drain your resources and reduce the potency of your efforts. One way to do this is to focus on those goals that relate to your key roles at a point in time. Another way to do this is to create a master plan—a 10- or 20-year plan—in which you map out the pursuit of specific goals according to your personal and professional mission.

5. *Allow for setbacks*—we are all human. If you get sidetracked or make a mistake while trying to accomplish your goal, forgive yourself and get back to your plan. If you do not move on, you will never accomplish your goals. When experiencing a setback, it may be an appropriate time to tap into your support network. Let's say you are midway in achieving your goal to quit smoking over a three-month period when your favorite uncle is diagnosed with a terminal illness. You might find it difficult to cope with this tragedy without returning to your pack-a-day habit. At this point, you might choose to reevaluate and adjust your goal; you might also seek out friends or relatives who can help you get through this crisis.

6. *Be honest with yourself*—evaluate objectively how well you accomplish your goals and objectives. The only way you can improve is to understand what you did wrong and focus on how you can change. Ask yourself, "Why did my last semester go so badly?" or "Why were my grades so low?" You might answer yourself, "Poor study habits, lack of time or discipline, and lack of priorities."

7. *Reward small accomplishments*—once you have reached an incremental, objective step or milestone, provide yourself with a reward.[11] Celebrating your continual accomplishments will help to maintain your optimism and belief in your abilities while refueling your commitment and motivation to goal achievement.

8. *Don't lose sight of the big picture*—make a habit of reviewing your goals on a daily basis. Use positive self-talk to reinforce your beliefs and reiterate the purpose behind

your actions. Remain flexible yet diligent. Allow for necessary changes and restructure as needed while still working toward the ultimate end. Understand how everything you do facilitates your ability to complete your goal.

9. *Revisit the process*—goal setting is not a one-time action; it is an ongoing process. Your values, roles, and dreams may change. Your resources may need to be reevaluated or you may need to make adjustments to overcome unforeseen obstacles. Goals should remain fluid, enabling you to plan, react, and adapt to changing circumstances as needed.

The Impact of Ethics

In light of the recent corporate scandals, the ethics of individuals and organizations is being more closely scrutinized. Increasingly, people are demanding that organizations and their employees act in accordance with high ethical and moral standards. In evaluating an organization's behaviors and actions, we must first examine the practices, guidelines, and corporate culture that impact ethical behavior. Individuals' actions, decisions, and practices are influenced by their values and ethics.[12]

What Are Ethics?

The word **ethics** comes from the Greek word *ethos,* which means a notion of character permeated with values that determine the identity and good or bad of an individual or group.[13] "Ethics [is] not so much a matter of right or wrong as it is a process by which an organization evaluates its decisions."[14] The difficulty with ethics is that the situations we face as managers are seldom black and white, with a clear understanding of which answer is the best for all concerned. Each person has a different world view (based on life experiences, education, family background, religious and political affiliations, perceptions, and values) that they bring into the decision-making process. Each person possesses a different **"ethical barometer"**[15] that stems from his or her experience and background. This diversity affects the ethical decision-making process, outcomes, and the ramifications of the decision.

Ethics and character reflect on our true inner self; they determine how we respond to managerial dilemmas. Many choices appear to be minor, but in reality these actions build up over time and set a foundation for more challenging decisions.[16] It is important to be aware of the guidelines we use for making small decisions. These guidelines can affect the way we approach larger, more significant decisions in other areas of life and work.

Ethical Dilemmas

Ethics play a part in our decision making whether we are acting as an individual, a group, an organization, or a member within an organization. **Ethical dilemmas** are situations where we are faced with making a decision that will be based largely on judgments and determinations rather than on indisputable facts. Ethical dilemmas can be the result of gross misunderstanding; value conflicts; cultural differences; conflicts of interest; differences based on gender, economic level, religion, age, sexual orientation, upbringing, race or ethnicity; or greed. Examples of ethical dilemmas are exchange of inappropriate gifts, making unwanted sexual advances, discovery of unauthorized payments or overpayments, and hiring an untrained person from a "name" family over a more qualified individual.

An ethical dilemma arises when a manager must choose between his or her own interests and the interests of someone else or some other group. Those with an interest in the outcome of the decision are referred to as **stakeholders.** As a manager in an organization, it is up to you to take into consideration the needs and interests of all key stakeholders—the employees, customers, suppliers, and shareholders who are affected by the decision—in addition to yourself. Decisions you make reflect not only your values but also the values of the organization you represent. Decisions you make on behalf of your organization carry consequences for the company's reputation and success in the community.

Factors Influencing Ethics

When evaluating the ethical actions of organizations, it is important to remember that three factors influence behaviors and actions: the individual ethics of organizational members, the corporate culture of the organization, and society as a whole. Individuals must work within the environment of an organization that reflects the pressures from the external environment.[17]

Individual Ethics

Ethical behavior, being aligned with personal values, moral reasoning, and personal ideology, has a direct impact on goals and actions.[18] Studies have shown that instrumental values can influence ethical decision making. Honesty was found to be strongly related to judgments made in the workplace. Another significant finding showed that the more ambition individuals had, the less ethical they were in their intentions.[19] Values reflected in a person's behavior and personality can be the basis for professional behavior.[20]

Kohlberg's Moral Maturity:[21] To understand personal ethics, we need to understand morality, or a person's belief about his or her obligations. Building on the work of psychologist Piaget, Lawrence Kohlberg identified six stages of **moral development** and reasoning, which he grouped into three major levels.[22] Each level represents a shift in the social–moral perspective of the individual which explains how judgments affect action. Each level is also comprised of two stages and as an individual advances through each level, the second stage of that level shows greater growth and ethical character.[23] (See Figure 3–1.)

At the first level, the **preconventional level,** a person's moral judgments are characterized by concrete, individual perspectives. Behaviors are guided by self-interest to obey the rules in order to avoid punishment. At this level, organizational members follow rules out of fear and managers tend to be autocratic. Individuals at the second level, or **conventional level** of reasoning, have a basic understanding of the need to conform to societal standards, realizing that norms and conventions are necessary to uphold society. These members tend to identify with the rules, uphold them consistently, and behave in ways society defines as "right." Within this level, members collaborate and understand the need to fulfill obligations laid out by the organization. Mangers at this level tend to encourage cooperation and productive working relationships.

Finally, the **postconventional level** is characterized by reasoning based on personal values and principles. At the final stage, individuals will make ethical decisions based on personal judgments and not on societal norms. When faced with a conflict between a law and a personal core value, the individual's internal beliefs will guide the decision rather

**Figure 3–1
Stages of Moral
Development**

Postconventional Level

Stage 6: Universal ethical principles—acts are consistent with personal moral principles, seeking the greater good

Stage 5: Social contract—attempt to get social consensus and tolerance

Conventional Level

Stage 4: Social accord and system maintenance—meet expectations of society as expressed in laws

Stage 3: Interpersonal accord, conformity to group norms—act to meet expectations of peers or organization

Preconventional Level

Stage 2: Instrumental purpose and exchange—acting in one's own interest

Stage 1: Obedience and punishment—act to avoid consequences

than the law. Individuals at this level seek out new solutions and work independently while managers focus on the needs of the employees and empower them to reason for themselves.

Most managers and individuals function at the conventional or second level. Very few function at the higher, postconventional, level.[24] Since most organizational members function at the level where they take their cue for behavior from the organization, it is critical that organizations examine and reexamine their practices and set ethical standards to guide decision making.

Organizational Ethics

An organization's culture and practices have an impact on the values, attitudes, and behaviors of its members. Studies show that the internal environment, the organizational constraints and pressures as well as systematic practices, have a strong link to managers' decision making and behaviors.[25] Since it has been shown that most individuals function at the second or conventional level of morality, it is clear that members will conform to the standards the organization deems acceptable. Organizational processes created by top management must reflect an ethical "philosophy that filters through all levels of the organization."[26] Managers and organizational members must be shown that they in turn can influence change and "make a difference" in organizational culture.[27]

Ethical Decision Making

Have you ever witnessed someone cheating on a test? Have you ever called in sick when you actually went skiing or to the beach? Have you ever been given too much change and kept it? Every day we face situations where we have to make decisions for which there are no apparent, clear-cut rules. For example, concerns about Internet security fraud are on the rise. Securities firms are constantly on the lookout for employees who are involved in insider training. Recent surveys suggest that increasing numbers of applicants lie about their backgrounds in employment interviews. Employees are creating "intellectual capital" during their day jobs and selling their expertise as consultants after hours. And ordinary employees are being entrusted with valuable financial and strategic information to help them make on-the-spot judgments about how to handle difficult situations. Managers and employees are constantly faced with challenges such as these. An ethical framework for decision making is needed.[28]

Ethical decision making involves applying principles or standards to moral dilemmas. Asking what is right or wrong, good or bad in business transactions is a basic business ethic.[29] Ethics guide people in making decisions that are not completely based on factors that have already been specified. Ethics can present a different perspective and give a new dimension to decision making. For example, it might be obvious—on paper—that opening a new manufacturing center in the remote areas of the Florida wetlands would be profitable due to low cost factors. Yet the detrimental environmental effects on the wetlands would be significant. Should the company open a wetlands plant? It's legal, but is it "right"? Who should make this decision? The company? Or the people in the area who are advocates for the wetlands? How should this decision be made? Is profitability the only criterion that should be used in making this decision? What should the decision be? Who will be affected by the decision? Who pulls the plug if it's the wrong decision? These are all ethical considerations that make the decision much more complex than it originally appeared on paper. Your own character, and that of the organization for which you work, are revealed by the types of decisions you make, how you make them, and to what end. Ethical decision making guides you in making decisions that are right not just for you but for those who are affected by the decisions.[30]

Benefits of Ethical Decision Making

Many companies today are providing ethical guidelines or codes of conduct for their employees to use when faced with a situation that is not covered by standard policies and procedures. This practice has several benefits listed as follows.

■ *Customer relations:* Employees in companies with ethical guidelines are better prepared to treat customers fairly if a conflict arises. This helps customers feel employees respect and understand them, resulting in higher levels of customer satisfaction.

■ *Goodwill:* By doing the "right thing" consistently, consumers, suppliers and others in the community at large see your organization as a desirable one with which to do business. The ethical reputation of a firm can actually increase its opportunities and sales, as shown by Anita Roddick's company, The Body Shop.[32] Her decision to buy ingredients that might have gone to waste (good for the environment) from countries that are economically depressed (good for society) has been widely praised. Employees and customers have noted that decisions like these positively impact their continued association with and patronization of The Body Shop. A company's goodwill also enhances its attractiveness and value to potential employees and acquiring businesses.

■ *Employee satisfaction:* Employees in companies with ethical guidelines experience high comfort levels—they are pleased and relieved when they see their organization acting in an ethical way and actively promoting ethical behavior.[33]

■ *Employee empowerment:* Employees in companies with ethical guidelines feel empowered to think clearly about dilemmas at hand, to make decisions clearly, to articulate the rationale for their decisions, and to have the support of senior management if their judgment is questioned.[34]

Figure 3–2
Eight Rules of Ethical Thinking[31]

1. Consider others' well-being and avoid actions that will hurt others. Before taking action, ask yourself if anyone stands to be hurt by the action, financially, emotionally, and other ways.
2. Think of yourself as a member of a community, not as an isolated individual. Before taking action, reflect on who will be affected by the decision, positively and negatively.
3. Obey—but don't depend only on—the law. An action may be legal yet unethical.
4. Think of yourself and your organization as part of society. What you do and how you think affect a larger entity beyond you and your immediate circle.
5. Obey moral guidelines by which you have agreed to live. Consider them "categorical imperatives" with no exceptions.
6. Think objectively. Be sure your action is truly ethical and not rationalized self-interest.
7. Ask, "What sort of person would do such a thing?" Or, "Will I be able to look at myself in the morning after doing X?"
8. Respect others' customs—but not at the expense of your own ethics.

Ethics-enhancing Tools

Unfortunately, it is a fact that workers often accept unethical actions as the consequence of doing business today. Lapses in ethics are viewed as standard—expected in today's diverse, complex, and fast-paced world. One survey reported that 48 percent of workers surveyed said they respond to job pressures by performing unethical or illegal activities.[35] The most common unethical behaviors cited were these:

■ Cutting corners on quality control (16 percent).

■ Covering up incidents (14 percent).

■ Abusing or lying about sick leave (11 percent).

■ Lying to or deceiving customers (9 percent).

It is not easy to raise the ethical consciousness of an organization. Organizations are made up of individuals who may behave in an unethical manner for what they believe are justified reasons. When people are faced with pressures at work and need to make fast decisions, they are not very likely to consult rules, regulations, and policies that often don't apply to the specific situation with which the employee is dealing.[36] This leads to many of the ethical lapses that occur in business today. In addition, organizations themselves might have policies that encourage employees to make unethical decisions. For example, a company might set unrealistically high sales targets, possibly leading some employees to engage in questionable tactics to increase sales to customers.

Making ethical decisions is more a matter of having the right values than a set of rules. To help employees cope with the need to make ethical decisions, organizations must raise the employees' level of ethical consciousness. This starts by first declaring the organization's values and expectations, and then laying out guidelines and a decision framework that employees can use when faced with decisions that require use of judgment in addition to adherence to company guidelines. The following are some tools that companies can use to educate employees about ethical decision making.

- **Code of ethics:** A written statement of values and guidelines for how to treat employees and customers. Codes of ethics provide a tangible description of what the company stands for, what it wants to achieve, and the means for achieving its goals. Codes are a good first step in raising ethical issues, although on their own they are insufficient to ensure that organizational ethical standards are followed.[37]

- **Ethics test:** A series of questions that aids employees in making well-considered judgments about a situation before making a decision. Using this test will not provide one "correct" answer. The test provides criteria to be considered when determining if a course of action is ethical.[38] The test has four components:

  - The test of *common sense:* "Does this action I am about to take make sense?"

  - The test of *one's best self:* "Is this action or decision I'm getting ready to take compatible with my concept of myself at my best?"

  - The *"light of day"* approach or making something public: "How would I feel if others knew I was doing this? Would I be willing to stand in front of my family, friends, and peers and be proud to tell them what I had decided to do?"[39]

  - The test of the *purified idea:* "Am I thinking this action or decision is right just because someone with appropriate authority or knowledge says it is right?" For example, if an accountant told you it was ok to claim certain entertainment and travel expenses as business expenses, although there is doubt in your mind about the fairness of this determination, do you abdicate responsibility for this decision since the accountant said it was acceptable?

- **Ethical audit:** A broad-based, agreed-upon system that lets an organization consistently focus and refocus on its values and whether its performance is meeting the standards it professes. An ethical audit analyzes the situational and environmental factors that have significant impact on ethical behaviors and internal policies. These audits encourage self-reflection across all levels of an organization and raise ethical consciousness, leading to less unethical or corruptive behavior.[40]

- **Decision-making model:** Frameworks that employees can use to help make decisions about ethical actions by following a short, step-by-step list of rules.[41] Models in ethical guidelines, such as those shown in Figure 3–3, aren't a guarantee that employees will

Figure 3–3
A Sample of an Ethical Decision-Making Model[42]

Step 1: Identify the facts and issues
  a. Who will be affected by my decision?
  b. What will be the short- and long-term consequences of possible courses of actions?

Step 2: Identify applicable values
  a. How will possible courses of action impact potential stakeholders?
  b. What consideration should I have with regard to:
    The rights of stakeholders?
    Justice among stakeholders?
    The short- and long-term balance of good among stakeholders?
    My gut feeling about what is the "right thing"?
    What I think those whom I respect for their virtue would judge to be "the right thing"?

Step 3: Seek help if needed
  a. Which course of action might keep me awake at night?
  b. Can my supervisor or human resources department provide guidance?

Step 4: Reach the best decision based on the available information
  a. Is my decision legal and within organizational policy?
  b. Do organizational values and my personal values support my decision?

always act ethically. They are a means to get employees to think through their actions and consider the ethical standards involved when making decisions that affect them and those around them.

■ **Ethics training:** For any of the above ideas to work in organizations, companies can offer their employees training about the company's policies and values and how to incorporate an ethical component into their decisions on an everyday basis. This training can be provided via a manual, a workshop, a Web-based self-directed program, or one-on-one mentoring and coaching sessions.

Summary

This chapter focused on goal setting (why it's important, how to set goals, and how to achieve goals) and the importance of values and ethics in the goal-setting process.

Having an understanding of our values and ethical beliefs is the foundation for the decisions we make in our daily lives. These decisions have an impact on our future as well as an impact on the organizations in which we work. Refer back to your definitions of success and satisfaction. Through the process of writing your goals and action plans, are you now on the right road to securing these values? If not, what changes should you make to get there?

The late management practitioner, W. Edward Deming, believed that approximately "two of 100 managers and 10 of 100 workers were happy in their work."[43] Since we spend almost a third of our time working, understanding our values and making our goals a reality become essential to living a fulfilled life. Use your goal-setting skills to enhance and guide your life. Consider incorporating goal setting as a fundamental part of your daily life. Challenge yourself to move to the next dimension. As Walt Disney said, "If you can dream it, you can be it."

Key Terms and Concepts

Code of ethics	Instrumental values
Conventional level	Intangible values
Decision-making model	Moral development
Ethical audit	Preconventional level
Ethical barometer	Postconventional level
Ethical decision making	SMART goals
Ethical dilemmas	Stakeholders
Ethics	Tangible values
Ethics test	Terminal values
Ethics training	Values
Goal setting	

Endnotes

1. Edwin E. Bobrow, "Goal Oriented Selling," *American Salesman* 41, no. 1 (Jan. 1996), p. 22.

2. Shawn K. Yearta, Sally Maitlis, and Rob B. Briner, "An Exploratory Study of Goal Setting in Theory and Practice," *Journal of Occupational and Organizational Psychology* 68, no. 3 (Sept. 1995), p. 237.

3. Douglas W. Lyon and Eric G. Kirby, "The Career Planning Essay," *Journal of Management Education* 24, no. 2 (April 2000), p. 279, in reference to a study by S. Courter, "Tomorrow's Captains of Industry Rate Gates Almost as High as DaD," *Wall Street Journal,* May 14, 1998, p. B1.

4. Milton Rokeach, *The Nature of Human Values* (New York: Free Press, 1973).

5. Rokeach, *Nature of Human Values.*

6. Robyn D. Clarke, "Going for the Goal," *Black Enterprise* 29, issue 6 (Jan. 1999), p. 83.

7. P. C. Earley, P. Wojnaroski, and W. Prest, "Task Planning and Energy Expended: Exploration of How Goals Influence Performance," *Journal of Applied Psychology* 72 (1987), pp. 107–114.

8. Yearta, Maitlis, and Briner, "Exploratory Study."

9. Wendy Warren, "First Step in Finding Success Is Deciding What Route You Want to Take," *Knight-Ridder/Tribune Business News,* Jan. 2, 1996.

10. Oriel F. Strickland and Mark Galimba, "Managing Time: The Effects of Personal Goal Setting on Resource Allocation Strategy and Task Performance," *Journal of Psychology* 135, no. 4 (July 2001), p. 357.

11. Susan B. Wilson, "How Good Are You at Setting Goals?" *Executive Female,* July–August, 1994, p. 73.

12. Sarath Nonis and Cathy O. Swift, "Personal Value Profiles and Ethical Business Decisions," *Journal of Education for Business* 76, no. 5 (May/June 2001), p. 251.

13. Tom Maddix, "The Essence of Ethics," *CMA Management,* Nov. 1999, p. 20.

14. Arthur Gross Schaefer and Anthony J. Zaller, "Why Ethics Tools Don't Work," *Nonprofit World,* March 1, 1999, p. 42.

15. Maddix, "Essence of Ethics."

16. Curtis C. Verschoor, "What's Ethical? Here's a Simple Test," *Strategic Finance,* March 2000, p. 24.

17. See Irene Roozen, Patrick DePelsmacker, and Frank Bostyn, "The Ethical Dimensions of Decision Processes of Employees," *Journal of Business Ethics* 33, no. 2 (Sept. 2001), p. 87; and Patrick E. Connor and Boris W. Becker, "Personal Value Systems and Decision-making Styles of Public Managers," *Public Personnel Management* 32, no. 1 (Spring 2003), p. 155.

18. B. S. Sridhar and Artegal Camburn, "Stages of Moral Development of Corporations," *Journal of Business Ethics* 12, no. 9 (Sept. 1993), p. 727.

19. J. Finegan, "The Impact of Personal Values on Judgements of Ethical Behavior in the Workplace," *Journal of Business Ethics* 13 (1994), p. 747.

20. Bruce L. Oliver, "Comparing Corporate Managers' Personal Values over Three Decades, 1967–1995," *Journal of Business Ethics* 20, no. 2 (June 1999), p. 147.

21. L. Kohlberg, "Moral Stages and Moralization: The Cognitive-developmental Approach." In T. Lickona (ed.), *Moral Development and Behavior: Theory, Research and Social Issues* (New York: Holt, Rinehart and Winston: 1976), pp. 31–53; and L. Kohlberg, *Essays on Moral Development,* Vol. 1: *The Philosophy of Moral Development* (San Francisco: Harper and Row, 1981).

22. Ibid.

23. Ibid.

24. James Weber and David Wasieleski, "Investigating Influences on Managers' Moral Reasoning," *Business and Society* 40, no. 1 (March 2001), p. 79.

25. Kelly C. Strong and G. Dale Meyer, "An Integrative Descriptive Model of Ethical Decision Making," *Journal of Business Ethics* 11, no. 2 (Feb. 1992), p. 89.

26. Jeanne M. Logsdon and Kristi Yuthas, "Corporate Social Performance, Stakeholder Orientation, and Organizational Moral Development," *Journal of Business Ethics* 16, no. 12/13 (1997), p. 1213.

27. Christine A. Hemingway and Patrick W. Maclagan, "Managers' Personal Values as Drivers of Corporate Social Responsibility," *Journal of Business Ethics* 50, no. 1 (March 2004), p. 33.

28. Ronald R. Sims, "The Challenge of Ethical Behavior in Organizations," *Journal of Business Ethics* 11, no. 7 (July, 1992), p. 505.

29. J. W. Weiss, *Business Ethics, A Stakeholder and Issues Management Approach,* Second Ed. (Philadelphia: The Dryden Press, 1998).

30. Maddix, "Essence of Ethics," p. 20.

31. Schaefer et al., adaptation from Robert C. Solomon and Kristine Hanson, *It's Good Business* (New York: Atheneum, 1985).

32. Joanne Martin, *Cultures in Organizations: Three Perspectives* (New York: Oxford University Press, 1992).

33. Schaefer et al., *It's Good Business.*

34. Curtis C. Verschoor, Lawrence A. Ponemon, and Christopher Michaelson, "Values Added: Rules and Values in Ethical Decision Making," *Strategic Finance,* Feb. 2000, p. 24.

35. Elaine McShulskis, "Job Stress Can Prompt Unethical Behavior," *HR Magazine,* July 1997, p. 22.

36. Verschoor, "What's Ethical?"

37. Schaefer et al., *It's Good Business.*

38. Verschoor, "What's Ethical?"

39. Ibid.

40. Schaefer et al., *It's Good Business.*

41. Verschoor, "What's Ethical?"

42. Ibid.

43. John Tschohi, "The Qualities of Successful People," *Managing Service Quality* 9, no. 2 (1999), p. 78.

Exercise 3–A
Values Inventory

1. From the list below, choose five items that are most important to you. Rank the top five items according to your current values. This is only a partial list; fill in the (other) blanks with items that are of personal value to you. Give the most important item a 1, the next most important a 2, and so on.

Values	Current	5 years	10 years	30 years
Security				X
Financial independence			X	
Having children		X		
Owning a home		X		
Free time		X		
Recognition or fame				
Friendships	X			
Helping others less fortunate than you	X		X	
Family	X		X	X
Travel		X	X	X
Having the respect of others				
Playing sports				
Having an interesting job or career				
Having good physical health	X		X	X
Being a knowledgeable, informed person				
Having a sense of accomplishment				X
Spiritual fulfillment				
Doing well in school	X	X		
(other)				
(other)				

Values
Family
Travel
Health
School
Helping Others
Priorities

2. From the same list, indicate in the columns which values would comprise your top five ranking in 5 years, 10 years, and 30 years. Look back over your rankings. Does anything surprise you? Were there any drastic changes from the present through 30 years?

3. In examining your current values, how do these fit in with the way in which you currently allocate your time? Do these values fit in with your dreams, goals, ambitions, and life principles?

4. What major, unanticipated event could cause you to modify your rankings (serious illness, business failure, marriage, etc.)? Discuss how this event would impact your rankings.

Exercise 3–B
"This Is Your Life"—A Personal Goal-setting Exercise

Fast-forward your life video and contemplate a celebration dinner (roast) to honor you. Imagine it is years into the future and we are celebrating your accomplishments at a retirement dinner. Assume that each of the following will deliver a speech: family member, close friend, business or professional associate, community or religious representative.

How would you prefer to have these people think about, see, and perceive you and your actions? Identify the main points each would make in your honor. What would you ideally like to have said concerning your accomplishments, relationships with others, contributions to society, and so on?

Family Member's Speech

_____

_____

_____

Close Friend's Speech

_____

_____

_____

Business or Professional Associate's Speech

_____

_____

_____

Community or Religious Representative's Speech

_____

_____

_____

From reviewing the speeches, is there a common thread or theme? Write a phrase or caption that would summarize your life principle.

_____

_____

_____

Source: Adapted from Stephen Covey, *Seven Habits of Highly Successful People: Powerful Lessons in Personal Change* (New York: Simon and Schuster, 1989).

**Exercise 3–C
Your Personal Mission
Statement**

1. Use the space below to write your personal mission. Your mission statement reflects your personal constitution, set of beliefs, and value system. In it, you should address such questions as these:

   a. What is my purpose? What do I believe?

   b. What do I value?

   c. What do I treasure?

   d. What is really important to me?

   e. How do I want to approach living my life?

   f. How do I want to approach life on a daily basis?

2. Answer these questions by first reviewing the speeches from Exercise 3–B to ensure a multifaceted mission statement. Use the space below to record insights and understandings that you have about yourself and your life plan.

   _____

   _____

   _____

   _____

   _____

   _____

   _____

   _____

   _____

   _____

   _____

   _____

   _____

   _____

   _____

   _____

Clarifying your mission is an ongoing process. Revisit and update your mission periodically.

**Exercise 3–D
Personal Goal Setting**

1. In the space below, brainstorm your goals in the following categories. Write down as many as you wish, including goals that are short-, mid-, and long-term.

Academic, intellectual

Health, fitness

Social: family, friends, significant other, community

Career, job

Financial

Other

2. Of the goals you have listed, select from each of the six categories the two most important goals you would like to pursue in the short term (next 6–12 months). Write these below.

1. _____
2. _____
3. _____
4. _____
5. _____
6. _____
7. _____
8. _____
9. _____
10. _____
11. _____
12. _____

3. From the 12 goals listed above, choose the 3 that are the most important to you at this time, the 3 you commit to work on in the next few months. Write a goal statement for each one, using the following guidelines:

■ Begin each with the word "To . . ."
■ Be specific.
■ Quantify the goal if possible.
■ Each goal statement should be realistic, attainable, and within your control.
■ Each goal statement should reflect your aspirations—not those of others such as parents, roommates, significant others, and the like.

1. _____
_____

2. _____
_____

3. _____
_____

4. On a separate sheet of paper, develop an action plan for each goal statement. For each action plan:

■ List the steps you will take to accomplish the goal.
■ Include dates (by when) and initials (who's responsible) for each step.
■ Visualize completing the goal and, working backwards, specify each step necessary between now and then to reach the goal.
■ Identify any potential barriers you might experience in attaining the goal. Problem-solve around these obstacles and convert them into steps in your action plan.
■ Identify the resources you will need to accomplish these goals, and build in steps to acquire the necessary information into your action plan.

5. Transfer the dates of each step for each goal in your action plan to a daily calendar.
6. Keep an ongoing daily or weekly record of the positive steps you take toward meeting each goal.

Exercise 3–E
Ethical Stance

Are the following ethical or unethical in your opinion? Why or why not? Consider individually and discuss in small groups.

■ Calling in sick when you really are not.
■ Taking office supplies home for personal use.
■ Cheating on a test.
■ Turning someone in for cheating on a test or paper.
■ Overcharging on your company expense report.
■ Trying to flirt your way out of a speeding ticket.
■ Splicing cable from your neighbor.
■ Surfing the net on company time.
■ Cheating on income tax.
■ Lying (exaggerating) about yourself to influence someone of the opposite sex.
■ Looking at pornographic sites on the Web through the company network.
■ Lying about your education on a job application.
■ Lying about experience in a job interview.
■ Making a copy of a rental video cassette before returning it to the store.

Exercise 3–F
The Gold Watch

The Situation

John is a 35-year-old salesman with Anderson and Sons, Inc., an established wholesaler of office equipment. He lives near Anderson's headquarters in Chicago with his wife and two adopted children.

On a recent sales tour abroad, John met J.R., an office-equipment supplier who was interested in a line of photocopiers worth $500,000. J.R. told John that he would give John an order for the photocopiers in return for a gold Rolex watch worth $13,000. J.R. showed John the watch he wanted in a catalog, and John said that he would see what he could do.

On returning to Chicago, John told Charles, his boss, about the proposition, asking if he could go ahead and buy the Rolex in order to obtain the order. Charles was outraged and said, "This is immoral! It's not decent business practice to offer bribes. We're living in a civilized society. If I find out that you've been bribing customers to get orders, I'll fire you on the spot! Have I made myself clear?"

After the confrontation with Charles, John left the office and drove to the home of Terry, his friend and colleague. He explained his plight and then said, "What can I do, Terry? It's an important order, and there's a chance of repeat business; J.R. is interested in office furniture and typewriters as well as more photocopiers in the future."

Terry thought for a moment and then said, "John, why don't you finance the deal yourself? Buy the stupid watch and land the contract. With your commission and any future business, you'll get a decent return on your investment. Don't even tell Charles; he's so ridiculously old-fashioned—he has no idea how to do business in this day and age."

John left Terry's home, went to his car, thought for a few minutes, and then drove to his bank. Mr. Gray, the bank manager and a close friend of John's father, listened to John's reasons for wanting the $13,000 loan. Despite the fact that John's checking account was overdrawn, he agreed to give John the loan immediately.

The next day John went to a jewelry store near his office and asked a clerk for the specific Rolex watch requested by J.R. While he was waiting for the clerk to bring him the watch, Jane, Charles' secretary, came into the store to buy a birthday present for her mother. Unobserved by John, she watched as the clerk gave the watch to John in exchange for the $13,000 cash. In her astonishment she forgot about finding a present for her mother, hurried back to Anderson and Sons, burst into Charles' office, and asked, "How can a salesman who earns $30,000 a year afford a $13,000 watch?"

Charles was furious. He rushed out of his office and found John just returning from the jewelry store. "You're fired!" he shouted.

"Let me explain . . .," muttered John.

"No excuses! I warned you!"

At that moment a Telex came through; it read as follows: "NO LONGER INTERESTED IN THE PHOTOCOPIER DEAL. FOUND ALTERNATIVE SUPPLIER. J.R."

Instructions

Rank order the following characters from 1 (least objectionable) to 6 (most objectionable):

6 John — least consistently ethical > 2x unethical
4 J.R. — suggestive : willing
1 Charles — most consistently ethical
5 Terry — suggestive : willing
2 Mr. Gray — know reason why money reqd = unethical
3 Jane — relaying what she saw

Source: From J. Pfeiffer, *Handbook of Structured Experiences for Human Relations Training*, vol. X. Copyright © 1983 by John Wiley & Sons, Inc. Reprinted by permission of John Wiley and Sons, Inc.

Exercise 3–G
Evaluating Goals
and Ethics

1. Watch a current TV show and answer the following questions:
   - What are some of the positive goal-setting behaviors exhibited by a primary character in the show? Describe these behaviors and the outcome achieved in the show.
   - Is there a character who offers a negative role model with respect to goal setting? Describe this person's behaviors related to goal setting (or lack thereof) and the outcomes.

2. View a movie in which achievement or goal setting is a theme, such as *Tucker, Braveheart, Don Quixote, Moby Dick, The Bridge on the River Kwai, October Sky, Mr. Holland's Opus, For the Love of the Game, Hoosiers, Remember the Titans, Top Gun, Cast Away, Lord of the Rings, Finding Nemo, Armageddon, Saving Private Ryan, E.T., Casablanca*, and answer the following questions:
   - Describe the main character's mission, its impact on that person's behaviors, and how he or she dealt with setbacks.
   - Identify elements of the character's behavior that you would like to apply to your own life. What would this look like?

3. Watch a TV show or a movie such as *Wall Street, Working Girl, Norma Rae, Silkwood, The China Syndrome, Saving Private Ryan, Nick of Time, Fail Safe, The Great Gatsby, The Hunt for Red October, Airforce One, Crouching Tiger, Hidden Dragon, Chocolat, Remember the Titans, The Negotiator*. What ethical dilemmas do the protagonist and antagonist face? How does each deal with the situation? What decision factors do they use to make decisions? How is the situation resolved to take into consideration the needs of all involved (or is it)?

4. The next time you're in a group situation and an ethical dilemma arises, watch the group to see how the decision is made. What factors are considered? Is an ethics test applied? How is the decision made? Is it the right one? How do you know?

Exercise 3–H
Reflection/Action Plan

This chapter focused on goal setting—what it is, why it's important, and how to acquire and increase the degree to which you possess it. We also discussed the role of values and ethics in setting goals that are aligned with your key priorities. Complete the worksheet below upon reading and finishing the experiential activities for this chapter.

1. The one or two areas in which I am most strong are:

_____

_____

_____

_____

2. The one or two areas in which I need more improvement are:

_____

_____

_____

_____

3. If I did only one thing to improve in this area, it would be to:

_____

_____

_____

_____

4. Making this change would probably result in:

_____

_____

_____

_____

5. If I did not change or improve in this area, it would probably affect my personal and professional life in the following ways:

_____

_____

_____

_____

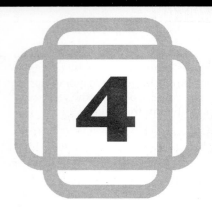

4 Self-management

Learning Points

How do I:

- Manage myself so that I can achieve more and feel better?
- Make better use of my time, that is, work smarter and not harder?
- Identify stressors in my life and find ways to reduce or change my response to them?
- Recognize and overcome barriers to self-improvement?
- Evaluate my emotional intelligence and identify areas for personal improvement?

"It is 8:05 and now I am going to be late!" Janet Smythe screamed, more to herself than anyone else. Just another typical morning of trying to get the kids off to school and get to work on time. "But Mom, I need you to sign my permission slip for the field trip. It needs to be handed in today or I can't go next week," her son yells back. Janet growls back, "Why didn't you have me fill it out last night?"

Somehow she makes it out the door, and heads to work. Of course the traffic is backed up and it doesn't look like she will be able to make up any lost time on the commute. When she finally gets into her office, her co-worker pops her head through the office door and asks Janet to send an electronic copy of their presentation for the 10:00 sales meeting. Janet then realizes that she left the disk containing the presentation in her home computer. With her frustration mounting, she takes her anger out on Mike, her assistant, who unfortunately chose that moment to remind Janet of the 10:00 meeting on her schedule. "I don't need constant reminding Mike, I do have a schedule and I can read!!" She slumps in her chair, not sure of how she should proceed to get out of this mess. She walks out of her office and finds Mike at his desk. "Sorry Mike. First I'm yelling at my kids, then you, and I have forgotten my work again. I'm losing my mind. Something has got to change."

1. What problems is Janet facing in self-management?
2. What are some strategies Janet could use to better manage the serious situation in which she finds herself?
3. If you were Janet, how would you handle the situation?

"It is not the mountain we conquer, but ourselves."

Sir Edmund Hillary

As many of us have heard before, if you don't take care of yourself, who will? In this chapter we explore the concept of self-management. Being able to manage oneself is a lifelong process and requires self-awareness and a continued willingness to make changes in our attitudes and behavior. The ability to manage oneself gives leaders credibility.[1] In order to be an effective role model, it is important to be an effective self-manager. Time and stress management along with emotional intelligence are concepts closely associated with self-management. We discuss how to overcome barriers to interpersonal effectiveness so that you can devote your full energies to doing what it takes to succeed and to be happy in life as well as in business.

What Are Time and Stress Management and Why Are They Important?

What distinguishes top performers from those who are just moderately successful? Naturally our genetic history, family background, education, and work history affect the opportunities that are available to us and our ability to seek and choose among these opportunities. And to be honest, plain luck, "being in the right place at the right time," is a factor in one's success. More and more, however, we are realizing that our ability to manage and allocate time and to handle our response to stress have a lot to do with the extent to which we ultimately succeed, in life as well as in business.

Time Management

Time management is the ability to allocate our time and resources to accomplishing our objectives. Skill in managing how we spend our time allows us to prioritize and accomplish more goals in life, resulting in a sense of well-being because we are able to see the fruits of our labors. It gives us a chance to achieve a balance between work and personal life that can be more satisfying, as opposed to restricting our activities to one arena at the expense of the other. Effective managers find that time management increases productivity. The popular saying, "work smarter, not harder" applies here. By focusing our energy on well-chosen activities, we can actually see our results. This in itself can be motivating, which can then increase our drive to achieve even more.

Managing our time also reduces stress levels. Taking control of our time means taking control of our life. This results in a feeling that we are in charge. "I exercised today, and now I can go back and study for the exam with a clear head" is an example of this, which is better than thinking subconsciously "I have no time, I have no life. I didn't exercise and now I don't even have the energy to study for this exam." Time management gives us more time to enjoy the activities that are important to us, such as spending time with family, socializing, reading, and favorite hobbies. This means we are better able to enjoy a varied, textured life. As human beings, we have many dimensions. We are not meant to simply work. Most of us have the need to be many things—a friend, a partner, a family member, part of a community. As we incorporate many elements of life into one, each of those elements is enhanced by our involvement in the others.[2]

Stress Management

Stress management is the ability to manage our response to situations that occur in our lives. Stress is a fact of personal and organizational life. Stress, when not understood or managed, can result in a variety of responses, including physiological, psychological, and organizational. A **physiological** response is one in which physical problems develop as a result of mental anguish.[3] Heart disease, high blood pressure, bulimia, anorexia nervosa, migraine headaches, cancer, gastrointestinal disorders, asthma, diabetes, allergies, skin disorders, cholesterol, and weakened body defenses are some examples of physical conditions that are often brought on by mental stress.[4] According to Crampton et al., physiological disorders have been recognized as one of the 10 leading work-related diseases in the country today by the National Institute of Occupational Safety and Health (NIOSH). **Psychological** effects are not always as readily identifiable as physiological responses.[5] Depression, sudden bursts of violence or anger, anxiety, chemical dependency, alcohol abuse, and phobias are examples of psychological reactions to stressful situations.

Organizational stress or work-related stress is the "adverse reaction people have to excessive pressures or other types of demands placed on them."[6] **Organizational** stress effects include job dissatisfaction, absenteeism, turnover, accidents, low morale, poor interpersonal relations, low productivity, and poor customer service. Stress caused by organizational problems is often difficult to manage, as the factors causing the stress are rarely under our control. Some jobs are highly stressful by design—air traffic controllers, dentists, and coal miners are extreme examples. Even businesses that are not commonly viewed as stressful are now prone to high stress levels, especially after so many businesses experienced drastic downsizing of staff in the early 1990s. In addition, employees are working more hours now than they were in the 1960s. The average worker now sends and receives about 190 messages per day (voice mail, e-mail, fax, etc.) and is interrupted an average of six times per hour, according to a study sponsored by Pitney Bowes.[7] These trends, coupled with the desire of many employees, male and female, to lead more balanced lives and spend time with their families and friends, are resulting in an increase in organizational-induced stress.[8]

Work-family conflict is another area associated with stress. The belief that we must "do it all" has led to high levels of stress. The changes in the U.S. labor force, with an increase in dual-worker families and single-parent families, has given rise to conflict over balancing the demands of work and the needs of the family. Over half of high-level executives surveyed ranked feeling "overextended" and concern for work–life balance as the top causes of stress.[9] Finding a balance between the roles of family caretaker (which includes taking care of spouse, parents, children, and/or siblings) and worker is necessary to reduce stress and its potential consequences (absenteeism, turnover, job dissatisfaction, family conflict, and life dissatisfaction).[10] Eliminating the potential for role conflict must be addressed by individuals as well as the managers and organizations for which they work.

These sources of stress can be problematic in personal life and in business. Stress is inevitable, but we can manage how we respond to stress. Managing stress is an important skill for both managers and their employees. Those managers who are able to understand their stressors and manage them—and who can help their employees do the same—will be more productive and successful than those who aren't.

Why Is Management of Our Time and Our Response to Stress Important?

The expression "time famine," or feeling that we have too much to do and not enough time to do it, is prevalent in a work environment that has increased employee responsibility through empowerment and autonomy.[11] Radical and lightning-quick changes are a permanent feature in today's contemporary business environment. Those managers who are able to stay current with these changes and adopt appropriate response strategies to these changes are more likely to succeed—and to help their employees succeed as well. Some of these response strategies—and the reasons why they are important—are described below.

Strategies for Time and Stress Management

Time Management Strategies

There are times in our lives when time doesn't seem to exist, or when it feels like we have no time to think or breathe. This is fine if it happens only periodically. But if you're constantly running from one high-priority task to another, it's likely you'll soon be either suffering from burnout (where you're too fatigued to have an interest in the things on which you're spending time) or doing everything only marginally. It's time to cut back. It's better to do fewer things with quality than many things poorly.

Time management is an important personal and managerial skill. It is a process of setting or taking on objectives, estimating the time and resources needed to accomplish each objective, and disciplining yourself to stay focused on the objective while completing it. It doesn't mean filling every minute. It means allowing for some "slack" time for the unexpected: those unforeseen circumstances that are inevitable.

It is an irony that we can't actually "manage" time. We can't change the amount of time we have. There are only 24 hours in a day, 168 in a week. We manage ourselves in order to be more efficient with our time. We can concentrate on the choices we make and be aware of what's motivating us to make the choices we make. We can focus on getting things done by being productive—getting the right things done . . . on time, on budget, and through the use of all our resources.

Figure 4–1

How to Manage Your Time

Use the chart below to evaluate your current usage of time, identifying your patterns of behavior and your current time wasters.

Typical Time Wasters	Degree to Which I Do These:			
	High		Medium		Low
Procrastination	1	2	3	4	5
Disorganization	1	2	3	4	5
Perfectionism	1	2	3	4	5
Visitors and interruptions	1	2	3	4	5
Telephone, voice-mail, e-mail, Internet	1	2	3	4	5
Daydreaming and distractions	1	2	3	4	5
Lack of focus or interest	1	2	3	4	5
Doing too many tasks at once	1	2	3	4	5
Accepting too much work	1	2	3	4	5
Paperwork and administrative tasks	1	2	3	4	5
Poorly planned meetings	1	2	3	4	5
Lack of necessary resources	1	2	3	4	5
Failure to use technology	1	2	3	4	5

If you scored less than 40, you may want to consider ways to reduce your wasted time. To do this, identify what is of value to you by determining what you consider to be important ways to spend your time. By referring to the personal and professional goals you established, you should be able to decide how to spend your time.

Other tips for time management include the need to do the following:

■ Plan and prioritize.

Planning is essential to effective time management.[12] The 10 or 15 minutes you spend organizing your schedule can save you hours of time during your week.[13] Heed the words of Benjamin Franklin: "Failing to plan is planning to fail."

■ Get in the habit of preparing "to do" lists. Make a list of everything you need to do for that day and prioritize the list according to the importance of completing each task. Bear in mind that most people will not complete every item on "to-do" lists; however you will accomplish more with a list than without one.

■ Follow the "80/20" rule. An estimated 80 percent of results are achieved from 20 percent of focused time. This includes spending more time doing useful activities, tracking what makes that 20 percent so productive, and making the transition of devoting more time to productive work.[14]

■ Plan for your time-specific activities and non–time-specific activities. For "time-specific" activities, determine in advance how close to completing the task you want to be by a certain time. This requires self-discipline and allows you to budget your time and accomplish more than you would in a non–time-bound scenario. Also plan your down time. Everyone needs a break to rest and recharge. Oddly enough, you can actually get more work done if you take several short breaks than if you don't.

■ Find your optimal working time—referred to as your biological "prime time"—and plan to maximize use of this time by scheduling and doing demanding jobs during these peak periods and less demanding tasks at other times.

■ Prioritize tasks by level of importance: vital, important, should be done today, or can be done tomorrow. Break complex tasks or projects down into manageable steps and set up a time line for completing each step.

■ Organize. Choose or set up the right environment for the task. This may require you to clear away unnecessary materials, reduce distractions (turn off phone or close door), and eliminate environmental interference (heavy traffic or neighbor's music). If all else fails, go to a place, such as a library, where you can work without distractions.

■ Delegate. Determine what tasks and activities would be possible to allocate to others. Clearly specify the task and the expected outcomes to ensure they will complete the task without requiring periodic coaching or redoing.

■ Differentiate between what's urgent and what's important. Most of us *expend* time on what's urgent—those unplanned events that are often thrust on us by others and beg for your immediate attention. Yet not enough of us *invest* time on what's important—those priorities that are meaningful and to which you are committed to spending time. Figure 4–2 illustrates the intersection between task and event importance and urgency. Be careful in deciding here. The interruption from one of your children or a roommate—a quadrant three activity—might be an investment if you are committed to spending time with your family and friends. The frequent interruption by a co-worker who likes to chat—also a quadrant three activity—is probably an expenditure. Responding to that

Figure 4–2
Time Management Matrix[15]

Quadrant 1	Quadrant 2
IMPORTANT AND URGENT	IMPORTANT BUT NOT URGENT
• Most problem-solving activities • Meeting immediate deadlines • Writing a report due in one hour • Exercise	• Reading a book related to your current priorities • Preparing for an upcoming event • Spending quality time with friends and family
Quadrant 3	**Quadrant 4**
NOT IMPORTANT BUT URGENT	NOT IMPORTANT AND NOT URGENT
• Answering the telephone • Checking e-mail • Dealing with interruptions, such as requests for info or help	• Worrying or being angry • Watching TV beyond time needed to unwind • Surfing the Internet for no reason

person every time she or he comes in unannounced takes time from the priority on which you're working and sends the message that it's OK to continue interrupting. Often when something comes up that was unplanned it takes away from what is important.[16] The more time spent on important but not urgent activities (quadrant two), the better you will be able to manage your time. If you devote time to the important, the urgent will often take care of itself. Learn to focus on the important and manage your ability to keep to the deadlines you have set; this will prevent the important from becoming urgent.

- Avoid postponing. Procrastination is one of the biggest time wasters. Unfortunately many times we "put off until tomorrow what we could be doing today." While some people enjoy the adrenaline rush this produces (e.g., waiting until the last minute to write a paper and having to stay up all night to get it done), rarely will you produce your best work operating this way. By waiting until the last minute, many procrastinators find they have been unrealistic about the time required to do the job right. For example, when writing a paper at the last minute, you're likely to have difficulty finding resource materials that are necessary to do a quality job.

  Waiting until the last minute also leaves little or no time to review your work, polish it, and ensure it's accurate and of sufficient quality. It's far better to plan ahead, leaving yourself some time toward the end of a project to take care of details that couldn't have been anticipated. Another negative consequence of procrastination is alienating co-workers. For example, your co-workers might think of you as one who always waits until the last minute. This not only causes stress for you but also for your co-workers, many of whom might wish they would not have to work with you again. Avoid this situation by planning and being realistic about what you can and want to achieve.

Procrastination can also cause an internal conflict over what a person should do and what he or she wants to do. It is usually associated with avoidance behavior—avoiding necessary action to complete a task—and can be used as a type of coping mechanism to delay an unpleasant task. So how can you overcome procrastination? You must first be aware of your tendency to procrastinate and evaluate the reasons for avoiding the necessary task. You can then work on changing your behavior by making the task more pleasant or less threatening. Planning and directing action to the long-term outcome may redirect your energy.[17]

Commit to evaluating periodically how you use your time. Do time audits—reexamine your goals and whether you allocate time appropriately to achieve them. To keep your schedule organized, reasonable, and attainable, incorporate tasks that are important to you. A balance between discipline and flexibility is key. Stay focused on your overall priorities (remember the 80/20 rule), while continually monitoring your progress and revising your plans as necessary.

Stress Management Issues

Stress is an upset in the body's balance, in reaction to an adverse or disturbing event. Hans Selye, a pioneer in stress research, defines stress as "the non-specific response of the body to any demand made upon it."[18] Stress comes about not from an event, such as failing an exam or winning the lottery, but from how we respond to it. Stress is found everywhere, in all aspects of life. It is inevitable and unavoidable. The sources of stress vary from person to person. Stress can be derived from external factors such as traffic jams or an ineffective or inefficient work environment. Stress also stems from internal factors such as our emotional state, our perspective on life, or the way we choose to respond to various situations or demands.

Types of Stress

There are two types of stress: "good" and "bad." Good stress, or **eustress,** is positive, presents opportunity for personal growth or satisfaction, and pushes people to higher performance. Bad stress, or **distress,** is negative and results in debilitating effects.[19]

Figure 4–3
Performance/Stress Graph

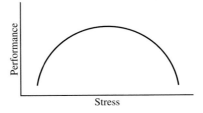

Surprisingly, too little stress can be as detrimental as too much stress. As Figure 4–3 demonstrates, when we lack any stress or pressure to perform, we may utilize minimal effort and achieve suboptimal performance. Conversely, too much stress might make it difficult to concentrate or perform effectively or efficiently. Whether a particular stress factor we are experiencing is "good" or "bad" depends largely on how we perceive the stressor and respond to it. In other words a situation can be termed "stressful" or not— depending on how we choose to look at and handle it.

Responses to Stress

Not all individuals respond in the same way to the same stressor.[20] Everyone has a unique level of tolerance. One person might be elated upon being promoted, while another might be traumatized at the prospect. We might find it impossible to work while children play noisily in the street, while our neighbor finds his concentration is actually improved by this external noise.

A variety of remedies or techniques is available for different types of stress. Psychological problems are much better understood today than in the recent past. Various drugs and other therapies are available for treating a wide variety of problems. Psychological problems are best dealt with by consulting a professional such as a counselor or therapist. These professionals can help individuals suffering psychological effects of stress by helping them understand these situations and manage their response to them more effectively.

Because of the likely connection between emotional or mental concerns and physical ailments, physiological problems are best dealt with through consultation with both a health professional and a mental health professional or wellness counselor. Typically an individual experiencing physiological stress will be given a test battery to diagnose the sources of the stress and potential solutions to the problems being experienced. A treatment program will be varied and might include regular exercise, better nutrition, relaxation techniques and, in some cases, prescription drugs as appropriate.

Organizational problems are complex. If you are suffering from job-related stress it is important to evaluate your work style; your level of job satisfaction; and the fit between you, your boss, your co-workers, and your organization. Those who feel the least (bad) stress are those who are in a work environment in which they can thrive, rather than one in which they are drained. Talking with your boss or co-workers about your concerns can help. But if change is not forthcoming, leaving the organization for one better suited to your personality is a good option.

Organizational Responses to Stress

Organizations need to respond to the causes of stress. Evidence shows there is an increasing link between work-related stress and negative individual and organizational outcomes.[21] Three types of intervention are required at the organizational level.[22] First, primary interventions need to be implemented by reducing the number of stressors present in the work environment. These strategies can include workload reduction, job redesign, or even flextime. The next step utilizes secondary interventions that aim at helping employees cope with stress and training to introduce stress management techniques. The third type of intervention focuses on rehabilitation of employees that are experiencing symptoms of stress. This final action usually incorporates the services of employee assistance programs.

Unfortunately, most organizations find that self-referral to employee assistance programs is not a common practice—usually only 5–15 percent of all stress-related cases are instigated by the employee themselves.[23] Intervention by an outside party usually starts the process. Therefore, it is important to train managers to be able to recognize symptoms of stress and to include assessment of stress levels in their personal observations of subordinates. Another important conclusion of recent studies is that most organizational policies focus on the secondary and tertiary strategies for dealing with stress. Organizations tend to ignore the first stage in which they would have the most control over removing the workplace stressors or at least attempting to reduce the impact of these stressors on its members. Organizations need better diagnosis of stress factors and a closer examination of stress-management practices.[24]

How to Manage Stress

There are a number of coping strategies that can be used to cope with stress. We'll never eradicate stress, but we can make choices about how we handle it.[25] Several suggestions follow; you'll be able to provide others from your own experience.

- Identify your stressors and stress levels. A **stressor** is a situation, activity, or person that causes you to feel stressed, out of control, or frazzled. **Stress levels** refer to the degree to which you let the source of the stress affect you. It is crucial to understand exactly what your stressors are; in other words, what your "hot buttons" are. What causes you to tense up, feel aggravated, or be angry or resentful? What causes you to get a headache or your blood pressure to rise? What causes you to think no one understands you or that there's no way out of a problem you're facing? It's also important to understand your own unique stress levels. How stressed do you get? What causes a severe versus just a regular headache? We cannot manage stress unless we know what causes stress, and how those causes are impacting us psychologically, physiologically, and organizationally. Look at the chart (Figure 4–4) and see if any of these signs of stress look familiar to you. Understanding your stressors—and being able to recognize them *before* they occur—is an essential skill in stress management. Understanding your stress levels—the degree to which you react to certain stressors—can help you manage your response to stress effectively.

- Implement time management skills. For some, feeling a lack of control over a situation causes stress. When this occurs, try to exert some influence over those aspects of a situation that are within your control. Making a change in your environment that reduces the impact of the offending stressor can often do this. For example, if you are feeling overwhelmed by a term paper assignment, you could find a quieter place in which to work, organize your work space by using files or piles for the various sections of the paper, or play soft music. These changes can help reduce stress levels.

Figure 4–4
Signs of Stress

Physical Signs	Emotional Signs	Mental Signs	Relational Signs	Spiritual Signs	Behavioral Signs
Appetite changes	Bad temper	Lack of humor	Isolation	A feeling of emptiness	Pacing
Headaches	Anxiety	Dull senses	Defensiveness	Apathy	Swearing
Fatigue	Nightmares	Lethargy	Intolerance	Inability to forgive	Substance abuse
Insomnia	Irritability	Boredom	Resentment	Cynicism	Nail biting
Indigestion	Depression	Indecisiveness	Loneliness	Loss of direction	Slumped posture
Colds	Frustration	Forgetfulness	Nagging	Doubt	Restlessness
Weight change	Oversensitivity	Poor concentration	Lower sex drive	Need to prove self	Risk aversion
Teeth grinding	Mood swings	Personality changes	Aggression	Negative outlook	Eating disorders
Tension	Fearfulness	Stuck in past	Abuse	Gloom	Headaches

■ Sharing and disclosure. Being open about your thoughts and feelings—with yourself and with others—is a surprisingly effective technique for reducing stress levels. Sometimes just being able to talk out loud about a situation and how it's affecting you can help you to process aspects of the situation in such a way that you develop a new attitude about or outlook on it. This changed understanding can result in a more positive perspective on the situation. For example, receiving a bad grade on a paper can be viewed negatively—as a disappointment—or positively—as a chance to get some useful feedback from the instructor that could improve your writing in the future.

■ Keep a journal. Journal writing involves setting aside some time on a regular basis to reflect on what's happening in your life. By writing your thoughts and feelings about and reactions to certain events and people, you can air your emotions about something of significance to you, enabling you to acquire a new perspective on the situation.

■ Talking to a trusted friend, relative, co-worker, or professional helper such as a resident advisor, counselor, physician, or minister can be enormously helpful in reducing stress levels. We all get extremely upset at times, making it difficult for us to see things objectively. An empathetic set of ears can help us to view things differently and adopt a perspective we might not have imagined on our own. Counseling and advisory services at work can have a positive impact on understanding and dealing with our stress. Saying you could use help does not mean you are ineffective at work. Seek ways to improve your stress management, and as a manager, be aware of when others need help.

■ Visualization and mental imagery are becoming increasingly popular techniques for reducing stress. "See yourself making the perfect putt on the green." "Picture where you want to be in five years." "See yourself finishing school and driving a new car." These are all examples of visualization and mental imagery—imagining yourself in a situation, playing out how you ideally see yourself behaving and looking, creating a mental picture of yourself and how you'll feel by achieving a goal you've set. The theory behind visualization is "success breeds success." By thinking positively we can at times will ourselves to act and behave in a way that gets us where we want to be.

■ Many people who are committed to reducing stress in their lives find that relaxation techniques can have a marked effect on stress levels. Some of these include:

Try This:

■ Take one or more slow, deep breaths. Often when we're becoming stressed we begin to take shallower breaths without even being aware of it. This causes us to be short of breath and to have difficulty concentrating. By taking a "time-out" and taking a few deep breaths, we automatically calm the body and the mind and are able to concentrate on the matter at hand. Try this technique before a presentation or during an emotional conversation.

■ Practice yoga or meditation. Yoga is a form of gentle exercise that positively influences the mind–body connection through the use of deep breathing, stretching, and slow but firm movements in a calm atmosphere. Meditation involves setting aside time on a regular basis to clear the mind of details and focus on being alert and calm. Usually meditation involves learning to concentrate on one image or sound, subduing other images and sounds. Practicing meditation for a few minutes each day can help reduce psychological and physical stress levels.[26] Health professionals and even some insurance companies have endorsed both yoga and meditation as proven methods for reducing stress.

■ Progressive muscle relaxation (PMR) and guided imagery. In PMR, you isolate various parts or muscle groups in your body, and then tense and relax these muscles several times before moving to the next muscle group. Typically, the pattern begins

(continued)

at one end of the body and concludes at the other. Guided imagery involves engaging our ability to recall a special place or memory (or imagining a fantasy place, such as floating in a cloud) and invite the same positive feelings or sensations to return. Both of these techniques can be done alone or with the use of an in-person or recorded facilitator or guide who can help you focus your thoughts on your body or your imagination in a powerful, stress-reducing way.

- Another important means for reducing stress is to eat healthily and exercise regularly.[27] Most scientists and nutritionists agree that proper nutrition and eating habits play a big role in keeping our systems fit. Three tips to consider include:

  - Try to avoid or restrict consumption of alcohol and caffeine, both of which deplete the system rather than replenish it. Most nutritionists who treat clients for a variety of stress-related ailments share this advice. One wonders why we care enough about our unborn children to instruct pregnant women to avoid alcohol and caffeine, yet once we are old enough to know better, we ignore this advice!

  - Eat for energy throughout the day, rather than simply eating for the sake of eating; this can also help you cope with stress. Comfort eating involves eating foods that bring immediate pleasant sensations yet yield little value long term. Comfort eating is hard to avoid since many of us find the process so, well, comforting! Unfortunately, comfort eating usually results in indulging in unhealthy foods and in undesirable quantities. Eating for energy is an entirely different mindset. It involves asking yourself throughout the day, how am I doing right now (physically, mentally, and emotionally), and what foods would be helpful? Which foods will help sustain me, and even help me thrive, versus which ones will drain me or fatigue me? An example is the midafternoon slump many of us face. Our first choice might be to eat a candy bar, although it would be better to eat a piece of fruit. Not only does fruit supply more energy over a longer period of time, it also provides valuable nutrients and fiber.

  - Create time for relaxation. This might seem impossible to the overworked student, the multitasking investment banker, the harried new parent, or the care giver of an aging parent or ill significant other. Taking at least some time out for you each day, away from the demands of others and the environment, can be rejuvenating and stimulating.

Overcoming Fear of Failure

No discussion of time and stress management is complete without mentioning a common obstacle to our being effective: fear of failure. Knowing the right course of action to take isn't always enough. Sometimes we run into obstacles. These obstacles shouldn't stop us. They can be addressed and, in most cases, overcome.

Figure 4–5

Hints for Overcoming Fear of Failure[28]
Look at failure as an event, not a reflection on you personally.
Remind yourself that everyone experiences failure.
Look for the "why" and find a solution.
Ask yourself what you learned.
Associate with positive people and abolish fear and failure statements.
Create a new environment.
Access new information; let adversity become advantage.
Create a new perspective or mindset—develop new "self-talk"—for instance, background thoughts.
Take one step at a time; keep moving forward.

One of the most common barriers to interpersonal effectiveness is fear of failure. **Fear** is an "emotion that occurs either as a response to external stimuli or as a result of an internal process that incorporates memory or introspections."[29] Fear can be good or bad. It can have negative or positive effects on people. **Good fear** maintains our alertness and vigilance. Based on knowledge, reason, and instincts, good fear keeps you from danger or harmful situations. Sometimes good fear can actually "adrenalize" you. For example, in public speaking, a little nervousness is actually good—it can enhance your vitality and enthusiasm. **Bad fear** holds you back instead of propelling you forward. It keeps you from applying your full energies to a situation. Some of the reasons for this are concern about rejection, making mistakes, taking risks, and failure. Negative fear stifles learning and interferes with decision making; it also prevents you from being yourself and discovering new talents and interests.

Don't let bad fear stifle creativity or self-expression. Giving in to fear can paralyze you, rendering you passive or unable to act. This can keep you from growing, developing, and ultimately succeeding. At its worst, bad fear can hinder your ability to take chances and be open to new experiences, threaten your existing relationships, and prevent new ones from developing. At its best, good fear can bring out new dimensions of your abilities and personality.

The Role of Emotional Intelligence

Effective self-management requires an awareness of our emotional and rational responses. Many of these elements associated with self-awareness are embodied in a new concept known as **emotional intelligence** or **EQ.** EQ is "a type of social intelligence that involves the ability to monitor one's own and others' emotions, to discriminate among them, and to use the information to guide one's thinking and actions."[30] As the ancient philosopher Aristotle said,

> *"Anyone can become angry—that is easy. But to be angry with the right person, to the right degree, at the right time, for the right purpose, and in the right way—this is not easy."*

Aristotle was a wise man. He recognized that as human beings we are able to experience a full range of feelings. Learning when, how, where, why, and with whom to share them is more complex than we might think at first glance. Emotional intelligence enables us to do this.

Emotional intelligence is a concept used to describe the levels we possess of key emotional responses. These include self-control, zeal and persistence, and the ability to motivate oneself to use our emotions, feelings, and moods and those of others to adapt and navigate in society. A guiding principle of emotional intelligence is that having and expressing emotions is a good thing. But expressing emotions, especially in the business world, requires an innate sense of what's appropriate to say, when, where, and with whom. EQ is developing an awareness of your feelings and emotions and using them in appropriate ways. Your level of emotional intelligence—the degree to which you are savvy about the use of emotions when communicating with others—is a huge factor in one's ability to be successful. EQ is considered to be just as important or even more important than IQ, one's "intelligence quotient." IQ and EQ involve different parts of the brain. IQ affects our ability to reason, to process information, to think analytically. EQ affects our ability to use emotions in relating to others at work and in our personal lives. Important criteria for professional success in any field are the "people" skills that are derived from understanding our emotions and responses to working with others. This type of self-knowledge is critical to our ability to relate to others and make decisions about our lives and work. The good news is that unlike one's IQ, which is determined primarily at birth, EQ is a quality we can actually learn about and improve.

There are six fundamentals for achieving emotional competency—a learned capability based on our EQ:[31]

- *Self awareness*—emotional awareness, accurate self-assessment, self-confidence, ability to recognize emotions and their effects on you and others.
- *Self-regulation*—self-control, trustworthiness, conscientiousness, adaptability, innovation, ability to manage disruptive emotions and impulses.
- *Motivation*—zeal, achievement drive, commitment, initiative, optimism, and the ability to remain persistent in the face of adversity.
- *Empathy*—understanding others, service orientation, developing others, leveraging diversity, political awareness, the ability to read and respond to others' feelings.
- *Social Skills*—interacting smoothly, managing interpersonal relationships, handling emotional responses to others, influence, communication, the ability to build bonds with others.
- *Group work skills*—collaboration and cooperation, team capabilities, conflict management, the willingness to work towards shared goals.

Understanding our levels of emotional intelligence is essential for our self-awareness. By knowing how we presently function when dealing with our emotions in situations with others, we can develop new goals, behaviors, and attitudes toward ourselves as well as others. The best managers have discovered it is essential for them to work on and demonstrate top-quality people skills.[32] Working to increase your emotional intelligence can help you do this. In the process, you can become a better manager as well as a better person.

Emotional Intelligence and Workplace Performance

Being able to understand and harness our emotions is just as valuable in the workplace as it is in our personal lives. Daniel Goleman, one of the foremost researchers on emotional intelligence, found EQ to be twice as important as IQ and technical skills at all job levels. Without it, a person can have the best training in the world, an incisive, analytical mind, and an endless supply of smart ideas, but he still won't make a great leader.[33] Goleman also concludes that EQ plays an even more substantial role in success at higher level positions.

On an individual level, self-regulation, self-awareness, and motivation have been positively associated with concern for quality, problem-solving ability, and ability to manage conflicts. Ranking high on these dimensions suggests that an individual would have effective behaviors at work. Being able to interpret the emotions of other, empathy, social skills, and group work skills would increase the effectiveness of organizational managers and leaders. Improving emotional intelligence allows managers to become primal leaders who positively influence others with commanding social skills.[34] Some key aspects of EQ for leadership include the following:[35]

- Reduced depression, greater optimism, and less impulsiveness—These behaviors help managers deal with difficult situations, improve decision making, and positively affect employees' work attitudes.
- Increased concern for mastering skills and tasks—Conscientious leaders strive for personal improvement and encourage "higher levels of thinking and increased capacity for self-learning in others."[36]
- Facilitation of adaptation and change—Emotional intelligence allows leaders to gain power and become catalysts for change.
- Influence on positive teaming—Emotionally intelligent individuals utilize social skills and can moderate their behavior and influence others to collaborate, build bonds and communicate on team-based efforts.
- Development of transformational leadership—Leaders that have a strong sense of self and have strong convictions in their beliefs are able to provide vision and encourage development and motivation in others.

The Manager's Role in EQ[37]

1. Assess "emotional impact" of jobs—Managers need to be aware of the emotional pressures associated with particular jobs when designing job assignments.
2. Create a positive and friendly emotional climate—Managers need to recognize that workers need a supportive environment; work should not be a cold place devoid of concern for its members.
3. Properly reward and compensate—Through appropriately developed reward and compensation systems, managers can encourage a positive emotional climate.
4. Select appropriate employees and team members—Managers need to base selection of employees and team members on their record of utilizing a positive emotional attitude.
5. Provide EQ training—Managers need to develop training to increase employee EQ and encourage positive emotional responses.

Summary

Management consultant and author Roy Zenger tells us that the only person who likes change is a wet baby. We can accept and even embrace change. By learning to adapt we can remain vibrant. With practice, managing our time and stress can become as much of a habit as brushing teeth or stopping at a red light. Understanding how emotional intelligence impacts our emotional responses and the responses of others will increase our effectiveness as peers, workers, and leaders. By managing ourselves, we are more likely to achieve success and satisfaction—in life as well as in business.

Key Terms and Concepts

Bad fear	Physiological stress
Distress	Psychological stress
Eustress	Stress
Emotional intelligence (EQ)	Stress levels
Fear	Stress management
Good fear	Stressor
Organizational stress	Time management

Endnotes

1. Grace K. Baruch and Rosalind C. Barnett, "Role Quality, Multiple Role Involvement and Psychological Well Being in Mid-life Women," *Journal of Personality and Social Psychology* 3 (1986), pp. 578–85.

2. Suzanne M. Crampton, John W. Hodge, Jitendra M. Mishra, and Steve Price, "Stress and Stress Management," *SAM Advanced Management Journal* 60, no. 3 (Summer 1995), p. 10.

3. Christine K. Nowroozi, "How Stress May Make You Sick," *Nation's Business* 82, no. 12 (Dec. 1994).

4. Crampton et al., "Stress."

5. John J. Sosik, "Self-other Agreement on Charismatic Leadership: Relationships with Work Attitudes and Managerial Performance," *Group & Organization Management* 26, no. 4 (Dec. 2001), p. 484.

6. Tim Cuthell, "De-stressing the Workplace," *Occupational Health* 56, no. 1 (Jan. 2004), p. 14, quoting definition by the Health and Safety Executive.

7. See Kim Bachman, "Feeling Stressed?" *CMA Management* 73, no. 3 (Nov. 1999), p. 14; and M. Goldstein, "Getting Out from under Successful Meetings," *Bill Communications* 48, no. 11 (October 1999), p. 28, in reference to a survey by Pitney-Bowes.

8. Ann Wilson Schaef and Diane Fassel, *The Addictive Organization: Why We Overwork, Cover Up, Pick Up the Pieces, Please the Boss and Perpetuate Sick Organizations* (San Francisco: Harper and Row, 1988).

9. Barry Adamson and Murray Axmith, "The CEO Disconnect: Finding Consistency between Personal Values and the Demands of Leadership," *Ivey Business Journal Online,* May/June 2003, p. 1.

10. Scott L. Boyar, Carl P. Maertz, Jr., Allison W. Pearson, and Shawn Keough, "Work-family Conflict: A Model of Linkages between Work and Family Domain Variables and Turnover Intentions," *Journal of Managerial Issues* 15, no. 2 (Summer 2003), p. 175.

11. L. A. Perlow, "The Time Famine: Toward a Sociology of Work Time," *Administrative Science Quarterly* 44 (1999), p. 57.

12. Patricia Buhler, "Time Management Is Really Self-management," *Supervision* 57, no. 3 (March 1996), p. 24.

13. Gary Izumo, Joyce Bishop, and Kathleen Cole, *Keys to Workplace Skills: How to Get from Your Senior Year to Your First Promotion* (Upper Saddle River, NJ: Prentice Hall, 1999).

14. Harry Plack, "Managing Time Can Be Crucial," *Baltimore Business Journal* 17, no. 40 (Feb. 18, 2000), p. 27.

15. Jeffrey Gitomer, "Difference between Urgency and Importance," *LI Business News* 46, no. 53 (Dec. 31, 1999), p. 21A.

16. Stephen R. Covey, *The Seven Habits of Highly Effective People* (New York: Simon and Schuster, 1989).

17. Wendelien Van Eerde, "Procrastination at Work and Time Management Training," *Journal of Psychology* 137, no. 5 (Sept. 2003), p. 421.

18. R. Kreitner and A. Kinicki, *Organizational Behavior* (Homewood, IL: Irwin, 1992).

19. Patricia M. Buhler, "Managing in the 90's," *Supervision* 60, no. 12 (Dec. 1999), p. 14.

20. Crampton et al., "Stress."

21. R. L. Murphy, "Occupational Stress Management Current Status and Future Directions," in C. J. Cooper and D. M. Rousseau, *Trends in Organisational Behavior,* John Wiley, Chichester (1995), pp. 1–14.

22. Phillip Dewe, "EAPs and Stress Management: From Theory to Practice to Comprehensiveness," *Personnel Review* 23 (1994), p. 21.

23. Tim Cuthell, "De-stressing the Workplace," quoting definition by the Health and Safety Executive.

24. Philip Dewe and Michael O'Driscoll, "Stress Management Interventions: What Do Managers Actually Do?" *Personnel Review* 31, no. 1/2 (2002), p. 143.

25. Buhler, "Time Management."

26. Herbert Benson, M.D. and Miriam Z. Klipper, *The Relaxation Response* (New York: Harpertorch, Feb. 2000).

27. S. Arbetter, "Handling Stress," *Current Health* (Oct. 1992).

28. Jeffrey Gitomer, "Tips to Getting over Biggest Fear: Failure," *Business Journal* 17, no. 19 (March 24, 2000), p. 41; Victor Parachin, "Eliminating the Fear of Failure . . . How to Fear Less and Hope More," *Supervision* 55, no. 2 (Feb. 1994), p. 7.

29. Mark Rodgers, "No Fear?" *Dealer News* 33, no. 2 (Feb. 1997), p. 74.

30. Peter Salovey and David J. Sluyter, eds., *Emotional Development and Emotional Intelligence: Educational Implications* (New York: Basic Books, 1997).

31. Daniel Goleman, "Emotional Competence," *Executive Excellence,* April 1, 1999, p. 19.

32. Goleman, "Emotional Competence."

33. Daniel Goleman, *Working with Emotional Intelligence* (New York: Bantam Books, 1998), p. 108.

34. Daniel Goleman, Richard Boyatzis, and Annie McKee, *Primal Leadership: Realizing the Power of Emotional Intelligence* (Boston: Harvard Business School Press, 2002), p. 3.

35. See John J. Sosik and Lara E. Megerian, "Understanding Leader Emotional Intelligence and Performance: The Role of Self-other Agreement on Transformational Leadership Perceptions," *Group & Organization Management* 24, no. 3 (Sept. 1999), p. 367; M. Afzalur Rahim and Patricia Minors, "Effects of Emotional Intelligence on Concern for Quality and Problem Solving," *Managerial Auditing Journal* 18, no. 1/2 (2003), p. 150; and Ceasar Douglas, Dwight D. Frink, and Gerald R. Ferris, "Emotional Intelligence as Moderator of the Relationship between Conscientiousness and Performance," *Journal of Leadership & Organizational Studies* 10, no. 3 (Winter 2004), p. 2.

36. John J. Sosik and Lara E. Megerian, "Understanding Leader Emotional Intelligence and Performance: The Role of Self-other Agreement on Transformational Leadership Perceptions," *Group & Organization Management* 24, no. 3 (Sept. 1999), p. 367.

37. N. M. Ashkanasy and C. S. Daus, "Emotion in the Workplace: The New Challenge for Managers," *Academy of Management Executive* 16, no. 1 (2002), p. 76.

Exercise 4–A Personal Time Management

I. "Where Does the Time Go" Survey

The following survey shows how much time you spend in current activities. When taking the survey, estimate the amount of time spent on each item. Once you have this amount for daily items you will need to multiply them by seven or five. After each item's weekly time has been calculated, add all these for a grand total. Subtract this amount from 168, the total possible hours per week.

1. Number of hours of sleep each night $7 \times 7 = 49$
2. Number of hours grooming per day $2 \times 7 = 14$
3. Number of hours for meals/snacks (including shopping and preparation) $1 \times 7 = 7$
4. Number of hours travel each workday $1 \times 5 = 5$
5. Number of hours travel time each weekend $= 4$
6. Number of hours per week for regularly scheduled activities (clubs, church, socializing, etc.) $= 5$
7. Number of hours per day for chores, errands, extra grooming, and so on $1 \times 7 = 7$
8. Number of hours of work per week $= 50$
9. Number of hours in class per week $= 6$
10. Number of hours per week socializing, dating $= 6$
11. Add the totals for items 1–10 $= 153$

Subtract the number from line 11 from 168: 168 – 153 = 15

These are the remaining hours you have each week for extra activities—studying, family, sports, hobbies, TV, relaxation. Surprised? Where does the time go!

Questions

1. How do you believe you spend your remaining hours?
2. How effectively do you believe you spend these hours?
3. What do you believe are your biggest time wasters?
4. In what areas of your life can you "gain" hours?
5. How can you redistribute your hours to have more time available for the things you want to do?

II. Weekly Tracker

Break down your weekly "extra" activities to identify where you actually spend your extra hours. Use the following time chart to track your activity for one week. Fill in all the hours with the activities you perform. Be honest with yourself to get an accurate picture and pattern of where your time is spent.

	Monday	Tuesday	Wednesday	Thursday	Friday	Saturday	Sunday
5 AM							
6 AM	Wake	Wake	Wake	Wake	Wake		
7 AM							
8 AM	Leave	Leave	Leave	Leave	Leave		
9 AM	Work	Work	Work	Work	Work		
10 AM							
11 AM							
12 PM							
1 PM							
2 PM							
3 PM							
4 PM							
5 PM							
6 PM	Home	Home	Home	Home	Home		
7 PM							
8 PM							
9 PM							
10 PM							
11 PM							
12 PM							
1 AM							
2 AM							
3 AM							
4 AM							

Questions

1. Is your actual weekly time consistent with the figures you put in your survey?
2. What are your extra time periods and your time wasters?
3. How can you manage your time more effectively?

Adapted from **http://www.gmu.edu/departments/csdc/time.html**

Exercise 4–B
Life Stress Test

The Holmes and Rahe Schedule of Recent Experiences Survey (with some author modifications)

Instructions:

Place a check mark next to each event you experienced within the past year. Then add the life change units associated with the various events to derive your total life stress score.

Life Event	Life Change Unit
_____ Death of partner	100
_____ Divorce	73
_____ Separation from mate	65
_____ Detention in jail or other institution	63
_____ Death of a close family member	63
_____ Major personal injury or illness	53
_____ Marriage	50
_____ Being fired at work	47
_____ Reconciliation with mate	45
_____ Retirement from work	45
_____ Major change in the health or behavior of a family member	44
_____ Pregnancy	40
_____ Sexual difficulties	39
_____ Gaining a new family member (e.g., through birth, adoption, oldster moving in)	39
_____ Major business readjustment (e.g., merger, reorganization, bankruptcy)	39
_____ Major change in financial state (e.g., a lot worse off or a lot better off than usual)	38
_____ Death of a close friend	37
_____ Change to a different line of work	36
_____ Major change in the number of arguments with partner (e.g., either a lot more or a lot less than usual)	35
_____ Taking out a mortgage or loan for a major purchase (e.g., for a home, business)	31
_____ Foreclosure on a mortgage or loan	30
_____ Major change in responsibilities at work (e.g., promotion, demotion, lateral transfer)	29
_____ Son or daughter leaving home (e.g., marriage, attending college)	29
_____ Trouble with in-laws	29
_____ Outstanding personal achievement	28
_____ Partner beginning or ceasing work outside the home	26
_____ Beginning or ceasing formal schooling	26
_____ Major change in living conditions (e.g., building a new home, remodeling, deterioration of home or neighborhood)	25
_____ Revision of personal habits (dress, manners, association)	24
_____ Troubles with the boss	23
_____ Major change in working hours or conditions	20
_____ Change in residence	20
_____ Changing to a new school	20
_____ Major change in usual type and/or amount of recreation	19
_____ Major change in church, synagogue, or mosque activities (e.g., a lot more or a lot less than usual)	19
_____ Major change in social activities (e.g., clubs, dancing, movies, visiting)	18
_____ Taking out a mortgage or loan for a lesser purchase (e.g., for a car, TV, freezer)	17

Life Event	Life Change Unit
_____ Major change in sleeping habits (a lot more or a lot less sleep, or change in part of day when asleep)	16
_____ Major change in number of family get-togethers (e.g., a lot more or a lot less than usual)	15
_____ Major change in eating habits (a lot more or a lot less food intake, or very different meal hours or surroundings)	15
_____ Vacation	13
_____ Christmas	12
_____ Minor violations of the law (e.g., traffic tickets, jaywalking, disturbing the peace)	11
Total score =	_____

Source: Reprinted from *Journal of Psychosomatic Research,* August 1967, T.H. Holmes and R.H. Rahe, "The Social Readjustment Rating Scale," p. 216. Copyright © with permission from Elsevier Science.

**Exercise 4–C
Emotional
Intelligence Test**

Answer the following questions by placing a check in the appropriate column; determine your results using the scoring instructions.

	Always	Usually	Sometimes	Rarely	Never
1. I'm aware of even subtle feelings as I have them.					
2. I find myself using my feelings to help make big decisions in life.					
3. Bad moods overwhelm me.					
4. When I'm angry, I blow my top or fume in silence.					
5. I can delay gratification in pursuit of my goals instead of getting carried away by impulse.					
6. When I'm anxious about a challenge, such as a test or public talk, I find it difficult to prepare well.					
7. Instead of giving up in the face of setbacks or disappointments, I stay hopeful and optimistic.					
8. People don't have to tell me what they feel—I can sense it.					
9. My keen sense of others' feelings makes me compassionate about their plight.					
10. I have trouble handling conflict and emotional upsets in relationships.					
11. I can sense the pulse of a group or a relationship and state unspoken feelings.					
12. I can soothe or contain distressing feelings so they don't keep me from doing things I need to do.					

Source: From *Emotional Intelligence,* by Daniel Goleman. Copyright © 1995 by Daniel Goleman. Used by permission of Bantam Books, a division of Random House, Inc.

Figure Your Score

For numbers 1, 2, 5, 7, 8, 9, 11, and 12:

> Always = 4
> Usually = 3
> Sometimes = 2
> Rarely = 1
> Never = 0

For numbers 3, 4, 6, and 10:

> Always = 0
> Usually = 1
> Sometimes = 2
> Rarely = 3
> Never = 4

Results

36 or above: You probably have superior emotional intelligence

25–35: Good level of emotional intelligence

24 or under: Room for improvement

Questions

1. What is your EQ? How accurate do you feel this score portrays you?
2. What if anything about your score surprised you?
3. What, if anything, about your score is most in sync with your view of yourself?
4. Evaluating the six fundamental components of EQ, in which area are you the strongest? Explain, citing a brief example.
5. In which area are you the weakest? Explain, citing a brief example.
6. What implications does your score have for your personal life? Professional life?
7. What steps can you take to increase your EQ?

Exercise 4–D
Reflection/Action Plan

This chapter focused on time and stress management—what they are, why they're important, and how to acquire and increase the degree to which you possess them. Complete
the worksheet below to reflect on what you have learned on these topics and to develop
plans for incorporating that learning into your work and life.

1. The one or two areas in which I am most strong are:

_____

_____

_____

_____

2. The one or two areas in which I need more improvement are:

_____

_____

_____

_____

3. If I did only one thing to improve in this area, it would be to:

_____

_____

_____

_____

4. Making this change would probably result in:

_____

_____

_____

_____

5. If I did not change or improve in this area, it would probably affect my personal and
professional life in the following ways:

_____

_____

_____

_____

UNIT 1

INTRAPERSONAL EFFECTIVENESS: UNDERSTANDING YOURSELF

1. Journey into Self-awareness
2. Self-disclosure and Trust
3. Establishing Goals by Identifying Values and Ethics
4. Self-Management

UNIT 2

INTERPERSONAL EFFECTIVENESS: UNDERSTANDING AND WORKING WITH OTHERS

5. Understanding and Working with Diverse Others
6. The Importance and Skill of Listening
7. Conveying Verbal Messages
8. Persuading Individuals and Audiences

UNIT 3

UNDERSTANDING AND WORKING IN TEAMS

9. Negotiation
10. Building Teams and Work Groups
11. Managing Conflict
12. Achieving Business Results through Effective Meetings
13. Facilitating Team Success
14. Making Decisions and Solving Problems Creatively

UNIT 4

LEADING INDIVIDUALS AND GROUPS

15. Power and Politicking
16. Networking and Mentoring
17. Coaching and Providing Feedback for Improved Performance
18. Leading and Empowering Self and Others
19. Project Management

Unit 2

The second leg of your journey features critical skills needed to interact with business associates, classmates, friends, loved ones, and people you don't already know. Having already filled up the intrapersonal effectiveness fuel tank, you are ready to sharpen your skills communicating in a variety of situations and overcome any challenges to effectively achieving common ground. As with any journey, you're likely to come across people of different shapes, colors, backgrounds, etc. How often have these differences challenged your ability to listen without judging, remain open to diverse viewpoints, or respect others whose beliefs, behaviors, or attitudes seem odd or even wrong. Even when such differences aren't apparent, you've probably experienced situations where you've asked someone to do (or not do) something, but somehow she or he doesn't come through. Or maybe you've been in a situation where you've stopped yourself from speaking up about a situation that's bothering you, choosing instead to drop hints or send telepathic messages. We discuss reasons why these situations may have occurred, and more importantly, provide opportunities to gain valuable knowledge and skills in the art of interpersonal communication.

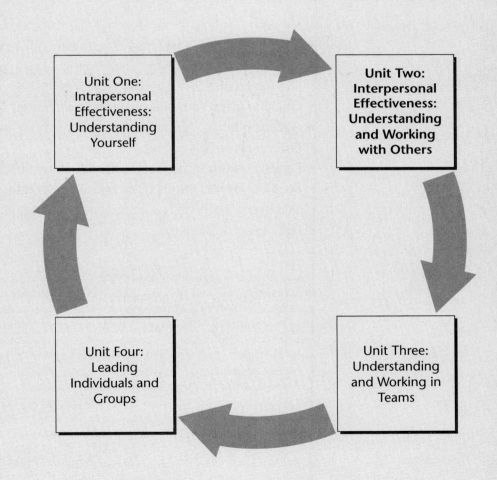

5 Understanding and Working with Diverse Others

Learning Points

How do I:
- Understand the biases I may have toward others who are different from me?
- Confront those biases by challenging stereotypes perpetuated by society and the media?
- Come to grips with others' biased perceptions toward me?
- Accept others' approaches and perspectives when they are completely different from my own?
- Learn to work effectively with others of different races, genders, ages?
- Seek out opportunities to increase the diversity and the benefits it brings to me personally and as a member of an organization?
- Help others do the same?

It was the summer before my senior year, and I was about to take part in the internship of a lifetime. I[1] was one of about 20 U.S. college students selected by a Fortune 500 corporation to be part of a very prestigious management internship program. All of us were to be flown into the area's largest airport, picked up by the human resources manager and taken to housing owned by the corporation. As part of our upcoming orientation, we were given the names of students with whom we'd be living in adjoining suites and encouraged to contact them in advance. After all, we'd be together for 12 weeks!

I remember the first time my suitemate and I spoke. It was about two weeks before we met. I called her to find out what things she was going to bring and, basically, to see what kind of person she was. I said, "Hello, my name is Reza Chamma and you and I are assigned suitemates." She then introduced herself and asked, "What are you?" Bewildered, I replied, "What do you mean?" Did she think I was an alien and she wanted me to assure her that I was a human being? Then she asked, "Are you Chinese or what?" My mouth gaped open in astonishment; I had never before been asked such an odd question. I guess she thought my last name was an Asian name, but still, what person comes out and asks such a direct question? Further, does it really matter where my last name comes from? In answer to her question, I told her that I was Middle Eastern. She replied with a curt and cold "Oh." So far, this girl struck me as stuck-up and politically incorrect.

I was one of the first interns to arrive. I was taken to my room and after unpacking for about an hour, I took a nap. I awakened to noises in the adjoining room. I walked through the bathroom and met my suitemate for the first time. As soon as I saw her, I hugged her. (In the Lebanese culture, we hug and kiss cheeks as opposed to shaking hands as in American culture.) My suitemate immediately pulled away after I hugged her; I was baffled by her reservation toward me. Was she still stuck on the whole "Oh, you are a foreigner" thing? Did she already form an opinion of me? Would we ever get along? Thoughts raced through my head as I imagined the dreadful relationship we were likely to have while sharing such close quarters. The rest of the day, my suitemate did not even acknowledge my presence.

The next morning, we walked down to breakfast together. We didn't speak until we sat down with our food. Here was my chance to find out a little about her. I had to know why she treated me the way she did. Was she rude to me because I was "different" from her? Or, was she rude to everyone? After chatting about "safe" subjects like our majors and hoped-for jobs upon graduation, we talked about our earlier school experiences. I found out that she went to private schools her whole life. All her classmates, teachers, and administrators were white. She had never interacted with anyone from a race other than her own. While she didn't verbalize her feelings about me, I could clearly detect her discomfort with me— as if she wasn't sure what to make of me or whether she could trust me. I was shocked!

After breakfast, we were moved into a large conference room. We were given activities to do that helped us learn more about our fellow interns. When we reassembled to talk about our experiences, my suitemate sat on the opposite side of the room. She didn't even make eye contact with me. We took turns sharing how we reacted to the activities; when it was my turn, my suitemate stopped paying attention and began whispering to another woman next to her. It was as if she had no interest in what I had to say. Boy, was this going to be an interesting summer!

1. Why was Reza so taken aback by her suitemate's reaction to her?

2. What could she have done to improve her relationship with her roommate?

3. We see that Reza is upset by her suitemate's reaction. In what ways does she contribute to the problem?

4. While there may be some hurdles that Reza and her suitemate will have to overcome, what are some benefits of living with someone who is "different" from you?

5. At this point, what would you do if you were in Reza's shoes? Why?

"To know one's self is wisdom, but to know one's neighbor is genius."

Minna Antrim (Author)

What comes to mind when you hear the word *diversity*? Many people, especially in the United States, think of diversity in a single dimension: race or ethnicity. In this chapter we discuss diversity more broadly. We address what diversity is, why it's important in business, how to build sensitivity to diversity, and how to manage diversity both as an individual and in the context of organizations.

What Is Diversity?

What is **diversity**? According to R. Roosevelt Thomas Jr., president of the American Institute for Managing Diversity, diversity is "dealing with the collective mixture of differences and similarities along a given dimension . . . [it] extends to age, personal and corporate background, education, function, and personality. It includes lifestyle, sexual orientation, geographic origin, tenure with an organization, physical and mental disability, exempt or nonexempt status, and management or nonmanagement."[2] Others extend this definition further to include diversity of individuals' values, beliefs, and opinions. As depicted in Figure 5–1, understanding and managing diversity for superior

**Figure 5–1
Primary and Secondary
Dimensions of Diversity[3]**

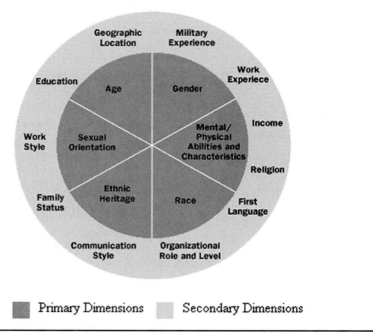

Primary Dimensions   Secondary Dimensions

organizational performance presupposes a broad definition, which includes both primary and secondary individual differences. In short, diversity reflects the sum total of individuals' uniqueness.

Managing diversity is a philosophy about how differences among individuals and organizations can be embraced rather than feared, encouraged rather than squelched. Empirical and anecdotal evidence tells us that organizations that are open to diversity—where people from different backgrounds and with diverse points of view are encouraged to be fully involved in the decision-making process—will "achieve a competitive advantage against organizations that are either culturally homogeneous or fail to successfully utilize their diversity."[4] As the makeup of the U.S. population changes, organizations must mirror those changes in order to reach and understand the changing needs, languages, and preferences of their clients and customers.[5]

Companies are finding that utilizing diversity in all aspects of the workforce makes not only strong moral sense, but also strong business sense as well.[6] By ensuring that diversity is built into various groups of organizational members, such as project teams, business start-up teams, customer service response teams, and top management and its sales force, businesses are able to achieve a number of goals:

- Access to a changing marketplace.
- Large-scale business transformation.
- Superior customer service.
- Workforce empowerment.
- Total quality.
- Alliances with suppliers and customers.
- Outsourcing partnerships.
- Continuous learning.

Numerous examples demonstrate the financial benefits that can accrue in companies that embrace diversity. Here are a few:

- Xerox plants using diverse work teams are now 30 percent more productive than conventional plants.[7]

- Through diversity and minority mentoring programs designed to manage personal growth, Dow Chemical and Texas Commerce Bank increased the number of minorities holding managerial positions, improved workforce attitudes, increased retention rates, and developed more effective teams.[8]

- Motorola beat its competition by producing the world's most efficient and high-quality cellular phones, which are produced almost exclusively by diverse work teams.[9]

- KFC experienced phenomenal success when it introduced its kosher line of chicken menus in Israel.[10]

- GE Power Systems experienced 13 percent productivity gains from cross-functional and multicultural teams versus homogeneous teams.[11]

- Numerous empirical studies of work teams demonstrate that when tasks are complex and not clearly defined, heterogeneous teams outperform homogeneous teams. "Super teams," those that were diverse in numerous respects and selected because of their differences, outperformed those that were homogeneous.[12]

In addition to the examples of positive effects of diversity listed above, there are some compelling statistics that should convince all of us of the importance of being open to and managing diversity.

- By the year 2050, the U.S. Bureau of Census estimates that 50 percent of the U.S. population will be non-Caucasian.[13]

- Estimates indicate that at least 10 percent of the workforce is homosexual.[14]

- Over half of the U.S. workforce is now between the ages of 34 and 54. Only 11 percent are over 55 years of age. However, workers 55 and older are the fastest growing segment of the workforce, a phenomenon known as the "graying of America."[15]

- Seventy percent of new entrants into the U.S. workforce are now women and minorities.[16]

- The spending power of African, Asian, and Hispanic Americans is now estimated to be more than $650 billion, up from $424 billion in 1994.[17]

Managing diversity is one of the primary business issues global companies and organizations face today. This reality means organizations are targeting their diverse customer bases in unique ways not previously seen. For example, the growth of online pharmacies can be explained by the explosive growth (and spending power) of the baby boomer generation and older relatives for whom they care. These progressive organizations have recognized the increased need for pharmaceuticals due to the aging population and growing acceptance and use of Internet technology among the U.S. population. Companies that embrace and adapt to changes in the workforce, and those whom they serve, will be better positioned to compete in the coming years.

Barriers to Accepting Diversity

Despite a general awareness in business that diversity is a positive factor, individuals still experience numerous personal barriers to accepting diversity. Those who came from homogeneous backgrounds are especially vulnerable to attitudes that prevent them from being more open to diversity—both in the workplace and in their personal lives. There are several barriers that sometimes prevent us from accepting diversity. These include

- **Prejudice**—unjustified negative attitude toward a person based on his or her membership in a particular group, such as not wanting to consider any college students for employment at your business because you believe they are all irresponsible, carefree partiers who will not be reliable workers based on what you have read about or seen on TV reports, or on one experience you had with a lazy worker who happened to be a college student.

■ **Ethnocentrism**—a tendency to regard one's own group, culture, or nation as superior to others,[18] such as what sometimes occurs in a selective club, religious sect, or political organization. People who are ethnocentric see their group-related customs or beliefs as "right" and evaluate others' beliefs or practices against this yardstick. Ethnocentrism tends to be consistent with all individuals. It is imperative for managers "to address and monitor cross-cultural settings so biases don't lead to detrimental behaviors or experiences."[19]

■ **Stereotypes**—set of beliefs about a group that is applied universally to all members of that group, such as "all poor people are uneducated" or "all Jews are cheap." While some stereotypes can appear to portray a group in a favorable light, such as "all Asians are good at math," stereotyping, whether positive or negative, is never a good idea because seldom does one statement hold true for all members of a group. Stereotyping is not always bad; it is a means to categorize and simplify a complex world. It is when stereotyping results in negative feelings or actions (such as discrimination or prejudice), leads to inaccurate perceptions, or results in closed-mindedness and myopic viewpoints that stereotyping can be a barrier.

■ **Blaming the victim**—making incorrect causal attributions, such as "she was asking for it" when referring to a young woman who is attacked while walking home after attending a friend's party. Sometimes we do this because of a common belief that people generally get what they deserve. However, these beliefs may prevent us from understanding and appreciating others' actions and perspectives. These beliefs may also falsely insulate us from the realities and challenges we all face.

■ **Discrimination**—barring an individual from membership in an organization or from a job because of her membership in a particular group. An example of unfair discrimination is the company that only interviews men for a position that requires a lot of travel.

■ **Harassment**—consciously shunning or verbally or physically abusing an individual because of membership in a particular group, such as individuals ganging up on a man because he's gay. Such harassment (and acceptance thereof) may start young, as in the case of the school bully who picks on the smaller or more studious children.

■ **Sexual harassment**—approaching a person in an unwanted, uninvited, intimate way, interfering with that person's productivity or advancement.

■ **Backlash**—negative reaction to the gaining of power and influence by members of previously underrepresented groups, leading to fear, resentment, and reverse discrimination.

How to Gain Awareness

We all have some prejudices. It's part of being human. We were all brought up with a certain set of values and experiences. We cannot deny who we are; the family, community, and country we come from; or the factors that make up our personality, beliefs, and personal characteristics. We can, however, commit to improving ourselves and our ability to understand and relate to others. There are some positive steps you can take to be more open to others and their perspectives. Some of these include reducing your prejudices and stereotypes, minimizing miscommunication, and building relationships with diverse others.

Reducing Your Prejudices and Use of Stereotypes[20]

■ Recognize that diversity exists and learn to value and respect fundamental differences.

■ Admit to your own biases and prejudices and commit yourself to reducing them.

■ Examine the stereotypes and actions that reflect your views of others, analyze your feelings based on these, and develop plans for changing your biases.

■ Dispel myths about diverse others when you are in a group of friends or associates.

Minimizing Miscommunication with Diverse Others

- Educate yourself about differences by reading, listening, and broadening your experience base.
- Practice effective communication skills (e.g., listening attentively, interpreting nonverbal cues, sending and receiving messages). When conversing with others whose first language is different from yours, pay careful attention to what they say and ask questions about what you don't understand.
- Use words that are inclusive rather than exclusive (for example, refer to "participants" rather than to a group by its primary gender).
- Avoid adjectives that spotlight certain groups and imply the individual is an exception (for example, the "female pilot" or the "black doctor" or the "qualified minority student").
- Be aware of current connotations of words; what seemed acceptable yesterday may be offensive to certain groups today. For example, the state of Virginia is now calling its upcoming year 2007 founding of Jamestown event a "commemoration" rather than a celebration, in deference to concerns raised by Native Americans who feel differently about the coming of "white people" than do Caucasians.
- Avoid forming an opinion as to the value of another's communication based on dress, mannerisms, accent, or eye contact. For example, northerners may perceive southerners to be ignorant and uneducated, while southerners may think northerners are pushy and rude. Concentrate more on the message than the messenger.

Building Relationships with Diverse Others

- Seek opportunities to interact with a wide variety of peers and associates.
- Form positive relationships with diverse others.
- Seek feedback from diverse others about how well you are communicating respect for them and valuing their diversity.
- Rather than treating diverse others as strangers, treat them as invited guests by showing interest in them. Share information about yourself and invite them to reciprocate.
- Encourage your peers to be candid by openly discussing their personal opinions, feelings, and reactions with you.
- Build trust by being open about yourself and being trustworthy when others share their opinions and reactions with you.
- Make goals to work with diverse others to achieve mutual goals.

Gender Differences

The face of the world's workforce is changing. Women will account for almost 50 percent of the American workforce by 2005, and this figure is expected to continue to grow.[21] Understanding the potential gender-based differences in communication styles, related traits, and work styles can allow members of both sexes to overcome stereotypes, biases, and behaviors that can hinder individual and organizational effectiveness.

Although men and women are equal, they are different. According to the latest research, so too is the way in which men and women communicate. John Gray, Deborah Tannen, and Kathleen Reardon are among the experts who have examined the reasons for and provided supporting evidence of these differences. In general, the research demonstrates that women tend to use communication to connect with others; they express feelings, empathize, and build relationships. In contrast, men tend to use communication to assert their status and request action; in so doing they tend to use more direct, succinct language. Women, however, tend to be more indirect, vague, and even apologetic when they speak. This language pattern demonstrates not only how women pay deference to others but also why some business associates view women as inferior to men.[22] There are many theories as to why this is so and how this tendency may evolve and change as more women assume managerial positions in the workplace.

Figure 5–2
Male/Female Communication
Differences[23]

	Male	Female
Content	Sports, money, business	People, feelings, relationships
Style	To resolve problems, denote status, and view conversation as a competition	To seek understanding, use conversation to connect with another individual
Structure	Get to the point without descriptive details	More detailed and descriptive, apologetic and unclear

Some surveys have shown that women managers are rated higher than their male counterparts in workplace communication, approachability, conducting performance evaluations, being a team player, and empowering others.[24] However, women are perceived to be unclear when giving instructions and also have a tendency to deflect the spotlight, making them appear "unleaderlike." Men may experience fewer task-related problems since their orders tend to be less ambiguous and subtle than their female counterparts. However, some employees might find their male co-worker or boss to be competitive and unsympathetic.

These differences between communication purpose and style (see Figure 5–2), along with cultural views on gender roles, have led to stereotypic beliefs about gender (see Figure 5–3), which may limit our ability to work closely and effectively with members of the opposite sex. Understanding that these beliefs are generally stereotypes will allow individuals and organizations to move away from discriminating or making false assumptions while managing and working with diverse others. Hopefully, the more exposure and knowledge we gain through working with members of the opposite sex, the better able we are to evaluate individuals based on all dimensions of their being, rather than the stereotypical traits associated with one's particular gender.[25]

So how can the sexes work more effectively together? Recognize that there are strengths in both the "female" and "male" styles. Men can learn from women's managerial style by using appropriate relationship building in the workplace, while women can learn from men's style to be less subtle and more assertive and direct, especially when giving instructions. Learn more about perceived differences between women and men both socially and in the workplace. Be aware that in many situations, gender might play a role in our ability to understand others. Be familiar with cultural gender stereotypes and avoid actions, language, and behaviors that perpetuate negative or hindering views. Figure 5–4 provides other suggestions for males and females.

Figure 5–3
Traits Associated with
Gender Stereotypes[26]

Male-associated Adjectives	Female-associated Adjectives
Aggressive	Affectionate
Autocratic	Complaining
Capable	Cooperative
Competitive	Emotional
Coarse	Easily Influenced
Decisive	Forgiving
Humorous	Indecisive
Individualistic	Illogical
Loud	Mild
Objective	Passive
Opportunistic	Sensitive
Reckless	Subjective
Tough-minded	Tactful
Unemotional	Weak

**Figure 5–4
Bridging the Gender Gap**

Means to Bridge the Gender Gap: For Women

- Maintain the strong "relationship" focus that women are known for. In today's team-based environment, the ability to relate to and work effectively with others is critical.

- Be more direct and assertive, less hesitant. Don't ask, "Can you complete this by Friday?" when what you mean is "I must have this report by Friday for my meeting with the client. Can I count on you?"

- Don't be afraid to speak up, especially in groups or meetings. Don't wait to be asked to speak. Come prepared with data or other information and share it confidently. If others interrupt you, politely request to finish.

- Be well read in areas sometimes thought of as the male domain, such as sports, finances, economics, science, and business. Part of being able to work effectively with diverse others requires understanding their perspective.

- Humor is fine but avoid self-deprecating humor; others may take the humor literally and reduce their faith in your abilities.

- Explain without apologizing. Men may interpret "I'm sorry" as an apology or acceptance of fault when women are communicating empathy, as in "I'm sorry that happened to you."[27]

- Avoid using vague terms and disclaimers, such as "You're welcome to disagree with me, but . . ." or "I'm not an expert, however, . . ." Express your views confidently; others will respect this quality.

- Avoid situations with co-workers that could be construed as intimate.

Means to Bridge the Gender Gap: For Men

- Maintain the direct, concise way of communicating that men are known for, especially in business situations. This increases the odds that others clearly understand your expectations and wishes.

- Add a relationship focus to your interactions with others at work. This is especially important in today's team-based, empowered environment.

- Encourage others to speak before you share your point of view. Others will listen more carefully to you if you first model this behavior.

- Be well read in areas sometimes thought of as the female domain, such as psychology, communication, interpersonal skills, relationships, group dynamics, self-improvement. The more you understand others' perspectives, the better you can understand and collaborate with them.

- Humor is fine but avoid stereotyping humor that is insensitive to members of certain groups.

- Avoid using the "fix-it" approach when others approach you about problems they are facing. Resist the urge to jump to a quick solution. Use active listening techniques to fully understand the problem and then ask if others want your advice or assistance.

- Avoid labeling. Refrain from using the words *girls, gals,* or *ladies;* these terms can be demeaning and labeling. Stick to the term *women* when talking to or about females.

- Be willing to make and admit mistakes; it helps humanize you in the eyes of subordinates and co-workers.

- Avoid situations with co-workers that could be construed as intimate.

Cross-cultural Diversity

In this increasingly global world, it is extremely important to understand the differences among cultures and how these differences can potentially affect communication between members of diverse cultures. Many communication barriers exist even when we speak the same language. Adding cultural and language differences to the mix can compound the potential for miscommunication. By understanding and acknowledging how the following elements vary across cultures, you can improve your ability to understand, and be understood by, others.

Semantics and Connotations

It is difficult at times to perfectly translate meaning from one language or culture to another. Many companies have found they made mistakes when trying to market a product made in one country to meet the needs of another. For example, Chevrolet experienced much difficulty marketing the Nova in Spanish-speaking countries. In Spanish, the phrase "no va" means "won't go!" While a boot is a type of footwear in America, in Australia and England it refers to the trunk of a car.

Social Conventions

Each culture has acceptable social conventions and norms that affect the communication process. What is considered rude in one culture is seen as perfectly acceptable in another. For example, in some cultures it is appropriate to use a stern, direct tone in admonishing strangers or in conducting business deals: Australians tend to be curt while Middle Easterners tend to talk very loudly. Acceptable levels of assertiveness are also an area of difference. In many Asian countries, businesspeople tend to be more indirect and vague in negative situations in order to maintain harmony in their business relationships. Gender status can determine roles and denote status, as is evident in many Middle Eastern cultures where women are expected to remain submissive and not speak or disagree with male counterparts in any way.

Nonverbal Communication

Nonverbal signals and gestures can be a source of embarrassment to an uninformed stranger. Direct eye contact in America and Latin America is expected in interactions, whereas some Europeans would experience discomfort with such lengthy, direct stares. Varying cultures view and utilize time differently. For example, North Americans and Japanese expect business meetings to begin on time—promptness is a virtue—but in South America it is not only accepted, but expected that you will be one to two hours late. In Latin America and southern Europe, standing close to others and touching are appropriate and expected, whereas in the United States people like their personal space and prefer not to be touched in business situations.

Dimensions of Cross-cultural Differences

There are many areas of difference between cultures. Language differences are the most pronounced, but other differences can be just as significant. According to Hofstede, there are five dimensions of cross-cultural differences: power distance, individualism versus collectivism, uncertainty avoidance, masculinity versus femininity, and long-term versus short-term orientation.[28] These differences can play a significant role in our ability to develop professional and personal relationships.

■ **Power distance** refers to the acceptance (or lack thereof) of unequal power distribution. In countries where power distance is high, citizens show deep respect for age and seniority and rarely bypass hierarchy in important decisions. Countries with high power distance are characterized by paternalistic management, where a supreme authority maintains tight control over policies and procedures. Latin America, Arab countries, and France are examples of high power distance countries.

In countries where power distance is low, competence is valued over seniority and status is less important. Countries with low power status are characterized by participative management, where decision making is shared across employee levels, and the opinions of many are considered before taking action. The United States, Australia, northern Europe, and Israel are examples of low power distance countries.

■ **Individualism versus collectivism** refers to how loosely or tightly integrated the society seems, the degree to which the people of the country prefer to act as individuals rather than as members of groups. In countries with an individualistic approach, individual achievement is emphasized and decision making is open to everyone involved. People who live in individualistic cultures are valued for their self-motivation and self-interest. Countries that can be characterized as individualistic include the United States, the United Kingdom, Canada, Australia, and the Netherlands.

In countries with a collectivist approach, the emphasis is on group harmony, total involvement in decision making, and a focus on decisions made in the best interest of the group. Countries that have a collectivist approach include Japan, many Latin American countries, and South Korea.

■ **Uncertainty avoidance** reflects the degree of threat felt when facing ambiguity and risk. In countries that are high in uncertainty avoidance, rules and procedures are preferred and followed, there is a limited display of emotion, and citizens have the expectation of lifetime employment. Examples of countries with high uncertainty avoidance are Greece, Guatemala, and Japan.

In countries with low uncertainty avoidance, risk taking is prevalent, entrepreneurship is encouraged, and citizens change jobs frequently. Countries with low uncertainty avoidance include Singapore, Hong Kong, and Ireland.

■ **Masculinity versus femininity** refers to the degree to which emphasis is placed on assertiveness, relationships, and quality of life. In countries that are more "masculine," individuals are encouraged to be assertive. Task orientation and competitiveness are valued qualities, and money and status are valued highly. Examples of countries that are more "masculine" in their approach include Japan and Italy.

In countries that are more "feminine," individuals are encouraged to work collaboratively and to be less assertive about their own personal needs. Job satisfaction as well as work–family balance are both considered to be very important. Examples of countries that are considered to be more "feminine" are Sweden, Norway, and Thailand.

■ **Long-term versus short-term** orientation refers to a culture's tendency to focus more on the future or the past, which includes economic success and values regarding savings and persistence. Long-term orientation implies a focus on the future, with trends toward delaying gratification, thriftiness (saving), and persistence. The top long-term countries are China, Hong Kong, Taiwan, Japan, and South Korea. These countries typically have higher savings rates and are more economically successful than countries with short-term orientation.

In countries where short-term orientation is common, there is a focus on values toward the past and present, with respect for traditions and fulfilling social obligations. These countries' values include the tendency to spend even if this means borrowing money. Countries with short-term orientation are Pakistan, the Philippines, Bangladesh, and all Western countries.

Strategies for Addressing Cross-cultural Issues

The challenge for working effectively with others in an increasingly diverse workforce is upon us. By implementing the following strategies, you can improve your ability to work with others from cultures different from your own.

For Individuals

■ Live and work outside of your home country. Be willing to take an overseas assignment whenever the opportunity arises.

■ Travel outside of your home country extensively.

■ While away, adapt to the customs of the new country. Get to know the local residents, rather than spending your time with people of your own nationality.

■ Develop friendships with people from nationalities other than your own. Make it a point to learn from them about their customs, about the way business is conducted, about the differences and similarities between their country and yours.

■ Learn another language or languages.

■ Work at developing a non-home-country perspective on world events. Subscribe to newspapers and periodicals that broaden your understanding of key issues from multinational perspectives.

■ When traveling outside your home country on business, learn in advance about cultural differences and customs that will affect the way in which you conduct business outside your home country.[29]

For Companies and Organizations

■ Offer language training to your employees.

■ Encourage your employees to accept non-home-country work assignments.

- Provide transition counseling to employees and their families both before and after a non-home-country assignment.

- Provide training to help employees learn about and be sensitive to cross-cultural differences.

- Examine your employment practices to ensure that your company is not intentionally or unintentionally discriminating against anyone due to his or her religion or ethnicity. For example, requiring employees to work on Saturdays precludes members of certain religions from joining your organization.

Cross-cultural differences are natural. These differences will be welcomed rather than feared and will not become a source of embarrassment if individuals and organizations accept responsibility for learning about other cultures. Those managers and companies that are knowledgeable about and committed to accepting a diversity of backgrounds and perspectives will be more open to and able to manage cross-cultural differences than those who adopt a narrow, one-culture perspective.[30] This multiple perspective will be useful not only in business but also in life.

Affirmative Action and Diversity

We have looked at the definition of diversity and why it is important, and we have examined diversity from the perspective of gender and cross-cultural differences. While acceptance of diversity seems to be on the rise among individuals and in organizations, many organizations are managing representation rather than managing diversity. This means companies are focusing on hiring good people through affirmative action programs but are not creating an environment that allows diverse individuals to feel free to be themselves, to be accepted for who they are, and, most importantly, to be promoted through the ranks of an organization.[31] The problem is evidenced by the high number of women and minorities who leave corporate America to start their own businesses, citing as a primary motivation the lack of advancement opportunities and a lack of acceptance by their bosses and co-workers.[32]

Companies are beginning to view the concept of managing diversity more broadly than simply bringing in diverse people. It is now viewed as "a 'way of thinking' toward the objective of creating an environment that will enable all employees to reach their full potential in pursuit of organizational objectives."[33] This broader view challenges us to improve conditions for and relationships among both members of "majority" groups as well as those who are members of "underrepresented" groups. In the United States, underrepresented groups include women, people of color, and those who are physically disabled. Traditionally companies did not make concerted efforts to recruit members of these groups, resulting in a dearth of women, minorities, and the disabled at senior levels of management in many organizations today. Recent laws now govern certain hiring practices, and companies are encouraged to hire members of underrepresented groups over members of majority groups when all things are equal. This notion is called **affirmative action.** Some of the resistance to this notion on the part of some people is due to their concern about the way in which affirmative action was implemented in their companies, which simply leads to fulfilling quotas. Some believe that affirmative action resulted in a form of reverse discrimination, where individuals from majority groups were overlooked in favor of less-qualified applicants from underrepresented groups.

In today's progressive times, the concept of affirmative action is being replaced by the concept mentioned earlier in this chapter, that of *managing diversity*. This notion challenges us to value the entire spectrum of individual experiences, abilities, and needs.[34] The more progressive companies have used the concept of managing diversity rather than affirmative action as a means to making their work environment more inclusive for all of their employees (including white males), not just those of a particular race or ethnic background.[35] The real innovators have gone beyond affirmative action to a focus on diversity that is voluntary, rather than government mandated, and is driven by an interest in

**Figure 5–5
Differences between
Affirmative Action and
Managing Diversity**[36]

Affirmative Action	Managing Diversity
Government mandated	Voluntary—Company driven
Legally driven	Productivity driven
Quantitative	Qualitative
Problem focused	Opportunity focused
Assumes assimilation	Assumes integration
Internally focused	Internally and externally focused
Reactive	Proactive

enhancing productivity, rather than a concern for the law. Figure 5–5 details the differences between the essence of affirmative action and the more proactive approach to managing diversity.

"No culture can live if it attempts to be exclusive."

Mahatma Gandhi

The Imperative for Diversity

Accepting and managing diversity is essential for managers who wish to succeed and for organizations that wish to be competitive in today's marketplace. Four change factors that make managing diversity imperative include:[37]

1. The global economic paradigm shift—The competitive global economy increases our interdependence on foreign and domestic markets for sources of labor, manufacturing, and customers. This global shift, which is consistent with living in the 21st century, increases the chances that individuals will work with or have contact with individuals from varying cultures.[38]

2. The "new worker" workforce—The numbers cited earlier indicate the increase in the number of women and minorities entering the workforce, the "graying" of the workforce not just in the United States but around the world, the lack of sufficient workforce entrants to staff the vast array of service and retail jobs that are available, the increased availability of technology that is enabling those with disabilities to enter the workforce, and the creation of new technologies that are affecting the way we work.[39]

3. The diversity of customers, clients, and suppliers—Marketplaces are becoming more diverse, and with this change comes the expectation that diversity will be reflected in the organizations that provide the goods and services. According to the U.S. government's Minority Business Development report, "multiethnic purchasing power may reach $4.3 trillion by 2045 in America."[40]

4. The shift to the empowerment model of management—This enables individuals to align their efforts with business objectives and gives employees greater involvement in decision making. "To empower all kinds of employees to perform at their best, organizational structure, systems, and policies must recognize and equally nurture the inputs of every group; integrate, rather than stifle, differences; and actively discourage both blatant and latent prejudice and discrimination."[41]

Benefits of Organizational Diversity

- Attracts and retains good people. Lack of diversity is stifling and causes good people to go elsewhere.

- Facilitates innovation. Anecdotal and empirical evidence clearly demonstrates that bringing together individuals with diverse talents and perspectives (and in a supportive atmosphere) results in greater innovation and creativity than that possible with a homogeneous group.[42]

(continued)

- Increases ability to manage external diversity. The best companies develop strategies to manage both their employees and external forces,[43] such as their corporate image and social responsibility agenda.
- Improves customer service by promoting respect for and open interactions between employees and other employees as well as between employees and customers.
- Improves organizational effectiveness. Teamwork, productivity, and work quality all increase when employees have or perceive they have the opportunity to contribute and have influence.
- Provides greater flexibility and readiness for change. Diverse organizations are better able to survive in changing environments.[44]

Organizations need to view managing diversity as a journey or opportunity rather than as a problem to be solved. When we focus on the positives, we open the doors to accepting diversity in practice rather than in theory. There will be more questions than answers. However, this is good; getting organizational members to embrace the issue is the starting place for true change.[45]

Tips for Managing Organizational Diversity

- Communicate diversity goals and expectations clearly to employees, spelling out the benefits for each of them as individuals as well as for the company and industry overall.[46]
- Communicate these goals through a wide variety of means such as in vision, mission, and value statements and written communications such as employee and shareholder newsletters, slogans, speeches, and vendor exhibits.
- Ensure that diversity is a top-down effort. Diversity must have visible support from the top if employees are to view it as real and credible.
- Remember that the vital link between successful and unsuccessful diversity initiatives is supervisors: If a supervisor supports and "lives" diversity in the organization, employees are more likely to accept it.[47]
- Avoid the "melting pot" technique—don't try to make everyone the same; respect both differences and commonalities.[48] Some refer to this as the "salad bowl" approach.
- Create a management plan—including assessing the situation, setting objectives, and involving employees in generating solutions and initiatives. Some successful initiatives include these:[49]
  - Aggressive hiring programs.
  - Early identification programs in the schools.
  - Partnerships with other businesses and community organizations.
  - Alliances with national advocate organizations.
  - Mentoring programs.
  - Minority employee networks.
  - Ongoing employee surveys.
  - Strict policies for dealing quickly and fairly with cases of prejudice, discrimination, and harassment.
  - Enhanced succession and promotion planning processes.
  - Tying manager pay increases to success in promoting diversity.
  - Accountability and reward programs.
  - Development of success measures.
  - Diversity awareness training programs.
  - Developing a comprehensive retention strategy.

Summary

We live and work in a diverse world. Diversity among our acquaintances, classmates, co-workers, neighbors, and friends is inevitable. How we interact with people who possess characteristics, values, and work styles that differ from ours plays a critical role in our ability to manage ourselves and help others achieve their goals. To work effectively with diverse others, we need to first understand and appreciate our own uniqueness. Use this information not to evaluate others' uniqueness, but as a starting point for building relationships. Seek opportunities to interact with diverse others. Share your insights, feelings, and values with them. Encourage them to do the same. The more you do this, the better you will accept and embrace diversity.

Key Terms and Concepts

Affirmative action	Long-term versus short-term orientation
Backlash	Managing diversity
Blaming the victim	Masculinity versus femininity
Discrimination	Power distance
Diversity	Prejudice
Ethnocentrism	Sexual harassment
Harassment	Stereotypes
Individualism versus collectivism	Uncertainty avoidance

Endnotes

1. Case is based on JMU student Randa Chamma; case submitted in COB 202 Interpersonal Skills, Fall 1999.

2. Genevieve Capowski, "Managing Diversity," *Management Review,* June 1996, p. 12.

3. Marty Loden, *Implementing Diversity: Best Practices for Making Diversity Work in Your Organization* (New York: McGraw-Hill, 1995).

4. Taylor Cox and Ruby Beale, *Developing Competency to Manage Diversity* (San Francisco: Berrett-Koehler, 1997).

5. Lee Gardenswartz and Anita Rowe, "Why Diversity Matters," *HR Focus,* July 1998, pp. 51–53.

6. Ibid.

7. J. Orsburn, L. Moran, E. Musselwhite, and J. Zanger, *Self Directed Work Teams* (Homewood, IL: Business One Irwin, 1990).

8. Anonymous, "Managing Diversity at Dow Chemical and Texas Commerce Bank," *Human Resource Management International Digest* 10, no. 6 (Sept.–Oct. 2002), p. 13.

9. Jon Katzenbach and Douglas Smith, *The Wisdom of Work Teams* (Boston: Harvard Business School, 1993).

10. Gail Robinson and Kathleen Dechant, "Building a Business Case for Diversity," *Academy of Management Executive,* Aug. 1997, p. 21.

11. Ibid.

12. R. M. Belbin, *Management Teams—Why They Succeed or Fail* (Woburn, MA: Butterworth-Heinemann, 1981).

13. U.S. Bureau of the Census, *Statistical Abstract of the United States: 1990* (110th ed.), Washington D.C.

14. Capowski, "Managing Diversity."

15. Ibid.

16. *Workforce, 2000: Work and Workers for the Twenty-First Century* (Indianapolis: Hudson Institute and U.S. Department of Labor, June 1987), p. xxi.

17. Robinson and Dechant, "Building a Business Case."

18. David W. Johnson, *Reaching Out: Interpersonal Effectiveness and Self-Actualization,* Sixth Ed. (Boston: Allyn & Bacon, 1997), p. 342.

19. Salma M. Al-Lamki, "Orientation: The Essential Ingredient in Cross-cultural Management," *International Journal of Management* 19, no. 4 (Dec. 2002), p. 568.

20. Portions of this are adapted from Johnson, *Reaching Out.*

21. U.S. Department of Labor, *The Glass Ceiling Commission, New Release* (Washington, DC: Office of Public Affairs, USDL 95-483, 1995).

22. Deborah Tannen, *You Just Don't Understand: Women and Men in Conversation* (New York: Ballantine Books, 1991).

23. Judi Brownell, "Communicating with Credibility: The Gender Gap," *Cornell H.R.A. Quarterly,* April 1993, pp. 52–61.

24. Sally Helgesen, *The Female Advantage: Women's Ways of Leading* (Garden City, NY: Double-day, 1990).

25. Gary N. Powell, *Women and Men in Management* (Newbury Park, CA: Sage Publications, 1993), p. 261.

26. Portions from J. E. Williams and D. L. Best, "Cross-Cultural Views of Women and Men," in *Psychology and Culture* (Boston: Allyn and Bacon, 1994), p. 193.

27. Deborah Tannen, "I'm Sorry I'm Not Apologizing," *Executive Female,* 1991, pp. 21–24.

28. Geert Hofstede, "Problems Remain, but Theories Will Change: The Universal and the Specific in 21st Century Global Management," *Organizational Dynamics,* July 1999, p. 34.

29. Barbara Pachter, "The Five Biggest Mistakes Americans Make When Doing Business Abroad," *Agency Sales Magazine,* Dec. 1997, p. 40.

30. Parshotam Dass and Barbara Parker, "Strategies for Managing Human Resource Diversity: From Resistance to Learning," *Academy of Management Executive,* May 1999, p. 68.

31. Cheryl Comeau-Kirschner, "Beyond Fair Representation," *Management Review,* Dec. 1999, p. 8.

32. Dayle M. Smith, *Women at Work: Leadership for the Next Century* (Upper Saddle River, NJ: Prentice Hall, 2000), p. 18.

33. R. Roosevelt Thomas, Jr., "The Concept of Managing Diversity," *The Public Manager: The New Bureaucrat,* Winter 1996, p. 41.

34. Loret Carbone, "Different Strokes," *Restaurant Hospitality,* Oct. 1995, p. 38.

35. Dinesh D'Souza, "Beyond Affirmative Action: The Perils of Managing Diversity," *Chief Executive* (U.S.), Dec. 1996, p. 42.

36. Adapted from Marilyn Loden and Judy B. Rosener, *Workforce America! Managing Employee Diversity as a Vital Resource* (Burr Ridge, IL: Irwin Professional Publishing, 1991).

37. Renee Bazile-Jones and Bernadette Lynn, "Diversity in the Workplace: Why We Should Care," *CMA—The Management Accounting Magazine,* June 1996, p. 9.

38. Al-Lamki, "Orientation."

39. Capowski, "Managing Diversity."

40. Linda Wallace, "Diversity: The Operating Manual," *Columbia Journalism Review* 42, no. 2 (July/Aug. 2003), p. 18, in reference to the U.S. Minority Business Development Agency's report "The Emerging Minority Marketplace."

41. T. Cox, "The Multicultural Organization," *Academy of Management Executive,* 1991, p. 34.

42. Susan G. Cohen and Diane E. Bailey, "What Makes Teams Work: Group Effectiveness Research from the Shop Floor to the Executive Suite," *Journal of Management,* 1997, p. 239.

43. Thomas, "Concept of Managing Diversity."

44. Roger D. Wheeler, "Managing Workforce Diversity," *Tax Executive,* Nov.–Dec. 1997, pp. 493–95.

45. Norma Bartum, "Diversity for All," *Association Management* 55, no. 7 (July 2003), p. 56.

46. Charlene Marmer Solomon, "Communicating in a Global Environment," *Workforce,* Nov. 1999, p. 50.

47. Matti Dobbs and Oliver Brown, "A Vital Link: The Supervisor's Role in Managing Diversity," *The Public Manager: The New Bureaucrat,* Summer 1997, p. 53.

48. "Conversing in a Diverse World," *Association Management,* Feb. 2000, p. 31.

49. Katherine Giscombe and Adrienne D. Sims, "Breaking the Color Barrier," *HR Focus,* July 1998, p. S9.

**Exercise 5–A
Personal Stereotypes**

Look at the words below. What stereotypes come to mind upon first seeing each word? Where did these stereotypes originate? What data or experience can be cited to dispel each of the stereotypes? From the list below, chose 5–10 groups for which you can identify common stereotypes. In the first column write a few adjectives that describe the stereotype (e.g., arrogant, emotional). In the second column list the probable origin of these stereotypes for you (e.g., my parent's beliefs, the media). In the third column, cite a statistic, known fact, or example from your personal experience that dispels the stereotype. Share (depending on your comfort level) your stereotypes, their origins, and ways to dispel the inaccuracies with others in your class or small group.

Group	Stereotypes	Origins	Inaccuracies
Whites/Caucasians			
Native Americans			
African Americans			
Asians			
Women			
Men			
Southerners			
Midwesterners			
Northerners			
Hispanics			
Jews			
Muslims			
Catholics			
Baptists			
Gays/Lesbians			
Elderly persons			
College students			
Teenagers			

Questions

1. What are some of the more common stereotypes?
2. Where do these stereotypes originate?
3. What facts can be cited to dispel the inaccuracies?
4. What, if any, stereotypes are you able to dispel as a result of this exercise?

Exercise 5–B
Personal Biases and Stereotypes in Employee Recruitment

Four volunteers serving as "candidates" will be given background profiles by the instructor to use while acting as potential employees. A fifth volunteer serving as "employer" reads a job description for a position to be filled. Individually, on a piece of paper, participants are to rank each of the four, from most likely to be hired (1) to least likely (4), citing reasons each candidate does or does not match the requirements for the job. Participants then vote for the person they think the employer is most likely to hire (out of the four candidates) for this position by going to that candidate. Participants should then explain to the candidate the reasons he or she was selected so candidates can compile a list. Participants are then to go to the candidate they believe would be the least favorable candidate and explain their reasoning for this decision. Candidates are to write on the board the characteristics or issues that made them appear more and less suited for the job.

Questions

1. What are some of the reasons certain candidates appear to be better suited for the position than the others?

2. What stereotypes emerged during the discussion of "fit" between the candidates and the position?

3. What are some of the legitimate factors used to differentiate among candidates, and what are some of the factors used to select one candidate over another that are less legitimate?

Source: This exercise is based on ideas from a JMU class presentation by Kim Aslen, June 1999.

Exercise 5–C
Cross-cultural Communication Simulation

In this simulation, you will play the part of a manager employed by one of three firms—a commercial bank, a construction firm, and a hotel development company—which are planning a joint venture to build a new hotel and retail shopping complex in Perth, Australia. They come from three different cultures: Blue, Green, and Red. Each has specific cultural values, traits, customs, and practices.

You are a manager in the company to which you have been assigned. You will attend the kickoff get-together for the three-day meeting during which the three companies will negotiate the details of the partnership. Your management team consists of a vice president and a number of other managers. Consider the types of topics that the various corporations would discuss at an initial meeting.

Your instructor will provide you with information pertaining to your culture. You will be given about 15 minutes to meet with your fellow corporate members, during which you should:

1. Select a leader.

2. Discuss what your objectives and approaches will be at the opening get-together.

3. Using the description of your assigned culture, practice how you will talk and behave until you are reasonably familiar with your cultural orientation. Be sure to practice conversation distance, greeting rituals, and nonverbal behavior.

You will then return to the kickoff meeting where you will meet with employees from the other firms. As the social proceeds, interact with the managers from the other companies. Maintain the role you have been assigned, but do not discuss it explicitly. Notice how other people react to you and how you react to them. We will discuss the experience after it is over.

Upon completing this activity, answer the following questions:

1. In what ways did your perceptions of others and their differences influence how you interacted with them and your ability to achieve your goals?

_____

_____

_____

_____

_____

_____

_____

2. What did you learn about yourself and others through this activity? Discuss your strengths and weaknesses in cross-cultural interaction.

_____

_____

_____

_____

_____

_____

_____

3. What were things you or others did or said that enabled or hindered you from adjusting to other people and their culture: (1) in this activity? (2) in similar real-life situations?

_____

_____

_____

_____

_____

_____

_____

4. What lessons did you learn from this activity? What steps can you take to improve your ability to understand and appreciate differences?

_____

_____

_____

_____

_____

_____

_____

Source: Daphne A. Jameson, "Using a Simulation to Teach Intercultural Communication in Business Communication Courses," *Bulletin of the Association for Business Communication (Business Communication Quarterly),* LV, no. 4, March 1993, p. 1–20.

Exercise 5–D
Diversity Squares

Move about the room and try to find people who can answer yes to your questions. This is just like BINGO in that you are trying to complete a row. Once you have found someone to answer yes to the question, you can cross off the square, placing that person's name or initials in the box. Each person who answers yes to one of your questions can only be used once. Continue to find others until you are able to complete a row.

Have you ever worked with anyone who is 20 or more years older than you?	Have you ever worked on a farm?	Do you speak more than one language?	Have you ever worked with anyone with a physical disability?	Have you ever worked with anyone who is a non-Christian?
Have you ever had a female boss?	Are you of Hispanic or Latin American heritage?	Do you have a family member or friend on welfare?	Have you ever had an African American boss?	Do you have a best friend of a different race?
Do you have a friend who is gay, lesbian, or bisexual?	Have you ever been discriminated against because of race or ethnicity?	Have you ever lived outside of your home country?	Have you ever known a convicted felon?	Did a single parent raise you?
Have you ever been sexually harassed at work?	Has either of your parents been in the military?	Are you of Asian heritage?	Are you a vegetarian?	Have you ever had a doctor whose race or ethnicity differs from yours?
Do you know someone with a chronic disease such as cancer or AIDS?	Have you ever dated someone who was less educated than you?	Have you ever been discriminated against because of gender?	Were your parents or grandparents immigrants?	Have you ever had a boss who was younger than you?

Source: This exercise is adapted from a presentation by Kari Calello, JMU student class presentation; and J. William Pfeiffer and Leonard D. Goodstein (Eds.), *The 1994 Annual: Developing Human Resources*, Pfeiffer & Company, 1994. Copyright © 1994 by John Wiley & Sons, Inc. Reprinted by permission of John Wiley and Sons Inc.

Questions

1. How did you feel asking individuals certain questions? What approach did you use to ask the questions?

2. Were some questions more difficult to ask than others (perceived to be potentially more sensitive or offensive)?

3. Why did you approach certain individuals for certain questions?

4. If you were approached by several people about the same question, how did it make you feel? Why did they select you for certain questions and neglect to ask you about others?

5. Would some of the questions be more difficult to ask or more likely to offend others if worded in the first person? For example, "Are you gay, lesbian, or bisexual?"

6. What did this exercise make you realize about stereotypes and prejudice?

Exercise 5–E
Gender Stereotypes

Part I

Your instructor will divide the group into smaller groups based on gender, resulting in male-only and female-only groups. Groups are to brainstorm a list in response to the following statements. It is not necessary for all members to agree with everything the group generates. Add all inputs to the list.

Female groups complete the following:

- All men are . . .
- Men think all women are . . .

Male groups complete the following:

- All women are . . .
- Women think all men are . . .

Part II

After generating your lists, your groups will present a role-play to the class based on the following scenarios by switching gender roles (females portray males, and males portray females):

Two friends (of the same gender) meeting each other back at school for the first time this year.

A person flirting with a member of the opposite sex at a party. (Females play a male flirting with a female; males play a female flirting with a male.)

Questions

1. What aspects of the role-plays were accurate, distorted, or inaccurate?
2. How did you feel portraying the opposite gender and how did it feel to see your gender portrayed?
3. On what stereotypes or experiences were these role-plays based?

Part III

Your group will now write its brainstorm lists on the board for discussion. Remember that these lists are a product of a group effort and are generally based on stereotypes and not necessarily the view of any one individual.

   Analyze the lists for positive and negative results in both personal and professional settings. Generate a list of ways to dispel, reduce, or counter negative stereotypes.

Source: Portions of this exercise are adapted from concepts in Susan F. Fritz, William Brown, Joyce Lunde, and Elizabeth Banset, *Interpersonal Skills for Leadership* (Englewood Cliffs, NJ: Prentice Hall, 1999); and A. B. Shani and James B. Lau, *Behavior in Organizations: An Experiential Approach*, Sixth Ed. (Chicago: Irwin, 1996).

Questions

1. What similarities, patterns, or trends developed from the groups?
2. How do you feel about the thoughts presented about your gender?
3. What implications do these thoughts have on actions and situations in the work environment?
4. What can you do to reduce the negative affects of these stereotypes? What can you do to help dispel these stereotypes? (Brainstorm with your group or class.)

Exercise 5–F
Diversity Awareness

1. Subscribe to a magazine or newspaper that provides you with a perspective that differs from your own (e.g., if you're Caucasian, subscribe to *Black Enterprise;* if you're from the United States, subscribe to the *International Herald Tribune*).

2. Invite someone you know who is from a country other than yours to your next party.

3. Attend service in a church, synagogue, or mosque that is different from your own.

4. Volunteer to work for a cause that helps children from a country other than your own.

5. Volunteer to work at a nursing home or at a home for physically or mentally challenged children or adults.

6. Watch a movie that deals with diversity issues such as *Courage Under Fire, GI Jane, Glory, Soul Man, Revenge of the Nerds, Pleasantville, Tarzan, In and Out, Philadelphia, The Godfather, The Crying Game, Guess Who's Coming to Dinner, Boyz 'n the Hood, West Side Story, Romeo and Juliet, Schindler's List, Thelma and Louise, Matewan, Remember the Titans, Chocolat, The Color Purple, The King and I, Dances with Wolves, Stand and Deliver, The Joy Luck Club, He Said She Said, Regarding Henry, Driving Miss Daisy, La Bamba, Simon Birch, Yentl.* Write a paper addressing these questions: What types and sources of prejudice were in evidence? How did diversity, stereotyping, prejudice, or discrimination affect the characters? What effective and ineffective strategies were employed to handle prejudice? What strategies did you learn to either overcome prejudice or manage diversity?

**Exercise 5–G
Reflection/Action Plan**

This chapter discussed the skill of understanding and managing diversity—what it is, why it's important, and how to improve your skill in these areas. Complete the worksheet below upon completing all readings and experiential exercises for this chapter.

1. The one or two areas regarding understanding or managing diversity in which I am most strong are:

_____

_____

_____

_____

2. The one or two areas of understanding or managing diversity in which I need more improvement are:

_____

_____

_____

_____

3. If I did only one thing to improve in this area, it would be to:

_____

_____

_____

_____

4. Making this change would probably result in:

_____

_____

_____

_____

5. If I did not change or improve in this area, it would probably affect my personal and professional life in the following ways:

_____

_____

_____

_____

6 The Importance and Skill of Listening

Learning Points

How do I:

- Ask a friend to be a good listener or sounding board for me when I have something important to discuss with him or her?
- Use behaviors that demonstrate that I am a good listener or sounding board?
- Differentiate between positive and negative listening behaviors?
- Ensure my verbal and nonverbal messages are congruent?
- Accurately interpret others' nonverbal messages?

It all started out well. I had been steadily increasing my client base for six months at the investment firm where I work as an analyst. Ron Sanders, the division manager, had recently asked me to handle a dozen accounts of long-established clients previously handled by a retired analyst. I had made a point to meet with all the owners of the transferred accounts to gain perspective on their portfolios.

I remember sitting with Mrs. Crenshaw, a wealthy widow in her late 60s. We discussed her past investments and possible changes for the future. She had the notion that 60 is old and she didn't believe she had enough money to last her through her final years. Mrs. Crenshaw stated she wanted to be more conservative in her investments, no longer willing to risk as much principle. After listening to her family stories and concerns for what I had thought was an acceptable length of time (to me it seemed interminable!), I finally said, "Sixty is young, you have plenty of years ahead of you, and the amount of savings you have is more than sufficient to allow us to combine higher risk investments with some of your more conservative investments." I continued to show her the opportunities she had for making high returns by redistributing her investments. She signed the papers for the new investment instruments and thanked me for my time.

Everything was set. That is why I was so surprised when Ron Sanders informed me that he had just come from a meeting with Mrs. Crenshaw's eldest son and I needed to complete paperwork to delay all changes to her account. I also needed to transfer all of Mrs. Crenshaw's files to Sharon Foster, a senior analyst at the firm. How could I have screwed this up? What was I thinking when I convinced her to make the changes? How could I have missed her discomfort with the changes? All of a sudden I realized I hadn't heard a thing she had been saying—not really heard, anyway.

1. Where did the analyst go wrong?
2. Why did the analyst have a difficult time reading Mrs. Crenshaw?
3. What verbal and nonverbal clues did the analyst miss?
4. What should the analyst do to improve his listening skills with clients?

"If you think you know it all, then you haven't been listening"

La Rochefoucauld

Communication is a two-way street. When done correctly, **communication** is a fluid, evolving process involving the sending and receiving of messages between two or more people. Communication is enhanced when all parties have the opportunity to both speak as well as listen, when all have a chance to check their perceptions of what they're hearing, and when principles of both verbal and nonverbal communication are followed. This chapter reviews the basic concepts of effective listening and how these principles can be applied in personal and professional life.

What Is Listening?

Listening, the process of taking in what we hear and mentally organizing it to make sense of it,[1] is an invaluable component of the communication process. No matter how accomplished a speaker is, if no one is listening the speaker is not reaching his or her audience. Listening is an essential skill for those who want to be successful in work and in life. Yet truly effective listeners are hard to find. When was the last time you truly felt listened to? When did you feel someone really made an effort to get to know you—to understand where you were coming from and why or to help you solve a problem without meddling and without shifting attention to *their* problems and away from yours? The challenge of listening is exemplified by Mark Twain's famous words:

"There's a reason why God gave us two ears and only one mouth."

How many of us were fortunate enough to be taught the skill of listening in school or on the job? Listening is critical for effective communication, yet few people have actually acquired training in this essential skill. Most of us have had exposure to the art of talking and presenting, but listening is a skill that is simply overlooked, perhaps because it is assumed that everyone can or will do this. Talking is one of the first skills we practice. Parents can hardly wait for their child to speak for the first time. Yet the most training we receive in listening is when someone says those infamous words "You're not listening to me" or "You had better listen to what I say!"

Many confuse the ability to hear or simply recognize sound with the skill of listening or the ability to comprehend what is heard. The act of simply "hearing" is a passive activity. The act of listening—truly listening—demands attention, concentration, and effort.

There are several different types of listening:[2]

Passive listening occurs when one is trying to absorb as much of the information presented as possible. The listener acts as a sponge, taking in the information with no or little attempt to process or enhance the messages being sent by the speaker.

Attentive listening occurs when one is genuinely interested in the speaker's point of view. The listener is aware something can be learned from the interaction. In attentive listening, the listener will make assumptions about the messages being relayed by the speaker and fill in gaps with assumptions based on what the listener wants to hear rather than on what the speaker is actually saying. At this level of listening, the listener doesn't check to see whether what she or he heard is what the speaker intended to say. Many barriers and biases can hinder this form of interaction.

Active or **empathetic listening** is the most powerful level of listening and requires the largest amount of work on the part of the listener. In active listening, communication is a vibrant, two-way process that involves high levels of attentiveness, clarification, and message processing. In active listening, the listener not only hears and reacts to the words being spoken but also paraphrases, clarifies, and gives feedback to the speaker about the messages being received.

Active listening follows the "70/30" principle: when in the role of listener, true active listeners spend almost 70 percent of their time listening and less than 30 percent of their time talking.

The Importance of Active Listening

Active listening shows the speaker that you are concerned. By paying full attention to the speaker, the listener is able to focus on the key elements of the message being sent, ask questions to clarify meanings, and offer statements that enhance both the speaker's and the listener's understanding of what is being said. Active listening leads to getting better information. By asking clarifying questions, the listener motivates the speaker to be more precise when explaining the nuances of a situation, enabling the listener to obtain details that otherwise might not have surfaced. Imagine the mother asking her teenage son how his day went. If she accepts his one-word answer ("fine"), she limits her understanding of his situation and might communicate that she really doesn't care to know more.

Active listening encourages further communication. In passive listening, a one-way form of communication, the listener simply takes at face value what the speaker says without processing or inquiring about the information. In active listening, it is common for the listener to be an active participant in the conversation, asking questions and probing for details in such a way that the speaker feels both supported and encouraged to share more information about a situation, enhancing both the speaker's and the listener's understanding of what is taking place.

Active listening also has the potential to enhance relationships. It takes more time to listen actively to someone else. Just taking this time to focus on a person and his or her issues can improve the relationship. Listening actively also involves offering mutual support and developing common understanding, both of which serve to strengthen trust and enhance interactions between the people involved. Returning to the mother and son example, if she took the time to listen and ask a few thoughtful follow-up questions, her son might begin to open up about his day. For example, he might talk about the fact he failed his geometry exam, won a wrestling match, or that his best friend was arrested for drug possession. When we take the time to truly listen—using our ears and eyes to take in a more complete story—others feel cared for. These feelings are usually reciprocated, resulting in an enhanced relationship.

Another benefit of active listening is that it can sometimes calm down another person who is feeling very upset about a situation. Think for a moment about airline ticket agents and how calm most of them are when confronted by an aggressive or just a tired passenger. Most airline ticket agents have received customer service training that emphasizes the importance of listening to the customer. While an agent can seldom do anything that would directly respond to the passenger's needs, such as change the weather or get the flight to leave on time, the best agents are skilled at focusing their attention on passengers in distress, hearing them out, and quietly helping the passengers problem-solve about the situation in which they find themselves. These agents use their training to make the passenger feel heard and understood. They listen, ask clarifying questions, empathize, and offer potential solutions for consideration by the passenger—all in a way that is intended to calm passengers.

Active listening invites others to listen to you. By listening actively you set a good example for others and remind them that listening is a valuable skill that they can also use. People who have been listened to actively are more likely to reciprocate. This benefit of active listening is echoed in one of Stephen Covey's best-selling *Seven Habits of Highly Effective People:* seek first to understand and then to be understood.[3] Typically, when two people disagree, one is likely to say something like, "OK, we don't agree. Let me tell you why you're wrong and how my way is superior." Perhaps that statement is a bit exaggerated, but it demonstrates the need of many of us to be right and have our say— first and foremost. Imagine how this exchange would differ if it sounded like this: "OK, we don't agree. Why don't you tell me your idea and why you think it will work." When we actively listen to another, chances are very high that they'll do the same in return.

Active listening leads to better cooperation and problem solving. We're all human and it's easy to make mistakes when we think we understand what someone is trying to say. By listening actively, asking questions, and probing for understanding, together the listener and speaker are generally able to develop more creative solutions than if the listener had remained passive, not offering any insight or support. Team members and employees report that when their team leaders and managers demonstrate real interest in them and their ideas by listening and paying attention to their concerns, their willingness to work collaboratively increases dramatically.

Active Listening and Organizations

Active listening can be a powerful competitive tool for organizations. Improving listening skills on an individual level will lead to higher levels of employee responsiveness, clearer understanding of organizational issues, and increased employee commitment to quality.[4] The opening scenario illustrates how the ability of organizational members to listen to the concerns and wants of the customer can have an impact on customer service. By listening to and understanding customers' needs, organizations can better serve these needs, thus providing the organization with a competitive edge.[5]

Active listening is also important for intraorganizational communication. Employees want and need to be listened to. Addressing employee concerns improves organizational effectiveness, reduces miscommunications and errors, and leads to a responsive work environment. Improving managerial listening skills raises performance levels through responsive and creative problem solving. Studies show that employees spend one-third of work time listening while top executives spend two-thirds of their work hours in listening activities.[6] The need for accurate information sharing in organizations is critical for strategic success. Successful organizations foster the need for active listening in the corporate culture.

Barriers to Effective Listening

University of Minnesota studies suggest people often have difficulty truly listening:[7]

- The average person remembers only half of what he or she has heard, even when the message came just a day or so ago.
- At all organizational levels, at least 75 percent of what we hear is heard incorrectly.
- Within two or three weeks, we remember less than 25 percent of the original content.
- An average person spends 80 percent of his or her waking hours communicating, and 45 percent of that time is spent on listening. However, adults typically practice listening at no better than 25 percent efficiency.

Barriers to Effective Listening

Despite its importance in promoting effective communication, active listening is often neglected. Many factors contribute to difficulties in listening.[8] These include:

- *Physiological limitations.* Poor listening can be partly blamed on our physiological process. Most individuals have the ability to speak at about 120 words per minute, while our brains have the ability to recognize words at the rate of 600 or more words per minute.[9] This gap creates a great deal of idle time for our brains to be wandering or processing other fragments of information from various sources. During the communication process, all our senses—sight, hearing, touch, taste, and smell—have the potential to operate, thereby stimulating our brain's simultaneous processing of both the speaker's words and everything else around us.

■ *Inadequate background information.* Most listeners hate to admit when they haven't heard all of the information necessary to engage in conversation, so they stumble along hoping to catch up. They seldom do.

■ *Selective memory.* Some employees treasure every accolade and never hear a single criticism. Others hear only the complaints and never the praise. We have a tendency to hear—and remember—what we want. There's a reason ad agencies run commercials over and over on TV and on the web. Without reinforcement of key messages, it's easy to forget entirely or to remember only selectively what a company has paid millions for you to remember. Interestingly, studies show that steps taken to increase viewers' recall, such as adding an attractive spokesperson or using flashy video, result in viewers remembering the attractive person and not the product or what it can do for them!

■ *Selective expectation.* If you expect dishonesty, poor work attitudes, or inattention, you'll probably get them. This is an example of the "self-fulfilling prophecy." Many employees expect not to be listened to. So many managers are preoccupied with immediate tasks and seldom have the time to devote to individual employee concerns that employees become accustomed to not being heard and understood. Often they'll just give up and resign themselves to the short, nonattentive interactions with managers to which they've become accustomed, or withhold information expecting it wouldn't be attended to anyway.

■ *Fear of being influenced or persuaded.* Some managers hold certain beliefs so dear to their hearts that they are biased—unable to entertain another's point of view about a matter. Typically managers who feel this strongly about an issue have a tendency to turn off speakers who dispute their cherished beliefs even before the position is fully explained.

■ *Bias and being judgmental.* When you don't like a person, it's hard to hear what he or she says. Sometimes this bias is based on wrong or incomplete information, such as "She's only 17, what could she know?" or "He's a bigot, so why should I listen to him?" When we make a negative judgment about the speaker, we typically stop or severely curtail our desire to listen to the speaker.

■ *Boredom.* Thought processes are four to five times the usual speed of speech. When you can guess what an employee is going to say seconds or even minutes before he or she speaks, your thoughts wander. When you return, the speaker may have gone on an unexpected track whose beginnings you lost and whose point you never do understand.

■ *Partial listening and distractions.* You may hear the literal words, but miss the connotation, facial expressions, or tone of voice. In essence, you get only part of the message. Perhaps you were trying to remember an important point when an employee interrupts to ask if they can leave to deal with an emergency at home. Chances are you didn't give that employee your full attention—even though your empathetic response to their situation would have gone a long way.

■ *Rehearsing.* Many of us use the time during another's talking to come up with a bulletproof rebuttal. If we are doing this, we aren't really listening. Sometimes we are so intent on winning an argument that the conversation veers in a different direction during our "rehearsal," resulting in our losing the segue for and impact of our carefully crafted rebuttal.

■ *Selective perception.* Perception is the process by which individuals take in and process stimuli according to their own experiences or attitudes. As such, we create our own reality, apart from what may actually be occurring. Since communication has a great deal of room for our individual interpretation, from the meaning of words to the interpretation of nonverbal signals, individual perception can easily distort the true message or its intent. Perception can be influenced by a number of factors such as our needs, opinions, personality, education, or environment. Selective perception is a process where we select or pay attention to only that information that adheres to or reinforces our own beliefs, views, or needs, causing severe distortion of messages.

■ *Interference from emotions.* Communication is susceptible to interference by emotions. Though we use communication to express our emotions, not everyone is able to understand, control, or explain their feelings adequately or fully. Emotions are neither right nor wrong but rather an expression of human reactions. By observing nonverbal cues, we are better able to interpret the true level and type of others' emotional states. We can then utilize empathy to neutralize emotional responses, paving the way to begin work on understanding the content of the communication. The emotional state of both the sender and the receiver must be considered in eliminating problems in the communication process.

Selective Perception   Most listeners hear what they want to hear. For example, many a manager has told a new employee that the organization gives "merit" pay increases. That new employee hears these words as "automatic" salary boosts, to which they feel entitled. Later, when the employee inevitably complains, the manager protests that the word "merit" means selective, and the employee will insist that to them the word "merit" means automatic. Who is right? Technically, the manager is. But in the interest of fostering good communication, it's up to the manager to be more explicit, give examples, and manage expectations by mentioning that only a small percentage of employees actually receive merit increases.

Characteristics of Active Listening

Active listening can be difficult for some people. Fortunately, listening skills can be developed and improved. Just as effective speaking is an acquired skill, so too is good listening. It requires a willingness to constantly practice, utilize various techniques, and evaluate progress.

Try This: Here are several strategies you can use to become an active listener.

■ Show interest and be sincere in listening. Use both verbal and nonverbal cues to demonstrate that you truly care about the speaker and his or her message.

■ Ask questions if you don't understand completely. Ask for clarification on points of contention ("Did he say that we would need to lay off employees or just cut costs?") as well as follow-up questions ("When will she have to start this process?").

■ Avoid distractions. Avoid doing two (or more) things at once. Make the speaker feel like she or he is the most important person in the world.

■ Use direct eye contact. Look away from the computer, the report, or your calendar while communicating with friends and associates. Also, be sensitive to cultural differences in interpreting the meaning that might be conveyed by making—or avoiding—eye contact with others.

■ Do not interrupt. To quote the American etiquette expert, Letitia Baldridge, "Good listeners don't interrupt—ever—unless the building's on fire."[10] Pause and count to three to make sure the speaker has completed his or her statements.

■ Read both the verbal and nonverbal messages. Good listening technique involves good detective work. Take the time and energy needed to understand the whole message and not just what is being spoken.

■ Be empathetic. Recognize and acknowledge the other person's feelings and emotions. If they're distressed, cracking a joke or making light of the situation might be interpreted as not caring about the speaker. The earlier example of the airline agent certainly applies here.

■ Paraphrase to correct misinterpretations, reflect the literal message, and improve retention. Repeat statements for clarification. Say, "If I heard you correctly . . ." or "So what you are saying is . . ."

(continued)

- Evaluate the message *after* hearing all the facts. A common habit of listeners is forming a response before the speaker is finished.[11] Avoid judgments by allowing the individual to complete the entire message before assessing the content and merit of the statements.

- Concentrate on the message as well as the messenger. Focus on the delivery as well as the content of the message itself, but be sure to check your potential biases about the messenger *before* you start the listening process.

- Give feedback to check accuracy, express your perspective, and broaden the interaction. For example, you might say, "So you want me to complete this report by Friday?" or "It sounds like we disagree; are there any elements of the plan on which we can both agree?"

- Listen with your entire body. Use direct eye contact, lean forward, nod your head, and use nonverbal communication to denote understanding or to get clarification.

- Don't talk so much! If you know you have tendencies toward verbosity, be on guard. As former U.S. President Calvin Coolidge said, "No one ever listened himself out of a job!"

Nonverbal Communication

Nonverbal communication is conveying meaning or expressing feelings consciously or subconsciously through means other than words. In a direct conversation between two individuals, up to 65 percent of the social meaning is sent through nonverbal means such as hand gestures, rolling the eyes, nodding the head, or looking away while someone is speaking.[12] How often have you experienced talking with someone who says they're listening even though they're watching television? Or having someone say they agree to something while shaking their head in disagreement? Conversely, have you experienced empathy from someone as evidenced by their nodding in support rather than sharing their agreement with you verbally? We often communicate nonverbally in ways that contradict what we're saying verbally. Nonverbal messages are often sent subconsciously, leading others to believe that they hold more of the true meaning than the verbal message.[13] Nonverbal communication is powerful. It is important to understand first how *we* communicate nonverbally, and then how to interpret correctly nonverbal messages that others send us.

The communication process involves much more than the spoken word. Key is sending verbal messages congruent with our nonverbal signals: Do they reinforce the message? Or do they contradict the intended message and confuse the receiver? For example, a boss who says he or she loves your ideas while rolling his or her eyes would lead you to believe that the boss might lack confidence in your suggestions.

There are several ways in which we communicate nonverbally. By increasing awareness of your own tendencies to communicate nonverbally, as well as the potential meaning of others' nonverbal communication, you can increase confidence in your ability to communicate effectively.

Non-Verbal Communication

Kinesics involves body movement, gestures, and posture. This includes eye contact, leaning, and body positioning. For example, we tend to use eye contact to provide information, express interest or intimacy, or facilitate the accomplishment of tasks. Many gestures are passed from one generation to the next without conscious effort. The way your dad looked at you when you did something wrong may be echoed in your behavior toward others. Check yourself and ask for feedback if you think others may find your gestures offensive. In addition, there are differences—some small, some vast—in the use, acceptability, and interpretation of gestures in other cultures. As said before, it is important to know your audience.

(continued)

Para-language refers to the tone of voice, volume, pitch, or speech rate. Is the sender using a strong, loud tone of voice or is he or she soft-spoken or timid in making an announcement? It is important to check both your message and how you deliver it to ensure that the receiver will interpret and respond to it as intended. The same message can have very different meanings depending on which words are emphasized. For example,

■ *Where* is your mother? might be used when another adult is helping a child locate his or her mother.

■ Where is *your* mother? might be said by a child's classmate at the start of the annual May Day parade.

■ *Where is your mother?* might be said by a neighbor staring alternatively between her newly broken window and a child wearing a baseball glove.

Environment refers to the layout of the space or room, lighting, color scheme, noise, decorations, and so on. The way in which you arrange your office may send a message to subordinates that may denote invitation or seclusion. For example, arranging your desk with your back to the door sends a very different message than arranging your desk facing the door. Also, placing chairs on the other side of your desk, facing you, places a barrier—figuratively and literally—between you and your co-workers. If you want to send a more egalitarian message, arrange your chairs next to your desk, or sit around a table with chairs when speaking with your employees or associates.

Chronemics is the study of how human beings use and structure time. Are you always late, early, right on time? What is the message you're sending, and how do your superiors, peers, or subordinates perceive it? If you are always late to meetings, what do others interpret about this behavior? What if you're always early? Is what your actions are communicating the message you intended to send? Again, there are cultural differences in how chronemics plays out in communication. Be aware of these differences to ensure mutual understanding.

Proxemics is the study of what you communicate by the way you use interpersonal space. According to anthropologist Edward T. Hall, we unconsciously use different distances or zones to communicate and interact with others.[14] You may notice that when talking to a close friend, you stand very near—perhaps a foot or less away. Conversely, when you go to the beach, you are more likely to look for a spot that is 10 or more feet from the next occupied space. How closely we stand to others with whom we communicate has a powerful effect on how we regard others and how we respond to them. For example, Americans prefer a "safe zone" when interacting with others, a space of a couple of feet or more. By contrast, many people in Latin American countries stand quite close and often touch those with whom they speak—in personal and even business conversations.

Haptics (tactile communication) refers to the use of touch. Touch can provide a strong nonverbal cue. Individuals tend to touch those they like or those with whom they have a close association, such as when a friend puts her arm over her friend's shoulder to express warmth and encouragement. Other types of touch can indicate varying degrees of aggression, such as pointing a finger or smacking another's hand. Touch-based communication varies depending upon the type of relationships, including functional/professional (dental examination, haircut), social/polite (handshake), friendship/warmth (clap on the back), and love/intimacy (kisses and hugs).

The old saying, "Actions speak louder than words" holds true. Figure 6–1 illustrates some common examples of nonverbal communication. Nonverbal messages tend to be ambiguous, so they may still need verbal clarification. Silence is probably one of the most misunderstood forms of nonverbal communication. Imagine you are at a team meeting and a major decision is about to be ratified. Some members vocalize their agreement while others remain silent. Are they in agreement, still thinking, bored, angry, tired, disinterested, or daydreaming? Interpreting nonverbal messages is a complex task; there is not one universal interpretation for each gesture or response. Before you interpret a nonverbal message, ask clarifying questions or get a verbal response to ensure a correct interpretation.

**Figure 6–1
Common Nonverbal
Behavior and
Interpretations
(in Western Industrialized
Countries)[15]**

Nonverbal Behavior	Common Interpretation
Darting eyes	Lying, bored, distracted, uninterested
Crossed arms	Closed to other's opinion, defensive
Tapping fingers	Impatient, nervous
Body lean (forward)	Interest, paying attention
Rubbing hands	Anticipation
Chin rub	Disbelief
Hands on hips	Anger, frustration
Steepling fingers	Authority, superiority
Rubbing nose	Lying, doubt
Quiet voice	Uncertainty, shyness, scared
Raised eyebrow	Amazement, disbelief

Summary

Listening is an essential skill for establishing and enhancing personal and professional relationships. If you are a good listener, you'll notice that others are drawn to you. Friends and associates confide in you and relationships thrive.

Listening also involves observing and interpreting nonverbal messages—yours and those of others. By concentrating on sending and receiving the whole message, verbal and nonverbal, we increase the likelihood for professional success and personal satisfaction.

Key Terms and Concepts

Active (or empathetic) listening

Attentive listening

Chronemics

Communication

Environment

Haptics

Kinesics

Listening

Nonverbal communication

Para-language

Passive listening

Proxemics

Endnotes

1. B. Goss, "Listening as Information Processing," *Communication Quarterly* 30 (1982), pp. 304–307.

2. Stephen Robbins and Phil Hunsaker, *Training in Interpersonal Skills* (Upper Saddle River, NJ: Prentice Hall, 1997).

3. Stephen R. Covey, *Seven Habits of Highly Effective People* (New York, NY: Simon and Schuster, 1989).

4. Marilyn M. Helms and Paula J. Haynes, "Are You Really Listening? The Benefits of Effective Intra-organizational Listening," *Journal of Managerial Psychology* 7, no. 6 (1992), p. 17.

5. Stephen B. Castleberry and C. David Shepherd, "Effective Interpersonal Listening and Personal Selling," *The Journal of Personal Selling & Sales Management* 13, no. 1 (Winter 1993), p. 35.

6. See J. D. Weinrauch and J. R. Swanda, Jr., "Examining the Significance of Listening: An Exploratory Study of Contemporary Management," *Journal of Business Communication*, February 1975, p. 25 and J. P. Kotter, "What Effective General Managers Really Do," *Harvard Business Review*, Nov.–Dec. 1982, p. 156.

7. G. R. Bell, "Listen and You Shall Hear," *The Secretary* 47, no. 9 (1984), pp. 8–9.

8. Adapted from John Morgan; revised by Beth Schneider in *Interpersonal Skills for the Manager*, Institute of Certified Professional Managers, Jan. 2000.

9. Max Messmer, "Improving Your Listening Skills," *Management Accounting (USA)*, March 1998, p. 14.

10. Winston Fletcher, "Good Listener, Better Manager," *Management Today*, Jan. 2000, p. 30.

11. Ibid.

12. M. Knapp and A. Vangelisti, *Interpersonal Communication and Human Relationships* (Boston: Allyn & Bacon, 1995).

13. Desmond Morris, *Body Talk* (New York: Crown Trade Paperbacks, 1994).

14. Edward T. Hall, *The Hidden Dimension* (New York: Doubleday, 1990).

15. Desmond Morris, *Body Talk*.

Exercise 6–A
Listening via the Rumor Mill

Five volunteers will be listeners. Four of the volunteers leave the room. All others in the room serve as observers, taking note of effective or ineffective listener behaviors (i.e., paraphrasing, eye contact, interrupting the speaker). The instructor tells the first listener (A) a brief story or reads a short passage. Another volunteer (B) returns to the room. The first volunteer (A) relates the story to (B). They then have a conversation. Another volunteer (C) returns and (B) relates the story to (C). This process continues through five volunteers. The final listening volunteer (E) writes on the board what (E) recalls of the story. The volunteers compare notes—and laugh at the distortions between the first version of the story and the last!

Questions

1. How much of the original story was retained? What implications does this have for our ability to communicate effectively?

2. What types of information were easiest to remember? Why?

3. What active listening techniques were used in helping to absorb the information?

4. Which techniques that weren't used could have helped in recalling information? Give examples of how you would have used these techniques.

5. What could the senders have done to encourage active listening?

6. In what ways did the listeners change the context of the information to make it more personal or memorable according to their own needs?

Exercise 6–B
Active Listening

This exercise involves triads. Each triad counts off into threes: 1, 2, 3, 1, 2, 3, and so on. In the first round, all the 1s in their respective triads take the pro position (see topics below), all the 2s take the con position, and all the 3s act as observers. After a topic is given, two individuals representing opposing viewpoints have one minute to collect their thoughts, and then five–seven minutes to arrive at a *mutually agreeable position* on that topic.

The observer should use the form below to capture *actual examples* of what the individuals said or did that indicated active and less-than-active listening. When time is called, the pro individuals share their opinion of which listening behaviors they performed well and which ones they'd like to improve. Then the con individuals do the same. Finally, the observers share their observations and insights, using examples to reinforce their feedback.

If additional rounds are used, rotate the roles so that each person plays a speaking role, and if possible an observing role.

Round 1:

Topic selected: _____

Notes:

Round 2:
Topic selected: _____
Notes:

Listening Feedback Form

Indicators of Active Listening	Pro	Con
1. Asked questions for clarification		
2. Paraphrased the opposing view		
3. Responded to nonverbal cues (e.g., body posture, tone of voice)		
4. Appeared to move toward a mutually satisfying solution		
Indicators of Less-than-Active Listening		
5. Interrupted before allowing the other person to finish		
6. Was defensive about their position		
7. Appeared to dominate the conversation		
8. Ignored nonverbal cues		

Potential topics to be used:

1. Gun control
2. Capital punishment
3. Race as a criterion for college admission
4. Prison reform
5. U.S. intervention in wars outside of the U.S.
6. Legalization of marijuana
7. Mandatory armed forces draft
8. Interracial adoption
9. Premarital and extramarital sex
10. Prayer in schools
11. Diversity or affirmative action in the workplace
12. Pornography on the Internet

Questions

1. Did you arrive at a mutually agreeable solution? What helped you get there?
2. What were some factors that hindered this process?
3. How comfortable did you feel "arguing" the position you were given? How did this influence your ability to actively listen?
4. If the position you were given was exactly opposite your values or beliefs, do you see this topic differently now than before the exercise?
5. What steps can you take to improve your ability to listen actively to friends or associates, especially when you don't agree with their viewpoint?

**Exercise 6–C
Tools of Active
Listening**

Instructions

A. *For each of the following active listening tools, write examples in the appropriate blanks.*

1. Empathetic Responses

Empathy is the ability to understand things from the other person's point of view. Empathetic responses communicate acceptance and your willingness to listen to the speaker.

Use empathetic responses when

■ You want to convey acceptance and establish rapport.

■ You want to encourage the speaker to continue talking.

Example   Speaker: I am really tired of being told I am empowered to do my job when the truth of the matter is what and how I work is still highly controlled.

Listener: _____

_____

2. Restatement

Restatement is a repetition of part of the speaker's own words, to show the speaker you have received the information being communicated.

Use restatement when

■ You want to "check out" the meaning of something the speaker has said.

■ You want to encourage the speaker to explore other aspects of the matter at hand and discuss these with you.

Example   Speaker: With these changes the report will have to be redone. It's going to take at least two or three days to do it.

Listener: _____

_____

3. Paraphrasing

Paraphrasing involves stating, in your own words, your interpretation of the speaker's message.

Use paraphrasing when

■ You want to confirm that you understand the speaker's feelings, and their relation to the content of the communication.

■ You want to help the speaker evaluate his/her feelings about the matter at hand.

■ You want to help the speaker reach a solution to a problem.

Example   Speaker: I'll be working on this project with Blackwell, and he's sharp technically, but he's not the easiest person in the world to work with.

Listener: _____

_____

4. Summative Statements

Summative statements condense large portions of what has been said, highlighting the key ideas.

Use summative statements when

■ You want to focus the discussion.

■ You want to confirm mutual understanding at a particular point in the discussion.

■ You want to get agreement on certain points that have been raised, in order to close the conversion.

Example   Speaker: I have some problems with this team effort. Few of us have been at every meeting, fewer still complete their action items, and we seem to be going nowhere.

Listener: _____

_____

5. Questioning Techniques

Questioning techniques are key tools in active listening. In particular, when the listener uses *open-ended* and *specifier* questions in combination, it can help the speaker express feelings and thoughts about a problem. Asking questions sends the message that you are willing to work at understanding.

Example   Speaker: The other day I heard that one of my major clients dropped us for another company.

Listener: Open-ended: *Why did they leave?*

Specifier: *Which client? Which*
competitor

6. Nonverbal Behavior

Use eye contact and a shift in posture to tell the speaker that you are listening. Anticipate and block interruptions/distractions. Observe speaker's nonverbal behavior and mentally note its message.

Example   Speaker: Sitting a few feet from the conference table with his body facing away from the others, the speaker gives input only when solicited and in short, one- or two-word phrases.

Listener: _____

_____

B. Match the following examples to their respective active listening tools.

Examples	*Active Listening Tools*
1. "As I understand it you feel . . ." "So the key ideas you expressed are . . ." "What we have agreed on is . . ."	a. Restatement
2. Face squarely, lean forward, uncross arms/legs, nod head, eye contact, facial expression	b. Summative Statements
3. "Two or three days?"	c. Empathetic Responses
4. "How did you feel about it?" "Which one?"	d. Paraphrasing
5. "You feel it would be difficult to get along."	e. Questioning Techniques
6. "Uh-Huh," "I see," "I understand"	f. Nonverbal Behavior

Source: S. de Janasz, L. Johnson, M. McQuaid, A. Paulson, D. Roccia, S. Stubblefield, P. Wahl, and C. Wojick, *Fundamentals of Facilitation,* Training manual created for Hughes Aircraft Company, 1992, pp. 4–28.

Exercise 6–D
Improving Nonverbal Observation Skills

1. Observe a TV talk show with interviews or watch a debate or speech (CNN, ESPN, David Letterman, *Meet the Press, The MacLaughlin Group,* etc.) to evaluate listening skills and nonverbal messages.

   - Facial gestures—look at their eyes, eyebrows, mouths.
   - Arm and hand gestures.
   - Feet, balance, and posture.
   - Breathing.
   - How can you tell if the moderator/facilitator is using active listening?
   - What nonverbal messages are they sending?

2. Go to a public place (shopping center, stores, fast food restaurant) and watch how employees (salespeople, cashiers) of certain establishments interact with the customers. Observe for approximately 15 minutes and make note of the nonverbal signals they send to the customers.

   - What nonverbal messages do the customers send?
   - Do the employees read the nonverbal messages?
   - How can you tell if the customers or employees are using active listening?

3. Stand in the middle of a room or empty space and have someone walk slowly toward you. Ask that person to stop walking as soon as you begin to feel uncomfortable. Instruct him or her to move closer and further away until you are at a comfortable distance. This is your personal buffer zone.

   - Does this zone change when different people walk toward you? Explain.
   - Compare your notes with one or two others who have done this exercise. Were there differences? To what can you attribute these differences?
   - Experiment with others' buffer zones. For example, stand "too close" while waiting in line, on an elevator, or in a bus. Observe that person's response to you. (Proceed carefully . . . possibly with members of your own gender.)

Source: Adapted from Matthew McKay, Martha Davis & Patrick Fanning, *Messages: The Communication Skills Book,* 2nd ed., Oakland, CA: New Harbinger Publications, 1995, p. 58.

Exercise 6–E
Nonverbal Role-Play

In small groups, create a role-play involving only body language with no talking. Pick a scene and characters and let the members improvise the rest. Do not overplay the scene; allow the audience to guess and make assumptions based on use of everyday nonverbal cues.

The group will present its role-play in front of the class. You may or may not set up the scene for the audience. Play out the scene for a few minutes.

Questions

1. Based on the body language, what was the scene depicting?
2. What was the relationship of the members to each other?
3. What were the personalities of the members?
4. What issues were affecting the group?
5. What emotions, behaviors, or feelings would you assume from the body language?

Source: Adapted from John Suler, Department of Psychology, Rider University, **www.rider.edu/users/suler,** 2000.

Exercise 6–F
Reflection/Action Plan

This chapter focused on listening and nonverbal communication—what they are, why they're important, and how to improve your skills in these areas. Complete the worksheet below upon completing all the reading and experiential activities for this chapter.

1. The one or two areas in which I am most strong are:

_____

_____

_____

_____

2. The one or two areas in which I need more improvement are:

_____

_____

_____

_____

3. If I did only one thing to improve in this area, it would be to:

_____

_____

_____

_____

4. Making this change would probably result in:

_____

_____

_____

_____

5. If I did not change or improve in this area, it would probably affect my personal and professional life in the following ways:

_____

_____

_____

_____

7 Conveying Verbal Messages

Learning Points

How do I:

- Improve my ability to send clear messages?
- Reduce barriers associated with ineffective communication?
- Determine which communication medium will best serve my needs in varying situations?
- Send messages that directly express and address my wants, needs, and opinions?
- Get my message across in a way that doesn't cause defensiveness on the part of the receiver?

David Jameson was in a bind. After years working as a technical specialist he was promoted to supervisor in his department. This required him to be responsible for people who had at one time been his co-workers, which created a good deal of resentment on the part of his co-workers. Yet he had business objectives to meet. Much was expected of him, and senior management was eyeing Dave for another promotion soon if all went well. After several weeks Dave discovered an unsettling communication pattern. Whenever he asked that something be done, his co-workers would nod in agreement. But when the time for the deadline came, the expected outcome hadn't happened. Just last Monday he met with Ann and Frank, telling them they needed to complete the computer drafts for the Winston project by the end of the business day on Thursday. However, the reports were still not on his desk on Friday morning. When he had finished talking to them on Monday, they gave him no response or indication that the project would not be complete on time. Dave thought he was communicating clearly. He had informed them of the deadline and simply left it at that when neither of them gave him a response. What was their problem? Dave didn't want to condescend to his subordinates by looking over their shoulders and checking on their progress, but he was afraid he might have to do this if things didn't change soon.

1. What issues are involved here? What's going on?
2. If you were one of Dave's co-workers, what would you think and how would you feel about the situation?
3. What ideas or suggestions do you have for Dave?

"The medium is the message."

Marshall McLuhan

aster communicator Marshall McLuhan said it best when he inferred that the medium used to send a message is just as important as the actual message, if not more so. Another way to say the same thing is "It's not just the message, it's the messenger." Both form and substance are important in the communication process. Everything we do or don't do, say or don't say, communicates something, and so does the way in which we send messages. Communicating effectively consists of both sending and receiving messages in ways that are both verbal and nonverbal. It's almost impossible not to communicate, unless, of course, we're sleeping! Studies show that we may spend as much as 80 percent of our time communicating.[1] In this chapter we look at verbal communication—what it is, why it's important, and how to both send and receive messages effectively.

What Is Communication?

Communication is a process in which information flows from a source to a receiver and back.[2] We communicate because we want something to happen or we want to satisfy a need. In fact, the majority of our work and life is devoted to communicating with others. For example, in business, the average supervisor spends about 80 percent of his/her time communicating, of which approximately 10 percent is spent writing, 15 percent reading, 30 percent speaking, and 45 percent listening.[3]

Because we communicate constantly, we need to communicate effectively—to do it right. It's not easy to be an effective communicator all the time. To do this takes work, effort, and practice.

The Communication Channel

When a message needs to be sent, a communicator (the *sender*) **encodes** a message according to her or his own perceptions, experiences, and abilities. The sender then determines which **communication channel**[4]—the method or medium—is most appropriate to use to convey the message. The message travels across the communication channel and is then decoded by the *receiver*(s) who interprets (**decode**) the message according to his or her own perceptions, abilities, and experiences.

Sending a message from source to receiver constitutes one-way communication. Adding the final stage, known as **feedback**, creates two-way communication (see Figure 7–1). Feedback is the process by which the receiver puts the message back into a channel to seek clarification, confirm what the receiver thought the sender said, or check for understanding and possible misinterpretation. Feedback can be verbal or nonverbal through the use of paraphrasing, questioning, nodding, gesturing, or even eye movement.

Feedback is an essential component of two-way communication. It allows the receiver to show the sender she or he is paying attention and clearly understands the messages being sent. By listening, repeating, reaffirming, and asking questions, it is more likely that the sender and receiver can understand fully what each is saying. This process doesn't guarantee that there will be agreement, but it does ensure understanding. Two-way communication is so essential that you should consider all your business communications to be two-way unless you are simply making an announcement or issuing an important directive that can't be challenged.[6]

Figure 7–1[5]
The Communication Channel

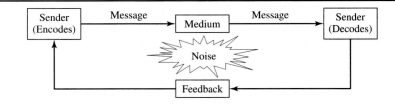

Effective Media Selection

As the quote at the beginning of this chapter implies, the medium you choose to convey your message is just as important as the content of the message itself. The advertising world has long understood this principle. In the business world it is just as true that "it's not just what you say but how you say it that counts." This saying has survived because it is so practical, so true. The medium (or media, if more than one medium is needed) selected to transmit a message can enhance or reduce the effectiveness of the message being sent. We have several choices available for communicating directly with others; they include oral, written, and electronic forms. Choosing among these forms of communication requires you to assess the message you need to send, your intended audience (from one to a hundred or more), and the response you hope to receive from the audience.[7] Each method has its advantages and disadvantages.

■ *Oral communication* or spoken communication tends to be the most preferred form of communication for managers. Oral communication should be used when it is important to engage in discussion and come to a consensus with one or more persons. One prominent benefit of oral communication (in person or via telephone or video-conference) is that it provides an automatic two-way exchange—both the sender(s) and receiver(s) can share information and obtain immediate feedback. This helps the sender shape the message as soon as a response is received on numerous points. Face-to-face contact is typically more effective than other types of oral communication, as both verbal and nonverbal signals are readily and simultaneously available.

On the other hand, oral communication does have its drawbacks. Communicating orally via a phone call, video conference, or meeting often results in people arriving at the exchange less prepared than if they were communicating in writing. In oral communication it is easy for the participants to forget the major points that were made soon after the meeting concludes. Without a common written record it is likely some of the promises made won't be followed up. Oral communication activities also tend to cause the participants to experience "information overload." Communicating orally is not the best choice when a large amount of complex information must be delivered. One way to improve oral communication as a medium is to add a written component. Taking minutes during a meeting, entering personal notes about follow-up actions in a day planner, and issuing a short e-mail summarizing agreed-upon action steps and deadlines are some of the ways oral contact can be strengthened as a medium of communication.

■ *Written communication* is the most effective method for sending precise or complex information. It is also appropriate when making an announcement that does not require two-way dialogue. Written communication should not be used when the subject is controversial and requires further input from others and decisions to be made. The written document, such as a letter, contract, memo, report, or presentation, has several benefits. Written communication is an effective way to get a message to a large number of individuals in a time- and cost-efficient manner. A written document or set of documents also ensures a "paper trail"—a record of exchanges made between individuals and groups. Written communication provides a formal or official document. Most of us prefer a legal, binding contract to be in written rather than in oral form. Written evidence is far more binding than is oral recall of events. Written information can also provide a reference for later use. For example, a work team that regularly records minutes for meetings will save time at each meeting by not having to recall what was said and agreed upon in previous meetings.

Written communication also has its drawbacks. It is too easy for us to write a long letter when a short memo would be sufficient. Written communication prevents a two-way dialogue, or results in a lengthier exchange if two-way communication is desired. In written communication it is nearly impossible to decode the nonverbals—those nuances, movements, and gestures that serve to reinforce and clarify a sender's message and intent.[8] Written communication is also prone to misinterpretation and inaccuracy. Just because something is written doesn't mean it's necessarily true or will be correctly interpreted! To improve the effectiveness of written communication, carefully evaluate messages sent or received to determine bias, misinterpreted connotations, and hidden agendas and seek verbal or written clarification to accurately encode or decode messages.

■ *Electronic communication* is effective for sending brief messages quickly to one or more persons. It is useful for clarifying agreements that have already been reached, when fast turn-around time is needed, and when members of a team are working "virtually" (meaning they're not all in the same location). Electronic communication should not be the primary medium when the message that needs to be sent is negative, controversial, or requires additional dialogue.

Much electronic communication in the workplace now takes place via e-mail, faxing, teleconferencing, cell phones, voice mail, and other means such as websites and Internet technology. While some of these means can be extremely fast, accurate, and efficient, they still require judgment, discretion, and "people skills" to be used correctly. New technology presents unique challenges in communication not only in speed and distance, but in evaluating the audience, which can comprise one or hundreds of individuals, with virtually little knowledge or understanding of the receiver(s).[9] Due to the relative ease of sending a message, many senders neglect the need for careful execution of their communication. How many of us have read about the guy who jilted his girlfriend in favor of another via e-mail—only to find he had sent the "jilt" e-mail to the new girlfriend, and the "amorous" e-mail to his old girlfriend! Or the CEO of a prominent entertainment company who confessed in a commencement speech that he had unintentionally sent the company's disappointing quarterly earnings report to representatives of the media rather than to his board.[10] Electronic communication should carry the same amount of professionalism as traditional communication forms, including proper spelling, punctuation, capitalization, and grammar.[11]

Thoughtful use of electronic forms of communication requires that we develop effective human communication skills in conjunction with new technology and equipment. One of the first rules of using electronic communication is to "remember the human." Do not lose sight that on the other end of the quick response to an e-mail is another human being who will interpret the message.[12] Our online actions and messages affect people.[13] Electronic messages can lose the emotional aspect of message in both content and tone, opening the door to miscommunications. Electronic communication also has the potential downside of reducing the quality and amount of human interaction. E-mail can reduce the amount of interaction between organizational members and promotes nonpersonal communication. Figure 7–2 provides some tips for using—and not using—electronic communication.

Figure 7–2
E-mail Communication: DOs and DON'Ts

- DO keep your address list up to date. DON'T set aside until "later" letters and messages you receive from colleagues giving you their new contact information.
- DO send business-related messages during work hours. DON'T send or receive personal e-mail during work hours.
- DO remember that anything you "say" in an e-mail can potentially be "seen" by many others besides those to whom you send the e-mail. DON'T send any e-mail that is personally negative about or potentially damaging to another person.
- DO have a personal e-mail account separate from your account at work or school. DON'T use your work account for both business and personal purposes.
- DO send brief messages to announce noncontroversial information or to confirm something that's already been agreed to. DON'T send lengthy announcements or messages about something that is best handled through face-to-face discussion or debate.
- DO send appreciative notes to people with copies to their supervisors. DON'T give negative feedback via e-mail.
- DO copy your boss on important messages that are relevant to them. DON'T leave your boss and significant members of your team out of the loop. DON'T go over your boss's head, even though you have access to the personal e-mail address of her or his boss.
- DO keep a hard copy of important documents for the record.
- DO clarify important details verbally. DON'T rely on e-mail communication on important matters (the person you're writing to might be out of town).
- DO batch your messages. DON'T send multiple messages throughout the day to the same people concerning the same project.
- DO send personalized e-mails. DON'T send mass e-mails, or if you do, don't include everyone's address at the top—that's giving away sensitive information. Send your message to yourself and blind copy it to the others.
- Do use proper grammar and syntax, and use capitalization and punctuation appropriately. Don't type in all caps—this is the equivalent of screaming.

Information Richness and Media Selection

Selecting the appropriate media used to send a message is a key component in communication effectiveness. You must take into consideration the complexity of the message to determine which media will be appropriate for disseminating your message. One means to evaluate which form of media to select is through examining **information richness** or the information capacity of data. Theorists Daft and Lengel define information richness as "the potential information-carrying capacity of data." They explain that an item of data that provides substantial new understanding would be considered rich. On the other hand, if the datum provides relatively little understanding or common information, it would be considered low in richness.[14]

As you consider what you intend to communicate and the amount of richness or information to be transmitted in the message, you need to evaluate the media by categorizing them in terms of four factors.

- *Feedback:* Do the media allow for two-way communication and contain the ability and speed necessary to provide the requisite feedback? The range of feedback would consist of immediate to very slow.

- *Channel:* Do the media allow for multiple cues ranging from combined visual and audio to limited visual?

- *Type of communication:* Do the media allow for emotional or personal connection; is it personal or impersonal?

- *Language source:* Is the source of the information from a natural source or body source (an individual) or is it from a purely data or numeric source?

These four characteristics will help you select the appropriate media. Face-to-face communication is the richest form of communication. It allows for immediate, two-way feedback and includes visual and audio cues. Face-to-face communication also is highly personal and its source is directly from the individual or natural source. When you need to convey more complicated or nonroutine information, a richer channel of media will be more effective. Written announcements or reports are some of the lowest channels of richness. They tend to discourage or slow the feedback process, are very impersonal, are sourced from pure data and information, and are limited to visual cues. Leaner channels are more appropriate when the information is routine or straightforward. Whatever channel is selected, it is important to remember that each has its advantages and disadvantages. Depending on the content of the message, multiple media may be necessary to ensure effective communication.

Barriers to Communication

As anyone who has ever been in an argument or had difficulty getting a message across knows, communicating is a complex skill. There are many obstacles to getting communication right. One of the reasons for this is that in communication, many potential areas for interference or "noise" exist. **Noise** is any distortion factor that blocks or disrupts the flow of information between sender and receiver, hindering the communication process. These distortion factors can range from emotional states or language differences to telephone static or a downed e-mail system. Using American slang (such as "cool," "bad," or "hot") when discussing the results of a new product design to a foreign counterpart could lead to a distortion of the interpreter's meaning, which would constitute noise.

Even good communication processes contain noise factors; it is inherent in all forms of communication. One way to improve our communication skills is to become aware of these barriers to communication and learn how to minimize or reduce their adverse effects.

Information Overload

As human beings, most of us have the ability to process only so much information. Some of the behaviors that can cause information overload for the receiver of your messages are listed below.

- *Presenting too much material:* Keep the information to an amount that is easily absorbed by the person or persons with whom you are speaking. Check for understanding and pause frequently, giving the person time to formulate clarifying questions and indicate to you that they understand what you are saying.

- *Presenting information that is overly complex:* When feasible, practice your main message or messages ahead of time, ensuring you deliver the message succinctly and coherently. If necessary, back up your words with visuals, or send data or a summary report ahead of time.

- *Presenting information too quickly:* Deliver your message slowly, in an organized fashion, focusing on just a couple of points at a time.

- *Presenting at a level of difficulty that goes beyond the person's understanding:* Always know your audience. If you don't, begin your message with a few overview comments and perhaps some questions to determine how much information the receiver already has on the subject.

- *Not giving the person sufficient time to process the information:* Give your listeners an opportunity to ask questions and to provide their perspective before asking for a decision. When possible, try to hold off on a decision until all the necessary information is available, perhaps at another time.

Trust and Credibility

Lack of trust is a huge barrier to effective communication. For example, if a company begins to lay off workers after having told them layoffs would not occur, those employees will be less likely to believe anything else their managers tell them. If you need to communicate with someone with whom trust has been broken, take the time to talk with the person, listening to his or her concerns, emphasizing the importance of the long-term relationship. If possible, wait until trust has been rebuilt before asking for a decision or insisting on their cooperation.

Lack of credibility prevents the listener from fully receiving your message. The receiver can hear your words but won't believe you or acknowledge your perspective because they question your knowledge base. New entrants into the workforce often experience this problem with more senior workers who may question their expertise. The best way to build credibility is to prepare, prepare, prepare. The more thoroughly you have done your homework before approaching someone with an issue or solution, the more likely you are to be well received.

Time

Lack of time is a major concern for practically all of us, whether we're a student, homemaker, parent, or manager (or all of the above!). Poor communication often results from lack of time. Being in a hurry does not lend itself to studied, thorough responses or decision making. Rushing to communicate often leads to errors, leaving out important details, or saying things that you later regret having said. The best way to approach this problem is to develop a habit of focusing on just one communication at a time. This flies in the face of the "multitasking" environment so favored in many industries today wherein employees are encouraged and expected to perform multiple tasks simultaneously. While not everyone can or prefers to multitask, studies suggest that multitasking causes a good deal of stress. When dealing with an important issue, person, or customer, focus your attention on one communication at a time. This will reduce errors and improve the quality of your communication. For example, when sending an e-mail message, take time to proofread it before sending it. When on the telephone, devote full attention to your listener and resist putting him or her on hold or call waiting (except in an emergency). When conducting a meeting, close the door to the meeting room to reduce distractions. You can't always adhere to these principles. But when what's being said or who's saying it is very important to you, it's worth doing it right.

Another communication problem that arises over the concept of time is today's increased expectation of speedy response. The use of e-mail, voice mail, and fax machines has resulted in a "just in time" mentality in the workplace. It used to take first-class mail three to four days to arrive at a destination. It wasn't uncommon for a manager to answer a letter within the next week or even two. Today that's hardly practical. Generally an e-mail message, phone message, or drop-by conversation in the office hallway carries with it the expectation of an almost immediate response. This can pose problems for you as the number of messages that need handling simultaneously mounts. Many successful managers are finding that it helps to batch their communications or group their responses by category. For example, you can attempt to set aside time each day for responding to and sending e-mail messages, a different time for responding to and making phone calls, and yet a different time of day for quick hallway conversations with co-workers. Of course this won't always be possible, but by setting some limits over the way you respond to these inquiries, you'll have a better chance of responding to each contact appropriately, accurately, and within a reasonable period of time.

Filtering

Filtering is the intentional manipulation of information to make it more favorable to the receiver. The way information is sent, the tone, and the framing of the material can greatly distort a message to serve an individual's or a group's needs. Filtering can make objective decision making difficult because the true message is never accurately sent or received. For example, a manager afraid of offending his subordinates may sugarcoat a message about the need to work overtime by leaving out information that clarifies why the work can't wait. Or an employee might inform a manager of errors, but leave out details on the extensive amount of damage that occurred. To resist filtering when you speak, present information based on the relevant facts. Deliver information sensitively but firmly and honestly. To prevent receiving filtered information, ask probing questions about a situation that's being presented to you. Ask follow-up questions about each detail that is of interest to you, focusing on results and outcomes, not just the facts that have been presented.

Emotions

Another factor that can hinder effective communication is **emotions** or emotional states. Emotions are strong feelings such as fear, love, hate, happiness, and anger. Because emotion is the opposite of reason, it is difficult to anticipate, predict, control, or read emotion in yourself and in others. Emotions are neither right nor wrong, but rather an expression of human reactions. However, communicating emotionally can prevent us from being objective about a situation. To reduce the potential for miscommunication, consider the emotional state of both the sender and the receiver in all interactions with others. In most business situations, it's best if both parties can remain as open and objective as possible. This is not to say that emotions will be nonexistent. However, it is wise to understand the potential effects emotional states can have on the communication process. A good rule of thumb is to stop and think. This might seem simple, but it requires an amount of self-discipline. Assess the impact of what you are about to say on the other person. Say things that won't offend others to avoid diverting their attention, which interferes with your ability to make a point. It is a good idea to leave a discussion and return to it later if you find yourself so emotional about the subject that your feelings are getting in the way of your being able to communicate. Similarly, if a person with whom you are speaking is reacting emotionally, it's a good idea to part and regroup later.

Message Congruency

The communication process is much more than just the spoken word. Studies have found that 55 percent of communication is transmitted through physiology (body language) while 38 percent of communication comes through the tone of voice and only 7 percent through words.[15] These statistics reinforce the need for sending verbal and nonverbal messages congruently. Communicators must carefully consider the potential message being sent nonverbally through gestures and body language. The nonverbals must reinforce the message, not contradict it. You may be misunderstood if you are rolling your eyes when you are confirming your acceptance of a suggestion. Are you trying to be sarcastic in your affirmative answer? If so, then confirm your opinion with congruent verbal and nonverbal statements. The goal is to make things clear for the receivers of your messages; don't send mixed signals. Practicing these techniques should improve your ability to have both you *and* your message taken seriously.

Assertive Communication

Assertive communication is a form of communication in which you speak up for your rights and take into account the rights and feelings of others.[16] Assertive communication includes these elements:

- Fairness
- Directness
- Tact and sensitivity
- Honesty

The purpose of assertive communication is to keep contact lines open and show respect for others while affirming your beliefs and preferences. Unfortunately, many of us feel uncomfortable being assertive; some falsely equate assertiveness with aggressiveness and instead use passive styles of communication.[17]

Passive communication includes indirectness, avoiding conflict, being easily persuaded/bullied, being overly concerned about pleasing others, and screening or withholding your thoughts and feelings to the extent that the person with whom you're communicating has no idea of your real opinion on the matter being addressed. We use passive communication when we are fearful of losing someone's affection or have low self-esteem, or when we have decided the issue isn't worth taking a stand. Frowning, crying, whispering under our breath, or simply saying nothing are all ways we demonstrate passive communication. Usually the primary purpose of responding passively to a person or situation is to avoid confrontation at all costs. Passive communication is usually not recommended, as it seldom results in getting what you really want. It can be useful, however, if avoidance is truly desirable, such as when you're in an organization where you have chosen not to speak up about everything with which you disagree.

Aggressive communication includes exerting control over others, humiliating others, dominating, being pushy, always needing to be right, using absolute terms, and blaming others.[18] We respond aggressively when we want to be in control, are insecure, are afraid, don't value the opinions of others, or have unresolved anger. The purpose of aggressive behavior is to win or dominate—to prove one is right and others are wrong. Aggressive communication is usually not recommended, as it results in a win–lose situation where you get your way at the expense of someone else. It can be appropriate, however, if you are in an extreme situation that dictates the need for an aggressive response, such as directions in crisis management or a physical attack.

Assertive communication is usually the most appropriate communication style.[19] There are times when we all feel somewhat passive or even aggressive. But for the most part, it's a good idea to learn to be firm about your needs and to insist on those needs being met. Have you ever had a roommate who ate your food or wore your clothes without asking? A boss who wouldn't give you a much-deserved raise? How did you handle this? Assertive communication will provide you with the ability to pass on information accurately and intelligently to accomplish objectives while still having respect for others and not making them feel "put down."[20]

How to Communicate Assertively

Nearly all of us have been involved in group projects, whether in school, business, or both. Many of us have also been in groups where one (or more) member contributes little or nothing to the task. What do you do? Do you ignore the situation, hoping that (1) it will improve, or (2) someone else will deal with the nonperformer? Using assertive communication may help you to remedy these and similar situations.

There are three parts to developing an assertive statement:[21]

- Your *perspective/perception* of the situation: In your own words, what is the issue or situation as you see it? For example, "I've noticed that the common areas are frequently messy and dirty."

- Your *feelings* about the situation: Describe how the situation makes you feel without placing blame on others. For example, "I feel frustrated since I am holding up my end of the deal yet others don't seem to do theirs."

- Your *wants* regarding the situation or outcome: Own your request for a resolution by using "I" instead of "you." "I would like to revisit our roommate agreement and come up with a plan that we all can live with regarding the cleanliness of our apartment."

Taking Responsibility and "I" Messages

An element of assertive communicating involves "taking responsibility." It is human nature to try to assess or make sense of our and others' behavior. However, the assumptions we make about the behavior of others are not necessarily consistent with reality; instead, our assumptions reflect our own values and beliefs. When conversing with another person, it is important to remember this fact, to clarify assumptions, and to be willing to accept at least some of the responsibility for any ambiguity in the communication. Among the ways to take responsibility and clarify assumptions are these:[22]

- Specify the behavior(s) on which the assumption is based: "Your facial expression suggests to me that I may not have made my point very clearly," rather than "Are you following what I'm saying?"

- If your assumption is based on your own expectation of the listener's behavior, state that expectation specifically; do not assume that the listener knows the details of your expectation: "I'm expecting that report next Monday at 4:00. Can we agree on that?" rather than "Is that report going to be done on time?"

- If your assumption compares the listener's behavior with that of other members of a reference group, clarify that group and exactly how the behavior compares: "The other members of the department always submit their weekly production reports on Monday, and each of your last four reports weren't submitted until Thursday," rather than "You didn't submit your weekly production reports promptly."

- Elicit feedback about your assumptions. Ask the listener to tell you whether the assumption is accurate: "Am I correct in assuming that you've already begun writing the report that's due next Monday?"

Another element of assertive communication is in the use of "I statements."[23] Most of the messages we send to people about their behavior are "you" messages—messages that are directed at the other person and have a high probability of putting them down, making them feel guilty, making them feel their needs are not important, making them defensive, and generally making them resist change. Examples of "you" messages are usually orders or commands ("Stop doing that! Get in the car!"), blaming or name-calling statements ("You are acting like a baby! You are driving me crazy!"), or statements that give solutions ("You should forget that idea. You better reconsider your plan"). Statements like these tend to remove the responsibility for behavior change from the other person. Morris Massey, a popular self-help author and coach, calls this being "should on."[24] Perhaps the worst example of a "you" message is the "if . . . then" threat: for example, "If you don't . . . then I will . . . "

Conversely, an "I" message allows a person who is affected by the behavior of another to express the impact it has on him or her and leave the responsibility for modifying the behavior with the person who demonstrated that particular behavior. An "I" message consists of three parts:

- The specific behavior.
- The resulting feeling you experienced because of the behavior.
- The tangible effect on you.

Thus a teacher might say to a student: "When you tap on your desk with your pencil, I feel upset because I get distracted and have difficulty teaching," rather than "You had better stop tapping your pencil!" Or a wife might say to her husband: "When I try to talk and you

Figure 7–3
Twelve Tips for Sending
Effective Verbal Messages

- Be direct: others may not pick up on your hints or may misinterpret them.
- Consider your audience: communicate with them in terms of their interests, values, and backgrounds.
- Be clear: don't ask questions when you need to make a statement. Focus on one thing at a time; know your purpose and have an objective; think and organize your thoughts before speaking.
- Watch the nonverbal aspects of communicating: make your facial expression and gestures congruent with your verbal statements.
- Pay attention to the receivers: watch for their nonverbal clues, not just what they're saying.
- As necessary, be redundant: repeat when needed or restate something to make it clearer to the receiver.
- Communicate bit by bit: make the pieces sufficiently understandable individually and as a whole.
- Use varying techniques to send your message; we all process information differently and have varying learning styles.[25]
  - Some are *auditory*—they have to hear it to learn it.
  - Some are *visual*—they need to read it or see it on paper.
  - Some are *kinesthetic*—they need to have hands-on use or personal practice to learn.
  - Some are *didactic*—they ask questions and get full background info before processing what others are saying.
- Cover your bases: write it, review it, demonstrate it, and defend it.
- Build in feedback and check for understanding. Encourage and incorporate means that allow others to know you want feedback. They are unlikely to do it automatically. Ask for feedback and clarification.
- Be straightforward with no hidden agenda or lies; deal with issues straight-on and in a timely manner, often, and openly.
- Be supportive: avoid labels, sarcasm, dragging up the past, negative comparisons, and "you" messages and threats.

don't say anything, I feel confused because I don't know how you feel about helping me," rather than "You never talk to me!" In effect, the "I" message removes the possibility of defensiveness and allows the sender to project, "I trust you to decide what change in behavior is necessary." "I" messages build relationships and don't place the sender in the position of enforcing a new behavior, as is frequently the case with the "you" message.

"Mend your speech a little, lest it may mar your fortunes."

William Shakespeare, *King Lear*

Sending Messages Effectively

We have all been talking and listening for so long that we tend to think we're experts. We have survived up to this point and gotten some results, so we must be doing something right. Despite the fact that most of the time we're probably somewhat or very effective, there's always room for improvement; the better your communication, the better your performance, interactions with co-workers, and relationships with others in your personal life. Studies show that up to 70 percent of business communication is ineffective in achieving its intended purpose.[26] Figure 7–3 provides some suggestions for increasing your skills in communicating effectively.

Summary

What and how we communicate affects our behavior as well as that of others. Effective communication is the means for developing better human relations and ultimately better organizational performance.

Verbal communication is not as easy as it might seem. Developing skills in communicating verbally with others is important for managerial success as well as success in our personal relationships. If you have a high degree of proficiency in communicating, people will be able to interpret your messages clearly. Part of communicating verbally is being able to communicate assertively. By sending messages clearly, seeking and giving feedback fairly, and working to overcome obstacles to effective communication, we increase the likelihood of personal and professional success.

Key Terms and Concepts

Aggressive communication

Assertive communication

Communication

Communication channel

Decode

Emotions

Encode

Feedback

Filtering

Information overload

Information richness

Noise

Passive communication

Endnotes

1. John R. Ward, "Now Hear This," *IABC Communication World,* July 1990, p. 20.

2. D. K. Berlo, *The Process of Communication* (New York: Holt, Rinehart and Winston, 1960), pp. 30–32.

3. G. R. Bell, "Listen and You Shall Hear," *The Secretary* 47 (1984), pp. 8–9.

4. Berlo, *Process of Communication.*

5. Ibid.

6. Duane Bazzett, "Communicating Effectively," *Supervision* 60, no. 12 (Dec. 1999), p. 3.

7. Ibid.

8. One notable exception to this would be tone—usually referred to in a verbal context (e.g., she spoke to me in an obnoxious tone), but possibly part of a written message through the choice of sarcasm and other nonverbal message amplifiers.

9. "Talking to the World," *Economist* (US), (Dec. 25, 1999), p. 83.

10. In case you were wondering . . . this was Disney's Michael Eisner!

11. Nelda Spinks, Barron Wells, and Melanie Meche, "Netiquette: A Behavioral Guide to Electronic Business Communication," *Corporate Communications* 4, no. 3 (1999), p. 145.

12. Paul Sturges, "Remember the Human: The First Rule of Netiquette, Librarians and the Internet," *Online Information Review* 26, no. 3 (2002), p. 209.

13. See Richard Gan Kon Guan et al., "The Impact of the Internet on the Managers' Working Life," *Singapore Management Review* 24, no. 2 (2002), p. 77, and Spinks et al., "Netiquette," p. 145.

14. R. L. Daft and R. H. Lengel, "Information Richness: A New Approach to Managerial Behavior and Organizational Design," *Research in Organizational Behavior* (Greenwich CT: JAI Press, 1984), p. 196.

15. Albert Mehrabian and M. Weiner, "Decoding of Inconsistent Communication," *Journal of Personality and Social Psychology,* June 1967, p. 109.

16. Matthew McKay, Martha Davis, and Patrick Fanning, *Messages: The Communication Skills Book,* Second Ed. (Oakland, CA: Harbinger Publications, Inc., 1995).

17. R. E. Albert and M. L. Emmons, *Your Perfect Right: A Guide to Assertive Behavior* (San Luis Obispo, CA: Impact Publishers, Inc., 1974).

18. Stephen Robbins and Phil Hunsaker, *Training in Interpersonal Skills* (Upper Saddle River, NJ: Prentice Hall, 1996).

19. E. Raudsepp, "Are You Properly Assertive?" *Supervision,* June 1992, p. 17.

20. Alfred Fleishman, "Going Back a Little Bit," *St. Louis Business Journal*, Jan 3, 2000, p. 29.

21. McKay et al., *Messages*, p. 128.

22. This is adapted from an exercise in J. William Pfeiffer and John E. Jones, *Structured Experiences Kit*, entitled "Taking Responsibility," C-CAE/0-15 (San Francisco, CA: Jossey-Bass Pfeiffer, 1980).

23. Ibid.

24. Morris E. Massey, *The People Puzzle: Understanding Yourself and Others* (Reston, VA: Reston/Prentice Hall, 1979).

25. Sharon Kay, "How Employees Process Information," *Supervision* (Dec. 1998), p. 6.

26. Robert N. Lussier, *Human Relations in Organizations*, Fourth Ed. (Boston: Irwin McGraw-Hill, 1999), p. 104.

Exercise 7–A Completing the Channel—Two-way Communication	The sender will sit or stand facing away from the group. (If the sender can be hidden from sight this would be helpful.) The sender will then proceed to describe a series of objects to the class. The participants are to draw what they believe is being described to them as accurately as possible. Participants are not allowed to ask questions or have any discussion with the sender. They are to work on their own and make no audible responses. (The instructor will record how long the first activity took, and participants are to write down how many objects they think they have drawn correctly.)

The sender will now face the group and proceed to describe another series of objects. The participants are to draw the objects the best they can from the description. This time participants are allowed to ask questions and discuss the objects with the sender. The instructor will write down the length of time the second activity took. |

Questions

1. What happened during the drawing of the first object? How did you respond? How did you feel doing the task? How many of the objects did you actually get right?

2. What happened during the drawing of the second object? How did you respond? Did you ask for any clarifications? How did you feel doing the task? How many did you actually get right?

3. From the class results, what assumptions can be made in comparing one-way versus two-way communication? Does it take more time to communicate effectively?

Source: Exercise is adapted from Harold J. Leavitt, *Managerial Psychology* (Chicago: University of Chicago Press, 1958), pp. 118–28.

Exercise 7–B
The Assertion Inventory

Many people experience difficulty in handling interpersonal situations requiring them to assert themselves in some way; for example, turning down a request, asking a favor, giving someone a compliment, expressing disapproval or approval, etc. Please indicate your degree of discomfort or anxiety in the space provided *before* each situation listed below. Utilize the following scale to indicate degree of discomfort:

1 = none
2 = a little
3 = a fair amount
4 = much
5 = very much

Then, go over the list a second time and indicate *after* each item the probability or likelihood of your displaying the behavior if actually presented with the situation.* For example, if you rarely apologize when you are at fault, you would mark a "4" after that item. Utilize the following scale to indicate response probability:

1 = always do it
2 = usually do it
3 = do it about half the time
4 = rarely do it
5 = never do it

*Note: It is important to cover your discomfort ratings (located in front of the items) while indicating response probability. Otherwise, one rating may contaminate the other and a realistic assessment of your behavior is unlikely. To correct for this, place a piece of paper over your discomfort ratings while responding to the situations a second time for response probability.

Degree of Discomfort	SITUATION	Response Probability
_____	1. Turn down a request to borrow your car	_____
_____	2. Compliment a friend	_____
_____	3. Ask a favor of someone	_____
_____	4. Resist sales pressure	_____
_____	5. Apologize when you are at fault	_____
_____	6. Turn down a request for a meeting or date	_____
_____	7. Admit fear and request consideration	_____
_____	8. Tell a person you are intimately involved with when he/she says or does something that bothers you	_____
_____	9. Ask for a raise	_____
_____	10. Admit ignorance in some areas	_____
_____	11. Turn down a request to borrow money	_____
_____	12. Ask personal questions	_____
_____	13. Turn off a talkative friend	_____
_____	14. Ask for constructive criticism	_____
_____	15. Initiate a conversation with a stranger	_____
_____	16. Compliment a person you are romantically involved with or interested in	_____
_____	17. Request a meeting or a date with a person	_____
_____	18. Ask for a meeting when your initial request was turned down	_____
_____	19. Admit confusion about a point under discussion and ask for clarification	_____
_____	20. Apply for a job	_____
_____	21. Ask whether you have offended someone	_____
_____	22. Tell someone that you like them	_____
_____	23. Request expected service when such is not forthcoming, e.g., in a restaurant	_____

Degree of Discomfort	SITUATION	Response Probability
_____	24. Discuss openly with the person his/her criticism of your behavior	_____
_____	25. Return defective items, e.g., store or restaurant	_____
_____	26. Express an opinion that differs from that of the person you are talking to	_____
_____	27. Resist sexual overtures when you are not interested	_____
_____	28. Tell the person when you feel he/she has done something that is unfair to you	_____
_____	29. Accept a date	_____
_____	30. Tell someone good news about yourself	_____
_____	31. Resist pressure to drink	_____
_____	32. Resist a significant person's unfair demands	_____
_____	33. Quit a job	_____
_____	34. Resist pressure to do drugs	_____
_____	35. Discuss openly with the person his/her criticism of your work	_____
_____	36. Request the return of a borrowed item	_____
_____	37. Receive compliments	_____
_____	38. Continue to converse with someone who disagrees with you	_____
_____	39. Tell a friend or someone with whom you work when he/she says or does something that bothers you	_____
_____	40. Ask a person who is annoying you in a public situation to stop	_____

Lastly, please indicate the situations you would like to handle more assertively by placing a circle around the item number.

Add the total scores for each column.

Degree of Discomfort _____   Response Probability _____

Assertiveness Inventory Scoring Grid

	Response Probability	
	Low (105+)	High (40–104)
High (96+)	UNASSERTIVE	ANXIOUS PERFORMER
Degree of Discomfort		
Low (40–95)	??? DON'T CARE	ASSERTIVE

Exercise 7–C
Communication Styles

For the following situations describe a passive, aggressive, and assertive statement or response. Discuss the potential consequences for each.

I. You've been standing in line at the bookstore for over an hour and someone cuts in front of you.

Passive response

- Say/Do nothing
- leave the line cout saying anything

Aggressive response

- Hey You
- say something – "I've been waiting – you can too"

Assertive response

- Excuse Me
- be courteous

II. You live in an apartment with three other people. One person is very messy and sloppy, leaving dishes on the table and in the sink, eating your food, leaving garbage in all rooms of the apartment.

Passive response

- clean up after them
- live with the mess

Aggressive response

- emotional, con frontation
- timing

Assertive response

- adjust expectations
- negotiate limits

III. A telemarketer calls you on the phone when you are in the middle of completing work for a deadline. She or he is going through the sales pitch for buying magazines.

Passive response

Aggressive response - hang up

Assertive response

IV. You go to an expensive steakhouse and order your steak medium rare and it is served to you well done.

Passive response

_____

_____

Aggressive response

_____

_____

Assertive response

_____

_____

Questions

1. From the above situations, which responses would you most likely give? What is your rationale?
2. Is there a pattern for your behavior? Describe.
3. If your approach to these situations is primarily passive, why is this so? Are you getting your needs met?
4. If your approach to these situations is primarily aggressive, why is this so? What impact might this have on others?
5. Which responses are the most effective and why?
6. What are some alternate responses that would work effectively in these situations?

Exercise 7–D
Taking Responsibility

For each of the following comments:

1. Write the underlying assumption(s) about the speaker's intent in making the statement.

2. Rewrite the comment to reflect efforts to take responsibility and to communicate assumptions clearly. Utilize the strategies discussed in the chapter.

1. "Can't you work under pressure?"

Assumption: _The environment is v. challenging._

Rewritten statement: _I want to ensure we all have a common understanding of expectations bec ...._

2. "You're not listening to me."

Assumption: _____

Rewritten statement: _____

_____

3. "Will you work overtime Friday?"

Assumption: _____

Rewritten statement: _____

_____

4. "Joyce, what have you done with the production figures?"

Assumption: _____

Rewritten statement: _____

_____

5. "Are you getting all this down in writing?"

Assumption: _No need t/b in writing_

Rewritten statement: _I'd prefer we track details - will you write this down for both of us._

6. "Why are you mad at me?"

Assumption: _You are mad./Confusion_

Rewritten statement: _I sense you m/b upset have I said/done something_

7. "You've never appreciated my work." _— acknowledgement gap_

Assumption: _Seeking recognition or feedback_

Rewritten statement: _I feel unappreciated._

Source: Exercise adapted from an exercise in J. William Pfeiffer and John E. Jones, *Structured Experiences Kit,* entitled "Taking Responsibility," C-CAE/0-15 (San Francisco: Jossey-Bass Pfeiffer, 1980).

Exercise 7–E
Reflection/Action Plan

This chapter focused on the skill of verbal communication—what it is, why it is important, and how to improve your skills in this area. Complete the worksheet below upon completing all readings and experiential activities for this chapter.

1. The one or two communication areas in which I am most strong are:

   _____

   _____

   _____

   _____

2. The one or two communication areas in which I need more improvement are:

   _____

   _____

   _____

   _____

3. If I did only one thing to improve in this area, it would be to:

   _____

   _____

   _____

   _____

4. Making this change would probably result in:

   _____

   _____

   _____

   _____

5. If I did not change or improve in this area, it would probably affect my personal and professional life in the following ways:

   _____

   _____

   _____

   _____

Persuading Individuals and Audiences

Learning Points

How do I:

- Persuade someone to do something they might not have considered?
- Persuade co-workers or team members even when I have no direct authority?
- Incorporate tactics and strategies to improve my persuasive skills?
- Influence others to change their behaviors, such as a roommate who . . . ?
- Use elements of persuasion to give an effective presentation?

Ed Garrett is a recently promoted senior-level manager in human resources at Titan Industries, a major industrial company in the Northeast. For years, Titan has been recruiting on college campuses for entry-level engineering and business hires. While the company has a good record, successfully hiring several students each year, it lacks a cohesive recruiting and retention strategy. The company is experiencing high turnover among its recent college hires. In addition, its image hasn't kept up-to-date with reality: it is a prestigious, global, high-tech organization, but it is viewed on campuses as just one of many traditional, solid but unexciting companies trying to compete for top talent. Lately, the company is experiencing even greater difficulty recruiting and retaining minority students from campuses across the country.

Ed has been given the specific charge of improving Titan's campus recruiting program in three areas: (1) recruiting effectiveness, (2) campus image, and (3) minority recruiting and retention. There's only one catch: Ed hasn't been given a staff to help him accomplish these goals. Instead, he's told to "work through others" to succeed. In other words, he has to get Titan's many major business units behind this change effort, including getting them to put up the necessary funding for Ed's new recruiting initiatives.

Ed is very bright and talented, and in previous positions has been able to effect significant change through his own efforts and those of his staff. But this is different. He is full of ideas and energy, but without a staff to help him he must rely on his own capabilities to motivate others to want to change. How does Ed do this? How does he get others who don't report to him to do the work that he knows needs to get done?

1. What is the nature of Ed's dilemma?
2. What resources does Ed have available to him to help him effect the changes that are necessary at Titan?

3. What strategies can Ed use to get people behind his change agenda? What about his boss?

4. If you were Ed, what steps would you take and why?

5. What barriers would you face in asking for time and financial resources? How would you overcome these barriers?

"Persuasion is a governing power. Those who have it use it to their advantage. Those who don't have it let it run their lives."[1]

Paul Messaris (Author)

The way we conduct business is changing as fast as the business world itself is. Organizations are becoming less hierarchical. Managerial levels have been flattened. Organizations are more diverse. Communication is increasingly electronic. Decision making is spread throughout all employee levels. What does this mean for you? As the power base has shifted to employees and they make decisions that affect their work environment, they need to convince others of the soundness of their decisions, often without any direct authority. Such is the case in work teams where members, not managers, make decisions about who does what, when, and how. This chapter is about persuasion—the ability to influence people through means other than issuing direct orders. We discuss the importance of persuasion in today's business world, provide an overview of persuasion theories, offer strategies for persuasion, and provide some tips for effective presentations.

What Is Persuasion?

Persuasion is a form of influence. It is a process of guiding people toward the adoption of a behavior, belief, or attitude that the persuader prefers.[2] It involves careful preparation and proper presentation of arguments and supporting evidence in an appropriate and compelling emotional climate. Unlike manipulation or coercion, persuasion does not rely on deceit or force, nor does it involve directly giving orders. As Allied Signal CEO Lawrence Bossidy explains:

The day when you could yell and scream and beat people into good performance is over. Today you have to appeal to them by helping them see how they can get from here to there, by establishing some credibility, and by giving them some reason and help to get there. Do all those things, and they'll knock down doors.[3]

Persuasion is an essential component of doing business. Persuasion does not mean telling someone what to do; it means presenting information and interacting with a person in such a way that you both fully understand the situation and come to an agreement about how to approach the situation. In this view, persuasion is more of a problem-solving activity than it is a convincing activity.

Effective persuasion ensures that the persuader is fully up to speed on the issues at hand. The persuader comes to the dialogue with an open mind, willing to change others' perspectives if the situation warrants. The persuader also works on developing an understanding of the situation as it is being experienced by the listener(s) prior to offering any proposals or solutions. Effective persuasion also means the listener is fully involved in a dialogue about the situation. The listeners are given the information necessary to make an informed decision; consulted about their opinions, experience, and insights; engaged in discussions that help to generate numerous options and solutions before a decision is offered; and given time before a decision has to be made.

Good persuaders have strong interpersonal skills. They:

■ Are good listeners.

■ Solicit and give feedback.

- Read other people and sense what's appropriate in a given situation.
- Think creatively about what's best for the common good.
- Are prepared.
- Are empathetic.

Why Persuasion Is Important

To be an effective manager, you must be an able persuader. Gone are the days when managers could delegate to others and have their decisions implemented without question. Employees today show little tolerance for unquestioned authority.[4] Even the military, where unquestioned authority has been a core value, is making changes that include giving officers and nonofficers alike input into key decisions, into the way the organization should be run. More and more companies are adapting a participative work style where employees at all levels are involved in formulating strategy, discussing business needs, making bottom-line decisions, and implementing workplace changes. In this nonhierarchical environment, the skill of persuasion is invaluable.

Another trend that makes persuasion a necessary skill in today's business world is the movement of work to teams and "virtual" work, or work done by employees who work off-site. In a team-based or team-supported workplace, seldom does a higher authority mandate decisions. More likely the work is divided between the work group members and overseen by the members of a self-managing team rather than by a higher-level manager. In this new business world, persuasion is now the way to get your—and others'—tasks accomplished. Employees and teammates cooperate with you because they want to, not because they have to. More often than not, you'll be working with others who are your peers rather than your subordinates. In this situation the skill of persuasion is not simply the best alternative, it's the only one!

While the primary focus of this chapter is on persuasion as it is experienced in the business world, the concept of persuasion can also be applied in your personal life as well. Whether running for office, discussing a salary raise with your boss, convincing your parents to let you have a car at school, deciding with your spouse or partner what movie to see, or resolving a roommate or family conflict, the skill of persuasion can be an effective means for achieving your objective.

Overview of Theories of Persuasion

One of the earliest theories of persuasion, advanced by Fritz Heider, is **balance theory**. He suggested that the success or failure of the persuasion attempt could be affected by whether the structure of the situation is balanced or unstable.[5] A balanced configuration is one in which the relationships among three elements—the person, another person, and an object or event—are all positive or contain one positive and two negatives. This relationship is illustrated in the triangle in Figure 8–1. *P* is the person, *O* is the other person,

Figure 8–1
Balance Theory Diagram

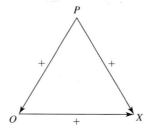

Figure 8–2
Balance Theory Example

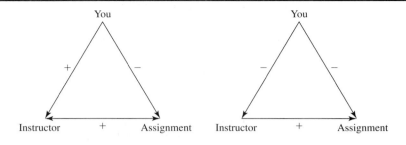

and *X* is the object or event. For example, if two people like each other and agree on an issue, the relationship is one that is in balance, and they are more likely to succeed at persuading one another. Heider also believed that we seek out balance, so in unbalanced situations (two positives and one negative) we attempt to change, avoid, or convince ourselves that the relationship between person, other, and thing is harmonious. So if you (*P*) like your instructor (*O*), and your instructor believes that a particular assignment is very important even if you don't (Figure 8–2), the instructor will have a better chance of persuading you of her view, in contrast to a situation in which you dislike your instructor. Imbalance exists when the three relationships are all negative or contain two positives and one negative. If two people dislike one another and disagree on a topic, there is an imbalance in the relationship. It will take more time for them first to find equal footing before they can begin the persuasion. Knowing where you and another stand on an issue, as well as your feelings toward one another, can help you determine a suitable strategy for effective persuasion.

Persuasion is also affected by the amount of dissonance, or tension, that is present in the relationship prior to the persuasion. Dissonance exists when the values or perceptions of the persuader and persuadee are different, or when conflict exists. For example, if the persuadee and persuader each come from a very different religious background, the chances of the persuader convincing the persuadee to change a religious belief are slim. This idea is central to Leon Festinger's **cognitive dissonance** theory.[6] He suggested that people are comfortable when their attitudes or beliefs are in concert with their behaviors, and uncomfortable when they are not.

To reduce the discomfort associated with this state, Festinger suggests that you are likely to increase the attractiveness of the chosen alternative, decrease the attractiveness of the unchosen alternative, create cognitive overlap, or revoke the decision.

Another theory that underpins the concept of persuasion is **inoculation theory.** Borrowing from the medical field, McGuire suggested that in the same way individuals receive a small injection of a disease-producing substance to increase immunity against that disease, persuaders can be effective when they anticipate the objections of the persuadee and address those objections before they arise.[7] For example, a firm could send information showing lower-than-expected profits prior to announcing a decreased merit pool. Other strategies for countering objections include presenting all points (for and against) and demonstrating how what's being proposed is the right solution, and broaching controversial subjects gently and early, before your audience has the chance to raise an issue that could become contentious or divisive.

A more recent model of persuasion effectiveness is Reardon's **ACE Theory.** She suggests that people use three criteria to determine whether to respond to a persuader's arguments: *appropriateness, consistency,* and *effectiveness.*[8] Trust and trustworthiness are essential for persuasion to be successful. The most successful appeals have these traits:

- **Appropriateness**—the right thing to do, based on generally accepted standards or norms, or in some cases, rules of law or morality. Appropriateness appeals are geared to the persuadee's or audience's belief system and interests.
- **Consistency**—the degree to which the action or belief proposed compares to that of similar others or to their own past behaviors or espoused beliefs. Appeals to consistency demonstrate that the persuader understands the beliefs or past behaviors of

similar others and presents arguments that make sense or track with these beliefs or behaviors.

- **Effectiveness**—the degree to which an action or idea leads to a desirable state or outcome. By knowing what the persuadee or audience wants or needs, a persuader can demonstrate how adoption of the proposed idea or action will help meet those needs.

According to Professor Jay Conger, persuaders are effective when they establish credibility, frame goals for common ground, reinforce their position, and connect emotionally with their audience.[9] These are described below.

1. **Establishing credibility.** To be persuasive, you must first be perceived as credible. You must be very knowledgeable about the subject matter and be able to present it in such a way that the listener(s) can be compelled to adopt a certain point of view. Credibility stems from four personal characteristics: expertise, trustworthiness, composure, and appearance.[10]

   - **Expertise**—acquired through developing an understanding or knowledge base about the subject matter or a track record of experience and prior success in the given area; demonstrated through passion or conviction, presenting reliable data, and giving nondefensive responses to questions or criticism.

   - **Trustworthiness**—acquired over time through personal and professional relationships in which others perceive you as consistent, reliable, and conscientious; demonstrated by showing empathy, humility, and solid emotional character; pursuing common ground; and looking out for the other's best interest.

   - **Composure**—acquired by practicing, having a plan and knowing what you're going to say and when; demonstrated by being confident and self-assured. When you are composed, you are solid and sure, even under pressure. "Never let them see you sweat" alludes to the contribution that composure makes to credibility.

   - **Positive Impression or Appearance**—acquired initially through one's appearance (attire, grooming), gestures (handshake, posture), and behaviors (etiquette), as well as through possession of credentials (title, reputation). Demonstrated over time through interactions with others, in particular taking a personal interest in the ideas and the people involved in the interaction and being enthusiastic and engaged with the process. Others' historical impressions of you can work to your advantage or disadvantage. If you are perceived as a remarkable leader, everything you say (for better or worse) will be accepted at face value. Conversely, if your reputation is inconsistent, others are likely to question and search for faults in your reasoning, creating an uphill battle for your persuasion attempts.

2. **Framing for common ground.** Effective persuaders develop a framework, or a plan for how to proceed, that involves describing their position in ways that identify common ground. Framing sets a collaborative tone and attains three interrelated objectives:[11]

   - Provides a perspective we would like the other party to consider. Sometimes, it's all in the packaging of the message. For example, if you need to introduce a new computer system to your company, you could present the technology as something new and exciting versus something that can free up time to be spent on more important tasks. Chances are, the latter approach will be more effective. This relates to knowing what makes the persuadee tick.

   - Provides an open-minded way for alternatives and ideas to be compared and contrasted. For example, "We need a solution for this problem. I've jotted down some benefits these improvements will likely bring and a few ideas for consideration. How do you think we can arrive at a solution?"

   - Creates a logical structure by which decisions can be made. By planning and creating a framework ahead of time, you provide a manner in which you and others can collaborate in the problem-solving process.

3. *Reinforce with* **logic and reasoning.** Presenting compelling evidence is extremely effective as a persuasion technique. Passion and emotion are important, but facts and data can make the difference between your audience supporting your argument or not.[12] Know the sources for your data; others might ask. Any errors in your reasoning can give the listener reason to doubt you. This does not imply that you must say everything you know about the subject. You must judiciously select the information regarding the subject that will have the most impact on your audience.[13]

4. *Establish an* **emotional connection.** While logic is essential, so too is appealing to people's feelings, fears, values, dreams, frustrations, egos, vanities, or desires. Many charismatic leaders, such as John F. Kennedy, Martin Luther King, Jr., and Mother Teresa, inspired others to support or join their cause not only because of its importance, but also because of their contagious passion and conviction to the cause.

By engaging yourself and your audience in the subject matter, everyone is vested in working together to find solutions to the problem at hand. Inspire others to "join the crusade" by applying the above principles of persuasion and by combining elements of both emotion and reasoning.

Strategies for Effective Persuasion

Persuasion is a complex two-way communication process that is most effective when the persuader has taken into consideration several elements regarding him or herself, the audience, and the issue or object at hand.[14] Figure 8–3 summarizes and highlights key behaviors and tactics to remember when you want to persuade others.

A Word of Caution

By adhering to many of the principles we've discussed, persuasion efforts are likely to be effective, resulting in positive outcomes for both the persuader and persuadee. Used incorrectly or for the wrong reasons, persuasion has the potential to be viewed as **manipulation**—convincing people to believe or adhere to something that is neither in

**Figure 8–3
Persuasion Tips and Tactics**

- *Believe in yourself.* Confidence, appearance, and attitude can help, especially if there is not enough time to solidify a relationship. When you believe you can accomplish something and it will benefit the organization, others sense this confidence and are more likely to back a "can-do" person than one who shows hesitation or reservation.
- *Show your own commitment and passion about the ideas being discussed.* Sense where the audience is on a subject (ask them if you have to) and show that you understand and can relate to their position.
- *Know your audience—start by examining their perspectives.* People are highly motivated by their own perceptions; arm yourself by using an overriding perception or belief of theirs that will be highly persuasive to them. When you understand what your audience believes and wants, you can better motivate them to work with you.[15]
- *Use facts, data, and logic.* Question your logic or propositions before presenting them. If there are holes, fix them. Be careful not to make mistakes when presenting data. This can be damaging to your credibility with the audience.[16]
- *Put your material in human terms rather than technical terms.* If you are trying to sell a computer, talk about the interesting things you can do and the ease with which you can do them as opposed to explaining the system configuration.
- *Use appropriate nonverbal communication:* lean forward, smile, keep your posture open, use good listening techniques.
- *Maintain your composure.* Show you are willing to discuss matters even if they are controversial. Appear reasonable; avoid yelling, insulting, belittling, or showing irritation.
- *Use props to enhance your story, not steal the show.* You can use data (charts or graphs) or samples and make them available later (if your audience is poring over data, they're not listening to you).
- *Provide reinforcement and follow through.* Once the interaction is over, offer praise and give the audience positive reinforcement to support their reasoning for being persuaded.[17]

their best interest nor something they would believe or do without the presence of the persuader. There can be a fine line between effective persuasion and manipulation.

To determine whether a speaker is positively persuading or negatively manipulating, ask these questions:[18]

- Who is really benefiting as a result of this act?
- Is the information being presented accurately?
- Does this interaction feel like a test of wills—a competitive game—or is it a healthy and positive debate—a two-way interchange?

Warning signals of manipulation include the persuader having more to gain from the exchange than the persuadee, discrepancies in the facts being presented as part of the argument, a war of words that heavily favors just one side, and a larger role for self-interest than public interest. If any or all of these conditions are present in an interaction, it's best to disengage and either discontinue or agree to resume the interaction when you can gain a more equal footing. To defend yourself against manipulation:

- *Be clear on your convictions and why you hold them.* Avoid being a victim of unscrupulous manipulators by being smart when interacting with them. Ask plenty of questions to ensure you understand clearly all sides of an issue. Analyze their intent and evaluate their argument before accepting what's being said, especially if your opinion is based primarily on the person's likability or reputation.
- *Think substance, not appearance.* Base your acceptance of a persuader on the strength of his reasoning, not simply because he has connected with you or the audience emotionally.
- *Doubt the truth of what's being said.* Do ask questions of speakers, before being convinced by the power of their words that they are right. Most of the time you will encounter presenters and persuaders who are truthful and honest. But it's a good strategy to be aware of the tactics that can be utilized by some whose self-interests override their interest in others.
- *Know the source.* Increasingly, people rely on the web for information and expertise. Yet much of the material readily available can't be attributed to a specific author, organization, or date. Out-of-context information is unreliable. Know the source before using content in personal or professional decision making. Otherwise, as A. Bostrom says in an article on future risk communication, "we may cross the divide from informal decision making to persuasion without reason."[19]
- *Consider the needs of others besides yourself.* When being courted by a persuader, consider not just your interests but those of others who may be affected by the action or perspective being advocated.[20] Is the action of benefit to the greater common good? Or will it benefit only a select few?

Making Effective Presentations

As persuaders, we often find ourselves making a formal presentation to others. Knowing how to create a persuasive presentation can increase sales, advance your career, enhance your reputation, and create professional opportunities along with personal satisfaction.[21] Being able to present, defend, and gain acceptance for your ideas is a critical skill in today's business environment. Persuasive presentations require the presenter not only to give information, but also to get the audience to accept, believe, and act on the ideas presented.[22]

Many individuals spend great amounts of time and energy creating and developing their ideas, but forget to learn the techniques necessary to sell the ideas. Selling the ideas is a critical component. A lack of "show and tell" ability can compromise a person's productivity, effectiveness, and opportunity to advance within an organization. Mastering these skills allows an audience to trust your expertise and your message, allowing you to sell your ideas and display your leadership ability.[23]

When creating persuasive presentations, it is crucial to determine your reason for giving the presentation and find the need behind your idea. This will provide the basis for your presentation. Once you have determined the information, shape the message to your audience. Your efforts will be more successful if you deliver the speech around the information needs of your audience. Imagine you need to make a presentation for a new product idea. You must first begin with the reason for the new product, the data and information necessary to show the projected demand for the new product. However, you will not get the rest of the team to buy into your product idea unless they have been shown the benefit it can provide to the organization. You must understand the group's concerns and its motivation for the new product development in order to create a persuasive pitch.

Elements of persuasion can be useful tactics when developing effective presentations. Figure 8–4 provides pointers for making persuasive business presentations successfully.

Figure 8–4
Tips for Effective Presentations

Before the Presentation

- *Research your intended audience.* What are their interests? Their beliefs? To what kind of presentation are they accustomed (i.e., length, format, and type of technology used)? Will they want to see your materials in advance? Will a handout or copy of the report being presented be expected?

- *Determine appropriate dress.* Many businesses are "business casual" every day of the week, while others reserve this for Fridays only or not at all. Find out what's appropriate in the environment in which you'll be speaking.

- *Prepare your remarks.* There are two kinds of presenters: those who are best when they have not prepared in advance, and those who are not. Those few who are blessed with the skill of relating to others extemporaneously, or "on the spot," can get away with minimal preparation. All the rest of us need to prepare, prepare, prepare!

- *Practice.* You don't have to write out the whole speech. Make a list of the key concepts you want to address and develop "talking points" that support each of these concepts. Practice saying these points in sequence, using a natural conversational tone.

- *Relax.* Just before the presentation, clear your head and focus on the task at hand.

During the Presentation

- *Begin with an anecdote or quote.* This ensures you begin with an attention-grabber that helps the audience focus on your presentation. Avoid the use of a joke—jokes can be offensive to members of a particular group. It's better to start with something of substance that relates to the subject matter or the audience.

- *Give your audience an organizing framework.* Begin your presentation by telling your audience the key concepts you'll be addressing. You could also present an agenda as a visual aid and means to reinforce key points throughout your remarks.

- *Present the core of your argument at the beginning.* This gives the audience a road map—they know where you're heading and why. "Tell them what you're going to tell them, then tell them." This also gives you a platform for demonstrating your enthusiasm about your subject, and for engaging them in that enthusiasm. Then build your case by presenting data or facts that support your argument.

- *Make your session interactive.* Take questions throughout. If there's no time for audience interaction, ask one or two rhetorical questions, or begin your presentation with a question that can focus their thinking even if a response is not expected. The more engaged they are, the greater the likelihood that they'll buy in to your arguments.

- *Use technology, but sparingly.* You want to be up on the latest cutting-edge methods—as appropriate for the message and audience—but you don't want to lose the personal connection with the audience or give the impression that you're more style than substance.

- *Be interesting but not necessarily entertaining.* It's important to engage your audience. Making people laugh can do this. Even more effective is making them think.

- *Summarize.* "Tell them what you told them." This helps focus the audience's attention on the essence of your presentation—the key take-aways or lessons of your message.

After the Presentation

- *Evaluate.* Ask yourself, and others who were present, what went well and what you can do differently in the future. It helps to debrief while your presentation is still fresh in your—and others'—minds. Debriefing is also helpful when recycling your presentation. If planned correctly, your presentation can serve as a "template" for your next one. The content will likely change but the format—opening, main concepts, key points that support your case, summary, close—can stay the same.

- *Follow up.* Prepare and send any materials or data you promised to the audience, and send a formal thanks to the organizer of the event at which you spoke.

Strategies for Dealing with "Stage Fright"

Many people, when asked, would say they dislike giving presentations. It's been suggested that public speaking is at or near the top of lists of people's greatest fears, even higher than death. Unless you're a natural salesperson or an expert on a topic, the prospect of giving a presentation can be a bit daunting. If you suffer from "stage fright," or find speaking in front of an audience difficult, consider the following pointers:

- *Prepare.* Begin preparation as soon as you find out about your presentation. Set aside 10–15 minutes a day, outlining what you will cover so it feels natural. Determine and practice your opening story or remarks in order to get through the highest-anxiety time of your presentation—the very beginning.
- *Visit the site.* Familiarize yourself with the speaking environment. Before the event, go to the place where you will be speaking so the setting won't surprise you and increase your anxiety. Find out who your audience is (their background, education, reason for attending) and how many will attend.
- *Visualize success.* Picture yourself in front of your audience in the place you will be speaking. See yourself being totally confident and in control of the situation, and your audience enjoying your speech. Avoid all negative thoughts during the visualization. This helps to reduce damaging self-thinking and substitutes a positive image for a negative one.
- *Maintain realistic expectations.* You don't have to be perfect. Just be the best you can be. Remember that you appear much more confident than you feel. You probably know as much or more about the topic than your audience does. They're there to learn from you, not to see you fail.
- *Gain experience.* The more you rehearse your speech, the better you feel about it. Present your speech to a group of friends to become more comfortable and get feedback on what you did well and what you can do to improve. "Rehearsal and preparation can reduce a speaker's fear by 75 percent."[24]
- *Talk about something that interests you.* You will feel more positive delivering your message if it is something that you believe and that is familiar to you.
- *Develop a relaxation routine.* Relaxing the body can eliminate or reduce physical discomfort that can add to levels of anxiety. Relieve the built-up tensions in your body in advance by exercising, meditating, or doing deep-breathing exercises.

  - Breathing deeply *before* a presentation relaxes the body and vents tension. Remembering to take breaths between sentences *during* a presentation can help you stay at a conversational level with the audience rather than quickening to a jittery "let's get this thing over" pace. Deep breathing can reduce stage fright by 15 percent.[25]

  - Tension restricts breathing and creates discomfort. Stand in a relaxed rather than a rigid position. Don't tense up your muscles or shoulders. Keep your shoulders low and relaxed, and your knees slightly bent. Before your presentation, stand in front of a mirror to get a visual and physical image of what a relaxed posture looks and feels like. Remember this image should tension creep in during your presentation.

- *Use visual aids.* They divert attention away from you so you can feel more relaxed and less like the center of attention. It's best to use them at the beginning of your presentation when the level of your anxiety is probably the highest.
- *Use gestures.* Don't be afraid to move. Be natural. When presenting, use the same gestures you would during a casual conversations. These movements will keep your body loose and relax your muscles. Smiles and other facial gestures convey confidence as well as engage the audience.

Summary

Persuasion is a skill that can benefit you in your personal and professional endeavors in many ways. Whether asking for an increase in salary, bidding on a project, or advocating for a significant organizational change, your ability to get what you want is influenced by your knowledge and application of persuasion theory and techniques. Knowing what influences your persuasiveness—including characteristics of you, your message, and those you hope to persuade—will enable you to influence others to act or believe in something that benefits them as well as you. These principles can be applied to making persuasive presentations, something you will probably be called upon to do many times in your work and life.

Key Terms and Concepts

ACE Theory	Expertise
Appropriateness	Framing
Balance theory	Inoculation theory
Cognitive dissonance	Logic and reasoning
Composure	Manipulation
Consistency	Persuasion
Credibility	Positive impression or appearance
Effectiveness	Trustworthiness
Emotional connection	

Endnotes

1. Paul Messaris, *Visual Persuasion: The Role of Images in Advertising* (Thousand Oaks, CA: Sage Publications, 1997).

2. Kathleen K. Reardon, *Persuasion in Practice* (Newbury Park, CA: Sage Publications, 1991), p. 2.

3. Jay A. Conger, "The Necessary Art of Persuasion," *Harvard Business Review,* May–June 1998, p. 84.

4. Conger, 1998.

5. Fritz Heider, *The Psychology of Interpersonal Relations* (New York: John Wiley, 1958).

6. Leon Festinger, *A Theory of Cognitive Dissonance* (Stanford, CA: Stanford Univ. Press, 1957).

7. W. J. McGuire, "The Effectiveness of Supportive and Refutational Defenses in Immunizing and Restoring Beliefs against Persuasion," *Sociometry* 24 (1961), pp. 184–197.

8. Reardon, *Persuasion in Practice,* p. 70.

9. Conger, "Necessary Art."

10. Reardon, *Persuasion in Practice.*

11. Lyle Sussman, "How to Frame a Message: The Art of Persuasion and Negotiation," *Business Horizons,* July–August 1999, p. 2.

12. Deborah C. Andrew, *Technical Communication in the Global Community* (Upper Saddle, NJ: Prentice Hall, 1998).

13. James P. T. Fatt, "The Anatomy of Persuasion," *Communication World,* Dec. 1997, p. 21.

14. Fatt, "Anatomy of Persuasion."

15. David Stiebel, "Getting Them to See Things Your Way," *Canadian Manager,* Winter 1997, p. 13.

16. Deborah Tannen, *You Just Don't Understand: Women and Men in Conversation* (New York: Ballentine Books, 1991).

17. Joseph D. O'Brian, "The Gentle Art of Persuasion," *Supervisory Management,* Feb. 1995, p. 14.

18. Perry Pascarella, "Persuasion Skills Required for Success," *Management Review,* Sept. 1998, p. 68.

19. A. Bostrom, "Future Risk Communication," *Futures* 35, no. 6 (Aug 2003), p. 553.

20. Richard Alan Nelson, "Ethics and Social Issues in Business: An Updated Communication Perspective," *Competitiveness Review* 13, no. 1 (2003), p. 66.

21. Bernard Rosenbaum, "Making Presentations: How to Persuade Others to Accept Your Ideas," *American Salesman,* Feb. 1992, p. 16.

22. Robert W. Rasberry and Laura Lemoine Lindsay, *Effective Managerial Communication,* Second Ed. (Belmont, CA: Wadsworth, 1994), p. 256.

23. Robert E. Kelley, *How to Be a Star at Work: Nine Breakthrough Strategies You Need to Succeed* (New York: Times Business, 1998), p. 225.

24. Debra Hamilton, "Prepare and Practice," *Officepro,* March 2000, p. 14.

25. Ibid.

**Exercise 8–A
Debate Persuasions**

Watch one political debate for the upcoming elections. The debate you choose to watch should be one for which you are already aware of the candidates and issues.

After watching the debate please answer the following questions.

Debate watched_____   Date of debate_____

1. Discuss the nonverbals used by the candidates. Did these support their verbal statements/positions?

2. Was one candidate more credible than the other? What made this candidate more credible? If both were equally credible, discuss why you thought this was the case.

3. What other forms of persuasion did the candidates utilize in the debate?

4. Choosing one of the candidates, what would you have done differently to make his or her debate performance more persuasive and effective?

5. How important was your own political ideology in assessing the relative performance of each candidate? How did your belief system affect your interpretation of the debate?

Contributed by Dr. David Kaplan, College of Business, St. Louis University.

Exercise 8–B
Deserted Isle

Your group has been stranded on a deserted island with an active volcano. There is a limited food supply and the future is uncertain. It is unknown how long the island will be able to sustain human life. A raft is available, but it is capable of taking only one team to safety.

In triads or small groups, you are to develop a persuasive argument to present to the instructor to convince him or her that your team should be the one rescued from the deserted island. Make up any information that will help support your arguments.

Groups will take turns presenting their arguments to the instructor, who will decide which team will be taken to safety.

Questions

1. How successful were you in devising and presenting a solid persuasive argument?
2. What areas of your argument were weak or lacking in support?
3. What could you have done differently to ensure greater success?
4. What objections were presented for which you were not prepared?

Exercise 8–C
"I Deserve a Raise"
Role-Play

"You have been employed in your first job after college for a little more than one year. When you were hired, you were promised a raise after the first year. However at your recent performance appraisal, there was no mention of a raise despite the fact that you received above average ratings on most performance criteria. You are considering leaving your employer to go to graduate school if you don't get a raise."

In your triad or small group, devise a persuasive argument to present to your boss to convince her or him you should get a raise. In each round, two of you play the roles of employee and boss, while the third and other persons are observers. In round one, person A is the employee, B is the boss, and C is the observer. In round two, person A is the boss, B the observer, and C the employee, and so on. Each round should last about 10 minutes and should include first the persuasion role-play and then a round of feedback in which the observer(s) gives feedback to the employee about his or her persuasion skills.

Questions for the Observer(s)

1. How successful was the employee in devising and presenting a solid, persuasive argument?
2. What areas of the employee's argument were weak or lacking support? Which were positive and supportable?
3. What did the employee do that contributed to her or his success? What could the employee have done to ensure greater success?
4. What, if any, objections did the boss present for which the employee was not prepared?

**Exercise 8–D
Back to the Future**

Your parents own a small print shop, one that had been passed down from one of their parents during the B.C. (before computers) period. Inventory and sales records are kept in notebooks or on cards filed in shoeboxes. Customers' names and numbers are listed on a Rolodex file. The annual Christmas card is sent by having one of the employees hand-address about 350 envelopes. While technology has changed, things in the print shop have not.

You are home over winter break and wish to apply some of your technology-based knowledge and skill to improve things in the print shop. You know of several computer systems and software applications that can keep track of customers, sales, and inventory all at the touch of a button. Send a letter to only those customers in a particular city? Piece of cake most anywhere else, but not at your parents' shop. You explain the value of computers to them, but they insist that all is well in the print shop. Besides, they tell you, "If it ain't broke, why fix it?"

To convince them to adopt (and use!) the kind of computer system you know will benefit them, you decide to apply Reardon's three-pronged approach. Use the worksheet below to develop a script for what you'll say and do to address each of these prongs:

Motivation: What do they want? How do I know this?

_____

_____

_____

Participation: How do I get them involved in the problem-solving process—get them to acknowledge how they would benefit from this change? How can I ease them into such a change?

_____

_____

_____

Reward: How will the change benefit my parents?

_____

_____

_____

**Exercise 8–E
Applying the ACE
Theory**

Scenario One

Your roommate will be spending a semester abroad. Just as you begin planning out a new and better arrangement of your room, you get a knock on your door from your RA. Standing beside him is someone who is, from the looks of it, likely not to be a lot of fun: the thick-rimmed glasses, the pocket protector, the skin color suggesting little if any time spent outdoors. You keep your stereotypes to yourself and hope for the best. Unfortunately, your expectations are met. Pat rarely talks, leaves the room, or spends time with anyone or anything besides the books and computer. You'd like to see Pat have a little bit of fun, but you're afraid that your offer will be declined, only adding to the tension in the room. Tomorrow night is movie night at your university, when a relatively recent film is shown for free in the main auditorium on campus. Perhaps, if your persuasion attempt follows the ACE Theory, you might be successful. Use the worksheet below to prepare a script for what you would say or do to convince Pat to take a break from the books and join you in a movie.

Appropriateness (What is typical, common, or accepted practice for similar others?)

_____

_____

_____

Consistency (In what ways might going to the movies align with Pat's behaviors or beliefs?)

_____

_____

_____

Effectiveness (How would going to the movie result in a positive outcome for Pat?)

_____

_____

_____

Scenario Two

You work at an insurance firm, consisting of approximately 150 employees, with most involved in desk work. You would like to convince the owner that an exercise/wellness program should be added to the workplace. The owner is a man in his mid 50s and is highly concerned with attendance and productivity. Use the worksheet to script out how the ACE Theory could help you in being successful in your persuasion attempt.

Appropriateness (What is typical, common, or accepted practice for similar others?)

_____

_____

_____

Consistency (In what ways might developing an exercise/wellness program align with the owner's behaviors or beliefs?)

_____

_____

_____

Effectiveness (How would developing an exercise/wellness program result in a positive outcome for the owner?)

_____

_____

_____

**Exercise 8–F
Reflection/Action Plan**

This chapter focused on persuasion—what it is, why it is important, and how to improve your skills in this area. Complete the worksheet below upon completing all reading and experiential activities for this chapter.

1. The one or two areas in which I am most strong are:

_____

_____

_____

2. The one or two areas in which I need more improvement are:

_____

_____

_____

3. If I did only one thing to improve in this area, it would be to:

_____

_____

_____

4. Making this change would probably result in:

_____

_____

_____

5. If I did not change or improve in this area, it would probably affect my personal and professional life in the following ways:

_____

_____

_____

UNIT 1

INTRAPERSONAL EFFECTIVENESS: UNDERSTANDING YOURSELF

1. Journey into Self-awareness
2. Self-disclosure and Trust
3. Establishing Goals by Identifying Values and Ethics
4. Self-Management

UNIT 2

INTERPERSONAL EFFECTIVENESS: UNDERSTANDING AND WORKING WITH OTHERS

5. Understanding and Working with Diverse Others
6. The Importance and Skill of Listening
7. Conveying Verbal Messages
8. Persuading Individuals and Audiences

UNIT 3

UNDERSTANDING AND WORKING IN TEAMS

9. Negotiation
10. Building Teams and Work Groups
11. Managing Conflict
12. Achieving Business Results through Effective Meetings
13. Facilitating Team Success
14. Making Decisions and Solving Problems Creatively

UNIT 4

LEADING INDIVIDUALS AND GROUPS

15. Power and Politicking
16. Networking and Mentoring
17. Coaching and Providing Feedback for Improved Performance
18. Leading and Empowering Self and Others
19. Project Management

Unit 3

A trip to Disneyworld would be fun, for sure, but the experience would be even more memorable if you shared this experience with others. Today's organizations are cognizant of the value of teams, and use them extensively in delivering and improving its products and services. In the same way you find value in sharing and comparing experiences with friends, organizations use work teams to support collaboration that often results in greater productivity, creativity, innovation, and fosters increased employee satisfaction and commitment. Along with these benefits, teams often face challenges, as many of you who have participated on teams—whether school, sports, work or other organization—have found. We discuss the team phenomena and offer opportunities for you to improve your skills in managing conflict, negotiating, persuading, and facilitating team process. Mastering these skills will help your team "accentuate the positive and eliminate the negative" aspects of team functioning.

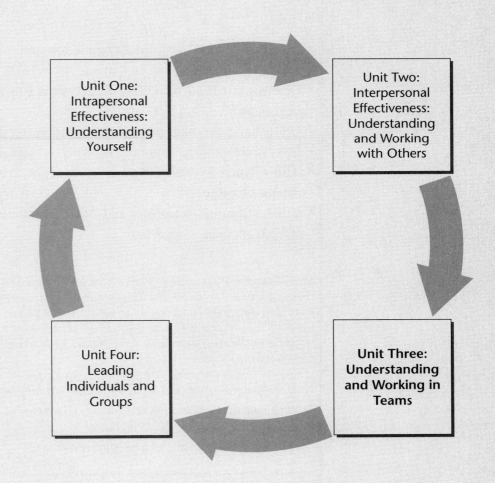

9 Negotiation

Learning Points

How do I:

- Determine what I want in a negotiation and make a plan to facilitate my ability to achieve this?
- Determine what I'm willing to accept if I don't get all that I want in a negotiation?
- Understand the other party's wants and needs in a negotiation?
- Involve the other person in a collaborative and interest-based negotiation?
- Know when to walk away from a negotiation if a resolution doesn't appear possible?
- Utilize framing, scripting, and other negotiation tactics to increase my effectiveness as a negotiator?

John Monroe is a senior vice president for one of the country's largest hotel chains. A competitor based in the United Kingdom is attempting to lure John away from his company. John has some concerns about his present employer but hadn't been actively looking for another position. In addition, he is concerned about how his wife and daughter would react to a move. John decides he'll accept the new position if it is "an offer he can't refuse."

1. At this point, what should John do? Is there anything he shouldn't do?
2. What kind of preparation should John do prior to his negotiation?
3. What are some specific arguments he could use to improve his chances of getting the opportunity package in which he is interested?

"You often get not what you deserve, but what you negotiate." [1]

John Marrioti

Everyone negotiates. Children negotiate to decide which games to play or which television show to watch. Students try to negotiate a higher grade from their professor. Employees negotiate for a certain salary, benefits, or perquisites. Corporations negotiate with other organizations on the sale or purchase of assets, materials, or operating units. Negotiations occur globally as in the case of the Mideast, the NATO treaty, and

NAFTA. Whether you're a diplomat or dignitary, spouse or salesperson, student or teacher, you negotiate almost daily. Sometimes the stakes are high, as in the case of a buyout of a firm; sometimes the stakes are low, as in the case of which movie you and your friends choose to see. In this chapter, we discuss the fundamentals of negotiation, benefits of doing it well, types and stages of negotiation, and principles and strategies for enhancing your skill in this arena. At the end of the chapter are several exercises to help you build your negotiating skills, as well as a list of references used that will help you pursue this important topic further.

What Is Negotiation and Why Is It Important?

Negotiation is a process in which two or more people or groups share their concerns and interests to reach an agreement of mutual benefit.[2] It occurs when all parties have both shared interests (meaning they're committed to a resolution) and opposed interests (meaning they don't agree on everything). This definition implies that both parties have an incentive for devoting energy to the negotiation and that they are willing to collaborate on reaching a shared agreement.[3] Sometimes we use the terms *bargaining* and *negotiating* interchangeably, although most associate bargaining with the type of haggling that occurs over items in a yard sale and negotiating with a more formal process in which parties attempt to find a mutually agreeable solution to a conflict situation.

Why Do We Negotiate?

We negotiate when what one party wants is not necessarily what the other party wants. The conflict of interests may be clear and simple. If the competitor offers John a significant increase plus a package that is attractive to John's wife and daughter, John may accept the offer. If the competitor doesn't have the latitude to offer a significant increase, or doesn't show an interest in the family's overall needs, John may turn down the offer. At other times, the conflict is more complex, consisting of multiple issues, competing interests, and unlimited potential solutions. Examples of this type of conflict include the merger or takeover of a company, a rift between a company's management and its unionized employees, or a divorce. While some conflicts wind up in court, most conflicts of this type, even those that appear to be quite complicated, can be negotiated and settled before trial.

Complex negotiation is a fact of life for anyone in business. Managers ensure work gets done on time and within a budget. To do this successfully, managers negotiate for the necessary resources. As long as there is a scarcity of resources, negotiation will always be an essential skill for businesspeople. Another factor driving the need for negotiation skills in business is the increased use of teams in the workplace. As individuals from "competing" business units are brought together on projects, the ability to negotiate with others—both inside and outside the team—is critical for the ultimate success of the project team. Global diversity is another factor motivating the need for acquiring skills in negotiation. As employees from a variety of countries and cultures are brought together to work on projects and joint ventures, an inevitable clash of customs and business practices results in almost constant negotiating that involves developing and modifying relationships and expectations over time. A backlash against the litigious tendency of our modern society is another reason why it is important for managers to develop skill in negotiating. As the court dockets fill with numerous (and often frivolous) lawsuits, the negotiation of differences has become accepted and valued as a cost-effective alternative to litigation. Witness the growth of the number of organizations dedicated to helping individuals and companies improve their negotiating skills. The increasing number and availability of books, audio and videotapes, and Internet sites devoted to this topic provide further testimonial to the importance of effective negotiating in today's world. All these factors build a compelling case for acquiring and enhancing your negotiating skills.

Benefits of Honing Negotiation Skills

Negotiating holds many benefits for individuals who strive to master this skill set. Studies show that those who have sound negotiating skills are able to maintain better control in business and personal situations.[4] In an effective negotiation, the parties focus on identifying each other's key interests and viewing the situation objectively, while putting their emotions aside. Over time, those who practice negotiating find they are better able to resist responding emotionally to a potential conflict.

Negotiation is a much better way to reach a solution than either a lawsuit or arbitration.[5] In a lawsuit, the adversarial nature of the environment pits one set of interests against the other. The goal is a "win–lose" situation, where one of the parties is clearly victorious over the other. In arbitration, both parties agree to a settlement reached by a third party, which may or may not reflect the interests of the conflicting parties. Arbitration occurs outside of the courtroom; however, the parties involved are bound by the verdict—one that may or may not bring satisfaction. Verdicts resulting from arbitration often resemble "win–lose" or even "lose–lose" resolutions, where either one party is victorious or both parties must compromise so severely that the final agreement is perceived as losing by both parties. In contrast, negotiation, when handled properly, typically results in identifying the primary interests of both parties and generating an agreement that addresses key issues of both parties. This can result in a "win–win" solution where both parties feel their primary interests have been listened to if not addressed.

If a resolution can't be reached, arbitration or litigation may be necessary. However, these options tend to require more time and effort than negotiation. In a lawsuit, attorneys spend many hours doing research and preparing. In arbitration, an outside third party (an arbitrator) spends numerous hours getting up to speed on a case before being able to rule on it. In negotiation, both parties are involved from the outset. Each party serves as the chief spokesperson for her or his point of view. Naturally others are involved, principally the negotiator or negotiators. But they work in partnership with the two parties, not as surrogates. The principal work is performed by the two parties themselves, resulting in a saving of time and energy spent on the negotiation process.

Another benefit of negotiation is that when it works, it helps both parties not only to achieve a workable resolution, but also to help preserve and improve their relationship, reputations, and sense of professional achievement. Conversely, after an arbitration or lawsuit has concluded, the parties involved often experience lingering feelings of resentment and anger that preclude them from being able to continue working together.

Lastly, negotiation reduces stress and frustration, and often results in a reduction in the number of potential future conflicts. When a negotiation is conducted properly, most if not all of the major and minor issues involved are surfaced and addressed. They are not placed on the "back burner" in deference to a narrow set of key issues, as is often the case in a lawsuit or arbitration. Being able to clear the air and deal with all legitimate concerns results in a clean slate—a feeling that both parties have been fully listened to and understood. This reduces frustration and the chance that these issues will resurface and generate additional conflict.

Integrative and Distributive Bargaining Strategies

Once we decide to negotiate,[6] our approach to negotiation or bargaining will generally fall into one of two categories or strategies: integrative, or "win–win," and distributive, or "win–lose."[7] Both strategies have their benefits and disadvantages and can be used depending on the needs inherent in a specific situation.[8]

Negotiators use an **integrative bargaining strategy** when they believe that a win–win situation exists and can be reached. This means that there's a chance both parties can achieve their primary objectives, without either feeling they lost. In integrative bargaining, the goal is to collaborate and generate one or more creative solutions that are acceptable to both parties. A simple example would be a couple trying to decide on a movie to rent. Taking an integrative approach, they would begin their discussion by drawing up a list of only those movies that were acceptable to both parties. They would discuss the available choices and choose a movie to see from that list, rather than arguing in favor of a movie that only one of the two parties wants to see.

A more complex example involves the creation of a "preferred supplier" agreement. Many firms seek to formalize the arrangements they may have with a particular supplier or vendor in order to reduce the uncertainty of changes in price and other market conditions. Should both organizations take an interactive approach to this solution, they would look beyond price—after all, the supplier's likely interest to maximize price is at odds with the organization's need to minimize it—to understand both the short- and long-term needs of both organizations. Issues of availability, reliability, quality, and prompt delivery and payment all enter into the equation in which price is but one factor. It's in both parties' best interests to find a workable solution, one that meets these multiple criteria. The supplier wins because it has a consistent customer for its product, ensuring a positive cash flow, steady employment, and predictable operations. The organization wins because it can rely on receiving the supplier's product consistently, when it's needed, at a fair price, and in the requested quantity. It doesn't need to search for additional options to save a few pennies; when all factors are considered, a preferred supplier arrangement benefits both parties.

Integrative bargaining only works when both parties are committed to preserving the relationship that exists between them. Integrative bargaining requires a great deal of creativity, problem-solving ability, and time, as well as a set of ultimate goals on which both parties can agree. Arriving at a truly integrative or collaborative solution requires that those involved gain the skills, knowledge, and attitude (including patience) necessary for this approach to resolving conflicts to work. Another requirement for integrative bargaining to work is a climate that supports and promotes open communication. Both parties need to be willing to change and to confront their conflict directly rather than run from it, resolve it through brute force, or pretend it will go away. The parties must be open to establishing longer-term goals on which they can both agree. For example, the couple choosing a movie must recognize that their relationship is more important than the choice of a movie and must be willing to collaborate or, if necessary, compromise for the sake of the overall relationship.

A **distributive bargaining strategy** is based on an attempt to divide up a fixed "pie" or amount of resources, resulting in a win–lose situation.[9] Negotiators taking a distributive approach typically take an adversarial or competitive posture to dividing a fixed amount of resources. One improves its lot at the expense of the other. This scarcity mentality implies that only one of the two parties can have the conflict resolved to its satisfaction. In distributive bargaining, the focus is on achieving immediate goals, with little or no regard for building future relationships. Little time or energy is expended in resolving the conflict in a distributive negotiation, resulting in the generation of few if any creative solutions. Generally, one or two fixed solutions are presented and a decision or choice is expected almost immediately, with possibly some consequence if a choice is not made soon. If distributive bargaining were used to resolve the movie decision mentioned earlier, the couple would likely not be very close, and one or both parties would not care whether the relationship was a good one or lasted much longer. In this example, one member of the couple would say something like "This is the movie I want to see. Take it or leave it." There would be no real discussion of the wants and interests of both parties. The "agreement" would be reached either by dictate or after some fierce arguing.

While win–lose is not a recommended strategy for resolving issues, it can be used in situations where achieving short-term goals is more important than maintaining or building longer-term relationships. Distributive bargaining is also appropriate to use in situations that are so contentious there is no possibility of a win–win solution, when there's a sense of urgency and time is short, and where the relationships involved are relatively unimportant compared to the issue at hand. Forcing children to wear protective gear when bicycling is an example of this. "Aw mom, do I have to wear my helmet? What if I promise to be really careful?" Allowing the child to negotiate on this issue is a waste of

**Figure 9–1
Comparing Bargaining
Approaches**

Considerations	Integrative Bargaining	Distributive Bargaining
Likely solution or end result	Win–win	Win–lose or lose–lose
Importance of continued relationship with bargaining partner	High	Low
Goal	Collaborate and generate multiple options or solutions; expand the pie	Winner takes all (scarcity mentality); distribute a fixed pie
Bargaining climate	Open, communicative, creative, willing to change	Determination to win, willingness to walk away, cards held close to the chest, ends justify the means
Amount of time needed	More	Less
Time horizon in consideration	Current and future	Immediate only

time, as his or her safety is paramount in this situation. Despite the intuitive appeal and apparent societal acceptance of the "winner take all" or "ends justify the means" approach to negotiation, distributive bargaining generally tends to be ineffective and counterproductive and should be used only in certain circumstances. Figure 9–1 summarizes these two approaches.

Five Stages of Negotiating

We've discussed why people negotiate and the types of negotiation. Now we turn to the how, or the process of negotiating. Keep in mind that all negotiations are different. Simple negotiations, such as choosing which movie to rent, need not require an extensive negotiation process. However, when negotiations involve significant or complex issues, you should consider using the five-stage process model depicted in Figure 9–2. As illustrated, negotiating consists of five stages: (1) preparation and planning, (2) defining ground rules, (3) clarifying and justifying your case, (4) bargaining and problem solving, and (5) closure and implementation.[10] These stages are described below.

1. *Preparation and planning.* Without question, preparation and planning are the keys to successful deal making. While some may think they can negotiate effectively "on the fly," all negotiators benefit from thorough advance thought and preparation. Be clear about what you want and why. Gather data to support your position. Consider ways to present your arguments persuasively. Consider what the other party wants and why. What data or tactics might they use? How will you counter? Answer these questions when preparing your negotiation strategy. Understand your and the other party's strengths and weaknesses, and take these similarities and differences into account in your strategy. If negotiating is new to you, learn and practice the basics of negotiating well in advance of a planned negotiation. Build new skills that are appropriate to this particular situation.

Another important component in preparing for negotiations is determining your **bottom line.** Identify what you ideally want and what you'd be willing to accept. The range between these two points gives you an indication of how much flexibility you have going into the negotiation. Lastly, prepare for a negotiation by learning as much as you can about the other party prior to the negotiation. In addition to the questions above, see what you can uncover about their negotiating style by talking with others with whom they've negotiated. If possible, try to become acquainted with the other party before the planned meeting. By establishing your willingness to get to know the other party, you will be better able to begin the negotiation with a positive, relationship-based tone rather than on an adversarial note.[11]

Figure 9–2
The 5 Stages of Negotiation

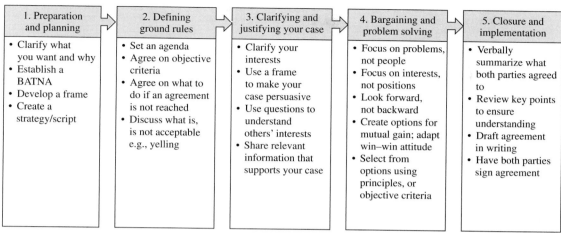

Many of the strategies or tips discussed in the chapter that should be considered during each phase are listed under the corresponding stage.

2. *Definition of ground rules.* Determining your own guidelines or rules for the negotiation helps you to plan a strategy that can be successful.[12] Establish who will or should be present and at what part of the negotiation. Decide where the meeting will be held and offer a possible agenda for how the time will be allocated and for which issues. The location has implications in terms of who's in charge. While there may be a benefit to having the negotiation at your office—the home court advantage—agreeing to have the negotiation at the other party's office might show flexibility and willingness to negotiate on your part. When the topic covered is potentially divisive or difficult, a neutral location might help level the playing field for both parties—an important consideration when an integrative solution is desired.

Set enough time in the negotiation to deal with the critical issues that are involved. Getting two opposing parties to agree, especially when multiple issues are being simultaneously considered, requires more time than you might imagine. Shortening the time available for the discussion serves as a conversation stopper and is counterproductive. Prior to the negotiation, establish a flexible, reasonable plan that outlines what you hope to accomplish, how you intend to talk about the topic, how you plan to introduce the topic, and how you will handle any responses from the other party. Set clear parameters for the discussion and the process such as no name calling, it's ok for either party to call a time out, additional issues may be set aside for a later discussion, and you both must agree. Finally, seek agreement on standards and criteria to use when discussing the various alternatives that are generated as part of the discussion.[13]

3. *Clarification and justification.* As the negotiation begins, state what you want and why. Being clear about your interests and expectations sets the stage for the other party to be similarly honest about their needs and hopes for the negotiation. Allowing the other party to state what they want and why they want or need it offers them a chance to become fully engaged in the process. Clarifying to one another your proposals and the rationale behind them enhances both your and the other party's understanding of the key issues that are involved. Clarifying and justifying require sound communication skills. Some of the verbal tactics that can be used in effective negotiations appear in Figure 9–3.

4. *Bargaining and problem solving.* In the fourth stage, both parties are actively and constructively engaged in working toward solutions. Once the interests and criteria are clearly communicated, it is time for a creative, idea-generating process. This requires skill in finding solutions that might address one or more of the parties' collective needs, as well as "expanding the pie" and generating even more creative solutions that may not be readily apparent. At this stage, it is best to remain open-minded, considering options

Figure 9–3
Verbal Negotiation Tactics[14]

Tactic	Description	Example
Promise (conditional, positive)	I will do something if you will do something I want you to.	I will lower the price by $5 if you will order in bulk.
Threat (conditional, negative)	I will do something you do not want me to do, if you do something I don't want you to do.	If you don't give me a good price, I'll take my business elsewhere.
Recommendation	If you do something I want you to do, a third party will do something you want.	If you give me a good deal on this item, I will get my friend to buy one too.
Warning	If you do something I don't want you to, a third party will do something you do not want.	If you do not replace this item, the government will investigate your operation.
Reward (unconditional, positive)	I will give you something positive now, on the spot.	Let's make it easier on you tomorrow and meet closer to your office. I have appreciated your meeting at my building.
Punishment (unconditional, negative)	I will give you something negative now, on the spot.	I refuse to listen to your screaming. I am leaving.
Normative appeal	I will appeal to a societal norm.	Everybody else buys our product for $5 per unit.
Commitment	I will do something you want.	I will deliver 100 units by June 15.
Self-disclosure	I will tell you something about myself or important information.	We have had to lay off 100 employees this month. We really need to sign a major contract by the end of the year.
Question	I will ask you something about yourself.	Can you tell me more about your foreign operations?
Command	I will order you to do something.	Lower your price.

without making value judgments or critiquing them. Judgment curtails creativity. By exploring all possibilities for solutions, rather than trying to focus too quickly on one fixed solution, interesting ideas and combinations of ideas may emerge.

Consider for example the aging patriarch who is looking for a potential suitor to buy his company. It would be easy to argue over dollars and cents—what the company is worth—and never arrive at a mutually agreeable solution. First, the assumptions or models both parties used to estimate the company's value are likely different. Second, there is a great deal of hidden "value." The business is not just a collection of assets, employees, customers, patented processes, and accounts receivable; it is, in the founder's mind, a child he nurtured for years and years. Putting yourself in the shoes of the founder, think about what he really might want, besides money. Recognition for his business acumen? A position as chairman emeritus and consultant? A monthly stipend and benefit package? An opportunity to share in the profits for the years he remains as a consultant to the new owner? When you look outside the box of the calculable solution, you might find something even better.

Once a number of alternatives have been put forth, analysis and discussion of each can begin. Take the time to assess carefully how well each alternative meets the interests of both parties, the benefits and disadvantages, and its relation to the key issues involved in the negotiation. At this stage, it is appropriate to begin narrowing the options to the one or few that appear to best solve the initial problem in a way that is satisfactory to both parties. Don't worry about "dotting all the i's and crossing all the t's" at this point. Details like the exact percentage of the profit-sharing plan described above can be worked out later. Structure a deal on which you can both agree by recording key terms of the agreement and the steps necessary to complete the details and maintain the agreement.

Sometimes, you don't have all the data available to finalize a decision. For example, you might agree to provide a benefits package to the founder of the company for a period no longer than three years and at a price no greater than 30 percent of his monthly draw. Determining which insurance company and whether it covers monthly chiropractic visits is more detail than is necessary at this point. Other times, you might have to end the discussion with some terms still up in the air. Perhaps a key piece of information will only be available at year-end. Record the terms to which you've reached agreement, and agree to postpone deciding on the remaining issues until a specified future date. This approach is generally preferable to one in which the last few details are quickly and perhaps forcibly pushed through. If the deal is likely to stipulate how two parties will work together over the next 5, 10, or more years, isn't it worthwhile to invest a proportionately similar amount of time and energy to ensure that the partnership will be successful?

5. *Closure and implementation.* In this final stage, the terms of the agreement that has been reached are formalized. Unfortunately, many overlook or ignore this step, thinking that once an agreement is reached it will be implemented automatically. Leaving out this step can lead to future misunderstandings. No two people will leave a communication with the same perceptions. The only way to ensure that both parties know what they're agreeing to is to

- Document what you agreed on.
- Review the key points to avoid misunderstanding.
- Discuss issues that were hedged on, describing clearly all stipulations of the agreement.
- Get it in writing.
- Read the written agreement before signing to ensure clarity and commitment to what was negotiated.[15]

Every negotiation is likely to present you with different challenges and opportunities. By following these five steps and the advice contained therein, you can increase the likelihood of arriving at an agreement that meets the needs of all parties involved in the negotiation.

Strategies for Negotiating Effectively

The process model we described provides a helpful template for preparing for and participating in a negotiation. Within these stages, and as depicted in Figure 9–2, there are a number of tips and techniques that can improve the likelihood of achieving success. Because of their importance in the negotiation process, three of these concepts—scripting, framing, and managing—are discussed in greater detail below.

Scripting

There is no substitute for adequate preparation in negotiation. Unlike other business interactions that can be handled simultaneously, negotiation is a serious enterprise that requires focus, attention, time, research, and planning. The more prepared you are, the greater the chances that you'll get what you deserve and bargain for.

One of the best ways to ensure adequate preparation time is to develop a **script** (see Figure 9–4). Take some time to think about the negotiation situation in which you find yourself. What are your interests and those of the other party? What would you each ideally like to see come out of the negotiation? How would you each like things to end up? What are some ways in which that might be possible? What can you do to make this

**Figure 9–4
Negotiation Script**

Goals:

■ Develop an interest-based strategy/approach prior to a face-to-face negotiation
■ Identify potential options/plans that can be proposed

Topics to Consider:

1. The other person's probable strategy. What do they want (goals) and why (interests)?
2. My strategy. What do I want and why? What am I willing to accept (my BATNA—best alternative to a negotiated agreement)?
3. How I'll begin the negotiation. What can I say to position the negotiation positively, and to express my desire to arrive at a solution that is mutually rewarding and satisfactory?
4. The core issues, and any assumptions about those issues, include the following: (remember to focus on the problem and not the person.)
5. The primary focus, or the real problem(s) to be resolved is:
6. What might get in the way of achieving the desired outcome? How can I overcome this?
7. How I'll react to . . . (list several potential proposals that may emerge during the negotiation and how you feel about those proposals):
   a)
   b)
   c)
8. Potential creative options or integrative, win–win solutions that I might suggest:
9. Components of a plan and/or objective criteria on which we can both agree:

happen? By thinking through the issues, objectives, options, and solutions from both your and the other's perspective, you are better able to handle almost anything that develops during the negotiation. Preparing ahead doesn't prevent surprises. But it can certainly lessen the number of surprises and make it more likely you can handle the unexpected if and when it happens.

Framing

Another important element to consider when preparing for or managing a negotiation is a **frame.** A frame is a point of view or perspective we bring to an interaction such as a negotiation. How we view a situation can impact how willing we are to engage in a negotiation and even our goals. Negotiation experts Max Bazerman and Margaret Neale offer the following example.[16] You and a friend go to the beach. After a few hours, your throat becomes dry and you'd like a sparkling water—if the price is right. Your friend offers to investigate the options, and you consider your limits. In one scenario, you're about a mile from town and notice a small, run-down market about a block away. How much are you willing to pay for a bottle of water? In another scenario, you and your friend are lying on the beach owned by a four-star resort. The waiter is about to approach and ask if he can get you anything. Now, how much are you willing to pay for that sparkling water? Chances are, you'll pay more in the second scenario—for the same bottle of water.

When we use frames in negotiation, we provide a perspective that helps others understand where we are coming from and manages expectations. When proposing a plan for downsizing an organization to shareholders, one possibility is to frame this move as a means to minimize costs or losses. Another possibility is to frame this move as a means to maximize competitiveness. While both frames involve the use of downsizing, the frames—posed as either losses or gains—will likely have differing effects on the perceivers. Similar to framing a picture, the frame highlights the points you want to make in negotiation and provides a filter for the other party to assess your position and supporting evidence. This is done by selecting a perspective believed to be credible, compelling, and appropriate to your intent. Frames can also provide a rationale for the evidence presented and a sequential pattern for presenting the evidence. This is done by creating a structure for organizing and presenting the evidence.[17]

Framing has several benefits. It focuses attention on the priorities you want to emphasize—on data and premises within the frame. Framing establishes a "big picture" context for the listener to use in perceiving and sorting through various options.

Extending the picture analogy, since a picture is worth a thousand words, a frame that paints a picture can not only enliven the goals you are pursuing, but it can also save time and words. Imagine two CEOs discussing a potential merger of their companies. One uses a metaphorical frame and alludes to a "melting pot of employees" in describing his hoped-for outcome for the merger. This frame paints a picture that both parties understand. The second CEO is a bit more creative. She recasts the frame and refers to the "mixed salad of employees" her plan is designed to create. Both plans highlight employee diversity, but the second frame recognizes the individual talents and skills of employees who can collaborate and work together while the first plan may be interpreted as a homogenization of all employees.

As negotiators we can use frames to recast the other party's notion of what is desired in a negotiation. We do this by reframing the discussion—describing it differently to ourselves. By reframing we're able to see it in a new light and approach the negotiation in a different way. A frame can be used to sell a proposal and overcome objectives others might raise. To do this,

- Develop a frame based on *both* your needs and those of the other party.

- Construct a set of messages that influence the other party's perception of these needs.

- Provide the other party with a filter to interpret your message—such as "half-empty or half-full," "good or bad," "profit or loss," "cost or benefit."

Managing

The last strategy to consider when preparing for and in the thick of the negotiation is *managing*. Every negotiation is an opportunity for you to manage: yourself, your expectations, the timing of the event, the way in which you approach the situation, your feelings toward the other person. The more you respond to a negotiation as a management challenge, the more proactive you can be in looking at it positively. A negotiation can be a learning experience, a chance to acquire some new skills, and maybe even a way to get what you want! Or it can be something you dread, fear, and avoid if possible.

The adage "practice makes perfect" really applies here. Negotiation doesn't come naturally to most people. Practicing negotiation greatly improves your ability to manage a negotiation situation successfully. Start small, with minor events day-to-day, such as negotiating an earlier lunchtime with co-workers. The more you negotiate—paying attention to your needs and speaking up for them—the better prepared you will be for significant negotiations in business and in life. Only negotiate when you're ready—when you have the time, have had the time to prepare, and are in an appropriate state of mind. Thorough negotiations can be exhausting; you have to be ready to persist. You can ensure you're ready by managing the circumstances under which you'll negotiate. Only agree to terms that are acceptable to you. For example, where, when, and with whom you'll negotiate are all things that make a difference and things over which you have some control. Assert that control so that you are at your best at the time of the negotiation.

Manage your emotions. Demonstrate exceptional listening and clarifying (communication) skills. This helps you focus on the issues at hand, not on how you are responding emotionally. Plan to engage only in discussions or arguments that are constructive. Be prepared to walk away or take a "time-out" if necessary. Sometimes called a caucus, this time could be used alone (or with a negotiating partner in a team negotiation) to gather your thoughts, adjust your strategy, and discover new frames or solutions.

Agree to disagree. Sometimes issues are unsolvable at that moment. It's better to quit while you're ahead and set another time to continue discussing remaining issues. Don't put anyone on the defensive. When we're upset, we often blame or label others, causing them to strike back in kind. This kind of negotiation will go nowhere. Make statements that are factual and "I" based rather than "you" based. For example say, "I am upset about the amount of raise I got," rather than "You're unfair for giving me such a low increase."

Other techniques for managing negotiations include the use of agendas, questions, and summarizing techniques. A negotiation is a meeting and should be treated as such. If an agenda was not created in advance, and the negotiation is getting off-track, spend a few minutes establishing an agenda. Decide key issues to discuss, and allocate time accordingly. Post the agenda and refer back to it to keep the discussion on track. Periodically summarizing what's been discussed and agreed upon not only helps to keep the discussion focused, but can also help reduce redundancy (i.e., beating a dead horse). Sometimes, negotiators revisit issues that have already been resolved because they forget or are unsure whether a point was resolved or deferred for later discussion. By saying, "Okay, let's review. We agreed to points *a*, *b*, and *d*, but are still working out the details on points *c* and *e*. Does that track with how you see it?" you can manage time and stay focused on the negotiation.

Finally, questions can be useful in many ways. Aside from helping you understand others' viewpoints and needs, questions can help steer the discussion toward desirable issues in a more subtle way. Depending on the goals of the negotiation, consider using various types of questions as appropriate from the list shown in Figure 9–5.

Figure 9–5
Questioning[18]

Questioning is recommended in negotiation when it is necessary to clarify communication. **Manageable questions** start thinking, get information, and prepare the other person for additional questions. **Unmanageable questions** cause difficulty by bringing the discussion to a false conclusion. Manageable questions can produce dialogue and creative approaches, while unmanageable questions may produce defensiveness and/or anger.

Manageable Questions

Type of question	Example
Open-ended	Could you explain the reasons for your decision?
Open (to get the other person thinking)	What is your feeling on the matter?
Leading (point toward an answer to the question)	Do you feel our proposal is fair?
Cool (without emotion)	How much would be charged for the additional work?
Planned (follows an overall sequence of questions)	After the additional work is completed, may we begin our phase?
Treat (flatters the opponent while soliciting information)	You are an expert in this area; what is your opinion?
Window (assists in seeing what the other person is thinking)	What brought you to that conclusion?
Directive (focus on a specific point)	How long will it take to complete the job?
Gauging (assists in determining how the other person feels)	What do you think about our proposal?

Unmanageable Questions

Close-out (forces your opinion on the opponent)	You wouldn't want to make us look bad, would you?
Loaded (puts opponents on the spot regardless of answer)	So, you are not willing to negotiate further?
Heated (triggers an emotional response)	Haven't we spent enough time on this crazy idea?
Impulse (tends to get the conversation off track)	While we are on the subject, is there anyone else who might care about this?
Trick (appear straightforward, but are actually "loaded")	What are you going to do—agree to our position, or go to court?
Reflective "trick" questions (direct the opponent into agreeing with your point of view)	Here is the way I see it, don't you agree?

Additional Tips for Effective Negotiating

What else can you do to ensure that you not only reach an agreement but also maintain or enhance your relationship with the other party? The following principles of successful negotiation should help ensure that negotiations are integrative, objective, and potentially relationship enhancing.

■ *Determine the importance of the outcome for you.* What do you want and why? Only negotiate when the matter is something you truly care about and when you have a chance of succeeding. Identify what you really need from the deal, not what you assume you need. Identify several items of interest to you and rank them in descending order of importance.[19] Do your homework. If the negotiation includes a financial outcome, consider several options or scenarios and the economic implications of each. This information will serve to eliminate the guesswork and strengthen the rationale of your proposal during the negotiation. Will you lease or buy the car? What if you put 10 percent, 20 percent, or nothing down? How does the financing rate change when the loan period changes or if you decide to buy a used instead of a new car? Calculating the implications in advance can also increase your confidence and strengthen your position in the negotiation.

■ *Look forward, not backward.* It's easy to get caught up in who did what and who is to blame. We sometimes do this to avoid having to resolve the problem or just out of habit. While it may be easy to get into long discussions about the past, it is clearly unproductive. Focus on where you want to be and not where you've been. There's no harm in brief discussions of the conditions that led to the current problem, but move on to what to do now and in the future.[20]

■ *Separate people from problems.* To negotiate effectively, separate the people involved in the discussion from the issues that are being addressed. Remain objective. Avoid personalizing issues, and don't allow yourself to be drawn into an emotional debate.[21] If the negotiation veers in this direction, request a time out. After you reconvene, remind the negotiators of the ultimate goal and the ground rules previously set. If emotions are still running high, consider deferring the remainder of the negotiation to another time. Focus on the problem, the issue at hand. Avoid personal attacks, criticism of style or personality traits, and placing blame. Negotiate in such a way that the people on the other side know they will not lose face if they have to back down on something. For example, match the other's concession with one of your own. A good rule of thumb is to be hard on the problem, soft on the people. Throughout the negotiation constantly ask, "Am I dealing with the person or the problem?" Entangling people, issues, and relationships with the problem dooms the negotiation to failure.[22]

■ *Adopt a win–win attitude.* Negotiation is a collaboration between parties with common interests and objectives. Think in terms of helping, not hindering; of listening, not ramming something down someone's throat; of a team and partnership, not competition. Take the perspective that both parties can win and it's in your best interest to want the other side to thrive, as future cooperative ventures may be possible.[23]

■ *Know your best alternative to a negotiated agreement* (**BATNA**). Renowned negotiators and authors Roger Fisher and William Ury introduced this concept. They showed that results from a negotiation can be improved by identifying your best alternative for each of your goals. For example, if you want to sell your house by June, what will you take if it hasn't sold by then? This is one way to determine a BATNA—the outcome you can accept that is better than never having negotiated at all.

Don't set your BATNA too low. When you go to a job interview with no other offers or prospects, you go in with a low BATNA—this job or nothing. Sometimes you have to do this. But whenever possible, it's better to have options in mind to avoid being or appearing desperate. For example, in the absence of job offers, you could consider living with family for a while rather than taking a job you don't want. This alternative gives you flexibility and a sense that you don't have to take whatever is offered.[24]

■ *Focus on interests, not on fixed positions.* A **position** is a stance—typically a firm one—taken by a negotiator. "I'll give you $4,500 and that's my final offer." An **interest** is the explanation behind the position, the ultimate need or desire that expresses

**Figure 9–6
Principles of the
"Power of Nice"**[25]

1. To get what you want, help the other side get what it wants.
2. Aim for win–win: a substantial win for your side, a satisfactory win for the other side.
3. Negotiation is a process, not an event.
4. Practice the three P's: Prepare, Probe, Propose.
5. Listen to the other side: They are trying to tell you how to make the deal.
6. Build relationships rather than make one-time deals.

why a negotiator wants what he or she wants. Fisher and Ury argue that negotiators ought to be problem solvers who explore interests as opposed to refusing to change or compromising only slightly on their positions. When a negotiation is a test of wills, it is destined to fail. By locating compatible interests, you can build a bridge from your goals to the others.[26]

■ *Go into the negotiation with* **objective criteria.** This leads to principled negotiation—negotiations based on principles, or objective criteria on which both parties agree. Bringing standards of efficiency, fairness, scientific merit, for example, can facilitate agreement and final satisfaction with an agreement. Rather than struggling for dominance, locate objective criteria both of you can agree to apply in determining goals and actions. Sometimes objective criteria are readily available. Other times, the negotiators will have to research, present, and jointly decide on these criteria.

Objective criteria should be independent of each side's will and should be legitimate and practical. For example, you can find published data on industry salaries, comparable house sales prices, and area bank or finance company mortgage rates. Once you have determined objective criteria, you can frame each issue as a joint search for the solution that best fits the criteria.[27]

■ *Respond, don't react.* When the other party throws their power around, don't react negatively or emotionally. When this happens, Fisher and Ury recommend you invite feedback and input with regard to the problem. Ask them their opinion. You can also reframe or recast their objections as attacks on the problem, not on you—attacks that are understandable given the circumstances or pressure they might be experiencing. When the other party attacks, ask questions. Avoid getting bullied into battle.

■ *Use a* **third party**—someone who is objective and has no vested interest in the outcome of the discussions. When two parties can't arrive at a mutually agreeable resolution, it can be helpful to involve a third party. Consider using the one-text procedure. Let someone draw up a plan that considers your interests and those of the other party. Then each of you does some editing. The third party redrafts it and perhaps requests additional feedback from both of you. By involving everyone in the development of a single text and having the parties involved edit it several times, at the end there is a feeling on the parts of both parties that they have been included in the solution. At the end all that is left to do is make a simple yes–no decision, not enter into a long discussion or argument over details.[28]

Special Situations in Negotiations

Not all negotiations involve two individuals who meet face to face in an effort to reach a resolution or sign a contract. Some negotiations involve teams of individuals, are done virtually (using teleconferencing, telephones, e-mails, and faxes), include third parties, or involve global negotiating partners.

Third-Party Negotiations

Often serious negotiations—such as high-stakes strike threats—require the use of a third party to gain an agreement. Other times, it is simply a wise idea to bring in an objective third party to help two opposing sides develop a shared agreement. Bringing in a third party has several advantages. A third party offers each party a chance to "vent" in a nonthreatening environment. By venting out of earshot of the other party, you have a chance to disclose your feelings about the situation. By sorting through your emotions with a third party, you can then begin to uncover what's really important and why, and address these issues in the negotiation.

Another advantage of bringing in a third party is that you and the other party can both benefit from the third party's expertise and experience. Assuming they have helped others negotiate before you, they have models and templates to offer—ways to structure the negotiation—that can help you arrive at an agreement faster than if you were starting from scratch on your own. They won't have had the exact same situation presented to them in the past. But their experience with other cases can help them advise you on a strategy for which there is probably a successful precedent.

Lastly, bringing in a third party helps the negotiating parties organize their thoughts and develop options that may be acceptable to both parties. The negotiator won't take sides, but will offer wise counsel about the potential benefits and pitfalls of each of the alternatives being considered. Part of what enables third parties to do this successfully is that they are just that, a third party. Third parties are able to help the negotiating parties develop criteria and solutions from an untainted, and therefore unemotional, perspective. This can be invaluable when it comes time to develop an agreement that is satisfactory to both parties. There are several types of third-party negotiators.[29]

■ A **mediator** is a neutral third party who has no stake in the outcome of the agreement. Many private training programs are now available for ordinary citizens to become mediators. Mediation is a very popular, low-cost option that is being used more and more as an alternative to costly litigation.[30] In schools, mediators are used to help children (and faculty) resolve conflicts with each other, and in many businesses, employees are encouraged to work out conflicts (e.g., grievances) with a trained mediator when possible.

■ An **arbitrator** is a neutral third party who has the legal power to bind both parties to an agreement determined by the arbitrator. Both parties submit information to arbitration and then are subject to whatever decision is made. Arbitration is mandated frequently as a cost- and time-effective alternative to litigation. One disadvantage is that neither party is involved in generating the solution that the arbitrator ultimately provides.

■ A **conciliator** is a trusted third party whose role is to ensure that a steady flow of accurate information exists between the negotiating parties. A conciliator does not rule on an agreement but merely counsels the parties about ways to approach the agreement and ways to view the information that is being presented as part of the negotiation.

■ A **consultant** is a neutral third party who teaches and advises the negotiating parties on skills and techniques of negotiation. The consultant hears out both parties, suggests an operating plan and strategy, assists both sides in identifying their chief concerns, aids the parties in arriving at a mutually satisfying resolution or agreement, and assists the parties in writing up this agreement.

Global Negotiations

Identity and culture are dynamic factors affecting negotiations.[31] This means negotiations between domestic and foreign firms (**global negotiations**) are on the rise. Those involved in global business need to have a solid understanding of the practices and customs of their foreign counterparts, in addition to basic negotiation skills.

To be effective when negotiating across borders, prepare carefully and be familiar with cultural differences and expectations.[32] The basics of negotiation still apply: You will still need to clarify what you want and why; you should still develop your BATNA. However, your strategy and the way in which you implement it will likely vary based on what you know about the practices and customs of your global negotiating partner. For example, an American firm sent a business proposal bound in pigskin to a country in which pigs were considered unclean. The proposal was never opened.[33]

Start by doing background research on the organization's culture, practices, and business. Some information can be found on the Internet by searching government pages from the State Department. Other information can be obtained by identifying other firms who have done business with this organization or individuals who were born or spent time in the country. Salacuse suggests knowing the eight **elements of international**

Figure 9–7
The Essential Rules of
"Winning with Integrity"[34]

Align yourself with people who share your values.

Learn all you can about the other party.

Convince the other party that you have an option—even if you don't.

Set your limits before negotiating begins.

Establish a climate of cooperation, not conflict.

In the face of intimidation, show no fear.

Learn to listen.

Be comfortable with silence.

Avoid playing split-the-difference.

Emphasize your concessions; minimize the other party's.

Never push a losing argument to the end.

Develop relationships, not conquests.

protocol for any country with which you do business.[35] These eight elements are listed below. Note that special gender-based differences may also apply.

1. Name (how individuals prefer to be addressed).

2. Rank/title (how these titles compare with those in your organization, the importance of using titles in interaction).

3. Time (whether punctual or casual, preferred time of day to do business).

4. Dress (formal or casual, whether special or sacred articles are worn).

5. Behavior (greetings, rituals, how decisions are made).

6. Communication (verbal or nonverbal differences, such as the meaning of the words *yes* and *no*, proxemic differences).

7. Gift giving (whether gifts are appropriate, size of gifts, public versus private opening, importance of reciprocation).

8. Food and drink (which foods [e.g., pork] and drinks [e.g., alcohol] are forbidden).

For example, in certain countries (e.g., Japan) silence is very common, whereas that is not typical in the United States. Businesspeople in many parts of South America prefer establishing a relationship first and will take much time to build an emotional bond—through dinners and other social gatherings—before talking business. The French often negotiate multiple issues simultaneously, while Americans prefer a linear approach, discussing and agreeing upon one issue at a time.[36] The Chinese often engage in gift giving, but you would be wise not to present your Chinese counterpart with a clock—it symbolizes death.[37]

Global negotiations are admittedly complex and uncertain. Planning is crucial to the process. Gathering information about a country and its practices and customs is a necessary step to understanding how to approach your negotiating partner. Understanding differences (and similarities!) between your and your foreign counterpart's communication style, behaviors, and practices can help you manage the negotiations and increase the likelihood that both parties leave the global negotiating table with satisfactory outcomes and a desire to continue the business relationship.

Summary

In this chapter we discussed the definition, importance, and benefits of negotiating. We reviewed the different types of negotiation strategies and the stages of negotiating. In addition, we provided strategies for negotiating effectively and tips for negotiating successfully. Lastly, we covered special situations in negotiating. Negotiating is a fact of life for all of us—in personal as well as business situations. Following the suggestions in this chapter will help you to be effective in developing negotiation strategies that meet your and others' needs.

Key Terms and Concepts

Arbitrator

BATNA

Bottom line

Conciliator

Consultant

Distributive bargaining strategy

Elements of international protocol

Frame

Global negotiations

Integrative bargaining strategy

Interest

Manageable questions

Mediator

Negotiation

Objective Criteria

Position

Script

Third party

Unmanageable questions

Endnotes

1. John Mariotti, "Are You an Effective Negotiator?" *Industry Week,* Sept. 7, 1998, p. 70.

2. Roger Fisher, William Ury, and Bruce Patton, *Getting to Yes,* 2nd ed. (New York: Penguin Books, 1991).

3. Ibid.

4. Darl G. Williams, "Negotiating Skills—Part I," *Professional Builder,* Jan. 2000, p. 155.

5. Danny Ertel, "How to Design a Conflict Management Procedure That Fits Your Dispute," *Sloan Management Review,* Summer 1991, pp. 29–42.

6. It is important to note, however, that one or both parties may choose to avoid negotiations or defer them until a future date. Doing so may serve a number of purposes. For more information on deferral, see Roy Lewicki, David Saunders, and John Minton, *Negotiation: Readings, Exercises, and Cases,* 3rd ed. (Burr Ridge; IL: Irwin McGraw-Hill, 1999), pp. 45–46.

7. R. E. Walton and R. B. McKersie, *A Behavioral Theory of Labor Negotiations: An Analysis of a Social Interaction System* (New York: McGraw-Hill, 1965).

8. Stephen Robbins, *Organizational Behavior,* 8th ed. (Upper Saddle, NJ: Prentice Hall, 1998).

9. Max Bazerman and Margaret Neale, *Negotiating Rationally* (New York: Free Press, 1992).

10. R. J. Lewicki, "Bargaining and Negotiation," *Exchange: The Organizational Behavior Teaching Journal* 6, no. 2 (1981); and Robbins, *Organizational Behavior.*

11. Janine S. Pouliot, "Eight Steps to Success in Negotiating," *Nation's Business,* April 1999, p. 40.

12. Ertel, "How to Design."

13. Pouliot, "Eight Steps to Success."

14. Nancy J. Adler, *International Dimensions of Organizational Behavior,* 3rd ed. (Cincinnati, OH: Southwestern College Publishing, 1997), p. 214.

15. Mariotti, "Are You an Effective Negotiator?"

16. Margaret A. Neale and Max H. Bazerman, "Negotiating Rationally: The Power and Impact of a Negotiator's Frame," *Academy of Management Executive* 6, no. 3, pp. 42–51.

17. Lyle Sussman, "How to Frame a Message: The Art of Persuasion and Negotiation," *Business Horizons,* July–August 1999, p. 2.

18. Adapted from R. J. Lewicki and J. A. Litterer, *Negotiation* (Homewood, IL: Richard D. Irwin, Inc., 1985).

19. Ron Shapiro, Mark Jankowski, Leigh Steinberg, and Michael D'Orso, "Powers of Persuasion," *Fortune,* Oct. 12, 1998, p. 160.

20. Fisher et al., *Getting to Yes.*

21. Terry Neese, "Negotiations Should Not Be a Contest of Wills," *LI Business News,* August 13, 1999, p. 30A.

22. Fisher et al., *Getting to Yes*.

23. Shapiro et al., "Powers of Persuasion."

24. Danny Ertel, "Turning Negotiation into a Corporate Capability," *Harvard Business Review,* May 1999, p. 55.

25. Ron Shapiro, Mark Jankowski, and James Dale, *The Power of Nice—How to Negotiate So Everyone Wins, Especially You!* (New York: John Wiley & Sons, 1998).

26. Harvey Mackay, "Flexibility Is a Word for the Wise," *Providence Business News,* August 9, 1999, p. 30.

27. Fisher, *Getting to Yes*.

28. Fisher *Getting to Yes*.

29. J. A. Wall, Jr., and M. W. Blum, "Negotiations," *Journal of Management,* June 1991, pp. 283–87.

30. Robert D. Benjamin, "Mediation: Taming of the Shrewd," *Commercial Law Bulletin,* Jan.–Feb. 2000, pp. 8–10.

31. Anthony Wanis-St. John, "Thinking Globally and Acting Locally," *Negotiation Journal,* 19, no. 4 (Oct. 2003), p. 389.

32. Robert Rosen, Patricia Digh, Marshall Singer, and Carl Phillips, *Global Literacies: Lessons on Business Leadership and National Cultures: A Landmark Study of CEOs from 28 Countries* (New York: Simon and Schuster, 2000).

33. Ibid., p. 176.

34. Leigh Steinberg and Michael D'Orso, *Winning with Integrity—Getting What You're Worth without Selling Your Soul* (New York: Villard, Sept. 1998).

35. Jerald W. Salacuse, *Making Global Deals: What Every Executive Should Know about Negotiating Abroad* (New York: Times Books, 1991).

36. Dean Allen Foster, *Bargaining across Borders: How to Negotiate Business Successfully Anywhere in the World* (Burr Ridge, IL: McGraw-Hill, 1995).

37. Ibid.

Exercise 9–A
Negotiation Role-Play

Working in groups of four or five persons, choose one of the scenarios below and develop a script to prepare for a negotiation you are about to enter. Role-play the script with another member of your group and get feedback from the other members on your skill as a negotiator. When all in the small group have taken a turn as a negotiator, discuss the activity with the class or group as a whole, using the discussion questions below.

Negotiation Scenario 1

You have worked in your current assignment for two years. During that time, your company initiated a new bonus system. However, neither you nor other employees know very much about the new system. Your employer cautioned everyone to keep their salaries and bonuses confidential, so you have little information about how others in your company are compensated. At year-end, you received a bonus, but it's significantly smaller than you anticipated. You want to approach your boss to ask for a larger bonus, but without information on what everyone else got, you have little information on which to base your argument. How do you prepare to negotiate with your boss?

Negotiation Scenario 2

You have been working hard on the job for five years. Your wife recently gave birth to your first child. She has an opportunity for a promotion at work and has asked if you would be willing to work part-time for a time while she pursues her career. You support the idea and agree to switch to part-time status on your job, pending your boss's approval. How do you prepare to negotiate with your boss to get his approval on this request?

Negotiation Scenario 3

Your parents have told you that you cannot have a car at school. They are concerned about your safety (you have already been in one car accident that was your fault), your grades (you have a C+ average), and your ability to keep up with the payments financially (your part-time job earns you enough just to cover your expenses while at school). How do you prepare to negotiate with your parents?

Questions

1. What was your strategy going into the negotiation? Was it effective? What worked? What didn't?
2. What ideas did you get from other group members about how you could improve your negotiating skill?
3. What was difficult about negotiating (other than having to role-play!)?
4. What did you learn about yourself as a negotiator from this exercise?

**Exercise 9–B
Negotiation Scripts**

1. Think of a situation you've been involved in recently where you wish you had negotiated. Using the script outline in this chapter, develop a script for how you would approach the situation if you had a second chance. Comparing this script to what actually happened, what aspects of your actual negotiation were positive? In need of improvement? What impact would the changes alluded to in your script have had on the actual outcome? Explain. Discuss this situation with a partner.
2. Use the script outline to prepare for an upcoming negotiation—with a friend, relative, significant other, current or prospective boss, or co-worker. Role-play with a partner who will play the person with whom you'll negotiate. Request your partner's feedback on what worked well and what you could do differently in the future. Make adjustments to your script outline.

**Exercise 9–C
Negotiating a Home
Purchase**

The Situation

You and your family have been renting a house for the last eight months. During a recent visit from your landlord, he mentioned his desire to sell some of his properties. "Not this one," he tells you, "but I have another house a few miles away." Hmmmm. You love the area, the school district is great, and you've been thinking about buying, although there have been few if any properties available in your price range. Your landlord, who lives in another state, gives you the address and his phone number. "Call me if you're interested and we'll talk," he says. You and your spouse drive by the house the next day. Not your dream home, but it is a possibility—if the price is right.

The Players

The landlord (additional information available from your instructor)

The renter (additional information available from your instructor)

An observer

The Process

Decide who will play which role in your triad. Read the situation and additional information, create a plan, and then negotiate. The observer should take notes on effective and less-than-effective negotiating behaviors. The observer will then lead a feedback discussion after the negotiation is complete.

Exercise 9–D
Negotiating a Raise

The Situation

You have worked hard at your job for three years. During that time, you also went to school at night and completed your MBA degree. You have discovered that your company is bringing in newly minted MBAs at a salary that is 25 percent higher than yours. You want to ask your boss for a raise. How do you prepare to negotiate with your boss?

The Players

The boss (additional information available from your instructor)

The subordinate (additional information available from your instructor)

An observer

The Process

Decide who will play which role in your triad. Read the situation and additional information, create a plan, and then negotiate. The observer should take notes on effective and less-than-effective negotiating behaviors. The observer will then lead a feedback discussion after the negotiation is complete.

Exercise 9–E
Rolling Hill Turkey Company

Your instructor will distribute instructions and materials related to this exercise.

Overview

Rolling Hill Turkey Company has been in business for well over 50 years and is located in Tinytown, USA. Rolling Hill is well known in its community, as it is one of the biggest employers in the area, employing 50 full-time workers. The relationship between management and the workers of Local 731 has traditionally been good. This fact was illustrated in contract negotiations three years ago.

In the last five years, competition in the turkey slaughter and packaging market has become brutal. In response to this situation, at the last contract negotiation, the workers of Local 731 agreed to a salary freeze for the length of the contract. Since that time, Rolling Hill has made the company profitable again, and the workers of Local 731 believe they were an integral part of this recovery.

At one time the union workers at Rolling Hill were among the best paid in their industry. Now they substantially lag behind the industry average. The contract negotiated three years ago is due to expire in a few days. Union workers believe that it is time for the company to pay them back for their loyalty. Management is still concerned about containing costs because many competitors are automating their plants, leaving Rolling Hill with higher costs, primarily due to labor.

Rolling Hill is an S-corporation with less than 50 shareholders. Most shares are tightly held by the family that started the company and other relatives.

Questions

1. How did you go about preparing for your negotiation (how did you come up with your final offers, etc.)?

2. How effective was your lead negotiator? Why? How effective was the other team's lead negotiator? Again, why?

3. Was your negotiation a success? Why or why not? Factors to consider: Did you achieve your goals? Was the union–management relationship strengthened or weakened?

4. How did you go about getting what you wanted for your constituency? Did you use threats or demands? Cooperation? Logic and reason? Other tactics?

5. Did you use distributive or integrative bargaining? Give examples. If the opposing team used a different strategy than you did note this and give examples to support your view.

6. If you called in an arbitrator, were you satisfied with the arbitrator's decision or did you wish you had kept negotiating on your own?

7. Did your negotiation follow the five steps of negotiation in the chapter? Explain.

Exercise contributed by Christine Roeder, MBA, Management Program, College of Business, James Madison University, Harrisonburg, Virginia, 2004. Reprinted with permission.

**Exercise 9–F
Reflection/Action Plan**

This chapter focused on negotiation—what it is, why it is important, and how to improve your skills in this area. Complete the worksheet below upon completing all reading and experiential activities for this chapter.

1. The one or two areas in which I am strongest:

   _____

   _____

   _____

   _____

2. The one or two areas in which I need to improve:

   _____

   _____

   _____

   _____

3. If I did only one thing to improve in this area, it would be to:

   _____

   _____

   _____

   _____

4. Making these changes would probably result in:

   _____

   _____

   _____

   _____

5. If I did not change or improve in these areas, it would probably affect my personal and professional life in the following ways:

   _____

   _____

   _____

   _____

10 Building Teams and Work Groups

Learning Points

How do I:

- Form a team and help it progress through developmental stages?
- Form or join a high-performance work team?
- Ensure that all members of a team contribute equally?
- Handle differences in values and work styles in a team setting?
- Allocate team roles and responsibilities?
- Motivate a team to achieve its objectives?

Jeremy was perplexed. He had been looking forward to the first team project in his new job. He had heard how much his new employer valued teamwork. At his previous job, he hadn't encountered teams. He had done virtually all his work on his own, as an individual contributor. This job was going to be different.

At the outset of the project, the group was given a series of projects on which to work. Over the course of the quarter, the group was supposed to evolve into what the team leader called a high-performance work team. But now, at the project's midpoint, Jeremy felt his group was anything but high-performance. Things had started out great. Right away, Jeremy hit it off with his fellow teammates. While the team was diverse in terms of gender, ethnicity, and function, most members had similar interests and got along well with each other. They had even gotten together socially a couple of times during the quarter. At the beginning, the group was very task oriented. They seemed to communicate well and were able to clarify their objective, determine their topic and research priorities, allocate roles and responsibilities, and set up a planning schedule working backwards from their project due date at the end of the quarter.

After a few initial organizing meetings, the group members were left to work on their own. That's where the problems started occurring. In preparation for an interim project due date, Jeremy and his team had planned a team meeting the day before to combine everyone's work and produce the deliverable that the team leader expected the next day. To his chagrin, Jeremy discovered that only he and one other team member were ready. The others had procrastinated and thought they could "wing it." He was contemplating pulling an all-nighter to make up the others' work. "This project is going nowhere," he thought. "Why didn't I just do everything on my own? I could have done better working on my own. This team stuff isn't all it's cracked up to be."

1. What is the situation Jeremy faces? What are the core issues here?

2. How did this situation develop? What could have been done to achieve a different outcome?

3. How would you feel if you were Jeremy? Has a similar situation happened to you?

4. What would you do if you were Jeremy?

5. What should Jeremy do?

"We are a pack animal. From earliest times we have used the strength of the group to overcome the weakness of the individual. And that applies as much to business as to sport."[1]

Tracey Edwards
(Skippered the First Women's
Crew to Circumnavigate
the Globe)

From the popular NBC reality show *The Apprentice* to most of the *Fortune* 500 and many high-tech start-up firms to competitive sports, teams are an everyday occurrence in our personal and work lives. As the nature of work progresses from individually based work to group settings, understanding teams and how to work in team settings and in work groups has become a crucial interpersonal skill. Not everyone is convinced that teams are more effective than individuals working on their own. But the reality is that many organizations are attempting to set up a team-based structure when tackling particular issues or processes, and the ability to work as a team is one of the most commonly required skills in the work environment.[2]

This chapter covers the basics of teamwork. We define teams and detail their importance in business today. We discuss strategies for forming teams and tips for making teams effective and successful. We also include several exercises at the end of the chapter for you to further enhance your team skills, and list resources available for further exploration.

What Is Teamwork?

A team is a formal work group consisting of people who work together to achieve a common group goal.[3] The word *team* is not synonymous with *group*. A **group** is a collection of people who work together but aren't necessarily working collectively toward the same goal. A **team** is composed of three or more interdependent individuals who are consciously working together to achieve a common objective, such as product development, service delivery, or process improvement. A group becomes a team when members demonstrate a commitment to each other and to the end goal toward which they are working. In a team, there is a higher degree of cohesiveness and accomplishment than in a group.[4]

From earliest times, human beings have used teams or groups to overcome the limitations of individuals. Collections of nomads in search of food and land, kingdoms composed of villagers and their leaders, native settlements, wagon trains and pioneers, the crews of ships—all were formed with the idea that more could be accomplished together than by an individual.[5] Even Adam and Eve decided to band together, as do the quasi-"alliances" on the CBS television show *Survivor*. Aside from gains in sheer horsepower, as in the case of a ship's crew, teams exist because few individuals possess all the knowledge, skills, and abilities needed to accomplish all tasks. Simply put, two heads are often better than one.

Within many professional sports teams, we can find shining examples of teamwork. Michael Jordan, one of the world's greatest basketball players and author of the book, *I Can't Accept Not Trying,* writes, "One thing I believe to the fullest is that if you think and achieve as a team, the individual accolades will take care of themselves. Talent wins games, but teamwork and intelligence win championships." He says he never forgot that he was only one-fifth of the effort at any time.[6] Staying with sports for a moment, consider the differences between a gymnastics team and a football team. In gymnastics, the members of a team may work together, but the ultimate achievement of a team is based on the collective efforts of the individual gymnasts. A winning team has the highest combined score. In football, a great quarterback is nothing without a great wide receiver, tight end, or offensive line that can keep him or her from getting sacked. The football team wins when all members work interdependently toward the same goal—passing and rushing their way toward touchdowns.

Returning to the workplace, it is estimated that between 70 and 82 percent of U.S. companies use the team concept, making teamwork skills one of the most commonly required skills in the work environment.[7] Many businesses are adopting a collaborative management approach that encourages sharing ideas and strategies throughout the organization. This collaboration provides many benefits to the organization as well as to the individuals who make up the teams.[8]

Why Teams?

Teaming is more than a phase or a buzzword. If it didn't work, organizations would abandon this strategy for getting work done. There is much evidence that teams can be effective, especially when tasks are complex and task interdependence is high. It is not always appropriate, of course, for work to be done in teams. But when a team structure is employed, and those teams work effectively, many benefits accrue to the organization and to the team members themselves.

Benefits of Teams

- Increased creativity, problem solving, and innovation.
- Higher-quality decisions.
- Improved processes.
- Global competitiveness.
- Increased quality.
- Improved communication.
- Reduced turnover and absenteeism and increased employee morale.

- *Increased creativity, problem solving, and innovation:* Bringing together a group of individuals who possess a wealth of ideas, perspectives, knowledge, and skills can result in a synergy through which new ideas can be entertained. We each have a unique set of skills. Working with others allows us to combine our skills and talents to create new approaches to solving problems.[9] An example is a team of marketers where each person applies his or her strengths to the issue at hand. One person who is very creative can lead the process of coming up with ideas; another who is detail-oriented can do the initial research; a third person who is skilled in graphic applications can put together a great sales presentation.

- *Higher-quality decisions:* Teamwork enhances the quality of the outcomes. Teamwork involves the collective effort of a group of people who represent diverse backgrounds and experiences. As more ideas are produced and alternatives are considered, the team gets closer to optimal decisions—decisions that are stronger because they have been made with various perspectives and interests in mind.

- *Improved processes:* Teamwork results in a systematic approach to problem solving. Because of the necessary coordination between and transfer of learning among team members, teamwork results in organized approaches to the situation at hand. For example, a team is more likely than an individual to set up project checkpoints and planning systems to enable all team members to contribute to the project as it unfolds. Teamwork also permits distribution of workloads for faster and more efficient handling of large tasks or problems.[10] When members representing different organizations work together to improve a process that cuts across multiple organizational functions, more glitches and interdependencies will be uncovered and addressed than would be by individuals working independently.

■ *Global competitiveness:* Teamwork enables companies to compete globally. Firms in the United States are relying increasingly on diverse teams to compete in the global economy.[11] Diverse teams have skill sets and perspectives that are superior to what a single individual can bring to the table. For example, when Clairol marketed its popular Mist Stick in parts of Germany, it flopped. Had the Clairol marketing team included someone of German origin, they could have informed the group that *mist* was a slang word for "manure." As we continue developing and marketing our products in a global marketplace, combining diverse perspectives is essential.

■ *Increased quality:* Studies show that those large, complex, global companies that have moved to teams show increases in productivity, employee ownership of and accountability for their work, timeliness, efficiency, and customer service.[12] This results in higher-quality standards than are possible when individuals or groups of individuals, who lack a common goal, are doing the work.

■ *Improved communication:* The use of teams in the workplace enhances employee communication. In a traditional, hierarchical organization, communication tends to flow primarily in one direction—downward. In a team-based organization, communication flows laterally, upward, downward, and even outside the organization's boundaries (e.g., customers and suppliers). Teamwork requires collective action that is grounded in words and actions. It's not sufficient for one person to determine how he or she wants to work. Each person must get others on board before proceeding. In effective teams, there is rich sharing of information and ideas that improves communication within the team and between the team and the organization.[13]

■ *Reduced turnover and absenteeism and increased employee morale:* Teamwork results in changes in employee behaviors and attitudes. Teamwork fosters a camaraderie that helps many employees to feel more a part of the organization than when working independently. They feel ownership of the problems on which they work, get immediate feedback from teammates, see the fruits of their labors, and feel they have an impact on their job and the organization. Compared with the alienation employees often experience in traditional firms, employees in team-based organizations are happier, more committed, and more loyal to their organization.

The chart below contains examples of the positive outcomes that resulted when organizations embraced and encouraged team-based work:

Examples of Successes by Self-managed Teams[14]

Organization	Reported Successes
Harley-Davidson	Returned to profitability in six years.
Hallmark	200 percent reduction in design time. Introducing 23,000 new card lines each year.
Liberty Mutual	50 percent reduction in contract process time. Saving of more than $50 million per year.
Johns Hopkins Hospital	Patient volume increased by 21 percent. Turnover reduced, absenteeism reduced by 20 percent.
Monsanto	Quality and productivity improved by 47 percent in 4 years.
Saab and Volvo	4 percent increase in production output. Inventory turnover increased from 9 to 21 times a year.

Potential Limitations of Teams

While this chapter focuses primarily on the effectiveness of teams and work groups and how-tos for being a productive team member, there are some concerns about teams and their ability to make the most effective decisions. Some of these concerns are expressed briefly below.

Limitations of Teams

- **Groupthink. Groupthink**[15]—or individuals agreeing reluctantly with a group's decision—is a potential problem for teams. Groupthink can happen when a decision is made in a hurry, when one or a few members are extremely dominant in a group setting, or when one or more members present believe they haven't had a chance to air their concerns before an action is taken.
- **Social loafing.** By definition a team is a collection of three or more people. Invariably, a team will be composed of members with different work ethics and work styles, and this can result in some individuals doing more work than others.
- *Quality concerns.* Ironically, although there is much evidence that teams produce quality outcomes, the fact is that some individuals have the expert knowledge necessary to be able to make decisions independently without the benefit of a team.
- *Timeliness.* Individuals can make decisions more quickly than teams, especially if gaining buy-in from others is not an essential component of the action under consideration.
- *Diversity.* In general, diversity of background and thought process is a good way to ensure that multiple perspectives will be incorporated into a particular decision. Sometimes, especially when expedience is desired or when management has a clear preference for a particular course of action, a homogenous group can make decisions more quickly and easily than can a more diverse group.

Organizing work into teams is the wave of the future. In fact, many organizations now have "virtual teams," in which much or all of the work is done by group members who may be dispersed geographically and communicate with each other primarily via e-mail and the Internet. But like any new phenomenon, it is important to understand that teams have both upsides and downsides. Teams may not be optimal for every business situation. When you are placed in a team, be aware of the potential problems and develop strategies early on to overcome these challenges.

Types of Teams

In the same way sports teams differ in function, makeup, and ultimate goal or purpose, so do teams in the workplace. The more commonly used team types are described below.

Cross-functional Teams: These include members from various departments or business specialties such as marketing, information systems, communications, public relations, operations, human resources, accounting, finance, planning, research and development, and legal. Cross-functional teams are usually charged with developing new products or investigating and improving a companywide problem such as the need to increase speed and efficiency across departmental lines or the need to adopt a new companywide computer system. Cross-functional teams derive their strength from diversity. By including representatives from all or most of an organization's primary functional areas, the team can diagnose a problem from multiple perspectives simultaneously, ensuring that all relevant points of view are taken into account. This can speed up the problem-solving process and result in an outcome that the various departments affected by the change more readily accept.

Case in point: Prior to producing its LH line of cars, Chrysler followed what most would call a serial design process. Engineering would design a car and throw it over the wall to manufacturing. "We can't build this," manufacturing replied, and sent it back over the wall to engineering. This would continue for months or years until marketing was charged with marketing a car that no one wanted. From product inception to market, this process could take as long as six years or more. By that time, technologies were obsolete and other companies easily stole market share. Realizing this, Chrysler moved to a simultaneous, cross-functional team-based design process. Everyone who had a stake in or was affected by the design of a new product was on a team that hashed it out—together. This included people from marketing, sales, engineering, design, and many others. These meetings had conflict, but the conflict was actually helpful. Chrysler was able to reduce the cycle time from over six years to less than 18 months!

Another example of a cross-functional team is a top management team. In many large organizations, the CEO typically makes strategic decisions in collaboration with the leaders of the major functional areas. Even at this level in the organization, top management recognizes their individual strengths and weaknesses and the value that diverse perspectives can add when making key organizational decisions.

Self-managed Teams: These are "groups of employees who are responsible for a complete, self-contained package of responsibilities that relate either to a final product or an ongoing process."[16] Also known as self-directed, self-maintained, or self-regulating, self-managed teams are typically given a charge by senior management and then are given virtually complete discretion over how, when, and what to do to attain their objective. Self-managed teams are expected to coordinate their work without ongoing direction from a supervisor or manager. Self-managed teams set their own norms, make their own planning schedules, set up ways to keep relevant members and others informed of their progress, determine how the work is going to be accomplished, and are held accountable for their end product or "deliverable." Many of these teams are responsible for hiring, training, and firing team members. The flattening of organizational structures, resulting in less hierarchy and fewer managers, makes self-directed teams a popular concept in business today. Of course, it's not as if management flips a switch and a team becomes self-managing. It's a long process of team building and teamwork combined with sufficiently greater responsibility and accountability gained through the team's demonstrated capabilities and performance.

Task Force: This is an ad hoc, temporary project team assembled to develop a product, service, or system or to solve a specific problem or set of problems. Companies are always faced with the challenge of getting ongoing, day-to-day work done while utilizing available resources to work on various change processes or product innovations. For example, a technology company might designate a group to study the next wave in software development while others are maintaining and servicing existing software programs. Often task force members are individuals who have demonstrated interest or skill in the area being examined by the task force, so the members are enthusiastic about the project and its potential. The task force process is very common in business today. It is lower in cost than hiring an outside consultant or group of contract workers and allows for management to allocate resources at will to various projects as the needs of the company and the interests of its employees change.

Process Improvement Teams: These teams focus on specific methods, operations, or procedures and are assembled with the specific goal of enhancing the particular component being studied. Process improvement teams are typically composed of individuals with expertise and experience in the process being reviewed. They are assigned the tasks of eliminating redundant steps, looking for ways to reduce costs, identifying ways to improve quality, or finding means for providing quicker, better customer service.[17] Process improvement teams are often given training on problem-solving tools and techniques to help them map processes, identify root causes of problems, and prioritize potential solutions.

To analyze a system and make recommendations for changes, process improvement team members diagnose the current state of a process and chart how it occurs step by step. They review customer or internal data and collect data from other sources such as managers, competitors, and others as needed. They identify ways the process can be enhanced, make their recommendations, and sometimes assist the operating units involved in implementing the changes. Process improvement teams are usually temporary and disband once the process being studied has been changed to the satisfaction of management.

Team Developmental Stages

Groups typically pass through a series of stages as they grow and evolve into teams. Theorists postulate that a team goes in and out of at least five stages in its life cycle:[18] forming, storming, norming, performing, adjourning. This process is fluid—teams may revisit a stage, or skip one or more altogether. Each phase has distinguishing characteristics and presents particular challenges to team members and their managers.

Stage One—Forming

In this stage, a team is established to accomplish a particular task. Typically the group members will not know each other, and even if they do, there is a feeling of uncertainty and tentativeness because people haven't had a chance yet to get to know one another and set group objectives.[19] In the **forming** stage, members will engage in behaviors such as defining the initial assignment, discussing how to divvy up the necessary tasks, understanding the broad scope and objectives of the project, and learning about the resources (time, equipment, personnel) available to the team as it works to complete the project. In this stage, there is some testing by members of leadership roles, some discovery of personality similarities and differences, some initial disclosure, and usually relatively little progress on the task.

As a team member or team leader, your role in stage one is to encourage the group to establish its mission and purpose, set up a work schedule, get to know one another, and establish some initial norms for working together.

Stage Two—Storming

In this stage, a group experiences differences over factors such as direction, leadership, work style and approach, and perceptions about the expected quality and state of the end product or deliverable. As is true of any relationship, conflict is inevitable. Many couples feel bad when they experience their first fight, and teams are no exception. When the first conflict among group members emerges, some or all of the members begin to feel less enthusiastic about the group and might even doubt the group can come together and achieve its objective. There may be struggles over leadership ("my way is best"), power ("if you don't agree we'll leave you behind") and roles ("who appointed you chief?"). In the **storming** stage, feelings emerge such as resistance to the task or approach being taken by the group, resentment about differences in workload, anger about roles and responsibilities, and changes in attitude about the group or toward individual group members and concerns. Typically in the storming stage, the group is in conflict and chaos, as the group has not yet established ways to communicate about these differences. During this stage, few if any processes and procedures are in place, as the need for them wasn't anticipated due to the lack of prior conflict. All of this can result in arguing among members, emergence of subgroups, and disunity. If and when a group in which you are working enters this stage, what can you do?

In the storming stage, your role as a group member or leader is to refrain from taking sides. Encourage the group to develop communication channels. Help your group members focus on the task and not on personal differences. Promote an environment of open communication to ensure that the inevitable conflict is healthy and results in improved communication and commitment to the group's task. Remember that an appropriate level of tension motivates a team, but too much or too little can affect productivity.[20] If your group cannot resolve or work effectively with conflict, request the assistance of a trained process consultant or facilitator. A group that can't learn how to handle conflict may never achieve its deliverable.

Stage Three—Norming

In this stage, the group faces its issues, conflicts, and power and leadership struggles openly and directly. The members establish and adhere to patterns of acceptable behavior and learn to incorporate new methods and procedures into their working together. In the **norming** stage, members feel a new ability to express constructive criticism; they feel part of a working team and a sense of relief that everything will work out.[21] In this stage, members attempt to achieve harmony by avoiding unnecessary conflict, acting more friendly toward and trusting of each other, and developing a sense of team unity ("together, we can solve this"). Norms don't have to be established about every single decision or policy, only those that are particularly significant to team members.[22]

As a team member or leader, your role is to encourage team members to take on more responsibility, work together to create means acceptable for solving problems, set challenging goals, and take personal responsibility for team success. As a leader, you set the tone. Don't expect others to "do as you say, but not as you do." If you are seen bickering with colleagues and secretly plotting political moves, team members are less likely to emulate the helpful norming behaviors and may regress to the storming stage.

Stage Four—Performing

In the **performing** stage, teams have worked through their differences. Their membership is stable, the task is clear, and eyes are on the prize. Team members are highly motivated to accomplish their task and focused on team objectives rather than individual interests. Through working closely together, team members have developed insights into each other's strengths and weaknesses (many even finish each other's sentences), feel satisfied with the team's progress, and believe the team will successfully reach or even exceed its goals. In this stage, members engage in constructive self-change for the good of the group; experience greatly enhanced ability to communicate with and give feedback to each other; are able to anticipate, prevent, or work through group problems; and, as a result, develop a close attachment to the team.[23]

As a team member or leader, your role at this stage is to encourage members to provide support to and serve as resources for each other. Make sure the team continues with its progress and maintains its cohesion and morale, and guide it toward success. Do remain vigilant, however. It's easy to kick back and relax, believing that once a team gets to this phase of development, it stays there. That may or may not be true. Changes in membership, scope of the task, or broader organizational changes can cause a team to regress developmentally. In addition, the close attachments members have to a team could possibly blind them to other developing problems.

Stage Five—Adjourning

After successfully completing the task or objective, teams may disband permanently or take a temporary break. Some may get new members or receive a new objective. This stage is usually brought on by an imminent deadline. At the **adjourning** stage, members are likely to feel disappointment—if the experience was positive—or gratitude—if the experience was negative. The task at this stage is to tie up loose ends and complete final follow-up on projects.

As a team member or leader, your role at this end stage is to encourage the team members to debrief the project, discussing the lessons learned that members can take with them to new projects and convey to new teams tackling similar issues. It is also helpful at this stage to recognize the team for its efforts. This could take the form of public recognition (a blurb on the team's accomplishments in the monthly newsletter), a reward (some organizations reward teams with a percentage of the savings or revenues realized as a result of the team's work), or other benefit (use company funds to take the team out for lunch). By providing encouragement and recognizing accomplishments, hard work, and efforts, you help to continue momentum and build motivation.[24] Of course, ongoing work project teams may not physically adjourn. They may remain intact, continuing with a new set of objectives once a particular project is complete. In this case, rather than adjourning, the team members may choose to debrief at certain checkpoints along the way, evaluating their processes and communication efforts to ensure they're keeping current and are as productive as they can be.

It is healthy for groups to move through some or all of these stages as they evolve into a team. Not all groups go through all the stages, and some go through them at different paces. For example, if a group's members knew each other previously and had similar values and goals—as well as a tight deadline—they might be able to move almost immediately to the norming stage. In another case, where the group members don't know each other well and they have some time before the deliverable is due, they might take longer to reach the norming phase and coalesce as a real team just before the deliverable is due. Some may get stuck in one of the stages and disband before progressing to the next stage or perform at a lower level than what might have been possible. A group stuck in the storming stage but facing an imminent deadline has to continue performing. In this case, it is likely that its performance will suffer due to the inability to function cohesively. In some extreme cases, a group will be dysfunctional and will require outside intervention in order to complete its task. As is true with relationships, teams have developmental cycles. Understanding this ahead of time can help you develop strategies for helping your group evolve into a team and to increase its effectiveness every step of the way.

Characteristics of High-Performance Teams

As former Notre Dame coach Lou Holtz said, "Winning is never accidental. To win consistently you must have a clear plan and intense motivation." As we have said, not all teams are alike. As a team member or leader, your primary goal is to encourage your group to evolve into a motivated, goal-oriented, successful team; we refer to these types of teams as high-performance teams. In **high-performance teams,** there is a commitment to quality and a dedication to producing the best outcome possible. Research shows that most high-performance work teams possess the following characteristics:[25]

■ *Common purpose and goals:* High-performing teams have a clearly defined mission, purpose, and goals. Individual team members understand why the team has been formed and what is expected from the team.[26]

■ *Intention:* According to researcher Barry Ekman, the best teams are not ad-hoc or unstructured. Instead, they are planned or structured to achieve a specific goal or address a specific challenge. In structured team building, the importance is on intentionally striving to achieve sustainable outcomes by matching team psychology with change and technology.[27]

■ *Clear roles:* High-performing teams have clarity about roles and responsibilities. Team members understand their roles and assignments and how they impact the group, have clear and stable boundaries, are aware of how their work affects other members, and know the direction that is needed to get there.[28]

■ *Communication processes:* High-performing teams have extensive communication mechanisms. They communicate regularly with each other either in person, via telephone, or through e-mail and keep those unable to attend meetings informed of the group's progress. They constantly update their planning calendar and communicate about adjustments, as they are needed.[29]

■ *Accepting and supportive leadership:* Studies have found that team leaders who function more as coaches than managers facilitate the development of participative, motivated teams.[30] These leaders were proactive and committed to the team, and they provided encouraging, positive influence over the team and its members. A manager pulls a group along; a coach gently pushes it from behind. A manager works to maintain control; a coach works to give up control.[31]

■ *Small size:* The size of the team can be essential to a team's success. The optimal size is between 6 and 10. This is large enough to accomplish the work and provide enough human resources and ideas, and small enough for a team to coalesce and reach consensus on major issues.[32]

■ *High levels of technical and interpersonal skills:* High-performing teams are composed of members who have a breadth of both specialty and people skills. Understanding how to work with and through others, problem solving, managing project work flow, giving and receiving feedback, goal setting, time management, and conflict management are some of the most valuable skills in team settings.[33]

■ *Open relationships and trust:* In high-performing teams, the members develop cooperative behaviors including understanding what is needed from one another; defining the interrelated activities necessary to complete the project; volunteering to assist each other in doing what's needed; and completing assigned tasks competently, on time, accurately, and with quality. Trust is built through behaviors such as being dependable, doing what is agreed upon, being kept informed and informing others of necessary facts and information, keeping confidential information private, and allowing others to use their specialized knowledge and abilities.[34]

■ *Accountability:* High-performance team members understand for what (and to what degree) they and others are held accountable. The team receives the message from the organization that performance matters—that it makes a difference whether goals are achieved or not. Expectations are clarified, and members are held responsible as individuals as well as members of the team.[35]

■ *Reward structures:* High-performing teams are rewarded for team accomplishments in addition to individual recognition. Organizations that support the team concept organize their recruiting, training, development, sales, business development, strategic planning, compensation, performance appraisal, and promotion strategies to support and reward teamwork.[36] When these strategies don't match with or undermine team processes or philosophies, the organization sends a mixed message and members find ways to "game" the system—often at the expense of their team. If an individual team member who "saves the day" for the department is rewarded for individual behavior, it sends the message that collaboration is not as valued as individual contributions or heroics, even if management's rhetoric suggests teams are truly valued.

Tips for Effective Teams

As a member of a team, it is important to be self-directed and work for the betterment of your team. You and your team members will be working with minimal supervision, and it is everyone's responsibility to make the team work. As athletes have learned, if one team member doesn't come through, the quality and performance of the entire team is affected. Teamwork requires full dedication and participation by all members of the team.

The following tips can help make your next team experience more positive and successful.

■ *Be focused.* Cooperate with your team members in concentrating on the current issues they face. Cooperation builds trust and mutual respect. Be willing and dedicated to working toward the common purpose.

■ *Handle conflict directly* and be willing to compromise. Be willing to explore conflict in a constructive, win–win fashion. Stand up for things that are important to you, but don't insist on getting your way in every discussion. When working together, put personalities aside and confront issues that arise. Resolve conflicts and walk away from sessions with regard, respect, and esteem for yourself and your team members.[37]

■ *Focus on both process and content.* Pay attention to the *process* of becoming and working together as a team as well as the *result* or end goal expected from the team. Teamwork is more than producing a deliverable. It also entails the approach or process used when people are working together.[38] The ends don't necessarily justify the means if team members despise and lack respect for team members because of the way decisions and outcomes were rammed through when teams fail to use a consensus approach. At team meetings, review both the processes being used as well as the status of the project.

■ *Actively participate,* and encourage others to do the same. At the beginning of a project, talk about roles and responsibilities. Also talk frankly about team members' schedules and their availability to participate fully in the project. Set up checkpoints to ensure that all are contributing equally.

■ *Keep sensitive issues private.* At the beginning of a project, discuss the importance of confidentiality. All teams engage in discussions that could be hurtful if made public. Have a pact that private information and views shared will be just that—not relayed to others outside the group. "What's said in the room, stays in the room."

■ *Communicate openly and positively.* In order to have full team participation, and for the team to learn and develop, it is essential that team members do not embarrass, reject, mock, or punish someone for speaking up and sharing ideas and perceptions. Foster a climate of psychological safety in order to motivate members to participate, admit errors, and share ideas and beliefs openly and comfortably.[39]

■ *Take time to establish operating guidelines* and clarify expectations. Make sure everyone is present for initial discussions of roles, responsibilities, and operating guidelines. For these guidelines to work, it is best that everyone participate in establishing and agreeing to uphold them. Put them in writing and have everyone sign them.

■ *Monitor what's going on with the team.* Watch for reactions, nonverbal cues, level of participation (or lack thereof), and general changes in the group's dynamics. Develop observational skills to help the team reach its full potential. A side benefit of doing this is that you increase your own interpersonal skills as you try to set a tone that is conducive to all members enjoying and participating in the team experience.[40]

■ *Practice giving (and receiving) effective feedback.* Express support and acceptance by praising and seeking other members' ideas and conclusions. If you disagree with others' viewpoints, criticize ideas but not the people. Be specific about the ideas that concern you and accept others' concerns about your ideas.

■ *Work with underperformers* to keep them in the flow of the project and prevent them from becoming excluded from the group.[41] If slackers are an issue in your team, talk with them immediately, preferably one on one. Find out if there is a personal problem preventing the member from being more engaged. Offer to be supportive but don't carry the workload. Give that team member specific, manageable tasks and hold him or her accountable. If the underperformance continues, talk with your manager or instructor. The person may need to be removed from the group or reassigned to a different team.

■ *Energize the team* when motivation is low by suggesting new ideas, through humor or use of enthusiasm. Encourage a time-out, if one is needed, or suggest a work or coffee break.

■ *Be reliable and conscientious.* Respect other members by honoring deadlines, commitments, and project milestones.[42] If you are having difficulty making a deadline, don't wait until the last minute—discuss the problem immediately with a team member or with the team. There might be a different way of approaching it. It's easier for a team to be flexible when there is adequate time to review the situation and come up with a different plan.

■ *When needed, give direction to the team's work* by stating and restating the purpose of assignments, setting or calling attention to time limits, and offering procedures on how to complete the assignment most effectively.

■ *Be supportive of your team members.* Always ask how you can help. It's a great way to remind everyone you're a team with collective objectives, not a group of individual contributors competing against each other.

Why Teams Fail

A note of caution: for teams and teamwork to succeed, there must be ample time in which to complete an assignment. Also needed are adequate resources to achieve the stated objectives and full management support of the team's effort. While the concept of teamwork is prevalent in both work and nonwork settings, not all situations warrant or are conducive to teams. Teams may be faced with tight deadlines; merging of processes and responsibilities; technological challenges; mismatched skills and abilities; unresolvable personality clashes, styles, and behaviors; limited work or teaming experience; or power struggles. In these situations, or in cases where there is no interdependence or need for collaboration, teamwork is going to be difficult if not impossible. These issues should be addressed early so that modifications can be made if necessary.

For example, if a team lacks the proper skill sets, additional members or training sessions can be added. If a power struggle is unfolding, a facilitator can be appointed. Inexperienced team members can be assigned informal mentors or coaches. Sometimes, if it's in the best interests of an organization, a team can be disbanded altogether. Perhaps the mission wasn't clearly defined at the outset of a project and the team members find they are unable to devote the time necessary to do the job. Or perhaps management requested individuals to work on a team project but made no allowances for mandatory day-to-day tasks. In situations such as these, it's appropriate for the team to be reconfigured (or disbanded) so that the original objective can be attained through either a different team or a different approach. Oftentimes, teams ignore early problems—perhaps believing such problems can be overcome—and become dysfunctional.[43] Intervening early, in a proactive way, can turn a team around or cause the organization to consider other, non-team-based approaches to solving a problem.

How can you deal with team members who aren't performing? Following are some tips.

Dealing with Problem Team Members

■ **Absentee member:** A member can become distracted by a work or personal problem that prevents him or her from following through on commitments made to the team. In this case, the best strategy is to be direct immediately. Discuss the situation with the team member in a way in which the person does not feel he or she is being put on the defensive. Explain the problem and find out the team member's perception of the situation. Ask specifically if the team member still has the time necessary for the team. If not, part ways if possible. If this is not possible, determine a way for the team member to make contributions outside of the normal meeting times and make the person accountable for a specific segment of the work that limits reliance on the team.

■ **Social loafer:** As mentioned earlier, it is not uncommon for one or more persons on a team to be able to "hide" the fact they're not contributing. This typically happens when the team members' work ethics differ and one or more team members "step up to the plate" and take on additional responsibility to ensure the work gets done, effectively covering for the less productive team members. Work standards will always vary from person to person. A strategy for dealing with this is to raise the issue at the onset of the project. Divide the responsibilities and set up checkpoints to ensure each member is contributing roughly equally. If a discrepancy appears, try to quantify it and re-allocate the workload so all members are contributing roughly equally.

■ **Procrastinator:** We're all human, and a seemingly human tendency is to "put off until tomorrow what we should be working on today." This is particularly problematic for work teams. Teams are composed of individuals with different work schedules and work styles. Some people thrive on the pressure of imminent deadlines while others find waiting until the last minute to be overly stressful. In this situation it is best to do two things: (a) set up interim checkpoints, or minideadlines, to ensure the work progresses at a reasonable pace, and (b) be realistic when work schedules are drawn up and deadlines determined. Prior to establishing deadlines, ask all team members to check personal and work calendars to catch any problems before they occur. At each meeting reclarify the commitments that might affect a person's inability to adhere to a deadline set earlier. And build in some slack: set the final deadline for a few days before the *actual* deadline—just in case!

Teams may not be a cure for all that ails an organization. But, teams can be very effective if the team structure makes sense and members practice the suggestions outlined in the chapter. Other steps team members and their managers can take to improve the likelihood of team success are summarized in the chart below:

Tips for Managing for Outstanding Results

■ Care about the people you work with—understand them, know what's important to them, and be able to motivate them.

■ Don't worry about who gets the credit—emphasize team effort and rewards; use the "whatever is best for the team" approach.

■ Respect individual differences—accept individuals and work to emphasize strengths and minimize weaknesses.

■ Subordinate yourself to a higher purpose—keep the common goal in the forefront.

■ Know yourself—be aware of your strengths and admit your weaknesses; surround yourself with people who can compensate for your weaknesses.

■ Don't be afraid to follow—some of the best teams are those where the leader doesn't call all the shots.

Source: Stephen Covey, "Team Up for a Superstar Office," *USA Weekend,* Sept. 4–6, 1998, p. 10.

Summary

Workplaces in the United States and abroad have embraced teaming. This is no accident. Organizations that implemented work teams as a way to improve products, services, and processes have witnessed tremendous measurable benefits. Some of these benefits accrue because of synergies—the notion that teams produce more and better solutions than individuals—gained from combining various skill sets, perspectives, abilities, and work styles on a single team. Not all teams produce phenomenal outcomes. By understanding the normal phases of group development and ways to gain and maintain group productivity and motivation, you can help your teams reach their full potential.

Key Terms and Concepts

Absentee member	Performing
Adjourning	Process improvement team
Cross-functional teams	Procrastinator
Forming	Self-managed team
Group	Social loafing/loafer
Groupthink	Storming
High-performance team	Task force
Norming	Team

Endnotes

1. Quote by Tracey Edwards in "Teaming with Talent," by Jim White, *Management Today,* Sept. 1999, p. 56.

2. Lillian Chaney and Julie Lyden, "Making U.S. Teams Work," *Supervision,* Jan. 2000, p. 6.

3. Karl L. Smart and Carol Barnum, "Communication in Cross-Functional Teams: An Introduction to This Special Issue," *Technical Communication,* Feb. 2000, p. 19.

4. Kevin McManus, "Do You Have Teams?" *IIE Solutions,* April 2000, p. 21.

5. Jim White, "Teaming with Talent," *Management Today,* Sept. 1999, p. 56.

6. Harvey Mackay, "Get on the Team and Be a Winner," *Providence Business News,* August 16, 1999, p. 38.

7. Chaney and Lyden, "Making U.S. Teams Work."

8. McManus, "Do You Have Teams?"

9. Ibid.

10. Smart and Barnum, "Communication in Cross-Functional Teams."

11. Chaney and Lyden, "Making U.S. Teams Work."

12. Mohsen Attaran and Tai T. Nguyen, "Succeeding with Self-managed Work Teams," *Industrial Management,* July–August 1999, p. 24.

13. Larry Cole and Michael Scott Cole, "Teamwork is Spelled Incorrectly: Teamwork = Communication," *Communication World,* April 2000, p. 56.

14. Attaran and Nguyen, "Succeeding with Self-managed Work Teams." Reprinted by permission of the Institute of Industrial Engineers, 25 Technology Park, Norcross, GA 30092, 770–449–0461. Copyright © 1999.

15. Irving I. Janis, *Groupthink,* 2nd ed. (Boston, MA: Houghton-Mifflin, 1982).

16. Attaran and Nguyen, "Succeeding with Self-managed Work Teams."

17. David Rohlander, "Building High-Performance Teams," *Credit Union Executive,* March 2000, p. 36.

18. Bruce W. Tuckman, "Developmental Sequences in Small Groups," *Psychological Bulletin* 63 (1965), pp. 384–99. The stage theory of team development was first identified by Tuckerman. Subsequent research has found the stages occur in a slightly different order. While the original model is reflected in this chapter, some researchers have found that teams more likely progress through conforming before entering the storming stage. See R. E. Quinn and K. S. Cameron, "Organizational Life Cycles and Shifting Criteria of Effectiveness," *Management Science* 29 (1983), pp. 37–61. Also see K. S. Cameron and D. A. Whetten, "Perceptions of Organizational Effectiveness in Organizational Life Cycles," *Administrative Science Quarterly* 27 (1981), pp. 525–44.

19. Peter R. Scholtes, *The Team Handbook* (Madison, WI: Joiner and Associates, 1988).

20. John R. Myers, "What It Takes to Make a Team," *Purchasing,* Sept. 2, 1999, p. 91.

21. Scholtes, *The Team Handbook.*

22. Daniel C. Feldman, "The Development and Enforcement of Group Norms," *Academy of Management Review* 9, no.1 (1984), pp. 47–53.

23. Scholtes, *The Team Handbook.*

24. Rona Leach, "Supervision: From Me to We," *Supervision,* Feb. 2000, p. 8.

25. Ruth Wageman, "Critical Success Factors for Creating Superb Self-Managing Teams," *Organizational Dynamics,* Summer 1997, p. 49.

26. Rohlander, "Building High-Performance Teams."

27. Barry Ekman and Emmanuela Ginngregorio, "Establishing Truly Peak Performance Teams—Beyond Metaphoric Challenges," *Human Resource Management International Digest,* 11, no. 3 (2003), p. 2.

28. American Management Association, "HR Update: Creating Real Teamwork at the Top," *HR Focus,* Jan. 2000, p. 2.

29. Smart and Barnum, "Communication in Cross-Functional Teams."

30. Paulo Vieira Cunha and Maria Joao Louro, "Building Teams That Learn," *The Academy of Management Executive,* Feb. 2000, p. 152.

31. Renee Evenson, "Team Effort: Beyond Employees to Team, beyond Manager to Coach," *Supervision,* Feb. 2000, p. 11.

32. Chaney and Lyden, "Making U.S. Teams Work."

33. Avan R. Jassawalla and Hemant C. Sashittal, "Building Collaborative Cross-Functional New Product Teams," *The Academy of Management Executive,* August 1999, p. 50.

34. Cole and Cole, "Teamwork Is Spelled Incorrectly."

35. Russ Forrester and Allan B. Drexler, "A Model for Team-Based Organizational Performance," *The Academy of Management Executive,* August 1999, p. 36.

36. Becky L. Nichol, "Top Ten Reasons Teams Become Dysfunctional," *National Public Accountant,* Feb. 2000, p. 12.

37. Jassawalla and Sashittal, "Building Collaborative Cross-Functional New Product Teams."

38. Cole and Cole, "Teamwork Is Spelled Incorrectly."

39. Cunha and Louro, "Building Teams."

40. Myers, "What It Takes to Make a Team."

41. Ted Gautschi, "Strengthen Your Team," *Design News,* Oct. 18, 1999, p. 158.

42. Myers, "What It Takes to Make a Team."

43. Smart and Barnum, "Communication in Cross-Functional Teams."

Exercise 10–A
Bridge Building

Groups of four to six are tasked with creating a bridge out of the materials provided. You have 30 minutes in which to complete this task. When the project is complete or time is called—whichever comes first—your instructor will roll a ball across your bridge to ensure it meets the project specifications. Following this activity, discuss these questions in your group.

Questions

1. How did your group decide how to build the bridge? Did it make a plan or did it just start building?
2. Did anyone play a leadership role in the task? Explain.
3. What made building the bridge as a group, rather than as an individual, more difficult?
4. In what ways did the group make the project easier? Explain.
5. Was your group a group or team? Explain.

Exercise 10–B
The Story: A Team Exercise

Read the instructions and story below and answer the corresponding questions. Next, complete the same task in your assigned group.

What Does the Story Tell?

Instructions

Read the following story and take for granted that everything it says is true. Read carefully because, in spots, the story is deliberately vague. Don't try to memorize it since you can look back at it at any time.

Then read the numbered statements about the story and decide whether you consider each one true, false, or questionable. Circling the "T" means you feel sure the statement is definitely true. Circling the "F" means you feel sure the statement is definitely false. Circling the "?" means you cannot tell whether it is true or false. If you feel doubtful about any part of a statement, circle the question mark.

Take the statements in turn and do not go back later to change any of your answers. Do not reread any of the statements after you have answered them.

Story

The owner of the Adams Manufacturing Company entered the office of one of his foremen where he found three employees playing cards. One of them was Carl Young, brother-in-law of foreman Henry Dilson. Dilson, incidentally, often worked late. Company rules did not specifically forbid gambling on the premises, but the president had expressed himself forcibly on the subject.

Statements about the Story

1. In brief, the story is about a company owner who found three men playing cards.	T	F	?
2. The president walked into the office of one of his foremen.	T	F	?
3. Company rules forbade playing cards on the premises after hours.	T	F	?
4. While the card playing took place in Henry Dilson's office, the story does not state whether Dilson was present.	T	F	?
5. Dilson never worked late.	T	F	?
6. Gambling on the premises of the Adams Manufacturing Company was not punished.	T	F	?
7. Carl Young was not playing cards when the president walked in.	T	F	?
8. Three employees were gambling in a foreman's office.	T	F	?
9. While the card players were surprised when the owner walked in, it is not clear whether they will be punished.	T	F	?
10. Henry Dilson is Carl Young's brother-in-law.	T	F	?

11. The president is opposed to gambling on company premises.   T   F   ?

12. Carl Young did not take part in the card game in   T   F   ?
    Henry Dilson's office.

Questions

1. What process did you use to come up with the group answers?

2. Did anyone act as a leader or facilitator in the exercise? Explain.

3. In what ways was it difficult to achieve a group decision?

4. Which behaviors blocked the group's process? Which ones helped?

5. What are the advantages or disadvantages of working in a group compared to working as an individual?

**Exercise 10–C
Case Study on Gaining Appropriate Membership on Teams**

This is the team's third meeting. The team's task, deliverables, and membership have been dictated by a steering committee that oversees the division's teaming efforts. Members represent different areas and management levels within the division. A new team member who missed the first two meetings enters the room. Let's eavesdrop:

SCRIBE: "Okay. Here's our agenda. Does this sound ok to everyone?"

NEW TEAM MEMBER: "Well, not exactly. I have a question regarding the team's task. I know I missed the first two meetings, but I'm unclear about our purpose. I mean, without a well-understood purpose, are we ready to talk about membership? I'm not even sure if I should be here!"

SCRIBE: "Well, I suppose we can add "team purpose" to the agenda. How much time should we allot?"

TEAM LEADER: (Feeling strained by all the necessary structure.) "Could we hold off with the agenda for a few minutes . . . I know we need the agenda, but I think we should talk about purpose for a few minutes at least; then we can get back to the regular agenda. She (the new team member) brings up a good point."

Some discussion ensues. It becomes clear that the team's purpose *is* unclear. Other additional information is revealed, such as the fact that there had been three other team members who, shortly after being appointed by the steering committee, decided to excuse themselves from the team. Also, the team leader brought a new person in (call her Possible New Member), who is not really a full-fledged member until the steering committee approves it.

SCRIBE: "Back to the agenda. Were there any corrections to the minutes? (No response.) Okay, now for today's meeting roles . . . oh, our timekeeper isn't here today."

NEW TEAM MEMBER: (Looking at Possible New Member) "Would you like to keep time?"

TEAM LEADER: "Well, we're not sure if she is an official team member yet. Remember, the steering committee hasn't okayed her yet. Should she keep time if she's not?"

NEW TEAM MEMBER: "What's the difference? And why do we need the steering committee's blessing? Let's just do it."

TEAM LEADER: "Actually, there are some other names, in addition to Possible Team Member, that we've submitted to the steering committee. After all, we've lost three people since the team began."

NEW TEAM MEMBER: "Do we need additional people? Why? Again, doesn't it depend on what we're trying to accomplish?"

Questions

1. Why is it important to clarify a team's purpose? Once the task is given, why is clarification necessary?

2. What role does this purpose play in defining team membership? Why do you suppose others have "excused themselves" from the team?

3. How effective is the team leader? Explain.

4. Meeting management techniques—using agendas, having a scribe and timekeeper—are intended to make meetings more effective. In what ways could these techniques have the opposite effect?

5. If you were asked to participate in this meeting, what would you do to get the process back on track? Explain.

Exercise 10–D
The Case of the Take-Charge Team Leader

You are a member of a team that is meeting for the third time. Your goal is to reduce the number and dollar amount of workers' compensation claims. The team consists of members from safety, human resources, legal, and medical (e.g., staff nurses and doctors) departments. The team leader—a senior level manager—demonstrates a "take-charge" approach in that he or she believes he or she knows more about the task and assignment than anyone on the team. Early in the team's existence, the leader shared a project milestone chart that the team accepted. While the group has kept up with its assignments and is working rather effectively, the team leader seems impatient with the team's progress. In fact, the leader would like to exert greater control over the team's activities because he or she already has supporting data from outside groups and departments about the task and wants to complete the project in record time. However, you and other team members are concerned that (1) there may be other issues that have not yet surfaced, and (2) if his or her ideas are accepted, one of the team members may lose his or her position in the firm.

Questions

1. What issues are at play? How would you feel in this situation?

2. If the leader is so capable, why do you suppose management created a team to address this particular (and highly visible) problem?

3. At this point, what would you do and why?

4. If no changes were made, what do you think the final outcome would be?

Exercise 10–E
Reflection/Action Plan

This chapter focused on teams in the workplace—what they are, why they are important, and how to improve your skill in this area. Complete the worksheet below upon completing all the reading and experiential activities for this chapter.

1. The one or two areas in which I am most strong are:

2. The one or two areas in which I need more improvement are:

3. If I did only one thing to improve in this area, it would be to:

Managing Conflict

Learning Points

How do I:
- Deal with unresolved anger in a constructive way?
- Identify the source of conflict as it's occurring?
- Understand what my natural conflict style is and know which strategy to adopt in a conflict situation?
- Change my attitude toward conflict and treat it as a normal and potentially beneficial part of relationships?
- Prevent conflict when appropriate?
- Learn how to manage conflict personally and professionally?

I am so angry with my boss I can't even speak to him. We had always been pretty close. Only a few years older than me, he was a member of my fraternity when he was in college. We met at a chapter career networking event. He said I would fit right in at the investment bank where he worked and that hired me as I graduated from college. For the first few years he was always there for me. I was placed in another department, but he stayed in touch, informally providing me with information and tips. People knew that we were close, and I have to admit I didn't mind being affiliated with him in people's heads. As his stature and reputation at the bank grew, I felt lucky and proud to have been taken under his wing. Don't get me wrong. I worked hard and earned my promotions on merit. But it didn't hurt to be associated with him and to get useful advice from him. At least, not until now.

Last year he was placed in charge of all campus recruiting for the bank. He was the senior person in charge, and people in all departments who recruited for the bank, like me, had a dotted line reporting relationship to him for our recruiting results. That's where things began to go wrong.

As soon as he was put in charge, he made me his lieutenant. I worked closely with him to ensure his strategic recruiting objectives would be implemented. I began to travel extensively with him and with the other recruiters—line people like myself who had been "lent" to the function for just one season. It was an honor to be selected. The opportunity to recruit at top-tier campuses is only offered to people who are "up and comers" at the bank. I was proud of his belief that I could contribute to the effort and do a good job.

Plus the added visibility couldn't hurt when it came time for my next bonus and promotion. Or could it?

One night after our firm's presentation at a top-tier school, he and I ended up the only recruiters left at the bar from our team of eight. Everyone else had retired for the evening. We were the diehards, left with a group of students who didn't seem to want to leave. I noticed my boss, Bob, over in a corner of the bar with one of the students. A female student. Uh-oh. I was worried how this might look and thought I'd better saunter over and join in. I got there just in time to hear the student, who sounded like she had already had enough to drink, order a drink whose name I hadn't heard since back in college on spring break in Florida. Bob told the waiter to charge it to his room. He also politely told me to scram. I left, slightly worried about what might be happening but figuring he knew how to handle himself.

To make a very long story short, a few weeks later, I found out that Bob had propositioned this student and that she had filed a complaint against him, and by association, against me and our firm's entire recruiting team. Apparently she thinks it was wrong of us to have sent the wrong signal to the students by staying out so late with them. She says she stayed because she thought we were interested in her as a potential hire. And that one of the reasons she didn't get invited back (for an interview the next day) is she refused to sleep with Bob.

Now both Bob's job and mine are on the line. Since he's the senior person in charge of recruiting and the one who made the pass, he's almost certain to lose his job. And since I'm his lieutenant, I'm vulnerable too. The rest of the team will probably get reassigned.

I am so angry I can't even talk to anyone about this. Not him. Not his boss. Not my fiancee. Not human resources. It's humiliating, childish, and shouldn't be involving me. All my hard work at the bank is about to go down the tubes. I'm so angry. I thought we were friends. I thought he would look out for me, not get me in trouble. I don't know what to do. I just want this all to go away.

1. Is this a solvable conflict? Why or why not?

2. By choosing not to speak to his boss or boss's boss, what impact does this have on the parties involved?

3. What options are available, assuming a resolution is desired?

4. While the bar scenario might not have been predicted or avoided, in what ways could the boss–subordinate conflict have been ameliorated before it progressed to this point?

5. What role do personal style and comfort with conflict play in our response (and resolution) to situations like these?

We're told that conflict is inevitable, that it's part of human nature to have conflicts with others. Yet seldom do we as human beings get comfortable with conflict. Many of us would prefer to avoid it at all costs. As we can see from the opening case, avoiding it doesn't make it go away. It bothers us emotionally whether we confront the source of the conflict or not. Managing conflict is one of the toughest yet most rewarding skills to acquire. Foremost, it is a skill that does not come naturally; it is learned. In this chapter we discuss conflict, what it is, and why learning to manage it is important. We discuss common sources of conflict and present a model for approaching conflict. We also include strategies and tips for dealing with conflict as well as suggestions for preventing conflict when possible and for being selective about which conflicts you choose to tackle. Exercises to help you process and build skills in managing conflict are at the end of the chapter, as is a list of references for further exploration.

"Speaking without thinking is like shooting without aiming."

Ancient Proverb

What Is Conflict?

Conflict is any situation in which there are incompatible goals, cognitions, or emotions within or between individuals or groups that lead to opposition or antagonistic interaction. It is the struggle between incompatible and opposing needs, wishes, ideas, interests, or people. Conflict is a form of interaction among parties who differ in interests, perceptions, goals, values, or approaches to problems. Conflict arises when we begin to feel that the other person is interfering with our ability to attain a certain objective. It begins when we believe the other party is interfering or standing in the way of an action we want to take, an idea we want to pursue, or a belief we hold. Conflicts may involve individual or group disagreements, struggles, disputes, quarrels, or even physical fighting and wars. Because human beings are unique—possessing a variety of physical, intellectual, emotional, economic, and social differences—conflict is inevitable.

Conflict is a fact of life in organizations. Each organization is composed of people, and each person has a set of goals that is likely to be distinct from the goals of others in the organization. When individuals with different interests compete for the same resource pool, dissension is sure to follow.[1] That tension can be dealt with constructively, in a way that stimulates creativity and positive change. In fact, lack of creative tension sometimes reflects an "I don't care" attitude that can lead to stagnation on the job. Effective managers are not afraid of conflict. They have been trained to deal with conflict and have trained their employees to deal with conflict constructively. They accept that conflicts must be faced and strive to find constructive means to manage them. Effective managers are those who are selective as to which conflicts they choose to pursue. Sometimes the best course of action in a difficult situation is to take "the path of least resistance"—to be silent!

Is Conflict Normal?

Society's view of conflict and conflict management has evolved substantially over the last century. These views can be summarized in three perspectives on managing conflict:[2]

1. **Traditional View**—This view was predominant in the early 20th century when it was believed that conflict was always bad and should be avoided at all costs. This perspective posited that conflict was a result of dysfunctional managerial behavior and therefore should and could be stopped at the source. Presumably, if the dysfunctional behavior was stopped (i.e., the manager is fired), the conflict would cease to exist.
2. **Human Relations View**—This was the overriding perspective for the three decades spanning 1940 through 1970. In this view, conflict was viewed as a natural and inevitable part of human existence and was accepted as a normal part of group interaction and relationships. Sometimes the conflict was functional, other times dysfunctional, but it was always present.
3. **Interactionist View**—The contemporary view holds that not only is conflict inevitable, but maintaining a degree of tension can actually be helpful in keeping a group energized and creative. In this view, conflict is seen as a positive force for change within organizations, groups, and relationships. The challenge is finding constructive means for managing conflict while still maintaining some differences that energize a group toward continued discussion and innovation.

Although managerial mistakes do sometimes cause unnecessary and even unhealthy conflict, it is important to discard the traditional notion that conflict automatically means one performs ineffectively. Conflict is a certainty for any manager, or any person, for that matter. The best managers recognize this and learn how to manage conflict in such a way that it has positive and fair outcomes for all involved.[3]

Why Is Conflict Management Important?

Conflict is a normal part of life. In every organization, family, relationship, and community, there are conflicts of ideas, values, thought, and actions. Conflict is a given. What isn't given is how we choose to react to conflict. As Marcus Aurelius says in *Meditations:*

> *If you are distressed by anything external, the pain is not due to the thing itself, but to your own estimate of it; and this you have the power to revoke at any moment.*

We can successfully face and resolve conflicts if we take a few steps: recognize conflicts are normal and inevitable,[4] train ourselves not to overreact when conflicts arise, and have a strategy to use when conflicts—some of which are predictable—arise.

Conflict can be either positive or negative. The outcomes of conflict depend on how the conflict is managed or resolved. **Positive conflict** is functional and supports or benefits the organization or person's main objectives.[5] Conflict is constructive when it leads to better decisions, creativity, and innovative solutions to long-standing problems. Conflict is viewed as positive when it results in

- *Increased involvement*—Organizational members have the opportunity to develop goals, share ideas, and voice opinions, gaining greater insight into others and situations.

- *Increased cohesion*—Members build strong bonds from learning how to resolve differences; "if we can survive this, we must have a true relationship" embodies this benefit of conflict.[6] In some cases conflict initially reduces cohesion that can in turn reduce the likelihood of "group think" occurring. In this case conflict is positive.

- *Increased innovation and creativity*—Members are encouraged to "put their ideas on the table";[7] this can lead to more discoveries, improvements, and creative solutions. "Two heads are truly better than one" when conflict brings about synergy instead of chaos.

- *Positive personal growth and change*—Individuals learn their strengths and weaknesses; conflict of ideas challenges individuals to learn and grow by expressing their ideas and thoughts through self-disclosure and sharing of important concepts with others.

- *Clarification of key issues*—Through discussion, members reduce ambiguity and focus energy on the real sources of conflict, then work together to target remaining issues that need to be addressed.

- *Values clarification*—Members clarify who they are and what they stand for, understand who the other party is and what his or her values are, and learn when to sublimate personal interests to the larger needs of the group or organization.

Negative conflict is dysfunctional and hinders the organization's or the person's performance or ability to attain goals or objectives. Conflict is destructive when it leads to stress and anxiety, inability to take action, and loss of esteem or purpose.[8] Conflict is viewed as negative when it results in

- *Unresolved anger*—Members leave the interaction believing they have legitimate concerns that have not been addressed appropriately or goals that cannot be achieved; companies can be slowly poisoned by anger and hostility.[9]

- *Personality clashes*—Members lack understanding of their style differences and how to work cooperatively and are more tied to their own interests than those of others.

- *Low self-esteem or self-confidence*—Members have a diminished sense of self-worth or identity as a result of the conflict. Often this results from impulsive things said or done in the heat of the conflict.

- *Unclear or opposing views on who is or should be responsible for what*—Members have different expectations of each other and their roles; the conflict was unresolved, unproductive, or ended too soon, leaving ambiguity in its wake.
- *Problems of efficiency*—Members decide they are unwilling or unable to work together, resulting in redundancies and poor use of existing resources.
- *"Unfinished business"*—Members are still unclear about the issue or have remaining concerns that will get in the way of being able to move forward.

The benefits of positive conflict far outweigh the time it takes to manage conflict well. As managers, it is our responsibility to learn how to manage conflict effectively and how to help others manage conflict. This is done by creating a climate and culture at work that support constructive conflict—encouraging the clash of ideas (not personalities) and developing processes, training, and tools that help people work through their inevitable differences with each other. This requires a collaborative approach and a commitment to eliminating or at least reducing the occurrence of destructive conflicts.

Sources of Interpersonal Conflict

Not everyone within a group or organization will have the same goals and objectives. By definition, different groups, business units, functions, operating companies, or locations within one organization will each have a set of expectations and operating principles that differs from the others. Each specific entity within an organization may have a unique customer set, employee profile, product orientation, management style, business niche, set of tasks and procedures, and culture or work environment. Business units in the same organization differ significantly in such areas as primary role, task assignments, workloads, vacation scheduling, pay or promotion policies, chain of command, work flow process, and others. For example, within General Motors are very different entities—separate organizations whose primary business is financing (cars and homes), production (building or assembling cars), sales and service (dealership and warranty organizations), and research and development (making continuous improvement on existing car lines as well as developing new ones such as GM's electric vehicle). Employees in these different units likely work together, sharing expertise as well as information. A variety of situational or organizational factors lead to conflict.[10]

Limited Resources

Despite clear differences between units within an organization, one commonality remains. In general, all are vying for the same resource pool. This pool is usually limited, causing the various units within an organization to compete against each other for finite resources. No matter how prosperous an organization might appear from its facilities, salary levels, or private jets and limousines, few if any organizations have infinite resources. This usually results in competition among business units for the restricted resources available through the parent organization. People in organizations compete for what they consider to be their fair share of resources such as money, time, senior management attention, technology, supplies, equipment, and human talent. This inevitably results in conflict.

Differences in Goals/Objectives

A common source of conflict within organizations is differences in personal and/or professional goals and objectives. If we are working on a project with someone whose objective is different from ours, tension or conflict is likely to occur. For example, perhaps one team member wants to "coast" or do as little work as possible toward the team's expected output or deliverable. If this person is on a team of individuals who are committed to a high-quality output, there will be differences between them on a host of items, such as approach to the work, ways to get the work done, and standards of work quality and quantity. This tension can be from **intragroup conflict**, differences between members of one group, or from **intergroup conflict,**[11] differences between competing subgroups of an organization. For example, the marketing department might have a different goal than the finance department. Marketing folks might push to increase spending on advertising and promotion in order to improve sales, while finance folks push for increased cost-cutting efforts.

Miscommunication

Many times, personal and professional conflicts arise due to poor communication. Seldom is miscommunication intentional. More often than not, it's the result of our not taking time to clarify our understanding of something, or gender or cultural differences, or errors in semantics. Often we say one thing and mean another. Or in our haste, we speak quickly and cryptically in hopes that others know what we want. Or perhaps we speak clearly but our nonverbal communication contradicts the verbal message. Or, in the case of e-mail communication, sometimes conflict arises because e-mail doesn't permit you to "read" the other person's verbal or nonverbal cues as you might in telephone or face-to-face communication.[12] In any case, misunderstanding is likely to occur. These communication issues are further compounded by the jargon shared by and understood within specific groups of people, such as engineers and military personnel. The processes and principles of communication may also differ between work groups. For example, one group might have a division newsletter, through which employees are kept informed of important organizational changes, while another group might rely on word of mouth to spread key bits of information. This results in each group having a very different understanding of what's going on in the organization. Interaction between these groups could lead to numerous miscommunications, each one a potential source of conflict.

Differing Attitudes, Values, and Perceptions

Many conflicts are the result of differences in attitudes, values, and perceptions. Sometimes, without even realizing it, we bring feelings or concerns into an interaction that predisposes us to react in a certain way. For example, if you are afraid of dogs and encounter a neighbor with a dog while out walking one morning, you may react with fear or even hostility. Upon reflection, you realize this fear is due to a fear of animals you've had since you were a child. But the neighbor, without knowing this background, might misinterpret your strong reaction and conclude you dislike the neighbor rather than fear the dog. Without a chance to communicate—for the neighbor to share his or her perception with you and for you to explain the background behind your reaction—it is likely that you will each emerge from the interaction with a vastly different understanding of what just occurred, and with different, possibly negative, opinions of each other.

Conflicting values are a common and difficult-to-resolve source of conflict between people. Differences in religious beliefs, attitudes toward diverse others, clashes in family values, or work ethic might result in interpersonal differences that surface in the work environment. For example, a young consultant who must leave work by Friday afternoon is viewed by her colleagues as a slacker when they are left to work late on a client deliverable. The fact is she is an Orthodox Jew. Her manager knows this but her colleagues do not. In this case it would be preferable for her colleagues to be aware of her beliefs. This way the team could make accommodations for her early departure on Fridays, and she could perhaps offer to work late on Thursdays. Fear, confusion, anxiety, and hostility are common attitudes and perceptions and a frequent source of conflict between individuals and groups, and these feelings are often magnified when the individuals are demographically different. As the above example shows, these attitudes toward and perceptions about others can be long lasting and self-fulfilling. When such feelings are allowed to develop, conflict is bound to occur.

Style Differences

Another common source of conflict is differences in personal style or personality. An obvious example of this is the predictable tension between two roommates who are on different "body clocks." The early riser who gets up at dawn and the night owl who sleeps until noon are almost certain to get into conflict with each other. Conflicts likely occur between the "slob" and the "neat freak." The manager who is task-oriented and the employee who is a perpetual socializer will probably encounter much tension and conflict in their boss–subordinate relationship. In some instances differences may be attributed to gender. Some might say, for example, that some men are more likely to pursue a conflict and some women less likely to deal with conflict. Recent research, however, points to style differences rather than gender as an explanation for much of the conflict that occurs in organizations today. In her work with teams, Klenke postulates that gender does not account for differences in team decision making among senior executives. Four constructs, including conflict management style, explain an individual's effectiveness in making decisions involving conflict.[13] Personality conflicts can result in unproductive behaviors at work including gossip, jealousy, insults, taking sides or playing favorites, slowing work speed, forming cliques, and even looking for another job.

Conflict Management Strategies

Knowing what causes conflicts is half the battle. Knowing what to do when conflicts arise, as they inevitably do, comprises the other half. Those who are effective at conflict management recognize that sources of conflict (for example limited resource) will probably always be present and seek ways to live with it, minimize its effect, and manage it. When deciding on a strategy for dealing with a specific conflict, keep two factors in mind: your goals, or what you hope to accomplish through the interaction, and the importance of the relationship to you.[14]

The first consideration when selecting a strategy is assessing your goals: What personal or organizational goals are to be accomplished, and how important is it to achieve those exact goals? Remember that conflicts often exist because of opposing goals. The nature and importance of a particular set of goals for you will determine which strategy is most appropriate for the situation. The second consideration when choosing a conflict resolution strategy is the depth, quality, and duration of the relationship.

Before selecting a strategy, work through answers to the following questions:

- Is this relationship long term or passing?
- Is the relationship substantive (goes beyond business issues to more personal matters) or narrow?
- Is the relationship more important to me than the matter under discussion?
- How important is it to maintain a working or friendly relationship with those with whom I am in conflict?
- What possible ramifications will surface after the dust settles?

How you answer these questions will impact the conflict strategy you ultimately select.

Research on conflict management suggests five possible strategies based on the intersection between relationship and goal importance.[15] Figure 11–1 helps illustrate how each conflict management strategy maps with the assessed importance of the goal and the relationship. Each option has advantages and disadvantages. The appropriate option depends on your preferences and on the context of the specific situation.

- **Avoiding**—in an avoidance or withdrawing strategy, you choose not to deal with the issues or the people involved. You retreat from the situation, hoping it either goes away or resolves itself. This strategy is suitable for situations in which the issues are trivial or of only minor importance to you, when emotions are high, when you feel you have no chance of satisfying your concerns, or when others could resolve the conflict more effectively. Avoiding is dangerous if the matter under discussion requires your attention. It may resurface if not dealt with effectively. What's worse, conflicts that are set aside or ignored can fester due to lack of communication and clarification, making it

**Figure 11–1
Conflict-Handling
Strategies**

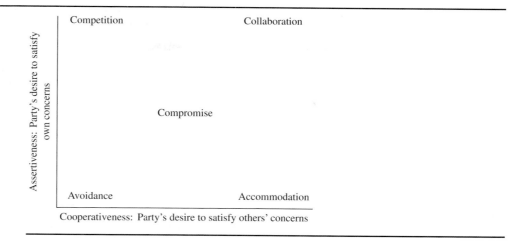

more difficult—and necessary—to address at a later time. If the conflict is one that must be addressed, save time and emotional energy by speaking up soon after the conflict is recognized. Avoidance can lead to a "lose–lose" scenario; goals may not be addressed or achieved and the relationship may not be able to progress beyond its current state.

■ **Accommodating** (smoothing)—when you use an accommodation strategy to resolve a conflict, you are more concerned with maintaining the relationship than in accomplishing a specific goal through the interaction. This strategy is appropriate when the issue is not that important to you or when harmony is of greater importance to you than "winning" on the issue. For example, if your children challenge your decision to take them to Burger King for lunch (McDonald's has the better toy this week), it's ok to give in to their wishes if both choices are equally suitable. It saves time and emotional energy, and it can be used in a later conflict negotiation ("I did what you wanted; now I want you to do . . . for me"). If you are always accommodating, as in "you win and I lose," it might signal that you are possibly sacrificing some important goals for the sake of the relationship. You might wonder why others never seem to do the same for you. Sometimes we do this because we want to be "nice" and have others like us. However, over-reliance on accommodating in conflict situations could be harmful to you and the relationship in the long term as you are likely to build up resentment over your unmet needs.

■ **Compromising**—when you compromise or "split the difference" in a conflict, you agree to give up part of your goal and part of the relationship in order to reach an agreement. This strategy is effective for achieving temporary solutions, when both parties are at a comparable level, when there are time pressures, or as a backup when collaboration or competing is neither possible nor successful. This strategy is the political equivalent of "win some, lose some." In other words, you consciously agree to accept that sometimes in the relationship you'll get your way and other times you won't. This is possible in a long-term relationship where there's time for give-and-take exchange. However, many people and groups jump to this strategy too quickly without pursuing synergy or collaboration. Perhaps it's our feelings about risk: I'm better off getting half of what I want than risking it and getting nothing. Whether this is true or appropriate depends on the situation.

■ **Competing** (forcing)—in a competing strategy, you work to achieve your goals at all costs, even if it means sacrificing the relationship. This is an "I win, you lose" strategy. Forcing may be appropriate when you have severe time restrictions, are in a crisis situation, need to issue an unpopular decision, or have to take an action that is vital to an organization's welfare. Some salespeople are guilty of forcing sales. They care about the commission they earn if they sell you a car—today—and use techniques (this is the last one [or day]; if you leave now, the deal expires) that make buyers feel pressured into the sale. More successful salespeople realize that future sales from this person and others in his or her network are likely if agreements are reached collaboratively rather than through a forcing approach. However, forcing children out on a specific path when the fire alarm rings is not only appropriate but also safer than discussing or arguing over other options.

■ **Collaborating** (integrating)—the ultimate "win–win" strategy—involves energy, commitment, and excellent skills in communication, problem solving, and negotiation. Collaboration is appropriate when there is plenty of time, when all want a solution that satisfies all parties' objectives and maintains the relationship, and when the issue is very important to all parties involved. It is also critical when the conflicting parties are responsible for implementing the solution. If you feel a solution was only partly effective or was forced on you, you will be less likely to put your heart and soul into its implementation. Coming to a consensus or finding an integrative solution takes considerable problem-solving effort and time. In collaboration, both parties don't necessarily agree, but both feel comfortable enough to express their disagreement and opinions and can work toward an optimal solution.[16]

Although collaborating or the win–win option appears to be the ideal strategy, it is not appropriate in all cases. Each of the strategies has strong and weak points. No one solution is best suited for all situations. The best managers are those who can move fluidly from one style to the next depending on the situation and circumstances. As a manager, you will find yourself using all these strategies. The choice of one over the other depends on the situation and persons involved as well as your own personality. Each of us has a style with which we're naturally most comfortable. (You'll have an opportunity to identify yours using one of the chapter exercises.) Be aware of your natural tendency and develop proficiency in using other, less comfortable styles, depending on what a situation dictates.

Figure 11–2
Gains and Losses Associated with Conflict Styles[17]

		Competition	Avoidance	Accommodation	Compromise	Collaboration
	Gains	Chance to win everything Exciting, games-manship Exercise own sense of power	No energy or time expenditure Conserve for fights that are "more important"	Little muss or fuss, no feathers ruffled Others may veiw you as supportive Energy free for other pursuits	No one returns home empty-handed "Keeps the peace" May or may not encourage creativity	Both sides win Better chance for long-term solutions Creativity in problem solving Maintains relationship New level of understanding of situation Improves quality of solution and commitment
	Losses	Chance to lose everything Alienates others Discourages others from working with you Potentially larger scale conflicts in the future (or more avoidance of conflict)	Less stimulation Less creative problem solving Little understanding of the needs of others Incomplete comprehension of work environment	Lowered self-assertion and possibly self-esteem Loss of power Absence of your unique contribution to the situation Others dependent on you may not feel you "go to bat" for them	Since neither side is totally satisfied, conflicts are likely to recur later Neither side realizes self-determination fully	Time, in the short run Loss of sense of autonomy

Tips for Managing Conflict

- *Control your temper and emotional response.* Demonstrate your respect for the other party's feelings. Validate that the conflict is real to them no matter how trivial it may seem to you.[18] Embracing conflict builds honest relationships. By validating both parties' feelings about a situation you can then move into a problem-solving mode.

- *Understand the issues.* Don't react impulsively when faced with a conflict situation. Take the time needed to fully assess the scope of the situation: the key players, the source of the conflict, the issues involved, the goals, and the dynamics of the relationship(s) involved.[19] Accept the faults of the parties involved and be willing to admit to them. Focus on changing behaviors, not people. Then select a conflict strategy from the above choices and apply it to the situation as appropriate.

- *Pick your battles.* Not all conflicts are manageable. Get all the facts before making any judgments. Choose the time and place carefully. A good manager will carefully choose the battles worth handling and select an appropriate strategy for handling them. In the same way small children bring their conflicts to grown-ups to solve, employees frequently do the same with their manager. Sometimes, in the interest of developing the skills of and relationships between employees who report to you, it's wise to determine if it is best to ignore a particular conflict so the individuals responsible for the conflict can address it.

- *Search for a common goal or ground.* Know your options, and select your best option. Attempt to work for win–win solutions that will be acceptable to both parties.[20] Do this by asking open-ended questions and demonstrating you've heard and understood others' goals or objectives. When this is not possible or time is short, try to accommodate as many of the others' interests as possible and then make the decision that is ultimately the most fair and helpful for the organization. Sometimes a compromise solution will have to suffice.

Conflict Prevention Techniques

While conflict can be healthy in an organization or relationship, it still makes sense to eliminate some sources of friction before they even begin. By effectively managing conflict, managers can gain the benefit of conflict without the costs.[21] Following are some techniques that can be used to minimize or deflect conflict.

Team Building: As organizations have gotten flatter and less hierarchical, individuals are working in teams dedicated to specific project goals. Providing training and coaching on team-building skills can reduce the amount of conflict that occurs in the team setting. Some of these skills include

- Setting clear objectives.
- Developing shared goals.
- Establishing team norms.
- Understanding the stages through which teams progress.
- Clarifying expectations.
- Planning projects and meeting deadlines.

Diversity Training: As organizations have become more diverse, individuals find themselves working more and more with people who vary in terms of background, physical ability, culture, ethnicity, gender, religious beliefs, education, economic status, sexual orientation, political view, values, goals, ideas, and knowledge base.[22] Diversity training is now offered by many large companies as a way of ensuring that employees understand the importance of differences among individuals and how to manage them effectively.[23]

This training often includes components such as these:

- Self-awareness of personal prejudices and stereotypes.
- Individual differences and how they develop.
- Valuing differences.
- Maximizing each person's strengths and capabilities to the advantage of the organization.
- Understanding and reducing discrimination.
- Legal guidelines for dealing with issues such as sexual harassment.
- Cross-training and cross-functional team training.

Open Communication: Companies are beginning to adopt more informal and personalized ways of connecting with their employees. By exchanging information freely and keeping people informed, companies find they are able to reduce some of the conflicts that arise from lack of information. Companies with open communication systems encourage:

- Regular staff meetings.
- Internal newsletters.
- Employee attitude surveys.
- 360-degree feedback (programs in which employees and managers receive performance feedback from subordinates, peers, and superiors).

Conflict Management Training: Many companies have discovered the benefits of providing their employees with training in dealing effectively with conflict. These programs teach participants to:

- Handle conflict constructively.
- Respect the legitimacy of others' points of view, feelings, and perceptions.
- Listen actively.
- Communicate assertively.
- Problem-solve collaboratively.
- Support conflict constructively.
- Help others avert unnecessary strife.
- Use communication skills to influence the way in which conflict is handled.[24]
- Anticipate and act accordingly.
- Be aware of potential problems and deal with them while they are still minor.[25]

Resource Allocation: As long as resources need to be shared among various departments within an organization, conflict will be a part of organizational life. While some conflict can be healthy and constructive, conflict also has negative side effects. Unresolved and continuous conflict can lower productivity and morale and lead to high turnover. One technique effective managers use to reduce the possible effects of negative conflict is to seek new ways in which resources can be obtained and allocated. If internal resources can be increased or reallocated, the number of win–lose situations is likely to drop. Of course, it still might not be possible to increase resources sufficiently to allow all parties to become winners. Related to this issue is the process by which resources are allocated. The more secretive this process, the greater the likelihood that organizational members will perceive inequity and take steps to reduce it. To the degree possible, organizations should establish rewards at the highest level—to encourage collaboration across departments and units—and involve key players in resource allocation decision processes to increase the fairness and effectiveness of these decisions.

The techniques just described focus primarily on what managers can do in their organizations to reduce sources and consequences of conflict. Following are a few additional techniques that individuals can use when interacting with others in a personal or professional setting.

Communication: Two communication techniques helpful for avoiding conflicts are using "I" language and paying attention to nonverbal cues. When we say things like "you just don't understand," or "your idea will never work," we put others on the defensive. They feel attacked and strike back, causing conflict to escalate. Take responsibility for your communication—"I'm not sure I've clearly stated my objection," or "I have a concern about the marketing part of this plan. Can we discuss this?"—and conflicts are less likely to occur.

On the other hand, there are times when we add to conflict by communicating. We flame the fires by paying too much attention to issues that would be better dealt with via the reinforcement technique of "extinction," providing no reinforcement at all by simply ignoring the event. Much as we would prefer this to be the case, things don't always get better by communicating openly. Sometimes it's best simply to express your opinion, "agree to disagree," and table the matter.

Managing Others' Expectations: Two techniques worth mentioning are setting limits and communicating consequences. Imagine your boss provides you with yet another project. You can do it, for sure, but not today, or this week for that matter. At least not with everything else on your plate. Most managers can't read minds. If you won't be able to complete the project when and how it is expected, let your boss know now instead of waiting until a critical deadline has passed. Setting limits—"I'm happy to do this project, but I need to let you know that the other project you wanted me to do will have to be placed on hold"—can help manage your boss's expectations and avoid a future conflict. Similar to setting limits, sometimes we need to communicate consequences. Returning to the lazy teammate scenario, realize that saying nothing is akin to approving this behavior. If you've tried reasoning, clarifying the issue, and asserting the team's needs but nothing has changed, it may be time to use consequences. "We've tried several times to get you to do what we've asked. If your part of the project is not up to the standards we've agreed to by Friday, we're going to ask the team leader to have you reassigned off the team."

Focusing on Others First: Often when we disagree with another person, we rush to explain why our ideas are superior. Like "you" language, this tendency can motivate others to defend themselves. One effective technique for preventing conflict involves anticipating another's disagreement or objection and explaining how your proposal takes this issue into account. "I know you're concerned about *x*, so let me tell you how I think this can be overcome." Even helpful advice could be taken the wrong way, implying that the listener is performing ineffectively. When you are looking to change or improve organizational processes, consider first how others might benefit from the change. Since most people dislike change, you can increase their willingness to listen to your idea if they feel doing so can benefit them and their organization. You can avoid conflicts by appealing to another's self-interest; for example, "I know that the current reimbursement process works. However, if we can reduce the number of approval signatures needed, you'll reduce time spent on your inbox and show us that you trust us to act appropriately."

Summary

Conflict is inevitable. People are unique and have different interests, goals, perspectives, values, and needs. For this reason, conflict can and does occur. Not all conflict is dysfunctional; some conflict can actually increase innovation, creativity, and the bond between conflicting parties. Practicing conflict prevention techniques can help you eliminate or diffuse conflicts before they surface. By knowing likely sources of conflict and appropriate strategies for dealing with different types of conflict, you can manage your response to conflict and improve your interactions with others.

Key Terms and Concepts

Accommodating

Avoiding

Collaborating

Competing

Compromising

Conflict

Human relations view (of conflict)

Interactionist view (of conflict)

Intergroup conflict

Intragroup conflict

Negative conflict

Positive conflict

Traditional view (of conflict)

Endnotes

1. James H. Keil, "Coaching through Conflict," *Dispute Resolution Journal,* May–June 2000, pp. 65–69.

2. Stephen Robbins, *Organizational Behavior,* 8th ed. (Upper Saddle, NJ: Prentice Hall, 1998), pp. 435–36.

3. Kathleen M. Eisenhardt, Jean L. Kahwajy, and L. F. Bourgeois III, "How Management Teams Can Have a Good Fight," *Harvard Business Review,* July–August 1997, p. 77.

4. Alfred Fleishman, "Going Back a Little Bit," *St. Louis Business Journal,* Jan. 3, 2000, p. 29.

5. F. Rees, *How to Lead Work Teams* (San Diego: Pfeiffer, 1991).

6. Jeri Darling and Diane Russ, "Relationship Capital," *Executive Excellence,* May 2000, p. 14.

7. Shari Caudron, "Productive Conflict Has Value," *Workforce,* Feb. 1999, p. 25.

8. Personnel Decisions International, "Five Steps to Mediating Conflict," *Workforce,* Oct. 1999, p. 30.

9. Michael Barrier, "Putting a Lid on Conflicts," *Nation's Business,* April 1998, p. 34.

10. John S. Morgan, revised by Beth Z. Schneider, *Interpersonal Skills for the Manager,* Fifth ed. (Institute of Certified Professional Managers, 2000), pp. 139–45.

11. J. K. Barge, *Leadership Communication Skills for Organizations and Groups* (New York: St. Martin's Press, 1994).

12. Raymond A. Friedman and Steven C. Currall, "Conflict Escalation: Dispute Exacerbating Elements of E-mail Communication," *Human Relations* 56, no. 11 (Nov. 2003), p. 1325.

13. Karin Klenke, "Gender Influences in Decision-making Processes in Top Management Teams," *Management Decision* 41, no. 10 (2003), p. 1024.

14. David Johnson, *Reaching Out,* 6th ed. (Boston: Allyn and Bacon, 1997), p. 240.

15. Kenneth Thomas, "Conflict and Conflict Management," in *Handbook of Industrial and Organizational Psychology* (Chicago: Rand McNally, 1976), pp. 889–935.

16. Shari Caudron, "Keeping Team Conflict Alive," *Training and Development,* Sept. 1998, p. 48.

17. Adapted from work of Ronald Fry, Jared Florian, and Jacquie McLemore, Department of Organizational Behavior, Weatherhead School of Management, Case Western Reserve University, Cleveland, Ohio, 1984.

18. Ted Pollock, "When Conflict Rears Its Head: A Personal File of Stimulating Ideas, Little Known Facts and Daily Problem Solvers," *Supervision,* Oct. 1999, p. 24.

19. Ed Rigsbee, "Conflict Management and Resolution," *Business Forms, Labels and Systems,* Feb. 20, 2000, p. 62.

20. Robert F. Pearce, "Developing Your Career Skills," *Compensation and Benefits Management,* Winter 2000, p. 15.

21. Allen C. Amason, "Distinguishing the Effects of Functional and Dysfunctional Conflict on Strategic Decision Making: Resolving a Paradox for Top Management Teams," *Academy of Management Journal* 39, no. 1, pp. 123–48.

22. Scott Sedam, "Why Muddle through Conflict?" *Builder,* June 1999, p. 148.

23. Caudron, "Keeping Team Conflict Alive."

24. Joseph Eby Ruin, "Six Factors in Conflict Management," *New Press Times,* June 14, 1997, p. 1-EX.

25. Pollock, "When Conflict Rears Its Head."

Exercise 11–A
Conflict Case Study

Case Study

My boss and I are having some interpersonal problems. There are several things that he does that I find really annoying. To start, he is not considerate of my employees or me. I often find myself thinking that I would be reluctant to do the things he does around me that annoy me. Yet he's my boss so what can I do? He comes in late to the office, after my co-workers and I have been working for a while and have our day planned. Inevitably he'll come in, interrupt, and lay on us a whole new set of priorities for the day. To be fair, he does stay late (we have flextime in our office) and he has a good reason to be late—he has child care responsibilities to fulfill on school mornings. But his habit of coming in and interrupting the schedule for our day is really off-putting. By the time I've listened to his concerns, reprioritized my and my staff's work, and gotten back on track, it's almost lunchtime and I feel I've wasted almost a half day trying to respond to his concerns. I'm afraid to confront him—he's a good guy and it would only put him on the defensive. And wouldn't really change anything. But I'm also tired of not feeling productive. I just wish he would be a little more sensitive to our situation and be better organized and more aware of our time constraints. Is that asking too much?

1. What is your immediate reaction to the scenario? How would you feel if you were the person writing about this situation?
2. How could this situation have been avoided?
3. What approaches to resolving this conflict are appropriate?
4. What are some things that, if done, would make this approach successful?
5. What are some things to avoid when attempting to resolve this conflict? Why?

Exercise 11–B
Conflict Role-Plays

In small groups, role-play one or more of the following scenarios. Perform them in the small group or in front of the large group or class. For each scenario acted out, analyze and discuss the following:

- What strategies were used?
- What attitudes were depicted?
- What worked and why?
- What didn't and why?

Scenarios

1. One of your co-workers is accepting gifts from a supplier; this is forbidden by your company's policy.
2. Two of your employees are unable to agree on anything in staff meetings.
3. You think one of your employees is harassing another employee sexually.
4. You think a fellow swimmer is cheating in competitions.
5. You and your roommate disagree over how clean to keep the apartment.

**Exercise 11–C
Conflict Assessment**

1. Briefly describe one conflict situation in which you found yourself recently (in the past couple of years). What were the reasons for and outcomes of this conflict? _____

_____

_____

_____

_____

2. Using the five conflict styles discussed in this chapter, describe the style you used in resolving the conflict discussed in number 1, pointing to specific behaviors and communication patterns that are evidence of this style. In what ways was this style effective and/or ineffective in this situation? _____

_____

_____

_____

_____

3. What style did the person with whom you were in conflict use? Evidence? In what ways was she or he effective and/or ineffective in this situation? _____

_____

_____

_____

_____

4. If you could replay this scenario, what things would you do the same, and why; what things would you have done differently, and why? _____

_____

_____

_____

_____

5. What conflict style are you most comfortable using? Why? _____

_____

_____

_____

_____

**Exercise 11–D
Humpty Dumpty's
Spaceship Challenge**

In teams of three to six, create a spaceship for Humpty Dumpty (an egg) that can withstand the gravitational forces that occur during a three-foot drop. The spaceship that withstands the highest drop will be the winner. If there is a tie, then the winner will be the spaceship fabricated out of the greatest number of materials. Each spaceship must be fabricated out of at least three materials. Each team only has possession of one material, so you will need to negotiate with other teams to acquire new materials.

Your team will have 10 minutes to plan your spaceship design. Decide what material your spaceship will be made from and determine which teams you will need to negotiate with for materials.

Next, your team will have 20 minutes to negotiate material and construct the spaceship. Negotiate as effectively as you possibly can; use any strategies or tactics.

Questions

1. Before approaching your opponents, how did you prepare for the negotiation process?
2. Did you use the same conflict-handling styles for all opponents that you negotiated with? Explain.
3. In this situation, which conflict-handling styles were most successful? Why?
4. Did every negotiation work out exactly as you planned and hoped? Why or why not?
5. What factors helped you in the negotiation process? What could you have done differently to make your negotiations more successful?
6. In performing this exercise, what lessons did you learn about negotiation? How does this exercise relate to negotiations in the "real world"?

Source: Used with permission of the author, Kim Eddleston, doctoral student, University of Connecticut, Storrs, CT. This exercise was presented at the 2000 Eastern Academy of Management/Experiential Learning Association Conference.

**Exercise 11–E
Reflection/Action Plan**

This chapter focused on conflict management—what it is, why it is important, and how to improve your skills in this area. Complete the worksheet below upon completing all reading and experiential activities for this chapter.

1. The one or two areas in which I am most strong are:

2. The one or two areas in which I need more improvement are:

3. If I did only one thing to improve in this area, it would be to:

4. Making this change would probably result in:

5. If I did not change or improve in this area, it would probably affect my personal and professional life in the following ways:

12 Achieving Business Results through Effective Meetings

Learning Points

How do I:
- Decide whether a meeting is necessary?
- Invite the appropriate people to a meeting?
- Get everyone prepared for the meeting?
- Keep meetings from exceeding the agreed-upon time allocation?
- Keep the meeting running smoothly?
- Keep team members on task during meetings?
- Ensure the next meeting will be effective?

Paul Atkins sold luxury new and preowned vehicles at a dealership on the East Coast. The money was pretty good, but there were some aspects of the job that always left him wondering what else he should do with his time and talents. One thing he hated was the hours—salespeople were typically scheduled for a minimum of 50 hours per week. This was especially bothersome since many hours, if not days, would go by with not a single customer walking in the showroom. Added to the boredom was another problem—the Monday morning all-hands sales meeting.

Going to a meeting wouldn't be so bad if it was useful. But this was rarely, if ever, the case. Ted, the general sales manager, would seemingly decide what he would do for the half-hour meeting on his way in. Some weeks he couldn't decide on an objective for the meeting (or chose instead to play golf), and the meeting was canceled—without notice to anyone. Other weeks, most participants left feeling their time was wasted. Paul, who sold only Mercedes and other European imports, would sit through videos on the Toyota Corolla—a car that the dealership next door, owned by the same person, sold. Still other times, the meetings were focused on selling techniques, some of which were about as archaic as you can imagine. Yet everyone was required to be there, even salespeople who were off or not scheduled to begin their day until noon (the dealership was open 9 A.M. to 9 P.M. Monday through Friday and until 6 P.M. on Saturdays).

When the European import dealership got its own sales manager (who reported to the general sales manager), the salespeople were relieved, believing that they would no longer have to waste their time at the Monday morning meetings. Unfortunately, that was not the case. In fact, the sales manager and the general sales manager frequently butt heads on this issue. After two successive weeks of last-minute meeting cancellations, the

European import car staff decided enough was enough. They boycotted the meetings.
Eventually, the general sales manager put pressure on the sales manager and made them
attend.

1. Many organizations have standing meetings. What benefits could be obtained from these meetings?

2. What are some potential downsides of a standing meeting?

3. Who should be required to come to the "all-hands meeting"? If you answer "it depends," on what should this depend?

4. Assuming the general sales manager is unwilling to change this requirement, what would you recommend he do to improve the meetings?

5. When you rate a meeting you've attended as "useless" or just "bad," what characteristics of the meeting caused this rating?

6. When caught up in a "bad" meeting, what are some things you can do to improve the situation?

M eetings are an important part of the business world. Meetings occur within organizations and between members of different organizations, for example, customers and suppliers. Managers use meetings to share necessary information and to train and coordinate efforts of their employees. Project teams, either school- or work-based, use meetings to set objectives, allocate resources, make decisions, schedule individual components of complex projects, discuss project progress, share needed information and status reports to ensure all are "on the same page," and solve problems. Many firms and campuses even have the capability for **virtual meetings,** where members are not physically in the same place but are connected via video conferencing technology or e-mail. In this chapter we discuss the importance of meetings, the how-tos of running effective meetings, and tips and suggestions for making the most of meetings. At the end of the chapter is a series of exercises and activities to help you assess and enhance your skill in running meetings.

Types of "Virtual" Meetings

- Video conferences
- Chat groups
- Conference phone calls
- Meetings via e-mail
- Project intranets and extranets

The Importance and Benefits of Meetings

Meetings serve an important function. In the increasingly complex and competitive business environment, members of a team or organization need to be kept abreast of critical functional, political, technological, and legal issues facing the firm. This becomes especially important in an empowered and team-based environment. When more work and decision making is being spread to team members and employees at all levels of the organization, meetings are used to ensure good decisions are made and others are kept apprised of progress and problems.[1] The need for meetings typically increases as the number of teams and team-based projects increases.

Meetings are important in shaping organizational norms and improving work processes. Companies that focus on continuous process improvement find meetings to be an excellent way to train managers and develop shared norms about how to behave and act.[2] Meetings also play a psychological role in organizations. Meetings are a way to fulfill our need to be a part of a team, providing a sense of togetherness and trust.[3]

Finally, meetings are important when members are involved in complex projects, with multiple deadlines and sets of objectives. The project meeting is an essential tool for keeping projects—and project team members—on track.[4] Most project groups, even those that are exceptionally organized and managed, function best with a regular series of contacts between group members. "Virtual" (online, video- or phone-conference) meetings have their place, but most project groups benefit from regular face-to-face meetings to monitor progress, exchange information, make decisions, and build team cohesion.

Problems with Meetings

"A committee is twelve men doing the work of one man."

John F. Kennedy

This quote underscores a common question contemplated by students and employees alike, namely, "Wouldn't it be easier to fly solo?" A recent study found that in the average eight-person committee, each individual member wished that three of the other seven weren't there.[5] And according to a *Harvard Business Review* study, the average executive spends three and a half hours weekly in formal committee meetings and at least a day each week in informal meetings and consultations.[6] Some suggest this figure is understated—that meetings take up more than half of executives' working hours.[7] As you climb higher on the corporate ladder, meetings become more frequent and lengthier.[8] A survey of middle managers showed the top three reasons for failed meetings: they get off subject, they lack agendas or goals, and they last too long.[9]

A big cause of ineffective or useless meetings is the lack of preparation and planning. How many times have you walked into a meeting having no idea what the meeting was about or why it was called? Perhaps it's a standing meeting, as in the case of the all-hands meeting chronicled in the opening scenario. Perhaps you have a general idea of what to expect; after all, it's always been done this way. For example, it may present the weekly status report, provide a pep talk, or communicate the sales objective. In either case, meetings are doomed to fail when participants (and the person calling the meeting) neither know what to expect nor what to prepare for a meeting.

Have you ever come to a meeting only to find it's been canceled, rescheduled, or moved to another room? What if the goal of the meeting is to discuss complicated technical information, yet no one received any reports or documentation ahead of time? Valuable time is wasted getting individuals up to speed. More time still is wasted when the goal of the meeting—plus any previous decisions made—is not or has not been clearly communicated. If you walk into a meeting and can't answer the question "Why am I here?" within the first few minutes, this meeting will probably not be optimal. If you meet because you've always met, that may not be a sufficient reason to have a meeting. What is the point of meeting? What do you want attendees to think, do, or feel as a result of the meeting?[10] If there is simple information to transmit to a group of employees, a meeting may not be the best use of everyone's time. For example, if human resources decides to add another provider to the list of HMOs currently available through employees' health benefits plan, this information could be transmitted easily via a paper memo. If, however, human resources is leading a charge to modify the current performance appraisal and merit pay system toward one that accounts for not only individual performance but also individuals' contributions in the many teams in which they work, a memo would likely be insufficient.

Meetings may be unnecessary and even costly, in terms of employees' time and productivity taken away from other tasks and objectives. Work becomes more complicated when you have to interact with others. You're probably not alone if you've felt that you could do the work assigned to your group more easily alone than as one of five or six people working together on a project.

**Figure 12–1
Strategies for
Effective Meetings**[11]

The Four P's of Effective Meetings	
Purpose	Determine if a meeting must be held Decide what the objective or outcomes of the meeting should be
Participants	Determine the appropriate size and the composition of the participants Consider the skills, knowledge base, and background of the participants Have a balance of task and process oriented members
Plan	Make logistical arrangements: time, place, equipment needs, visual aids, space Prepare and circulate an agenda Consult with participants before the meeting Decide on decision-making process
Process	Begin with review of past progress and clarify purpose of the meeting Establish ground rules Use visuals (flipchart or board) and denote progress and ideas Summarize meeting's accomplishments and review assignments

Source: From David A. Whetten and Kim S. Cameron, *Developing Management Skills*, 4th Edition, © 1998. Reprinted by permission of Pearson Education, Inc., Upper Saddle River, NJ.

There are several explanations for this.

■ First, there's the issue of interpersonal dynamics. When we work with others, our uniquenesses—work style, personality, preferences, values, and attitudes—often clash with those of others. Others may have important information to offer, but if they're combative, overly analytical, or just plain critical, you might prefer they just send the needed information via interoffice mail!

■ Second, the more people involved in making a decision, especially a consensus decision, the more time it takes. Despite the benefit of others' input and the existence of **synergy**—the belief that two heads are better than one[12]—some wonder whether the costs (individuals' time and energy) overshadow the benefits.

■ Third, there may be redundancies of people and effort. Someone might wonder, "If other members of my group are represented, why must I be here too?"

These three reasons underlie why meetings are the source of frustration and loss of work time[13]—an increasingly valuable resource. In one study, 70 percent of American executives surveyed considered many of the meetings they attend to be a waste of time.[14] Given the preponderance of poorly planned and executed meetings, it is easy to see why many view meetings as a necessary evil. Not surprisingly, the lack of a clear objective or purpose is a main reason for failed meetings, as evidenced by 89 percent of American executives who blame meeting failure on lack of proper planning and organization.[15]

If managed effectively, however, meetings can be useful for dispensing or gathering information, building morale, making decisions, creative brainstorming, and encouraging group action.[16] As much as we might want to be left alone to do our work, many of us appreciate being in the fold—knowing what's going on and being involved in decisions and problem-solving efforts. Meetings don't have to be a waste of time or necessarily evil. By learning a few principles and practicing several techniques, meetings can be more efficient, productive, and possibly even enjoyable.

Strategies for Effective Meetings

Before the Meeting

The first principle in running effective meetings is clarifying the purpose. Whether or not a meeting should be held depends on the goal to be achieved. Employee input should be sought, and discussions—at multiple levels and parts of the organizations—need to occur.

Clarify the Purpose of the Meeting

Legitimate purposes for calling a meeting include generating ideas for a project, discussing the pros and cons of potential solutions to a problem, gaining employee input and buy-in for a program or company point of view, or deciding on a strategy or course of action.[17] By clarifying the purpose or goal of a potential meeting, you will be able to determine whether the objective could be accomplished just as easily in a memo, e-mail, or article in the weekly newsletter. Consider whether the potential benefits of getting members together outweigh the costs.[18]

Evaluate whether a meeting should be held based on its stated purpose. Even if this evaluation is made, don't assume that invitees know the purpose unless it has been clearly articulated before (and clarified during) a meeting. To say, "to have our all-staff sales meeting," is not clear enough, especially when this is a standing meeting. Without a clear understanding of why there's a meeting and how they can contribute, employees waste time contemplating the purpose and reason for being at a meeting instead of doing their normal work. Worse still, when a meeting is held without a clear, stated purpose, discussions meander about endlessly and with minimal if any closure. To ensure a successful meeting, decide on a clear achievable task[19] and communicate it before the meeting begins. This task should support a project or task team's overall objective, which could come from management, the team members, or a combination thereof.

Four General Types of Meetings

■ **Information Sharing**—several or all members share gathered information or report status on group or individual progress. For example, a team designing a new minivan may include members from engineering, manufacturing, marketing, quality assurance, and legal. Subcommittees tasked with specific goals (e.g., gather data on consumer satisfaction, quality tests) may be asked to update the rest of the team on their findings to ensure the group that the subcommittees are on track as well as to furnish the entire group with information needed for group decisions. These meetings tend to be relatively short, in that the purpose is to share information and not solve problems or make decisions.

■ **Information Dissemination**—used when critical information must be conveyed and shared with members. Typically, such information is too important for a memo and may require more in-depth explanation or discussion, as in the case of introducing a new reward system. Information dissemination meetings focus primarily on relaying information to the members or employees, with some time allocated to address the audience's questions and ensure they have a full and clear understanding of the information.

■ **Problem Solving/Decision Making**—employees or members are assembled to solve a problem or make a decision. In contrast with the information dissemination meeting, a problem-solving meeting typically requires full participation of all members present, particularly if the outcome or disposition of the problem affects them. You might also include subject matter experts—those who have specific knowledge in a related area but may not be a member of the group that is meeting. Because of the time needed to make well-informed, consensus decisions, it's important to carve out sufficient time for this type of meeting. Decision-making meetings require more time than information-sharing meetings.

■ **Symbolic/Social**—used to celebrate a special event or share recognition for a job well done. When long-time or key employees retire, for example, it would be appropriate to invite those people with whom they have worked to recognize the retiree's contributions publicly. Or perhaps one of the customer service teams just completed one year of complaint-free service. A meeting or social event may be just the thing to recognize this accomplishment. Finally, meetings could be valuable when social interactions are needed and encouraged. One example is the holiday meeting or party. Another example is the case when two firms merge. It would be easy for each firm to continue operating autonomously (while gossiping about "the other guys" behind closed doors). However, if one of the reasons behind the merger is to gain synergy, it behooves the merged firm to encourage the kind of interaction that will increase trust and lead to cooperation among employees of the previously separate firms.

Decide Who Should Participate in the Meeting

The second principle for running effective meetings is to spend time considering who needs to be at a meeting. Whom do we invite? The answer: those who can best contribute to the objective.[20] Returning to our opening case, if all you are planning to do is show a video and hand out updated brochures, perhaps all 40 salespeople should come. But if the purpose of the meeting is to get employees to generate creative ideas, 40 may be too many people. For this type of activity, the optimal size would be between 5 and 7, and no more than 10.[21] Breaking up the group into four or five smaller groups, or having several smaller meetings, may better serve your purpose.

What if your top salesperson can't attend the meeting? Should you have the meeting anyway? If part of the meeting is being used to share and discuss sales tips and techniques, it might be best to postpone the meeting or, if deemed necessary and cost-effective, use videoconferencing to include a key person if he or she is in a different location.

What about support staff and people from a business function such as finance? Again, this depends on the purpose and intended benefit for those who attend. If the receptionist is interested and feels he can contribute based on his experience with call-in customers, perhaps support staff should come. Multiple perspectives can help; they can also lead to communication challenges. Other considerations in answering the "whom to invite" question are organizational politics, need for objectivity, and potential for problems.[22] Sometimes individuals are invited to meetings for political reasons; for instance, because they hold a particular title or have access to other important individuals in the organization. However, their presence could stifle lower-level employees' creativity. Evaluate the trade-off, and consider whether a one-on-one meeting with the politically connected individual would do the trick.

Another consideration is the need for objectivity. Sometimes it is effective, depending on the meeting's purpose, to have outsiders come to the meeting. While they might not be directly affected by the meeting's outcome, they may be able to offer valuable, unbiased, and novel perspectives to the group. Finally, consider potential problems that may result from or during the meeting. For example, consider the company "troublemakers." These are the individuals who have a knack for stirring up the pot needlessly or turning every issue into a power struggle. Perhaps their perspective is valuable, but the way in which they share it is not. If possible, you might want to exclude these persons from the meeting but schedule a time to meet with them one-on-one.

Inviting the right people—those who have a stake in the outcome or who own the problem, those affected by the outcome, subject matter experts, problem solvers, and idea people[23]—helps ensure that the purpose is served and time-wasting diversions are minimized. For example, if you suspect that the meeting's objective and discussion centers on financial impacts, you might invite representatives from accounting or finance and meet them in advance to gain insight into their attitudes, opinions, or hidden agendas.[24] In addition, it is a good idea to know the participants ahead of time. If you know that Mary in accounting has experience in a particular industry and that her insights would be valuable if shared, you can plan when and how to solicit that input should she not share without prodding.

Develop a Plan for the Meeting

Next, develop plans that will ensure the success of the meeting. First, create and distribute an **agenda** or specific plan for the meeting. The meeting agenda (see Figure 12–2 for a guide) clarifies the goal and lists the points of discussion and their priority for the meeting. A well-defined agenda spells out the tasks, estimated time allocated to each task, the decisions to be made, and expected outcomes or deliverables.[25] It also includes logistical information, such as where and when the meeting will be held and the roles individuals will play.

Circulating a specific agenda to invitees prior to the meeting is important, but it's also important to be flexible about potential changes. By soliciting their input on potential additions or modifications to the agenda, you can increase participants' ownership in the meeting and its purpose.

In planning the meeting and preparing the agenda, decide on a time and place that is likely to suit the schedules and needs of the invited participants. If manufacturing is typically busy with month-end inventory, it might be best to wait a week, if possible, to ensure manufacturing can and will participate in a meeting in which their input is necessary. If you are planning a lengthy planning or team-building meeting, for example

Figure 12–2
Sample Agenda

Start and End Time: _____
Place: _____

Stage one (# of minutes): _____

- Clarify objective
- Agenda overview, vision and goal clarification
- Introduction of members and facilitator

Stage two (# of minutes): _____

- Review of last meeting's minutes
- Review of roles for today's meeting
    - Facilitator—
    - Timekeeper—
    - Scribe—
    - Other—
- Set ground rules or operating guidelines
- Continuing business
    - Progress reports from committees, etc.
    - Activity goals and deadlines
- New business
    - Information to be shared
    - Decisions to be made

Stage three (# of minutes): _____

- Review accomplishments
- Summarize

Stage four (# of minutes): _____

- Process check
- Preparation for the next meeting
    - Action items
    - Roles, next agenda
    - Time and place verification
- Future meeting

a half-day or full-day session, you might want to consider having the meeting at another location to minimize distraction and interruptions. Based on the purpose of the meeting, select a site that has adequate space, visual tools, and resources (e.g., copy machine, clerical staff). Select a temperature (a little cooler is better than too warm), seating arrangement (discussions are best when all participants can see one another), and schedule (i.e., include breaks and beverages) that will facilitate lively participation.[26] Include specific directions and a meeting location phone number to ensure everyone makes the meeting—and on time.

During the Meeting

"Be sincere . . . be brief . . . be seated."

Theodore Roosevelt

Pay Attention to Process

When you preside over a meeting, your role is to make the discussion lively, proactive, creative, and focused. To make this happen, think of the meeting as a collection of tasks or services—communicating, facilitating, documenting[27]—and consider who can assist you in performing those services. The more you do to control the meeting, the more other participants will look to you for this control. Instead, encourage the participants to take an active part in contributing to and controlling the meeting. There are many ways you can do this during the meeting. To simplify matters, we'll divide the meeting into four stages,[28] shown in the meeting flowchart process that follows.

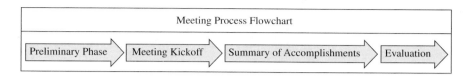

Meeting Process Flowchart

Preliminary Phase → Meeting Kickoff → Summary of Accomplishments → Evaluation

1. The **preliminary or initial phase.** In the first few minutes of the meeting, clearly articulate the meeting purpose and objectives. Then proceed with a general overview of the agenda to set the tone and give members a feel for how the meeting will be conducted. Next, explain why the participants were selected and invited to the meeting. These three steps help establish clear expectations for what will occur.[29] If members do not know one another, briefly allow members to introduce themselves and the department for which they work.

2. Meeting kickoff or the heart of the meeting. If a group of individuals will be meeting on a regular basis, it is important that they establish operating guidelines, or the standard or set of norms to which they will be held, collectively. Operating guidelines are the rules of engagement for meetings.

These guidelines establish how meetings should be run, how members will interact, and what kind of behavior is acceptable.[30] A sample set of operating guidelines appears in Figure 12–3. While some of the guidelines may sound like common sense or common courtesy, the fact that the group collectively believes in and articulates the importance of starting and ending meetings on time and not interrupting others makes the implied explicit. It also gives members the ability to "call each other" on behaviors that violate the operating guidelines and therefore undermine the group's ability to effectively operate and achieve its goals. After the guidelines are created, post them where members can see them. By helping the group establish operating guidelines, you help create common expectations among members, encourage desirable behavior, and enhance the group's ability to be self-managing.[31] Good managers not only plan and run effective meetings, they also teach and encourage their employees to do the same.

Encouraging individuals to perform meeting roles also facilitates self-management. Early in the meeting (or in the previous meeting), establish who will play which role—scribe, timekeeper, facilitator, or meeting leader. Typically, groups rotate these roles so that all members develop each of these skills. The recorder or scribe publicly takes notes—using a flip chart or white board—on issues discussed, key decisions made, and action items assigned. The timekeeper keeps track of the time as it relates to the agenda and reminds the group when it is about to exceed the agreed-upon time allotment for a particular topic or discussion. The group should then decide whether the time should be extended (and for how long) or the discussion tabled for a future meeting. The meeting

---

**Figure 12–3
Sample Operating
Guidelines**

- We will use an agenda, timekeeper, and meeting leader for each meeting.
- Meetings will start on time (with a review of the agenda) and end on time (with a process check), unless there is team consensus to extend it.
- Team members who have been absent or tardy must take measures to "get up to speed."
- Team members will practice active listening.
- It is OK to talk about/address the inappropriate use of power by team members.
- A time-out can be called if the meeting is off track or otherwise ineffective.
- Items identified as sensitive will be kept confidential.
- Silence by team members indicates a need for further inquiry.
- The meeting's facilitator should remain neutral but may formally step out of the role to contribute to the discussion.

leader is tasked with keeping the discussion task oriented and in line with the agenda. The facilitator helps ensure that participation is balanced, communication is effective, and the process is smooth. Many problems are avoided when members take responsibility for using these meeting roles.[32]

The purpose of the meeting is what the team is attempting to accomplish. The process describes how members go about their task. Do members yell and scream when they don't get their way? Do they belittle others who offer opposing views? Does the group go off on tangents, discussing items that are neither important nor on the agenda?

Some Meeting Process Suggestions

■ Encourage the clash of ideas, not personalities. One way to do this is alternate pros and cons. After hearing a proponent's views on a subject, ask for any other or opposing views.[33]

■ Maintain focus and stick to time frames. When appropriate, stick to the agenda—it's the plan to which all members agreed. While there are times when unforeseeable issues arise between meetings and must be addressed at the meeting, it is important to bring the potentially divergent discussion to the attention of the group and check whether adjustments should be made. If the group decides that an issue is important but does not require immediate discussion, make use of a "parking lot" or a visual bin (such as a piece of newsprint on a blackboard) where issues are collected and stored for future use. Alternatively, you can ask the scribe to record the issue under "next meeting." By taking one of these steps, as opposed to just noting an issue's irrelevance, you demonstrate to the person who suggested that idea that it was heard, noted, is important to the group, and will be discussed in the next meeting or handled outside of the meeting.[34]

3. The **summary of accomplishments** or wrap-up stage. In this stage, the team leader—with the help of the scribe's notes—will review decisions made and summarize the key points discussed. This can be done during the meeting, as you move through and complete agenda items, as well as near the end of the meeting. By summarizing each point before moving to the next item, you help ensure that everyone is in agreement, members remain focused, and the scribe takes clear meeting notes.[35] By summarizing at the end, you allow another opportunity for clarification or agreement, help bring closure to the meeting, and clarify the group's accomplishments. Knowing you've completed all or most of the agenda items often gives group members a sense of satisfaction.

4. **Evaluation** and closing remarks. This step is often missed in meetings and could negatively impact future meetings. First, determine whether the meeting objective has been met. One way to do this is by having members do a **process check.** Each person might share a comment or two on how she or he felt about what was accomplished and how it was accomplished. What did the team do well? For example, "We got through all our items, we kept focused, and we came to agreement on a tough issue." What can the team do better next time? One person may note that despite all that was accomplished, he felt his input wasn't valued when he was frequently interrupted. Another may note that the meeting lasted longer than the agreed-upon hour. By having an opportunity to air concerns like these, issues are more likely to be nipped in the bud before they escalate into full-blown conflicts. If the person who didn't feel valued didn't say so, and if no one else noticed and addressed the interrupting behavior, this person is likely to dislike the group, find ways to avoid coming to the meeting, or give the appearance that she or he is on track while secretly planning to sabotage the team's efforts. Process checks also tend to minimize the need for the meeting after the meeting. These are the impromptu, out-in-the-hallway, or in-the-bathroom exchanges in which real feelings and issues are discussed. Again, these processes may undermine the team's objective by weakening the trust and confidence members have in each other's ability and desire to achieve the objective.

**Figure 12–4
Meeting Behaviors**

Encourage	Discourage
Listening	Talking too much; dominating
Supporting	Criticizing
Staying on track/timekeeping	Sidetracking/getting off track
Encouraging discussion	Shutting people down or out
Posing solutions	Complaining
Taking and sharing notes	Relying on memory and rehashing decisions made previously
Clarifying	Proceeding without asking questions

After the process check, plan the next meeting. While the discussion and decisions are fresh, decide what should be covered in the next meeting, as well as the logistics of when, and where, and meeting roles. If parking lot items neither made it to the current or next meeting, capture their contents in a section known as "future meetings" or "future action outside of these meetings." At this point, review the action items. Will there be sufficient time to complete them? Should resources be made available to the actionee? Bring closure to these items to ensure that members are sufficiently prepared for the next meeting. Figure 12–4 summarizes some meeting behaviors to encourage and discourage.

After the Meeting and between Meetings

By following the tips and techniques we've shared, you're likely to plan and run meetings that are effective in accomplishing the objectives you've set. Follow-up after the meeting and before the next meeting is essential in maintaining effective meetings and active progress toward the group's goals.[36]

To maximize the group's effectiveness, consider implementing the following after- or between-meeting strategies:

■ Immediately after the meeting, *have the minutes* (summary of key points and decisions) and *next meeting agenda typed up and distributed* in advance of the next meeting. Request that members review these immediately to ensure accuracy and again just before the next meeting to be prepared for and ready to contribute to the next meeting.

■ As appropriate, *send out checkpoint memos or e-mails,* especially if external team issues may impact the team's objective or ability to achieve the goals set. Offer support resources for actionees, such as whom they might contact or where they might get certain information.

■ Make sure members have *phone, fax, and e-mail lists of all members.* When things come up that may preclude someone's attendance, contacting other members of the team should be easy. Also, by having the list, members are able to contact others for clarification or assistance with action items.

■ If appropriate, *use the time between meetings to meet with individual members* to ensure they are clear about and committed to the goals of the team. Depending on the work or communication styles of some group members, it may be hard to gauge whether or not this is the case from their meeting behavior. Outside of the meeting you may get a different response. Depending on the experience level and track record of members, it may be necessary to ensure that action items are carried out. If not, offer assistance. Tread carefully however. It is important to show members you trust them and have confidence in their abilities. Saying you do is not the same as showing it. If the individual comes to the next meeting without a completed action item, the lack of progress—for whatever reason—may deter the progress of the group. Talk to the person about this and ensure he or she understands the need to follow through on commitments made to the group so this doesn't happen again.

■ Minutes may not always be the best way to disperse important information about a meeting. Perhaps the team can design a *meeting summary form* that meets its particular needs. It might include places in which to capture what tasks were decided on, who is going to do the tasks, and the deadlines for these tasks, as well as a running record of key points made throughout the meeting. If the form is simple to use, it may be possible to complete it during the meeting and make copies members can take with them upon departing the meeting. Doing this helps confirm everyone's responsibilities, clarifies assignments, and establishes accountability.

■ Be sure to *send meeting notes to those members who could not be present* and let them know of any action items they may have been assigned in their absence. Taking this important step helps ensure that those who missed the meeting can get up to speed, provides them with a record of what was done, and lets everyone have equal access to the process.

■ *Have subcommittee meetings if necessary.* Remember, not all work needs to be done by every member of the team. In fact, this is rarely the case in effective teams given time and expertise constraints. Typically, a subcommittee may go off to develop a draft—a suggested process, a working set of objectives—as a starting point for other members' input and ideas. Using subcommittees can be a highly effective use of time and energy.

■ *Track progress* against a milestone chart. The process checks can help you determine how the team is doing relative to its task. It can also uncover potential problems or deficiencies. By examining the trend of evaluations, you can strategize and plan for corrective action, if necessary, before the group gets irrevocably off course.

■ *Keep key stakeholders informed* of team progress and setbacks. Perceptions of a team's effectiveness (or lack thereof) are not only impacted by what and how they accomplish their objectives; they are also a function of how well informed those external to the process are kept.[37] In an environment where teaming and empowerment are the norm, it is easy to take the ball and run with it—and never inform others who may have a need to know. This may include other departments, top management, customers, or suppliers. By ensuring that communication flows freely within the team, as well as beyond the team's boundaries, perceptions and support of the team are likely to remain positive.

Other Helpful Meeting Hints

■ Write down the cost per minute of the meeting (total all salaries of those present and divide by the number of participants) on a flipchart. This can have a focusing effect; it is an effective way to illustrate that time is money, so let's not waste either!

■ Announce the adjournment time right when the meeting starts. This clearly informs participants how long they will need to focus and will help them adjust their comments to fit the schedule.[38]

■ Set rules for debate if one is likely to ensue. For example, "No one can speak for more than five minutes," or "No one can speak twice until everyone who wants to speak has had a turn."[39] It's easy for a meeting to denigrate into a one-person show or a case where "those who talk the longest and loudest win." By establishing these rules up front and encouraging all members to adhere to them, this problem is less likely to surface.

■ Try to schedule all internal meetings for 30 minutes or less, unless a key decision must be made. This relatively short meeting period forces members to be prepared if they plan to accomplish anything and puts pressure on members to focus.[40]

■ Have a meeting standing up. Researchers at the University of Missouri's College of Business and Public Administration found that meetings involving creativity and judgment held with members standing up were 34 percent shorter than those in which members were seated. This, and their finding that the shorter, stand-up meeting resulted in the same quality of and satisfaction with decisions made,[41] suggests that shorter meetings may be more efficient and effective.

(continued)

- Preestablished timetables should be followed unless the situation warrants change. Start and end the meeting on time, but be open to change if needed. If you run a tight ship but it runs aground, you have not achieved your objective. Be firm but flexible and get member input on proposed time changes.
- If possible, complete the meeting summary and send it out the same day while it is fresh in everyone's mind.[42] This aids closure and ensures that action items are completed and members are prepared for subsequent meetings.
- Demonstrate management support and commitment to the team and its tasks. Ask if you can come to team meetings periodically. Remove or reduce impediments (policies, individuals, insufficient resources) to show your commitment to a team's success. Provide the team with adequate time and logistical arrangements to have effective meetings.
- Have fun. When the goal of a meeting is for people to be creative and innovative, they need to loosen up to think in different ways to gain better perspectives.[43] To do this, encourage an off-site meeting and casual dress, have food, and intersperse activities (appropriate physical or experiential exercises) to lighten up the mood and reenergize the members.

Summary

So many people find meetings to be a waste of time. It's not surprising. If you've ever been in workplace meetings, or perhaps had meetings for a class project assignment, you're likely to agree. When done well, meetings can fulfill multiple, important purposes. When poorly planned and executed, meetings become the source of wasted time, humorous water cooler talk, and plain old misery. With so much to do in such little time, wasting time in useless meetings is not an option. Today's manager must be skillful not only at running meetings, but also in deciding whether a meeting is necessary. Planning is essential and can prevent many problems from occurring. If they do occur, you'll be better equipped to resolve these problems and help groups have and run their own effective meetings.

Key Terms and Concepts

Agenda

Evaluation (meeting stage)

Information-dissemination meeting

Information-sharing meeting

Meeting kickoff (meeting stage)

Preliminary or initial (meeting stage) phase

Problem-solving/decision-making meeting

Process check

Summary of accomplishments (meeting stage)

Symbolic/social meeting

Synergy

Virtual meeting

Endnotes

1. Frank Basil, "Advance Planning Is Key to Successful Meetings," *Indianapolis Business Journal,* March 13, 2000, p. 21.

2. Timothy J. Kloppenborg and Joseph A. Petrick, "Meeting Management and Group Character Development," *Journal of Management Issues* 11, no. 2 (Summer 1999), p. 166.

3. Mark T. Chen, "Project Meeting Cost Analysis," *AACE International Transactions,* 2003.

4. Ibid.

5. Winston Fletcher, "The Meeting Game and How to Win," *Management Today,* Dec. 1999, p. 32.

6. Fletcher, "Meeting Game."

7. Charlie Hawkins, "First Aid for Meetings," *Public Relations Quarterly,* Fall 1997, p. 33–36.

8. Fletcher, "Meeting Game."

9. Basil, "Advance Planning."

10. Anonymous, "Making Your Short Meetings More Productive," *Agency Sales,* Oct. 1992, p. 15.

11. David A. Whetten and Kim S. Cameron, *Developing Management Skills,* 4th ed. (Reading, MA: Addison Wesley, 1998), pp. 522–27. Reprinted by permission of Addison-Wesley Educational Publishers, Inc.

12. Jan Smith, "If Meeting Is Necessary, at Least Keep It Controlled," *Sacramento Business Journal,* Nov. 5, 1999, p. 42.

13. Becky Jones, Midge Wilier, and Judy Stoner, "A Meeting Primer: Tips on Running a Successful Meeting," *Management Review,* Jan. 1995, p. 30.

14. Basil, "Advance Planning."

15. Ibid.

16. Ibid.

17. Hawkins, "First Aid."

18. Roy Woodard, "Meeting, Bloody Meetings," *Credit Control,* 1993, p. 14.

19. David Dunning, "Steer Clear of Pitfalls That Can Doom Meetings," *Puget Sound Business Journal,* Jan. 21, 2000, p. 29.

20. Hawkins, "First Aid."

21. Ibid.

22. Ibid.

23. Ibid.

24. Jones et al., "Meeting Primer."

25. Luis G. Flores and Janyce Fadden, "How to Have a Successful Strategic Planning Meeting," *Training and Development,* Jan. 2000, p. 31.

26. Jones et al., "Meeting Primer."

27. Stacey R. Closser, "Creating Memorable Meetings Is Key," *Triangle Business Journal,* Feb. 18, 2000, p. 37.

28. Mark J. Friedman, "How to Run a Problem-Solving Meeting," *Training and Development,* Oct. 1996, p. 11.

29. Schlegel, "Making Meetings Effective."

30. Peter R. Scholtes, *The Team Handbook* (Madison, WI: Joiner and Associates, 1988).

31. Ibid.

32. Hawkins, "First Aid."

33. Jim Slaughter, "How to Keep Discussions Short," *Association Management,* Jan. 2000, p. 123.

34. Hawkins, "First Aid."

35. Smith, "If Meeting Is Necessary."

36. **www.sna.com/switp/between.html**

37. D. G. Ancona, "Outward Bound: Strategies for Team Survival in an Organization," *Academy of Management Journal* 33 (1990), pp. 334–65.

38. Slaughter, "Keep Discussions Short."

39. Ibid.

40. John R. Brandt, "Time's Up (Limiting Business Meetings)," *Industry Week,* Jan. 10, 2000, p. 2.

41. Tricia Campbell, "Speed Up Your Meetings," *Sales and Marketing Management,* Nov. 1999, p. 11.

42. Jones et al., "Meeting Primer."

43. Hawkins, "First Aid."

Exercise 12–A
Committee Meeting

You are the chairperson of the social event committee for your school or community-based organization. Much is riding on you and your committee as you begin making preparations for the annual dance/celebration. This annual event is one of the biggest in your town and typically brings in between $10,000 and $20,000 that can be spent on resources, travel, and outreach efforts. It's very important that the dance go smoothly. It has for the last 15 years.

You are about to call a meeting of the social event committee to discuss arrangements for the dance. In this meeting, which is about six weeks away, you'll have to decide on location, food, music/entertainment, tables and chairs, decorations, and admission fee. You might even look for corporate sponsors to help fund the event.

1. What needs to be handled in your meeting? _____

   _____

   _____

   _____

   _____

2. Who should be invited? _____

   _____

   _____

   _____

   _____

3. What preparation work should be done? _____

   _____

   _____

   _____

   _____

4. What could you do before the meeting to ensure that everyone will come with ideas and enthusiasm? _____

   _____

   _____

   _____

   _____

5. What should you do during the meeting to ensure that you get closure on the key issues? _____

   _____

   _____

   _____

   _____

6. After the meeting, what can you do to ensure that other committee members follow up on their promises to complete certain tasks? _____

   _____

   _____

   _____

   _____

Exercise 12–B
Prepare an Agenda for a Team Meeting

Prepare an agenda for your next project group meeting.

Exercise 12–C
Plan and Have a Meeting

Working in groups of four to six, you will be given a topic and a block of time in which to plan and have a meeting. Consider the meeting's topic (see list below) and complete the following:

1. Prepare an agenda. Be sure to include these points:
   - Issues to be discussed.
   - The amount of time allocated to each issue.
   - Role assignments (e.g., scribe, timekeeper, leader, facilitator).
   - Time for a process review.
2. Have the meeting. Record key points and decisions on a flip chart or other "public" device. Plan to have one or more members present the findings of your group.
3. Do a process review. Discuss what worked well and could be improved in this meeting.
4. Report out on your group's outcomes (what recommendation or conclusions your group offers) and processes (how your group got to that point).

Topics

- Feedback on this course: What elements are effective in terms of your ability to learn and apply what's being taught, as well as suggestions for strengthening elements that could be improved.
- The role of technology in your team's next presentation. What options are available? What are the strengths and weaknesses of the options? What recommendations would you make for future team-based presentations?
- Add your own.

Exercise 12–D
Reflection/Action Plan

This chapter focused on meetings—why they're important and strategies for planning and running effective meetings. Complete the worksheet below upon completing all reading and experiential activities for this chapter.

1. The one or two areas in which I am most strong are:

_____

_____

2. The one or two areas in which I need more improvement are:

_____

_____

3. If I did only one thing to improve in this area, it would be to:

_____

_____

4. Making this change would probably result in:

_____

_____

5. If I did not change or improve in this area, it would probably affect my personal and professional life in the following ways:

_____

_____

13 Facilitating Team Success

Learning Points

How do I:
- Recognize when a team's process is ineffective?
- Help team members work cohesively and effectively with one another?
- Teach and guide teams in utilizing effective process skills?
- Use interventions at the appropriate time and in the appropriate manner?
- Deter the eruption of dysfunctional behaviors of team members?
- Create an environment that allows teams to achieve goals effectively?

Dick Wilson is on a creative team that is putting together an advertising campaign for a major pet food company. One member, Jennifer Smith, has had several years' experience working with pet food company clients—and she lets the team know it frequently during team planning meetings. In fact, she often volunteers to do more than her share in putting together both the campaign and the presentation of the campaign. While you appreciate her efforts, you feel that it's hard for you and the rest of the team to get their voices heard in these meetings since Jennifer always seems to "have the floor." Dick is worried that the team leader will think Dick and the others aren't carrying their weight. If this is the case, Dick's bonus will be affected.

1. What are some of the main issues in this situation? From Dick's perspective? Jennifer's? The team leader's?
2. Why is it a problem for Jennifer to be so dominant?
3. What should Dick do?
4. What should the team do?
5. What should the team leader do?

"Our chief want in life is somebody who will make us do what we can."

Ralph Waldo Emerson

n this chapter we define facilitation and why it's important. We describe key facilitative behaviors and strategies and provide tips for facilitating teams. At the end of the chapter are exercises that help you enhance your facilitating skills and a list of resources for further exploration.

What Is Facilitation?

Bostrom, Anson, and Clawson[1] define **facilitation** as "activities carried out before, during, and after meetings to help a group achieve its own outcomes." There are two types of facilitation. **Process facilitation** is defined as "the provision of procedural structure and general support to groups through the meeting process."[2] **Content facilitation** involves interventions that relate directly to the problem being discussed.[3] Miranda and Bostrom's research[4] has found the first type, process facilitation, to be more effective in contributing positively to the overall process of group meetings. While both types are common and can be useful depending on the situation, this chapter focuses primarily on the use of process facilitation as a strategy for improving the effectiveness of meetings and teams.

   Facilitation is a process in which a team is assisted in improving internal processes, such as how members communicate, make decisions, or resolve conflict, that are essential for achieving team goals. Effective processes (the means) are critical to achieving successful outcomes (the ends).[5] The diversity present on the team challenges team members to actively and objectively listen to and search for agreement among their diverse counterparts. The team's ability to listen effectively or to communicate with one another represents a critical process or means by which desired outcomes can be achieved.

Why Is Facilitation Important?

Teams have become an important vehicle for organizations to develop and improve products, services, and processes. However, "simply bringing together a group of professionals does not ensure that this group will function effectively as a team or make appropriate decisions."[6] Team members' varying beliefs, backgrounds, personalities, and work styles can hinder a team's ability to get work done. With such diversity comes the likelihood that individuals will misunderstand or undervalue the contributions of their team members. Some teams find it hard to reach agreements and solve problems. Just sprinkling pixie dust over a group of individuals does not necessarily result in the kind of team outcomes organizations expect. Therein lies the need for team facilitation.

What Facilitators Do

A **facilitator** formally or informally takes on the role of monitoring a team's process for effectiveness. The facilitator focuses more on how a team is working than on what the team is doing. The responsibilities of a facilitator vary from team to team, depending on the goals, technical requirements, duration, and employee makeup of that team. Employees or students who have worked on teams before, or who have been working with one team for a long time, may require less facilitation than would members of a newly formed team. In general, facilitators attend to such team processes as communication, meeting management, decision making, problem solving, and conflict resolution.[7]

   The facilitator's role may not be confined to what happens during meetings; many work outside meetings to further group cohesion or help gain sponsorship or support from key groups or individuals external to the team.[8] While facilitators' responsibilities may vary with respect to teams' expected outcomes, technical requirements, and employee makeup, they often do whatever it takes to help the team improve its processes and outcomes. This might start with helping a team clarify and buy into its goals and objectives, and progress through coaching a team to present its recommendations to management and eventually implement these recommendations.

Finally, facilitators model and educate team members in the use of facilitative skills. It would be very easy for a facilitator to provide continual assistance in improving team processes and outcomes. However, team members would likely become dependent on that help, rendering themselves unable to function effectively without the aid of a facilitator. When a facilitator not only helps the team use meeting management techniques, for example, but also teaches the team why and how to use them, the team will eventually become self-facilitating.[9] In other words, good facilitators often work themselves out of a job.

In summary, facilitators do whatever it takes to help the team improve its processes (and outcomes). Facilitators may do many things, from helping create a safe and receptive environment in which to effectively communicate and make decisions to coaching a team to present its findings and recommendations to management or other stakeholders.

Facilitation Skills and Behaviors

Three specific types of role behaviors are typically exhibited in team meetings. A skilled facilitator will be equipped to recognize all three.[10]

- **Task-related behaviors** focus on the *content* of the meeting—the actions necessary to complete a task or goal. These task-related behaviors include contributing to, asking for, summarizing, and clarifying information. The facilitator will monitor these behaviors and intervene if the team's attention to task precludes them from paying attention to process or group dynamic issues. For example, a team might be so focused on their deadline that they will overlook the fact that one member has resigned from the group and is not attending meetings. In this case, a member or the facilitator can ask clarifying questions and help the team acknowledge and deal with this problem, rather than ignore it.

- **Maintenance-related behaviors** relate to the *process* of how the group works together. Some quiet or shy members may need encouragement to participate. Tensions arising from conflicts need to be reduced. Other issues, particularly those that may not be obvious to some, must be diagnosed and resolved. Members of an effective team are likely to exhibit both task- and maintenance-related behaviors during meetings. If conflict surfaces, members may use these behaviors to resolve it. If unsuccessful, the facilitator can raise the issue and provide a model for team members to later emulate should another conflict emerge.

- **Dysfunctional behaviors** are actions taken by members that may hinder or even undermine the team's progress. When members intentionally block the team's progress by refusing to budge on their position on an issue, the facilitator can try to address the issue by using an intervention, such as asking justifying questions.

Figure 13–1 lists some examples of each type of role behavior.

Team facilitators, as opposed to team leaders, should focus primarily on group process (how the team is going about achieving its formal tasks, including who talks to whom, how decisions are made), with much less focus on team content or outcomes (reasons for the team's existence, what the team is talking about). Facilitators assist the team with its process (as opposed to the content) by intervening when necessary, such as refocusing a divergent discussion, ensuring balanced participation, or clarifying whether all options have been objectively evaluated.

In addition to process expertise, some facilitators may possess specific content or technical knowledge such as an engineering background, which might potentially benefit a team. However, since a facilitator's primary responsibility is to ensure the open and objective discussion of diverse perspectives, facilitators will typically downplay content knowledge for fear of being perceived as nonobjective or vested in a particular outcome.[11]

**Figure 13–1
Role Behaviors**

	Behavior	Explanation	Examples
Task Related	Initiating	Proposes a task	"Why don't we start by . . ."
	Giving/seeking information	Offers/asks facts, ideas	"In our department, we were able to cut costs by . . ."
	Clarifying and elaborating	Clears up confusion	"So you're saying . . . "
	Summarizing	Restates, offers conclusion	"We've covered all but the last item on the agenda"
	Consensus testing	Checks on group position	"It sounds like we agree on points 1 and 2, but not 3 . . . "
Maintenance-Related	Harmonizing and compromising	Reduces tension, looks for middle ground	"It doesn't have to be either x or y . . . why don't we use the best elements of both?"
	Gatekeeping	Facilitates balanced participation	(To silent member) "What's your opinion?"
	Diagnosing	Shares observations of group process	"It seems a few of us are unhappy with the decision . . . shall we revisit . . .?"
	Standard setting	Helps set norms, test limits	"Let's agree to brainstorm, then evaluate"
Dysfunctional	Blocking	Prevents consensus	"I'm not going to agree to a solution which . . ."
	Dominating	Talks more than his/her share	Often talks the longest and loudest, overshadowing others' potential contributions
	Withdrawing	Silent, distracted	(Check body language)
	Self-seeking	Oppresses with personal needs	"The only way I'll agree to this is if you'll do . . . for me"

Key Facilitation Strategies

A facilitator can do many things behind the scenes or before meetings begin that might help prevent problems from occurring or diminish their impact on the team should such problems surface. The list of strategies, shown in Figure 13–2, ranges from premeeting planning (e.g., working on the agenda with the team leader, ensuring quality of meeting logistics), to start-of-meeting process clarification (e.g., establishing ground rules), to things you could say or do during a meeting (e.g., suggesting or getting agreement on the process, educating the group) to ensure all members of the team are on the same page and working toward a common goal.

Key Facilitative Interventions

Even the most skilled facilitator cannot prevent all problems from surfacing on a team. Sooner or later, one or more group members may decide to take a stand on an issue that is opposed to the position supported by other group members. Or, management may decide to change the scope of a team's goals and objectives, add or delete team members, or shorten the time in which completion is expected. Or, a team member may decide that his or her time is too valuable to be "wasted" at these "frivolous" team meetings. Any of

Figure 13–2
Facilitative Strategies[12]

General Approach	Specific Things You Can Say or Do
Establish ground rules—define roles (make your social contract)	Up front (and ongoing) discussion of your role and the ground rules of your involvement with the team leader and later the team members.
Get agreement on process	"Before we begin to evaluate the alternatives, are we agreed that we'll begin by saying what we like about each alternative, and then go on to our concerns about each one?"
Get agreement on content/outcome	"Which issue are you going to discuss first?" "What's the purpose of this meeting? To design the agenda for the full commission next Wednesday? Does anybody have a different conception of this meeting?"
Be positive (win–win attitude)	If you really believe a win–win solution can be found, you will increase the chances of it happening.
Build an agenda	By working with the team leader to plan an agenda for your meetings, you can anticipate and prevent many potential meeting problems from occurring.
Get permission to enforce the process agreements	"If you want to get through all these reports by 11:00, I'm going to have to hold you to your five-minute time limit. Is that OK? Any objections?"
Get the group to take responsibility for its actions	"This is your meeting. What do you want to do?"

these situations, combined with the diversity challenges mentioned earlier in the chapter, provides ample opportunity for you to intervene in an effort to aid the team.

Some of the **interventions,** or things a facilitator can say or do to help a team assess and deal with what is going on in the present moment (see Figure 13–3), are fairly simple, straightforward, and innocuous. For example, the use of "say what's going on" is perfect for the team that is experiencing the formation of factions with respect to a particular issue. By sharing your observations with the team, you clarify what is happening while (hopefully) motivating them to reach a resolution. This intervention might sound like, "It seems we have two perspectives on this decision; John's approach would be to . . . while Mary's approach would involve. . . . Half of you seem to agree with John while the other half prefer Mary's approach. . . . Am I correct?" A similar intervention, which is simple yet powerful if not overdone, is the "play dumb" intervention. When a team has lost its focus or has become sidetracked on another topic, a facilitator might say something like, "I'm confused. What were we supposed to be discussing now?" This technique can help get the group to focus on its own process and how to improve it. Both of these interventions are fairly easy to do while having the dual benefit of regaining the team's focus and simultaneously improving its members' ability to be self-facilitating.

Another set of interventions involves the use of well-timed questions to help uncover important reasons behind a position (e.g., justifying questions), move the team into a different direction (e.g., leading questions), or get the team to take a leap outside the proverbial box (e.g., hypothetical questions). In the latter case, questions that cause the group to move beyond the "That'll never work here" or "We've tried that before and it didn't work then" types of responses can be really effective. For example, if a team member were to say something like "That's a great idea but management would never go for it," a facilitator might ask a justifying question, such as "Why do you think that is the case?" to clarify underlying reasons. If the team member responds with "Well, when the team in the finance department tried to . . . , management apparently shelved their recommendations," the facilitator might respond with the following hypothetical question: "If you had some assurance management is going to listen and take action this time, what specific recommendations should we make about implementing . . .?"

Figure 13–3
Facilitative Interventions[13]

General Approach	Specific Things You Can Say or Do
Boomerang	Don't get backed into answering questions the group should be answering for themselves. Boomerang the question back to the group.
Maintain/regain focus	"Wait a second. Let's keep a common focus here."
Play dumb	When the group has gotten off track or the meeting has broken down in some way, playing dumb is a way of getting the group to focus on its own process by having to explain to you. It's a form of boomeranging and is easy to do when you're really confused.
Say what's going on	Sometimes, simply identifying and describing a destructive behavior to the group is enough to change that behavior. Be sure to "check for agreement" after your process observation.
Check for agreement	Almost any time you make a statement or propose a process, give the group an opportunity to respond. Don't assume they are with you.
Accept/legitimize/deal with, or defer	This is a general method of intervening that works well for dealing with problem people and emotional outbreaks of all kinds.
Don't be defensive	If you are challenged, don't argue or become defensive. Accept the criticism, thank the individual for the comment, and boomerang the issue back to the individual or group.
Use justifying questions	When team members disagree on an issue, a facilitator can use justifying questions to help bring out discussions by uncovering facts and reasons behind team members' opinions.
Use leading questions	Use when the team has too narrow a focus and you want to gently guide them into another direction or if the team needs a "jump-start."
Use the group memory	The group memory (i.e., the easel/notepad on which minutes or key points are being recorded) can also be used to reinforce many of the interventions and preventions.
Don't talk too much	The better facilitator you become, the fewer words you will have to use. When you have really done a good job, the group may leave thinking that the meeting went so well it could do without you next time.
Use hypothetical questions	When a team appears to be stagnant or more interested in maintaining the status quo, the facilitator could use hypothetical questions to spur creativity, innovation, etc.
Use a reality check	Use when a team needs to reexamine or modify its direction, progress, process agreements.
Use a time-out	When team members are fighting, losing sight of the big picture, or becoming uncooperative for some reason, try calling for a time-out. Ask that members take a five-minute break, after which the meeting will resume.
Call a team member's bluff	Use when a team member threatens to do something unless or until the team changes direction. (This intervention is risky; you must be willing to accept a team member's decision.)

Another set of interventions has the facilitator taking an active and perhaps directive role. Doing so is necessary in certain situations. It is important to remember that the more directive the facilitator is, the more the team members come to expect such behaviors from the facilitator as opposed to developing their own facilitative skills. One example is the use of "time-out." If members are fighting or unusually uncooperative, continuing the meeting might prove unproductive if not harmful. In such a situation, the facilitator might end the meeting early or call a time-out—a 5- or 10-minute break—after which the meeting resumes. A more risky intervention might be necessary when a team member threatens to leave the meeting or to do something that might sabotage the team's progress should the member not get his or her way. This team member may be waiting for others to cajole him or her back into the meeting or change their way of thinking. In such a situation, it might be appropriate for a facilitator to "call the person's bluff," for example, "No one can make you stay . . . you can leave if you want to, just as long as you realize . . ." This intervention is risky in that the facilitator must be willing to accept the outcome (e.g., a team member's departure) and its impact on the team.

Facilitation Tips

- Keep an open mind about what you think needs facilitating. Your perceptions may or may not match those of the team, leaving open the possibility that the facilitator could do more harm than good.

- Wait and see if team members can resolve their own conflict. Remember that the more a facilitator takes an active role in facilitating a group's process, the more likely the team is to become dependent on the facilitator doing so now and in the future.

- Share your observations in order to check with team members whether your observations are correct (i.e., check for understanding). If you were to skip this step and actively promote a certain path to resolve the situation, you may cause more problems than you fix. If your observations are correct, evaluate which approach would work best in this situation and then suggest these options to the team.

- Focus primarily on the process or how the team goes about achieving its goals. However, early in the team's existence, it might be appropriate for you to be somewhat directive or task-oriented; it might help give direction when the team's start seems slow.

- As teams move through their developmental stages and members learn and use effective process skills, facilitators should move toward being more nondirective, using questioning and reflecting behaviors to help the team help itself.

Identifying and Dealing with "Problem People"

Some people, with or without ill intent, can single-handedly hinder even the best teams. We call these **problem people.** Figure 13–4 summarizes some of the more common behavioral descriptors, clarifies the problem, and suggests possible solutions for handling these people or situations. You may encounter a team member who always complains and turns the conversation to an unrelated topic that is irritating them, leading the team astray. For example, the team may be working on a new computer system for the human resource department and every time the company or budget is discussed, a member begins to complain how the company should be spending funds on giving raises and benefits instead of upgrading the computer system. How would you deal with this individual? What preventive techniques might you use? What interventions might you use?

Some Barriers or Limitations to Facilitation

Not all organizations or teams use or recognize the value of facilitators. The costs may be prohibitive, preventing work teams from having the luxury of adding (even temporarily) an outside member to facilitate them. If there are no employees with facilitation skills available in the organization, the organization may not want to pay for services of an

**Figure 13–4
Dealing with
Problem People**[14]

Problem Person	Problem	Solution
The Silent One	Withdrawn. May be bored, indifferent, timid, or insecure.	Ask for her opinions. Give positive verbal and nonverbal reinforcement.
The Heckler	Combative individual who wants to play devil's advocate.	Stay calm. Don't lose your temper. Appeal to him or her for cooperation.
The Fighters	Two or more persons clash at the personality level.	Interrupt politely but firmly. Stress points of agreement, minimize points of disagreement.
The "Stand Pat"	Won't budge. Refuses to accept the group's decisions. Often prejudiced. Unable or unwilling to see your point or those of others.	Toss his view to the group: "Does anyone else feel as Pat does about this?"
The Sidetracker	Off the subject or agenda.	Take the blame for sidetracking her: "Something I said must have led you off the subject. This is what we should be discussing . . . (restate point)."
The Verbal Stumbler	Lacks ability to clearly express himself. Has the ideas but finds it difficult to put into words.	Help the person out. Rephrase his statements.
The Whisperer	Engages nearby people in side conversations while someone else has floor.	Interrupt politely and ask if they could share their information with the group.
The "Eager Beaver" (talker/monopolizer)	Monopolizes the conversation.	Interrupt politely with "That's an interesting point. What do the rest of you think about it?"
The Mistaken	Member is obviously incorrect.	To bring out correction tactfully, say "I see your point, but how can we reconcile that with . . . (state correct point)?"
The Latecomer	Comes late and interrupts meeting.	Announce an odd time (8:46 AM) for the meeting to emphasize the necessity for promptness.
The Early Leaver	Announces, with regret, that they must leave for another important activity.	Before the meeting begins, announce/confirm the ending time and ask if anyone has a scheduling conflict.

outside facilitator. Even if internal employees with the necessary skills can be identified, there are costs associated with pulling them out of their normal duties and reassigning them—even temporarily—to work with one or more teams. In the absence of a trained facilitator, individual team members will be called upon to use facilitative skills as appropriate. In this case, **objectivity**—the ability to view a situation without personal bias and one of the benefits perceptually bestowed upon an "outside" facilitator—is not present. When such is the case, some of the problems inherent in culturally and functionally diverse teams (e.g., misunderstanding or devaluing others' opinions, fighting over scarce resources) are not likely to be overcome by an "inside" facilitator.

Even when outside facilitators or process consultants are offered to a team, other problems may exist. First, teams can see the job of process facilitation resting squarely and solely upon the facilitator. Such dependence precludes team development toward self-management. Second, at the other extreme, team members may not trust the outsider or "allow" him or her to intervene. This is especially likely when a team has existed for a period of time and resists the presence and questions the value of this appointed outsider. This problem can be exacerbated if management appoints a facilitator to a team without communicating the reasons or objectives for this step. Team members might become suspicious and choose to be less forthcoming in team meetings and discussions. Facilitators can only facilitate what they see and hear; if the team's work goes "underground," there is not much a facilitator can do to help, should help be needed.

As a facilitator you can reduce these effects by introducing yourself at the first meeting and discussing with the group how they see your role. Check out the team's expectation of the facilitator and discuss the importance of everyone's role in the process.[15] The members' perceptions and expectations will depend on their previous experiences. This role can then be negotiated over time. Example: "Hi, I'm Jan Smith. Your manager asked me to come to help you map your manufacturing process to find ways to decrease defects and cycle time. My background is in . . . and I see myself doing (list role or responsibilities) for you." Listen and honor their opinions and perspectives, further reinforcing that each person has an important role to play in the process.

Another problem facilitators may face is resistance due to a lack of familiarity with or credibility in a part of the organization,[16] despite the fact that such unfamiliarity may underlie valuable objectivity. Since facilitators often work between a team and its management, a facilitator who is seen as ineffective or incredible (or a deterrent to some "master plan") might be "blocked" from helping the team achieve its goals by other organizational stakeholders.

While team facilitation is not a panacea for all organizational challenges, benefits can be gained through the use of a trained process facilitator.[17] Facilitative skills can be learned and should be used either formally as a trained facilitator or informally whenever you are part of a team. Whether a facilitator is utilized or not, having all team members trained and skilled in facilitation techniques will greatly enhance the teaming experience and output.

Summary

Facilitation helps team members work cohesively and cooperatively to effectively achieve organizational and individual goals. Through the use of facilitation, teams will function more effectively, members will be more satisfied with the team experience and learn new skills, and output will be enhanced. Facilitation is a skill that can increase the effectiveness of all members of teams and organizations. Even if your team does not have the benefit of a process facilitator, having knowledge and skills in facilitation will make you a valuable contributor to your team and organization.[18]

Key Terms and Concepts

Content facilitation	Maintenance-related behaviors
Dysfunctional behaviors	Objectivity
Facilitation	Problem people
Facilitation strategies	Process facilitation
Facilitator	Task-related behaviors
Intervention	

Endnotes

1. R. P. Bostrom, R. Anson, and V. K. Clawson, "Group facilitation and group support systems," in L. Jessup and J. Valacich (eds.) *Group Support Systems: New Perspectives*. New York: Macmillan (1993), pp. 146–68.

2. C. Eden, "The unfolding nature of group decision support—two dimensions of skill," in C. Eden and J. Radford (eds.), *Tackling Strategic Problems*. London: Sage, 1990, pp. 48–52.

3. Eden (1990).

4. Shaila M. Miranda and Robert P. Bostrom, "Meeting Facilitation: Process versus Content Interventions," *Journal of Management Information Systems.* Armonk: Spring 1999, Vol. 15, Iss. 4: p. 89.

5. E. Cooley, "Training an Interdisciplinary Team in Communication and Decision-Making Skills," *Small Group Research* 25 (1994), p. 6.

6. Ibid.

7. R. Sisco, "What to Train Team Leaders," *Training,* February 1993, pp. 62–63.

8. Ibid.; and D. G. Ancona, "Outward Bound: Strategies for Team Survival in an Organization," *Academy of Management Journal* 33 (1990), pp. 334–65.

9. The idea that effective modeling leads to mastery is consistent with A. Bandura, "Self Efficacy: Toward a Unifying Theory of Behavioral Change," *Psychological Review* 84 (1997), pp. 191–215.

10. E. Schein, *Process Consultation* (Menlo Park, CA: Addison-Wesley, 1988).

11. Sisco, "What to Train."

12. This chart is adapted from S. de Janasz, L. Johnson, M. McQuaid, A. Paulson, D. Roccia, S. Stubblefield, P. Wahl, and C. Wojick, *Fundamentals of Facilitation,* Training manual created for Hughes Aircraft Company, 1992, pp. 6-38 to 6-40.

13. This chart is adapted from and expands on de Janasz et al., *Fundamentals of Facilitation,* pp. 6-42 to 6-46.

14. This chart is adapted and compiled from two sources (1) de Janasz et al., *Fundamentals of Facilitation,* pp. 13-4 to 13-10; and (2) Peoples, *Presentations Plus* (New York: John Wiley & Sons, 1988), pp. 147–55.

15. American Business Women's Association, "The Art of Facilitation," *Women in Business,* Jan.–Feb. 1999, p. 38.

16. Sisco, "What to Train."

17. Tom Terez, "Can We Talk?" *Workforce,* July 2000, pp. 46–55.

18. Kathryn Tyler, "The Gang's All Here . . ." *HRMagazine,* May 2000, pp. 104–13.

Exercise 13–A
Case Study: Dealing
with Team Conflict

You've been asked to facilitate a team that has not been doing too well lately. This cross-functional team is composed of eight members from various disciplines, including materiel, engineering, program management, operations, and finance, and has been working together for about six weeks. Its task: to reduce the time necessary to procure materials for use on a particular program/line of business. Things were going well in the beginning, as everybody's job can be simplified if there weren't so many delays in the process. However, in the last meeting, the group identified three key causes that, in essence, suggest that one or more of the represented disciplines are to blame for the delays. These causes included:

1. Undependable suppliers (if it wouldn't take "them" so long to get the needed materials and deliver them on time, things would be fine).

2. Lengthy and cumbersome signature cycle (members of finance and program management are among those who must sign each request).

3. Too many engineering changes (when engineering makes design changes, new materials have to be ordered and "old" materials have to be returned).

Most members of the team, including managers and technical personnel, are hesitant to expose their organization's part (if any) in the delays.

Questions

1. Do you think it's possible to help this team achieve its goal? Explain.

2. As a facilitator, what specific things would you do and say to ensure an effective process? Why?

3. What impact would this likely have on the outcome?

4. What, if anything, can be done "behind the scenes" to improve the team's chances for success?

Exercise 13–B **Video Case:** *Twelve* *Angry Men**	Your instructor will be showing a clip from the classic *Twelve Angry Men.* In this movie, members of a jury are about to decide the fate of a young boy charged with murdering his father. Answer the following questions after viewing this clip.

1. In the beginning of this clip, we see the foreman suggesting a process (e.g., why don't we take a straw vote) and clarifying instructions related to this process. Using the role behaviors in Figure 13–1 as a guide, which behaviors did the foreman use and what effect did they have?

2. During this initial or straw vote, we see hesitation on the part of some members when casting their votes. What explains this hesitation, in your opinion, and if you were the foreperson, what might you have done differently?

3. After this vote, some members can be seen pressuring the single dissenting member. If this were to happen in a team you were facilitating, what intervention would you use and why?

4. Midway through the clip, the foreman suggests one process ("Let's all go around the table and convince this man why he's wrong"), and immediately thereafter, another jury member suggests a different process ("It seems to me that he—the dissenter—should be the one who tries to convince us"). Both processes have value. How would you help the group choose between the processes? What, specifically, would you say or do?

5. Periodically, throughout the clip, we see jury members treat one another harshly (e.g., remarks that are ethnically or age discriminatory). If you were to facilitate this group, would you intervene during these moments? Why or why not? If you would intervene, what would you say or do and why?

6. The foreman is actually one of the 12 jury members. At times, he plays a leaderlike role; other times, he is facilitative. Cite examples of each. Should he play both leader and facilitator? Why or why not?

7. Different jury members have different personality styles. Such is also the case on most teams. What are some ways to point out these differences in a way that enables members to benefit from instead of being aggravated by these differences?

8. The jury member played by Jack Klugman, who admits that he "grew up in a slum" and identifies with the defendant, speaks infrequently and only when requested by others to do so. Even then, he seems to lack confidence in sharing his ideas and concerns. If you were to facilitate this "team," what techniques might you use to help this character contribute? Identify at least one "prevention" and one "intervention," and describe how you would use them.

9. Another jury member, played by E. G. Marshall, is intelligent, articulate, and very confident in his opinions. You could see this when he tries to point out the defendant's guilt on the basis of the boy's inability to recall the name of the movie he saw. These qualities can both benefit and hinder a team's process. What impact did his behavior have on you? If you were to facilitate the meeting, what might you have said or done to facilitate this member and why?

10. Which of the four stages of teaming did this "team" go through? Identify the stages and cite evidence to support your answer.

*Distributed by MGM Home Videos, 1957 (Sidney Lumet, director; Henry Fonda, star).

Exercise 13-C
Alternative Exercise for *Twelve Angry Men*

View the portion of the film shown in class by the instructor. As you watch the movie, record examples of dysfunctional behaviors demonstrated in the film on the chart below. Cite the actor (describe his role or appearance if you don't know the name) and the specific action or statement that is evidence of a particular dysfunctional behavior. For each behavior, describe strategies that were or could be used to counteract each of the dysfunctional behaviors listed.

Dysfunctional Behaviors and Related Facilitation Strategies: *Twelve Angry Men*

Behavior	Actor/Evidence	Strategy Used or Suggested
Whisperer—periodically engages team member(s) in side conversations		
"Eager beaver" (talker/ monopolizer)—always has something to say		
Heckler/complainer—combative; tells team members why what they're working on will never work		
Silent member—withdrawn; doesn't participate		
Sidetracker—dicusses items not on the agenda		
Fighter—picks a "fight" and/or argues with another team member		
"Stand pat"—won't budge; hostile; unwilling to look at situation from others' perspective; often prejudiced		
Verbal stumbler—unable to express self clearly		
Early leaver—announces they must leave for another activity		

Exercise 13–D
Facilitation Assessment

The following questions relate to the facilitation activity you did in your class. Please answer them completely yet concisely.

1. What interpersonal skills covered in our class (e.g., listening, problem solving) did you find yourself using when you played the role of facilitator during this activity? Name at least two skills and share an example for each.

2. When you facilitated, what do you believe to be the things you did particularly well? Please describe at least two instances when you felt your facilitation was effective.

3. When you facilitated, what do you believe to be the things you did not do particularly well or that resulted in an outcome different from what you had anticipated? Please describe at least two instances when you felt your facilitation could have been improved.

4. What lessons did you learn about yourself and about the challenges of doing work in teams from this activity? What steps can you take to improve your skills as a facilitator and as a team member?

Exercise 13-E
Observing Group Process

Using one of the scenarios below, form a small group. Conduct a meeting on the topic and generate a list of recommendations within a specified period of time. While your group is conducting the meeting, a second small group will be arrayed in a circle around your group, observing your group process.

Scenario 1:

The CEO of a large, Fortune 500 company that has just embraced "teaming" has assembled your team. Customer complaints about your products and services have risen over the last few years and it is your hope that "teaming" can turn that trend around. Your task is to come up with recommendations for how to implement teaming in the customer service division, one of 10 divisions in this company. Mr. Smith, the executive vice president in charge of this project, would like your recommendations by the end of the semester.

Scenario 2:

Your team has been assembled by the Athletic Director to enhance the quantity and quality of the undergraduate recreational athletics at your university. Dr. Jones expects your team's report and recommendations by the end of the semester.

Using the chart below, the observing group will note at least one behavior each group member exhibits. When time is up, the other small group will share their impressions with your group as to which behaviors they observed and did not observe while your group was meeting.

Observing Group Process

Instructions: Enter the names of team members along the top. Enter comments in the appropriate boxes when you see any or all of the behaviors.

Initiating: Gets a conversation going.						
Information or opinion seeking/ giving: Drawing out/ sharing relevant information.						
Clarifying and elaborating: Clears up confusion.						
Summarizing: Pulls together what's been said.						
Consensus testing: Moves the group toward decision.						
Harmonizing and compromising: Reduces tension, works out disagreements.						
Gatekeeping: Helps communication channels open.						
Diagnosing: Looks at the process, how people are feeling about the group.						
Standard setting: Looks at the group structure.						

"Observing Group Process Chart" from Peter R. Scholtes, *The Team Handbook,* (Madison, WI: Joiner Associates, 1988), pp. 7–43.

Questions

1. Which behaviors were observed most frequently? Least?
2. Which behaviors had the greatest positive impact on the team's ability to succeed in its task?
3. Which behaviors, had they been used, would have helped the group to move forward?
4. Did the group appoint a timekeeper? Scribe? Facilitator?
5. What else did the group do to operate effectively?

**Exercise 13–F
Reflection/Action Plan**

This chapter focused on facilitation—what it is, why it is important, and how to improve your skill in this area. Complete the following questions upon completing all readings and experiential activities for this chapter.

1. The one or two areas in which I am most strong are:

   _____

   _____

   _____

   _____

2. The one or two areas in which I need more improvement are:

   _____

   _____

   _____

   _____

3. If I did only one thing to improve in this area, it would be to:

   _____

   _____

   _____

   _____

4. Making this change would probably result in:

   _____

   _____

   _____

   _____

5. If I did not change or improve in this area, it would probably affect my personal and professional life in the following ways:

   _____

   _____

   _____

   _____

14 Making Decisions and Solving Problems Creatively

Learning Points

How do I:

- Decide between competing options and interests?
- Make a decision before having all of the necessary information?
- Make a decision that won't change?
- Evaluate potential options?
- Think creatively about alternatives?

Ashley was torn. She looked at the materials the executive search firm had sent her. Fortunately, she had performed well in her interviews for a senior management position, and had not one, but three job offers from which to choose. Now, she didn't know which one would best suit her personal and professional needs. One of the offers was exactly what she wanted for her next step professionally, but it was in a city far away from her aging parents, whose needs she and a sibling attended to. The second offer was in a location more conducive to her lifestyle needs, but professionally it wasn't quite the "step up" she was seeking. The third was in a different location altogether, and was in a new career field unrelated to her previous background and experience. She had to make a decision soon, but didn't know what to do.

1. Why is Ashley in this situation?
2. What issues is she facing?
3. What options does she have available to her?
4. What should she do?

(Alice standing at the crossroads), "Cheshire-Puss," she began . . . "Would you tell me please which way I ought to go from here?"[1]

Alice in *Alice in Wonderland*

Making decisions—and being able to live with them rather than second-guessing them—is one of the most difficult tasks we face in life and in business. Deciding what major to choose can be just as difficult for a college student as deciding which company to acquire for an ambitious CEO. In this chapter we discuss what decision making is, why it is important, and strategies to use to make effective decisions. At the end of the chapter, we've included some exercises to help you improve your skills in decision making.

What Is Decision Making?

Decision making is a process by which several possibilities are considered and prioritized, resulting in a clear choice of one option over others. Decision making is a fact of life personally and in business. We make dozens of decisions each day. Some decisions are simple, while others are complex. Decision making aids managers in identifying and selecting among potential opportunities, helping them solve immediate problems and make future problems more manageable.[2] Good decision makers are those who are effective at processing information, assessing risks, and making choices that will have positive outcomes for their organization.[3] While at times intuitive or "gut" decision making is appropriate, in this chapter we focus our attention primarily on the rational decision-making process, as it is most relevant to working in organizations and as part of a group.

Why Is Decision Making Important?

Effective decision making is essential for both organizations and individuals. Changes in organizational structures, processes, technology, and the availability of data have increased the need for members at all levels of organization to make decisions—and make them effectively.

■ With the change from hierarchical to flatter, more participative organizational structures, it is crucial for employees at all levels of the organization to have the information and authority they need to react quickly to customer concerns, business issues, and changing market trends. Having a decision-making frame of reference enables employees to react quickly and make decisions that are in the best interest of the organization.

■ Today more business decisions are being made in team environments. Group decision making is even more complex than decisions made by one or two individuals. Employees in team environments need to understand how to gain buy-in for their positions and how to work with others to arrive at a consensus about a preferred course of action. A decision-making framework can provide the basis for identifying mutual interests. This can serve as the foundation for healthy discussion and eventual selection of one option over others.

■ Technology is literally speeding up the pace of business. Quick decision making is not only desired, it is expected.[4] Poor or slow decision making can result in failure or a lack of competitiveness. In our fast-paced business environment, the ability to identify potential problems and opportunities, collect the data needed to analyze their limitations and merits, and make expedient determinations based on the information available has become one of the most important managerial skills. Companies that train their employees to be good decision makers and encourage smart decision making can increase efficiency and boost profits. By eliminating unnecessary steps, combining knowledge, and simplifying processes to help speed up decisions, managers with honed decision-making skills can have a tremendous impact on a company's bottom line.[5]

■ The vast amount of information available today through the media, Internet, and other outlets makes decision making an essential—rather than a "nice to have"—skill. The most effective managers are those who are able to scan quickly a wide variety of data from numerous sources and determine which information is relevant for their needs. Through decision-making processes, managers learn to translate, assimilate, and activate the information they receive.[6] Decision-making skills play a vital role in managerial success.

The Decision-Making Process

Figure 14–1 represents a straightforward **decision-making process** for almost any type of decision. This framework can be used for decisions you face in your personal life, at school, and in the workplace.

**Figure 14–1
The Decision-Making
Process**

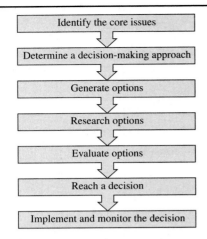

Identify the core issues

Determine a decision-making approach

Generate options

Research options

Evaluate options

Reach a decision

Implement and monitor the decision

Step One—Identify the Core Issues	What is the concern you are addressing? What is it you're trying to change or react to? In the first step of decision making, you need to determine your objective, stating clearly and specifically what you want the end result to be.[7] You want to select a movie everyone can agree on. You want to choose a major that makes you happy. You want to acquire a business that will increase your share of the market. By specifying the end goal or desired state, you have a logical foundation for making a good decision—for sorting through options and determining which one or ones best meet your overall objective.[8]
Step Two—Determine a Decision-Making Approach	How will you (and your group) make the decision? What options are available to you? What are the possible ways in which you can respond to a situation? What are the different steps that can be taken?
	Establish a course of action before attempting to make the decision. This sounds simple. But often people rush to make a decision before agreeing on how the decision will be made. The very act of discussing a potential process paves the way for consideration of options that might not otherwise have surfaced.
Step Three—Generate Options	By definition, making decisions implies that more than one option is available to you. It is very rare and unusual for any problem or situation to have only one solution or possibility. People who only consider one alternative or solution are setting themselves up for failure or marginal success. Often the initial solution presented is not the best one.
	The best decisions are those made after consideration of varied or multiple options. Be creative and brainstorm as many potential alternatives or solutions as possible (more about this later in this chapter).
Step Four—Research Options	For virtually all decisions in teams and in organizations, this is a crucial step. Often one of the reasons we're unable to move forward and make a decision is we simply don't have the information needed to make a good decision. By taking the time to gather data, you are able to increase your confidence that once the decision is made it will be the right one, as it is based on the information available at the time.
Step Five—Evaluate Alternatives	At this point, a little healthy pessimism is needed. Once you've been creative and non-judgmental in generating options and gathering information about them, you can assess the pros and cons of each option.[9] Assess the gains that would be derived from each and any limitations that are inherent in each option. Also consider other factors that are important to you when making the decision and evaluate the degree to which each option relates to the factors of importance.

Many times we work with incomplete or imperfect information in the decision-making process. We can reduce the risk factors by hypothesizing potential scenarios. For each option, ask questions such as, What would happen if I decided to do option X? How would I feel if I were to implement option X? How would option X affect other areas of my life or the business? At this stage, it's also appropriate to narrow the alternatives. Only consider the options that are truly realistic and fulfill the goal or desired end state you defined in step one.

With the availability of so much information in today's technology age, it is possible to get caught up in having too many alternatives, too many ideas, and too much work. This can lead to a lack of focus and momentum, which can lead to indecisiveness and a loss of power.[10] We may become overwhelmed by the options and never proceed to selecting one, a condition known as **analysis paralysis**.[11] Prioritizing the factors that are important to you and evaluating your options against these priorities can help you to narrow the options to those that are the most viable given the circumstances and your goals in a specific situation.

Step Six—Reach a Decision

Once all the information is in and you've had a chance to consult with others as necessary and weigh the alternatives, it's time to make a decision. Determine which option best meets your overall needs and resolve to act on that option. But before taking the plunge, envision taking the plunge first. Do a self-visualization to make sure the decision you're making is one you can live with. One way to do this is to make a decision, but take 24 hours to think about it. Let your subconscious act as though you've made the decision, but don't let anyone know and don't act on the decision yet. The next morning, before you even rise, ask yourself how you feel about the decision you made yesterday. Listen to what your heart tells you. Do you feel positive? Calm? Like it was the right choice? Or do you feel negative? Panicked? Like it would be the wrong choice? If you feel fine about the choice you've made, it's an intuitive sign you've made the best decision given the information available and you can probably act on it. If you still have serious reservations about your decision, then you're not ready to act and you should defer action until you've had a chance to resolve the conflict you're experiencing.

Step Seven—Implement and Monitor

Once you've reached a decision, it's time to act on your decision and monitor it to make sure it's resulting in the outcome you expected. Develop a plan that specifies the steps you'll take, a time frame, and the key players. Then, monitor the plan to see if it is following the direction you wanted. Also observe whether external factors have changed or if you're receiving information that might affect your decision, and adapt your plan accordingly. Taking the time to plan and to monitor the decision after making a decision ensures that you'll do the follow-through necessary for the decision to be successful.

What Kind of Decision Maker Are You?

What kind of decision maker are you? You may be more methodical, pondering your situation and analyzing options before deciding on one. You may be more impulsive, reacting quickly and intuitively. Or perhaps you are somewhere in the middle, acting based on your intuition, after taking some time to explore the situation. Whatever your natural style, when considering a life or career decision or change, it is important to incorporate elements of all of these approaches.

- If you are usually organized, analytical, and deliberate in making decisions (often referred to as "left-brained,") be somewhat creative and see what your intuition can contribute to your decision.
- If you are intuitive and tend to approach things in a roundabout way (often referred to as "right-brained,") or make decisions hastily based on your past experience, take the time to develop and implement a plan in consultation with others who can help keep you on track.

Whether we act intuitively, analytically, or through a combination of the two, it is important to take time to make a decision with which we can live. The chart below offers pointers about steps to take before making a decision.[12]

The "Readiness for Change" Test: Don't Make a Decision Until . . .	• You've assessed your risk-taking ability, clarified your options, and generated creative options • You've communicated with and obtained full support from those who are affected by the decision • You've gathered the information you need • You've predicted the "best and worst" outcomes and developed contingency plans • You're ready to follow through, and stick with, your choice • You've "slept on it" and your intuition is telling you it's the right thing to do • You have an exit strategy for "just in case"
Collaborative Decision Making	One of the reasons it's often difficult to make decisions is we're not the only one involved in making the decision. When you're in a significant relationship with someone else—whether a spouse or partner, team member, employer, customer, or client—it's useful to know how to take into consideration the best interests of the other party or parties who will be affected by the outcome. **Collaborative decision making** involves identifying your and the other parties' priorities and determining the option(s) available that meet both sets of needs. This can be possible by careful attention to your and the others' ability to handle risks; thorough assessment of each of your primary needs and motivators; continuous, positive communication; and a willingness to be creative in generating options rather than taking a stand for one fixed option. See the chart below for tips for collaborative decision making.
Tips for Collaborative Decision Making[13]	• Consider you and the person(s) involved as one unit. Do what's ultimately best for the unit (e.g., the team, the organization, the couple, the family, etc.). • Be open to new ways of looking at the situation. Establish what's important to you and the other(s). • Sharpen your communication skills. Making decisions as though others mattered requires shifting focus from one's own interests to a set of joint interests—those of self and others. In particular, skills in self-disclosure, value clarification, assertiveness, sending verbal and nonverbal messages, active listening, persuasion, conflict management, and interest-based negotiation are particularly helpful in collaborative decision making. • Rely on your intuition. The analytical process described in this chapter is useful and important. But don't rely solely on a logical approach in decision making. Your feelings (and those of the others involved in the decision) are just as important as the pragmatic facts of the situation. • Have a "veto" rule. Some teams and couples rely on a "veto" guideline to prevent them from moving forward before all involved are "on the same page." A veto guideline gives each party the freedom to "call time" and request that a decision not be enacted until all issues are resolved.

In the next section we discuss problem solving, why it's important, strategies that can be used to solve problems, and tips to make your problem solving efforts more productive. We also include information on creativity to aid in innovative thinking. At the end of the chapter are some exercises to help you enhance your skills in rational and creative problem solving as well as suggestions for further resources.

What Is Problem Solving?

Dr. Walter A. Shewhart suggests that **problem solving** is a cyclical process composed of four steps: Plan, Do, Check, Act **(PDCA)**.[14] This process was introduced to Japan by W. Edwards Deming, one of the most highly recognized gurus of quality management techniques. As you can see from Figure 14–2, the most important step in the process is the *plan*. It is in this stage that we define and identify potential solutions for problems. This is easier said than done. What looks like the problem might actually be a symptom. Correctly defining the problem can be a challenge; with the remaining elements in this step we validate whether we identified the real problem and create a plan for fixing it.

Once the plan is complete, the next stage is to *"do"*—or implement—the plan. Next, we *"check"* to see if the changes made resulted in lasting, measurable improvements. If not, we may need to take a step back. Did we solve the right problem? Did we unknowingly create a new one? Did we implement a short-term fix that will need modifications in the future? Based on our check, we then *"act"* by taking appropriate steps to adjust or ensure the problem is solved.

Figure 14–2
PDCA Cycle

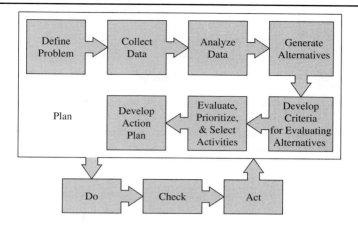

Why Is Problem Solving Important?

Organizational problems come in many forms—whether in processes (how managers lead, how employees communicate, how work flows, how conflicts are solved, how employees deal with customers or suppliers) or outcomes (inadequate or unsatisfactory products or services, excessive employee absenteeism or turnover, insufficient profit margins). Problems such as these can significantly hamper an organization's ability to operate and succeed in the long term. The ability to solve problems—and apply problem-solving techniques to improve processes that work—can significantly and positively impact an organization's bottom line, as well as its long-term viability.

All too often, managers and employees rush to fix what they do not completely understand, in effect relieving symptoms temporarily. Often the problem resurfaces, possibly with greater intensity and impact than during its initial appearance.[15]

Problem-Solving Techniques

These techniques can be used individually or in combination depending on the nature of the problem and resources available.

Brainstorming

Brainstorming is a tool used to stimulate and capture creative thoughts and ideas. It involves the creative generation of many ideas to solve a problem. There are several variations of brainstorming, yet they all have in common the following ground rules:

Brainstorming Guidelines

- Articulate the theme or the question (e.g., Why are sales down? How can we cut costs in the manufacturing area?).
- Set a time limit (usually 5 or 10 minutes, depending on the size of the group and the complexity of the theme or question).
- Record the ideas for everyone to see (using a flipchart or whiteboard).
- Quantity is important (generate as many ideas as possible).
- Everyone should actively participate (no benchwarmers!).
- All ideas are good ideas (positive or negative critiquing is *not* permitted).
- Piggyback or build on ideas of others.

If the pace begins to slow, or participants seem stifled by constraints, the leader or facilitator of the brainstorming session may ask a hypothetical question such as "What if money were no object?" or "What if you could wave a magic wand to get rid of these problems . . . which ones would disappear?" During the process, it is important to enforce the ground rules should they be broken. Many people can't seem to resist evaluating others' ideas—it's human nature. However, such evaluation can stifle creativity or cause participants to censor their ideas before sharing them with the group.

After the flow of ideas slows, and all useful hypothetical questions have been used, it is time to ask questions and clarify and consolidate ideas. Evaluation should still be kept to a minimum, as the craziest of ideas may spawn other creative but useful ideas or solutions. Be careful not to remove or downplay ideas prematurely.

A normal or open[16] brainstorming session tends to result in the most ideas, the most creative ideas, and the most synergy among group participants and their ideas.[17] However, those who are introverted or feel inhibited by senior members of the organization may be overshadowed by those who are more verbal or dominant. To ensure that all members present fully participate in the idea-generating process, consider using variations on brainstorming, such as round robin, nominal group technique, and Post-It Note brainstorming.

- In **round robin** brainstorming, group members participate in a structured order, for instance, starting with the person at the head of the table and moving clockwise. Using this technique helps equalize the verbal and less verbal participants, but may inhibit some of the creative disagreement that comes when participants can shout out ideas as they come.

- The **nominal group technique**, or NGT, is another variation on open brainstorming that ameliorates the negative impact that status differences may have on a problem-solving group. The technique "nominalizes" or equalizes hierarchical or status differences among members of a group, enabling individuals to speak out without concern for such differences or fears of being ridiculed.[18] To brainstorm NGT style, all team members are given index cards or pads on which to write their ideas. After the theme or question is posed, each person in the group must write down as many answers to the question as they can. After the silent writing of ideas slows, you ask each member in sequence to share one written idea, recording all ideas on the flip chart for everyone to see. Keep going around the group, asking for and recording one unique idea from each person until all written ideas are recorded. If individuals note that their idea was already listed, underline or put a check next to the idea.

- When using the **Post-It Note brainstorming** variation,[19] participants' brainstormed ideas are written on Post-It Notes—one idea per note—instead of on a flip chart. For the open method, this variation requires one scribe to record each idea on a Post-It Note and then stick it to a wall or whiteboard. Post-It Notes can also be used in the nominal group technique; all participants are given a pad of Post-It Notes (instead of cards or slips of paper) on which to write their ideas. Scribing ideas on Post-It Notes may take a bit longer than using the traditional method, but one benefit is the ability to easily manipulate the idea in subsequent problem-solving steps or techniques such as affinitizing, which is described next.

Using Affinitizing to Synthesize Brainstormed Ideas

The **affinitizing** method provides a useful means to organize and produce agreement on categories of ideas; doing so facilitates a group's ability to address organizational problems.

The process is fairly simple. After brainstorming ideas on Post-It Notes (or cards), group members use the following steps:

Affinitizing Steps

1. Stick the notes on a wall or whiteboard so that each note can be seen (or spread out cards on a large desk).
2. Silently (no talking allowed!), group related ideas by moving notes into categories.
3. Discuss, clarify, and modify groups as necessary once the movement slows.
4. Brainstorm a title that encapsulates or expresses the theme for each group of notes. When all agree on the titles for each grouping, they are written on Post-It Notes (one per grouping) and placed at the top of each grouping.

At this point, instead of working with 20 or 30 unmanageable ideas, the group has pared down the ideas into 3–8 manageable groups of ideas. As an added bonus, the highly participative nature of brainstorming and affinitizing helps build consensus among team members on identifying problems.

Building Consensus through Multivoting

Multivoting can be used with a brainstormed list of topics or a pared down list of affinitized categories. The process is as follows:

Multivoting Steps

1. Begin with the brainstormed list. As appropriate, combine overlapping items. Another option is to use the categories that emerged from the affinitizing process.

2. Number each idea or category.

3. Divide the total number of ideas or categories by 3; this is the number of votes each member gets. If there are 13 ideas, each member picks his or her top 4; if there are 8 categories, each member picks 3. (Individuals may only give one vote per idea or category.) It might be useful to discuss selection criteria before members make their selections. For example, instruct members to consider those with the greatest potential impact or least time to implement when making their choices.

4. After members have had time to select and jot down their top choices, have a recorder tabulate the results. An easy method is to jot down the numbers and, for each number, ask which members had this as one of their top choices. Another method is to go around the room and ask each member their choices, placing hatch marks adjacent to the appropriate number.

5. The idea or category with the highest number of votes wins. In the event of a tie, utilize the multivoting process once more to arrive at a winner.

Because participants each pick their top choices, the winning idea or category tends to be on almost everyone's list. While multivoting does not by itself produce consensus, it gets the group closer, quickly.

At this point, you should be familiar with an assortment of tools and techniques to use when attempting to solve a problem. While you may think that all organizations use a logical, rational approach similar to the problem-solving process we've outlined, this is not necessarily the case. Other approaches are available, and depending on the problem at hand and the people involved, other approaches to solving problems may be warranted. In the next section, we describe several intuitive or creative approaches that can be used to complement or substitute stages in the problem-solving process.

What Is Creativity and Why Is It Important?

Carol Goman, well-known creativity author and consultant, defines **creativity** as "bringing into existence an idea that is new to you."[20] She cites research done in the late 1940s by a group of psychologists attempting to prove that by age 45, few individuals could think creatively. By testing subjects at various ages, they found that 90 percent of five-year-olds were highly creative; by age 17, that number dropped to 10 percent; and by 20, the figure dropped and stayed at about 5 percent.[21]

What makes individuals and businesses ultimately successful is creativity and innovation.[22] Consider this: a plain iron bar is worth $5. If you take that iron bar and forge horseshoes from it, the value increases to $11. If it is made into needles, the price rises to $3,285. And if you make watch springs from it, it is then worth $250,000. The difference between $5 and $250,000 is creativity.[23] When we see things differently, we break with tradition and find solutions and often new problems. Creative problem solving helps us to view a situation from a new perspective and increases the likelihood that we will generate innovative, cost-effective ways to do business. Imagine coming to work one day and pretending you were a customer or competitor. What are your reactions? How could you use those observations to find new ways of solving old problems? How do our assumptions about how things have always operated constrain us from changing and finding more innovative ways to operate?

Strategies for Increasing Creativity in Problem Solving

Creative problem solving requires the use of both convergent and divergent thinking. **Convergent thinking** is starting with a problem and working to move toward a solution. Most of us take this approach. If you walk into your apartment and notice a foul odor, you're likely to first check to see if the trash needs to be taken out. Then you'll look in the refrigerator, and so on. Eventually, you may find (and eradicate) the problem. Another approach to solving problems is **divergent thinking.** This involves generating new ways to view a problem and seeking out novel alternatives to the problem.

Let's say your manager informs you that the incidence of shoplifting has been increasing at the apparel store in which you work as a salesperson. The convergent approach involves the usual—install video cameras, post warning signs, install antitheft tags on the clothing. Taking a divergent approach, you might first create analogies for the problem statement, how do we keep people from stealing? Trying to keep people from shoplifting is *like:*[24]

- Trying to keep kids from sneaking cookies out of the cookie jar.
- Trying to prevent people from jaywalking.
- Trying to keep flies away from cow manure.

Next, you solve the analogy. How do you keep kids from sneaking cookies out of the cookie jar? Hide the jar, put a lock on the jar, or give the kids cookies. How do you prevent people from jaywalking? Post warning signs, increase police presence, increase the number of tickets issued, or create physical barriers along the street. How do you keep flies away from cow manure? Cover the manure, move the animals to another site, or create a fly-friendly haven.

Finally, transfer the analogy solutions to the problem. To keep people from stealing, we could hide the expensive clothing or put it in a special room, give out free samples of apparel (something very cheap), give out free clothes for those who turn in shoplifters, or move the store to another area (or venue, such as catalog or Internet sales).

Four Stages of Creative Problem Solving[25]

- Preparation—gather info, define the problem, generate alternatives, examine all available info.
- Incubation—involves mostly subconscious mental activity in which the mind combines unrelated thoughts in pursuit of a solution.
- Illumination—occurs when insight is recognized and a creative solution is articulated. This is sometimes called the AHA! stage.
- Verification—involves evaluating the creative solution relative to some standard of acceptability. In this phase, you test to see if the idea can work. You might do a reality check (pulling the creativity down to fit within constraints and boundaries), ask for feedback from others (is this feasible or how can we make it feasible?), or try a pilot project.

Some Methods for Generating Novel Ideas

Not everyone gets to the illumination phase in the same way or time. Some people are naturally creative—they are tinkerers. Others either haven't developed this skill, have had it "beaten out of them," or could benefit from some techniques. Several methods and examples for generating novel ideas are below.[26]

- Part Changing—list parts or attributes that can be changed. Think about the first laptop computer. It did everything a desktop PC could do, only it was lighter and portable. How about the popular fruit smoothies? Before that, if you wanted something cold and thick, you'd get a milkshake. If you want to improve a product or service, list the parts or attributes. Brainstorm possible changes—even ones you think could never work. How about online banking and loans, online brokerage services, virtual real estate or vacation tours, or online doctors?

■ Checkerboard—make a grid with parts or attributes listed on the vertical and horizontal axes to find new interactions or combinations. By considering "forced" combinations, new ideas could emerge—if you let them. How about the all-in-one office machine (printer, scanner, fax, copier)?

■ Checklist—make lists to make sure nothing is left out or forgotten. Using questions such as those below can serve as a checklist for ensuring that all possibilities are considered:

  ■ What else can this be used for?

  ■ What could be used instead? What else is like this?

  ■ How could it be adopted or modified for a new use?

  ■ What if it were larger, thicker, heavier, or stronger?

  ■ What if it were smaller, thinner, lighter, or shorter?

  ■ How might it be rearranged or reversed?

■ **Analogy Method**—fix a problem or create something new by thinking of other products, people, animals, or social units that perform similar acts to make analogies. The shoplifting example we discussed is one application of the similarity method; another example is waiting for you to try at the end of the chapter. What follows is an actual situation in which this method was successfully used to solve a business problem.

A cosmetics manufacturer watched as sales of its lipsticks declined. They weren't sure why this was occurring, so they decided to investigate. Using customer information cards filled out at various cosmetics counters, they contacted customers and asked if they would be willing to participate in a focus group. It turns out that the customers liked the lipsticks—the colors, the texture, the staying power, the options (sheer, frosted, and matte), and the price were all judged satisfactory. What customers didn't like was the metal tube into which the lipstick was placed when not in use. Within weeks of purchase, the tubes looked old and tarnished. This made customers think that the lipsticks were perhaps old. After buying the product the first time, few customers made repeat purchases.

The manufacturer undertook several experiments to respond to this problem, but was unable to find a material that wouldn't tarnish. Employees were challenged to solve this problem. One employee, a hunting enthusiast, noticed that ammunition was always bright and shiny—even cases that had been in his closet for years. He contacted the ammunition manufacturer, explaining his dilemma, and requested a visit. While there, the employee learned what materials were used for the ammunition casings. These materials were then used for the lipstick cases. It worked! Within a short period of time, the trend toward declining sales was reversed. The moral of this story is to be willing to challenge assumptions about where to look for clues to solving problems.

Management's Role in Supporting and Stimulating Creativity

Many of the ideas we've discussed seem simple enough. With practice, we can all use analogies, checkerboards, or other approaches to find creative solutions to enduring problems. What happens when employees are creative but the rest of the organization is not? Unfortunately, this is often the case. How many of the following statements have you heard before in your organizations?

Idea Killers

- We tried it before.
- It would cost too much.
- That's not my job.
- That's not how we do things here.
- You may be right, but . . .
- That'll never work.
- You can't do that here.
- Our customers would never go for that.
- It's good enough.
- If it ain't broke, don't fix it.

Goman calls these and similar statements **idea killers.**[27] When creative suggestions or ideas are met with these responses, creativity is killed—not just now, but in the future as well. Statements such as these send the message that any idea that "breaks the rules" will not be accepted, let alone listened to. If you are on the receiving end of one of these statements, chances are you'll learn to keep your mouth shut. Who wants to be ridiculed? Even when employees are told to be creative and innovative, any encouragement coupled with idea killers is likely to be canceled out.

Instead, as a colleague and manager of other employees, you can play a role in creating an environment that truly encourages and stimulates creativity. How you respond to others' creative ideas sends a strong message for future attempts. Statements such as the following show that you are listening to another's idea and are open to continued discussion.

Idea Growers

- How could we improve . . . ?
- How can (that suggestion) build on (a previous idea)?
- What have we missed?
- Who else would be affected?
- What would happen if . . . ?

- Who else has a suggestion?
- I don't know much about that. How about you?
- How many ways could we . . . ?
- May I ask a question?

Idea growers, as Goman calls statements like these,[28] really help continue conversations focused on creative problem solving and stimulate further creative ideas. Saying you value creativity isn't the same as demonstrating it! Think about it. If an employee were to come to you with an idea you believe is ill-conceived, how would you respond? We're not suggesting you should lie and treat employees like the two-year-old who managed to eat her food without plastering the walls with it. At the same time, you can give feedback in a way that encourages the employee to keep working at the idea while addressing concerns you may have.

One technique that you could use is called **P-P-C,** which stands for *Positives, Possibilities, and Concerns.*[29] It works like this. Imagine you manage the women's wear section of a major department store. You have solicited the input of your employees on ways to improve customer service. One employee, Nancy, suggests clearing enough space to place comfortable chairs, a table, and reading material to increase the spouses' and boyfriends' willingness to wait while their partners try on clothes. She further suggests serving coffee or wine. You have some reservations, but there are some strengths in the idea. Using the P-P-C approach, you respond:

- Positives: "I like your concern regarding the spouses."
- Possibilities: "We could even include merchandise catalogues (e.g., automotive, tools, stereo) for them to read while they wait."
- Concerns: "I'm not sure we could take down the display area to make enough room to implement the idea. How do you think it could be handled?"

You might take this idea a step further. Since most thinking in organizations is logical and rational, set aside a room (or part of another room or basement) and call it the **innovation chamber.**[30] Even if creativity is not totally valued in other parts of the organization, this is one place where it is not only valued but also desired. This chamber will become a safe haven for generating innovative, creative ideas. You might even decorate it in a way that stimulates creative thinking (i.e., neither white walls nor a linoleum floor). For example, paint the walls with abstract designs, use colored lights (pink, purple), play soft music, use floor pillows instead of a table and chairs, and have plenty of space for writing (or use flip chart paper taped to the walls). Put a sign on the door and send an official memo to employees about the purpose and use of this room. Post rules in the room, such as these:

- The innovation chamber is a criticism-free space.
- All ideas—even crazy ones—are welcomed, discussed, and credited to the individual and the group.
- All who enter must participate.
- If no really deviant ideas emerge, then the session is less than successful.

Strategies for Increasing Individual Creativity

We mentioned earlier that as we age, we lose our capacity to be creative. There are many reasons why this occurs, but more importantly, how can you get this lost creativity back? Here are a few suggestions:

- Do creative exercises: Challenge your mind. Resist the temptation to opt for quick, tried and true solutions. Experiment, play, and search out new solutions. Like any other muscle in the body, the mind becomes weak and rigid in the absence of exercise.[31]
- Break some rules. Write in your books, order off the menu, question the validity (and objectivity) of news reports, challenge your religious beliefs, vote differently from your parents or how you might have voted 10 years ago.
- Learn your language (or a new one). Commit to learning one new word a day. Ensure you pronounce it correctly.
- Keep an open mind. When you meet someone new, take in all aspects of that person's personality and don't label them as a ditz, lazy, and so on.
- Keep a journal. Writing down your thoughts helps you remember key discoveries, such as feelings, emotions, and beliefs. One of your most creative moments is right when you wake up. This is one of the best times to jot down your thoughts, especially if you can remember key aspects of a dream you had that night.
- Develop confidence in your senses.[32] Don't wear a watch; guess the time given available clues. Guess the temperature before looking at the sign above the bank. Guess your friends' heights and weights using your own as a comparison, and if you're brave enough, ask for confirmation. Cook something without a recipe or measuring devices. Use your sense of smell and taste to make needed modifications.
- Expose yourself to new perspectives. Take an elevator to the top of a tall building; what do you see that you couldn't see before? Read a novel or see a movie that you would ordinarily never read or see. Eat a type of food that you've never eaten before. Travel outside your comfort zone—this may be different for different people. For some, it's outside the town; for others, it's outside the continent. An excellent illustration of this is the scene in the film *Dead Poet's Society* in which Robin Williams's character has his students stand up on their desks to get a different perspective of the world. A bit unusual for a conservative school, but that was the point![33]

Being creative is not just a workplace skill; it's a life skill as well. How we approach situations is a function of how many possibilities we can see. Have you ever tried to buy a car and found out that your credit was less than perfect? Did you give up or begin looking for a creative way to finance this purchase? How about when you and your significant other are planning a date. Do you stop after suggesting movies or dinner? What about a picnic in the mountains? A lesson in ballroom dancing? Bungee jumping? When you exercise your creative potential, you can benefit both professionally and personally.

Summary

We face decisions every day. Some of these are tough—mired in ambiguity, complexity, and ethical considerations—while others are easy. The process by which you make decisions can significantly impact whether the decision is right—effective and successful in the long term—for you and those affected by the decision. While simple decisions, such as whether to wear a blue or red shirt, may not require a multistep decision process, more complex and consequential decisions do.

Organizations face problems (or opportunities) on a daily basis. Those firms that take a disciplined approach to problem solving—clearly defining the problem, identifying potential and creative solutions, selecting solutions based on appropriate criteria, and creating a detailed plan to implement the solution—are likely to succeed and prosper. Finding solutions—especially creative ones—to problems or inventing new products and processes requires creative employees and the right environment. Your effectiveness as a manager can be greatly enhanced by your ability to make effective decisions and solve problems creatively.

Key Terms and Concepts

Affinitizing	Idea growers
Analogy method	Idea killers
Analysis paralysis	Innovation chamber
Brainstorming	Multivoting
Collaborative decision making	Nominal group technique
Convergent thinking	PDCA cycle
Creativity	Post-It Note brainstorming
Decision making	P-P-C technique
Decision-making process (steps)	Problem solving
Divergent thinking	Round robin

Endnotes

1. Lewis Carroll, *Alice in Wonderland* (NJ: Castle Books, 1978).

2. Raymond Suutari, "Tale of Two Strategies: How Does Your Company Make Its Strategic Business Decisions," *CMA Management,* July–August 1999, p. 12.

3. Rosemary Kane Carlough, "From the Publisher (The Importance of Communicating Decisions)," *HR Focus,* July 1999, p. 1.

4. Sal Marino, "Rely on Science, Not Your Gut," *Industry Week,* Jan. 24, 2000, p. 18.

5. D. Keith Denton and Peter Richardson, "Making Speedy Decisions," *Industrial Management,* Sept. 1999, p. 6.

6. A. Read, "Managers Making Dicey Decisions," *Internal Auditor,* Dec. 1999, p. 14.

7. Winston Fletcher, "It's Make Your Mind Up Time," *Management Today,* Sept. 1998, p. 31.

8. Ralph L. Keeney, "Foundations for Making Smart Decisions," *IIE Solutions,* May 1999, p. 24.

9. Fletcher, "Make Your Mind Up Time."

10. Jennifer White, "Maintaining Focus: The Best Way to Overcome the 'Too Much Syndrome,'" *Business Journal,* March 10, 2000, p. 39.

11. Joel Barker, *Paradigms: The Business of Discovering the Future* (New York: Harper Business, 1993).

12. This material and the chart below adapted from Karen O. Dowd and Sherrie Gong Taguchi, *The Ultimate Guide to Getting the Career You Want (and What to Do Once You Have It)* (New York: McGraw Hill, 2003).

13. Dowd and Taguchi, *The Ultimate Guide.*

14. Paul Kiesow, "PDCA Cyle: An Approach to Problem Solving," *Ceramic Industry,* Oct. 1994, p. 20.

15. Quinn Spitzer and Ron Evans, "New Problems in Problem Solving," *Across the Board,* April 1997, p. 36.

16. R. Glenn Ray, *The Facilitative Leader: Behaviors That Enable Success* (Upper Saddle River, NJ: Prentice Hall, 1999).

17. Ibid., p. 103.

18. Larry Hirschhorn, *Managing in the New Team Environment: Skills, Tools, and Methods* (Reading, MA: Addison Wesley, 1991).

19. Ethan M. Rasiel, "Some Brainstorming Exercises," *Across the Board,* June 2000, p. 10.

20. Carol Kinsey Goman, *Creativity in Business: A Practical Guide for Creative Thinking* (Menlo Park, CA: Crisp Publications, 2000), p. 46.

21. Ibid., p. 11.

22. Oren Harari, "Turn Your Organization into a Hotbed of Ideas," *Management Review,* Dec. 1995, pp. 37–40.

23. Goman, *Creativity in Business,* citing a "Ripley's Believe It or Not" column.

24. This example is adapted from Goman, *Creativity in Business*, pp. 62–63.

25. J. W. Haefele, *Creativity and Innovation* (New York: Reinhold, 1962); Max H. Bazerman, *Judgment in Managerial Decision Making* (New York: Wiley, 1986), pp. 89–91.

26. G. David and S. Houtman, "Thinking Creatively: A Guide to Training Imagination" (Madison WI: Wisconsin Research and Development Center for Cognitive Learning, 1968); and Goman, *Creativity in Business.*

27. Goman, *Creativity in Business,* p. 76.

28. Ibid., p. 77.

29. Example adapted from Goman, *Creativity in Business,* p. 82.

30. Floyd Hurt, "Creativity: A Hole in Your Head," *Agency Sales Magazine,* June 1998, pp. 58–60.

31. Tom Wujec, *Pumping Ions: Games and Exercises to Flex Your Mind* (New York: Doubleday, 1988).

32. Marilyn vos Savant and Leonore Fleischer, *Brain Building in Just 12 Weeks* (New York: Bantam Books, 1991).

33. The authors thank Robert A. Herring of Winston-Salem State University for making this suggestion.

Exercise 14–A
Decision-Making
Matrix

- **Step 1:** Use the table below to choose four mutually exclusive options to pursue in the first year after your graduation from college. In other words, what will you do with your life after you graduate? At the bottom of this page, succinctly describe each option.
- **Step 2:** In the column entitled, "Decision Factor," briefly describe the aspect or criterion that differentiates your choice of one option over the other. For example, one decision factor might be "income in first year." Another might be "intellectual challenge," and so on. Bear in mind that each decision factor must be applicable (but not necessarily the best) for each outcome. For example, if one outcome option is to join the Army, you cannot use a decision factor like "overcome fear of guns." If you did, the only possible column that could get the check mark would be the one for "Join the Army."
- **Step 3:** Using the criteria in step 2, place an X in the column for each row that will most thoroughly fulfill that criterion/factor. That is, which option is the best for that decision factor?
- **Step 4:** Add the number of X's in each column and record that number at the bottom of the table in each column.
- **Step 5:** For the time being, ignore the left-hand column.
- **Step 6:** Your instructor will debrief this exercise with the class.

Where to Live 2006

	Decision Factor	Options			
		A	B	C	D
	Price	✓		✓	
	Neighbourhood	✓	✓	✓	
	Commute	✓	✓		✓
	Access to ammen.	✓	✓		
	Lifestyle Impacts				✓
	Maintenance Fees	✓		✓	
	Visitor Parking	✓		✓	✓
	TOTALS:	6	3	4	3

Option A: North Burnaby

Option B: Yaletown

Option C: East

Option D: North Vancouver

This exercise was developed and contributed to this book by Dr. Brian K. Miller, Assistant Professor, Management Program, College of Business, James Madison University, Harrisonburg, Virginia, 2004.

**Exercise 14–B
Weighted Average
Decision Making**

Sometimes it's difficult to make a decision in which many variables are involved that are all important to you. But since it's unlikely you'll be able to make a decision that satisfies all your needs, weighted averaging gives you a way to differentiate those factors that are more important to you than others and to weigh these differences when analyzing the factors. Working on your own, think of a decision that you need to make now or that you will face in the near future.

1. On a separate sheet of paper, list all of the variables or factors (up to 10) that are important to you in making a specific decision. These factors determine what you want to achieve from the decision's outcome.

2. In the left column below, list these factors in priority order, #1 = most important.

3. Across the top of the page, list each alternative you are considering (up to four alternatives).

4. Start with the first factor. Working across this row, determine which option best meets this factor and assign the number 1 to that option. Then determine the option that next best meets the factor, assigning it the number 2. Continue with this determination using the numbers 3 and 4.

5. Move to the second (and subsequent factors) and repeat step 4.

6. Multiply each cell (#1–4) by the priority number in the corresponding row (#1–10). Note these numbers in each cell.

7. Sum each column. The column with the *lowest* sum below is the option that *best* meets your higher-priority needs (your top priority is #1).

Factor/Priority	NorBurn Option A	Yaletown Option B	East Option C	NorVan Option D
1. Price	2 / 2	4 / 4	1 / 1	3 / 3
2. Neighbourhood	2 / 4	1 / 2	4 / 8	3 / 6
3. Commute	2 / 6	1 / 3	4 / 12	3 / 9
4. Access to ammenities	2 / 8	1 / 4	3 / 12	4 / 16
5. Lifestyle impacts	2 / 10	3 / 15	1 / 5	4 / 20
6. Maintenance Fees	2 / 12	4 / 24	1 / 6	3 / 18
7.				
8.				
9.				
10.				
Sum	12 / 42 #1	14 / 52 #3	14 / 44 #2	20 / 72 #4

Exercise 14–C
Brainstorming—A
Warm-up

How creative are you? Using the space below, brainstorm as many ideas as you can in five minutes on the *alternative uses of a paper clip*. Write down all ideas, even outlandish ones. If you get stuck, switch your point of view—what if you were lost at sea, in a desert, in a snowstorm, or on the moon? Challenge your assumptions about the paper clip—how can it be changed to produce different purposes?

Questions

1. How did you do?
2. Did you use the entire time? Could you have continued writing after time was up?
3. How could this technique be applied in the workplace?

Exercise 14–D
Binge Drinking
Problem Solving

The following questions pertain to the problem-solving exercise you were led through in class.

1. Did your problem-solving group arrive at a workable plan for implementing a solution? If yes, to what do you attribute the group's success? If not, what precluded you from generating a workable solution to the problem presented?

2. In what ways did solving the problem as a group instead of individually improve the process and outcome?

3. In what ways did solving the problem as a group instead of individually hinder or undermine the process and outcome?

4. How did you overcome these hindrances?

**Exercise 14–E
The Lawn: A Problem-
Solving Exercise**

1. Each group will receive 25 statements of data concerning a situation: the goal is to define the problem from the data given. Each member of a group gets *five* of that group's statements. The rules for the activity are listed below:

   a. The members are not permitted to exchange cards or to show their cards to other members of their group.

   b. All data must be communicated orally to the other members of the group; these statements may be repeated as often as the group feels is necessary.

   c. If all members of the group feel that a statement (data) is not relevant to arriving at the definition of the problem, the statement is to be placed face down and not repeated.

   d. Group members may *not* take notes during the process.

   e. Only one problem definition may be presented from each group.

2. At the end of the allotted time, your group must write a definition of the problem on a sheet of blank paper and submit it to the instructor. After doing so, discuss:

   a. Your reactions to the experience.

   b. Any difficulties you had in separating irrelevant from relevant data.

   c. How your groups decided which data were relevant.

   d. How the use of only verbal communication affected the difficulty of the task.

Source: J. William Pfeifffer, Handbook of Structured Experiences Kit, University Associates, 1983, #GTB PS/A-17. Copyright © 1983 by John Wiley & Sons, Inc. Reprinted by permission of John Wiley and Sons. Inc.

**Exercise 14–F
Developing a New
Team Sport**

You are part of a team charged with creating a new team sport that will increase the use of some of the sporting equipment that your company produces. Your new sport must use at least two items from your company's product list (you may use other equipment or props if necessary):

Baseball bat	Soccer ball
Football	Tennis ball
Frisbee	Tennis racquet
Horse shoes	Swimming goggles
Volleyball net	Boxing gloves
Pogo stick	Hula-hoop
Jump rope	Bike helmets

Your team must provide the following criteria in developing the sport:

- The equipment that will be necessary.
- The playing surface or field dimensions and type.
- The number and type of team players, any specialized positions.
- The time frame for the sporting activity (innings, periods, etc.).
- The point systems and means for measurement; how to determine a winner; how to obtain a score; differentials in scoring, penalties, and so on.
- All rules that are required in playing the sport.
- The process for playing the game—sequence, format, instructions, or training.
- Name of the game.

Questions

1. Did your team go through the four stages of creative problem solving? Explain.
2. What method or techniques did you use to generate novel and creative ideas?
3. What was difficult about this exercise? Easy? Explain.
4. Based on your experience, how would you express a team's ability to be creative as compared with an individual?

Exercise 14–G
Creative Groups

Without lifting your pencil, draw no more than four straight lines to connect all nine dots to one another.

• • •

• • •

• • •

Now try to find other ways to connect the dots with three lines, two lines, and even one line. Compare your answers with others sitting near you.

Now join with another team. Your task is to pass an object (e.g., a ball, hat, notebook) so that every team member's hands have touched the object. Do an initial run, and then discuss and try process improvements that will shorten the time needed to complete a single process (passing through all members' hands once).

Questions

1. Discuss the creative process. How does it happen for you, as an individual? Compare your answer with that of your teammates.
2. Discuss the creative process in a group setting. What behaviors or actions helped and hindered your group when it tried to find new or better solutions?
3. What did you learn about yourself and others from this exercise?
4. How can you apply this to work groups at school? In the workplace?

Source: Based on J. L. Adams, *Conceptual Blockbusting: A Guide to Better Ideas,* 2nd ed., New York: Norton, 2001, pp. 25–30.

Exercise 14–H
Solving "Real" Problems

1. Select a problematic operation or process in your school or organization, perhaps one about which students or employees complain (e.g., too cumbersome, too time consuming, inaccurate).
2. Brainstorm (alone or with a group) potential causes for this problem. Why does this problem exist or what has caused this to be problematic?

3. Select a key cause by using affinitizing and or multivoting (see chapter for explanation if needed).

4. Focusing on this key cause, brainstorm as many potential creative solutions as you can in five minutes. Write them in the space below.

5. Which of these ideas, if implemented, is likely to result in a lasting improvement? Why? Support your answer with logic.

6. What barriers are you likely to face if you were given the green light to implement this improvement? What are your plans for overcoming these barriers?

Exercise 14–1
Reflection/Action Plan

1. The one or two problem-solving or creativity areas in which I am most strong are:

   _____

   _____

   _____

   _____

2. The one or two problem-solving or creativity areas in which I need more improvement are:

   _____

   _____

   _____

   _____

3. If I did only one thing to improve in this area, it would be to:

   _____

   _____

   _____

   _____

4. Making this change would probably result in:

   _____

   _____

   _____

   _____

5. If I did not change or improve in this area, it would probably affect my personal and professional life in the following ways:

   _____

   _____

   _____

   _____

UNIT 1

INTRAPERSONAL EFFECTIVENESS: UNDERSTANDING YOURSELF

1. Journey into Self-awareness
2. Self-disclosure and Trust
3. Establishing Goals by Identifying Values and Ethics
4. Self-Management

UNIT 2

INTERPERSONAL EFFECTIVENESS: UNDERSTANDING AND WORKING WITH OTHERS

5. Understanding and Working with Diverse Others
6. The Importance and Skill of Listening
7. Conveying Verbal Messages
8. Persuading Individuals and Audiences

UNIT 3

UNDERSTANDING AND WORKING IN TEAMS

9. Negotiation
10. Building Teams and Work Groups
11. Managing Conflict
12. Achieving Business Results through Effective Meetings
13. Facilitating Team Success
14. Making Decisions and Solving Problems Creatively

UNIT 4

LEADING INDIVIDUALS AND GROUPS

15. Power and Politicking
16. Networking and Mentoring
17. Coaching and Providing Feedback for Improved Performance
18. Leading and Empowering Self and Others
19. Project Management

Unit 4

It's been a long and enlightening journey. Along the way, you've had opportunities to fuel your tank (assess and manage intrapersonal effectiveness), have enlightening conversations with a wide range of diverse individuals (interpersonal and communication effectiveness), and work collaboratively and effectively with individuals who share the same goals as you (working in teams). These skills will help you interact effectively and build relationships with colleagues, supervisors, co-workers, subordinates, faculty, parents, significant others, and even your children! What about when others look to you for leadership? In this fourth and final stop in our personal development journey, we take a look at the characteristics and skills of effectively leading individuals and groups. Today's leaders mentor, coach, and provide feedback to others. They manage projects. They empower employees and they influence others through networking and the appropriate use of power and politics. By mastering these skills, you can focus on developing others, and in turn, focus your energies on charting your course toward new and different destinations.

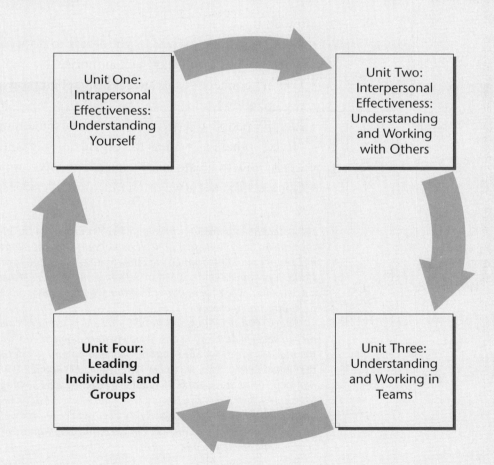

15 Power and Politicking

Learning Points

How do I:

- Acquire and use power to get others to do what I want them to do even when my position lacks such authority?
- Use my connections to successfully champion a cause within an organization?
- Identify people to go to if I want to get something done in an organization?
- "Read" others as well as the organization's culture?
- Learn how to create and manage a positive impression of myself?
- Consider the negative or unethical implications of my actions?

Eddie has been a member of a high-performing team for the last six months. During that time, he has distinguished himself as not only a consummate problem solver, but also a masterful communicator. His teammates seem to value his contributions. Lately, however, Eddie has noticed a bit of distance from some of them. This change in their behavior started three weeks ago, about the time when the team made its first crucial presentation to senior management.

Faced with declining sales and increasing customer complaints, management hand-picked several star employees from various departments to work together to determine the reasons for the decline and recommend potential solutions. Five months after their first meeting, the team was ready to present its plan for how it would restore the company's position as a market leader in designing and hosting Web pages for national catalog companies. Not surprisingly, the team elected Eddie as the primary presenter. And, boy, was he impressive! Eddie deftly covered the team's well-planned presentation and provided clear, rational answers to each and every question raised by members of the senior management team.

After the presentation, Eddie's boss, Carla, and her manager, Raymond, invited Eddie to lunch. While flattered by the invitation, Eddie wondered why the rest of the team wasn't invited. He was going to say something . . . but by then, his teammates had scattered. "I'll be sure to mention the team's efforts at lunch," Eddie thought.

When the threesome arrived at the executive dining room, Eddie looked around and noticed all of the company's most senior players. Vice presidents, directors, even the chief technology officer, were there, enjoying the company-subsidized food and ambience. Smiling on the inside, Eddie noted to himself, "I could get used to this . . ."

Moments later, Carla, Raymond, and Eddie were escorted to their table. Raymond turned to Eddie, "Nice job in there, Eddie. You really have what it takes to be a leader in this organization. That's why we've asked you to join us . . . so we can talk about your new position." Eddie was floored! Carla looked happy, but a bit uncomfortable, particularly when Raymond noted that "some details still have to be ironed out . . . like what role Carla and her organization will have in supporting you and your new team."

1. How would you respond to this situation if you were Eddie? Explain.
2. How would you respond to this situation if you were Carla? Explain.
3. Eddie had had solid performance appraisals in the past, yet this was to be his first major promotion. What characteristics of Eddie or the situation were most influential?
4. Why were Eddie's teammates distancing themselves from him? What could Eddie have done to prevent this?
5. Why did Carla appear uncomfortable at this meeting? What could Raymond have done to prevent or reduce Carla's discomfort?

Have you ever experienced or witnessed a situation such as this? Maybe you've seen an opposite situation—one where a manager uses his or her influence to get an employee demoted or fired. Perhaps you've wondered why certain individuals become the lucky (or unlucky) recipients of powers exerted by high-ranking members of an organization. In this chapter, we discuss power and politicking, why they're important in organizations, and how to assess situations and effectively use power and politicking to achieve your goals and those of your organization.

What Is Power and Why Is It Important?

Power is the ability to get someone to do something you want done or the ability to make things happen in the way you want them to.[1] Some use the power of their position to influence or control others' actions, while others use personal power. In the current environment, where managers must compete for scarce resources and achieve goals that require the actions and abilities of others, understanding and utilizing various types of power becomes a critical skill.

Position or Formal Power

Have you ever had a boss (or parent for that matter) command you to complete a task that didn't appeal to you? As much as you may have wanted to ignore his or her wishes, you probably realized that as a boss, he or she has the right to make such demands as well as to carry out consequences should you not comply. This set of power mechanisms or processes are conferred on the basis of one's position or managerial level in the organization and are referred to as **position power** or **formal power**. Descriptions and examples of these three bases of power[2] are described below:

Power Base	Description	Example
Legitimate	Based on a person holding a formal position or title. Employees comply because they accept the legitimacy of the person in charge.	A manager who uses his position or title to get battling employees to sit down and discuss their differences.
Reward	Based on a person's ability to provide (or withhold) rewards. Others comply because they desire the rewards available from the person in power.	A sales manager who tells her employees that if each one makes his or her monthly sales goals, the entire department will receive a lump sum bonus of 2% of monthly sales generated.
Coercive	Based on a person's ability to punish or harm. Others comply because they want to avoid punishment.	A manager who warns her department that if productivity doesn't improve, layoffs will ensue.

Another source of power that often but doesn't always come with one's position is **information power**—the access to vital information and control over its distribution to others.[3] Typically, by virtue of their position, managers get access to information that is unavailable to peers and subordinates (e.g., financial and operational measures). With the opportunity to distort or frame the information, managers can use information power as a means for influencing others' goal-directed behaviors.[4] Some subject matter experts or those with networks that expand beyond the immediate organization have the opportunity to obtain and wield information power.

Person or Informal Power

What happens when you aren't a manager or supervisor? Due to the delayering and downsizing in many organizations, there are proportionately fewer employees in positions of formal authority. Influencing peers or teammates to comply with your wishes can be a more challenging, and likely more important, proposition. Power of the person, or informal power, comes from the qualities of a person or how she or he is viewed by others. Two well-established bases of "person" power—expert and referent power—are described below.

Power Base	Description	Example
Expert	Based on a person possessing knowledge or superior skills in an area of expertise. Employees comply because they respect and trust their knowledge or skill.	Someone who gets management to recall a product because of new knowledge gained in testing the product under extreme conditions.
Referent	Based on a person's ability to influence because of others' desire to identify or associate with him or her. Others comply because they like, believe in, or want to emulate the person and what they represent.	An employee who gives up an opportunity to transfer to a more exciting department or project because she or he is deeply attached to remaining in the midst of his or her role model.

These two power bases can be as powerful as formal ones[5] but unlike formal or position power, informal or person power engenders commitment as opposed to compliance. Put another way, individuals who are influenced more by a person's qualities than his or her position willingly accept the assignment requested and put their "all" into achieving a positive result, as opposed to doing the bare minimum to "get by." The table below offers tips for increasing your referent and expert power.

Some Tips for Increasing Power[6]	
Referent	**Expert**
Develop your people skills. The better you get along with others, the more referent power you'll have.	Take advantage of any training or educational opportunities provided by your organization.
Improve your relationship with and gain confidence from your manager and peers. Their success is influenced by you and your performance.	Attend trade and professional association meetings. Use networking skills to increase your connections and visibility.
Use personal appeals and sincere flattery to make a connection with and befriend others.	Let others know about your expertise by volunteering for projects that will allow you to showcase your skills or talents. Also, consider displaying diplomas or awards in your office.

Remember that the use of power is situational, meaning that any power base can be effective if used appropriately and positively. Consider the situation, as well as your personal and position power, and choose wisely. The right power base can provide the necessary fuel to support your position or goals. In the next section, we discuss politicking, or how to turn power into influence.

What Is Politicking and Why Is It Important?

Politicking is the use of power and information to move resources toward preferred objectives.[7] It is speaking up on behalf of our and our employees' or company's interests and is part of the process of rule making and decision making in organizational life. People use political behavior to affect decisions, obtain scarce resources, and earn the cooperation of people outside their direct authority.[8] Simply put, politicking is advocating for your interests in a way that meets your and your company's objectives. One who is effective at politicking in business is fully engaged in the life of the organization, understands the key issues and drivers within the organization and the industry, and exercises sound judgment when making decisions that affect the people in and resources of the organization. One who is politic is cautious, not rash, and makes decisions carefully, not impulsively. To some, the word *politicking* may conjure up negative connotations, as the term can be used to define behavior that is motivated primarily or even exclusively by self-interest. Organizations, like people, can have a "dark side." It is not uncommon to find people willing to put their needs above those of others, to do whatever it takes to get what they want. In this chapter we prefer to focus on the positive view of politicking.

Politicking is important because of the complexities involved in being in business today. The global marketplace, the changing attitudes and growing diversity of employees, the intense competition for profits, the explosion of technology, the constant changes in business strategy, and the changing cast of characters who run companies are just a few of these intricacies. Politicking is a way to strengthen and expand your existing network of contacts within your organization. It can be used to learn about available resources and how to get them allocated to objectives that support your and your employees' interests.[9] In one study, 53 percent of those interviewed noted that organizational politics enhanced the achievement of organizational goals and survival.[10] Developing skills in politicking enables managers to understand the changing nature of their business, obtain needed information and resources, adapt as needed, and even reduce workplace stressors.[11]

Engaging in Politics: Considerations

Effective politicking requires forethought before being put into action. Three dimensions to consider when determining if and how to engage in politicking are analyzing yourself, reading others, and assessing the organization.[12]

Analyzing Yourself

Politicking begins with a clear understanding of yourself and the politicking qualities you possess naturally. What are your strengths and limitations, and how do these help or hinder your ability to be political within an organization? What strengths can you bring to your interactions with others, and what limitations might make it difficult for you to influence others, particularly within an organizational context? Several personal characteristics, such as being confident, articulate, and sensitive, make it easier for a person to be an effective politicker (see "How Political are You?"). Having an honest assessment of your goals, and your capability for achieving them, will help in utilizing your positive aspects while diminishing or controlling your negative factors. For example, if you have a tendency to dominate conversations, try to focus on listening intently to others while they are speaking.

Another aspect of self-understanding with regard to politicking is the role of power. Understanding the power base from which you are working and determining the power base that would best match a specific situation or person with whom you are interacting will increase the effectiveness of your politicking.

How Political Are You?[13]

Take a look at the list below. Circle the number that most describes the degree to which each word describes you.

	Agree		Neither		Disagree
Articulate	1	2	3	4	5
Sensitive	1	2	3	4	5
Competent	1	2	3	4	5
Extroverted	1	2	3	4	5
Self-confident	1	2	3	4	5
Assertive	1	2	3	4	5
Collaborative	1	2	3	4	5
Intelligent	1	2	3	4	5
Logical	1	2	3	4	5
Socially adept	1	2	3	4	5

Total the numbers circled. If your score is less than 30, you have a natural ability to be political in organizations.

Reading Others

Effective managers who are good at politicking within their organizations know the importance of being able to "read" people,[14] or understand others' perceptions, reactions, and motivations. To be effective in politicking, it is important to understand others quickly: their power base; their perceptions regarding their position, the situation, and organization; and their stance on the issues at hand. This requires attention to what is known (others' position, experience, previous decisions), as well as what lies beneath the surface (e.g., goals, values, fears).

In some instances there is insufficient time to form impressions and check our understanding of these perceptions with the person or with a trusted colleague. In these cases, we have to rely on our instincts about the person—understanding where they're coming from and what they want to obtain from the situation. Let's say your star employee just left for an overseas assignment and you need to find a temporary replacement. There's no time for a formal search, especially given the temporary nature of the assignment, so you'll have to rely on your hopefully accurate impression of potential candidates in your network. You'll do this by identifying a potential applicant or pool of applicants, asking a few respected others for their opinions, talking with those you are considering, and offering the position to the person who you think best fits your profile.

Some Tips on Reading Others

- *Listen intently.* Listen for what is said and how it is said, not for what you think the person *should* be saying. Use pauses frequently; silence often encourages a person who wants to say more.
- *Observe aggressively.* Interpret others' body language and check for consistency (or lack thereof) between what's being said verbally and what's being displayed nonverbally.
- *Turn up your sensitivity.* Be aware of more than simply the conversation that is taking place. Use all your senses to pick up the nuances that are occurring within and between groups of people in the room.
- *Analyze first impressions.* Think about what the person is trying to present or hopes to gain before accepting what you see. If something seems inconsistent, ask.

Assessing the Organization

People who use politicking strategies effectively are likely to be those who have a good handle on the way an organization is structured, how it operates, how things get done, and how its people and culture function. They use their connections to people and information to obtain resources, get decisions made and implemented, navigate through complex bureaucracies, and generally facilitate processes in a way that meets organizational objectives.[15] Often, politicking behaviors are used by managers to influence people and processes when they lack formal direct authority. The following tactics can help you determine whether and how to politic appropriately.

- *Observe and listen.* Pay close attention to the organizational norms. Know what type of behavior is acceptable and what is frowned upon by individuals and by the organization. Pay attention to successful and unsuccessful practices and actions: Do employees speak up in meetings when their managers are present? What time do employees usually arrive and leave the organization? Do they work on Saturdays? One employee at Microsoft, a company known for its intense work culture, decided to come in early to get work done so he could leave early to pick up his children from school. Others paid little attention to the time he arrived, but were quick to point out his "early" departure. He earned an unfavorable perception, despite the fact that he worked as many hours as his co-workers, and eventually was asked to leave.[16] Although this employee eventually won a lawsuit against his employer, it's a good example of the role that politicking can play in organizations. Unfair? Perhaps, but we have to know and follow both the written and unwritten rules to succeed in an organization.

- *Evaluate the organization.* You may know who reports to whom on the organization's chart, but this may not represent how authority actually flows or the way in which certain practices are carried out. Know the formal roles individuals play in the organizations, as well as the informal roles. For example, don't overlook departmental clerical and administrative staff members. To the politically astute, these individuals can be a wealth of information. When treated with respect, they can help get you what you need, whether access, information, or "insider" tips.

Once you've assessed the organization, you can increase the odds that your efforts at politicking are successful. The following section describes three broad strategies you can use to develop your political skill: choosing wisely, managing impressions, and managing information.

Choosing Wisely

Do you remember the children's story about the boy who cried wolf? After several trial calls—just to see if others would come—the townspeople ignored subsequent calls, figuring it was yet another trial or joke. When the call was real, no one came. Similarly, if you were to wield your power (or political influence) for each and every "cause," others may eventually reduce the attention they pay to subsequent causes. You'd be better off conserving your "political capital"—your reputation, influence, energy, and resources—for more important actions or causes. In addition, consider the most appropriate time to wield power. Sometimes waiting is helpful, as you might get what you want without asking. Or, you might get a portion of what you want. Be gracious, and then determine whether and how to get the rest.

Just as it is important to determine which situations warrant politicking, it is also crucial to decide how you will approach the situation. Various politicking strategies (see the following box) can be utilized to achieve your goal. You should carefully select a strategy based on the organization, the situation, and the individuals involved, and you should weigh the potential consequences of your political action. Each strategy can have elements of effectiveness if used appropriately and negative repercussions when used in haste.

Politicking Strategies[17]

Assertiveness—being able to speak up for your and your employees' rights without interfering with the needs of others in your organization.

Upward Appeals—demonstrating that more senior and powerful people in your organization support the decision for which you are advocating.

Exchange or **Bargaining**—using the "give and take" or compromise approach; e.g., "I do this for you if you do this for me."

(continued)

Reciprocation—offering something to someone else and then expecting them to support your stance on a topic.[18]

Coalition Building—gaining support for a position from others.

Ingratiation—putting the other in a friendly mood before approaching, or building a friendly rapport first before transacting business.

Rationality—using logic and reasoning to support your appeal.

Inspirational Appeals—using emotional appeals based on values and ideas to gain support.

Consultation—seeking participation and input in the process before making a decision about a position to support.

Managing Impressions

Another important politicking strategy relates to influencing others' impressions of you. You've heard the saying "You only have one chance to make a first impression." This saying stems from our human tendency to form opinions about others before we've actually gotten to know them. Whether this is fair or not, we form impressions about others—consciously or subconsciously—based on subtle factors such as their dress, speech, handshake, phone manner, writing style, prior reputation, and behavior and mannerisms. **Impression management** is a process by which we attempt to influence the reactions and images people have of us and our ideas.[19] We do this when we wear our best suit on a job interview or when we send a copy of a congratulatory e-mail or note to our boss. We also do this when we choose words we say in public carefully. Never say anything in private that you can't defend in public. A good rule of thumb is to not say things behind a person's back.[20] People tend to confide things to others, sharing information or opinions they hope will be kept private. But in business, seldom can anything be kept private. Only share those items about yourself and others that you wouldn't mind hearing from someone else. Keep your private thoughts about someone to yourself. Only talk publicly about things that are job-related.

Through impression management, we become aware of all the ways in which we convey an initial impression of who we are to others and make a conscious choice about what parts of us we want to display to others. In the same way networking can help others take notice of your resume and invite you to an interview, impression management can get you noticed—and keep you noticed once you've been hired.

Finally, try to adopt a "win–win" attitude. When making a request for organizational resources (e.g., staff, budget, time, project approval), it's best to frame your request in terms of the "greater good" and show that you've thought through the impact of your request on other areas and departments within your organization.

Managing Others' Impressions of You

- *Be punctual*—demonstrate self-control and respect for others' time.
- *Dress appropriately*—inquire ahead whether business or business casual is the norm. Dress to impress—err on the conservative side—but don't overdress. It could make others feel uncomfortable.
- *Flatter legitimately*—say positive things about the person based on fact or personal observation. Be genuine. Others can sense when you're not.
- *Have a good sense of humor*—it helps put people at ease. Do try to use humor appropriately—as a lead-in to, not as a replacement for, substance. Beware of humor that can be construed as prejudiced against a certain group.
- *Be friendly and approachable*—talk about things you have in common with the other, such as experience, hobbies, or views on current events. One way to do this in a business setting is to stay current with business periodicals, e.g., *The Wall Street Journal, Fortune, Business Week, International Herald Tribune,* and others.
- *Make friends*—and value all contacts.

Managing Information

Managers who are effective at politicking stay well informed about the organization and the industry and use information they gather to help them make better business decisions.[21] **Information management** involves obtaining useful information and managing the information received so that it is accessible and available as needed. As technology advances and we are bombarded 24/7 by all kinds of information, the ability to manage information is becoming even more critical. The most effective managers are those who understand the importance of information and know how to access, sift through, store, and use information to their advantage. In high-tech fields, innovations become old news by the time they are available to end users. Knowing what's coming, what's in the works, and who's involved in these efforts can make the difference between success and failure. Relying solely on the information easily accessible, or worse, ignoring such information, is a recipe for disaster.

Being able to effectively organize current and emerging information that relates to your work is important in many professions. In sales, for example, when your customer has indicated particular likes or needs and has asked you to contact her in six months, or has referred you to another potential customer, this information is vital to your success. Does your information management technique rely on numerous nondescript piles of paper on your desk? If so, you may want to come up with a different system. It doesn't have to be formal. For example, a series of Post-It Notes stuck to your bulletin board might work.

Tips for Managing Information

- *Set up a simple, user-friendly file system* (both print and electronic).
  - The system should include both specific project folders as well as general "resource" folders that are topical rather than pertain to a specific assignment. Resource folders might include technology, reports, or current events that may affect your organization or career.
  - Cleanse these folders on a regular basis to ensure they are current.
  - File the folders from past projects in a place separate from your active files. Limit the clutter in your active pile.
- *Glance briefly at all information* that comes to you either electronically or in print.
  - Quickly make "importance" decisions: must handle, handle if time, or discard.
  - Decide who else should see this information and arrange for them to be copied or informed.
  - Discard items that are not relevant or can be obtained later. Process or file the remaining items immediately. One rule of time management is to handle each piece of paper only once.
  - Make printouts of sensitive e-mails and file them in your personal files. Then, remove them from your electronic in-box.
- *Refer to your project and related resource files prior to attending a meeting about the topic.* These few minutes can help get you up to speed and reduce wasted time in meetings.
- *Keep written notes on all meetings attended.* Date the pages and jot down key issues discussed and decisions made. Bring these notes with you to subsequent meetings to prevent having to revisit topics that have already been addressed.
- *Keep a telephone log* to track phone messages received and follow up calls needed or made.
- *Manage your e-mail.* Respond to professional e-mail messages during the day, preferably during one or two blocks of time set aside for this task. Only respond to

(continued)

personal e-mail after hours, or better still, maintain a separate personal account. Many Internet service providers (ISPs) offer this service for free.

■ *Keep running "to do" and "tickler" lists.* Maintain all "to do" items on one master list, and a separate "tickler" list to remind you of upcoming deadlines and activities. Related folders can be kept in the current file until you work on a specific "to do" item.

Ethical Issues in Politicking

When engaging in political behaviors, it is important to keep in mind any ethical implications of your actions. As physicists tell us, "For every action, there is an equal and opposite reaction." Before taking action, ask yourself whether the action you're considering might cause an imbalance in your or someone else's area of the organization. For example, if you are advocating salary raises for your staff, what are the implications for the staffs of other managers? It's also important to consider whether you are achieving your objective at the expense of someone else's objectives. Always think through the implications of your objectives on the work of others. You don't want to "win the battle but lose the war," an old saying that reminds us to consider the long-term implications of a change effort as well as the short-term benefits or implications. While your staff might appreciate the raises you were able to obtain for them, the other staff with whom they work might perceive inequity and reduce their cooperation and effort to equalize the situation.

Is Your Politicking Ethical?

■ Why am I considering doing this?
■ Who will be benefited by this action? Am I doing this for my own exclusive benefit?
■ Who (if anyone) might be harmed?
   ■ How can I adjust my strategy to ensure others' needs will be taken into account?
   ■ What alliances can I form that will make this action more likely to meet my own as well as others' needs?
■ Is this request in the best interest of my colleagues and organization?
■ Are the tactics I'll use and the outcomes that will result fair and equitable?
■ Would the tactics I use and words I convey be acceptable if known publicly?

When done correctly, politicking can be a powerful tool for achieving your objectives and being successful within an organization. Asking yourself the questions listed above should help you to reduce or prevent potential negative side effects from developing from your efforts. As a manager, it is your role to create an environment that supports a healthy level of politicking, one that helps others understand the power and appropriate use of politicking within the organization.

Keeping Organizational Politics in Check

Sometimes organizations experience unfair or negative politicking—devious, self-interested efforts to sway opinion or a decision toward one point of view, at the exclusion of all others. While politicking will always exist at some level in organizations, you can ensure your staff's use of fair, positive politicking and work to reduce the level of unfair, negative politicking. Some tips for doing this follow.

■ *Reduce Task Ambiguity*—Employees need to be clear on what they can and cannot do and how tasks are prescribed. There should be no misunderstanding about what's expected of employees, their role, the amount of authority they have, and the level of work in which they're expected to get involved. For example, make it clear if they will be doing routine things in addition to more creative work. This will reduce the inevitable "infighting" that develops when people feel they're being taken advantage of in the workplace.

■ *Increase Communication Channels*—Open up two-way communication. Ensure that all involved have input into key decisions and resource allocation requests before they're made. Be clear on where everyone stands, and ensure that all have the equivalent amount and quality of information needed to make informed decisions. This will prevent employees from feeling left out of important decisions and increase the degree to which they support or buy into your company's change efforts.

■ *Ensure a Clear and Consistent Reward and Promotion Structure*—Have a reward system that is well organized, fair, and clearly communicated. One of the best ways to reduce unfair politicking is to put careful thought into designing a compensation structure that is understood by all current and new employees, accessible and beneficial to employees at all levels within the organization, and motivating to current as well as to potential employees. This increases employee motivation, reduces concerns about potential inequities, and helps to focus attention on business objectives rather than on an individual employee's or department's perceived salary inequities.

■ *Provide Sufficient Resources*—A scarcity of resources leads to a high degree of politicking within organizations. It's not always possible, but managers should try to the best of their abilities to offer a work climate in which the staff has the resources necessary to do a job well. For example, as a hospital administrator, you would want to make sure that as the occupancy rate at your hospital increases, sufficient additional staff will be called in to accommodate the increased patient volume.

■ *Formalize the Structure*—The more formal the structure, the more reasoning and performance-based data will be used for politicking.[22] In informal work settings that are less established, such as in some high-tech and dot-com start-ups, reasoning and performance-based data are supplemented with personal contact, emotional appeals, and future-oriented thinking.

Summary

Your ability to understand and use power and politics can give you an important edge in the current business environment. With fewer layers of management and greater competitive demands, supervisors and non-supervisors alike are challenged to marshall the necessary resources to get things done in a positive and effective manner. By following the power and politicking strategies and tips offered, you can facilitate your success and that of those who work with and for you.

Key Terms and Concepts

Bargaining	Ingratiation
Coercive power	Inspirational appeals
Consultation	Legitimate power
Expert power	Person power
Formal power	Politicking
Impression management	Position power
Informal power	Reciprocation
Information management	Referent power
Information power	Reward power

Endnotes

1. J. R. Schermerhorn, Jr., J. G. Hunt, and R. N. Osborn, *Core Concepts of Organizational Behavior* (Hoboken, NJ: John Wiley & Sons, 2004), p. 256.

2. J. R. P. French and B. Raven, *The Bases of Social Power* (Ann Arbor, MI: University of Michigan Institute for Social Research, 1959) pp. 150–167.

3. A. Pettigrew, "Information Control as a Power Resource," *Sociology* 6 (1972), pp. 187–204.

4. L. N. Lussier and C. F. Achua, *Leadership: Theory, Application, Skill Development* (Cincinnati, OH: South-Western College Publishing, 2001).

5. D. Krackhardt, "Assessing the Political Landscape: Structure, Cognition, and Power in an Organization," *Administrative Science Quarterly* 35, no. 2 (1990), pp. 342–369.

6. Lussier and Achua, *Leadership.*

7. D. Farrell and J. C. Petersen, "Patterns of Political Behavior in Organizations," *Academy of Management Review,* July 1982, p. 405; and D. J. Vredenburgh and J. G. Maurer, "A Process Framework of Organizational Politics," *Human Relations,* Jan. 1984, pp. 47–66.

8. Joseph E. Champoux, *Organizational Behavior: Using Film to Visualize Principles and Practices* (South-Western: Cincinnati, OH, 2000).

9. Runzheimer International, "Enhance Your Networking Skills," *Agency Sales Magazine,* March 1999, p. 52.

10. B. E. Ashforth and T. R. Lee, "Defensive Behavior in Organizations: A Preliminary Model," *Human Relations* 43, no. 7 (1990), pp. 621–648.

11. P. L. Perrewé, G. R. Ferris, D. D. Fink, and W. P. Anthony, "Political Skill: An Antidote for Workplace Stressors," *Academy of Management Executive* 14, no. 3 (2000), pp. 115–123.

12. Stephen P. Robbins and Phillip L. Hunsaker, *Training in Interpersonal Skills: Tips for Managing People at Work* (Upper Saddle River, NJ: Prentice Hall, 1996), p. 128.

13. R. W. Allen, D. L. Madison, L. W. Porter, P. A. Renwick, and B. T. Mayes, "Organizational Politics: Tactics and Characteristics of its Actors," *California Management Review,* Fall 1979, pp. 77–83.

14. Iris Randall, "The Key to Networking: Knowing How to 'Read' a Person Makes Networking Easier," *Black Enterprise,* March 1996, p. 56.

15. David Krackhardt, "Assessing the Political Landscape."

16. Video case, "Joys and Risks of the Daddy Track," *Nightline,* August 14, 1991.

17. Reprinted from D. Kipnis, S. M. Schmidt, C. Swaffin-Smith, and I. Wilkinson, "Patterns of Managerial Influence: Shotgun Managers, Tacticians, and Bystanders," *Organizational Dynamics,* Winter 1984, pp. 58–67. With permission from Elsevier Science.

18. John Mariotti, "Understanding Influence and Persuasion," *Industry Week,* April 5, 1999, p. 126.

19. Asha Rao, Stuart Schmidt, and Lynda Murray, "Upward Impression Management: Goals, Influence Strategies, and Consequences," *Human Relations* 48, no. 2 (1995), p. 147.

20. Marcia A. Reed, "Through the Grapevine," *Black Enterprise,* July 1999, p. 62.

21. Thomas H. Davenport, Robert G. Eccles, and Laurence Prusak, "Information Politics," *Sloan Management Review,* Fall 1992, pp. 53–65.

22. Rao et al., "Upward Impression Management."

**Exercise 15–A
Assessing Your Views
of Power**

Indicate your opinion on each question by using the following scale:

5 strongly agree

4 somewhat agree

3 neither agree nor disagree

2 somewhat disagree

1 slightly disagree

Strongly disagree

Statements	Your score
1. It is important for a leader to use all power and status symbols that the organization provides in order to be able to get his or her job done.	2
2. Unfortunately, for many employees, the only thing that really works is threats and punitive actions.	1
3. In order to be effective, a leader needs to have access to many resources to reward subordinates when they do their job well.	1
4. Having excellent interpersonal relations with subordinates is essential to effective leadership.	5
5. One of the keys to a leader's influence is access to information.	5
6. Being friends with subordinates often reduces a leader's ability to influence them and control their actions.	2
7. Leaders who are reluctant to punish their employees often lose their credibility.	4
8. It is very difficult for a leader to be effective without a formal title and position within an organization.	1
9. Rewarding subordinates with raises, bonuses, and resources is the best way to obtain their cooperation.	2
10. In order to be effective, a leader needs to become an expert in the area that he or she is leading.	1
11. Organizations need to ensure that a leader's formal evaluation of subordinates is actively used in making decisions about them.	5
12. Even in the most enlightened organizations, a leader's ability to punish subordinates needs to be well preserved.	2
13. The dismantling of formal hierarchies and the removal of many of the symbols of leadership and status have caused many leaders to lose their ability to influence their subordinates.	4
14. A leader needs to take particular care to be perceived as an expert in his or her area.	1
15. It is key for a leader to develop subordinates' loyalty.	2

Scoring: Reverse score for item 6, then add your scores on each item as follows:

Legitimate power	Add items 1, 8, and 13:	Total:	7
Reward power	Add items 3, 9, and 11:	Total:	8
Coercive power	Add items 2, 7, and 12:	Total:	8
Expert power	Add items 4, 6, and 15:	Total:	9
Referent power	Add items 5, 10, and 14:	Total:	7

The higher your score in each category (maximum of 15) the more you believe in utilizing that source of power.

Questions

1. For each base of power, discuss an appropriate situation for its effective use.
2. Did the outcome of this assessment surprise you? Why or why not?
3. What are the pros and cons of using your dominant source/s of power?
4. How does the outcome of this assessment match up to the dominant source of power used by your supervisor (parent, team leader, etc.)?

Source: A. Nahavandi, *The Art and Science of Leadership,* 3rd edition, © 2003 (Upper Saddle River, NJ: Prentice Hall), p. 95. Used with permission.

Exercise 15–B
Power and Its
Consequences

Working with a partner, you will be asked by your instructor to get your partner to do something that he or she may not want to do. Your mission is to utilize each of the five bases of power (legitimate, reward, coercive, expert, referent)—one at a time—to accomplish this task. Then, reverse roles and do the same thing.

Questions

1. Which of the bases of power were easiest for you to use to accomplish your task? Explain.
2. Which of the bases of power resulted in the most immediate compliance from your "subordinate"? Why do you think this was the case?
3. Once the tables were turned, how did you feel about being the one toward whom power was being used?
4. Which of the bases of power did you feel most comfortable complying with?
5. Which of the bases of power did you feel least comfortable (or most bothered by) complying with?
6. Discuss the applications and implications of this exercise in team or organizational settings.

Source: This exercise is adapted from S. Meisel, "Quick Tips and Energizers for OB Classes," presented at the 2001 OBTC annual conference in Carrollton, GA.

Exercise 15–C
Recognizing Effective
and Ineffective
Political Behavior

Analyze the following situations and determine whether the behavior utilized in each demonstrates effective or ineffective politicking. Explain the reasons for your assessment.

1. Julio is taking golf lessons so he can join the Saturday golf group, which includes some higher-level managers.
   Effective or Ineffective (circle)? Explain. _____
   _____
   _____

2. Paul tells his manager's manager about mistakes his manager makes.
   Effective or Ineffective (circle)? Explain. _____
   _____
   _____

3. Jasmine realizes that her team will not be able to complete its task by the deadline. She asks her boss for a meeting to give her a heads-up on the situation.
   Effective or Ineffective (circle)? Explain. _____
   _____
   _____

4. Sally avoids spending time socializing so that she can be more productive on the job.
   Effective or Ineffective (circle)? Explain. _____
   —can impact team cohesion

5. John sent a very positive performance report to three higher-level managers to whom he does not report. They did not request copies.
   Effective or Ineffective (circle)? Explain. _____
   —taking liberties c̄ someone else's time
   —presumptuous

6. Tamika has to drop off a daily report by noon. She delivers the report at around 10 A.M. on Tuesday and Thursday so that she can run into some higher-level managers who meet at that time near the office where the report must go. On the other days, Tamika submits the report around noon on her way to lunch.

Effective or Ineffective (circle)? Explain. _____

(handwritten: — ingratiating / respectful s — efficient of time)

Source: This exercise is adapted from R. N. Lussier and C. F. Achua, *Leadership: Theory, Application, Skill Development* (Cincinnati, OH: South-Western College Publishing, 2001), p. 355. Used with permission of South-Western, a division of Thompson Learning: www.thompsonrights.com. Fax 800 730-2215.

**Exercise 15–D
Politicking—Elevator
Role-Play**

1. Divide into pairs or small groups.
2. Role-play the following scenarios, each time playing a different role. Ad lib as appropriate. When you finish, discuss in your pair or small group the questions printed below the scenario.

Role-Play I: You find that you are on an elevator for a few minutes with an important superior, one who can potentially open doors for you in the organization. You decide to use this time to try to establish an important connection with the superior. What do you say to this person? How do you strike up a conversation, and about what? What topics do you raise to steer the conversation toward either making connections, obtaining recognition, or making an important point? (2–3 min.)

Roles

Person A—Employee

Person B—Superior

Persons C–F—Observers

Questions for your small group:

- What effective and ineffective behaviors were displayed?
- What strategies were successful in getting the boss's attention?
- How did the employee feel and react (before and during the interaction with the superior)?
- How did the superior feel and react when approached by the employee?

Role-Play II: Switch roles, giving two others in your small group the opportunity to play a role. You are an employee and once again have a chance to ride an elevator for a few minutes. This time it's with a colleague with whom you have been having a disagreement but whose cooperation you need on a team project. Specifically, this person has some information you need to be successful on this project. How do you approach this person? What do you say? What topic(s) do you raise? How do you turn the conversation toward the information you need? (2–3 min.)

Roles

Person A—Employee

Person B—Colleague or Associate

Persons C–F—Observers

Questions for your small group:

- What effective and ineffective behaviors were displayed?
- What strategies were successful getting the attention of the colleague with whom you were having the conflict?
- How did the employee feel and react (before and during the interaction with the colleague)?
- How did the colleague feel and react when approached by the employee?

3. Now, discuss the exercise in your large group or class using the questions below. (10–15 min.)

Questions

1. How many of you got your point across (to the superior in Role-Play I or the colleague in Role-Play II)?

2. What happened to the observers on the elevator when the employee approached the superior/colleague?

3. How do these role-plays relate to politicking in organizations?

4. What did you learn about yourself and others from this exercise?

Exercise 15–E
"Powers" of
Observation

Observe a business meeting being held. Record the effective and ineffective politicking behaviors you observe being performed by members of the group.
 Following your instructor's guidelines, write a paper that addresses:

1. What makes the behaviors effective or ineffective?

2. What role does someone's authority (or power in his or her position) play in his or her use and effectiveness of political behaviors?

3. What steps could be taken to regulate or reduce the need for politicking in future meetings attended by this group?

Exercise 15–F
Reflection/Action Plan

This chapter focused on power and politicking—what they are, why they are important, and how to improve your skills in these areas. Complete the following worksheet upon completing all readings and experiential activities for this chapter.

1. The one or two areas in which I am most strong are:

_____

_____

_____

2. The one or two areas in which I need more improvement are:

_____

_____

_____

3. If I did only one thing to improve in each of these areas, it would be to:

_____

_____

_____

4. Making these changes would probably result in:

_____

_____

_____

5. If I did not change or improve in these areas, it would probably affect my personal and professional life in the following ways:

_____

_____

_____

16 Networking and Mentoring

_____ **Learning Points**

How do I:

- Identify a job opening or arrange an interview through a friend or a friend of a friend?
- Reach out to and connect with others when I am a newcomer in an organization?
- "Work a room"—meet many different people in a short amount of time?
- Overcome my reluctance or discomfort with networking?
- Build a diverse network of mentors who can provide insight and assistance on career-related issues?
- Develop effective relationships with, and provide value to, others in my network?

Mr. Zaven Yaralian is a prime example of how networking can help individuals progress through their careers (see chart diagramming his career below). Yaralian was a professional football coach for the New Orleans Saints. Like most other professions, success in obtaining coaching jobs relies on both technical expertise and networking skills. Yaralian's career has benefited time after time from contacts he made at the beginning of and throughout his career. He acquired his former position directly as the result of networking.

Coach Yaralian played football for the University of Nebraska, a highly recognized program that produces outstanding players as well as coaches. He honed his game through one of the best college coaches, Tom Osborne. After graduation, he kept in close touch with Coach Osborne. Following his unsuccessful attempt at pursuing a career in the NFL, Yaralian contacted Osborne. Osborne, who knew Yaralian's heart belonged to football, suggested coaching. Coach Osborne gave Yaralian his first job in coaching, as a graduate assistant in his own program.

Yaralian then began moving up in his profession. He began his first full-time job in football at Washington State University. He got the job through a referral and recommendation from Coach Osborne. From there he progressed to other schools including the University of Colorado. While in Colorado, Yaralian's team made a bid for the national championship. His boss and well-respected head coach, Bill McCartney, helped Yaralian reach the next level of performance in his career. Through recommendations from him and Osborne, Yaralian was offered and accepted a position to join Mike Ditka of the Chicago Bears. Ditka then helped Yaralian obtain an offer from Dan Reeves of the New York Giants. Yaralian then reunited with the Hall of Famer, Mike Ditka, five years later in New Orleans, where Yaralian became the defensive coordinator for the New Orleans Saints. The once unknown defensive back coach was given the opportunity to coach with some of the best coaches and teams in the NFL because of a network of key relationships he had made and cultivated throughout his career.[1]

Mr. Zaven Yaralian's Career through Networking

Top: Career opportunity
Bottom: Connection used

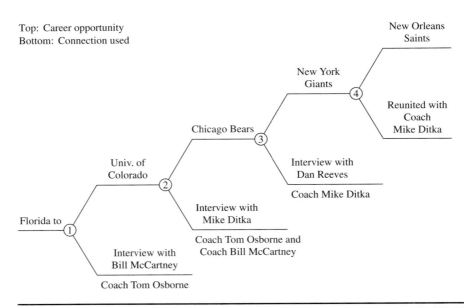

Source: B. Yaralian, et al. "Networking," unpublished student paper, James Madison University, COB 202, fall 1999.

1. In business, neither technical skills nor networking abilities are sufficient by themselves. Do you agree with this statement? Why or why not?

2. When Yaralian proves he is an effective coach, why would others help him move up—and out—of their organization? Wouldn't you prefer keeping outstanding performers as opposed to helping them leave?

3. What are some benefits of networking?

4. What are some potential downsides of networking?

5. In what ways have you used networking to get a leg up on a job or other opportunity?

"It's not what you know, it's who you know."

The old adage about the valuable role others can play in opening doors for us has stuck because often it's true. As illustrated in the above case, moving up successfully can happen as the result of both acquiring knowledge and fostering important relationships with others who can be helpful to you as your career progresses. While we wouldn't say that credentials aren't important, the fact is that having the credentials to do a job is just the first step. Equally important is getting access—to information, people, and jobs—and other people are often the conduit through which this access is obtained. In this chapter, we discuss the definition and importance of networking and mentoring, how they are used, and tips for effectively building mentor networks to increase your social capital and that of others.[2]

What Is Networking?

Networking is the building and nurturing of personal and professional relationships to create a system or chain of information, contacts, and support. In the business world, the goal of networking is to develop and maintain relationships with people who can be helpful to you, your employer, or your organization.[3] Successful networking requires a certain mindset or philosophy: an attitude of giving advice, information, and help rather than expecting this from others.[4] Effective networking is most likely to occur between two or more people who build rapport by finding common interests through meaningful, balanced, two-way communication. A networker who appears too needy or self-centered might face resistance from others who might otherwise be able to help him or her.

Whether through face-to-face, phone, written, or electronic means, the networker attempts to connect with others who can provide needed information and opportunities. A person's network is evolving constantly. Studies estimate that over a lifetime, a person will have several thousand acquaintances. Moreover, as age and income increase, so too will the number of acquaintances. Some contacts are cultivated deliberately and others evolve naturally.[5] The largest portion of a person's network actually consists of secondary contacts—friends of friends who are close to the situation about which you need information.

The Importance and Uses of Networking

Creating a personal network and developing networking skills can provide numerous professional benefits for individuals and organizations. Networking is invaluable for those who are seeking advancement within an existing organization as well as those who are seeking a new career opportunity. Building a network of contacts can keep you current with industry trends and expedite your career advancement from one position to another, either within an existing organization or in a move from one organization to the next.[6]

Networking within an Organization

Networking while on the job increases your access to available resources and information.[7] Networking with others helps you augment your thoughts and ideas with those of others, creating a concept that incorporates "best practice" thinking from the outset of its development. Networking helps you increase your effectiveness when researching a new concept, starting a new project, or developing a new product idea.[8] By consulting with others who are experts in the topic in which you are involved, you incorporate the thoughts of others into your knowledge base in the given area. For example, when charged with developing or testing a new product, an important first step is to identify internal and external experts who can serve as sources of information on the relevant topic, preventing you from "reinventing the wheel" and building allies who can later advocate for the change you are proposing.

Networking is essential when taking on a new assignment or project. It is a good habit to get to know others, both inside and outside your department, and at all levels—peers, subordinates, and superiors. By networking with co-workers as well as with individuals at more junior and senior levels of the organization, you can learn about the broader business in which your organization is involved and about the challenges and opportunities that lie ahead.[9]

Staying in touch with people and trends in your company enables you to prepare for and adapt to organizational changes. Access to information and "connectedness" enables you to acquire a more strategic view of the business, one that is holistic rather than limited to your specific functional area. This helps you to position your department and organization to respond strategically to marketplace changes as they inevitably occur.[10]

This heightened understanding can increase your effectiveness as a businessperson and your value to the organization as you learn to make decisions from multiple rather than one-dimensional business perspectives. For example, an aerospace firm during the early 1990s found defense budgets shrinking substantially. The CEO's directive—cut 30 percent across the board—could have spelled disaster if not for the willingness of division and department managers to network. Some programs were nearly dead, while others—early in the life cycle though potentially a financial success—were struggling to make ends meet. Managers met and discussed the directive, deciding that cutting costs by one-third did not necessarily mean firing one-third of the employees, and that cutting all programs or departments at the same rate did not make sense. They networked, shared information and resources, and found ways to meet the directive in a way that met the needs of the organization.

Organizations may be represented on charts as groups of self-contained work units, such as marketing, finance, research and development, purchasing, information systems, planning, logistics, communications, public relations, human resources, and legal counsel, but in fact, most departments rely heavily on outputs of other departments. Most decisions made by one segment of an organization affect other segments of an organization. What happens between the boxes on the organization chart—the "white spaces"[11]—could mean the difference between failure and success of the organization. Managing the white spaces through organizational networking not only facilitates organizational synergy but also helps you when you're promoted to positions elsewhere in the company or when you move to other companies and industries.

Networking to Find a Job or Change Careers

Networking can also help you learn about new job opportunities. In today's fast-paced, global, high-tech environment, your attitude about and comfort with networking can significantly impact your ability to establish contacts, get interviews for jobs, and identify and cultivate mentors within organizations.[12] By improving your ability to sell yourself, you can benefit in terms of a new job as well as increased skill in selling and promoting— useful skills in any business today. Networking skills are crucial for career and personal success. Career specialists estimate that 70–80 percent of the best jobs come from effective and consistent personal networking with others rather than through executive search firms (commonly referred to as "headhunters"), sending in blind resumes, posting a resume on the web, or responding to job ads.[13]

Effective networking leads to a ripple effect. Like a stone thrown in the water, creating numerous waves and movements, one personal contact can lead to others that eventually result in knowledge about multiple career opportunities.[14] You might recall the commercial for Fabergé Organics shampoo ("I told two friends, and they told two friends, and so on"). Another way of explaining the value of networking is the premise of "six degrees of separation,"[15] the notion that most of us can find a connection to anyone else in the world through six levels of contacts. This is referred to as the "**secondary network**" and validates the importance of not relying solely on those you know when doing research, getting to know an organization, or searching for a job.

An effective technique for finding the right job or career for you is informational interviewing. This means interviewing people about their own careers and jobs. In **information interviews,** the goal is to learn from the person with whom you're speaking, not to obtain a job. This can be done by asking what they like and dislike about their job, getting advice from them about how you might embark on a similar career path or join a similar organization. A sample set of questions to ask during information interviews appears in the box on the next page. When used early in the job search process, networking for information, rather than for specific jobs, can help you clarify your job goals and improve your interviewing skills. Wouldn't it be better to realize that you are not cut out to spend eight hours a day in front of a computer than to take a job and quit? This focused task will help you to achieve your short-term goal as well as clarify your interest or compatibility with a particular job or career field.

Questions to Ask in Information Interviews

1. How did your interest in this career develop?
2. How did you prepare for this career?
3. What do you like and dislike about this career?
4. What are the current and future trends in this career?
5. What are the key issues with which you're working right now?
6. Describe a typical day in this job.
7. If you could change one thing about this career, what would it be?
8. What advice do you have for someone like me?
9. Would you have a few minutes to critique my résumé?
10. Who else can I talk to about a career in _____?

This principle can be applied both as a student and as a manager. As a student, it is important to identify key resource people who can help you attain your goals. Through networking with your resident advisor, upper-class students, coaches, and teachers, you can learn the names of people you can consult or organizations that can be of benefit to you on school projects or when dealing with personal problems. Those students who are willing to reach out to others rather than trying to solve all their own problems are better able to make changes and solve problems than are those who refuse assistance from others and try to fix or change things on their own. Students who utilize their contacts are more likely to get internships and jobs than those who do not.

Other Uses of Networking

Networking is a great way to locate providers of goods and services. This can serve individuals and organizations by helping them to identify good deals or valuable savings to help reduce costs. Have you ever wanted to buy a car, needed to find office supplies at a discount, or relocated to a new area and needed a doctor, a dentist, or hairdresser? A network of friends, peers, and acquaintances can help you streamline your search.

Networking can be instrumental in helping managers find key people to hire.[16] Firms in high-growth areas, such as information security and wireless or digital technologies, experience great difficulty in recruiting and retaining talented professionals. Even with promises of signing bonuses and stock options, some firms come up empty handed. Often, the personal recommendation from a friend—alone or combined with a signing bonus—can help entice a prospective employee to accept a job offer. Also called **reverse networking,** this practice offers numerous benefits to firms over traditional recruiting strategies.

Small business owners and entrepreneurs benefit greatly from networking. For example, how would real estate agents, independent financial planners, and consultants find leads and turn them into paying customers? How do entrepreneurs locate venture capitalists to invest in their businesses? By nurturing relationships with individuals in the profession (e.g., peers in other organizations, former employees, or people you meet at conferences or in trade associations) and in your community (e.g., volunteer organizations, religious groups, city or school councils, athletic teams), you can increase your contacts exponentially.[17] More importantly, the likelihood of gaining new business from a referral is 60 to 70 percent as opposed to 10 percent from a nonreferral.[18]

Simply put, networking is an important and valuable skill for those who want to succeed within an organization, find a new employer, or expand a customer base. Networking enables us to break out of old patterns and find new, more efficient solutions to fulfill our organizational and career-related needs.

Developing an Appropriate Mindset for Networking

There is more to networking than just understanding the tactics and techniques for developing and practicing the skill. Networking involves building and maintaining relationships.[19] Successful networking requires a positive, cooperative mindset. So far, we have discussed networking as a way to use your connections to get your needs met. This sounds rather one-sided. The most successful networkers have an attitude derived from viewing relationships as opportunities to give to, rather than take from, others.[20] There are two kinds of networkers: those who are self-oriented, and those who are focused on others.

■ The "self-oriented" networker approaches a room and surveys it for potential customers or clients, thinking, Who can I sell? Who might be able to give me a job lead? What can I get them to buy? How do I convince them they need me or what I offer?

Networking in Action[21]

Met Mrs. Gonzales at Trade Fair June 7. She suggested I contact Mr. Kerne at Trim Tech.

June 11
Took Mr. Kerne to lunch. Discovered we had much in common. He made an appointment to see a John Grant at Jaco Co.

June 18
Mr. Grant, a vice president, took me to their human resource director. Two interviews followed.

June 30
Accepted position with Jaco.

Contact Record[22]

Here is a good format to use to keep up with your contacts. You can keep track of your contacts in an organizer, rolodex, notebook, or computer database. This will allow you to access all the pertinent data when you need to and to keep it current.

Name: _____

Contact: _____

Company/Organization: _____

Address: _____

_____

Phone: _____

E-mail address: _____

How do I know this person? _____

_____

_____

_____

Why are they a good first contact? _____

_____

_____

Contact record. List date(s) of all contacts and brief subject/nature of contact. Keep track of items sent and "to do" items here. _____

_____

_____

■ The "other-oriented" networker approaches a room and identifies people who need to be connected with others in the room, thinking, Who in this room could use my help? Who can I introduce to whom? How can I help you? I know someone who might be able to help you; can I have them contact you?

Those who are approached by the self-interested networker might feel taken advantage of. A relationship was not formed; instead, pleasantries were exchanged as a way of getting some need met. Should this networker contact the person at a later date, there's a possibility that the person will be less willing to help.

Barriers to Networking

Networking may sound simple enough, but for some the prospect of networking can be intimidating. For many people, the skill of networking does not come naturally. Meeting others, making small talk, and especially marketing or promoting oneself are processes that require practice in order to be performed successfully. Some reasons why people fear or avoid networking include:

■ Lack of self-esteem or confidence in personal skills and abilities. Networking can be achieved through means other than face-to-face meetings, such as an e-mail or letter. Once your confidence and competence increase, try combining these approaches with more direct, face-to-face methods, such as through meetings and conferences.

■ Difficulty in asking others for help and being unable to reciprocate the favor immediately. Realize that networking goes beyond a single interaction; you may have the opportunity to return the favor at a later time. Moreover, you'll be helping your contact by connecting him or her to your network.

■ Wanting to reach goals without any special help from others. While this is a noble cause, refusing to network can negatively impact your career as well as the value of the social capital you can offer. Furthermore, it is unlikely that networking alone will get you a job. It opens doors. If you don't possess the necessary knowledge, skills, and abilities, any "special help" from others would reflect poorly on them. From the organization's perspective, when two candidates are equally qualified, a "known quantity" is preferred to hiring an "unknown."

■ Concern about sharing sensitive or competitive information. The nature and amount of information you share is up to you and your contact. Specific expectations can and should be discussed early in the relationship. Over time, trust—a key ingredient of effective relationships—will build and this concern will likely lessen.

Whatever your personal barriers or discomfort with networking might be, it is important to resolve the issues that can prevent you from becoming an effective networker. Those who do not learn how to network will fall behind in today's competitive and global environment.[23] Luckily, these skills can be learned and applied in a variety of contexts. Networking takes conscious effort. It is very much like working out: If you do not continue to work at it, you will lose what you have already gained. Also, once the habit has been established, it becomes a natural (and beneficial) part of your routine.

Strategies for Building an Effective Network

The following steps will help get you started in developing and maintaining a beneficial network:

■ *Organize your current network.* Identify people you already know and enter their names and contact information into a database. See "What If I Don't Have Any Contacts?" for ideas.

■ *Expand your network:* After assessing your network, think about how you want to expand it. Realize that diversity and reciprocity are two key principals to building a successful network.[24] It's best to seek out people in different groups, companies, and industries as the occupational world is diverse. Begin by asking your co-workers for names of people they know or have heard about in your fields of interest. At the same time, check the Internet and other publications to identify other people and organizations to add to the list. Professional associations that are related to your field of expertise or interests are an excellent source of names of people with whom to network. You or someone you know might already be a member of one or more of these organizations. Using associations as sounding boards can help you to get the needed information, as well as to assess the strengths and weaknesses of the information you receive.[25]

Review the list with anyone involved in the project to obtain additional names. Then contact each name on the list (via phone, e-mail, or memo), one at a time, introducing yourself, explaining the reason you're making the contact, and describing where you found the person's name. Explain why you need the information and offer a little background that helps them understand why you're contacting them. It helps to say something positive about why you're contacting each person specifically—such as you know they're an expert, you heard good things about them, or you know they have the experience that could benefit your project.

■ *Nurture the relationships.* Commit to spending time, one-on-one, to get to know your contacts. The more they know you and your goals, the better they can help you. Similarly, find out their wants and needs. End every conversation with people in your network by asking how you can help them. Finally, keep in touch periodically with your friends, contacts, and associates to maintain these relationships.

What If I Don't Have Any Contacts?

Everyone has contacts! A contact is simply a person who is willing and able to help you. Below are a few examples of who your contacts might be. If you're having trouble identifying names of potential contacts, you might be overlooking the obvious— friends, relatives, and neighbors. Remember, these people may not have the information you need but they may know others who do. Another strategy for meeting potential contacts is to get involved in organizations—community service, career, professional, recreational, civic, fraternal, academic, religious—where you are likely to meet people who share an interest or commitment to a cause with you.

Who Are Contacts?[26]

Friends, relatives, neighbors, sorority/fraternity members

Co-workers of parents, spouse or significant other, and other family members

Current and former classmates

Priests, ministers, rabbis, and fellow church or synagogue members

Fellow club members

Personal lawyer, insurance agent, realtor, accountant, doctor, dentist, beautician

Teachers and former teachers

Employers and former employers

Co-workers and former co-workers

Members of your employer's human resources department

Grade school, high school, college, and graduate school alumni and alumni associations

Business associates and members of professional organizations

To prepare mentally for a networking meeting, follow these three steps:

1. Analyze the *process*. Ask yourself with whom you'll need to network—the types of individuals you will be seeking, and for what purpose.[27] Be sure to identify what you hope to gain as well as ways in which you can contribute. Remember that networking is a two-way street. Others will be more apt to help you when you show your willingness to help them.

2. Identify the *place* where the networking might or will occur. Identify community organizations; professional associations; clubs; social, professional, or fraternal organizations; alumni associations; and chambers of commerce—any source that might be a good place to meet others interested in topics similar to your interests.

3. *Practice* networking. Focus on the specific steps and techniques of networking. Practice these steps and learn to be comfortable with networking. Success breeds success. The more you practice, the better you'll be at networking. You might begin practicing and build up your confidence by using a "safer" method to network, such as a letter or e-mail.

Before, During, and After a Networking Meeting

We've discussed the importance of networking and ways for you to increase your network and networking skills. The following table is organized chronologically, highlighting key things to do or consider before, during, and after a networking meeting.

Before	During	After
■ Make networking a high priority; allot time in your weekly or monthly planner for networking activities.	■ Focus completely on the others' needs initially when establishing professional relationships.	■ As you walk away, jot down a few notes on the back of the person's business card to jog your memory when writing a follow-up note.[28]
■ Set specific networking goals (why, with whom, about what, when, where, how).	■ Get all vital information (name, title, address, company, phone number, e-mail address, etc).	■ Follow up with new contacts within 48 hours, and again when you achieve a goal they helped you attain.
■ Start with a small circle of well-known associates and friends; small goals will lead to big goals.	■ Verify how to pronounce the person's name correctly.	■ Send thank-you notes (by mail, not e-mail). Be sure to maintain professionalism in all follow-up correspondence (phone messages, e-mail), including proper grammar, pronunciation, etiquette.
■ Practice small talk—develop conversation starters before entering a room or attending a conference or meeting.	■ Be visible, not pushy. Check nonverbal language for cues.	■ If you follow up by phone, consider writing a script or key ideas to mention. Be organized—sketch out in advance how you plan to approach the conversation.
■ Know the organizational culture—the norms, customs, dress.	■ Respect the other's time—if you ask to chat for 10 minutes, don't exceed that.	■ Assess yourself; how did you do? What kind of impression do you think you made?
	■ Refrain from praising, fawning, self-deprecation, flirting, or cuteness.	■ Follow through on your promises and be conscious of how you can help others in your network.
	■ Be sincere; give only genuine, specific compliments. Instead of "You were great" try "The lead you gave me on the consulting job was very helpful. I was able to . . . Thanks!"	

What Is Mentoring?

"Mentoring is an enduring phenomenon that has survived several major, historical paradigm shifts. The fact that it has endured, documented, for millennia . . . suggests that mentoring fulfills some deep, important yearnings for connection between the generations."

James Clawson[29]

We may have dozens or even hundreds of individuals in our network. Some of these people rise to the level of mentor. In this next section, we discuss mentoring, its importance, and strategies for building effective mentor networks.

Mentoring has been traditionally defined as a unique interpersonal relationship between two individuals, a *mentor* and a *protégé*. The **mentor** is generally a higher-ranking employee who has advanced organizational (or industry) experience and knowledge and who is committed to providing guidance and support to the **protégé's** career development.[30] Recently, mentoring has been described in more reciprocal terms, indicating the belief that benefits of such relationships accrue to mentors as well as to protégés.[31] Even organizations benefit from mentoring, as mentoring facilitates the socialization process and helps acculturate junior members of the organization.[32] In fact, in one of *Fortune* magazine's issues on the 100 best companies in the United States, 60 of 100 companies had implemented formal mentoring programs.[33] Similar examples are shown in Figure 16–1.

**Figure 16–1
Formal Mentoring in
Action[34]**

IBM—Executive Resource Program has been particularly helpful to retain women—it helped increase the number of women in executive positions by 27 percent from 1998–1999.

Digital Consulting Software and Service (Houston)—formalized mentoring has helped them achieve an 80 percent retention rate for female employees.

Coca Cola Co.—developed mentoring programs to help with diversity training for all employees.

Hewlett Packard—developed an Accelerated Development program to combine mentoring, planning and leadership workshops, helping them save on the cost of hiring new employees. Recently augmented this program with an e-mentoring program.

Lucent Technologies—actively recruit employees to participate in mentoring programs to help attract and retain talented employees.

Hewlett-Packard, Intel, and National Semiconductor—developed mentoring programs for high schools, colleges, and grade school students and teachers to encourage interest in IT careers.

We all know that teaching through experience can be one of the most effective methods of transferring knowledge. Which would you prefer, being handed a company's five-inch-thick manual, or having someone "show you the ropes"? In addition to teachers, mentors play many roles, including role model, confidant, coach, advisor, counselor, encourager, and friend. These roles fall into two broad categories of mentor functions, career and psychosocial:[35]

Career functions: Aspects of the relationship that enhance career advancement such as sponsorship, exposure, visibility, coaching, protection, challenging assignments, and career strategizing.

Psychosocial functions: Aspects of the relationship that enhance a sense of competency, identity, and effectiveness in a professional role, including role modeling, acceptance and confirmation, counseling, friendship, support, and personal feedback.

When done well, mentors can help protégés gain needed job information and experience, as well as support and encouragement (or psychosocial support[36]) to advance in their job and career.

The Importance of Mentoring

Why are we interested? First, trends in the business environment make mentoring not only desirable but also essential for the success of both organizations and employees.

Second, because those involved in a mentoring relationship gain indisputable benefits. We'll begin with the business trends.

One trend responsible for the increasing reliance on mentoring is the fact that more organizations are viewing their people—as opposed to their products, services, or assets—as the chief source of sustainable competitive advantage.[37] Peter Drucker asserts that knowledge is the only meaningful resource in today's economy; knowledge and the people within which knowledge resides have become the primary assets and sources of competitive advantage. As the competition for highly skilled and dedicated professionals heats up, firms are focusing more attention on developing their current employees. If sharing knowledge provides added value in the knowledge economy, then involvement in productive mentoring relationships should benefit both individual participants and the organization.[38]

Another trend is the dramatic changes in the nature of individual career development. Bidding farewell to the days when employees climbed the same corporate ladder over the course of 30 years, we now see new career patterns described as "Protean" or "boundaryless," meaning that individual careers can change shape or form at any time.[39] Part of what is driving these changes is organizational downsizing and rapid technological change that can cause previously valuable skills to suddenly become obsolete, necessitating changes in an individual's career path. Add global marketplace dynamics to these challenges and it's easy to see why not just one, but multiple mentors are needed to assist protégés in learning specific skills, establishing connections with influential decision makers, and navigating the less secure waters of today's careers.[40]

Benefits of Mentoring

One reason for the popularity of mentoring is that it can provide benefits to both protégé and mentor. Anecdotal evidence suggests that protégés may be assisted in many ways, both professionally and personally. Figure 16–2 explains many of the benefits that can be derived from obtaining a mentor.

Recent research on mentoring's effects confirms much of what has been expected. Studies that empirically examined the impact of mentoring compare protégés and nonprotégés, and confirm that protégés receive more promotions, have higher incomes, have higher career satisfaction, have higher job satisfaction, and are less likely to express an interest to leave than their nonmentored counterparts.[41]

Effective mentoring programs can bring about benefits for the mentor as well, some of which are listed in Figure 16–3. Mentoring has been found to be a reciprocal process: "in learning you teach and in teaching you learn." Through their relationship with a protégé, mentors have been able to hone their interpersonal skills, gain insight into their ideas and perceptions, and increase their awareness through diverse experiences.[42]

Another reason mentoring is being offered by more and more corporations is its applicability to company diversity programs. Mentoring programs, which have been proven to bolster a person's chances for advancement, are now being offered by many

---

**Figure 16–2
Mentoring Benefits
for Protégés**

- Career and leadership development—career preparation and leadership training.
- Increased self-confidence, self-awareness, and growth.
- Mutual sharing and enhancement of relationship.
- Development of friendships that can provide valuable contacts and expand associations in related networks.[43]
- Development of interpersonal skills—by working with a more experienced individual, protégés learn by observation[44] and practice.
- Protection for the individual and the organization against potentially damaging experiences.
- Gaining valuable inside information into the workings of the organization for movement in the organization, insight into informal workings.
- Saving time. By allowing protégés to learn from others' experience, they don't have to reinvent the wheel; they can speed up the advancement process and get a jump on the learning curve.[45]

**Figure 16–3
Mentoring Benefits
for Mentors**

- Experience shared learning and positive results.
- Gain personal satisfaction from helping another.
- Develop patience, insight, and understanding.
- Are exposed to cultural, social, or economic characteristics different from their own.
- Improve their leadership and communication skills.
- Gain personal experience for future career options, including training, teaching, or counseling.
- Train employees in ways that will meet future needs for their organization, thereby ensuring its future competitiveness.
- Receive help to revitalize and redefine their own careers through reflection.[46]

corporations to all employees, with an emphasis on minorities and women, who have long been underrepresented in many industries and organizations. Companies are finding that offering mentoring programs is an excellent way to boost the performance and advancement rates of minorities and women, as well as build confidence and boost morale.

Given the tangible benefits available to both individuals and organizations, it is easy to see why mentoring has been integrated into the structure and processes of numerous and diverse types of organizations, including higher education, law firms, police departments, and large corporations such as Douglas Aircraft, Motorola, and Coca Cola.

Qualities of an Effective Mentor

What makes for effective mentors? What characteristics or qualities facilitate their ability to help others—inside and outside their firm or industry—reach their full potential? Mentoring expert Kathy Kram compiled a list (see Figure 16–4) of characteristics or skills—ranging from willingness and desire to be a mentor to possessing highly developed interpersonal skills—that aid in a mentor's effectiveness. Whether you are a mentor or looking for a mentor, it is important to develop these skills.

**Figure 16–4
Characteristics of
Effective Mentors[47]**

- Expertise and experience in their profession, successful in their professional endeavors.
- Enthusiasm and genuine interest for the profession.
- Desire and energy to help others.
- Available time to help others.
- Ability to relate to others in all types of settings.
- Good interpersonal skills; good listening skills; a high level of emotional intelligence or ability to read others and situations and act appropriately.
- Skilled in giving honest and detailed constructive feedback.
- Supportive in their work for others.
- Ability to work well with a diverse group of people.
- High yet achievable standard of performance for themselves and others.
- Worthy of emulation.
- Willingness to expose their protégé to a broad-based network of professionals and to share information about organizational norms.
- Ability to separate personal needs and concerns from professional demeanor when interacting with a protégé.

Types of Mentoring Relationships

Many of us have functioned as mentors at one time or another, perhaps without the formal designation. We might have a kid brother or sister whom we taught how to ride a bicycle, or perhaps we helped a new classmate or employee learn the rules of the game. Mentoring, and mentoring relationships, can be formal or informal. **Formal mentors** (also called *organizational* or *managerial mentors*) are relationships officially designated by the institution through a formalized mentoring program. Mentors' relationships with protégés are arranged through a formal matching process and with the assistance of an external organizing force (for example, human resources). Formal mentoring relationships usually have a specific time frame, a method for termination, and one or more checkpoints for goal setting and meetings.

Most of us have been involved in the other type of relationship, known as an **informal or peer relationship.**[48] These relationships often develop spontaneously and without a specific plan. They occur when a mentor and protégé find each other (either when a potential protégé seeks another's advice or a potential mentor notices another's potential and offers to take the protégé under his or her wing) and negotiate terms of their relationship. Many informal or peer relationships develop over time and are very effective and rewarding if there is a consistency with needs, goals, and resources. Based on the level of commitment, intensity, types of issues, and needs addressed by those involved in a peer relationship, three types of relationships can be identified and represented on a continuum:[49]

- **Informational peers** benefit most by exchanging information about their work or organization. The relationship is characterized by low levels of self-disclosure and trust and demands little in terms of time and support.

- **Collegial peers** tend to trust more and share more, delving somewhat into issues beyond work, including family and personal. Peers request and receive direct and honest feedback.

- **Special peers** exhibit high levels of trust, self-disclosure, and self-expression; they share ideas and advice on a multitude of issues and allow for the exchange of dilemmas, fears, and concerns.

As a peer mentoring relationship deepens toward the "special" category, we find a greater number and depth of mentoring functions being served. In addition to the formal and informal types of relationships, we see the development of a new form: co-mentoring.[50] In this type of relationship, each person is both mentor and protégé. The newer or less experienced members share their technology skills or what's considered the latest thinking in a field, while the more experienced members share their expertise and experience in the organization and industry.

Four Stages of Mentoring Relationships

Most mentoring relationships evolve through four stages. They are described below:[51]

1. Orientation and initiation. In this phase, the mentor and protégé are assigned or select one another, disclose information, and begin to build trust. This phase usually lasts between 6 and 12 months, during which time initial wishes become realized (e.g., coaching is provided) and the relationship takes on significance for both parties. Traditional relationships begin face to face and within a single organization; however, technology has enabled such relationships to occur virtually, using e-mail and other methods (e.g., phone, and videoconference) to connect geographically distant partners.[52] (See Online Mentoring, Exercise 16–F).

2. Cultivation. During this phase, which may last between one and five years, the relationship becomes more rewarding for both parties. There is continued growth and development in career and psychosocial support functions, mutual trust, sharing and challenging of ideas, and learning—for both protégés (who gain knowledge and insight) and their mentors (who gain loyalty and a sense of helping another).

3. Separation. Most mentoring relationships typically fade after a few years. At this point, the protégé is ready to assert more independence and work more autonomously, or perhaps the mentor experiences a significant change in his or her career (for example, retirement). Or, one or both may change jobs, creating geographical and psychological distance to the relationship. When opportunities to interact are constrained, mentor and protégé may step back from the formal relationship, or they may continue, depending on their commitment to the relationship.

4. Redefinition. Depending on the nature of the separation, the mentor and protégé will often redefine their mentoring relationship. Typically, the mentor's job is "done" and peer status is achieved. Protégés express appreciation for their mentors, who now see their protégés as equals, similar to peer colleagues or friends.

How to Find a Mentor

If your company does not have a formal mentoring program, you can find a potential mentor or mentors through informal channels.

- Clarify your career goals and coaching needs. Ask yourself why you're seeking a mentor, what your objectives are, and how someone more senior in the organization (who's not your boss) can be helpful to you.

- Identify potential candidates. Have you served on a committee or task force with someone who's a few levels above you and whose ideas you respect? Did you have a chance to develop a rapport with that person? If so, approach the person directly, indicating your interest in succeeding at the organization and ask whether he or she would be willing to meet with you from time to time to offer career advice and insights into the company and industry.

- Involve your boss. Often your boss will be supportive of your interest in being mentored, especially if your boss is people-oriented and understands the importance of developing staff.

- Network with others. If you're relatively new and haven't had the chance to develop your own network, your associates and co-workers might have some contacts that could be helpful to you.

Limitations of Mentoring

It's hard to deny the value of mentoring, especially in this environment of continuous, complex, and transformational change. However, mentoring may not always have the positive impact it is designed to have. Mentoring partners and organizations should be aware of the limitations or possible roadblocks associated with building and maintaining mentoring relationships. As much as we would like to believe otherwise, mentoring relationships don't always work. Just as relationships with friends and loved ones can become dysfunctional, so too can those with a mentor. When dysfunctions arise (e.g., codependence, abuse of power, inappropriate intimacy), it is important for organizations and individuals to take steps to redefine or dissolve the relationship when it is not working for one or both of the parties involved.[53]

Another issue in mentoring is that mentors, despite their desire to help, may not have adequate time to devote to a protégé. Formal programs typically take the time commitment into account when designing and implementing mentoring. However, mentors may be promoted or become involved in projects that require additional time. This forces the mentor to choose between job-related needs and those of the protégé. When the former is chosen, mentors might feel guilty, and without the benefit of an explanation, protégés might wonder why their support system is suddenly unavailable. By contrast, a protégé might become promoted or be given greater responsibility or visibility. Some mentors, feeling threatened by the protégé's success and seeing the protégé as a competitor or rival who could threaten their professional or personal image, might subtly (or not so subtly) attempt to sabotage their protégé's career. This is more likely to occur when a mentor is in the same function and organization as the protégé and is compounded when the mentor lacks personal or organizational assurance of his or her role in the organization.

Mentoring may result in a mismatch of resources or a mismatch between the mentor and protégé in goals, perceptions, and personality. For example, a mentor may be selected on the basis of his or her position in the organization, yet may lack the specific skills or resources desired by the protégé. Similarly, a protégé may feel that the mentor has delivered less time or attention than what was expected or promised. Finally, despite their strengths, mentors may inadvertently display weaknesses, such as a negative work style and bad habits, which are then emulated by the protégé.

Mentoring relationships can also suffer when protégés become overly submissive to the mentor. This is especially likely when both parties are in the same chain of command. A protégé may become submissive to the mentor, unwilling to disagree with the mentor's viewpoints or share pertinent information that might be damaging (e.g., concerns about performance), when a protégé fears power inherent in the mentor's position. In such a situation, the benefits of mentoring are not realized because of the protégé's concerns about how their true views or beliefs could impact performance appraisals or desire for retribution.[54] What starts out well may not remain so. The dynamics of a mentoring relationship can become destructive if interests of the parties change. This may be especially problematic in a formal mentoring program where there is inertia supporting the status quo and possibly fear of loss of prestige or reputation should either party request the dissolution of the relationship.

These limitations can exist in any type of mentoring relationship or in any context. Other limitations might be specific to the organization as a whole. Even in organizations that formally support and implement mentoring, such support may be more lip service or marketing hype than reality. This could happen for several reasons. First, should an organization suddenly face a severe market threat, it is likely to respond in a reactionary mode. That is, short-term thinking and shortcuts take precedence over planning and long-term fixes. While mentoring may be seen as valuable, the current "fire" may need immediate attention, whereas the long-term building of human capability is relegated to the back burner. Another possibility is the potential disconnect between the leaders' espoused philosophy about mentoring and a reward system that runs counter to it. Related to this are fears or mismanaged expectations that reduce managers' willingness to carry out the mentoring policy or philosophy. Mentoring will fail if the environment does not support it.

A limitation for mentoring facing many organizations is a lack of sufficient female and minority role models.[55] The glass ceiling effect, argued by Kanter and others, explains why so few women have positions at the most senior organizational level. For female and minority employees hoping to partner with someone who understands them and their challenges, finding a high-ranking female or minority—especially one who is willing to devote the time and attention necessary—might be difficult. Discouraged, they may ignore their desire for a mentor or look outside the organization or industry for a mentor. It is suggested that gender of the parties involved may impact the functionality of a mentoring relationship. Sexual harassment or improper behaviors have been reported in cross-gender partnerships. There is also the potential for improper behaviors, such as abuse of power and discrimination, in cross-racial relationships.[56]

Despite these challenges, mentoring—whether formal or informal, one-on-one or group, internal or external—offers benefits to the individuals involved. The list below provides some keys for making the most out of mentoring.

Keys for Protégés to Make Mentoring Work

- Respect the mentor's time and manage expectations. Focus on just a few quality meetings rather than numerous surface discussions. If you need additional time or attention, discuss this up front to determine if he or she can address these needs.

- Be mindful of the mentor's credibility and reputation. Act professionally at all times and be willing to confess mistakes and acknowledge the mentor's assistance.

- Be realistic. Having a mentor doesn't guarantee you'll receive promotions and advancement opportunities. Mentoring does offer you insights into how an organization operates and helps you understand decisions that are made—both about the company overall and about you and your career. Also, realize that as the situation changes, so too will your need for different mentors.

- Be selective. Choose mentors who are respected in their organizations and who have a reputation for being effective collaborators or developers. Selecting mentors on the basis of title alone may lead to disappointment.

- Make mentoring a two-way street. Seek out opportunities to provide mentors with technical information, new knowledge, or emotional support, as "the goal of building networks is to contribute to others."[57] Helping others increases the likelihood of

(continued)

receiving assistance in the future as well as increasing the trust and credibility of the relationship.[58]

■ Demonstrate your trustworthiness. Always treat as confidential any sensitive company information the mentor shares with you. Demonstrate your trust as well. If you don't honestly share your fears or concerns, your mentor won't be able to help you.[59]

■ Be willing to accept gracefully all feedback mentors are willing to provide you. Encourage feedback by requesting it. Show your appreciation by acknowledging how their feedback proved helpful.

■ Seek out multiple mentors: A collection of mentors is invaluable, providing different perspectives, knowledge, and skills while serving multiple mentoring functions.[60] They can provide emotional support or protection from political enemies in a way no one individual can.[61]

Summary

Networking and mentoring do not guarantee that our careers will advance. But they are extremely effective tools for individuals interested in building their social capital. In this chapter we have seen how networking and mentoring can benefit individuals and organizations, and we discussed strategies for effective networking and mentoring. Those who actively network and seek out mentoring relationships will reap benefits, as will their contacts and their organizations. Following are some exercises designed to help you improve your skills in both areas.

Key Terms and Concepts

Career functions	Networking
Collegial peers	Orientation and initiation stage
Cultivation	Protégé
Formal mentors	Psychosocial functions
Informal or peer relationships	Redefinition stage
Informational peers	Reverse networking
Information interviews	Secondary network
Mentor	Separation stage
Mentoring	Special peers

Endnotes

1. Blake Yaralian, "Networking," unpublished student paper, James Madison University, COB 202, Fall 1999.

2. W. Baker, *Achieving Success through Social Capital: Tapping the Hidden Resources in Your Personal and Business Networks* (San Francisco: Jossey Bass, 2000).

3. M. Forret and T. Dougherty, "Correlates of Networking Behavior for Managerial and Professional Employees," *Group and Organization Management* 26, no. 3 (2001), pp. 283–311.

4. Deb Haggerty, "Successful Networking," *The National Public Accountant,* Sept. 1999, p. 30.

5. Moshe Even-Shoshan and Tamar Gilad, "Network Your Way to Better Recruitment," *Workforce,* June 1999, p. 106.

6. Frank Sonnenberg, "The Professional (and Personal) Profits of Networking," *Training & Development Journal,* Sept. 1990, p. 55.

7. Catherine M. Petrini, "Building a Chain of Contacts," *Training & Development Journal,* Jan. 1991, p. 27.

8. Dorothy Riddle, "Networking Successfully," *International Trade Forum,* July–Sept. 1998, p. 13.

9. Marcia A. Reed, "Through the Grapevine," *Black Enterprise,* July 1999, p. 62.

10. Baker, *Achieving Success.*

11. Geary A. Rummler and Alan P. Brache, "Managing the White Space," *Training,* Jan. 1991, pp. 55–67.

12. A. Andrew Olson, "Long-Term Networking: A Strategy for Career Success," *Management Review,* April 1994, p. 33.

13. Laura Koss-Feder, "It's Still Who You Know . . . In the Boom Economy, Job Hunting Is a Way of Life. Here's How to Do It," *Time,* March 22, 1999, p. 114F.

14. Brian Kreuger, "Job Hunter," **www.collegegrad.com,** May 2000.

15. David Berman and Sean Silcoff, "Have Rolodex, Will Go Far," *Canadian Business,* Nov. 13, 1998, p. 50.

16. Baker, *Achieving Success.*

17. M. Forret and S. Sullivan, "A Balanced Scorecard Approach to Networking: A Guide to Successfully Navigating Career Changes," *Organizational Dynamics* 31 no. 3 (2002), pp. 245–258.

18. Marc Parise, regional president of First Midwest Bank, as cited in Forret and Sullivan, "Balanced Scorecard Approach."

19. Jeffrey Gitomer, "Building Good Relationships Puts the Work in Networking," *The Kansas City Business Journal,* Feb. 25, 2000, p. 24.

20. Haggerty, "Successful Networking."

21. Mike Godwin, Megan Fandrei, Josh Bare, Scott Longendyke, Cheryl Morgan, Brian Sweet, "Politicking and Networking," unpublished student paper, James Madison University, COB 202, Fall 1999.

22. M. Godwin et al., 1999, adopted from Tom Irish and Peter Grassl, "How to Build Your Network," **www.smartbiz.com/sbs/arts/irish5.htm.**

23. Riddle, "Networking Successfully."

24. M. Tosczak, "Career Strategies to Weather Unpredictable Times, *Kenan-Flagler Business Magazine,* Fall 2002, pp. 12–16.

25. Forret and Sullivan, "Balanced Scorecard Approach."

26. Andrea Nierenberg, "Masterful Networking," *Training and Development,* Feb. 1999, p. 51.

27. Jeffrey Gitomer, "Networking Not Working? Try Smart-Networking," *Birmingham Business Journal,* Jan. 7, 2000, p. 10.

28. Ibid.

29. Quote by James Clawson, Professor at University of Virginia Darden School, 1996.

30. Ellen A. Fagenson, "The Mentor Advantage: Perceived Career/Job Experiences of Protégés versus Nonprotégés," *Journal of Organizational Behavior,* 1989, pp. 309–320; Kathy E. Kram, *Mentoring at Work* (Glenview, IL: Scott Foresman and Co., 1985); Raymond A. Noe, "An Investigation of the Determinants of Successful Assigned Mentoring Relationships," *Personnel Psychology,* 1988, pp. 457–479; and Terri A. Scandura, "Mentorship and Career Mobility: An Empirical Investigation," *Journal of Organizational Behavior,* 1988, pp. 169–179.

31. Kathy E. Kram, "A Relational Approach to Career Development." In D. T. Hall (ed.), *The Career Is Dead—Long Live the Career,* pp. 132–157 (San Francisco: Jossey Bass, 1996); B. R. Ragins, "Diversified Mentoring Relationships in Organizations: A Power Perspective," *Academy of Management Review,* 1997, pp. 482–521.

32. D. M. Hunt and C. Michael, "Mentorship: A Career Training and Development Tool," *Academy of Management Review,* no. 3 (1983), pp. 475–485.

33. S. Branch, *Mentoring at Work.* "The 100 Best Companies to Work for in America." *Fortune,* 139, no. 1 (1999), pp. 118–130.

34. Jade Boyd, "Firms Work to Keep Women—Flextime, Mentoring Programs Interest Retention Efforts in IT," *Internetweek,* Nov. 27, 2000, p. 90; and Talila Baron, "IT Talent Shortage Renews Interest in Mentoring," *Information Week,* April 24, 2000.

35. Terri A. Scandura, "Dysfunctional Mentoring Relationships and Outcomes," *Journal of Management,* May 1, 1998, p. 449.

36. Kathy E. Kram, *Mentoring At Work: Developmental Relationships in Organizational Life* (Glenview; IL: Scott Foresman, 1985).

37. Peter F. Drucker, *Managing for the Future: The 1990s and Beyond* (New York: Dutton, 1992); J. Pfeffer, T. Hatano, and T. Santalainen, "Producing Sustainable Competitive Advantage through the Effective Management of People," *Academy of Management Executive,* 1995, pp. 55–72.

38. Troy R. Nielsen, "The Developmental Journey of Mentoring Research and Practice," paper presented at the annual Academy of Management Meeting, Chicago, 1999.

39. M. B. Arthur and D. M. Rousseau, "The Boundaryless Career as a New Employment Principle." In M. B. Arthur and D. M. Rousseau (eds.), *The Boundaryless Career* (New York: Oxford University Press, 1996), pp. 3–20; D. T. Hall, "Protean Careers of the 21st Century," *Academy of Management Executive* 10 (1996), pp. 8–16.

40. S. de Janasz, S. Sullivan, and V. Whiting, "Mentor Networks and Career Success: Lessons for Turbulent Times," *Academy of Management Executive,* 17, no. 4 (2003), pp. 78–91.

41. List of benefits confirmed in the following studies: Dreher and Ash, 1990; Scandura, 1992; Whitely, Dougherty, and Dreher, 1991; Turban and Dougherty, 1994; Chao, Walz, and Gardner, 1992; Fagenson, 1989; Scandura and Viator, 1994.

42. Patricia M. Buhler, "A New Role for Managers: The Move from Directing to Coaching," *Supervision,* Oct. 1, 1998, p. 16.

43. Ibid.

44. A. Bandura, *A Social Learning Theory* (Englewood Cliffs, N.J.: Prentice Hall, 1977).

45. Buhler, "A New Role for Managers."

46. S. Sullivan, D. Martin, W. Carden, and L. Mainiero, "The Road Less Traveled: How to Manage the Recycling Career Stage," *Journal of Leadership and Organization Studies,* 10, no. 2 (2003), pp. 34–42.

47. Kram, *Mentoring at Work.*

48. Kram, *Mentoring at Work,* pp. 134–139.

49. Kram, *Mentoring at Work.*

50. Andy Hargraves and Michael Fullan, "Mentoring in the New Millennium," *Theory into Practice* 39 (2000), p. 50.

51. Kathy E. Kram, "Phases of the Mentoring Relationship," *Academy of Management Journal* 26, (1983), pp. 608–625.

52. V. Whiting and S. de Janasz, "Mentoring in the 21st Century: Using the Internet to Build Skills and Networks," *Journal of Management Education,* no. 3 (2004), pp. 275–293.

53. Scandura, "Dysfunctional Mentoring Relationships."

54. Ibid.

55. Gary N. Powell, *Women and Men in Management,* Second Ed. (Newbury, CA: Sage Publications, 1993), p. 207.

56. Scandura, "Dysfunctional Mentoring Relationships."

57. Baker, *Achieving Success.*

58. Forret and Sullivan, "Balanced Scorecard Approach."

59. de Janasz, Sullivan, and Whiting, "Mentor Networks."

60. Ibid.

61. J. A. Wilson and N. S. Elman, "Organizational Benefits of Mentoring." *The Academy of Management Executive* 4, no. 4 (1990), pp. 88–94.

Exercise 16–A
Your Personal Network

1. Working on your own, write down all your primary contacts—individuals you know personally who can support you in attaining your professional goals. Then begin to explore their secondary connections. Make assumptions about possible secondary connections that can be made for you by contacting your primary connections. For example, through one of your teachers (primary), you might be able to obtain some names of potential employers (secondary).

2. Then meet with your partner or small group to exchange information about your primary and secondary networks and to exchange advice and information on how to best use these connections, as well as how you could be helpful to them.

3. Add names or types of names to your list based on ideas you get by talking with others in your group.

Primary and Secondary Connections

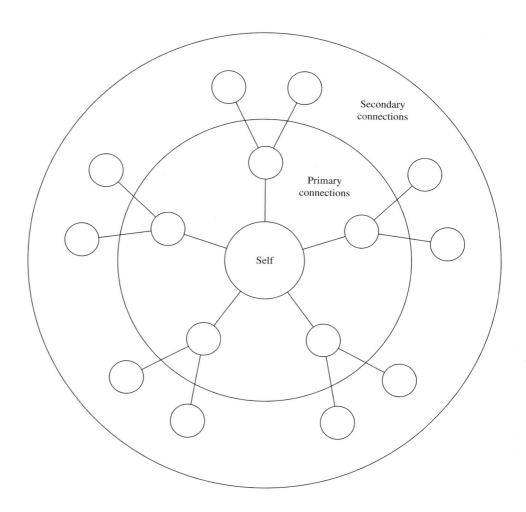

Secondary connections

Primary connections

Self

Questions

1. What were some of the best primary sources identified by your group?

2. What were some of the best sources for secondary contacts identified by your group?

3. What are some suggestions for approaching primary contacts?

4. What are some suggestions for approaching secondary contacts, and how is contacting secondary sources different from contacting primary contacts?

5. What did you learn about yourself and others from this exercise?

**Exercise 16–B
Networking Scenarios**

Working on your own, develop a networking strategy for the following three scenarios.
   Next, collaborate with a partner or small group to identify the best strategy for dealing with each of the three scenarios. Each group should develop one best strategy for each scenario and be prepared to report its findings.

Scenarios

   I. You are running for student government president. What steps would you take to make your candidacy a success?

   1. _____

   2. _____

   3. _____

   4. _____

   5. _____

   6. _____

   II. You are working as an intern and are interested in becoming a permanent full-time employee at the organization. What people would you approach and what steps could you take to obtain an offer?

   1. _____

   2. _____

   3. _____

   4. _____

   5. _____

   6. _____

   III. You just moved to a new community and your company's business growth relies heavily on referrals. How do you make contacts in a place where you don't know anyone? How can you build a client base?

   1. _____

   2. _____

   3. _____

   4. _____

   5. _____

   6. _____

Questions

1. What was difficult about this exercise?
2. What creative means were devised to build networks of contacts in these scenarios?
3. Which of these ideas would be easy to implement? Which would be difficult? What makes some strategies easier to do than others?
4. What personal qualities are needed to actually use these strategies?
5. How can someone who is shy about approaching new people use (some or all of) these strategies successfully?

Exercise 16–C
It's a Small World

1. Find someone in the room whom you barely know. Discuss people and connections you have to see if you can find common ground (e.g., shared personal interests or viewpoints, acquaintances you have in common).

2. Determine whether you have any acquaintances in common and determine how many levels or layers of connections it will take you to arrive at a commonality. Discuss organizations you belong to, classes you have been in, where you grew up, sports you play, and so on.

3. Mention a goal you would like to achieve, such as an internship connection you would like to make, a contact in a particular industry in which you are interested, or a person you would like to meet. Work with the other person to see if he or she might know someone who has a valuable connection for you.

Questions

1. Was it difficult or easy to approach someone relatively new with whom to discuss this topic? Why?

2. Did the exchange get easier as it proceeded? Why and how?

3. Did you establish a connection to a person of interest to you such as a potential summer employer? If so, with whom, and how did you make this connection?

4. What is your plan for following up on the contacts you made through your discussion(s) with your teammate(s)?

Exercise 16–D
The 30-Second
Commercial

Imagine you are going to a career conference. Representatives from a few hundred firms known to recruit at your school will be there. Your job is to network—meet as many people as practical while attempting to find what would be the perfect job and organization for you. To do this it is crucial to be able to communicate quickly and neatly what contribution you can offer to a prospective employer. Each new person you meet will want a thumbnail sketch of who you are, what skills and experience you offer, and any other special information. They don't have time for your life story, nor will they want to ask 20 questions to get the information they need to decide whether to continue talking to you about possible opportunities.

1. To network effectively in this situation, you will need to create a 30-second commercial, possibly in response to, "So, tell me about yourself." Think about how you'd like to present yourself to this particular audience. Create a script—one that will take between 20 and 30 seconds to verbalize—that you can use in this setting. Focus on a short, *genuine* appraisal of your capabilities.

2. Now, practice your script. How long does it take? How does it sound—confident but not arrogant? What changes might you make?

3. Now pair up with someone in the class. Practice meeting each other (take turns playing student and potential employer) and using your introduction. Exchange feedback and advice to refine both "commercials."

Questions

1. How did it feel pitching yourself? Why?

2. How did it feel being pitched to? Explain.

3. Why is it important to have this commercial rehearsed and ready?

4. What are the benefits and downsides to using this commercial?

Exercise 16–E
It's Not What You Know . . . It's Who You Know: A Hands-on Networking Exercise

Participants will be given role assignments (available from your instructor). Consistent with the practice of networking, these role assignments (and potential combinations thereof) contain three possible outcomes as described below.

- "I help/need you, you help/need me." In this scenario, two people each have something the other wants.

- "I help you now, you help me later." In this scenario, two people can each help each other in the near future.

- "I can't help you directly, but I know someone who knows someone who can possibly help you." In this scenario, three or more people are involved.

1. Read the following role descriptions. Take a few minutes to think about how you would market yourself and your "needs." Think about creative, yet not necessarily obvious or "in-your-face," ways to make your needs and wants known.

2. You now have approximately 15–20 minutes to network. Take your time and make a positive impression—even if the person with whom you first connect is of no immediate use to you. You can politely ask the unuseful participants to direct you to others whom you may have met who may be able to provide what is being requested.

3. Continue until you find the person or persons who can help meet your needs. Along the way, make note of others' needs and make a conscious effort to direct those people to each other.

Questions

1. How did you find who you were looking for? What interpersonal skills were helpful in enabling you to achieve your objective? Explain.

2. What were some of the lessons you learned about networking—what works well and not so well (e.g., role of eye contact, being persistent, being positive)?

3. How did it feel when you approached someone new with your need?

4. What was most difficult for you to do in this exercise?

5. In real life, what would be most difficult for you in approaching someone new about something you needed?

6. What did you learn about yourself and others from this exercise?

Source: Suzanne C. de Janasz and Stephen C. Davis, "It's Not What You Know . . . It's Who You Know: A Hands-on Networking Exercise," presented at Organizational Behavioral Teaching Conference, Carrollton, GA, 2000.

Exercise 16–F
Online Mentoring

You will identify and develop an online business mentor relationship with a current business manager, with whom you will correspond periodically on course-related topics.

Start thinking about who might be an appropriate mentor for you. Consider professional and personal acquaintances of your family and friends—lawyers, accountants, doctors, owners of small businesses, executives. It is not necessary that the mentor you select is in the field in which you are majoring; however, such "matching" may be helpful in establishing rapport with your mentor and providing you with insight into your chosen field. For example, those students with an interest in international business may want to select an online mentor who currently works overseas or who is employed by a domestic branch of an international corporation.

Getting Started

1. Select a mentor. Your instructor will provide you with criteria for mentor selection. In addition to professional and personal acquaintances of your family and friends, consider former bosses, fraternity/sorority colleagues (preferably those who have graduated several years ago), and neighbors.

2. Contact the potential mentor, discuss the assignment, explain their potential role, and clarify the time commitment (about 15 minutes for each of three e-mail exchanges during the semester). Explain why you have selected the mentor or believe he or she would make a good mentor; for example, you have similar career interests, you are aware of his or her success/expertise, and so on. Ascertain the mentor's ability to commit to providing you valuable feedback in a timely fashion.

3. Develop your first set of questions. Please give your questions careful thought. A few things to consider about your questions:

(a) You are making an impression, so ask intelligent questions, and ask them in an appropriate format. The question: "Do you use empowerment in your workplace?" is a closed question which is likely answered with a simple yes or no. Rewording the question, "In what ways do you empower your employees?" is likely to result in a more thoughtful and complete response. You might want to go a step further and establish a context for your question, such as "In class, we discussed some of the benefits and pitfalls of empowerment, which is a way to give employees greater discretion over their work environment. To what extent do you empower your employees and what impact has that had on their productivity and satisfaction?" Typically, if the answers your mentor gives you are less than satisfactory, the question was too vague, ambiguous, or closed-ended.

(b) Try to ask questions that help clarify topics currently under discussion. You are welcome to ask questions that relate to topics not yet covered, but you may find it more difficult to compose such questions.

(c) Ask questions that are personally meaningful to you. If you chose a mentor who has experience in a field you would like to enter, fashion questions that are industry specific, such as "Given the rapid rate of change in the computer industry, how do you keep abreast of both technology and management issues?" or "In what ways does managing technical professionals differ from managing nontechnical or administrative employees?"

(d) Don't assume that your mentor understands all the terms you discuss in class. If you are interested in interpersonal style differences and would like to know your mentor's style, do not ask "Are you a Theory X or Theory Y manager?" (explained in Chapter 18) without some context or explanation of these styles. Even more commonly used terms like empowerment may not mean the same thing to people at different levels in the organization or in different types of organizations. Instead try a question like: "In class, we learned that individuals have different preferences in the way they handle conflict. The five styles we discussed are (briefly describe each). Which style is most (least) comfortable for you and why? Share an example where your style did (or did not) accomplish your intended goal."

(e) Feel free to build on previous questions, especially if you feel your mentor's answer was incomplete or you would just like to delve deeper. The goal is that you find value in the exchanges with your mentor.

Source: Vicki R. Whiting and Suzanne C. de Janasz, "Mentoring in the 21st Century: Using the Internet to Build Skills and Networks." *Journal of Management Education,* 28, no. 3 (2004), pp. 275–293. Copyright © 2004 Sage Publications, Inc. Reprinted by permission of Sage Publications, Inc.

Exercise 16–G
On Becoming a Master Mentor . . .

Become involved as a mentor. There are multiple opportunities to do this, including

- Junior Achievement.
- Big Brothers, Big Sisters.
- Literacy program.
- School-based mentoring program.
- Community organizations—contact information available through local campus service learning office.
- Working as a counselor for a day camp.

Prior to beginning your work as a paid or volunteer mentor, decide which skills you want to concentrate on most.

At the conclusion of the first month or 15 hours of service, evaluate your mentoring abilities—what's working well and what could be improved. If you developed a trusting relationship with a peer or supervisor, ask him or her for feedback on your strengths and opportunities for improvement. You might even ask the people whom you mentor two simple questions: In my role as your mentor (Big Brother, teacher, counselor), what are some things I'm doing that are helpful for you? What are some things that I don't do or should stop doing? In other words, how best can I help you achieve what you want to achieve?

Following your instructor's guidelines, write a reflection paper summarizing your experiences and providing an in-depth assessment of your strengths and opportunities for improvement as a mentor. Utilize the feedback you've received from others as well as your personal experiences prior to and including this experience.

Exercise 16–H
Reflection/Action Plan

This chapter focused on networking and mentoring—what they are, why they are important, and how to improve your skills in these areas. Complete the worksheet below upon completing all reading and experiential activities for this chapter.

1. The one or two areas in which I am most strong are:

_____

_____

_____

_____

2. The one or two areas in which I need more improvement are:

_____

_____

_____

_____

3. If I did only one thing to improve in each of these areas (coaching and mentoring), it would be to:

_____

_____

_____

_____

4. Making these changes would probably result in:

_____

_____

_____

_____

5. If I did not change or improve in these areas, it would probably affect my personal and professional life in the following ways:

_____

_____

_____

_____

17 Coaching and Providing Feedback for Improved Performance

Learning Points

How do I:
- Identify characteristics of effective coaches and feedback?
- Help others set and achieve goals?
- Utilize techniques and strategies to coach others with whom I work?
- Praise someone for giving extra effort?
- Give constructive feedback without making the recipient feel defensive?
- Let others know I am open to receiving constructive feedback?
- Give myself feedback and check these perceptions with others?

Susan Dougherty was a "high potential" manager at a global industrial company. She had been with the company for 10 years. During that time she had excelled as a technical specialist. A year ago, she was promoted to a managerial position. She didn't really want it, as she was very happy where she was. This new position required her to be more involved in internal politics than desired. She had solid credentials—bachelor's and master's degrees in engineering from a top school. She had an excellent performance record and was respected by all who worked with her.

The reason Susan was promoted is that her company wanted to have more women in prominent leadership roles. To help her make the transition, they gave her an opportunity to participate in the company's management development program. Through the program she was learning a lot about herself, including her strengths and weaknesses as a manager. As part of the program, she was invited to sit down for about an hour with a senior member of the human resources staff to discuss her progress.

As Susan prepared for this meeting, she was full of self-doubt. She had been told by her manager that there were some concerns about her ability to do the job. Not about her technical expertise—that was unquestioned—but about her ability to be a manager, to supervise and relate to others. She was a bit abrupt in her interactions with others, and typically more task oriented than those she supervised. Also she seemed to be more comfortable when she was working alone rather than as part of a team. Susan also disliked "schmoozing with the higher-ups," a "necessary condition for anyone here on their way up," as her manager explained to her.

Susan was confused. She wasn't sure how she should handle the upcoming meeting. She hadn't really wanted the job in the first place, yet she did want to do well. She was

307

confident of her technical abilities but unsure she had what it takes to be a good manager. She wasn't sure how much to divulge to the HR representative, or if that person would be able to help her. She was really shaken. This was the first time in her professional career she had received some potentially damaging feedback. And she didn't know what to do.

1. We learn that Susan's manager had some concerns. Do you feel her manager provided adequate support for Susan to improve? Why or why not?

2. What are the key issues involved here?

3. What kind of feedback and help should she elicit from her manager? From the HR representative? From her co-workers? From close friends?

4. What can Susan do on her own to prepare for the meeting—and to make a decision about how to proceed within the company?

"Good management consists of showing average people how to do the work of superior people."

Ron Zemke[1]

Good managers are in business to help their business succeed—and they know that the way to do this is to help those around them succeed. Good managers and team leaders take regular employees and team members and give them the advice, guidance, and information necessary to become exemplars in their work—people who are superior workers. Long reserved for athletes or top performers in business, coaching is a technique recently adopted and formalized by organizations as a way to motivate employees to superior performance. Coaching involves guiding, instructing, and training,[2] with a focus on teaching individuals, groups, or teams specific skills needed to improve their performance. Coaches also provide feedback to let employees know how they're doing and whether adjustments need to be made to succeed in an organization. In this chapter we look at both coaching and feedback—what they are, why they are important to individuals and organizations, and ways you can develop your skills in coaching and providing feedback to others.

What Is Coaching?

"Coaching is unlocking a person's potential to maximize their own performance. It is helping them to learn rather than teaching them."

Harvard Educator Timothy Gallwey

Coaching is a means for managers to provide guidance, insight, and encouragement to their employees for improved work performance through frequent interactions. It is designed to strengthen and enhance learning through a continual day-to-day process going beyond the once-a-year appraisal system.[3] Coaching conveys a set of beliefs, values, and vision and enables goal setting and action steps for the realization of extraordinary results.[4] Because of the interdevelopmental nature of the coaching process, both coaches and the individuals whom they coach benefit by building skills and developing as people. Traditionally, coaching is recognized as a term and process used in sports. In athletics, coaches demonstrate or encourage the effective use of skills, reinforce positive behaviors, and identify and correct negative behaviors. The term *coaching* is now seen as a useful concept in other walks of life, such as business.

In response to merger mania, the proliferation of dot-coms, ever-changing technology, and calls for downsizing and cost cutting, organizations are expecting their employees to do more with less. With fewer employees and frequent changes in job roles, managers cannot watch over every aspect of the job (and employees don't want them to!). Instead, managers need to use their sideline vantage point to empower their employees to perform at high levels when the "coach" is off the field.[5] This notion that managers act as coaches—instead of traditionally top-down oriented supervisors—is especially important given the demands that the globally competitive, technologically complex environment places on organizations' educated and adaptable employees.[6] By acting as a coach (like a facilitator or enabler), rather than a supervisor (like a director or superior), employees' abilities and creativity can be unleashed instead of controlled, resulting in increased morale, productivity, and enhanced interpersonal working relationships.

The Importance and Benefits of Coaching

Traditionally, employees looked to their supervisors for direction, decision making, and control. Today's more fluid, less hierarchical working environment calls for a different philosophy or mindset. To remain competitive, organizations need to harness the creative and synergistic capacity of all their employees, not just the ones in leadership positions. The very capabilities that led an organization to success a few years ago could cause its undoing if it refuses to engage in continual learning and renewal. By adapting and creating a new environment where there are leader–employee partnerships—where leaders are more like coaches and less like bosses—individuals thrive and organizations remain competitive and survive.[7] Coaches are leaders who focus their energy on helping others improve their performance and achieve goals.[8] A coaching philosophy and process benefits both individuals and the organization. Specific benefits for individuals and teams include:[9]

■ Coaching reduces employees' fears related to their (and others') status in the organization. By emphasizing collaboration, partnership, and mutual growth, the perception of "manager versus worker" is replaced with a more team-oriented view of "Together we can . . ."

■ Coaching enables workers to feel they are part of the organization rather than used by it. They take ownership in and contribute to organizational performance and success. Employees enjoy working in a healthy environment, one where relationships are rooted in mutual respect and rapport, and constructive and respectful language is encouraged. While some employees are used to and respond to fear and threats, the outcome of the management by fear approach is compliance, not commitment.

■ Effective coaching endorses rather than diminishes people's skills and abilities. Imagine the Little League coach who publicly scolds or belittles a child upon making an error. Now imagine another coach who encourages children to play to their potential, scolds parents for their unhealthy and belittling remarks, and utilizes not only the best players but those who have yet to develop their full potential. For which coach would you rather play? When managers coach effectively, they "accentuate the positive and eliminate the negative," to quote a popular 1940s song. They see more possibilities than limitations in the individual and the organization and take personal responsibility for overcoming those limitations.

■ Coaching helps people overcome personal obstacles to their success. Good coaches use goal setting and constructive feedback.[10] When good coaches help employees set and achieve goals, they feel a sense of accomplishment. World class athletes Tiger Woods and the Williams sisters (Venus and Serena) didn't fit the traditional mold for American golf and tennis stars. As racial minorities, they sometimes faced prejudice from competitors and detractors. They could have accepted a lesser fate, but the sense of self-worth and self-esteem facilitated by their coaches, their fathers, helped them put concerns about acceptance aside and achieve phenomenal success.

■ When used in team settings, coaching improves team communications and provides a structure for managing conflict. Coaching helps reinforce team goals and commitments by providing external support and insight into effective team processes.

■ Coaching behaviors encourage others to coach. In essence, coaching behaviors beget coaching behaviors. With greater trust and support, employees are more likely to take risks and suggest creative solutions to organizational problems.[11] As employees feel supported and trusted, they become more supportive of other employees and more trusting of management.

Beyond individual and team benefits, coaching provides many benefits for the organization as well.[12] Coaching helps to improve workforce recruitment and retention. People want to join and stay in an organization where they will be respected, trusted, listened to, and valued. It also reduces misunderstanding and mistakes by resulting in a more positive and supportive climate at work through the use of a common language to which everyone can relate. Coaching emphasizes the unique potential of individuals to evoke hidden talents, thereby increasing their ability to contribute to the organization's success.

Effective coaching can help enhance organizational communication with internal and external customers. As employees are more involved in decisions and communications, they play a more active role in relationships with customers both inside and outside of the organization. This will lead to improved performance management, positively affecting external customer service while internally promoting focused performance discussions, the development of new skills, and planning for personal career advancement.

Another important result of coaching is seen in the expansion of entrepreneurial thinking within organizations. Coaching fosters creativity and helps build a shared vision. Building on the benefit of trust and support of individuals, coaching creates an atmosphere in which individual creativity is not only supported but also deeply encouraged. Coaching provides organizational members with the opportunity to start new projects or initiate partnerships with suppliers or customers.

Skills and Characteristics of Effective Coaches

Effective coaches acquire a mindset, skills, and values that will help build employee commitment to the organization. Coaching skills or techniques are not seen as genuine when accompanied by an attitude or behaviors that run counter to the goals of coaching. Merely possessing a coaching philosophy is not enough; it is also necessary to have good skills in communication, feedback, and goal setting. Effective coaches have all the following characteristics or abilities:

- *A desire to bring out the best in others' performance.* Effective coaches support employees' needs, create choices, seek commitment, and provide means for self-expression.[13]

- *Ability to give constructive and positive feedback.* Coaching enables employees to understand their mistakes and how to improve or develop their skills. Effective coaches are able to talk face-to-face with others about performance problems, and they also affirm and acknowledge others' contributions to the organization.

- *Honesty and trustworthiness.* Effective coaches are keenly aware of themselves and how they impact others. Through their actions, they demonstrate their trustworthiness, high personal standards, ability to develop mutual relationships, and willingness to share their wisdom.[14]

- *Willingness to NOT assign blame.* "Blame the process, not the person." Good coaches are process- and problem-oriented; they focus on how to solve problems rather than on the personality of the people. To do this, they get involved and collaborate to find solutions.

- *Good communication skills.* Good coaches create an environment in which communication is open and two-way, encouraging employees to bring forth problems as well as opportunities without fear of blame or retribution. Such dialogue builds mutual trust and commitment.

- *A parallel style of thinking and acting.*[15] Good coaches attend to both human and business needs. They realize that in order to accomplish the organizational goals, they must balance the need for learning with the need for results.

- *Responsibility and accountability.* Good coaches accept full responsibility for their actions and for what occurs in their environment and encourage others to do the same.[16]

- *Constructive conflict management.* Effective coaches encourage the clashing of ideas for creativity and innovation and discourage personal conflicts. They stress the team approach and facilitate mutual understanding among all parties involved.

- *A personal level of caring.* For employees to respect the coach and his or her knowledge, the coach must show genuine care and concern toward them.[17]

Effective Coaching Behaviors

Now that you know the benefits of coaching and what makes coaches effective, you might be wondering exactly what to do when planning to call an employee (or teammate) in for coaching. Situations vary and call for different strategies. The following represents findings of a study of a major service organization in which Stowell examined the behavior of effective and ineffective coaches and their coaching sessions.[18]

- Coaching sessions require managers to use face-to-face discussions of performance problems. For many managers, this is considered an unpleasant task and is therefore avoided. The best sessions last between 35 and 45 minutes.

- Effective coaches don't legislate quality; they model it. "Do as I say, not as I do" does not work in this environment. For the leader–employee partnership to work, there has to be mutual respect and trust.

- Effective coaches and their sessions contain high levels of **supportive behaviors** (words or actions that denote concern or acceptance) and moderate levels of **initiating** or *problem-solving* **behaviors** (words or actions that encourage problem solving/resolutions). Coaches should avoid using nonsupportive behaviors (words or actions that express aggression or power). (See Figures 17–1 and 17–2.) The leader establishes a framework for the coaching discussion, which might look something like: "We have a situation that deserves some attention. What can we do to solve it? I'm confident in your ability. I'll support you. What do you think would help in this situation?"

- Successful coaches use supportive behaviors far more frequently than unsuccessful coaches. These behaviors fall into three categories: verbal (statements that indicate the coach's commitment to and backing of the employee), tangible (statements that offer help, resources, links to other people and information), and active (behaviors and actions that indicate complete and empathic listening including asking questions, acknowledging,

Figure 17–1

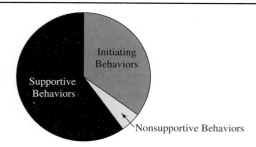

Source: Reprinted with permission from Steven J. Stowell, "Coaching: A Commitment to Leadership," *Training & Development Journal,* June 1988, vol. 6, pp. 34–38.

Figure 17–2
Key Leadership Behaviors for Successful Coaching and Coaching Sessions[19]

Supportive Behaviors—A leader's words and actions showing concern and acceptance of employees.

- Collaboration regarding solutions to problems.
- Help and assistance through training and resources.
- Concern over the employee's needs and objectives.
- Empathy for the employee and attention to obstacles and problems.
- Expressions of the value of the employee and his or her contribution to the work.
- Acceptance of responsibility in situations.
- Interaction that provides time for the employee to air his or her feelings.

Initiating Behaviors—Initiating and structuring actions and discussions.

- Feedback and analysis of issues and concerns.
- Clarification of leader expectations and requirements.
- Exploration of impact and effects of employee's actions.
- Action planning around solutions and desired changes.
- Seeking commitment to the action plan.
- Clarification of positive and negative consequences connected to future action and plans.

using appropriate body language, showing genuine interest). This last category might be most important; it demonstrates the coach's willingness to understand before trying to be understood.

- The best coaches ask questions that enable the employee to discover how to improve. They collaborate with the employee to analyze situations and performance and jointly find solutions.

- Successful coaches challenge employees and stimulate resolutions. This is done through initiating action-oriented problem analysis discussions. These problem-solving discussions are best when focusing on one or two issues. Any more would be overwhelming.

- The best sessions were those in which the coach planned, prepared, and rehearsed prior to the coaching session. Because many find such sessions difficult to do, this preparation can be key to reducing the coach's discomfort with the process, enabling him or her to do the same for their employee.

Counseling

Coaching should not be mistaken for counseling. Some situations call for counseling rather than coaching. It is important for managers to understand the difference between the two. (See Figure 17–3.) **Counseling** is used to address personal or attitudinal problems rather than those related to an individual's ability (or lack thereof). Counseling is a complex task and is best reserved for professionals. It involves listening skills, feedback skills, trustworthiness, and a good deal of patience.

Two methods facilitate the counseling process. The choice of method will be determined by the manager's comfort and ability with counseling and the severity of the problem being addressed in the session. **Directive methods** include probing, questioning, and discussing specific problems and possible solutions. In addition, a manager may have the person discuss her behavior, beliefs, and perceptions in order to help the manager put the individual's emotions and attitudes into perspective.

Another method, the **nondirective approach,** involves being a good listener and sounding board. Listening may be the most valuable and helpful means for identifying the source and solution for counseling-related problems. Sometimes people just need to disclose the way they are feeling to relieve stress and gain a new perspective on a situation. In so doing, they often find solutions to their own problems.

Seldom should a manager get involved in counseling an employee. Good managers recognize their limitations in helping others and refer employees with personal or emotional problems to other professionals or resources, such as the organization's employee assistance program. Many organizations have employee assistance and wellness

Figure 17–3
A Comparison between
Coaching and Counseling

	Coaching	Counseling
Objective:	To reinforce positive behaviors and correct negative behaviors, to gain positive work outcomes and enhance relationships.	To facilitate understanding of behaviors and to obtain a willingness to change.
Means:	Pass information, set standards, and provide insight, encouragement, direction, and guidance.	Two methods: Directive—assuring, probing, and questioning. Nondirective—listening and supporting.
Employee problems stem from:	Lack of ability, information, or understanding and incompetence.	Attitudes, defensiveness, personality clashes, and other emotional problems.

programs to assist with personal and health problems ranging from mental illness, substance abuse, day care, and family issues to physical health issues and financial planning.

Helping Others Set Goals

A major component of coaching is helping others set goals. Receiving performance feedback through coaching can be difficult for employees. By incorporating goal setting into the coaching activity, a manager can motivate an employee to set a new course or direction.

Managers and organizations can have a dramatic impact on subordinate goal attainment.[20] To increase employees' chances for attaining goals, the organization's environment must be conducive to individual growth and development in the context of organizational goals. Underscoring this philosophy with managerial support via coaching—both in setting the example and supporting others to do the same—also facilitates the goal-setting process. Managers need to be aware of behaviors that can positively impact others in setting and achieving personal and organizational goals.

Goals you set for yourself are more likely to be achieved when they are SMART (specific, measurable, achievable and attainable, realistic, and time bound). This is also true of goals set by your teammates or employees. Coach others to ensure their goals conform to and contain SMART elements. Work with them to ensure that the desired outcome is clear and that they have the necessary skills and resources to accomplish their goals. Good managers help others set "stretch" goals—those that require total effort but are not so unrealistic that subordinates avoid committing to what is perceived to be impossible. Studies demonstrate that performance increases with the level of goal difficulty, providing that the individual is committed to achieving it and has the ability to do so.[21] Goals should be challenging yet realistic.

Once SMART goals are set, your work isn't done. As a coach, you might need to provide periodic feedback and encouragement, especially if the goal is particularly complex and long-term. Encourage others to break up large, complex goals into smaller objectives, and set checkpoints and processes to follow up. Some employees may prefer feedback initiated by the manager, while others prefer to provide periodic updates. There may even be employees who are accustomed to the "no news is good news" approach. Use your judgment and assessment of their capabilities and past performance to determine how often and by what mechanism interim performance is checked and modified, if necessary. In addition, goal setting is an ongoing process. Your work helping others set goals is likely never done, though your level of involvement may change over time. Encourage employees to establish and update goals periodically, annually at the minimum.

Goals that are SMART are more likely to be achieved. The same can be said for goals that are personally meaningful or externally rewarding. When employees set goals that advance personal needs and desires for growth and development, their intrinsic motivation to achieve those goals will be high. Employee commitment can be increased further when they stand to gain recognition, perquisites, or other financial rewards when goals are achieved. Managers or coaches can clarify the existence of such organizational rewards or create new ones. A perfect example of this is in sales organizations. Top sellers within a specified period of time are likely to be awarded bonuses, priority parking spaces, minivacations, or other special treatment, like access to desirable training opportunities. These rewards can encourage individual commitment to (and healthy competition between co-workers in obtaining) rewards in such organizations. When such rewards are not available, managers can increase goal commitment and achievement by using an informal chat or note to express their satisfaction and appreciation for the employee's positive efforts and improvements.

Finally, commitment to goals will vary directly with the amount of participation and input from the employee in setting the goals. You cannot set someone else's goals and expect to have high commitment and motivation.[22] In addition, some researchers have hypothesized that allowing participation in the goal-setting process increases a person's perception of control and fairness.[23] Have you ever been asked by someone else to get high grades, quit smoking, or lose weight? Were you successful? Chances are, unless and until the goal is yours, you're likely not to give it your all. Depending on the employees'

**Figure 17–4
Five Steps for
Helping Others
Set Goals**[24]

PREPARE—Be informed on the organization's goals and direction to ensure a match between these and the goals of the individual. Also be sure to review the individual's past performance and accomplishments to ensure goals are attainable and challenging.

CLARIFY—Provide an overall picture on how the individual's goals and objectives fit with the organizational objectives. Ensure that they know their part in the whole.

DECIDE—Work together to decide what would be attainable, desirable, and challenging goals. Put the goals in writing and make them public.

COMMIT—Determine how you can commit to support, assist, and facilitate others in achieving their goals. Such support might include making phone calls, arranging for training, coordinating with the efforts of other individuals or departments, and obtaining needed equipment.

PARTICIPATE—Schedule regularly planned meetings to discuss progress, revise goals if necessary, and set higher or additional goals. Make goal setting a part of the process, continue the cycle on a regular basis.

understanding of organizational goals and their role in achieving those goals, managers can trust employees to set their own goals or managers can solicit employee input and set goals participatively. Extend the notion of participative goal setting to include goal checking. In other words, jointly develop a system that will enable individuals to gauge their performance to jointly established goals and know whether (and why) they have successfully completed them.[25]

Effectively helping others to set goals is a key element in managerial coaching. Figure 17–4 summarizes and highlights steps and behaviors necessary for helping others set and achieve goals.

What Is Feedback?

Many receive advice, only the wise profit from it.

Syrus

Today's companies are being pressured by the marketplace to come up with the best ideas and the most innovative products. How do these companies and their employees know whether their efforts are successful? Ultimately, consumers indicate their approval of a company's products and services through their purchasing behavior and other company-initiated mechanisms, such as customer satisfaction surveys. By asking for and responding to this "advice," organizations remain viable competitors in our continuously changing environment. The old adage "no news is good news" no longer suffices. Organizations—and the employees within them—need to know how they're doing so they can continually develop and improve. Whereas customers provide this information to organizations, managers are responsible for letting employees know how they're doing and whether adjustments need to be made. This section discusses **feedback:** why it's necessary for organizations and individuals, how to give and receive it effectively, and benefits gained for doing so.

Feedback is information that enables individuals or groups to compare actual performance with a given standard or expectation. Feedback involves offering your perceptions and describing your feelings in a nonjudgmental manner and supplying data that others can use to examine and change behaviors.[26] It also assists in goal setting and performance improvement.

Most people are eager to know how they are doing. As a student, you receive much feedback on your schoolwork. Grades on exams and assignments, written suggestions for improvement, and face-to-face meetings with faculty provide you with feedback on your performance or how well you are doing relative to others in your class or your teacher's expectations. Through feedback, you receive direct information about how you are performing and how to direct your future efforts in terms of corrective action (do more of this, stop doing that). If the feedback is constructive—it is truthful, fair, and not given as a personal attack—the information gained can be invaluable in enhancing our performance and helping us grow personally and professionally.[27]

Why Giving Job Feedback Is So Important . . . in Organizations

The importance of giving, receiving, and incorporating feedback into organizational life is increasing today due to heightened competition and shifting requirements. Workplace change is now a constant. Positions and roles are continually being reengineered, often with little or no additional training offered to employees as they start new jobs or new roles within their organization. As a result, seasoned employees are expected to give feedback to new employees or team members on company expectations and requirements. This is beneficial because it ensures that employees experience many aspects of the business and become successful at teaching, coaching, and mentoring others. On the other hand, continual adaptation to new roles can be a mentally and emotionally taxing experience for new and existing employees. Knowledge of effective feedback mechanisms can reduce the strain caused by having to continually train new people.

In this new environment, feedback also travels upward from employees to managers. Feedback mechanisms are put in place for employees to share progress toward goals, relay current problems, and inform management about how they feel about their jobs, co-workers, and the organization in general.

Why Feedback Is Important . . . for Individuals

The ability to give, receive, and ask for feedback is important to us personally. Giving feedback greatly benefits those with whom you work. When information about performance is given in such a way that the person can learn and grow from the feedback, it can be an enormous boost for professional confidence and competence. Helping others to better understand the company and how to excel at their jobs can result in enhanced employee morale, improved employee relations, greater teamwork, and enhanced productivity.

By receiving feedback, we learn how others perceive us. Because it isn't unusual to find that our behaviors are interpreted differently than we intended,[28] feedback provides us with information needed to change our behaviors and attitudes (if we desire to do so). Feedback highlights what we need to do to be more efficient or effective. It adds to our understanding of our strengths and weaknesses and aids us in developing self-improvement plans through which we can learn new skills and evaluate our use of these skills. Through enhancement and improvement, we can reinforce positive actions and correct insufficient or disruptive behaviors.

Asking for feedback has many benefits. By asking for feedback, we demonstrate our commitment to improve and our dedication to do things right. This strengthens our affiliation or sense of belonging with an organization. If we see ourselves as temporary or short-term employees, we won't care what others think of us. When we ask for feedback, we signal a desire to remain involved with an organization in a longer and more meaningful capacity. Asking for feedback also builds and enhances our esteem. Through feedback we can receive reinforcement of the things we do well. This is a confidence-builder and critical for developing a positive self-identity. Even feedback that is constructive can be beneficial. Constructive feedback enables us to find out—in a nonthreatening way—how we can change and ways to improve. When offered appropriately, constructive feedback can also result in significant behavior changes. Feedback can have a strong impact on our actions and on our attitude. We all have blind spots. The better we understand our behaviors and their impact on others, the better equipped we will be to choose alternative behaviors.[29]

Sources of Feedback

Feedback typically comes from one of three primary sources:[30] (1) others—superiors, peers, customers, friends, contacts, and parents; (2) the task itself—feedback can be directly built into the task we are attempting; and (3) self—honest, realistic appraisal of how we're doing relative to others' and our own expectations.

- *Others*—As we interact with others, we receive much input as to how we are doing. This can be an excellent source of feedback. While it is helpful to ask for and obtain feedback from others, overly positive and overly negative feedback should be treated with care. Your self-identity and self-awareness should be strong enough that you can assess your own behavior and evaluate judgments about you against your own perceptions about yourself. When you receive feedback that is overly positive (e.g., "You did a great job today") from someone who is not aware of mistakes you made in your performance, accept the feedback gracefully but don't "believe your own press." Vow to make changes so that the next time you receive this feedback, you will feel it is richly deserved. Sometimes we receive negative feedback (e.g., "Why can't you ever do anything right?"). When this happens, use your self-awareness to evaluate this feedback. If there's a kernel of truth, accept it and make changes. If not, forget about it and focus on the positives you know you have to offer instead.

- *The Task Itself*—When developing project plans, it is a good idea to build in mechanisms through which you evaluate the progress of the project and the people responsible for getting the work done. As a member of a project team, you might suggest building in regular checkpoints—periodic points during which the team evaluates the progress made to date and makes needed changes—and continually monitoring the project until its end. The team can also discuss and debrief the project throughout and at the end as a means for getting feedback about which elements went well and which ones could be improved the next time around. Evaluating a completed project provides an excellent source of feedback, as the actual project output is tangible evidence of the quality (or lack thereof) with which a project was done. For example, a quality improvement team will know whether their project is successful if the number of defective parts declines. Similarly, a customer service team can evaluate their progress by tracking the ratings given by customers in customer satisfaction surveys.

- *Self*—Our own thoughts and perceptions can be good sources of feedback, although it is difficult for us to be completely objective when self-evaluating. While we can sometimes be our own worst critics, studies show that workers often overestimate their own performance. Few employees or even students think they are just average. Giving feedback to yourself is easy, but doing it objectively can be difficult. Generally, if self-esteem is an issue, you'll be harder on yourself than others would be. However, this may not apply to people from cultures whose values differ from yours. It is helpful to supplement your own evaluation with comments from others. Take for example the student who asked his close friends for some feedback about himself. His actions showed intelligence as well as courage. It must have been a good strategy—that student is now president of a major consumer products company! When giving yourself feedback, it helps to assess yourself relative to others in similar roles, rather than making your assessment in a vacuum. Evaluate honestly those things you're doing well and those areas in which you can improve, and make plans to make the necessary changes. You can also check your self-evaluations with those of others.

> *To know what to do is wisdom. To know how to do it is skill. But doing it, as it should be done, tops the other two virtues.*
>
> Anonymous

Characteristics of Effective Feedback

Effective feedback provides both instruction and motivation.[31] A supervisor who demonstrates the proper sequence of steps in responding to a customer's technical questions has provided instruction to an employee. When the employee performs these steps correctly in a subsequent call, the boss responds, "Nice job! I really liked how thorough you were in asking questions to discover the best solution." This kind of feedback reinforces desired behavior and motivates the employee to continue to improve performance. To ensure that your feedback fulfills these two objectives, it should possess the following characteristics:

---

12 Characteristics of Effective Feedback

1. Specific	7. Timely
2. Nonpersonal	8. Frequent
3. Work related	9. Purposeful
4. Documentable	10. Constructive and balanced
5. Descriptive	11. In the appropriate setting
6. Nonprescriptive	12. Interactive

■ *Specific:* General comments like "You did a good job" or "That is all wrong" tend not to be helpful. Instead, focus your comments on a specific activity or behavior so others know exactly how they can improve their performance in the designated area. "That was a tough decision. I'm impressed with how you weighed the pros and cons and selected the best course of action." "I'd like to talk with you about your proofing of these reports."

■ *Nonpersonal:* How you deliver feedback is as important as what you say. Avoid blaming ("You're the reason we have mistakes around here") and referring to assumed personality traits ("How come you're so lazy?"). Direct your feedback at the behavior itself and not the worker. An example of this is, "I am concerned about the fact you've been late every night this week."[32] Focus on what people do, not who they are.[33]

■ *Work related:* When giving feedback to someone on the job, only refer to behaviors that are directly related to the job. "We need to talk about your absences," rather than "I understand you've been going nightclubbing every night this week."

■ **Documentable:** When giving specific work-related feedback, make sure it is based on fact rather than hearsay. "Our records show you've been using company phones for making personal calls" will be accepted more readily than, "Betty tells me you're on the phone a lot." Also keep a written record of any conversations you have when using feedback to help employees correct undesirable behaviors. This could be important if in the future you need to fire a poor-performing employee.

■ **Descriptive:** Focus your feedback on a specific behavior that the recipient can change or control, describing behavior rather than evaluating it—for example, "I've noticed the filing system is getting a bit disorganized." Discuss what the person did and the feelings aroused by those actions rather than labeling or name-calling. "You interrupted me and I get frustrated when I lose my place" rather than "You're inconsiderate."[34]

■ **Nonprescriptive:** Avoid moralizing or giving feedback that is judgmental or prescriptive. When you lecture employees about what you think they should do, they are likely to become defensive and tune out your feedback.

■ *Timely:* Give feedback promptly, immediately after the event or incident, if possible. While promptness is important, it is OK to wait briefly if it means delivering feedback in a private setting and once emotions have cooled. "Let's debrief how the meeting went tomorrow, after we've both had a chance to think about it." Don't delay giving feedback, as it will reduce the likelihood that others will understand and learn from their mistakes. In addition, don't withhold the feedback. Saying nothing when performance is inadequate or when someone treats you inappropriately is equivalent to indicating your acceptance of his or her behavior.

■ *Frequent:* The best performance feedback is given frequently and on an ongoing basis. Ideally, there should be no surprises at your formal performance appraisal (typically once each year); feedback about specific incidents should have already been delivered. This allows the formal review to focus more proactively on the future, on clarifying and reinforcing personal strengths and development goals.

Figure 17–5
Benefits of Giving, Getting, and Asking for Effective Feedback

Benefits of:

Giving Feedback	Getting Feedback	Asking for Feedback
■ Ensures that individuals focus on meeting organizational goals and objectives.	■ Builds our confidence by reinforcing our strengths.	■ Demonstrates our commitment to improve.
■ Reinforces positive and effective actions and behaviors.	■ Directs us toward areas needing improvement.	■ Demonstrates our dedication to doing things right.
■ Provides corrective action of ineffective or problematic behaviors.	■ Helps us understand our blind spots—weaknesses of which we're unaware.	■ Shows our commitment to continued service in an organization.

■ *Purposeful:* Focus feedback on only one or two specific topics. "Let's talk about what happened during the last week of the project." As they say in marriage counseling, "Don't throw in the kitchen sink." If you're discussing a team member's lack of follow-through on a project, don't take the opportunity to offer a laundry list of other unrelated concerns.

■ *Constructive and balanced:* Feedback is more likely to be accepted when it contains a balance of positive and negative comments. When giving feedback, it's helpful to start the conversation with positive feedback. This reinforces to the employee that she has strengths and is valued by you and the organization. Initial positive feedback reduces employees' defensiveness and increases their openness to any constructive criticism that follows. "I am really pleased with the quality of your work on the Miller project. I'm wondering if there's a way you could bring others from the team into more phases of the Genovese project."

■ *In the appropriate setting:* While there are some cultural exceptions, it is appropriate to give positive feedback to employees either in private or public. Constructive feedback should always be shared in a private setting to avoid embarrassment, resentment, and defensiveness. "I'd like to talk with you. Let's go somewhere where we're out of earshot."[35]

■ *Interactive:* Good feedback takes into account the needs of both the giver and the receiver. Feedback is best when it is a two-way interchange. One way to do this is to solicit an employee's perspective on a subject or incident before deciding how to handle it. "I've shared your teammates' view of the situation. What is your perspective on what occurred? How do you think we should approach this situation?" By asking for and integrating the employee's perspective with your own, you can reduce misunderstandings, develop better solutions, and most importantly, gain their commitment to a solution—*their* solution.

Challenges in Providing Feedback

Giving performance feedback, especially constructive feedback, is one of the most difficult things for a manager to do well. Studies show that many managers dread feedback sessions with their employees and often resist or avoid them. Giving feedback is one of the toughest managerial responsibilities, yet it is one of the most important. Anxiety over giving feedback exists for several reasons:

1. Managers are uncomfortable giving negative feedback and discussing performance weaknesses. While many of us can and do give out compliments and praise, few look forward to doling out criticisms and therefore avoid or delay giving feedback. Research suggests that women are particularly uncomfortable giving critical feedback due to their preference for "saving face" for others.[36]

2. Employees tend to have an inflated view of their own performance; most people rate themselves above average when, statistically, about half will be below average. The perceptual differences between a manager and employee underscore the difficulty in and conflicting nature of giving feedback.

3. Managers are afraid of the reaction they might get when delivering negative feedback to some employees. They fear that employees will respond defensively, perhaps even with hostility.[37] Recent research on workplace incivility demonstrates that such behaviors have become more commonplace and of concern in the workforce.[38]

4. As organizations have downsized and increased spans of control, managers have less time available to provide effective feedback to greater numbers of employees. With other more pressing matters tugging at them, managers may feel unable to make "time for all those intimate, eyeball-to-eyeball encounters"[39] amidst all the other things for which they are accountable.

Despite how difficult giving feedback might appear to be, it is important for managers to give constructive feedback. Feedback—and the lessons derived from it—are the lifeblood of an organization. Without feedback, employees are left in the dark, frustrated over not knowing where they stand. This can lead to interpersonal conflicts, absenteeism, and turnover.[40]

Tips for Preparing and Leading a Feedback Session

By following the tips and techniques below, you'll find it easier to **give feedback** and ensure that employees accept and act upon it positively for improved performance:

■ *Prepare a script.* If possible, identify in advance the situation that will be discussed and develop a "script" for how you intend to approach the situation, using an outline such as the one in Figure 17–6. Most people fear the unknown and unexpected. By preparing a script and thinking through possible responses, you are likely to reduce the discomfort associated with providing constructive feedback. See Figure 17–7 for a sample script.

■ *Examine your motives.* Evaluate why you need to give feedback and the outcome you hope to achieve by doing so. Getting something "off your chest" is not a sufficient reason. Assess potential barriers or obstacles, the strength of your relationship with the intended recipient, competitive pressures that might impact the situation, the perceived imbalance of power, and the credibility you both possess in the organization. This assessment can bring to the surface problems that could arise when giving (or receiving) feedback. Understanding your reasons and the factors affecting the potential feedback session aids in developing a successful strategy for giving feedback.[41]

■ *Ask for input.* Get the employee's or team member's opinion about and perspective on the situation. This enables others to examine their own perspective and allows you to determine whether a situation is completely understood. It also paves the way for getting their ideas on how to proceed, making them feel part of the process and the organization instead of isolated or victimized by it. By ensuring two-way communication, both parties confirm data and perceptions, assuring the dialogue meets expectations on both sides.[42]

■ *Offer help, support, and suggestions.* If appropriate, offer to be of assistance by meeting with the employee periodically to check progress or, if appropriate, by recommending internal or external resources that might be available (e.g., an employee assistance program). Be supportive of the employee as a person. Make clear it is only his or

**Figure 17–6
Outline for Feedback
Session**

Brief Description of Situation:

Opening: Overview/Purpose of Meeting (state why you are meeting and what you hope to accomplish)

Feedback (explain the situation objectively, using facts to back up your assertions about a specific behavior and its impact on fellow employees or team members)

Interaction/Clarification (invite a response—what the employee's perception of the situation is)

Suggestions (offer a suggestion for change or brainstorm a solution with the employee)

Clarify Expectations/Close/Next Steps (agree to meet again at a specific time to review progress)

**Figure 17–7
Sample Script**

The situation: As Director of Marketing, you have been receiving some signals that your star salesperson, Margaret, has been ruffling the feathers of some of her customers and peers. John, a buyer for Belk's (a department store), sent you a letter detailing the harsh treatment he received from Margaret when he requested to change his current order. You also heard from another of your employees that Liz, a co-worker of Margaret's, was seen crying in the employee lounge immediately following a heated discussion with Margaret. Stories like these are out of the ordinary when it comes to Margaret; however, you have also heard through the grapevine that Margaret may be experiencing some personal problems. Margaret has been an outstanding performer for the last four years; however, you are concerned about an emerging pattern of interpersonal issues involving her. You plan to approach Margaret in the following way:

Opening: "Margaret, I'd like to talk with you about your performance over the last two months. My goal is to get some clarity about two specific situations and offer assistance in improving your current performance."

Feedback: "Margaret, for the last four years, you've had steadily increasing sales and have been a star performer. Lately, however, I've received some distressing information about how harshly you treated a Belk's buyer, and of a strained discussion with Liz."

Interaction/Clarification: "I'm not sure what to make of these instances; could you help shed some light on what's going on?" (Listen to her response.)

Suggestions: "Margaret, I am committed to helping assist you in removing whatever's in the way of you performing at your peak . . . is there anything I can do to help?" (Wait for her suggestions. If none are forthcoming, offer some, such as additional training, time off.)

Clarify Expectations/Close/Next Steps: "Sounds like we have a good plan. So we're both on the same page, what changes should I expect to see over the next few weeks?" (Listen to her response.) "Let's plan on meeting again in three weeks . . . how about Friday the 19th at 2:00 P.M.?"

her behavior that is of concern to you. Explain the impact of desired results—how the requested change will benefit them as well as others. Emphasize joint problem solving. This reduces their defensiveness and resistance to your suggestions.

■ *Clarify expectations and specify next steps.* Ask the employee for feedback on your feedback. Have you made your expectations clear? Have you provided adequate resources or information? Once the situation and options for improvement are understood, it's time to discuss suitable next steps and a plan to follow up. As a manager, you demonstrate the seriousness of the situation and signal your commitment to the requested change by asking the employee to meet with you, call, or send you a progress memo on a regular basis.

Constructive feedback can have positive results if handled and presented properly. Start the session positively, discuss what needs to change, and involve the employee in developing action steps he or she can focus on and work toward for development. This ensures ending the feedback session on a positive note.[43]

Tips for Receiving Feedback

When **receiving constructive feedback,** it is important to demonstrate an openness to hearing the information and benefiting from it. Try to understand the speaker's point of you—even if you don't agree with his observations—rather than argue your views. While it may feel a bit uncomfortable having the attention focused on you and your behavior, try to be objective and not take things personally. Check your body language. Even if you don't think you feel defensive, crossing your arms over your chest and interrupting may communicate otherwise. Listen carefully, and if something is unclear, ask for specific examples that support the speaker's feedback. Finally, summarize key points to demonstrate that you've understood the feedback.[44]

If the person giving you feedback is well trained, she'll deliver the information fairly and effectively. If the person lacks this training, there are a few steps you can take to ensure things go well.

■ *Keep an ongoing performance folder.* Keep letters or e-mails that commend your performance in the folder. If a problem surfaces, keep careful documentation of whom you talk to and what is said. Keep a running list of projects in which you've been involved, noting your contributions to each. This is a good idea to do even if you don't receive constructive feedback. But if you do, this record might provide you with information that can be useful when asked to share your perspective on the situation.

■ *Evaluate your own progress on a regular basis.* Whenever assigned to a new project, task force, or work group, make it a habit to request feedback early on and throughout the project. This makes it easier for co-workers and teammates to approach you with concerns if any surface and often prevents a formal feedback session from being necessary.

■ *Let someone know if a change in your personal circumstances is affecting your work.* We are often reluctant to bring personal problems to work or school. Yet if something serious is happening and is affecting the quality of our work, it's better to talk with someone before the problem gets out of hand. This way, co-workers can manage their expectations about and make allowances for what is hopefully a temporary downturn in your performance.

Asking for Feedback

As we have discussed, it is important for employees and team members to receive feedback. This inspires us to improve, grow, and develop both as people and as professionals.[45] However, many teammates, managers, and organizations are reluctant or fail to provide feedback. Feedback is a two-way process. If feedback is not forthcoming, it is up to you to request it. Questions such as "How am I doing?" "How can I improve?" and "Can we debrief—what worked and what didn't?" demonstrate your willingness to receive feedback, and might also provide you the opportunity to give feedback. As a manager, you must show that you value feedback and input from all affected by your performance. As renowned management author and consultant Peter Drucker said, "The leader of the past was a person who knew how to tell. The leader of the future will be the person who knows how to ask." Studies show that managers who requested feedback, analyzed it, and made action plans based on the information were perceived to be more effective than those who didn't.[46]

Often a manager will be relieved when you bring up the need for feedback. He or she might have been too busy, or perhaps was avoiding the situation because of the fears mentioned earlier. Whatever the reason, there are times when you might need to empower yourself by requesting a feedback session. Below are a few suggestions to ensure things go smoothly:

■ Demonstrate you're open to continual change and learning.

■ Learn why you're not getting the feedback. Do most employees in the organization not get feedback, or are you the only one? By understanding why feedback has been absent, you will be better able to devise a plan for requesting and receiving feedback more regularly.

■ Assess why you want feedback before you request it. Make sure you're not overly dependent on someone else's view of you. According to Deborah Tannen, some women tend to seek more feedback than men, on a continual basis, and see it as more important.[47] Regular feedback is useful. Requesting it too frequently is not, as it may send a message that you lack confidence in your abilities.

■ Ask for suggestions on how you can improve. End any feedback session with a question about ways in which you can improve. This assures the giver of the feedback that you are listening and taking the feedback seriously. Restate or clarify their suggestions to show the giver that you understand and are committed to making the needed changes.

Summary

Coaching is an effective way to facilitate personal and organizational performance improvement and success. By providing feedback and support, coaches let individuals and groups know how they're doing so they can determine whether to modify current strategies, actions, and behaviors. Simply put, if it's not working, then why do it! Despite the benefits of coaching and giving feedback, many lack the skill and confidence to do so effectively. By following the tips and techniques for effectively providing, accepting, and asking for feedback, you will improve your performance and that of your co-workers, teammates, and subordinates.

Key Terms and Concepts

Asking for feedback

Coaching

Counseling

Descriptive

Directive methods

Documentable

Feedback

Giving feedback

Initiating behaviors

Nondirective approach

Nonprescriptive

Receiving constructive feedback

Supportive behaviors

Endnotes

1. Ron Zemke, *Coaching Knock Your Socks off Service* (Amacom: New York, 1997).

2. Brian Walker, "Debunking the Five Myths of Coaching," *Training and Development,* March 2000, p. 2.

3. Gary S. Bielous, "Effective Coaching: Improving Marginal Performers," *Supervision,* July 1998, p. 15.

4. Corporate Coach University International, **www.ccui.com,** May 2000.

5. Jeremy Lebediker, "The Supervisor as a Coach: Four Essential Models for Setting Performance Expectations," *Supervision,* Dec. 1995, p. 14.

6. Bruce Hodes, "A New Foundation in Business Culture: Managerial Coaching," *Industrial Management,* Sept.–Oct. 1992, p. 27.

7. Ibid.

8. Clinton Longenecker and Gary Pinkel, "Coaching to Win at Work," *Manage,* Feb. 1997, p. 20.

9. Corporate Coach University International, **www.ccui.com,** May 2000.

10. Robert W. Lucas, "Effective Feedback Skills for Trainers and Coaches," *HR Focus,* July 1994, p. 7.

11. K. T. Dirks and D. L. Ferrin, "Trust in Leadership: Meta-analytic Findings and Implications for Organizational Research," *Journal of Applied Psychology,* 87 (2002), pp. 611–628.

12. Corporate Coach University International, **www.ccui.com,** May 2000.

13. Steven J. Stowell, "Coaching: A Commitment to Leadership," *Training & Development Journal,* June 1988, pp. 34–38.

14. Ibid.

15. Ibid.

16. Corporate Coach University International, **www.ccui.com,** May 2000.

17. Longenecker and Pinkel, "Coaching to Win," p. 21.

18. Stowell, "Coaching."

19. Ibid.

20. Gary P. Latham and Edwin A. Locke, "Goal Setting—A Motivational Technique That Works," *Organizational Dynamics,* Autumn 1979, pp. 68–80.

21. Shawn K. Yearta, Sally Maitlis, and Rob B. Briner, "An Exploratory Study of Goal Setting Theory and Practice: A Motivational Technique That Works?" *Journal of Occupational and Organizational Psychology,* Sept. 1995, p. 237.

22. R. H. Axelrod, *Terms of Engagement: Changing the Way We Change Organizations* (San Francisco: Berrett-Koehler, 2000).

23. M. Erez and F. H. Kanfer, "The Role of Goal Acceptance in Goal Setting and Task Performance," *Academy of Management Review,* 1983, pp. 45–46.

24. Cynthia A. Mulhearn, "Seeking New Heights: How and Why Goal-Setting Works," *Managers Magazine,* June 1994, p. 13. Reprinted with permission of LIMRA.

25. Yearta et al., "An Exploratory Study."

26. A. R. Cohen, S. L. Fink, H. Gadon, and R. D. Willits, *Effective Behavior in Organizations,* Fifth Ed. (Boston, MA: Irwin, 1992), p. 295.

27. C. R. Zemke Bell, "On-Target Feedback," *Training,* June 1992, p. 36.

28. S. D. Carr, E. D. Herman, S. Z. Keldsen, J. G. Miller, and P. A. Wakefield, *The Team Learning Assistant Handbook* (New York: McGraw Hill, 2005).

29. J. Luft, *Group Processes* (Palo Alto, CA: National Press Books, 1970).

30. Cohen et al., *Effective Behavior,* p. 295.

31. Angelo Kinicki and Robert Kreitner, *Organizational Behavior: Key Concepts, Skills and Best Practices* (Boston, MA: Irwin/McGraw-Hill, 2003), p. 159.

32. Harriet V. Lawrence and Albert K. Wiswell, "Feedback Is a Two-Way Street," *Training and Development,* July 1995, p. 49.

33. Carr et al., *Team Learning Assistant,* p. 45.

34. Cohen et al., *Effective Behavior,* p. 295.

35. Robert W. Lucas, "Effective Feedback Skills for Trainers and Coaches," *HR Focus,* July 1994, p. 7.

36. Deborah Tannen, "The Power of Talk: Who Gets Heard and Why," *Harvard Business Review,* Sept/Oct 1995, pp. 138–148.

37. J. Jackman and M. Strober, "Fear of Feedback," *Harvard Business Review,* April 2003, pp. 101–106.

38. L. Andersson and C. Pearson, "Tit for Tat? The Spiraling Effect of Incivility in the Workplace," *Academy of Management Review* 24, no. 3 (1999), pp. 452–471.

39. Richard Nemec, "Getting Feedback," *Communication World,* March 1997, p. 32.

40. Bill Yeargin, "If You Criticize, Make It Constructive," *Boating Industry,* Oct. 1997, p. 24.

41. Lawrence and Wiswell, "Feedback."

42. Ibid.

43. Crain Communications, "Tips for Providing Feedback to Employees," *Investment News,* Nov. 23, 1999, p. 34.

44. Carr et al., *Team Learning Assistant,* p. 46.

45. Richard Koonce, "Are You Getting the Feedback You Deserve?" *Training and Development,* July 1998, p. 18.

46. Dick Sethi and Beverly Pinzon, "The Impact of Direct Report Feedback and Follow-Up on Leadership Effectiveness," *Human Resource Planning,* Dec. 1998, pp. 14–16.

47. Koonce, "Are You Getting the Feedback."

**Exercise 17–A
Coaching Clinic**

Think of a coach you have had in the past—from sports, school, clubs, or work. Draw upon your experiences with this coach to answer the following questions.

What about their coaching style made them effective (characteristics, behaviors, attitudes)?

_____

_____

_____

_____

_____

What about their coaching style made them less than effective? _____

_____

_____

_____

_____

From your observations, and using the grid that follows, make a list of characteristics that you believe are necessary for effective coaching. Compare and supplement your list with characteristics provided in the chapter. Next, evaluate yourself as to your level of competency with the skill, trait, or characteristic. Then determine an action plan on how you can improve this characteristic, trait, or behavior.

Necessary Characteristic	Your Level of Competency (Low, Medium, High)	Action Plan for Improvement
1.		
2.		
3.		
4.		
5.		
6.		
7.		
8.		
9.		
10.		

**Exercise 17–B
I Need a Coach**

In groups of three you will conduct a coaching session. One person will serve as the observer, one as the coach, and the third will be coached with regards to an ability issue.

1. One participant is to explain a trait, skill, or ability in which they would like to become more proficient.

2. The coach is to devise a coaching session and use various coaching techniques to help the other person.

3. The observer should note characteristics of the coach and techniques used to help the other person. Discuss with the pair tactics used, what might have been effective, and what areas need to be improved upon. This is an opportunity for all members to give feedback.

Observation

1. What coaching techniques were utilized? _____

_____

_____

_____

2. In what ways were they effective? _____

_____

_____

_____

3. In what ways could the coaching have been improved? _____

_____

_____

_____

As a trio, discuss the aspects of coaching or of being coached that were most difficult and why.

**Exercise 17–C
Everyone's a Coach**

We're all coaches, whether we realize it or not. Those who are younger or less experienced than us may look to us for guidance, information, and ideas about how to do things better. Reflect on your role as a coach in others' lives and complete the worksheet below. With a partner, discuss this or a current coaching relationship in which you're involved.

1. Describe the situation and the key players.

_____

_____

_____

_____

2. In what ways are others relying on you to be a role model or advice giver or teacher?

_____

_____

_____

_____

3. In your capacity as informal coach, what things are you doing well?

_____

_____

_____

_____

4. In what areas could you improve? Explain, citing examples.

_____

_____

_____

_____

**Exercise 17–D
Helping Others Set
Goals—Modeling
Exercise**

In groups of three or four, you will be role-playing the following scenarios. For each role-play, there will be two participants and at least one observer. After each role-play, the observer should provide feedback and lead the group in a discussion based on the following questions.

Observer Questions

1. What techniques were used in helping others set goals? Which ones were effective and why? Which ones were ineffective and why?

2. What could have been done differently? What impact would that have had on the outcome?

3. Evaluate the goals that were set. Are they "SMART" goals? How can they be improved upon?

4. How will completion be ensured? What type of control or check-up system has been put in place?

5. In what ways have the goals been tied to rewards? How clear is the goal measurement system?

Scenario One

The roles include:

Mother and/or father (Mom and Dad)
College-level son or daughter (Terry)
A silent observer

Using the following scenario, help Terry set "SMART" goals:

Terry is about to leave for his/her sophomore year at college, where he/she is hoping to major in marketing in the College of Business. By the end of this semester, Terry has to apply to the College, but is concerned that his/her GPA may not be high enough.

Mom and Dad have talked with each other and have concluded that Terry was unfocused in virtually every area of life during his/her freshman year. They would like to help Terry to become more serious about his/her performance and bring up his/her grades. So, before Terry leaves for college, they want to talk with Terry and get him/her to set some goals for sophomore year.

Scenario Two

The roles include:

Jamie Harper—the supervisor
Pat Phillips—the subordinate
A silent observer

Using the following scenario, help Pat set "SMART" goals:

Pat is a researcher for a marketing firm and is assigned to do background research on various projects. At any given time, Pat may be assigned as many as three projects.

Jamie is having a feedback session (in Jamie's office) with Pat regarding his/her inability to meet project deadlines. In the past six months, Pat has met only one of eight deadlines. Pat is consistently two to three days behind schedule, and works extra hours (in a panic) just before every deadline. Pat always seems to be busy and very disorganized; he/she is frequently taking on side projects from various people in the organization who need a little extra help or favor. Jamie would like to help Pat set some goals to help him/her start creating and achieving realistic deadlines and work schedules.

**Exercise 17–E
Giving Positive
Feedback**

Positive feedback is as important as constructive feedback. This activity provides an opportunity for you and your teammates to give and receive positive feedback.

1. Working first on your own, on small pieces of paper or index cards write one team member's name on each card. On the other side, write a positive statement about the team member.

2. Working in teams or small groups, each team member takes a turn sharing his or her positive feedback with the other team members, handing the person the card on which they've written the positive statement. Repeat the process until all feedback is shared and all cards have been received.

3. As a group, discuss the feedback. What surprised you? What did you learn about yourself? What are some things you heard about others that you'd like to improve? What are some qualities you would like the team to improve?

4. As a group, summarize the feedback without revealing names. Elect a scribe to record a list of the positive qualities most mentioned, and a list of things team members have said they'd like to work on as a group.

5. Each group reports their findings to the large group.

6. Discuss the qualities that make for effective team leadership and how one can improve these qualities.

**Exercise 17–F
Peer Feedback**

In this activity, you will use feedback forms (pages that follow) to provide feedback to each of your teammates.

1. Divide into working teams.

2. Complete a "peer feedback sheet" on each team member. On the back of the sheet, offer examples that back up the two most outstanding behaviors and the two most in need of improvement that have been identified in the checklist. Complete a feedback sheet for each member of the team, including yourself.

3. Share the positive aspects of each team member with the group. Distribute the papers so each individual can read in private about areas in which he or she can improve.

4. Discuss the findings and determine ways you can work together to support each other in developing exemplar characteristics as a team.

Peer Feedback

To:
From:

Behavior	Outstanding	Satisfactory	Needs Improvement
1. Enthusiasm/attitude	_____	_____	_____
2. Motivation/willingness to work	_____	_____	_____
3. Responsibility/accountability	_____	_____	_____
4. Effort	_____	_____	_____
5. Completion/quality of assigned tasks	_____	_____	_____
6. Punctuality	_____	_____	_____
7. Ability to meet deadlines	_____	_____	_____
8. Dedication to team	_____	_____	_____
9. Attendance/participation	_____	_____	_____
10. Sharing of ideas and feedback	_____	_____	_____
11. Communication with team	_____	_____	_____
12. Creativity	_____	_____	_____
13. Accuracy	_____	_____	_____
14. Respect for others	_____	_____	_____
15. Flexibility	_____	_____	_____
16. Ability to get along with teammates	_____	_____	_____
17. Organization	_____	_____	_____
18. Ability to create group "synergy"	_____	_____	_____
19. Leadership	_____	_____	_____
20. Other (specify): _____	_____	_____	_____

Peer Feedback

To:
From:

Behavior	Outstanding	Satisfactory	Needs Improvement
1. Enthusiasm/attitude	_____	_____	_____
2. Motivation/willingness to work	_____	_____	_____
3. Responsibility/accountability	_____	_____	_____
4. Effort	_____	_____	_____
5. Completion/quality of assigned tasks	_____	_____	_____
6. Punctuality	_____	_____	_____
7. Ability to meet deadlines	_____	_____	_____
8. Dedication to team	_____	_____	_____
9. Attendance/participation	_____	_____	_____
10. Sharing of ideas and feedback	_____	_____	_____
11. Communication with team	_____	_____	_____
12. Creativity	_____	_____	_____
13. Accuracy	_____	_____	_____
14. Respect for others	_____	_____	_____
15. Flexibility	_____	_____	_____
16. Ability to get along with teammates	_____	_____	_____
17. Organization	_____	_____	_____
18. Ability to create group "synergy"	_____	_____	_____
19. Leadership	_____	_____	_____
20. Other (specify): _____	_____	_____	_____

Peer Feedback

To:
From:

Behavior	Outstanding	Satisfactory	Needs Improvement
1. Enthusiasm/attitude	_____	_____	_____
2. Motivation/willingness to work	_____	_____	_____
3. Responsibility/accountability	_____	_____	_____
4. Effort	_____	_____	_____
5. Completion/quality of assigned tasks	_____	_____	_____
6. Punctuality	_____	_____	_____
7. Ability to meet deadlines	_____	_____	_____
8. Dedication to team	_____	_____	_____
9. Attendance/participation	_____	_____	_____
10. Sharing of ideas and feedback	_____	_____	_____
11. Communication with team	_____	_____	_____
12. Creativity	_____	_____	_____
13. Accuracy	_____	_____	_____
14. Respect for others	_____	_____	_____
15. Flexibility	_____	_____	_____
16. Ability to get along with teammates	_____	_____	_____
17. Organization	_____	_____	_____
18. Ability to create group "synergy"	_____	_____	_____
19. Leadership	_____	_____	_____
20. Other (specify): _____	_____	_____	_____

Peer Feedback

To:
From:

Behavior	Outstanding	Satisfactory	Needs Improvement
1. Enthusiasm/attitude	_____	_____	_____
2. Motivation/willingness to work	_____	_____	_____
3. Responsibility/accountability	_____	_____	_____
4. Effort	_____	_____	_____
5. Completion/quality of assigned tasks	_____	_____	_____
6. Punctuality	_____	_____	_____
7. Ability to meet deadlines	_____	_____	_____
8. Dedication to team	_____	_____	_____
9. Attendance/participation	_____	_____	_____
10. Sharing of ideas and feedback	_____	_____	_____
11. Communication with team	_____	_____	_____
12. Creativity	_____	_____	_____
13. Accuracy	_____	_____	_____
14. Respect for others	_____	_____	_____
15. Flexibility	_____	_____	_____
16. Ability to get along with teammates	_____	_____	_____
17. Organization	_____	_____	_____
18. Ability to create group "synergy"	_____	_____	_____
19. Leadership	_____	_____	_____
20. Other (specify): _____	_____	_____	_____

Peer Feedback

To:
From:

Behavior	Outstanding	Satisfactory	Needs Improvement
1. Enthusiasm/attitude	_____	_____	_____
2. Motivation/willingness to work	_____	_____	_____
3. Responsibility/accountability	_____	_____	_____
4. Effort	_____	_____	_____
5. Completion/quality of assigned tasks	_____	_____	_____
6. Punctuality	_____	_____	_____
7. Ability to meet deadlines	_____	_____	_____
8. Dedication to team	_____	_____	_____
9. Attendance/participation	_____	_____	_____
10. Sharing of ideas and feedback	_____	_____	_____
11. Communication with team	_____	_____	_____
12. Creativity	_____	_____	_____
13. Accuracy	_____	_____	_____
14. Respect for others	_____	_____	_____
15. Flexibility	_____	_____	_____
16. Ability to get along with teammates	_____	_____	_____
17. Organization	_____	_____	_____
18. Ability to create group "synergy"	_____	_____	_____
19. Leadership	_____	_____	_____
20. Other (specify): _____	_____	_____	_____

Peer Feedback

To:
From:

Behavior	Outstanding	Satisfactory	Needs Improvement
1. Enthusiasm/attitude	_____	_____	_____
2. Motivation/willingness to work	_____	_____	_____
3. Responsibility/accountability	_____	_____	_____
4. Effort	_____	_____	_____
5. Completion/quality of assigned tasks	_____	_____	_____
6. Punctuality	_____	_____	_____
7. Ability to meet deadlines	_____	_____	_____
8. Dedication to team	_____	_____	_____
9. Attendance/participation	_____	_____	_____
10. Sharing of ideas and feedback	_____	_____	_____
11. Communication with team	_____	_____	_____
12. Creativity	_____	_____	_____
13. Accuracy	_____	_____	_____
14. Respect for others	_____	_____	_____
15. Flexibility	_____	_____	_____
16. Ability to get along with teammates	_____	_____	_____
17. Organization	_____	_____	_____
18. Ability to create group "synergy"	_____	_____	_____
19. Leadership	_____	_____	_____
20. Other (specify): _____	_____	_____	_____

Exercise 17–G
Practicing Giving
Performance Feedback

In your triad or small group, you'll participate in a performance feedback session. Person A is the listener—the one who's receiving the feedback. Person B is the talker—the one who's giving the feedback. Person C is the observer/recorder—the one who observes and comments on the interaction between Persons A and B.

1. Choose a scenario from the list below. Person B prepares a script using the outline in Figure 17–6 as a guide.

2. Person B gives feedback to Person A. Person A practices the tips for accepting feedback given in the book. Person B practices the tips for giving feedback given in the book. Person C observes the interaction and evaluates Persons A and B using the feedback observation sheets below.

Observation Sheet: Listener

1. _____ The Listener asked the Talker to cite specific examples of the behavior being discussed.

2. _____ The Listener asked clarifying questions and paraphrased the Talker.

3. _____ The Listener actively listened—asked probing questions of the Talker.

4. _____ The Listener appeared nondefensive and open to improvement suggestions.

5. Other examples of effective feedback behaviors of the Listener (specify):

Observation Sheet: Talker

1. _____ The Talker offered balanced feedback (positive feedback followed by constructive feedback and suggestions for improvement).

2. _____ The Talker was not judgmental or evaluative.

3. _____ The Talker focused on specific behavior.

4. _____ The Talker asked the Listener for input and suggestions.

5. Other examples of effective feedback behaviors of the Talker (specify):

Feedback Role-Play Scenarios

1. A roommate conflict (e.g., due to messiness, playing loud music, not paying their bills).

2. A problem with your significant other (e.g., due to always being late, not being a good listener, overspending).

3. A subperforming employee (e.g., due to lateness, frequent absences, distracted by non-work issues). Another option is to use the example in Figure 17–7.

4. A serious employee offense (e.g., concerns about possible theft, potential sexual harassment, potential discrimination).

Questions

1. What was the hardest thing you faced in developing this script?

2. Can you see this script working in real life? Why or why not?

3. What about the script makes it easier to give appropriate feedback?

4. How does the Talker's preparation affect the ultimate goal of improving performance?

5. What would you do if the Listener gets defensive or argumentative?

6. Was there satisfactory closure at the end of the session? Explain.

**Exercise 17–H
Giving Feedback: A
Reflection Worksheet**

We often give feedback to others without thinking about it. Recall two recent occasions when you gave others feedback. By answering the following questions, you can increase your understanding of and skill at giving feedback.

Think about a time when you gave feedback to another person and the outcome was positive.

1. Describe how you gave the feedback (what you said and did to convey your message).

_____

_____

_____

2. How did the recipient react to your feedback?

_____

_____

_____

3. What made your feedback effective? Was there anything you could have done differently to make the feedback even more successful? Explain.

_____

_____

_____

Recall a time when you gave feedback and the recipient responded negatively or did not change his or her behavior.

4. In what way did you give feedback—what were specific things you said or did to convey your message?

_____

_____

_____

5. How did the recipient react to your feedback? Did the reaction surprise you?

_____

_____

_____

6. Evaluate your feedback, using the tips and techniques shared in the chapter. If you could relive this moment, what would you do differently, and what might you leave unchanged? Explain.

_____

_____

_____

Source: This exercise is adapted from William Gudykunst, Stella Ting-Toomey, Sandra Sudweeks, and Lea Stewart: *Building Bridges: Interpersonal Skills for a Changing World*, p. 236. Copyright © 1995, Harcourt Brace and Company. Copyright © 1995 by Houghton Mifflin Company. Reproduced by permission of the publisher.

**Exercise 17–I
Giving Self-feedback**

1. Working on your own, complete the self-feedback worksheet below. The sheet concerns your involvement in project teams. (Alternatively, you can conduct a self-evaluation of your own performance as an employee, student, or roommate, focusing on two questions: What do you do well? In what areas can you improve?)

2. At the bottom of the worksheet, describe your positive team qualities and areas you'd like to improve. Give specific details on how you intend to make changes.

3. Share the results with a partner.

4. Discuss the activity with the large group using the questions below:

   - In what areas are you stronger? Weaker?
   - What can you do to improve in those areas?
   - What suggestions do you have for others who wish to improve?
   - In what ways have these behaviors helped keep previous teams on track?
   - Discuss a situation where the lack of these qualities hindered a team from being effective.
   - What did you learn about yourself as a team member from this exercise?

Self-feedback Worksheet

In team projects:

1. _____ I participate willingly.
2. _____ I stay with the task assigned.
3. _____ I start by clarifying the assignment with the group.
4. _____ I try to encourage the group to get back on track when needed.
5. _____ I use the experience as a potential learning activity.
6. _____ I try consciously to be aware of my own behavior style and the styles of others.
7. _____ I try to engage in active listening.
8. _____ I try to provide positive feedback to group members.
9. _____ I help the group keep track of time.
10. _____ I help the group summarize results and action items.
11. _____ I volunteer to record for the group.
12. _____ I raise concerns openly rather than ignore or avoid them.
13. _____ I volunteer to be a group spokesperson.
14. _____ Other (specify):

Things I do well:

Ways I can improve:

Exercise 17–J
Reflection/Action Plan

This chapter focused on coaching and feedback—what they are, why they're important, and how to improve your skills in these areas. Complete the worksheet below upon completing all reading and experiential activities for this chapter.

1. The one or two areas in which I am most strong are:

   _____

   _____

   _____

   _____

2. The one or two areas in which I need more improvement are:

   _____

   _____

   _____

   _____

3. If I did only one thing to improve in this area, it would be to:

   _____

   _____

   _____

   _____

4. Making this change would probably result in:

   _____

   _____

   _____

   _____

5. If I did not change or improve in this area, it would probably affect my personal and professional life in the following ways:

   _____

   _____

   _____

   _____

Leading and Empowering Self and Others

Learning Points

How do I:

- Identify the skills and characteristics of effective leaders and develop these skills to increase my ability to lead?
- Provide leadership to others, even when I'm not an official leader?
- Adopt a mindset that allows employees to take responsibility for their work, as opposed to controlling their every move?
- Reduce any fears I have about mistakes made by my empowered subordinates?
- Empower myself when an organization or manager does not provide it?
- Motivate others to take risks and do what they think is best?
- Give responsibility of doing a task to another while ensuring quality of work?

You drive up to your hotel, exhausted after a long, protracted plane ride and subsequent taxi ride. After a full day of traveling, you are looking forward to settling into a comfortable night's sleep at the residence hotel your assistant booked for you. Tomorrow is a big day. You will be making an important presentation to a potential client—one that could be worth millions of revenue to your consulting organization.

One of the hotel's desk clerks, Derek, happily greets you and gets you checked in. One small problem, Derek informs you, the nonsmoking room you requested is unavailable. "Will this be a problem?" Derek asks. You are visibly upset. "I don't understand what the problem is. My assistant made the arrangements and he confirmed that the room is nonsmoking. I have terrible allergies and must be in a smoke-free room. You must have another room available! Please do something! It's 1 A.M., I'm tired, and I want to go to bed." Derek apologizes, "Sorry, I can't help you, but perhaps my manager can. I'll page her for you. She should be here in a few minutes."

While you wait, your anger and resentment deepen. You think to yourself, "How hard could it be to scrounge up a nonsmoking room? Where else could I go? By the time I find another place and take a taxi there, it'll be at least 2 A.M.! This is ridiculous . . . I'll never stay at this hotel again!"

Derek is also feeling very uncomfortable while waiting for his manager to appear. He knows that they keep a few rooms in reserve at all times for emergencies. However, he does not know what qualifies as an emergency. An error resulting in overbooking, a VIP showing up unannounced, or this person who demands a nonsmoking room? What is taking the manager so long to come to the desk? He can feel the heat from the glare of the customer's gaze.

1. Why was Derek unable to fix the problem?
2. What impact did his inability to deal with the issue have on you?
3. What role did his manager play in the unfolding of this situation?
4. Has something like this ever happened to you before? How did you react?
5. Have you ever been in a position similar to Derek's—one in which you wanted to help a customer but were neither trusted nor trained to make decisions like these? If so, how did it feel?
6. Have you ever been in a position similar to Derek's manager—one in which you didn't trust your subordinate to make the "right" decisions? Explain.

Leadership is as delicate as Mozart's melodies. The music exists and it doesn't. It is written on the page, but it means nothing until performed and heard. Much of its effect depends on the performer and the listener. The best leaders, like the best music, inspire us to see new possibilities.[1]

If you were asked to think of someone who has made a positive impact on society, who would that be? Mother Teresa? Martin Luther King, Jr.? Thomas Jefferson? Gandhi? Nelson Mandela? Rosa Parks? Most likely, the person you thought of would be considered a leader. But what exactly is leadership, and why is it important?

Throughout history, civilizations have focused on their leaders.[2] Whether elected or appointed, the kings, queens, chiefs, and presidents of their nations are entrusted with decisions that affect all whom they serve. Leading armies, creating new lands (and destroying existing ones), and defining what is and isn't acceptable are among the many responsibilities of leaders.

Leaders of organizations face similar challenges. While they need not bring their troops to the battleground, organizational leaders must understand the environment in which they operate, establish goals and objectives, and motivate their employees to achieve excellence to "battle" in the global marketplace. Moreover, these leaders must lead the "troops" in a way that enables them not only to do necessary tasks, but also to participate in day-to-day decisions that affect them. Employees expect to play a more meaningful role in the business of the organization than in the past, rendering the command and control approach to leadership useless. We begin this chapter by discussing leadership, what it is, why it's important, and how to develop self-leadership even if you don't hold an official title. Next, we examine empowerment and delegation—two tools that leaders can use to keep themselves and their colleagues motivated and involved in their work. We also look at the benefits, challenges, and strategies of implementing them in organizations.

What Is Leadership?

"Great leaders often inspire their followers to high levels of achievement by showing them how their work contributes to worthwhile ends."

Warren Bennis and Burt Nanus,
Leaders

As a field of study, leadership has been around for centuries. We have been intrigued by the magical, illusive power of certain individuals to move nations of people, inspire others to follow their lead, or bring about complex social change. Scholars have offered numerous theories as to what leadership is and what makes individuals successful in leadership roles. As it would be almost impossible to offer a single definition of leadership, we present a compilation. **Leadership** is:

- A process of social influence to move individual and groups toward goal achievement.[3]
- Sharing a vision and engaging followers in that vision.[4]
- The ability to move an organization to a higher level of performance by transforming vision into significant actions.
- A relationship, as opposed to the property of an individual.[5] Leadership exists only where followers exist, and its effectiveness varies in direct relation to the level of trust present in the relationship.[6] Similarly, while some individuals may be more or less trusting than others, trust exists (and evolves) in relationships.[7]
- An observable, learnable, set of practices and skills—many of which fall into the interpersonal arena.[8] Anyone who wants to lead can significantly improve their ability to do so through training, practice, and feedback.[9]
- An integration of theory, process, and practice, and the realization that what is effective in one situation may be ineffective in another.[10] Effective leadership requires the ability to size up the situation (and people involved), compare it against prior experiences and practices, and develop an approach that would fit but remain flexible enough to adjust as the situation requires.[11] Effective leaders also take the time to reflect on their actions and behaviors to objectively assess what worked and what didn't. In short, effective leaders are continuous learners.

Characteristics of Effective Leaders

Each of us has the ability to become a great leader. Even those who came from humble beginnings, like Abraham Lincoln and Bill Clinton, rose to positions of leadership and influenced many people and nations. You might be thinking, "But I'm only a student," or "What can a single mom do" or "I'm not that smart." Great leaders do not fit a singular mold. They are women and men, young and old, able-bodied and physically challenged, and come from all nations and socioeconomic backgrounds. What does it take to be a great leader? According to Kouzes and Posner, effective leaders are characterized by their ability to:[12]

- *Challenge the process.* Some of the most successful leaders bucked the system. They took risks, challenged convention, and ignored rules. For example, in 1955, Rosa Parks broke the law by refusing to give up her bus seat to a white passenger while riding a bus in Montgomery, Alabama. She was jailed, but her spirit wasn't broken. Her strong belief in the rights of all humans, regardless of their skin color, coupled with her role as secretary of the local National Association for the Advancement of Colored People (NAACP), helped prompt a bus boycott that lasted nearly a year. Shortly thereafter, the Supreme Court struck down segregation laws.

Figure 18–1

Effective Leaders Are Those Who[13]
Challenge the process
Inspire a shared vision
Enable others to act
Model the way
Encourage the heart

■ *Inspire a shared vision*. Rather than dictate direction, effective leaders appeal to group members' values, beliefs, and emotions, motivating them to align themselves with a mission that reflects the greater good. Leaders who passionately believe in their teams, products, or services exude enough fervor to "infect" others with this passion. In 1980, enraged over the death of her 13-year-old daughter at the hands of a repeat drunk-driving offender, Candy Lightner enlisted some friends and founded Mothers Against Drunk Driving—MADD. Through Lightner's inspiring vision and tireless efforts, MADD has grown to approximately 600 affiliates and 2 million members and supporters nationwide, has helped to pass more than 2,300 anti–drunk driving and underage drinking laws and is credited with saving more than 268,000 lives through research-based programs, policy initiatives, exemplary victim services, and public education.[14]

■ *Enable others to act*. Effective leaders share information and power with their collaborators, empowering them to set and achieve cooperative goals. Employees need to know where they fit in the bigger picture and have the ability to make decisions in order to contribute in meaningful ways. By listening to and supporting all employees—regardless of their rank—leaders create an atmosphere of mutual trust and respect and enable others to perform to their potential.[15]

■ *Model the way*. A leader is "a part of, not apart from" the group.[16] In other words, leaders' power exists not so much in their role but from that which is granted by those who follow. To be effective, leaders must "walk the talk" by exhibiting the behaviors they expect in others and ensuring consistency between their words and deeds. For example, leaders who expect their managers to empower subordinates must do the same by sharing power, accepting mistakes, and involving managers in decisions large and small. Similarly, leaders who expect persistence and dedication must not give up, even amidst adversity.

A young boy followed in the footsteps of other great peacemakers by utilizing his poetic talents to promote peace. By the age of 13, Mattie Stepanek had published several best-selling poetry books in support of this mission, despite his severe muscular dystrophy and reliance on a ventilator and wheelchair.[17] Shortly before his death in 2004, Mattie realized another of his dreams, to meet and spend time with former President Jimmy Carter, whom he idolized for his efforts in promoting peace in several of the world's war-torn countries.

Moving to the business arena, when Procter & Gamble first premiered Bounce™ fabric softener sheets, many questioned whether the product would appeal to customers. Even the patent was turned down until someone in the company championed it. Bounce™ became one of P&G's most successful brands.[18]

■ *Encourage the heart*.[19] Last but not least, leaders must find ways to reward individuals and groups that achieve success and progress toward common goals. Along the way, effective leaders provide coaching, feedback, and recognition to show others appreciation for their efforts.

As you can see from these characteristics and examples, even those without a formal leadership position can lead others successfully. Perhaps you can recall a time when others hung on your every word, asked for your advice, or looked to you for direction. Or, perhaps you were in a situation where someone should have taken the lead but didn't. In situations like these, you can bemoan the lack of direction or vision . . . or you can practice self-leadership.

Self-leadership

Self-leadership is what happens when individuals act on their own to achieve the organization mission, vision, purpose, values, and goals.[20] It occurs when you challenge yourself to muster the self-direction and self-motivation you need to perform a task or achieve a goal.[21] Imagine you come up with an idea for a new product—one that would revolutionize the way individuals brushed their teeth. You pitch the idea to your boss, but she gently dismisses the idea, noting that the dental hygiene market is already saturated with products manufactured by your and competing organizations. You work evenings and weekends perfecting the design, even doing a patent search to determine the patentability of your innovative design. You pitch the idea to your boss's boss, and while intrigued, he intimates that management would never commit the necessary resources to develop the product and bring it to market. Frustrated, you decide to discuss the idea with family and friends, searching for support—both emotional and financial. Your enthusiasm is contagious, and they agree that your new product idea has the potential to revolutionize dental hygiene and produce substantial revenues. You develop your business plan while simultaneously planning your eventual departure from your organization.

Sound like a fairy tale? Actually, this scenario approximates the path many successful entrepreneurs took in leaving relatively secure jobs with established organizations to pursue their passion. It's easy to see how important it is for organizations to support and reward this kind of self-leadership. By expanding their view of work control to reconfigure the important role of self-influence,[22] organizations and the individuals who practice self-leadership can reap significant benefits.

First and foremost, self-leadership helps create an ideal organization. Employees who practice self-leadership perform because they believe in and enjoy what they're doing, not because of threats.[23] In this way, the organization's goals become the employees' goals—the creation of meaning[24]—and are sought with the same energy and conviction. While it may be easy to envision such a situation in a nonprofit organization such as MADD, Doctors Without Borders, Greenpeace, or UNICEF, for-profit organizations whose mission goes beyond raising shareholder value to include socially responsible actions[25]—including The Body Shop, Patagonia, and Ben & Jerry's—have been able to attract, motivate, and retain employees on the basis of such alignment.

In addition, employees who practice self-leadership are more productive because they have more control and decision-making power.[26] Returning to our opening story, had Derek been allowed to determine an appropriate solution for the weary traveler, he would have been able to move on to the next task, rather than wait for and watch his manager handle the situation. Because of their ability to exert control over their environment, employees are more satisfied with their jobs[27] and more committed (loyal) to their organizations.

What Is Empowerment?

In simple terms, **empowerment** is the process by which a leader or manager shares his or her power with subordinates.[28] This definition provides a starting point for understanding empowerment, yet you might be asking yourself: Power to do what? In the traditional workplace, which was centered on manufacturing, all you needed was obedience to get work done.[29] Workers' tasks were preplanned and simplified; managers observed employees closely to ensure adherence to prescribed ways of completing tasks.

The current environment—characterized by increasing turbulence, complexity, speed, competition, and change—renders the old command-and-control system useless. Shortened product life cycles and constant focus on change create a need for the "**knowledge worker.**"[30] Knowledge workers are employees who need and use information to perform their work. This category can include everyone from product developers or producers to programmers to consultants to clerks who deal with customers. Knowledge-focused companies recognize that people are their greatest assets and keep their workforces involved and informed.[31] The environment demands workers who are adaptable and self-managing, flexible and autonomous, and enabled and motivated to accomplish what they choose.

Why Is Empowerment Important?

One reason empowerment has been embraced lies in its ability to provide motivation. Managers realize that employee motivation facilitates the achievement of organizational goals. According to Maslow's **hierarchy of needs theory,**[32] people are intrinsically motivated in direct relationship to their needs, beginning with the most basic needs and progressing up the hierarchy as these needs are met. (See Figure 18–1.) According to Maslow, physiological needs are among the most basic of needs; they relate to sustaining

**Figure 18-2
Maslow's Hierarchy**

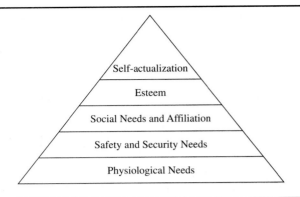

life (e.g., food, shelter, oxygen). Safety needs relate to security, stability, and freedom of the fear of no longer meeting the physiological needs. Once these needs are satisfied (which is usually accomplished by obtaining a job and earning wages), they tend to lose their motivating potential. Individuals then move up the pyramid, striving to satisfy the needs on the next higher level. For example, once an employee has taken care of his physiological and safety needs, he will seek ways to fulfill social, esteem, and self-actualization needs. While empirical support for this theory is lacking,[33] the needs hierarchy helps clarify why many workers are no longer simply motivated to just work; they want to be challenged, become satisfied with their accomplishments, and contribute to personal and organizational goals.[34]

Through empowerment, organizations are able to support the motivating potential inherent in satisfying higher-level needs. Managers facilitate employee motivation through empowerment and thus increase autonomy, respect, power to make decisions, status, and freedom to grow and develop within the organization. Thus, an empowered worker is a satisfied worker.[35]

Now return to the opening case scenario to extrapolate the benefits of empowerment. If you were the owner of the hotel chain, would you be satisfied knowing that your client's needs were unmet at first? If you were the clerk, would you feel you did everything in your power to ensure customer satisfaction? Chances are, you answered no to both questions. Thanks to the ubiquity of technology and information, many of us have become quite proficient at identifying the best value when purchasing products and services. We can "name our own price" for anything from groceries to airline tickets. One might conclude that as a result, the need for good customer service has declined. In fact, it has increased. Once price and ease of obtaining a good or service no longer matters, how do successful firms differentiate themselves in the eyes of their customers? How do organizations build customer loyalty to current and future products and services? They do this through their human assets—their employees.

When employees feel aligned with an organization's mission and goals, supported to target such outcomes, and rewarded when they and the organization achieve desired performance and outcomes, they do whatever it takes to produce a deliverable or satisfy a customer.[36] Contrast this philosophy with one in which employees are closely monitored, given information on a need-to-know basis, and rewarded randomly, if at all. When workers are empowered, they are involved in decision making, asked to suggest new services and processes, and encouraged to solve problems creatively and effectively. Derek, our hotel clerk, is not empowered. He is not able to problem-solve or suggest potential solutions to the weary traveler. Such decisions are better left to someone in charge, right? Wrong!

Had Derek been given the power to satisfy his customer, a different, more positive outcome would have emerged for the customer, Derek, and, ultimately, the organization. However, giving employees power, or empowering them, may not be as easy as it seems. Many managers view sharing power and authority as risky and question the notion that empowerment is beneficial. We'll discuss why shortly. We'll also help you understand why today's leaders need to recognize that empowering their workforce is an opportunity, rather than a threat.[37] In addition, an organization that empowers its employees may be better suited to attract and retain its highly skilled and trained professionals, thus maintaining its competitive edge.

Benefits of Empowerment

There are numerous benefits to empowerment. After reading the list of benefits below, you might wonder whether you or the organization for which you work can afford *not* to empower its employees!

■ Empowerment reinforces member participation and growth, commitment to quality, and a more open, honest environment. This results in greater job satisfaction, motivation, and commitment—a sense of achievement.[38]

■ With empowerment, people have a greater sense of achievement, improved confidence and self-esteem, and a sense of belonging.[39] Mary Kay cosmetics exemplifies empowerment in how its representatives do business. They are provided support and training through conventions and other educational materials, they are able to control their schedule and the amount of effort they wish to exert, and they receive recognition and rewards for their efforts. Because they are treated as owners of their businesses, Mary Kay employees feel confident and have a sense of belonging and control over their work. This empowerment helps release their energies toward even greater achievements.

■ Empowerment speeds up reaction time and decision making and provides speed and flexibility, allowing quicker response to customers. Empowered employees who deal directly with customers will be able to better meet their needs and demands, leading to more satisfied customers.[40] Imagine you are boarding a plane when you realize you have been ticketed for a seat that is already "rightfully" occupied. Some airlines would have you deplane and wait until all passengers are seated and then consult a supervisor about fixing the problem. In an empowered airline organization, the agent, who is likely part owner in the airline, immediately takes the problem into his or her hands and finds a solution. Perhaps you are bumped to first class, or perhaps you are given another option or compensation. Either way, the problem is solved quickly and without management intervention, and the customer is satisfied. Empowerment is often cited as a key reason for the phenomenal success of Herb Kelleher's Southwest Airlines.

■ Empowered employees are more likely to offer ideas, exercise creativity, and develop more innovative processes and products than those who are not.[41] In an empowered organization, employees are encouraged to take risks and are not afraid of failure. They look for opportunities to improve products, processes, and services that seem to work well, in addition to reacting to problems that need immediate attention. Because they have the authority to act in the best interests of their work unit and organization, empowered individuals positively affect their environment through proactive behaviors.[42] An example of an empowering organization is 3M. When the scientist created the failed glue that eventually became the key ingredient in Post-It Notes, he was not "punished" by his management. Instead, he was encouraged to see if he could come up with a use for his "failure." Wouldn't you want to get a percentage of Post-It Notes' revenues?

■ With empowerment, employees are more responsible, which leads to greater loyalty, trust, and quality.[43] By transferring power and authority to employees, they become accountable and responsible for their decisions and actions. Since they solve their own problems and find their own solutions, empowered employees will be more committed to a quality outcome and to stay long enough to see the fruits of their labor. This kind of loyalty is invaluable to an organization's ability to attract and retain talented personnel.

■ Empowerment reduces operational costs by eliminating unnecessary layers of management, staff, quality control, and checking operations.[44] The traditional hierarchical design assumes that employees cannot be trusted to make sound organizational decisions. Each successive layer of management has a role in ensuring that employees representing the previous layer follow the stated rules and procedures and, if not, they are to be corrected by their management. For example, at one large aerospace company, the process of ordering a $2 package of pencils could cost as much as $75 when accounting for the seven layers of management and approval all orders had to go through before being placed. However, by defining parameters, the ordering process was streamlined to a single individual ordering products within certain reasonable limits, without the need for management consent. In terms of quality control, empowered workers take responsibility and receive rewards for the quality of their product and are therefore committed to producing products and services of the highest quality possible. In many empowered organizations, employees not only take responsibility for their operations, but they also engage in activities designed to streamline and improve processes—building in quality from the start. This eliminates the need for surveillance or inspection by a "big brother" or quality assurance engineer.

- ■ Empowerment reduces turnover and aids in retention. In 2000, when the economy was booming, employee turnover was near a 20-year high. Schellenbarger reports that due to the costs of replacing an employee—about 1.5 times a year's pay—companies are pouring millions of dollars into efforts designed to increase employee loyalty.[45] By tending to such issues as fair pay, involvement in decision making, and trust in leadership—all elements associated with an empowered workforce—employees remain more committed and loyal to organizations.

Disadvantages or Costs of Empowerment

At this point, you might be thinking to yourself, if empowerment is all this and more, then why don't we see more organizations doing it? Many managers and organizations want to empower their workforce but are not sure how to do it without jeopardizing achievement of the jobs and organizational goals. Truth is, many managers and organizations resist empowerment for a number of reasons.[46] For one, empowerment results in greater costs in selection and hiring. Little difficulty is likely to be encountered finding individuals capable of performing simple, controlled tasks. When employees are to be empowered—trusted with organizational information and the means to improve it—selectivity in hiring is necessarily increased.

Empowerment can also result in lower and inconsistent delivery. In the control model, employees follow a specific script and set of instructions, eliminating any inconsistency (and creativity, for that matter). Employees in an empowered environment have a different experience. In their efforts to satisfy the customer, empowered employees may take more time and personalize the service for the customer's needs. Depending on the business and strategy, this could be good or bad. A recent article suggests that fast-food franchises do significantly more business in their drive-through windows than through their walk-up counters. Reducing the service delivery time by a small increment can have a substantial positive impact on profits.[47] There is also the possibility for giveaways and bad decisions.[48] What if Derek were empowered to satisfy the weary traveler and, to compensate for the hotel's error, gave the traveler an upgraded room for the same price? Would this be a bad or a good decision? One such decision is likely not to impact an organization's profits; however, empowered employees may go too far in satisfying customers, to the point that profits are affected. Giving away products and services—while it increases customer satisfaction—reduces revenues. Empowered employees may also make changes in their environment that improve their work unit yet negatively impact another work unit. Hopefully, this is not likely to happen when employees have information about how all the pieces fit together. However, such freedom could result in a costly error.

Empowerment typically comes with boundaries. While an organization gives empowered employees the authority to make decisions, these decisions must generally be made within certain broad operating principles. However, what if employees were to stray beyond those boundaries? What if employees abuse their power? For example an empowered and overzealous employee, acting without regard for company guidelines, might satisfy one customer in the short term but damage relationships with the home office in the long term. An example of this would be Derek the desk clerk. He could overcompensate, not only offering the guest a room upgrade but also coupons for free stays at any location within the hotel chain for the next three months. Organizations that empower employees must give their employees authority, responsibility, and guidelines or parameters within which they perform.

An important dimension that hinders empowerment is the fact that some individuals cannot handle or do not want the responsibility. Despite the intrinsic and extrinsic benefits of empowerment, some employees prefer to show up, be told what to do, get their paycheck, and go home. Empowerment may be perceived as freedom by some but as ambiguity by others. Some prefer keeping things simple and known. They fear the responsibility inherent in thinking about and making decisions that could change, and possibly improve, the way things have always been done. It's important to remember that just because you value empowerment, others may not.

Finally, one reason some managers avoid empowerment—even when their organization embraces it—is fear of change and the unknown. "It's working now, so why should I change? What if my empowered employees mess up; will I be fired? What if they do so well—become self-managing—that I'm no longer needed? How can they know better than me; I've been here longer and have more experience than they do." It takes a certain mindset or philosophy to empower successfully. What makes some leaders more willing and able to empower their subordinates than others? Some individuals possess a leadership style or proclivity toward empowering (or disempowering) behaviors while others understand that empowerment can actually expand their power base, that more might be gained than lost.

To Empower or Not to Empower?

It seems clear that empowerment is an important and necessary element, at least in some form, in today's global environment. Only the fittest and most innovative companies will survive; empowerment increases the energy level of the workforce and channels it into good use.[49] Is empowerment a one-size-fits-all proposition? Luckily, no.[50] There are multiple approaches to empowerment, and there are several criteria worth considering when determining the degree to which empowerment should be implemented in your workplace.

Different levels of empowerment can be used in empowering your workforce; deciding which level will be appropriate for your situation or workforce can facilitate successful implementation.[51] These approaches differ in terms of the degree to which ingredients of empowerment are present.

■ In **suggestion involvement,** the organization makes a small shift from the production line or control model. Employees are encouraged to contribute ideas, possibly via an anonymous suggestion box. In general, day-to-day activities remain unchanged, unless a manager decides to implement a suggestion. This step is helpful in that employees are encouraged to be creative and think about ways to improve products and processes; however, employees may not know whether their ideas are acknowledged or may not be asked to get involved in implementation.

■ In the **job involvement** approach to empowerment, employees are given greater freedom in their job and tasks. Their responsibilities become more open or fluid, such as a team in which all employees are cross-trained to perform a variety of tasks. Their jobs become enlarged and enriched,[52] and they receive feedback on their performance. This can aid in increasing employee satisfaction and productivity. Managers' roles in this approach are more like advisors; they give some choices to employees but must be kept apprised, especially if problems surface.

■ Employees in a **high involvement** organization have much greater voice and discretion over their work environment. Managers provide the necessary resources, information, and rewards to employees while acting as coaches or facilitators of employees and teams. Because they understand their role in the organization and its success, empowered employees are in the best position to redesign their work, solve problems (or find new ones!), and share in the profits realized by their innovative and productive efforts. Employees take ownership in their work unit and the organization, and often manage themselves.

Is empowerment an appropriate strategy for your organization? Certain considerations or contingencies (see Figure 18–3) should be evaluated in deciding whether a low level of empowerment (production-line approach) or a high level of empowerment is more appropriate.

The production line approach works effectively when the primary business value is speed and efficiency, for example, in a fast-food restaurant. Empowerment takes time. The production line approach breaks tasks out into noncomplex, predetermined components,

**Figure 18–3[53]
Empowerment
Considerations**

Contingency	Production Line vs. Empowerment Approach
Basic business strategy	Efficient high volume vs. customized differentiated
Tie to the customer	Transaction vs. relationship
Technology	Routine vs. nonroutine
Business environment	Predictable vs. dynamic
Type of people	McGregor's Theory X managers vs. Theory Y managers

whereas empowerment is needed where employees require time to process varying situations and generate appropriate solutions.

The production line approach works well when employees' ties to the customer are secondary to the product or service being delivered, for example, a gas station attendant. Organizations that value longer term customer relationships, for example, a four-star resort or a wealth management firm, will find empowerment more beneficial for both employees and customers.

The production line approach works in environments where technology enables workers to perform many of the most important tasks routinely. In organizations with a lot of variety and complexity, where employees perform tasks that are primarily nonroutine, empowerment will be required.

The production line approach works well in business environments that are predictable, where most of the problems that may arise can be anticipated, prepared for, and responded to in a prescribed manner. Empowerment is preferred in unpredictable environments, such as the airlines, where weather and mechanical issues can require a variety of responses that would be difficult to specify in a manual.

Lastly, the production line approach is best when an organization's managers are primarily hierarchical, "top-down" **Theory X[54] managers.** An X manager believes subordinates dislike work and shirk responsibility, leading them to be more directive with the tendency to dictate work efforts. An organization predominated by participative, open **Theory Y managers**—holding the belief that people enjoy work, crave responsibility, and strive for excellence—is the perfect environment for an empowerment approach to problem solving. These managers, and the employees, are more comfortable with higher levels of employee involvement.

Guidelines for Implementing and Improving Empowerment[55]

1. Walk the talk—managers need to "practice what they preach."
2. Set high performance standards—set standards that force others to excel, and show that you have confidence in their ability to reach them.
3. Empowerment must be recognized (in the structure of the organization)—empowerment must be reflected in attitudes and in processes within the organization.
4. Change old habits—managers must be ready to relinquish power, and subordinates must be ready and able to accept new responsibilities.
5. Start small—changes need to be made little by little; empowerment does not happen overnight.
6. Build trust—managers must emit confidence and be open and honest with their co-workers.

**Implementing
Empowerment**

So, exactly how does an organization empower its workforce? According to Bowen and Lawler, four ingredients of empowerment must be present in an environment for effective employee involvement. They include:[56]

■ Information about the organization and its performance. Unlike the old model, in which only top management is interested in and can understand an organization's financials, operating costs, and competitive position, empowered employees are given this information and the training to understand what this information means to their work unit and how their actions can and do impact the bottom line. If you don't know where you are, how will you know if you're improving?

■ Rewards based on the organization's performance. Many organizations still reward employees for nonperformance-related criteria such as tenure. While there are some benefits to employee loyalty, what message does an organization send when it rewards employees who are less productive but more senior than those who actively and productively contribute to the organization's bottom line? In an empowered organization, employees engage in collaborative efforts—for the collective good—and share in the organization's success through profit sharing and stock ownership. Recall the slogan for Avis: "We're the employee owners of Avis . . . we work harder!"

■ Knowledge that enables employees to understand and contribute to organizational performance. Along with the training to understand organizational performance, empowered employees are given training and access to resources to fix problems and improve processes. This knowledge may come in the form of education (problem-solving and quality classes) or resources (bulletins for charting progress, meeting times, outside experts).

■ Power to make decisions that influence organizational direction and performance. This ingredient brings us back to our original definition of empowerment. Training, knowledge, and rewards are great, but if all employees can do is recommend—rather than implement—solutions, commitment to the outcome will be constrained. Empowered employees are given the authority, usually within defined parameters, to make decisions and implement changes that improve the performance of individuals, teams, work units, and the organization.

Through these ingredients, we can see that empowerment is more than just sharing power. Empowered employees are enabled. They are provided with the freedom to successfully do what they want to do, rather than getting them to do what you want. Whetton and Cameron refer to this as a pull strategy, rather than a push strategy; this means that employees accomplish tasks because they are internally meaningful or motivating, not because someone or something external to them deems it important.[57] To make empowerment work, managers have to believe in and want empowerment, and employees must feel empowered—perceive that there is a liberating rather than constraining environment. It is their perception of the environment that shapes the empowerment.[58] Spreitzer discusses four psychological attributes of empowerment: meaning, self-determination, competence, and impact.[59] This view holds that it is essential for organizations to be empowering. Organizations need to provide the right climate, tools, training, and support for empowerment to exist. However, for empowerment to actually exist, it must be felt or experienced by employees. In other words, only through acts of empowerment, as carried out by employees, can empowerment come alive and be more than just words on a page in a company brochure. It is the manager's role to engender the four psychological attributes in those they intend to empower.[60] However, individuals can still refuse to accept empowerment or feel empowered.

Six Social Structural Characteristics That Create an Empowering Environment[61]

Low role ambiguity—a clear set of responsibilities and duties, defined guidelines, and standards for accountability.

Wide span of control—decentralization to allow for greater contribution to overall operation; to avoid micromanagement.

Sociopolitical support—the existence of relevant support networks of bosses, peers, subordinates, and members of the work group.

(continued)

Access to information—Availability of information on operations and procedures to determine strategy and frameworks for the accomplishment of organizational goals; freely sharing information across levels and functions.

Access to resources—ability to marshal resources essential to tasks to eliminate dependency and powerlessness.

Participative unit climate—a climate and culture that emphasizes and encourages individual contribution and initiative rather than top-down command and control.

There are five stages to implementing empowerment.[62]

1. **Investigation**—analyzing whether empowerment should be implemented and in what form. In this phase, the organization evaluates its current business processes and strategies for success, and weighs the current situation against preferred goals. Using the chart in Figure 18–3, the company first identifies its core business strategy, its customer links, the prevalence of technology throughout the organization, the business and environment in which the business is operating, and the type of people currently working for the organization. Then it considers data such as employee morale, customer satisfaction, and industry best practices. After this analysis the organization can determine whether empowerment will bring the desired changes and outcomes needed to achieve greater success.

2. **Preparation**—setting the stage for generating and demonstrating organizational support. This is a crucial step. Changing from a production-line approach to a decision-making and problem-solving approach that is more empowering requires a significant culture shift. The way people act and are rewarded will change dramatically. In this phase managers and employees all receive information about the desired shift, why it's occurring, the changes that will result, the training and tools that will be available to help them through the change, the benefits of the change, and information on how and when the changes will take place.[63]

3. **Implementation**—assessing all current systems and adjusting to support an environment based on empowerment. In this phase job descriptions are redesigned, reporting relationships are examined, and reward systems are aligned with the changes. For example, an employee who was formerly paid on an hourly basis might be placed in a bonus pool and receive periodic recognition for "best practice" examples of excellent customer service. Operating procedures and policy manuals are updated, ongoing training is developed and offered, and information and communication systems are realigned to support the ongoing changes that will result from the empowerment initiative.

4. **Transition**—moving from the former system to the new one. This phase marks the end of the introduction or "roll out" of the new system and starts the permanent implementation of the new system. This phase involves receiving feedback on how the new system is working and making modifications as required. Numerous adjustments are made as employees and managers gain experience with the new guidelines and techniques. In this phase employees are also mobilized—allowed to have an impact, given the freedom to take action, supported in their decisions, and encouraged to take risks.

5. **Maturation**—the new system is firmly rooted. This phase involves maintaining the new system and continuously improving it. There is a constant need for reexamination of current processes to determine how changes or new adaptations need to be implemented to remain vital.

Self-empowerment

So far, we've discussed what empowerment is, why it's used, and its benefits and disadvantages. We've also discussed that in order for empowerment to result in increases in productivity, innovation, satisfaction, and commitment, organizations and their managers have to be empowering and individuals have to accept empowerment. Employees must demonstrate and prove that they have the ability and desire to handle the responsibility that empowerment brings. What if empowerment does not exist in your organization or your work group? Do you give up and wait for others to tell you what to do? Here's where self-empowerment comes in; follow these steps:

- Create a vision of preferred achievements for yourself and your group. Set high standards for performance and establish goals and deliverables needed to achieve that standard.

- Understand your need for dependency—and let go of your need. We all start out that way. As children, we look to our parents for rules and norms of accepted behavior. When we succeed—or fail—we look to others for recognition or acceptance. When you empower yourself, you set the goals and the rules and you evaluate your performance. No one will tell you what to do or whether you were successful. Believe in yourself and your capabilities to succeed. When you do, you can have pride in your accomplishments and the knowledge that you made it happen.

- Identify and manage your allies and adversaries, and network and politic where appropriate. Even the best-laid plans are subject to roadblocks. After setting a vision and goals, determine what and who can help—and hinder—your ability to achieve those goals. Find ways to reduce obstacles or enlist the support of others, including your peers and managers, to remove or reduce those obstacles. Who might champion your efforts? Maybe your boss is uncomfortable with empowerment, but her boss is not. This is not to say that you should skip the chain of command; rather, you do what you need to get the job done. Inform your boss of your plans and where they fit in. If your boss chooses not to get involved, don't let that stop you. Get others involved, and keep your boss informed of your progress. Persuade others to support you. Most people will offer help or resources to individuals and projects that have the potential to make a positive difference in the organization.

- Develop risk-taking strategies; find the courage and confidence to live out your vision. The old saying, "nothing ventured, nothing gained" holds true. Why be an average performer when you are capable of so much more? Why do only what others expect of you when your expectations and aspirations are higher? By accepting self-empowerment and daring to go where others may not have gone, you have to accept that failure is a possibility. Then again, so too is success. Evaluate the costs and benefits of taking on a self-empowered "adventure"; if the net result is positive, what have you got to lose? Former Chicago Bulls superstar Michael Jordan was cut from his high school varsity basketball team as an underclassman. What would have happened if he lacked the courage to persist when others told him he didn't make the cut? Luckily for his fans, he pursued his vision.

One final note about empowerment. Research suggests that empowered managers are more likely to empower their subordinates than managers who are not empowered.[64] Referred to as the falling dominos effect, this phenomenon suggests that beyond the benefits already mentioned, empowerment can be downwardly contagious. When you feel empowered, you are likely to take steps to do the same for those reporting to you, and so on. Because of this cascading effect, when empowerment starts at the top of the organization, the benefits are likely to be exponential!

Empowerment through Effective Delegation

As you progress in your career, you're likely to find that no matter how skilled and experienced you are, you can neither do everything nor make all necessary decisions. Even if you could—and that would probably make you superhuman—you would be preventing your subordinates from developing and reaching their full potential. One means of empowering others is through the technique of **delegation.** Delegation involves assigning work—and the authority and responsibility for the work—to others. Healthy environments are characterized by delegation; if done properly it can be one of the most effective management tools for getting things done, and it is considered a critical part of being a good leader.[65]

Delegation is not as simple as it sounds. In fact, many managers avoid delegation or do it poorly. Delegation involves transferring authority, responsibility, and accountability to others, typically subordinates. It is not abdication or "dumping"; rather, it can help create a positive, team-oriented environment. In this section, we discuss why delegation is important and how to do it effectively.

Benefits of Delegation

Benefits of delegation accrue to both the delegatee and the delegator. Some of these benefits are listed below.

- Delegation enables staff to handle specific tasks that are routine. This enables managers to observe and evaluate employee performance, as well as deal with tasks that are more complex.

- Transferring responsibility to staff aids in their development and increases staff readiness for promotions.[66]

- Delegation increases the delegatees' level of job satisfaction through greater autonomy and the feeling that they are making a contribution to organizational success.

- Delegation can lead to better decision making because people closer to the issue have input on decisions. This pushes organizational decision making downward, leading to better ways to do things and a more democratic or inclusive process.[67]

- Delegation allows for growth and development of the manager who's delegating. By giving responsibility for tasks to others, the manager's time is available for other tasks, for conceiving new ideas, or for innovation.

- Delegation demonstrates a manager's trust in his or her employees. It shows the manager's ability to manage and develop other individuals, to effectively communicate, and work through others.

Challenges in Delegating

Despite these benefits, many of us choose not to delegate or do it poorly. Delegating responsibility is easy to understand yet hard to do; however, not delegating can be disastrous.[68] Some reasons people fail to delegate include:

- *Lack of time:* Perhaps you feel you can do it yourself more quickly. While training will be needed to ensure a task is done correctly, not training means the next time the task needs to be done, you will be doing it. The biblical adage, "You can give a man a fish or teach him how," reminds us that delegation is important.

- *Perfectionism:* Perhaps you feel you can do it better, which may be true; however, letting others perform a task enables them to learn, grow, and develop. Let go of the idea that asking a less-qualified person to do a task seems illogical.[69]

- *Fear of surrendering authority:* Perhaps you fear a loss of power. If you believe that you are the only one who can do something, that belief reinforces your perception that you maintain control or power in a situation. Truth is, few employees are indispensable.

- *Lack of confidence in staff:* Perhaps you don't trust in the abilities of your staff or you fear they might purposely fail to make you look bad. Build trust by delegating a simple, low-risk task and progress from there.

- *Dual accountability:* Perhaps you feel that this task is your responsibility and that it's not right to share that responsibility with someone else. Certain tasks, such as personnel issues, should not be delegated; many other tasks can and should be delegated. By delegating, you *help* others build their skills and feel more satisfied about their contributions.

Activities Included in Delegation

To be effective, delegation requires three activities: assigning responsibility, transferring authority, and establishing accountability.[70] All three elements are needed and should occur simultaneously. These activities are described below.

   1. **The assignment of responsibility.** When assigning the responsibility to accomplish a task, the delegatee must understand exactly what is to be accomplished and accept

the responsibility for doing so. This requires two-way communication to ensure both parties clearly understand the task and the expectations that go along with it. Manager and subordinate might discuss and clarify all potential contingencies and ascertain whether the subordinate has the necessary skills and knowledge to perform the assigned task.[71]

2. The transferring of authority. The delegatee must have the proper authority to obtain the necessary resources to complete the task. This includes formal control over necessary resources, clarification of parameters or guidelines, and an understanding of the authority given and the limits therein.[72] As appropriate, others should also be apprised of the transfer of the authority. For example, suppose a manager is traveling for two weeks and he delegates the collection and processing of timecards to a subordinate. Before he leaves, he needs to make subordinates aware of this temporary change and make arrangements with the payroll office to ensure the acceptability of the subordinate's signature on the timecards.

3. Establishing accountability. Delegation is not complete without holding delegatees accountable for the completion of the assignments. They need to be aware of the rewards and consequences of their actions and must realize that they will have to justify decisions for the tasks for which they are responsible. If the delegatee forgets to turn in the timecards and her co-workers don't get paid, they are likely to become unhappy. When delegating tasks, it is important that consequences—both good and bad—are clearly understood. A word of caution: be sure to delegate both pleasant and less pleasant tasks. "Dumping" provides little variety and could lead to employee complaints.[73]

A Process for Effective Delegation

Effective delegation begins with an open, supportive environment. Create a work environment that has mutual support, mutual trust, and clear lines of communication.[74] Communication and delegation go hand in hand—most problems associated with delegation such as lack of motivation, dissatisfaction, and inferior work can be traced back to a lack of understanding.[75] Two-way communication—aided by effective speaking, listening, and feedback skills—is necessary throughout the entire delegation process.

Next, decide what to delegate. Examine tasks that can and should be delegated; determine why (i.e., what is the goal of the delegation) and how (the process) you will do this. Determine what will be required with the delegation, such as training, information, resources, and experience. Just because an employee lacks experience is no reason to avoid delegating or to only delegate mundane tasks to him or her.[76]

Assess and select capable individuals. To do this, you will need to match the person to the task, design a training program if necessary, make sure the person will be able to complete the task and goal, and work with him or her to anticipate any potential problems and ways to overcome them. Employees need to feel confident and competent to succeed.

Delegate over stages, allowing employees to work more and more on their own without constant supervision. In other words, start small. Show your support of and trust in them by allowing them to prove themselves and their ability to work with little or no supervision on simple tasks or on an initial task related to a larger project. For example, you can start with low levels of delegation where you ask someone to get baseline information. Then you can move the person to a medium level by asking him or her to get information, analyze it, and suggest options. This way you are able to assess the person's skills and decision-making abilities and determine their capacity to handle the next level or an entire assignment on their own.[77] This process allows you to maintain an appropriate level of control and responsibility over the task.

Next, you'll want to establish controls. While you are ultimately responsible for the task, delegation does not mean that you no longer are accountable or responsible for the end results. Make it clear at the time of delegation how and when checks will occur, and develop feedback mechanisms to ensure the task is on target and being performed properly.[78]

As needed and requested, provide help and coaching. Encourage a delegatee to complete the task by demonstrating your confidence in their abilities. Accept only finished work—do not allow for reverse delegation—and make others understand that their success depends on their contribution. Try not to give in to the fears associated with delegation or let others give you the work the delegatee took responsibility for. You can be a support factor—ask questions and give guidance, and teach employees to be problem solvers and decision makers.[79]

Finally, provide feedback. Give rewards and credit for jobs completed successfully, and provide constructive feedback for insufficient work. If you accept substandard work and fix or finish it, you deprive the delegatee of the opportunity to learn from mistakes, as well as send a message that mediocre (or worse) performance is acceptable.

Summary

In today's dynamic business environment, effective leaders are needed to help individuals and organizations succeed and achieve their full potential. Leaders establish a vision and, through their actions and behaviors, inspire others to embrace and achieve that vision. Effective leaders use empowerment to increase employee participation, creativity, and motivation in order to remain viable and competitive. By understanding the benefits and tactics for empowerment, along with being aware of the potential consequences of improper empowerment and delegation, you will be able to increase job satisfaction while effectively achieving organizational goals.

Key Terms and Concepts

Accountability

Assignment of responsibility

Authority

Delegation

Empowerment

Hierarchy of needs theory

High involvement

Implementation stage

Investigation stage

Job involvement

Knowledge worker

Leadership

Maturation stage

Preparation stage

Self-leadership

Suggestion involvement

Theory X manager

Theory Y manager

Transition stage

Endnotes

1. M. Kur, "Leaders Everywhere! Can a Broad Spectrum of Leadership Behaviours Permeate an Entire Organization?" *Leadership and Organization Development Journal,* 18 (1997), p. 271.

2. A. Nahavandi, *The Art and Science of Leadership,* Third Ed. (Upper Saddle River, NJ: Prentice Hall).

3. P. G. Northouse, *Leadership: Theory and Practice* (Thousand Oaks, CA: Sage, 1977).

4. Kur, "Leaders Everywhere!"

5. A. Shriberg, D. L. Shriberg, and C. Lloyd, *Practicing Leadership: Principles and Applications,* Second Ed. (New York: John Wiley & Sons, 2002).

6. J. M. Kouzes & B. Z. Posner, *Credibility: How Leaders Gain and Lose It, Why People Demand It* (San Francisco: Jossey-Bass, 1993).

7. D. W. Johnson, *Reaching Out: Interpersonal Effectiveness and Self-Actualization* (Upper Saddle River, NJ: Pearson Education, 2002).

8. Nahavandi, *Art and Science.*

9. Kouzes and Posner, *Credibility.*

10. Shriberg et al., *Practicing Leadership.*

11. D. Goleman. "Leadership That Gets Results," *Harvard Business Review,* March/April 2000, pp. 78–90.

12. Kouzes and Posner, *Credibility.*

13. Ibid.

14. J. Lord, "Really MADD: Looking Back at 20 Years," *DRIVEN* magazine, Spring 2000, **http://www.madd.org/aboutus/0,1056,1686,00.html,** accessed August 24, 2004.

15. R. Bommelje and L. Steil, *Listening Leaders: The 10 Golden Rules to Listen, Lead, and Succeed* (Minneapolis, MN: Beaver's Pond Press, 2004).

16. Kouzes and Posner, *Credibility.*

17. "Poems for Peace: Young Poet Tugs at Heartstrings with More Heartsongs," *ABCNews.com,* March 11, 2003, at **http://abcnews.go.com/sections/GMA/Living/GMA030311_MattiePoems. html? GMAad=true.**

18. Shriberg et al., *Practicing Leadership.*

19. Kouzes and Posner, *Credibility.*

20. Kur, "Leaders Everywhere!"

21. C. Manz and C. Neck, *Mastering Self-Leadership* (Upper Saddle River, NJ: Prentice Hall, 2003).

22. J. P. Kotter, *The New Rules: How to Succeed in Today's Post Corporate World* (New York: The Free Press, 1995).

23. S. G. Cohen, L. Chang, and G. E. Ledford, Jr., "A Hierarchical Construct of Self-management Leadership and Its Relationship to Quality of Work Life and Perceived Work Group Effectiveness," *Personnel Psychology* 50, no. 2 (1997), pp. 275–308.

24. G. M. Spreitzer, M. A. Kizilos, and S. W. Nason, "A Multidimensional Analysis of the Relationship between Psychological Empowerment, and Effectiveness, Satisfaction, and Strain," *Journal of Management* 23, no. 5 (1997), pp. 679–705.

25. For a broader discussion of social responsibility and organizations that practice it, check out A. B. Carroll, *Business and Society: Managing Corporate Social Performance* (Boston: Little Brown, 1981).

26. Kotter, *The New Rules.*

27. H. K. S. Laschinger, J. E. Finegan, J. Shamian, and P. Wilk, "A Longitudinal Analysis of the Impact of Workplace Empowerment on Work Satisfaction," *Journal of Organizational Behavior* 25, no. 4 (2004), pp. 527–543.

28. Jay A. Conger and Rabindra N. Kanungo, "The Empowerment Process: Integrating Theory and Practice," *Academy of Management Review* 13 (1988), p. 473. For a closer look at the relationship between empowering practices and the employees' psychological experience of empowerment, see Scott Seibert, Seth Silver, and Alan Randolph, "Taking Empowerment to the Next Level: A Multiple-level Model of Empowerment, Performance and Satisfaction," *Academy of Management Journal* 47 (2004), pp. 332–351.

29. Joanne Cole, "Building Heart and Soul," *HR Focus,* October 1998, pp. 9–10, quoting Hornstein, author of *Brutal Bosses.*

30. Peter Crush, "New Product Development: Letting Staff Be Creative," *Marketing,* July 13, 2000.

31. Larry English, "Information Quality Management: The Next Frontier," *DM Review,* April 2000, p. 38.

32. Abraham H. Maslow, *Motivation and Personality,* Second Ed. (New York: Harper and Row, 1970).

33. E. Lawler and J. Shuttle, "A Causal Correlation Test of the Need Hierarchy Concept," *Organizational Behavior and Human Performance* 7 (1973), pp. 265–287.

34. Realize that this theory is culture-bound. For example, in other cultures—e.g., Asian and Hispanic—the order of the hierarchy differs and social needs dominate other needs.

35. Laschinger et al., "Longitudinal Analysis."

36. See, e.g., David E. Bowen and Edward Lawler III, "The Empowerment of Service Workers: What, Why, How and When," *Sloan Management Review,* Spring 1992, pp. 31–39.

37. Gretchen M. Spreitzer, "Social Structural Characteristics of Psychological Empowerment," *Academy of Management Journal,* April 1996, pp. 483–504.

38. Rob MacLachian, "Regeneration X," *People Management,* April 2, 1998, p. 34.

39. Wong Pang Long, "Managing Problems: To Empower or Not, Is the Question," *The New Press Times,* Dec. 22, 1996, p. 32.

40. Ibid.

41. Ibid.

42. Spreitzer, "Social Structural Characteristics."

43. R. Forrester, "Empowerment: Rejuvenating a Potent Idea," *Academy of Management Executives* 14 (2000), pp. 67–80.

44. Bowen and Lawler, "Empowerment of Service Workers."

45. Sue Schellenbarger, "To Win the Loyalty of Your Employees, Try a Softer Touch," *The Wall Street Journal,* January 26, 2000, p. B1.

46. Bowen and Lawler, "Empowerment of Service Workers."

47. Jennifer Ordonez, "Next! An Efficiency Drive: Fast Food Lanes Are Getting Even Faster," *The Wall Street Journal,* May 18, 2000, p. A1.

48. Bowen and Lawler, "Empowerment of Service Workers."

49. Long, "Managing Problems."

50. Forrester, "Empowerment."

51. Bowen and Lawler, "Empowerment of Service Workers."

52. See, for example, Greg R. Oldham and J. Richard Hackman, "Relationships between Organizational Structure and Employee Reactions: Comparing Alternative Frameworks," *Administrative Science Quarterly,* March 1981, p. 66.

53. Bowen and Lawler, "Empowerment of Service Workers."

54. Douglas McGregor, *The Human Side of Enterprise* (New York: McGraw-Hill, 1964), pp. 68–78.

55. Leaders Direct, **www.leadersdirect.com/empower.html.**

56. Bowen and Lawler, "Empowerment of Service Workers."

57. David A. Whetton and Kim S. Cameron, *Developing Management Skills,* Fourth Ed. (Reading, MA: Addison-Wesley, 1998), p. 377.

58. Spreitzer, "Social Structural Characteristics."

59. Ibid.

60. K. S. Cameron, D. A. Whetton, and M. U. Kim, "Organizational Dysfunctions of Decline," *Academy of Management Journal,* 1987, 30, pp. 12–138.

61. Spreitzer, "Social Structural Characteristics."

62. Carol Yeh-Yen Lin, "The Essence of Empowerment: A Conceptual Model and a Case Illustration," *Journal of Applied Management Studies,* Dec. 1998, p. 223.

63. Carole Schweitzer, "Empowerment by Example," *Associate Management,* May 1998, p. 50.

64. Bernard M. Bass, David A. Waldman, Bruce J. Avolio, and Michael Bebb, "Transformational Leadership and the Falling Dominoes Effect," *Group & Organization Management,* 1987.

65. Carl Holmes, "Fighting the Urge to Fight Fires," *Harvard Business Review,* Nov.–Dec. 1999, p. 30.

66. Joseph H. Foegen, "Are Managers Losing Control?" *Business Horizons,* March–April 1998, p. 2.

67. Ibid.

68. Holmes, "Fighting the Urge."

69. Foegen, "Are Managers Losing Control?"

70. S. C. Bushardt, D. L. Duhon, and A. R. Fowler Jr., "Management Delegation Myths and the Paradox of Task Assignment," *Business Horizons,* March–April 1991, pp. 34–43.

71. William W. Hull, "Passing the Buck vs. Making an Assignment," *Supervision,* March 1999, p. 6.

72. Ibid.

73. Nahavandi, *Art and Science.*

74. Holmes, "Fighting the Urge."

75. Robert Rohrer, "Does the Buck Ever Really Stop?" *Supervision,* April 1999, p. 11.

76. Monique R. Brown, "Management by Delegation: Don't Be a Micro Manager: Share the Responsibility," *Black Enterprise,* Feb. 1998, p. 76.

77. M. E. Haynes, "Delegation: There's More to It Than Letting Someone Else Do It," *Supervisory Management,* January 1980, p. 9.

78. Hull, "Passing the Buck."

79. Pat Weisner, "Delegating Up," *Colorado Business Magazine,* Dec. 1997, p. 9.

**Exercise 18–A
Do You Know an
Effective Leader?**

Think of someone whose leadership skills you admire. It can be in any setting—work, school, family, and so on. Use the worksheet below to evaluate his or her effectiveness.

1. In what way/s did this person "buck the system," challenge the process, or ignore the rules in leading? Explain.

    _____

    _____

    _____

2. What was this person's vision for the organization or group she or he led? In what ways did she or he inspire others to embrace that vision?

    _____

    _____

    _____

3. What are some examples of ways that this person provided information, power, or support to those she or he led? How did this create an environment that enabled others to act? If you were a follower, what impact did this environment have on you?

    _____

    _____

    _____

4. Did this person "walk the talk"? Provide an example that demonstrates this important quality of effective leadership. How important was this consistency between his or her words and deeds to others' (your) trust in him or her?

    _____

    _____

    _____

5. In what ways did this person recognize and reward his or her followers or teammates? If you were one of these individuals, what impact did this person's efforts at encouraging the heart have on your motivation to succeed?

    _____

    _____

    _____

Questions

1. Which of these five abilities is most and least critical to leaders' effectiveness? Explain.
2. Which of these five abilities do you value most? Explain.
3. When a person leads in the absence of a formal position of authority, which of these five abilities is most difficult to exhibit? Explain.

Exercise 18–B
What Is Your Self-leadership Quotient (SLQ)?

Instructions: Read over the following items and, using a scale from 0 (never) to 5 (always), rate how characteristic each is of how you approach activities at work at play. When you're done, add up your score.

Not characteristic 0—1—2—3—4—5 Very Characteristic

Setting My Course—Determining Where I Aim to Go

Getting Centered
___ 1. I check my feelings.
___ 2. I clarify what is important to me.
___ 3. I get in touch with my personal power.

Identifying Purpose
___ 4. I seek problems to solve.
___ 5. I clarify my purpose.
___ 6. I assume responsibility to act.

Deciding on Direction
___ 7. I survey the situation.
___ 8. I brainstorm what is possible.
___ 9. I envision my purpose accomplished.

Setting Goals
___ 10. I match challenges to my ability.
___ 11. I align my personal goals with my purpose.
___ 12. I set specific targets.

Traversing My Course—Getting from Here to My Destination

Establishing Milestones
___ 13. I survey my resources.
___ 14. I map out action steps.
___ 15. I establish standards of achievement.

Getting Cooperation
___ 16. I create a network of allies.
___ 17. I build team spirit.
___ 18. I share my vision.

Motivating Myself
___ 19. I create meaning in what I do.
___ 20. I measure my progress
___ 21. I reward my progress.

Enjoying the Moment
___ 22. I accentuate the positive.
___ 23. I look for satisfaction in small things.
___ 24. I get absorbed in my activities.

Staying On Course—Correcting My Course and Bypassing Obstacles

Thinking Flexibly
___ 25. I maintain a "can-do" attitude.
___ 26. I adapt my thinking to the situation.
___ 27. I avoid perfectionism.

Correcting My Course
___ 28. I identify detours.
___ 29. I make contingency plans.
___ 30. I learn from my mistakes.

Bypassing Obstacles
___ 31. I accept the challenge.
___ 32. I view problems as opportunities.
___ 33. I do something differently.

Piloting my Adventure
___ 34. I focus my attention.
___ 35. I develop strategies.
___ 36. I follow my bliss.

Scoring

144–180: Excellent—Your ability to lead yourself is outstanding. By studying the qualities you can probably become an even better self-leader as well as an outstanding leaders of others.

109–144: Good—You employ most self-leading skills. With practice you can become an excellent self-leader.

73–108: Potential—You have many self-leading skills, but employ them inconsistently. With some skill training and practice you have the potential to be an excellent self-leader.

36–72: Needs Improvement—You have many self-leading skills, but use them infrequently. If you make the effort to learn and practice the skills you can greatly improve your self-leading ability.

0–35: Deficient—You demonstrate self-leading ability and will find yourself going in circles and looking to others for direction. You probably have the capability to become a self-leader but you will have to make acquiring the skills a priority.

Exercise 18–C
It's Plane to Me

Each group will consist of five production employees and one supervisor. You will be instructed to create a paper airplane. The instructor will supply the supervisors with their instructions for their production process. Production workers are to follow the instructions provided by their supervisor. Any questions or suggestions should be discussed with your supervisor.

Questions

1. How did you feel while doing your job?
2. How do you feel about your supervisor?
3. How did you respond or react to your supervisor's instructions?
4. Would you enjoy working for this company? Why or why not?
5. What was your productivity level? What was the quality?

Exercise 18–D
Case Study: "Am I the Manager?"

Gail was hired at the apparel manufacturing company to be the office and production manager. She was very excited about her new position; the job responsibilities seemed to be a perfect fit with her skills and strengths. Her responsibilities included running the office and the ordering department and coordinating the production facilities. Larry was the owner of the company and he handled all the financial aspects of the business. L.J. was the plant manager and was Gail's direct supervisor.

On the first day of work, Larry instructed Gail to make the order and production department more efficient. Gail soon began to realize that there were a few employees in the ordering department who were very inefficient and lacking in motivation. One employee in particular, Kathy, would come in 10–20 minutes late, have several personal calls that lasted anywhere from 5–25 minutes, and refuse to answer the phones when anyone else seemed to be free. She would simply say to the other order people, "I need you to get that call; I'm busy doing my account summaries." Larry had already warned her of Kathy's unacceptable behavior and informed her that Kathy had several documented violations and notations in her personnel file. Larry felt that Gail should try to work with her, but if she was not able to change her behavior, he wanted Gail to document one final complaint and terminate her.

Gail decided to have a feedback session with Kathy, during which Kathy was very defensive yet said she would try to change her behavior. Kathy insinuated that even though she did these things, Larry liked her and he was not really bothered by them. Over the next two weeks Kathy did not change her behavior, so, with the documented results of the feedback session and the other citations in her file, Gail decided she would terminate Kathy. Kathy caused a scene in the office and ran into Larry's office. After a considerable time period, Gail was called into Larry's office. He told Gail that Kathy was not fired and that "Gail just needed to help Kathy improve upon her behaviors." Gail left the meeting feeling like she had just been undermined in front of the entire staff.

Another situation that had been developing dealt with Gail's reorganization of the production department. To gain efficiency between the ordering staff and the production department, there needed to be an order and prioritization schedule. After developing a new system, Gail proceeded to explain the new system to both the ordering department and to Maggie, the production supervisor, and her staff. Not much was said and Gail felt confident her new system would work out. Soon she discovered that nothing had changed. Maggie was making her own determinations regarding production regardless of the orders put in and prioritized by the order department. Gail went to discuss it with Maggie and the reply she got from Maggie was, "This is my department, I have been here much longer than you, and I'll have them produce what I want them to. Go cry to Larry if you don't like it. Until I hear it from Larry I will do as I please." This dream job was starting to seem more like a nightmare.

The final straw came regarding ordering materials. Gail quickly realized that they did not have the necessary materials to make the high-demand products. She worked on an inventory count with L.J. and between the two of them they were able to come up with an accurate count and an order plan to get production back on schedule. Gail then proceeded to place an order for the necessary supplies. At least she had control over something around here. Two days later, Larry called her into the office furious about the orders. "How dare you order supplies," Larry stormed. "You do not have the right to requisition materials; I handle the finances and this just put me in a bad spot with a supplier I owe money to. I make the decision on when we purchase materials. Understand?" Gail was beginning to understand all too well. She was mad, frustrated, hurt, and disillusioned all at the same time. "What have I gotten myself into with this organization?" she thought.

Questions

1. What guidelines of empowerment did Larry or Gail violate?
2. What guidelines of delegation did Larry or Gail violate.
3. What should Gail plan to discuss with Larry? What issues need to be raised?
4. What does Gail need to do to obtain the necessary elements of empowerment and delegation? What does Larry need to do to facilitate Gail's success?
5. What advice would you give to Larry and Gail regarding their working situation?

**Exercise 18–E
Empowerment
In-Basket Simulation
and Self-assessment**

Your instructor will provide the materials needed to complete this in-basket activity. Playing the role of J. Carter, a newly promoted manager in General Software Systems, you will have approximately 20 minutes to respond to a stack of memos in your in-basket. You must provide a written response to each memo, keeping in mind the person and position to whom the response is targeted. After this activity is completed, answer the following questions completely but concisely based on your experience.

1. How did you feel about your job' (playing the role of J. Carter) and the organization for which you worked? What did you like and dislike about carrying out the functions of your role?

_____

_____

_____

_____

2. What characteristics of your job and organization made you feel empowered and/or disempowered? Explain, citing specific examples.

_____

_____

_____

_____

3. If, as researchers suggest, the characteristics and behaviors of empowered people are so functional, and those of disempowered people are so dysfunctional, why don't we see more empowerment in the workplace?

_____

_____

_____

_____

4. What specific things can you do to empower your co-workers or teammates? What steps can you take to overcome disempowerment that currently exists in your work-place or team?

_____

_____

_____

_____

Source: D. Eylon & S. Herman, "Exploring Empowerment: One Method for the Classroom," _Journal of Management Education_ 23, no. 1 (1999), pp. 80–94. Copyright © 1999 by Sage Publications, Inc. Reprinted by permission of Sage Publications, Inc.

Exercise 18–F
Delegating Tasks

From a past or present job, group project, or organizational task (from a fraternity, fundraiser, committee activity), think of a task you would like to or could delegate to another person.

The task to be delegated, including all contingencies and related activities: _____

_____

_____

The goal and benefits (to me, to the delegatee) of delegating the task: _____

_____

_____

The person or persons who will be chosen (What skills, abilities, and competencies do they possess?): _____

_____

_____

Assigning the responsibilities (How will I clearly communicate all the requirements for this task? How can I motivate them to do this task?): _____

_____

_____

Transferring authority (What power must they have? Who else will need to be informed? What parameters will be set for limitations?): _____

_____

_____

Establishing accountability (What are the rewards and consequences? How will comple-tion be measured? What are the standards for completion?): _____

_____

_____

Establishing responsibility (What degree of responsibility will I give? What level of delega-tion will I use and why?): _____

_____

_____

Establishing controls (What control mechanisms will I need to develop? When and how will I evaluate progress?): _____

_____

_____

Questions

1. What will be the most difficult aspect of this delegation for you?
2. What potential problems, barriers, or consequences can you foresee for this delegation?
3. What other steps or aspects must be taken into consideration to make this an effective delegation?
4. What unanticipated developments could occur to impact task accomplishment?

**Exercise 18–G
In Their Own
Words . . .**

Interview a manager about the way she or he empowers employees. (You might need to define the term for them.) Ask them questions such as:

- How many direct reports do you have?
- Do you consider them to be effective performers? Why or why not?
- Do you consider them to be trustworthy? Why or why not?
- In what ways do you empower your employees?
- Is this process successful? Why or why not?
- If you were called out on a two-week assignment, is there an employee you would feel comfortable putting in charge of your unit? Why or why not?
- What concerns would you have in doing so?
- In what ways does an empowering management philosophy help or hinder your success as a manager?

Based on his or her answers, would you say this manager used empowerment successfully? Defend your answer with examples shared in your interview.

**Exercise 18–H
Reflection/Action
Plan**

This chapter focused on leadership and empowerment—what they are, why they're important, and how to improve your skills in these areas. Complete the worksheet below upon completing all reading and experiential activities for this chapter.

1. The one or two areas in which I am most strong are:

   _____

   _____

   _____

   _____

2. The one or two areas in which I need more improvement are:

   _____

   _____

   _____

   _____

3. If I did only one thing to improve in this area, it would be to:

   _____

   _____

   _____

   _____

4. Making this change would probably result in:

   _____

   _____

   _____

   _____

5. If I did not change or improve in this area, it would probably affect my personal and professional life in the following ways:

   _____

   _____

   _____

   _____

Project Management

Learning Points

How do I:

- Keep projects on track?
- Help my team meet deadlines?
- Ensure project members agree on and maintain the necessary standards or quality?
- Handle multiple projects simultaneously?
- Incorporate my personal project time lines into my professional project time lines?
- Keep long-term objectives in mind while working on day-to-day objectives?
- Handle unexpected events that interfere with my preplanned schedule?

Carol Marshall is a bright young engineer in a large manufacturing facility. Although she's been out of college for three years, she's been promoted twice and is now in a supervisory position. She is very comfortable with projects in which she is the key contributor. She has high work standards and always goes the extra mile to bring projects in on time and budget. Working autonomously, she has developed good systems that allowed her to accumulate an enviable success record. Her managers, noticing her leadership potential, have given her a very important task force to oversee. A lot depends on the results of the task force.

Carol has devoted a lot of energy to the task force. She has helped them build confidence in and rapport with each other. She has involved the group in several social gatherings to strengthen their comfort level in working with each other. She has good communication with the group as a whole and with each of the five other group members. They've been together for four months, and the deadline for their task force deliverable is drawing near. Carol heard two weeks ago that they were on schedule and today she's expecting to see the final report.

In looking over the project report, Carol is shocked to discover the development subcommittee is behind schedule and needs more time to complete the final report. Carol is worried; she has a presentation to senior management scheduled for the end of the week. There's no way she's going to be ready by then. She wonders, "What happened? What could I have done differently? How come this always happens?" She concludes she's not cut out for supervision and thinks she needs to go to her managers and request a reassignment. "From now on," she mutters, "I'll just do important things like this on my own. I'm not going to depend on anyone else but me."

1. Why was Carol left in this situation?
2. What could Carol have done over the four months to ensure timely completion of the project?
3. Do you think Carol should give up supervision? Why or why not?
4. Has something like this ever happened to you before? How did you react? What did you learn from this experience?

"Plan the work. Work the plan."

This old saying is the cornerstone of management today. If you don't plan, you will be so busy reacting to situations that you will not have time to take advantage of new opportunities.[1] It's easy for most people to develop plans. What separates successful plans from unsuccessful ones is the implementation. For a plan to become reality, it needs to be operationalized—brought to life. This chapter introduces the concept of project management and discusses how this concept can be used to organize projects and assignments that are managed by teams. The definition and importance of project management, steps involved in managing projects, and strategies and tips for honing your project management skills are discussed. We also include information on tools available to help you manage projects.

What Is Project Management?

Have you ever been involved in a team project where team members had different definitions of quality? Or different interpretations of the phrase "on time"? Or where everyone procrastinated until the last minute? When used effectively, project management can help prevent or reduce the likelihood of these problems. **Project management** is the coordination of your work and that of others such that organizational objectives can be achieved while meeting time, budget, and quality standards or expectations.[2]

Project management is a systematic process through which almost all the steps involved in starting and completing a project are anticipated and outlined in advance.[3] We use the word "almost" because no one can predict everything that will happen between the present and the project deadline. In project management, the known steps are anticipated and accounted for; in addition, the schedule includes some "slack" to account for unforeseen difficulties or events that invariably arise. Project management involves tracking a project from its inception to completion. This includes scheduling steps, allocating tasks to various team members, creating and overseeing time and financial budgets for projects, monitoring progress made toward goals, and overall project resource management.

Why Project Management?

In today's rapidly changing and highly competitive workplace, managers are being asked to reduce costs while increasing productivity. This imperative forces managers to develop new models of operating for every aspect of the organization.[4] One way to "do more with less" is to encourage employees to be efficient in plotting their work flow, whether on independent or team-based projects. As employees work increasingly in teams, it is essential to have a system to help team members work collectively on a project that has multiple milestones or deadlines. This is especially true when individual members are involved in multiple projects. They, and their managers, must juggle many balls simultaneously. Being involved in multiple individual and team-based projects, project managers and project team members have a lot—perhaps too much—on their plates today. Project planning and management becomes essential as project managers attempt to adapt to changing technology, coordinate with multiple people and departments, meet financial goals, and manage business strategy while simultaneously monitoring multiple projects with day-, week-, or year-long or more time spans. And all of this must get done while getting the day-to-day work done![5]

Projects that encompass many tasks and run over several weeks or months require planning and coordination with other projects and activities, both personal and professional. As a manager or employee, your ongoing job priorities and commitments have to be factored in when planning new projects. The same is true for students. Coursework and extra assignments need to be incorporated into your plans, as do personal commitments. Vacations, medical appointments, sports competitions, community involvement, carpooling, child care, and elder care are examples of personal commitments that should be taken into account when planning project schedules either independently or with others.

Benefits of Project Management

Applying a project management approach to your work has numerous benefits for organizations and individuals. We've mentioned the need to "do more with less" or perhaps "work smart, not hard." Project management helps organizations do this and ensures that:

■ *Resources such as time, money, and personnel are appropriately allocated to the organization's numerous priorities and objectives.*[6] Through advance planning, individual project calendars can be adjusted to be in sync with other organization commitments. For example, in planning a major new product rollout, a company can ensure that it occurs at a time when other projects aren't absorbing needed time and energy of the managers and employees involved in the rollout effort.[7]

■ *Long-term objectives can be kept in mind while short-term objectives are being implemented.* Through thinking strategically about an organization's long-term objectives, short-term activities that help move the organization toward the longer-term goal can be planned and implemented. Using project management, a company can ensure that weekly or monthly tasks and objectives—in addition to those responsible for them—are included in plans that support a new marketing strategy. If a company strives to expand sales by 20 percent by adding an online business to complement its brick and mortar business within two years, it could set up multiple milestones that track this progress. Within 3 months, content for the website is researched; within 6 months, the website is up and running; within one year, sales should increase by 5 percent; within 18 months, sales should increase by 15 percent, and so on.

■ *Contingencies can be anticipated.* By articulating in advance the known steps to complete a project and building in some slack in the schedule, each unanticipated event that occurs during the project time line does not have to be treated as a crisis that affects the ultimate deadline or deliverable. Let's say a company is implementing a new integrated computer system that tracks inventory, sales, costs, and operations. The consultants who are installing the package estimate that complete installation and implementation will take eight months. This includes installation of software, training all employees, testing and debugging the system, and making modifications. For project planning purposes, it's best to add 10 to 20 percent additional time to each phase. This will ensure that slack is built into the schedule to accommodate the unexpected, such as incompatibility with previous hardware, heavier than usual sales, or vacations and holidays. By allocating extra time to projects at the outset, you have a better chance of getting ahead of your workload and staying there.[8] Sarah Gavit, an experienced project manager at NASA's Jet Propulsion Laboratory, notes, "Manage the risk. There always will be certain parts more susceptible to going wrong. Before we ever lay out a schedule, we look at four or five areas with high risk. We develop contingency plans and watch extra closely. Other project managers sometimes don't look until they're up against the wall."[9]

■ *Project output is made more consistent.* By developing quality standards in advance, team members, managers, and employees have the opportunity to discuss and clarify their perceptions of the project objectives and their expectations for the end product, or project deliverable(s). For example, when developing a new interviewer training program, a company can outline the legal requirements, research industry benchmarks or best practices, and develop a set of specifications for the project that all members of the planning team agree to in advance. By getting all involved on board before any project output is generated, the quality of the components comprising the end product will be higher and more harmonious than if everyone established his or her own quality standards independently.

Project management has numerous benefits for the individuals involved as well as the organization. In addition to enabling individuals to be more efficient and organized, through project planning and management:

■ *Collegiality is enhanced.* Through meeting with other team members and organizational employees who have a stake in the success of a project, you have the opportunity to build relationships that contribute to a sense of belonging in the organization.[10] Let's say you are part of a group tasked with implementing a new budget tracking system for the company. By meeting regularly as a team and with department heads and other stakeholders, you are able to form relationships that contribute to the success of the project at hand and last beyond the duration of the project. These relationships facilitate your knowledge and understanding of where you and your work fit with that of others in the organization. This enhances your perspective and enables you to think more globally in how you do your work. In addition, by being connected or networked with others in the organization, trust and helping behaviors—part of collegiality—are increased.[11]

■ *Morale is enhanced.* No one likes feeling that they're all alone in overcoming a mountain of work at the office. Planning work in advance and achieving the desired outcome successfully boosts your morale and the morale of others involved in the effort. For example, tackling a thorny problem such as designing a new budget monitoring system can be a tedious task. When the various components of the task are articulated, planned for, and carried out systematically and incrementally, what might be an overwhelming task appears more manageable. And when you are able to make progress on this task— even one small component at a time—your self-efficacy increases along with your morale. "Projects that succeed are just about the most satisfying work experience you can have. It's as much fun as you can have and still get paid," notes Steve McMenamin, Vice President of Customer Service at Southern California Edison Co.[12]

■ *Job satisfaction is increased.* Once we have mastered the basics of any job, many of us want more. Once we prove our capabilities, many people want to be involved in greater levels of responsibility, more variety of work, and more complex work.[13] Being involved in multiple projects or tasks affords you this opportunity to stretch and grow further and, as a result, experience enhanced job satisfaction. Let's say that in recognition for your outstanding capabilities as a waitress, the owner of a busy restaurant asks you to participate in a task force that is evaluating ways to improve customer service. Project management gives you the tools needed to juggle both roles simultaneously, facilitating your ability to take on both roles and, in so doing, increasing your ability multitask and contribute to the organization beyond your daily job.

■ *Learning is enhanced.* Project management results in learning about others' jobs and work styles, not just your own. Working with others on projects increases your understanding of how your and others' roles and responsibilities fit into the whole. This increases your knowledge of the complexities and interdependencies in the organization, enabling you to make more substantive and appropriate contributions to the organization's success. For example, you might be involved in a group project at school where the ultimate deliverable is a presentation on a cutting-edge business topic. By planning the project in advance with other team members, you exchange ideas about preferred ways to approach the project, manage time, communicate with each other, make decisions, and solve problems. This collaboration increases everyone's skills and knowledge base.

■ *Creativity and synergy are enhanced.* Through planning a project in advance with your manager and team members, you are more likely to envision a new way to approach the situation than if you simply did the work in the same way it's always been done. Imagine you are part of a team charged with implementing a membership expansion campaign for a fraternity. By planning the project in advance, you can ask big-picture questions such as, "What do we want to accomplish?" "How can we do things better than before?" "What worked and what didn't work previously?" "Ideally what would we like the new program to look like?" By brainstorming with other team members to answer these questions, you're likely to tap into the synergistic potential that resides in most diverse groups. This process energizes a group toward identifying more creative, innovative, and better solutions than could have been produced by any one team member working on his or her own.

Let's face it. Despite, or perhaps because of, all the technology that is now available, working today is harder and more pressure filled than ever. The average workday for today's white-collar worker is longer today than it was in the 1960s.[14] With the availability of e-mail, fax machines, and voice mail, our expectations for quick turnaround have changed from a week or so to an hour or two! Customers want service now. Managers want deliverables yesterday. With all this pressure, it's a wonder that any projects with a time line of more than a few days get done. Managing projects can be tedious and time-consuming work. The time that an organization or individual invests in planning will yield paybacks and returns through reduced implementation time and costs.[15] A project management mindset can serve as a way to spread the work around, making working on projects more effective and enjoyable.

Eight Steps to Managing Projects

The eight steps for managing projects (see Figure 19–1) can help you clarify, organize, and implement projects or complex tasks. First, we must define *what* we are managing before we plan *how* we manage it.

Step One—Define Project Objectives and Scope

As a group, discuss the goals of the project. What deliverables and outcomes are expected? What would you ideally like to accomplish? The answers to these questions may be different. If so, focus first on the essentials or must haves, and then, if there is room in the schedule, incorporate the optionals or nice to haves. For example an essential element would be to meet the deadline imposed by the instructor or manager. An optional element would be to have deliverables prepared a week ahead of time. After going through all the steps of project management, you'll then be able to assess whether getting done a week early is possible.

Figure 19–1
Steps to Managing Projects

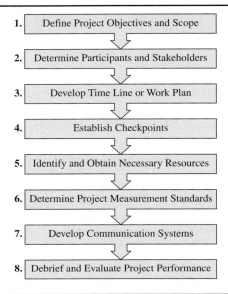

1. Define Project Objectives and Scope
2. Determine Participants and Stakeholders
3. Develop Time Line or Work Plan
4. Establish Checkpoints
5. Identify and Obtain Necessary Resources
6. Determine Project Measurement Standards
7. Develop Communication Systems
8. Debrief and Evaluate Project Performance

Project Management in Action[16]

Pam Statz, an analyst for HotWired—a company that creates and manages websites for other entities—used to struggle with reaching deadline until her department began using project management. Pam and her staff would continually fall short of expected deadlines because they were unable to work together toward stated objectives. They would also have to spend their weekends and late nights in the office to try and accomplish their goals. Once they installed and began using Microsoft Project, specific objectives were defined as was the person responsible for achieving them. It focused the department on using a time line and plan to follow. The project management tools and approach provided a means for the group members to communicate and share files without having to be physically together. Project management enabled Pam's department to become a cohesive unit that met their deadlines in a relatively stress-free manner. It also enabled HotWired to efficiently and effectively design websites—and satisfy their customers—often before project deadlines.

■ Relate the project goals to overall organizational goals and strategy. For example, if your team's goal is to produce a set of recommendations for consideration by senior management, determine your boss's objectives—as well as those of his or her boss—to ensure your project goals support the organization's broader goals. Without taking this step, you risk "doing things right" instead of "doing the right things."

■ Clarify the scope of the project. Making recommendations is not the same as implementing them. Aside from the time required, these differing outcome expectations can be a source of frustration and chaos for a team.

■ Clarify project objectives with the project manager or instructor to ensure everyone's on the same page about the expected outcome. This might surprise you, but the phrase "zero defects" means different things to different people. Quality of 99.9 percent is impressive, unless you consider that a .1 percent error rate equates, for example, to Americans consuming over 14,000 cans of "bad" soda in a single year. The clarification of project objectives and scope can be one of the most critical steps in the process of project management.

Step Two—Determine Project Participants and Stakeholders

Now that you are clear about what to do, it makes sense to consider who should be included in the project. Even though some people may not seem necessary at first, the fact that their work or organization is affected by the outcomes of the project, thereby making them **stakeholders,** may suggest that their inclusion is more important than you might think. Key considerations for this stage include the following:

■ Make sure that vital employees and teammates are made and kept a part of the project and that key stakeholders—those who have a stake in the outcome such as your manager or instructor—are either involved in or kept apprised of the group's efforts throughout the project.[17] For example, a functional organization charged with procuring materials for projects became frustrated with a system that took anywhere from four weeks to 18 months to obtain even simple, low-cost items. The group worked together and devised a new system designed to save countless hours and, hence, costs. But they weren't done. The proposed system required extensive changes in the way accounts payable did its work. The group presented their plan to their management as well as members of accounts payable, and then asked representatives from the latter to join their group to flesh out the details and then implement the new system. Had they not included this step, the group might have faced an uphill battle—even though their proposed new system could save valuable resources.

■ Once the project group has been assembled, begin a master calendar on which members' availability (and lack thereof) is noted. Indicate specific dates in which one or more of the team members will not be available to work on the project. Holidays, vacation days, anticipated personal days, travel days, meeting days, or commitments to other projects should be noted and accounted for when designating project steps and entering to do items on the project calendar. Some dates may have to be skipped completely if key group members are unavailable, while others may be okay to include as long as tasks performed by others are unaffected by individual absences.

- Discuss what the group members' interests are—their strengths and desired contributions to the project. One might volunteer to contribute by doing research, another by doing data entry, and a third by doing analysis, and so on. Two things for the team to consider: (1) if possible, allow members not only to do what they do best but also afford them the opportunity to develop other skills, and (2) if individuals don't volunteer, or if all members lack needed skills, roles will have to be assigned regardless of personal interest or strengths. For example, give someone with a computer background the chance to take on a marketing role if possible and if the person desires. While he or she may be better equipped to prepare the final report or presentation, allowing members to stretch and possibly cross functional lines builds their skills for future projects.

- Consider the team members' planning and organizing skills. Discuss expectations regarding meeting project deadlines as well as what each person can contribute to the task. When allocating project steps to specific team members, assign tasks that stretch but don't overextend any one team member.

Step Three—Develop a TimeLine or Work Plan

The next step is to create a specific plan that takes into account all the various steps—large and small—as well as the relationship among the steps. For example, in building a car, you would never install the headrests before installing the seats. Figure 19–2 shows a work plan for a five-member team presentation project. It includes all the steps necessary to complete the project, a time frame to allow for completion of the project, and assignment of responsibilities for individual team members. Some tactics for developing a timeline or work plan include these:

- Working with a large blackboard, whiteboard, easel and newsprint, or computer program (something that can be seen by all involved), begin brainstorming all the steps that will be needed to complete the project. If possible, start with the end goal and work backwards from there. This process is called **backscheduling** and involves looking backward from a target date, beginning with your goal or objective and then plotting out the means to achieve it. This is done by:

1. Identifying the individual tasks necessary to achieve the objective.

2. Estimating how long it will take you to complete each task and determining the best time to do it.

3. Listing each task on a calendar, appropriately backdating each task from the project due date.[18]

Figure 19–2 Sample Work Plan

Project: Team presentation on business topic of current interest

Due Date: December 3

Team Members' Names and Initials: James Smith (JS), Mary Conover (MC), Jesse Baron (JB), Nomi Hussein (NH), Maria Santanella (MS)

Step	Date	Initials
1. Meet with team; decide topic	10/8	All
2. Discuss key components of topic	10/12	All
3. Assign individual research topics	10/15	MS
4. Re-group to share results	10/29	All
5. Further research and develop outline	11/5	JS, MC
6. E-mail to group to solicit and incorporate feedback	11/12	JS, MC
7. Develop presentation and share draft with others, edit	11/19	JB, NH
8. Plan presentation, prepare slides, and share with group	11/26	MS
9. Rehearse	11/29	All
10. Prepare copies for distribution	12/1	JB
11. Present	12/3	All
12. Arrange, have debrief and lunch session	12/5	NH

Let's take you away from business to share an example of backscheduling. If you were preparing a meal, the Spanish *paella* to be exact, you wouldn't put all the ingredients in at the same time. This complex dish includes meats (sausage, chicken), seafood (fish, shrimp, mussels), and vegetables (carrots, peppers), each of which has an optimal cooking time. If you were planning to serve the dish in 40 minutes, you would put the meats in first, as they would take the longest to cook. Then you'd add the vegetables, and finally the seafood. Shrimp that has cooked for 40 minutes tastes mushy, and the fish would fall apart and taste dried out. If you put the meats in last, say with only 10 minutes to go, you may subject your guests to undercooked meats (and the problems that brings). When you backschedule, you determine what happens last, next to last, next to next to last, and so on. For the example in Figure 19–2, the team would need to start with the presentation date and work backwards to determine when they would need to begin the project to ensure quality and timely completion. By doing so, they would determine that they will need eight weeks to allow for successfully creating this particular presentation.

If the project is complex and it's easier to start at the beginning, do so. List each step and allocate all steps to specific dates on the calendar. Realize that some tasks are serial (one must precede another) while others are parallel (two noninterrelated tasks that can occur simultaneously).

■ Determine and specify the dependencies that exist between all the tasks, participants, and activities in a project plan. Each step relates to others in the plan. Understanding these interrelationships can help the group know where potential problems could arise or where a delay or lag could change the process.[19] If employees at the manufacturer supplying the upholstery material for the car seats are on strike, this impacts not only car seat readiness, but also the installation of the headrests.

■ As a group, clarify the objectives when specific tasks are assigned. Clearly communicate the expected deliverables and the desired results. Monitor tasks delegated and record to whom specific tasks are allotted. Set precise and realistic deadlines for short-term deliverables, adjusting the timeline as necessary throughout the project.

■ Build in time for the unexpected. Planning and communication with teammates are essential here. Watch for the tendency to try to make up losses late in the project cycle. It's not atypical for a project to stay on schedule for the first 80 percent of the time and then fall apart due to overconfidence ("We're practically done"), reduced attention to the schedule ("We know what we have to do . . . who needs to see the schedule?"), or just procrastination. Once group members recognize this slippage, they stress and rush to completion, resulting in lower quality output than would have been the case had the original timeline been adhered to. Many people and teams grossly underestimate the time needed toward the end to complete details that bring a final deliverable up to quality standards. Let's say your team is assembling a report based on a survey conducted over a six-month time period. Who's going to check the accuracy of the data? Who will proofread? Edit? Check for content? Run the report by the research and legal departments? Share a preview copy with a few stakeholders to ensure buy-in? Copy and prepare presentation materials, or ensure they're available online? All these minute details take much more time than most people imagine. It's wise to build them into the schedule from the outset of the project.

Talking through these kinds of details with a project group has several benefits. It helps the group become realistic about what can and cannot be accomplished. It helps individuals think of additional steps that might otherwise have been omitted from the planning phase. And it helps team members to begin defining in real terms the quality standards for the project.

■ Avoid the tendency to wait until late in the project to buy time for these important details. Budget for them up front. Stay vigilant and look at the whole project to determine where time can be bought earlier on in the process. Taking time for this discussion will pay off in a higher quality outcome, and with less stress than "winging it!"[20]

■ Some final advice from a veteran project manager. "Be very flexible. In this day where we're on these faster, better, cheaper programs, with very high turnaround and very high-risk technologies, you can come up with a great master plan, but things never go according to plan. You have to be flexible when changes come in to rapidly replan and not be discouraged by it."[21] The goal of your project is set, but the action plan or means of getting to your end result must constantly be adapted to address deviations from the original path. Effective project managers recognize when and how to change directions as well as to ask for help when extra resources are needed.[22]

Step Four—Establish Checkpoints and Control Mechanisms

Step four involves setting up a series of checkpoints, or points at which progress on the project will be checked, and entering these onto the project calendar. Even after your group lists all the tasks, identifies interdependencies, and assigns specific due dates, it is wise to establish periodic checkpoints. These may be progress meetings where members can check status, clarify expectations, or raise issues. If unanticipated problems arise, these checkpoint meetings can be used to problem-solve and make necessary adjustments to the schedule.

■ Evaluate your project for important steps or tasks to be completed and insert interim deadlines or checkpoints in the project plan. In step three, we broke the project into smaller tasks or objectives. In this step, break these down further into milestones or incremental steps in order to determine when checks and tests should be completed. For example, break a 30-day project into three 10-day subsections, instituting a checkpoint after each one. This will help to shorten the time between when an error or misunderstanding occurs and when it can be discovered and corrected.[23] It will also help to prevent or reduce the possibility of time line slippage.

■ Review and update the project plan regularly. Monitor other projects and events that might interfere with your project schedule and adjust accordingly. One suggestion is to post the project plan in an area visible to all group members. Don't confine the schedule to the conference room in which you meet only monthly. Instead, put it in a hallway that all members pass through, such as the hallway to the bathroom or breakroom. By keeping the plan highly visible, potential interferences and problems can be raised and dealt with before they impact the expected outcomes.

Step Five—Identify and Obtain Necessary Resources

Project managers and their teams must identify and obtain the resources that are needed to complete the project within the specified time frame, cost parameters, or budget in order to meet quality standards. It is therefore necessary to:

■ Look through the tasks and objectives and discuss what will be required to carry out the assignment. Be realistic about what can be accomplished given the resources available and time constraints inherent in the project; this will facilitate effective **resource management** over the course of the project. If your group anticipates a shortfall of personnel, budget, time, computer support, administrative support, or supplies, now is the time—before you roll up your sleeves and begin the project—to discuss these needs with your manager. If the resources can be provided, great. If not, it's important to "push back" on management and negotiate which elements of the deliverable can be achieved, given the resources available. Don't assume you can get these resources later. Get what you need before you start or, if the resources are not forthcoming, manage stakeholders' expectations about the group's ability to achieve a desired outcome.

■ Know when to let a project go or when to start over. Sometimes a project team discovers early on that the project expectation is unrealistic or the scope of the project is more complex than originally envisioned. Perhaps the team thought its job was to make recommendations when their manager saw the task as ending with implementation of the recommendations. These perceptions differ substantially. Or perhaps a pilot project is expanded to include the entire organization. The project team might need to reconsider its objectives and change course. If this happens to you, consult with your manager or instructor. Perhaps the task can be reconceived. Don't let politics, pride, or the thought of failure keep you from asking for help or from scrapping a project that is not going to contribute to the organization. Use active decision making throughout to help you make these determinations.[24] Communicate frequently and clearly about these determinations with appropriate stakeholders.

Step Six—Determine How Project Results Will Be Measured

Before the project starts, understand how the project will be evaluated and who will assess it. This will ensure that steps are built into the process to obtain the data needed to evaluate the success of the project. If your group's task is to improve customer satisfaction, how will you know whether you've done it? Are they happier? Do they file fewer complaints? Is the wait time for help shorter? Especially in a case like this, your group might first have to measure and establish a baseline. How do you know if the wait time is shorter after your recommendations are implemented if you don't assess the wait time before you begin? In some organizations, teams are rewarded with a percentage of total savings—another good reason to establish and assess results.

Step Seven—Set Up an Ongoing Communication System

There is no substitute for effective communication in project management. Typically, projects get in trouble when people are unsure of their role or responsibilities relative to other roles and responsibilities. To avoid confusion, members must see over the horizon and convey to others their ideas, perceptions, and the objective with clarity and confidence. It also requires listening skills. It's important to:

■ Communicate with team members and stakeholders. The ability to deal with people—using your interpersonal skills—can be the primary factor in the success of a project.[25] Important skills to use throughout the process are listening, giving and receiving feedback, persuasion, delegation, seeing things from another's perspective, and getting people to respond to you.[26]

■ Start the project with face-to-face or telephone contact if possible. This is important for both traditional and virtual teams. Research shows that e-mail contact can occur once the group is formed and people are clear on their roles and responsibilities. Misunderstanding is less likely to occur when members are able to meet and fully discuss project expectations and concerns in real time, with the benefit of nonverbal language.

■ Meet regularly (in person or virtually) to check on project status and progress. Meetings can keep a project on task by enabling members to check and recheck their understanding of dates and deliverables. To be effective, meetings should be primarily decision oriented. In addition to sharing status, meetings can be used to maintain agreed-upon deadlines, discuss changes that might be necessary in the plan or work schedule, address questions and issues, and clarify roles and expectations.

■ Revisit initial decisions made by the group if they are not working. An important aspect of project management is continuously reviewing the initial prioritization of steps. Continuously cross-check all interrelated project components to make sure that the critical aspects and requirements are being implemented. Constantly review and modify where necessary, ensuring your ability to deliver what is promised by your deadlines.[27]

■ Keep people informed by issuing progress reports. This can be done face to face, but written methods (e.g., an e-mail sent to the team) may provide an easier and more efficient means for tracking individual and collective progress. Err on the side of going overboard on updating people on how your objectives or tasks are measuring up to the goals of the project.[28]

Figure 19–3
Project Management
Tips from Bill Gates[29]

1. Choose carefully. Projects should be large enough to be worthwhile and should suit your skills and qualifications.
2. Establish a realistic time line.
3. Let employees know how important the project is.
4. Keep employees informed and involved so they understand the constraints under which they're operating.
5. Meet across boundaries—involve people from various parts of the organization if possible.
6. Keep in touch with the progress and morale of the crew.
7. Share bad news and information when things aren't going well—don't keep employees in the dark.
8. Make trade-off decisions crisply to minimize big changes, but be flexible to adjust to marketplace developments and changes.
9. Know when to give up.
10. Breed healthy competition.

■ Ensure a positive, open atmosphere. Provide encouragement throughout the project. If the project occurs over an extended period of time, plan some fun get-togethers to build camaraderie, trust, and rapport among team members.

■ Monitor performance and catch problems early on. If this is not done, you risk marginalization, wherein the poor performers bring down the group's standards rather than the other way around. Since a change to a single step can have a ripple effect on the whole project and system, communicating instantly is critical in keeping projects on time and on budget.[30] Providing constructive feedback as soon as possible can do this. A good project manager will be able to question others and give feedback without alienating the members.[31]

■ Give less experienced team members more initial attention and direction. As they acquire experience and confidence, you can be less involved in overseeing their work.

■ Be clear on accountability and clarify where overall responsibility for the ultimate quality of each deliverable lies. Make sure everyone understands and is held accountable for the responsibilities they assume.

■ Develop records that document the group's progress on the project. This will help the group stay on track without having to replicate earlier discussions. This also aids future groups working on similar projects. The records can be print or electronic and should include the original project plan and changes that are made, meeting schedules and minutes, team to-do lists, memos and e-mail correspondence, and samples of interim and final deliverables.

Step Eight—Debrief and Evaluate the Process and Results at Project End

Remember that all processes and efforts can be improved. Keep notes of lessons learned throughout the process and share them with group members at the end of the project. Discuss what worked well and what didn't. Discuss what everyone learned from the group's mistakes and how similar mistakes can be prevented in future team projects. This allows for all involved to offer feedback and to share ideas for improving group behaviors and processes in the future.

Project Management Tools

Several tools are available to help you track progress on projects. One of the more common and simple tools is the **Gantt chart.** Named after its developer, Henry Gantt, this chart describes the temporal relationships of events of tasks that unfold over time.[32] It can also show projected and actual schedules. Figure 19–4 shows how another project team engaged in project management when given the same task as the team in Figure 19–2. From this chart, the team can track the planned activities, control individual activities, and identify delays or deviations from the original plan. The team can see where they have lost time and can plan and make adjustments to complete the project on time. The Gantt chart will also be helpful when debriefing the project and team process for future improvements on their next assignment.

To make a Gantt chart,

1. Brainstorm all the tasks necessary to complete the final project.

2. Reorganize this list in order from beginning to ending tasks.

3. Create a grid (or use graph paper) wherein the columns represent weeks (or days if the project is very short) and the rows represent specific tasks. Plan to post this where all group project members can see it.

4. List each task in order and estimate the time needed to complete each task. Traditionally, this would be represented by a rectangle whose endpoints show the start and finish time of the task; the longer the rectangle, the longer it would take to complete this task.

5. You could also include two rows for each task—one that shows the projected or planned time (using an opaque rectangle) and one that shows the actual time (using a shaded rectangle).

While it may not be critical to have the planned and actual schedules on a Gantt chart, adding the actual schedule helps in at least two ways. First, you will be able to make

Figure 19–4
A Gantt Chart on the Development of a Team Presentation

		Week	1	2	3	4	5	6	7	8	9
1	Decide Topic	Plan	▓								
		Actual	░								
2	Research Topic	Plan	▓								
		Actual	░								
3	Meet to Share Results	Plan		▓							
		Actual		░	░						
4	Further Research and Develop Outline	Plan		▓							
		Actual			░	░					
5	Get Team Feedback and Incorporate Ideas	Plan			▓						
		Actual				░					
6	Develop Presentation and Discuss Draft	Plan				▓					
		Actual									
7	Plan Presentation, Develop Slides	Plan					▓				
		Actual									
8	Rehearse Presentation	Plan					▓				
		Actual									
9	Prepare Audience Handouts	Plan						▓			
		Actual									
10	Present	Plan						▓			
		Actual									
11	Prepare and Pass Out Evaluation	Plan						▓			
		Actual									
12	Debrief	Plan						▓			
		Actual									

real-time adjustments to the schedule, especially when a preceding, interdependent task was delayed in starting or finishing. Second, the comparisons will help in the overall project debrief and provide feedback and lessons learned for future projects and planning.

Another common tool used in project management is the **PERT (Program Evaluation and Review Technique)** chart. A PERT chart diagrams all the steps involved in completing a project and estimates the length of time needed in each phase of the project. By mapping out tasks in a flowchart pattern, the PERT helps identify sequences of dependent activities (see Figure 19–5).[33] It answers the questions of what are the most optimistic estimates of the time to complete the project under the best conditions, what's the most pessimistic under the worst conditions, and what is the most likely under normal conditions.[34] The PERT process can also determine the longest anticipated single line of activity from start to finish,[35] which is known as **critical path method (CPM).**

To make a PERT chart and determine the critical path:[36]

1. Define the project and all of its significant activities and tasks.

2. Develop the relationships among the activities. Decide which activities must precede and follow others.

Figure 19–5
PERT Chart for Development of Team Presentation

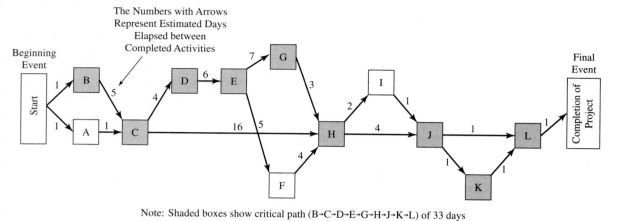

Note: Shaded boxes show critical path (B→C→D→E→G→H→J→K→L) of 33 days

3. Draw the network connecting all the activities.
4. Assign time and/or cost estimates to each activity.
5. Compute the longest time path through the network; this is called the critical path.
6. Use the network to help plan, schedule, monitor, and control the project.

The critical path represents tasks and activities that, if delayed, will cause the entire project to be delayed. Teams can use this information to identify noncritical tasks for replanning, rescheduling, and reallocating resources to gain flexibility and allow for alterations. Therefore, PERT and CPM can play a major part in controlling a project. Figure 19–5 illustrates a team presentation project showing the relationship between the activities and the estimated time needed to complete the presentation. The critical path shows that they will need a minimum of 33 days to complete all the steps and identifies which steps are critical and which ones have some slack time.

Both of these methods are immensely helpful in planning out a project. By creating either chart, most groups discover missing steps, clarify whether the anticipated time line is realistic (or not), and identify critical dependencies and resources. One recommendation for creating a first draft Gantt or PERT chart is to use Post-Its or other easily movable notes. Since so many hidden tasks or issues arise in the building of these charts, the use of Post-Its can reduce group members' frustration in the process. Software programs can also be used to create PERT charts; the team identifies the tasks and time estimates, and the programs prepare the charts.

Numerous Web-oriented software programs are available. These programs enable group members to enter tasks, estimate time lines and other dependencies, and create the project management chart.[37] One benefit of these programs is that changes—added tasks, modified time lines—create instant adjustments to the overall schedule, enabling members to see the immediate impact of a midterm slippage. Another benefit is that many of these programs can be "connected" to company systems, enabling stakeholders such as department heads and customers to access information on how a project that concerns them is progressing, while the project team maintains control over the project.[38] This allows for others, besides the team members, to participate and have easy access to project information. Of course, as is true of any computer program, their availability does not replace the need for human interaction. Keeping people informed through personal contact is an important complement to electronic communication about project status.[39]

Summary

In today's environment, company and individual success comes more readily to those who can do more with less while working smarter, not harder. One way to do this is to make effective use of project management skills and tools. This becomes especially important when you are involved in one or more complex projects. Taking time to clarify project expectations, determine contributors and stakeholders, establish specific objectives or milestones, create contingency plans, and communicate regularly with stakeholders are among the steps needed to make all your projects a success. In the final analysis, others expect project outcomes or deliverables—on time and on budget—not excuses or explanations!

Key Terms and Concepts

Backscheduling

Critical path method (CPM)

Gantt chart

Program Evaluation and Review
   Technique (PERT)

Project management

Project time line

Resource management

Stakeholders

Work plan

Endnotes

1. David L. Coles, "Step Back to Get Ahead; The Key to Completing Projects on Time Is Working Backward from Your Deadlines," *Coles and Associates,* March–April 1988, p. 14.

2. Joe E. Beck, Worley Johnson, and R. Steve Konkel, "Project Management Insights," *Occupational Health and Safety,* June 2000, p. 22.

3. Alexander Laufer, "Project Planning: Timing Issues and Path of Progress," *Project Management Journal,* June 1991, p. 39.

4. Robert D. Landel and J. Robb Dixon, "Assessing the Potential for Office-Productivity Improvement," *Operations Management Review,* Fall 1983, pp. 3–8.

5. Kathleen Melymuka, "Born to Lead Projects: Some People Have Innate Talents for Managing Projects," *Computerworld,* March 27, 2000, p. 62.

6. Howard Millman, "On Track and in Touch," *Computerworld,* June 26, 2000, p. 88.

7. Sonia Tellez, "Think Globally When Designing a PM Solution," *Computing Canada,* Dec. 10, 1999, p. 28.

8. Coles, "Step Back."

9. Quoted in article by Kathleen Melymuka, "Project Management Top Guns," *Computerworld,* Oct. 20, 1997, pp. 108–109.

10. Lawrence Todryk, "The Project Manager as Team Builder: Creating an Effective Team," *Project Management Journal,* Dec. 1990, p. 17.

11. M. C. Higgins, "The More the Merrier? Multiple Developmental Relationships and Work Satisfaction," *Journal of Management Development,* 19, no. 4 (2000), pp. 277–296.

12. Melymuka, "Project Management Top Guns."

13. See J. Richard Hackman, "Motivation through the Design of Work—Test a Theory," *Organizational Behavior and Human Performance,* Aug. 1976, p. 250; J. R. Hackman, "Is Job-Enrichment Just a Fad," *Harvard Business Review,* Sept.–Oct. 1975, p. 129.

14. See Frank Swoboda, "Workers Generally Worse Off Than a Decade Ago, Study Finds," *Washington Post,* Sept. 7, 1992, p. 25; and Susan Cartwright, "Taking the Pulse of Executive Health in the U.K.," *The Academy of Management Executive,* May 2000, p. 16.

15. Lloyd A. Rogers, "Project Team Training: A Proven Key to Organizational Teamwork and Breakthrough in Planning Performance," *Project Management Journal,* June 1990, p. 9.

16. Pam Statz (2001) "Wanna Be a Project Manager?" *WebMonkey.* (http://hotwired.lycos.com/webmonkey/01/18/index3a.html?tw=jobs)

17. Robert Thompson, "More Heads Better Than One in Project Management," *Computing Canada,* Dec. 10, 1999, p. 27.

18. Coles, "Step Back."

19. Paul S. Adler, "Never-Ending Mission to Find Magic Solution," *Computing Canada,* Oct. 1, 1999, p. 17.

20. Don Reinertsen, "The Best-Laid Plans Become the Enemy of Vigilance," *Electronic Design,* March 20, 2000, p. 57.

21. Quote attributed to Uwe Weissflog, manager of strategic planning Structural Dynamics Research Corp., as captured by Kathleen Melymuka, "Project Management Top Guns."

22. Rogers, "Project Team Training."

23. Don Reinertsen, "Projects Can Slip by More Than One Day at a Time," *Electronic Design,* March 6, 2000, p. 56.

24. Daphne Main and Carolyn L. Lousteau, "Don't Get Trapped," *Strategic Finance,* Nov. 1999, p. 74.

25. Melymuka, "Project Management Top Guns."

26. Melymuka, "Born to Lead Projects."

27. Yourdon, Ed, "The Value of Triage," *Computerworld,* March 20, 2000.

28. "Ask Bill Gates (Project Management Tips)," *Management Today,* Feb. 2000, p. 38.

29. "Ask Bill Gates." Reprinted with permission from "Ask Bill Gates," *Management Today,* February 2000, p. 38.

30. Tellez, "Think Globally."

31. Melymuka, "Born to Lead Projects."

32. Peter R. Scholtes, *The Leader's Handbook* (Washington, DC: McGraw-Hill, 1998), p. 205.

33. Scholtes, *The Leader's Handbook,* pp. 99 and 205.

34. Haidee E. Allerton, "How To," *Training and Development,* Nov. 1999, p. 15.

35. Scholtes, *The Leader's Handbook,* p. 205.

36. Barry Render and Ralph M. Stair, Jr., *Introduction to Management Science* (Boston, MA: Allyn & Bacon, 1992), p. 368.

37. "Get a Grip," *Fortune,* Summer 2000, Supplement, pp. 74–90.

38. Matthew J. Liberatore, "A Decision Support System Linking Research and Development Project Selection with Business Strategy," *Project Management Journal,* Nov. 1988, p. 14.

39. Thompson, "More Heads Better Than One."

**Exercise 19–A
Team Project
Worksheet**

1. As a team, use the following sheet to develop a work plan for your team project. Use the guidelines outlined in this chapter, and be sure to break down large objectives into smaller components.

2. For each project step, collectively decide on a due date as well as the persons ultimately accountable. Even if a task requires input from all team members, one person must accept the responsibility for coordinating this task.

3. Before approving the plan, each member should compare his/her project tasks with other requirements or deadlines listed in his/her day planner. Potential conflicts should be discussed and adjusted accordingly. Slack time should be incorporated as well.

4. Present your team's work plan to the class or group. Obtain feedback from them about steps that might have been overlookd or time lines that may be unrealistic. Adjust accordingly. Remember to make adjustments both on the team work plan and in your own day planner.

Team Project Work Plan

Project:

Due Date:

Names and Initials of Team Members:

Project Steps:	Date:	Initials:
1.		
2.		
3.		
4.		
5.		
6.		
7.		
8.		
9.		
10.		
11.		
12.		
13.		
14.		

(continue with additional steps on reverse or on blank sheet of paper)

Exercise 19–B
Individual Day Planner
Update

Each person should bring two sharpened pencils and his or her own personal day planner to this session.

1. Make a list of all activities and projects, personal and professional, in which you're currently involved. This can include work activities or classes in which you're enrolled, children's commitments such as carpooling or after-school activities, family, church or community obligations, exercise, planned travel (trip, vacation, holidays), and medical appointments.

2. Working through the list, enter all known dates for all commitments, activities, and appointments into your personal day planner, using a pencil. Be as thorough as possible. For example, if you are a student, enter all class sessions, exams, paper and project due dates, and vacation schedules. If you are unsure of a specific date, write the activity in the expected week, month, quarter, or semester in which it is likely to occur.

3. Make adjustments as you discover conflicts.

4. Keep this list up to date. As your schedule changes or as additional activities and deadlines are made known, add these into your day planner on a regular basis.

Discuss in small groups:

1. How does it feel to devote time to planning and scheduling activities and commitments?

2. What impact does planning have on our tendency to procrastinate or not devote ample time to what's really important?

3. What other tools or strategies are used to ensure the regular planning and achieving of goals and objectives?

Exercise 19–C
Personal Project
Time Line

You will need your up-to-date individual day planner and project sheet or computer project management program.

1. Working on your own, consider a project in which you're currently involved or in which you anticipate being involved soon.* The project can be personal, such as planning a trip; academic, such as preparing to give a class presentation; or professional, such as conducting an analysis of available products that compete against those of your company.

2. Develop a work plan for the project, following the steps outlined in this chapter. Starting backwards from the project deadline, list every step needed to complete the project. Use a pencil if working on paper. Be as thorough as possible. Assign initials and projected dates for each step.

3. Now transfer each of these dates (in pencil if using paper) to your personal day planner. If there are conflicts between this project and other classes, projects, or activities that are already in your planner, adjust the dates accordingly on both the project work plan and in your personal day planner.

4. Share your project work plan with a partner and obtain feedback on how realistic and how detailed your plan is, as well as on any suggested steps for adding or deleting. Modify your plan accordingly.

*If you can't think of a project, imagine it is the start of the fall semester and you are asked to prepare a 20-page term paper and presentation on a cutting-edge business topic by the end of the semester. You have 12 weeks in which to plan and complete this project. Other ideas: Building a new house, opening a retail store, producing a TV documentary, manufacturing and marketing a new product.

**Exercise 19–D
R & D Project
Planning***

You are part of a newly formed task team that is taking over a project presently being handled by Research and Development. You have been assigned responsibility and authority for planning the project, and then, after top management has reviewed and accepted your plans, for carrying out the project. How do you get (and keep) a project running smoothly from start to finish?

Your instructor will provide additional materials to complete this activity.

*Referenced with permission from Human Synergistics International's Project Planning Simulation #SM17101.

Exercise 19–E
Product Recall

The Scenario

You are part of the Yum Yum Bubblegum's management team. Yum Yum Bubblegum manufactures and sells bubble gum in the United States and Canada.
You have three manufacturing plants:

■ Chewing, Mississippi

■ Bubbleton, Alabama

■ Poppingsburg, South Dakota

The same products are manufactured at all plants and then sent to Yum Yum's distribution center in Shipit, Arkansas, where they are then shipped to customers via distribution trucks. Assume that the company has no contingency or preventive product recall plans.

The Problem

■ The company has just been notified that six people have been hospitalized for toxic poisoning related to substances found in Yum Yum Bubblegum.

■ Three of the hospitalized individuals purchased gum in Dallas, Texas; one in San Antonio; one in San Diego, California; and one is believed to have purchased the gum in an airport in Utah.

Questions and Task

Using the tips and techniques provided in the chapter, work as a team to manage the clean-up project.

1. How should you as managers attack this problem? What's your plan? Create a list of key steps and time frame for each.

2. Next, choose your project team. Who should be on this team? What is each team member's role? Who should be the leader?

3. Determine a contingent plan of attack that specifies how to approach the problem and how to control the process.

4. Finally, determine a preventive plan for the future, assuming that this fiasco does not *blow* the company's ability to continue to do business.

5. Discuss the importance of project management in preventing or dealing with crises.

Source: Permission provided by creator Sherry Ghodes, JMU MBA Student, presented Fall 2000.

Exercise 19–F
Tools of Project Management

1. Research existing project management tools and resources on the Internet, such as Microsoft Project. Bring an example of a new product that you think looks particularly effective to your class or group.

2. Contact your computer department and ask them for recommendations of new software programs that can be used easily for tracking projects. Try one out and report to your group on its effectiveness and potential applicability to your group's project.

3. Visit a local office supply or stationery store and investigate the current day planner systems that are available. Make a note of the particular strengths and limitations of each. Report to the class or group on the top one or two that you believe are the best available for your group's purposes.

**Exercise 19–G
Reflection/Action Plan**

This chapter focused on project management—what it is, why it's important, and how to improve your skills in this area. Complete the worksheet below upon finishing all the reading and experiential activities for this chapter.

1. The one or two areas in which I am most strong are:

   _____

   _____

   _____

   _____

2. The one or two areas in which I need more improvement are:

   _____

   _____

   _____

   _____

3. If I did only one thing to improve in this area, it would be to:

   _____

   _____

   _____

   _____

4. Making this change would probably result in:

   _____

   _____

   _____

   _____

5. If I did not change or improve in this area, it would probably affect my personal and professional life in the following ways:

   _____

   _____

   _____

   _____

Index